MW00637688

A Higher Law

Readings on the Influence of Christian Thought in Anglo-American Law

Second Edition

BY JEFFREY A. BRAUCH
REGENT UNIVERSITY SCHOOL OF LAW

William S. Hein & Co., Inc.
Buffalo, New York
2008

Library of Congress Cataloging-in-Publication Data

Brauch, Jeffrey A.
A higher law : readings on the influence of Christian thought in Anglo-American law / by Jeffrey A. Brauch. — 2nd ed.
p. cm.
Rev. ed. of: Is higher law common law? / Jeffrey A. Brauch. 1999.
Includes bibliographical references and index.
ISBN 978-0-8377-1694-7 (cloth : alk. paper)
1. Common law—United States—Philosophy. 2. Religion and law—United States. 3. Common law—Great Britain—Philosophy. 4. Religion and law—Great Britain. I. Brauch, Jeffrey A. Is higher law common law? II. Title.
KF380.B62 2008
340.5'7—dc22 2008022434

Printed in the United States of America

This volume is printed on acid-free paper
By William S. Hein & Co., Inc.

Dedication

To Becky, my true love and best friend

Table of Contents

Preface to the First Edition

I prepared this book to use in a course at Regent University School of Law entitled "The Common Law." At Regent, the course is required for first-year law students. In their other first-year courses students learn the legal rules and doctrines that govern various areas of the law (contracts, property, torts, civil procedure). The Common Law course encourages students to take a step back from those courses and ask "why?" Why do we enforce contracts? Why do we have the tort rules we do? Why do we punish crime?

The course introduces students to some basic principles of legal history and legal philosophy. It involves legal history by considering the development of the Anglo-American common law from the Middle Ages to today. The course involves philosophy by asking broad questions about the nature of law and about worldviews that have shaped the common law over time. The course also involves theology. In keeping with the mission of Regent University, it encourages students to recognize and seek the biblical foundations of law and legal institutions.

The course is a survey. Accordingly, this book is not exhaustive. It merely gives an introduction to the topics it covers. It is also selective. I chose the readings included here from books, articles and cases for one of two reasons. They are either historically or philosophically significant or they raise important issues that foster a thought-provoking class discussion. Some are both.

It is my hope that the readings will cause students to think more deeply about what the law is, where it has come from, and what it ought to be.

Preface to the Second Edition

Since the first edition of this book was published, I have enjoyed a great privilege. I have joined hundreds of students in a quest. A quest to ask questions that are often ignored in a traditional law school course. A quest to look beyond legal rules and institutions to the legal philosophies that shaped (and are shaping) them. We have questioned. We have disagreed. And we have grown.

This second edition, like the first, is designed to further this quest. Its overall purpose and most of the readings remain unchanged. Nonetheless, this edition reflects some important changes. First, some readings have been updated to reflect recent developments in the law. For example, Part A now includes critical race theory, a legal philosophy that increasingly plays an important role both in the legal academy and in the public arena. Similarly, the chapter regarding the jury trial includes the results of a very recent study that reveals significant jury reforms that have been enacted throughout the country since the first edition was published.

Second, the book reflects a slightly broader focus. The first edition looked almost exclusively at common law rules and institutions. While the second edition continues to emphasize those rules and institutions, it also addresses current issues regarding international and constitutional law. Readers will now consider the moral and legal arguments regarding preemptive war and whether transgendered individuals have a fundamental human right to change their sexual identity on their birth certificate. This broader focus, reflected in the revised title of the second edition, recognizes that many current clashes over legal worldview are taking place outside the realm of the common law.

Third, Part C of the book has undergone substantial updating. Its purpose has not changed. The readings in Part C still introduce the reader to Christian thinking on how higher law should influence human law today. But the readings are now organized to address two key questions: 1) What is the role of Old Testament law today?; 2) To what extent should higher law be applied in modern society?

Acknowledgements

I am deeply grateful to the following people for their significant contributions to this book:

My wife Becky and my children Cynthia, Melissa, Christina and Jeffrey for their patience and support;

Kelby Kershner for his superb research, editorial, and technical assistance with all aspects of this book;

Thomas DeBusk for his diligent, creative, and excellent editorial and technical assistance;

Christi Bittinger and Timothy Halpin for their helpful research assistance;

Julie Kershner for her helpful editorial assistance and Latin translation.

Derick Henderson for his helpful editorial assistance;

My co-teachers and colleagues Mike Hernandez, Brad Jacob, Ben Madison, Eric DeGroff, and Tom Folsom for their wisdom, support, and editorial and substantive guidance;

My colleagues Gary Amos, Doug Cook, Scott Pryor, Mike Schutt, and Craig Stern for their wisdom and valuable comments on the issues discussed in this book;

J. Nelson Happy and James Murphy for their support and encouragement.

Introduction

The basic problem of the Christians in this country in the last eighty years or so, in regard to society and in regard to government, is that they have seen things in bits and pieces instead of totals.

They have very gradually become disturbed over permissiveness, pornography, the public schools, the breakdown of the family, and finally abortion. But they have not seen this as a totality—each thing as being a part, a symptom, of a much larger problem. They have failed to see that all of this has come about due to a shift in worldview—that is, through a fundamental change in the overall way people think and view the world and life as a whole.

FRANCIS SHAEFFER, *A Christian Manifesto*

This book tells a story. It is a story about how we view the world, and how that view affects our legal system. It is a story about Anglo-American law, particularly the common law, the legal system that for over 800 years defined and governed most legal rights and duties of citizens first in England and later in the United States. The common law still forms much of the basis of our law today.

The thesis of this book is that Anglo-American law—and especially the common law—was once based on a particular view of the world. That view held that there was such a thing as truth. It was possible to say objectively that some things were true and that others were false, that some things were right and that others were wrong. Anglo-American law, too, was based on a particular view of human beings. That view held that humans were both created by God in his very image (and thus possessed of a dignity given by their creator) and yet fallen. And Anglo-American law was based on a particular view of law. That view held that there was a fixed law—a higher law—upon which all human law was based. The higher law was something by which all human law could be evaluated and through which justice could be attained.

In the last century and a half, however, our view of the world changed. We became skeptical. We became skeptical about the existence of God, or at least what place he holds in the universe. We became skeptical about the nature of human beings. Instead of seeing individuals created in the image of an infinite yet personal God, we began to view humans as simply the product of an impersonal evolutionary process. We became skeptical about truth—about whether anything is objectively right or wrong.

Naturally, our change in thinking affected our legal system. We became skeptical of traditional legal institutions and rules. We became skeptical about whether there really is a higher law or such a thing as true justice. In many ways, we began to view law as simply a means to exert power or to accomplish certain social welfare goals.

This book tells its story largely through the words of others. It consists of excerpts from books, articles, and cases written by some of the people who have most shaped the Anglo-American legal system. The worldview that was foundational to the development of Anglo-American law, particularly the common law, is described by the common law's most brilliant lawyers and judges: Henrici de Bracton, Sir Edward Coke, and William Blackstone. The great legal movements of the last century are described by the leading thinkers of those movements in works that explain and defend those movements. The book contains excerpts from the works of the world's greatest legal minds: Thomas Aquinas, Oliver Wendell Holmes, Karl Llewellyn, Richard Posner, and many others.

The book tells its story in three parts. Part A traces the shift in thinking largely at a philosophical level. It reveals how our thinking about the world and the law has changed from approximately 1050 A.D. to the present day. It begins by setting forth several views of the higher law and how that higher law should affect human law. It then demonstrates the powerful influence that belief in a higher law had on the development of the common law. Finally, it discusses the shift toward skepticism of the existence of a higher law that has taken place. It introduces influential legal philosophies that have largely replaced higher law thinking today: positivism, realism, law and economics, critical legal studies, and critical race theory. While many of the excerpts in Part A are philosophical, others ask very practical questions. For example, how does a belief in, or skepticism of, a higher law affect how I should live as a citizen or judge or lawmaker? Is civil disobedience appropriate? When?

Part B takes a step back and explores how the legal ideas from Part A have influenced specific legal institutions and doctrines. It focuses particularly on contemporary issues in which there is a clash over legal philosophy. The issues vary widely. Some involve traditional common law doctrines such as damages for contact breach or the right to a jury trial. Others involve some of the most controversial public policy questions of our day: Is preemptive war morally and legally justified? To what extent may we hold individuals responsible for criminal acts when those individuals were influenced by genetic or environmental factors? Should a woman's choice to have an abortion be protected as a fundamental constitutional right?

Part C addresses whether the higher law—if it even exists—has any relevance to human law today. It contains excerpts from books and articles by Christians who all believe in a higher law but disagree about whether and how it applies in a modern context. These authors address two fundamental questions: 1) What is the role of Old Testament law today?; 2) To what extent should higher law be applied in modern society?

Part A The Nature of Law and the Fundamental Shift in Legal Thinking

Chapter 1 Higher Law Thinking: Man's Law is Based on and Evaluated by the Law of God

A. The Origin of Modern Legal Thought in the Papal Revolution of 1050-1250 A.D.

Introduction

The author of the following piece, Professor Harold Berman, argues that the most significant event in the history of western legal thought occurred between the Eleventh and Twelfth centuries. He calls that event the Papal Revolution (it is also commonly known as the Gregorian Reform or Investiture Struggle).

At its heart, the Papal Revolution was a struggle by the church to free itself from control by secular authorities. The revolution had profound political, religious, and legal consequences throughout Europe. Berman argues that the revolution dramatically changed law, the study of law, the practice of law, and legal thinking itself. He believes that the legal developments coming out of the revolution formed the basis for modern law, including the common law.

Before his death in November, 2007, Berman was the Robert Woodruff Professor of Law at Emory University. He was also the James Barr Ames Professor Emeritus at Harvard Law School. He taught jurisprudence, comparative legal history, international trade law, and Russian law. He was a prolific writer of books and articles, particularly regarding the influence of religion on law. The piece that follows is an excerpt from Berman's award-winning book, *Law and Revolution*, published by Harvard University Press in 1983.

Harold Berman, *Law and Revolution*[*]

The Origin of the Western Legal Tradition in the Papal Revolution

Among the peoples of western Europe in the period prior to the eleventh century, law did not exist as a distinct system of regulation or as a distinct system of thought. Each people had, to be sure, its own legal order, which included occasional legal enactments by central authorities as well as innumerable unwritten legal rules and institutions, both secular and ecclesiastical. A considerable number of individual legal terms and rules had been inherited from the earlier Roman law and could be found in the canons and decrees of local ecclesiastical councils and of individual bishops as well as in some royal legislation and in customary law. Lacking, however, in both the secular and the ecclesiastical spheres, was a clear separation of law from other processes of social control and from other types of intellectual concern. Secular law as a whole was not "disembedded" from general tribal, local, and feudal custom or from the general custom of royal and imperial households. Similarly, the law of the church was largely diffused throughout the life of the church—throughout its structures of authority as well as its theology, its moral precepts, its liturgy—and it, too, was primarily local and regional and primarily customary rather than centralized or enacted. There were no professional judges or lawyers. There were no hierarchies of courts.

Also lacking was a perception of law as a distinct "body" of rules and concepts. There were no law schools. There were no great legal texts dealing with basic legal categories such as jurisdiction, procedure, crime, contract, property, and the other subjects which eventually came to form structural elements in Western legal systems. There were no developed theories of the sources of law, of the relation of divine and natural law to human law, of ecclesiastical law to secular law, of enacted law to customary law, or of the various kinds of secular law—feudal, royal, urban—to one another.

The relatively unsystematized character of legal regulation and the relatively undeveloped state of legal science were closely connected with the prevailing political, economic, and social conditions. These included the predominantly local character of tribal, village, and feudal communi-

---

[*] HAROLD BERMAN, LAW AND REVOLUTION, 85-88, 94-99, 103-06, 111-19 (1983). Reprinted by permission of the publisher from LAW AND REVOLUTION: THE FORMATION OF WESTERN LEGAL TRADITION by Harold J. Berman, pp. 85-88, 94-99, 103-106, 111-119, Cambridge, Mass.: Harvard University Press, Copyright © 1985 by the President and Fellows of Harvard College.

ties; their relatively high degree of economic self-sufficiency; the fusion of authorities within each; the relative weakness of the political and economic control exercised by the central imperial and royal authorities; the essentially military and religious character of the control exercised by the imperial and royal authorities; and the relative strength of informal community bonds of kinship and soil and of military comradeship.

In the late eleventh, the twelfth, and the early thirteenth centuries a fundamental change took place in western Europe in the very nature of law both as a political institution and as an intellectual concept. Law became disembedded. Politically, there emerged for the first time strong central authorities, both ecclesiastical and secular, whose control reached down, through delegated officials, from the center to the localities. Partly in connection with that, there emerged a class of professional jurists, including professional judges and practicing lawyers. Intellectually, western Europe experienced at the same time the creation of its first law schools, the writing of its first legal treatises, the conscious ordering of the huge mass of inherited legal materials, and the development of the concept of law as an autonomous, integrated, developing body of legal principles and procedures.

The combination of these two factors, the political and the intellectual, helped to produce modern Western legal systems, of which the first was the new system of canon law of the Roman Catholic Church (then regularly called for the first time *jus canonicum*). It was also at that time divided into "old law" (*jus antiquum*), consisting of earlier texts and canons, and "new law" (*jus novum*), consisting of contemporary legislation and decisions as well as contemporary interpretations of the earlier texts and canons. Against the background of the new system of canon law, and often in rivalry with it, the European kingdoms and other polities began to create their own secular legal systems. At the same time there emerged in most parts of Europe free cities, each with its own governmental and legal institutions, forming a new type of urban law. In addition, feudal (lord-vassal) and manorial (lord-peasant) legal institutions underwent systematization, and a new system of mercantile law was developed to meet the needs of merchants engaged in intercity, interregional, and international trade. The emergence of these systems of feudal law, manorial law, mercantile law, and urban law clearly indicates that not only political and intellectual but also social and economic factors were at work in producing what can only be called a revolutionary development of legal institutions. In other words, the creation of modern legal systems in the late eleventh, twelfth, and early thirteenth centuries was not only an implementation of policies and theories of central elites, but also a response to social and economic changes "on the ground."

Religious factors were at work, as well. The creation of modern legal systems was, in the first instance, a response to a revolutionary change within the church and in the relation of the church to the secular authorities. And here the word "revolutionary" has all the modern connotations of class struggle and violence. In 1075, after some twenty-five years of agitation and propaganda by the papal party, Pope Gregory VII declared the political and legal supremacy of the papacy over the entire church and the independence of the clergy from secular control. Gregory also asserted the ultimate supremacy of the pope in secular matters, including the authority to depose emperors and kings. The emperor—Henry IV of Saxony—responded with military action. Civil war between the papal and imperial parties raged sporadically throughout Europe until 1122, when a final compromise was reached by a concordat signed in the German city of Worms. In England and Normandy, the Concordat of Bec in 1107 had provided a temporary respite, but the matter was not finally resolved there until the martyrdom of Archbishop Thomas Becket in 1170.

The great changes that took place in the life of the Western Church and in the relations between the ecclesiastical and the secular authorities during the latter part of the eleventh and the first part of the twelfth centuries have traditionally been called the Hildebrand Reform, or the Gregorian Reform, after the monk Hildebrand, who was a leader of the papal party in the period after 1050 and who ruled as Pope Gregory VII from 1073 to 1085. However, the term "Reform" is a serious understatement, reflecting in part the desire of the papal party itself—and of later Roman Catholic historians—to play down the magnitude of the discontinuity between what had gone before and what came after. The original Latin term, *reformatio*, may suggest a more substantial break in continuity by recalling the sixteenth-century Protestant Reformation. Another term used to denote the same era, namely, the Investiture Struggle, is not so much an understatement as an oblique statement: by pointing to the struggle of the papacy to wrest from emperor and kings the power to "invest" bishops with the symbols of their authority, the phrase connects the conflict between the papal and imperial (or royal) parties with the principal slogan of the papal reformers: "the freedom of the church." But even this dramatic slogan does not adequately convey the full dimensions of the revolutionary transformation, which many leading historians have considered to be the first major turning point in European history, and which some have recognized as the beginning of the modern age. What was involved ultimately was, in Peter Brown's words, "the disengagement of the two spheres of the sacred and the profane," from which there stemmed a release of energy and creativity analogous to a process of nuclear fission.

* * *

The Dictates of the Pope

It was Hildebrand who in the 1070s, as Pope Gregory VII, turned the reform movement of the church against the very imperial authority which had led the Cluniac reformers during the tenth and early eleventh centuries. Gregory went much farther than his predecessors. He proclaimed the legal supremacy of the pope over all Christians and the legal supremacy of the clergy, under the pope, over all secular authorities. Popes, he said, could depose emperors—and he proceeded to depose Emperor Henry IV. Moreover, Gregory proclaimed that all bishops were to be appointed by the pope and were to be subordinate ultimately to him and not to secular authority.

Gregory had been well prepared to ascend the papal throne. He had been the dominant force in the reigns of the popes Nicholas II (1058-1061) and Alexander II (1061-1073). Also, in 1073 at the age of fifty, he was ready to exercise the enormous will and pride and personal authority for which he was notorious. Peter Damian (1007-1072), who had been associated with him in the struggle for papal supremacy since the 1050s, once addressed him as "my holy Satan," and said: "Thy will has ever been a command to me—evil but lawful. Would that I had always served God and Saint Peter as faithfully as I have served thee." A modern scholar has described Gregory as a man with an overpowering sense of mission, who pressed his ideas with "frightening severity and heroic persistence...regardless of the consequences to himself or to others [and who] had, to say the least, the temper of a revolutionary."

Once he became pope, Gregory did not hesitate to use revolutionary tactics to accomplish his objectives. In 1075, for example, he ordered all Christians to boycott priests who were living in concubinage or marriage, and not to accept their offices for the sacraments or other purposes. Thus priests were required to choose between their responsibilities to their wives and children and their responsibilities to their parishioners. As a result of opposition to this decree, there were open riots in churches and beating and stoning of those who opposed clerical marriage. One writer, in a pamphlet entitled "Apology against Those who Challenge the Masses of Priests," stated that Christianity was being "trampled underfoot." "What else is talked about even in the women's spinning-rooms and the artisans' workshops," he asked, "than the confusion of all human laws...sudden unrest among the populace, new treacheries of servants against their masters and masters' mistrust of their servants, abject breaches of faith among friends and equals, conspiracies against the power ordained by God?...and all this backed by authority, by those who are called the leaders of Christendom."

Lacking armies of its own, how was the papacy to make good its claims? How was it to overcome the armies of those who would oppose papal supremacy? And apart from the problem of meeting forceful opposition, how was the papacy to exercise the universal jurisdiction it had asserted? How was it effectively to impress its will on the entire Western Christian world, let alone Eastern Christendom, over which some claims of jurisdiction were also made?

An important aspect of the answers to these questions was the potential role of law as a source of authority and a means of control. During the last decades of the eleventh century, the papal party began to search the written record of church history for legal authority to support papal supremacy over the entire clergy as well as clerical independence of, and possible supremacy over, the entire secular branch of society. The papal party encouraged scholars to develop a science of law which would provide a working basis for carrying out these major policies. At the same time, the imperial party also began to search for ancient texts that would support its cause against papal usurpation.

There was, however, no legal forum to which either the papacy or the imperial authority could take its case—except to the pope or the emperor himself. This, indeed, was the principal revolutionary element in the situation. In 1075 Pope Gregory VII responded to it by "looking within his own breast" and writing a document—the *Dictatus Papæ* (*Dictates of the Pope*)—consisting of twenty-seven terse propositions, apparently addressed to no one but himself, including the following:

1. That the Roman church is founded by the Lord alone.
2. That the Roman bishop alone is by right called universal.
3. That he alone may depose and reinstate bishops.
4. That his legate, even if of lower grade, takes precedence, in a council, over all bishops and may render a sentence of deposition against them.

7. That to him alone is it permitted to make new laws according to the needs of the times.

9. That the pope alone is the one whose feet are to be kissed by all princes.
10. That his name alone is to be recited in churches.
11. That he may depose emperors.

16. That no synod should be called general without his order.
17. That no chapter or book may be regarded as canonical without his authority.

18. That no judgment of his may be revised by anyone, and that he alone may revise [the judgments] of all.

21. That the more important cases of every church may be referred to the Apostolic See.

27. That he may absolve subjects of unjust men from their [oath of] fealty.

This document was revolutionary—although Gregory ultimately managed to find some legal authority for every one of its provisions. In December 1075 Gregory made known the contents of his Papal Manifesto, as it might be called today, in a letter to Emperor Henry IV in which he demanded the subordination of the emperor and of the imperial bishops to Rome. Henry replied, as did twenty-six of his bishops, in letters of January 24, 1076. Henry's letter begins: "Henry, king not through usurpation but through the holy ordination of God, to Hildebrand, at present not pope but false monk." It ends, "You, therefore, damned by this curse and by the judgment of all our bishops and by our own, go down and relinquish the apostolic chair which you have usurped. Let another go up to the throne of St. Peter. I, Henry, king by the grace of God, do say unto you, together with all our bishops: Go down, go down [*Descende, descende*], to be damned throughout the ages." The letter of the bishops is in a similar vein, ending: "And since, as you did publicly proclaim, no one of us has been to you thus far a bishop, so also shall you henceforth be pope for none of us."

In response, Gregory excommunicated and deposed Henry, who in January 1077 journeyed as a humble penitent to the pope in Canossa, where, tradition has it, he waited three days to present himself barefoot in the snow and to confess his sins and declare his contrition. Thus appealed to in his spiritual capacity, the pope absolved Henry and removed the excommunication and deposition. This gave Henry a chance to reassert his authority over the German magnates, both ecclesiastical and secular, who had been in rebellion against him. The struggle with the pope, however, was only postponed for a short time. In 1078 the pope issued a decree in which he said: "We decree that no one of the clergy shall receive the investiture with a bishopric or abbey or church from the hand of an emperor or king or of any lay person, male or female. But if he shall presume to do so he shall clearly know that such investiture is bereft of apostolic authority, and that he himself shall lie under excommunication until fitting satisfaction shall have been rendered." The conflict between pope and emperor broke out again and the Wars of Investiture resulted.

The first casualties of the Wars of Investiture were in the German territories, where the emperor's enemies took advantage of his controversy with the pope to elect a rival king, whom Gregory eventually supported. However, Henry defeated his rival in 1080 and moved south across the Alps to besiege and occupy Rome (1084). Gregory appealed for help to his allies, the Norman rulers of southern Italy—Apulia, Calabria, Capua, and Sicily. The Normans' mercenaries drove the imperial forces from Rome, but then proceeded to loot and sack it with the savagery for which they were notorious. Henry continued to face revolts from the German princes; and when he died in 1106, his own son was leading a rebellion against him. That son, as Emperor Henry V, occupied Rome in 1111 and captured the pope.

The immediate political issue of the Wars of Investiture was that of the power of emperors and kings to invest bishops and other clergy with the insignia of their offices, uttering the words, "Accipe ecclesiam!" [Take the church!] Behind this issue lay the question of loyalty and discipline of clergy after election and investiture. These issues were of fundamental political importance. Since the empire and the kingdoms were administered chiefly by clergy, they affected the very nature of both the ecclesiastical authority and the imperial or royal authority. Yet even more was involved—something deeper than politics—namely, the salvation of souls. Previously, the emperor (or king) had been called the deputy ("vicar") of Christ; it was he who was to answer for the souls of all men at the Last Judgment. Now the pope, who had previously called himself the deputy of St. Peter, claimed to be the sole deputy of Christ with responsibility to answer for the souls of all men at the Last Judgment. Emperor Henry IV had written to Pope Gregory VII that according to the church fathers the emperor can be judged by no man; he alone on earth is "judge of all men"; there is only one emperor, whereas the Bishop of Rome is only the first among bishops. This indeed was orthodox doctrine that had prevailed for centuries. Gregory, however, saw the emperor as first among kings, a layman, whose election as emperor was subject to confirmation by the pope and who could be deposed by the pope for insubordination. The argument was put in typical scholastic form: "the king is either a layman or a cleric," and since he is not ordained he is obviously a layman and hence can have no office in "the church." This claim left emperors and kings with no basis for legitimacy, for the idea of a secular state, that is, a state without ecclesiastical functions, had not yet been—indeed, was only then just being—born. It also arrogated to popes theocratic powers, for the division of ecclesiastical functions into spiritual and temporal had not yet been—indeed, was only then just being—born.

Ultimately, neither popes nor emperors could maintain their original claims. Under the Concordat of Worms in 1122, the emperor guaranteed that bishops and abbots would be freely elected by the church alone, and he renounced his right to invest them with the spiritual symbols of ring and staff, which implied the power to care for souls. The pope, for his part, conceded the emperor's right to be present at elections and, where elections were disputed, to intervene. Moreover, German prelates were not to be consecrated by the church until the emperor had invested them, by scepter, with what were called the "regalia," that is, feudal rights of property, justice, and secular government, which carried the reciprocal duty to render homage and fealty to the emperor. (Homage and fealty included the rendering of feudal services and dues on the large landed estates that went with high church offices.) Prelates of Italy and Burgundy, however, were not to be invested by the scepter and to undertake to render their homage and fealty to the emperor until six months after their consecration by the church. The fact that the power of appointment had to be shared—that either pope or emperor could, in effect, exercise a veto—made the question of ceremony, the question of procedure, crucial.

In England and Normandy, under the earlier settlement reached at Bec in 1107, King Henry I had also agreed to free elections, though in his presence, and had renounced investiture by staff and ring. Also, as later in Germany, he was to receive homage and fealty before, and not after, consecration.

The concordats left the pope with extremely wide authority over the clergy, and with considerable authority over the laity as well. Without his approval clergy could not be ordained. He established the functions and powers of bishops, priests, deacons, and other clerical officials. He could create new bishoprics, divide or suppress old ones, transfer or depose bishops. His authorization was needed to institute a new monastic order or to change the rule of an existing order. Moreover, the pope was called the "principal dispenser" of all church property, which was conceived to be the "patrimony of Christ." The pope also was supreme in matters of worship and of religious belief; and he alone could grant absolution from certain grave sins (such as assault upon a clerk), canonize saints, and distribute indulgences (relief from divine punishment after death). None of these powers had existed before 1075.

"The Pope," in the words of Gabriel LeBras, "ruled over the whole church. He was the universal legislator, his power being limited only by natural [law] and positive divine law [that is, divine law laid down in the Bible and in similar documents of revelation]. He summoned general councils, presided over them, and his confirmation was necessary for the putting into force of their decisions. He put an end to controversy on many points by means of decretals, he was the interpreter of the law and granted privileges and dispensations. He was also the supreme judge and administrator. Cases of importance—*maiores causae*—of which there never was a final enumeration, were reserved for his judgment." None of these powers had existed before 1075.

Gregory declared the papal court to be "the court of the whole of Christendom." From then on, the pope had general jurisdiction over cases submitted to him by anyone—he was "judge ordinary of all persons." This was wholly new.

Over the laity the pope ruled in matters of faith and morals as well as in various civil matters such as marriage and inheritance. In some respects, his rule in these matters was absolute; in other respects, it was shared with the secular authority. Also, in still other matters which were considered to belong to the secular jurisdiction, the papal authority often became involved. Prior to 1075 the pope's jurisdiction over the laity had been subordinate to that of emperors and kings and generally had not been greater than that of other leading bishops.

The separation, concurrence, and interaction of the spiritual and secular jurisdictions was a principal source of the Western legal tradition.

* * *

The Rapidity and Violence of the Papal Revolution

In trying to comprehend the full dimensions of the changes that took place during the eleventh and twelfth centuries, one may lose sight of the cataclysmic character of the events that were at the heart of the Papal Revolution. These events may be explained, ultimately, only by the totality of the transformation; but they must be seen initially as the immediate consequence of the effort to achieve a political purpose, namely, what the papal party called "the freedom of the church"—the liberation of the clergy from imperial, royal, and feudal domination and their unification under papal authority. By placing that political purpose, and the events that followed immediately from the effort to realize it, in the context of the total transformation, one can see that what was involved was far more than a struggle for power. It was an apocalyptic struggle for a new order of things, for "a new heaven and a new earth." But at the same time, the political manifestation of that struggle, where power and conviction, the material and the spiritual, coincided, is what gave it its tempo and its passion.

Rapidity is, of course, a relative matter. It may seem that a transformation which began in the middle of the eleventh century and was not secured until the latter part of the twelfth century, or possibly the early part of the thirteenth century, should be called gradual. However, the length of time which it takes a revolution to run its course is not necessarily the measure of its rapidity. The concept of rapid change refers to the pace at which drastic changes occur from day to day or year to year or decade to decade. In a revolution of the magnitude of the Papal Revolution, life is speeded up; things happen very quickly; great changes take place overnight. First, at the start of the revolution—in the Dictatus Papae of 1075—the previous political and legal order was declared to be abolished. Emperors were to kiss the feet of popes. The pope was to be "the sole judge of all" and to have the sole power "to make new laws to meet the needs of the times." The fact that many of the features of the old society persisted and refused to disappear did not change the suddenness of the effort to abolish them or the shock produced by that effort. Second, new institutions and policies were introduced almost as suddenly as old ones were abolished. The fact that it took a long time—several generations—for the revolution to establish its goals did not make the process a gradual one.

For example, it was part of Pope Gregory VII's program, at least from 1074 on, that the papacy should organize a crusade to defend the Christians of the East against the Turkish infidels. Until his death in 1085 he promoted that idea throughout Europe, although he was never able to get sufficient support to bring it about. Only in 1095 did his successor and devoted follower, Pope Urban II, succeed in launching the First Crusade. One may say, then, that it took a long time—over twenty years—to accomplish this change, which literally turned Europe around and united it in a collective military and missionary expedition to the East. But in another sense, the change from a precrusading Europe to a crusading Europe came with shocking rapidity. From the first moment the crusade became a declared objective of the papacy, the reorientation proceeded, continually producing new hopes, new fears, new plans, new associations. Once the First Crusade was undertaken the pace of change accelerated. The mobilization of knights from virtually every part of Western Christendom, their journeys across land and sea and, finally, the innumerable military encounters, were a compression of events into a time span that came and went with extraordinary speed. Moreover, it was not only on the ground, so to speak, that the crusades represented an acceleration of the pace of events. It was also so in the realm of high politics. For example, the papacy tried to use the crusades as a means of exporting the Papal Revolution to Eastern Christendom. The pope declared his supremacy over the entire Christian world. The schism between the Eastern and Western churches, which had reached a climax in 1054 in the famous theological controversy over the *filioque* [Son] clause in the creed, took the form of violence and conquest. Also in 1099 Western knights entered Jerusalem and founded there a new kingdom, the Kingdom of Jerusalem, subordinate, at least in theory, to the papacy. History was moving very fast indeed! Although almost fifty years elapsed before the Second Crusade was launched, and another forty years from the end of the Second Crusade to the Third, these time spans, too, must be considered in the light of the continual agitation that was generated both by anticipation of them and by the remembrance of them. Throughout the twelfth century there was a widespread feeling that a crusade might come at any time.

And so with the principal aim of the revolution, expressed in the slogan, "the freedom of the church": it was not something that could be achieved overnight—indeed, in its deepest significance it was not something that could be achieved ever—yet the very depth of the idea, its combination of great simplicity and great complexity, was a guarantee that the struggle to achieve it would be, on the one hand, a prolonged one, over decades and generations and even centuries, and on the other hand, a cataclysmic one, with drastic and often violent changes occurring in rapid succession. For freedom of the church meant different things to different people. To some it meant a theocratic state. To others it meant that the church should renounce all its feudal lands, all its wealth, all its worldly power; this, indeed, was proposed by Pope Paschal II in the early 1100s, but was quickly rejected both by the Roman cardinals and by the German bishops who supported the emperor. Or it might mean something quite different from either of these extreme alternatives. The fact that its meaning kept changing from 1075 to 1122 was one of the marks of the revolutionary character of the times.

Apart from the crusades, the violence of the Papal Revolution took the form of a series of wars and rebellions. The papal and the imperial or royal sides used both mercenaries and feudal armies. There were many violent popular rebellions, especially in cities, against the existing authorities—against ruling bishops, for example, who might be appointees and supporters of either the emperor or the pope.

It is doubtful that the rapidity of the Papal Revolution can be separated from its violence. This is not to say that if the struggle could have been carried on without civil war—if Henry IV could have been persuaded not to resist Gregory by armed force, or Gregory not to summon his Norman allies in defense—the events would have lost their rapid tempo. Nevertheless, in the Papal Revolution, as in the great revolutions of Western history that succeeded it, the resort to violence was closely related to the speed with which changes were pressed as well as to their total or fundamental character. It was partly because of the rapidity of the changes and partly because of their totality that the preexisting order was unwilling and unable to make room for them; and so force, in Karl Marx's words, became "the necessary midwife" of the new era.

Force, however, could not give a final victory either to the revolutionary party or to its opponents. The Papal Revolution ended in compromise between the new and old. If force was the midwife, law was the teacher that ultimately brought the child to maturity. Gregory VII died in exile. Henry IV was deposed. The eventual settlement in Germany, France, England, and elsewhere was reached by hard negotiations in which all sides renounced their most radical claims. What can be said for force is that it took the experience of civil war in Europe to produce the willingness of both sides to compromise. The balance was struck, ultimately, by law.

* * *

Social-Psychological Causes and Consequences of the Papal Revolution

Ultimately, compromises were reached in the struggle between the papalists and their opponents. It was out of that struggle and those compromises that Western political science—and especially the first modern Western theories of the state and secular law—were born. As K.J. Leyser has written, "Political ideas in the classical sense only appear in the polemics of the eleventh and early twelfth centuries incoherently, in flashes.... There [was at that time] no theory of the secular state as such, but as a result of the great crisis it was all ready to be born."

The new meanings of secular were derived from the struggle between supporters of the secular and spiritual authorities, respectively. Those who denied altogether the papacy's distinction between secular and spiritual, and who insisted on maintaining the sacral character of imperial or royal rule, were generally defeated. But the actual boundaries between the two realms—the specific allocations of functions—were worked out by reconciliation and compromise between opposing forces. They could not, by the very nature of the problem, be defined abstractly.

Closely related to both the clergy's sense of corporate identity and its sense of mission to reform the world was a third aspect of the new social consciousness that emerged in the eleventh and twelfth centuries, namely, a new sense of historical time, including the concepts of modernity and of progress. This, too, was both a cause and a consequence of the Papal Revolution.

A new sense of time was implicit in the shift in the meaning of *saeculum* [the age] and in the new sense of mission to reform the world. A relatively static view of political society was replaced by a more dynamic view; there was a new concern with the future of social institutions. But there was also a fundamental revaluation of history, a new orientation toward the past as well as the future, and a new sense of the relationship of the future to the past.

* * *

The Rise of the Modern State

The Papal Revolution gave birth to the modern Western state—the first example of which, paradoxically, was the church itself.

As Maitland said a century ago, it is impossible to frame any acceptable definition of the state which would not include the medieval church. By that he meant the church after Pope Gregory VII, since before his reign the church had been merged with the secular society and had lacked the concepts of sovereignty and of independent lawmaking power which are fundamental to modern statehood. After Gregory VII, however, the church took on most of the distinctive characteristics of the modern state. It claimed to be an independent, hierarchical, public authority. Its head, the pope, had the right to legislate, and in fact Pope Gregory's successors issued a steady stream of new laws, sometimes by their own authority, sometimes with the aid of church councils summoned by them. The church also executed its laws through an administrative hierarchy, through which the pope ruled as a modern sovereign rules through his or her representatives. Further, the church interpreted its laws, and applied them, through a judicial hierarchy culminating in the papal curia [papal court] in Rome. Thus the church exercised the legislative, administrative, and judicial powers of a modern state. In addition, it adhered to a rational system of jurisprudence, the canon law. It imposed taxes on its subjects in the form of tithes and other levies. Through baptismal and death certificates it kept what was in effect a kind of civil register. Baptism conferred a kind of citizenship, which was further maintained by the requirement—formalized in 1215—that every Christian confess his or her sins and take Holy Communion at least once a year at Easter. One could be deprived of citizenship, in effect, by excommunication. Occasionally, the church even raised armies.

Yet it is a paradox to call the church a modern state, since the principal feature by which the modern state is distinguished from the ancient state, as well as from the Germanic or Frankish state, is its secular character. The ancient state and the Germanic-Frankish state were religious states, in which the supreme political ruler was also responsible for maintaining the religious dogmas as well as the religious rites and was often himself considered to be a divine or semidivine figure. The elimination of the religious function and character of the supreme political authority was one of the principal objectives of the Papal Revolution. Thereafter, emperors and kings were considered—by those who followed Roman Catholic doctrine—to be laymen, and hence wholly without competence in spiritual matters. According to papal theory, only the clergy, headed by the pope, had competence in spiritual matters. Nevertheless, for several reasons this was not a "separation of church and state" in the modern sense.

First, the state in the full modern sense—that is, the secular state existing in a system of secular states—had not yet come into being, although a few countries (especially the Norman Kingdom of Sicily and Norman England) were beginning to create modern political and legal institutions. Instead, there were various types of secular power, including feudal lordships and autonomous municipal governments as well as emerging national territorial states, and their interrelationships were strongly affected by the fact that all of their members, including their rulers, were also subject in many respects to an overarching ecclesiastical state.

Second, although emperor, kings, and other lay rulers were deprived of their ecclesiastical authority, they nevertheless continued to play a very important part—through the dual system of investiture—in the appointment of bishops, abbots, and other clerics and, indeed, in church politics generally. And conversely, members of the clergy continued to play an important part in secular politics, serving as advisers to secular rulers and also often as high secular officials. The Chancellor of England, for example, who was second in importance to the King, was virtually always a high ecclesiastic—often the Archbishop of Canterbury or of York—until the sixteenth century.

Third, the church retained important secular powers. Bishops continued to be lords of their feudal vassals and serfs and to be managers of their estates. Beyond that, the papacy asserted its power to influence secular politics in all countries; indeed, the pope claimed the supremacy of the spiritual sword over the temporal, although he only claimed to exercise temporal supremacy indirectly, chiefly through secular rulers.

Thus the statement that the church was the first modern Western state must be qualified. The Papal Revolution did lay the foundation for the subsequent emergence of the modern secular state by withdrawing from emperors and kings the spiritual competence which they had previously exercised. Moreover, when the secular state did emerge, it had a constitution similar to that of the papal church—minus, however, the church's spiritual function as a community of souls concerned with eternal life. The church had the paradoxical character of a church-state, a

Kirchenstaat: it was a spiritual community which also exercised temporal functions and whose constitution was in the form of a modern state. The secular state, on the other hand, had the paradoxical character of a state without ecclesiastical functions, a secular polity, all of whose subjects also constituted a spiritual community living under a separate spiritual authority.

Thus the Papal Revolution left a legacy of tensions between secular and spiritual values within the church, within the state, and within a society that was neither wholly church nor wholly state. It also, however, left a legacy of governmental and legal institutions, both ecclesiastical and secular, for resolving the tensions and maintaining an equilibrium throughout the system.

The Rise of Modern Legal Systems

As the Papal Revolution gave birth to the modern Western state, so it gave birth also to modern Western legal systems, the first of which was the modern system of canon law.

From early centuries on, the church accumulated a great many laws—canons (that is, rules) and decrees of church councils and synods, decrees and decisions of individual bishops (including the Roman Pontiff), and laws of Christian emperors and kings concerning the church. The church in the West also produced many Penitentials (handbooks for Priests), containing descriptions of various sins and the penalties attached to them. All these laws were considered to be subordinate to the precepts contained in the Bible (both the Old and New Testaments) and in the writings of the early church fathers—men such as Polycarp of Smyrna, Tertullian of Carthage, Gregory of Nyssa, and Augustine of Hippo.

These authoritative writings, in which the canons were merged, had contributed to the gradual establishment throughout Western Christendom, between the sixth and tenth centuries, of a common body of theological doctrine, a common worship service (in Latin), a common set of rules concerning major sins (such as killing, breaking oaths, stealing), and a common ecclesiastical discipline and structure. Everywhere priests heard confessions and dispensed the sacraments to their flocks; everywhere bishops ruled priests, consecrated churches, and arbitrated disputes within their respective dioceses; everywhere bishops were responsible to their primates (metropolitan bishops of provinces and regions), and all bishops owed loyalty to the Bishop of Rome as first among equals. There was, however, no book or series of books in existence in the year 1000 which attempted to present the whole body of ecclesiastical law or, indeed, systematically to summarize any part of it. There were, to be sure, a considerable number of collections of canons, and particularly canons of church councils and decrees of leading bishops. Usually these collections were simply arranged chronologically within broad categories of sources (canons of councils, letters of popes, sayings of the fathers), but in some collections there was also a division into a number of topics (Ordination, Church Courts, Liturgy, Marriage, Heresy, Idolatry). Hardly any of these collections were recognized as valid everywhere; almost all of them had only regional significance.

The decentralized character of ecclesiastical law prior to the late eleventh century was closely related to the decentralized character of the political life of the church. As a rule, bishops were more under the authority of emperors, kings, and leading lords than of popes; and even in those spiritual matters in which secular authorities did not intervene, a bishop usually had a considerable autonomy within his own diocese. The universality of the church did not rest primarily on a political or legal unity but on a common spiritual heritage, common doctrine and worship, and a common liturgy. Such political and legal unity as it had was connected, above all, with the preservation of its spiritual universality. In this respect the Western Church was like the Eastern Church. Its law, being largely interwoven with theological doctrine and with the liturgy and the sacraments, was concerned only secondarily with organizational matters and the authority of bishops, and hardly at all with rules of property law, crime and tort, procedure, inheritance, and the like. In these secondary and tertiary concerns the law of the church was often wholly merged with secular law, and secular law was itself largely diffused in political, economic, and social custom.

In the wake of the Papal Revolution there emerged a new system of canon law and new secular legal systems, together with a class of professional lawyers and judges, hierarchies of courts, law schools, law treatises, and a concept of law as an autonomous, integrated, developing body of principles and procedures. The Western legal tradition was formed in the context of a total revolution, which was fought to establish "the right order of things," or "right order in the world." "Right order" signified a new division of society into separate ecclesiastical and secular authorities, the institutionalization of the ecclesiastical authority as a political and legal entity, and the belief in the responsibility of the ecclesiastical authority to transform secular society.

The dualism of ecclesiastical and secular legal systems led in turn to a pluralism of secular legal systems within the ecclesiastical legal order and, more specifically, to the concurrent jurisdiction of ecclesiastical and secular courts. Further, the systematization and rationalization of law were necessary in order to maintain the complex equilibrium of plural competing legal systems. Finally, the right order of things introduced by the Papal Revolution signified the kind of systematization and rationalization of law that would permit reconciliation of conflicting authorities on the basis of synthesizing principles: wherever possible, the contradictions were to be resolved without destruction of the elements they comprised.

To summarize, the new sense of law and the new types of law that emerged in western Europe in the wake of the Papal Revolution were needed as means: (1) to control by central authorities a widely dispersed population with diverse group loyalties; (2) to maintain the separate corporate identity of the clergy and add a new legal dimension to their class consciousness; (3) to regulate relations between competing ecclesiastical and secular polities; (4) to enable secular authorities to implement in a deliberate and programmatic way their proclaimed mission of imposing peace and justice within their respective jurisdictions; and (5) to enable the church to implement in a deliberate and programmatic way its proclaimed mission to reform the world.

The most important consequence of the Papal Revolution was that it introduced into Western history the experience of revolution itself. In contrast to the older view of secular history as a process of decay, there was introduced a dynamic quality, a sense of progress in time, a belief in the reformation of the world. No longer was it assumed that "temporal life" must inevitably deteriorate until the Last Judgment. On the contrary, it was now assumed—for the first time—that progress could be made in this world toward achieving some of the preconditions for salvation in the next.

Perhaps the most dramatic illustration of the new sense of time, and of the future, was provided by the new Gothic architecture. The great cathedrals expressed, in their soaring spires and flying buttresses and elongated vaulted arches, a dynamic spirit of movement upward, a sense of achieving, of incarnation of ultimate values. It is also noteworthy that they were often planned to be built over generations and centuries.

Less dramatic but even more significant as a symbol of the new belief in progress toward salvation were the great legal monuments that were built in the same period. In contrast not only to the earlier Western folklaw but also to Roman law both before and after Justinian, law in the West in the late eleventh and twelfth centuries, and thereafter, was conceived to be an organically developing system, an ongoing, growing body of principles and procedures, constructed—like the cathedrals—over generations and centuries.

Questions

1. What is the Papal Revolution?
2. Describe western law as it existed before the Papal Revolution.
3. Describe the relationship between church and state prior to the revolution.
4. What were Gregory's claims?
5. What were the Emperor's claims?
6. Who won?
7. What was the impact of the revolution on church-state relations?
8. What was the impact of the revolution on western law?

B. Thomas Aquinas on Natural Law

Introduction

Thomas Aquinas was born into the Italian nobility in 1225. At a very early age, he decided to dedicate his life to the service of God. At age six he left home to live in a Benedictine monastery run by a relative. Aquinas stayed in the monastery until he was thirteen, when he left for five years of study at the University of Naples. There he was very influenced by a group of Dominican monks called the Order of Preachers. These monks traveled around the countryside ministering to people and working among them.

Aquinas' family was very unhappy with Aquinas' decision to join the Order of Preachers and opposed him joining any order other than the Benedictine. At first they tried to persuade him. But when Aquinas was preparing to depart for a missionary trip with the Order of Preachers, his mother sent his brothers to capture him and hold him until he came to his senses. But Aquinas would not come to his senses. Instead, he spent his time praying and studying scripture. Finally his family realized the case was hopeless and released Aquinas.

Upon regaining his freedom, Aquinas traveled through France and Germany studying at various universities. Aquinas was reserved, shy by nature, and rather large. It was during this time that he acquired his nickname: "the dumb ox." Aquinas' brilliance wasn't recognized until one day when he accidentally spilled his papers. Another student helped

Aquinas collect the papers, read some of them, and was impressed by the depth of learning and scholarship. Students began to talk to him and were amazed. One of Aquinas' tutors exclaimed, "We called Brother Thomas an ox, but I tell you he will yet make his lowing heard to the uttermost parts of the earth."

This prediction has certainly come true. Aquinas is one of the most renowned and brilliant theologians and philosophers in history. In the course of a life of teaching and writing, his most influential work is the one from which the following excerpts are taken, *Summa Theologica*, a summary of Christian doctrine. More specifically, the excerpts are from the "*Treatise on Law*." This particular reading is from an edited version of the *Summa* entitled, *Summa of the Summa*, by Professor Peter Kreeft, a professor of philosophy at Boston College. The text is Aquinas'; the numbered footnotes are Kreeft's.

Aquinas came out of the tradition of thinking and scholarship that followed the Papal Revolution. He attended universities that sprang up after the revolution. His work marked the high point of the attempt that followed the revolution to systematize both theology and law. In many ways, Aquinas was part of the intellectual fruit of the revolution. His works had a tremendous impact throughout Europe, including England. They continue to have a tremendous impact today worldwide.

Peter Kreeft, *A Summa of the Summa: The Essential Philosophical Passages of St. Thomas Aquinas' Summa Theologica Edited and Explained for Beginners*[*]

QUESTION 90

OF THE ESSENCE OF LAW

First Article

Whether Law Is Something Pertaining to Reason?

I answer that, Law is a rule and measure of acts, whereby man is induced[248] to act or is restrained from acting: for lex (law) is derived from

[*] PETER KREEFT, A SUMMA OF THE SUMMA: THE ESSENTIAL PHILOSOPHICAL PASSAGES OF ST. THOMAS AQUINAS' SUMMA THEOLOGICA EDITED AND EXPLAINED FOR BEGINNERS 500-12, 514-19, 523-27 (1990). Reprinted with the permission of Ignatius Press.

[248] I.e., led, moved, commanded. This is something stronger than merely "advised" or "requested" but weaker than "forced" or "necessitated". Law binds morally but not physically. It obligates but it

ligare (to bind), because it binds one to act. Now the rule and measure of human acts is the reason, which is the first principle of human acts, as is evident from what has been stated above (Q. I, A. I ad 3); since it belongs to the reason to direct to the end, which is the first principle in all matters of action....

Second Article

Whether the Law Is Always Something Directed to the Common Good?

*I answer that,...*the first principle in practical matters, which are the object of the practical reason, is the last end: and the last end of human life is bliss or happiness,[⌑] as stated above (Q. 2, A. 7; Q. 3, A. I). Consequently the law must needs regard principally the relationship to happiness. Moreover, since every part is ordained to the whole, as imperfect to perfect; and since one man is a part of the perfect community, the law must needs regard properly the relationship to universal happiness. Wherefore the Philosopher, in the above definition of legal matters mentions both happiness and the body politic: for he says (Ethic. v. I) that we call those legal matters just, which are adapted to produce and preserve happiness and its parts for the body politic....

Third Article

Whether the Reason of Any Man Is Competent to Make Laws?

I answer that, A law, properly speaking, regards first and foremost the order to the common good. Now to order anything to the common good, belongs either to the whole people, or someone who is the viceregent[252] of the whole people. And therefore the making of a law belongs either to the whole people or to a public personage who has care of the whole people....

---

does not necessitate. It appeals to free will to obey or disobey. Free will follows upon reason—where reason is, free will is too—therefore law appeals to reason.

[⌑] Earlier in his treatise, Aquinas defines happiness as follows:

> Happiness is the attainment of the Perfect Good. Whoever, therefore, is capable of the Perfect Good can attain Happiness. Now, that man is capable of the Perfect Good, is proved both because his intellect can apprehend the universal and perfect good, and because his will can desire it. And therefore man can attain Happiness.—This can be proved again from the fact that man is capable of seeing God...in which vision...man's perfect Happiness consists....

[252] A "vice-regent" is a *representative*. St. Thomas holds that the good state, whether ruled by one, a few, or many, should contain at least an essential element of democracy; even a king reigns for the people's good, not for his own.

Fourth Article

Whether Promulgation Is Essential to a Law?

I answer that, As stated above (A. I), a law is imposed on others by way of a rule and measure. Now a rule or measure is imposed by being applied to those who are to be ruled and measured by it. Wherefore, in order that a law obtain the binding force which is proper to a law, it must needs be applied to the men who have to be ruled by it. Such application is made by its being notified to them by promulgation. Wherefore promulgation is necessary for the law to obtain its force.

Thus from the four preceding articles, the definition of law may be gathered; and it is nothing else than [1] an ordinance [2] of reason [3] for the common good, [4] made by him who has care of the community, [5] and promulgated.

QUESTION 91

OF THE VARIOUS KINDS OF LAW

First Article

Whether There Is an Eternal Law?

I answer that, As stated above (Q. 90, A. I *ad* 2; AA. 3, 4), a law is nothing else but a dictate of practical reason emanating from the ruler who governs a perfect [complete] community. Now it is evident, granted that the world is ruled by Divine Providence, as was stated in the First Part (Q. 22, AA. I, 2), that the whole community of the universe is governed by Divine Reason. Wherefore the very Idea of the government of things in God the Ruler of the universe, has the nature of a law. And since the Divine Reason's conception of things is not subject to time but is eternal, according to Proverbs 8:23, therefore it is that this kind of law must be called eternal....

Second Article

Whether There Is in Us a Natural Law?

On the contrary, A gloss on Romans 2:14: *When the Gentiles, who have not the [Mosaic] law, do by nature those things that are of the law*, comments as follows: *Although they have no written law, yet they have the natural law, whereby each one knows, and is conscious of, what is good and what is evil.*

I answer that, As stated above (Q. 90, A. I *ad* I), law, being a rule and measure, can be in a person in two ways: in one way, as in him that rules and measures; in another way, as in that which is ruled and measured, since a thing is ruled and measured, in so far as it partakes of the rule or measure. Wherefore, since all things subject to Divine providence are ruled and measured by the eternal law, as was stated above (A. I); it is evident that all things partake somewhat of the eternal law, in so far as, namely, from its being imprinted on them, they derive their respective inclinations to their proper acts and ends. Now among all others, the rational creature is subject to Divine providence in the most excellent way, in so far as it partakes of a share of providence, by being provident both for itself and for others. Wherefore it has a share of the Eternal Reason, whereby it has a natural inclination to its proper act and end: and this participation of the eternal law in the [very nature of the] rational creature is called the natural law. Hence the Psalmist after saying (Ps 4:6): *Offer up the sacrifice of justice*, as though someone asked what the works of justice are, adds: *Many say, Who showeth us good things?* in answer to which question he says: *The light of Thy countenance, O Lord, is signed upon us*: thus implying that the light of natural reason, whereby we discern what is good and what is evil, which is the function of the natural law, is nothing else than an imprint on us of the Divine light. It is therefore evident that the natural law is nothing else than the rational creature's participation of the eternal law.[254]...

Third Article

Whether There Is a Human Law?

I answer that, As stated above (Q. 90, A. I, *ad* 2), a law is a dictate of the practical reason. Now it is to be observed that the same procedure takes place in the practical and in the speculative reason: for each proceeds from principles to conclusions, as stated above (*ibid.*). Accordingly we conclude that just as, in the speculative reason, from naturally known indemonstrable principles, we draw the conclusions of the various sciences, the knowledge of which is not imparted to us by nature, but acquired by the efforts of reason, so too it is from the precepts of the natural law, as from general and indemonstrable principles,[255] that the human reason needs to proceed to the more particular determination of certain matters. These particular determinations, devised by human reason, are called human laws.

---

[254] Thus the voice of conscience (natural reason judging good and evil) is the echo of the voice of God, and is therefore sacred and inviolable.

[255] Self-evident theoretical axioms like the law of non-contradiction. There are also self-evident practical axioms, both general ("Do good, avoid evil") and specific ("Be just"). These are "the precepts of the natural law", which, since it is in our nature, is also naturally *known*, just as first theoretical principles are.

Fourth Article

Whether There Was Any Need for a Divine Law?[257]

I answer that, Besides the natural and the human law it was necessary for the directing of human conduct to have a Divine law. And this for four reasons. First, because...man is ordained to an end of eternal happiness....

Secondly...on account of the uncertainty of human judgment....[¤]

Thirdly, because...man is not competent to judge of interior movements, that are hidden....

Fourthly, because...human law cannot punish or forbid all evil deeds....

Fifth Article

Whether There Is But One Divine Law?

On the contrary, The Apostle says (Heb 7:12): *The priesthood being translated, it is necessary that a translation also be made of the law.* But the priesthood is twofold, as stated in the same passage, viz., the Leviti-

---

[257] The divine law is that part of the eternal law which God made known by special revelation.

[¤] Earlier in his treatise, Aquinas answers the question,

> *Whether besides philosophy, any further doctrine is required?*
>
> * * *
>
> It is written (2 Tim 3:16): *All Scripture inspired of God is profitable to teach, to reprove, to correct, to instruct in justice.* Now Scripture, inspired of God, is no part of philosophical science, which has been built up by human reason. Therefore it is useful that besides philosophical science there should be other knowledge—*i.e.*, inspired of God.
>
> *I answer that,* It was necessary for man's salvation that there should be a knowledge revealed by God, besides philosophical science built up by human reason.
>
> Firstly, indeed, because man is directed to God, as to an end that surpasses the grasp of his reason: *The eye hath not seen, O God, besides Thee, what things Thou hast prepared for them that wait for Thee* (Is 66:4). But the end must first be known by men who are to direct their thoughts and actions to the end. Hence it was necessary for the salvation of man that certain truths which exceed human reason should be made known to him by divine revelation.
>
> Even as regards those truths about God which human reason could have discovered, it was necessary that man should be taught by a divine revelation; because the truth about God such as reason could discover, would only be known by a few, and that after a long time, and with the admixture of many errors. Whereas man's whole salvation, which is in God, depends upon the knowledge of this truth. Therefore, in order that the salvation of men might be brought about more fitly and more surely, it was necessary that they should be taught divine truths by divine revelation. It was therefore necessary that, besides philosophical science built up by reason there should be a sacred science learned through revelation.

cal priesthood, and the priesthood of Christ. *Therefore* the Divine law is twofold, namely the Old Law [covenant, testament] and the New Law.

*I answer that,...*In the first place, it belongs to law to be directed to the common good as to its end, as stated above (Q. 90, A. 2). This good may be twofold. It may be a sensible and earthly good; and to this, man was directly ordained by the Old Law: wherefore, at the very outset of the law, the people were invited to the earthly kingdom of the Chananaeans (Ex 3:8, 17). Again it may be an intelligible and heavenly good: and to this, man is ordained by the New Law....

Secondly, it belongs to the law to direct human acts according to the order of righteousness (A. 4): wherein also the New Law surpasses the Old Law, since it directs our internal acts, according to Matthew 5:20: *Unless your justice abound more than that of the Scribes and Pharisees, you shall not enter into the kingdom of heaven.* Hence the saying that *the Old Law restrains the hand by the New Law controls the mind* (3 *Sent.*, D. xl).

Thirdly, it belongs to the law to induce men to observe its commandments. This the Old Law did by the fear of punishment: but the New Law, by love, which is poured into our hearts by the grace of Christ, bestowed in the New Law, but foreshadowed in the Old....

QUESTION 92

OF THE EFFECTS OF LAW

First Article

Whether an Effect of Law Is to Make Men Good?[260]

Objection 1. It seems that it is not an effect of law to make men good. For men are good through virtue, since virtue, as stated in *Ethic.* ii. 6 is *that which makes its subject good.* But virtue is in man from God alone, because He it is Who *works it in us without us*, as we stated above (Q. 55, A. 4) in giving the definition of virtue. Therefore the law does not make men good.

Objection 2. Further, Law does not profit a man unless he obeys it. But the very fact that a man obeys a law is due to his being good. There-

[260] The question, in contemporary terms, is: Can you legislate morality? St. Thomas answers, Of course! What else is worth legislating? Of course, law cannot *guarantee* moral behavior, since man's will is free to disobey; but it can certainly make a great difference, and make men better. St. Thomas would agree, I think, with Peter Maurin's simple definition of the good society: the good society is a society where it is easy to be good (because of its good laws). But he would also agree with St. Thomas More that "the times (or the society) are never so bad but that a good man can live in them."

fore in man goodness is presupposed to the law. Therefore the law does not make men good.

Objection 3. Further, Law is ordained to the common good, as stated above (Q. 90, A. 2). But some behave well in things regarding the community, who behave ill in things regarding themselves. Therefore it is not the business of the law to make men good.

Objection 4. Further, some laws are tyrannical, as the Philosopher says (*Polit*. iii. 6). But a tyrant does not intend the good of his subjects, but considers only his own profit. Therefore law does not make men good.

On the contrary, The Philosopher says (*Ethic*. ii. I) that the *intention of every lawgiver is to make good citizens....*

Reply Obj. 1. Virtue is twofold, as explained above (Q. 63, A. 2), viz., acquired and infused. Now the fact of being accustomed to an action contributes to both, but in different ways; for it causes the acquired virtue; while it disposes to infused virtue, and preserves and fosters it when it already exists. And since law is given for the purpose of directing human acts; as far as human acts conduce to virtue, so far does law make men good. Wherefore the Philosopher says in the second book of the *Politics* (*Ethic*. ii) that *lawgivers make men good by habituating them to good works.*

Reply Obj. 2. It is not always through perfect goodness of virtue that one obeys the law, but sometimes it is through fear of punishment.

Reply Obj. 3. The goodness of any part is considered in comparison with the whole; hence Augustine says (Conf. iii) that *unseemly is the part that harmonizes not with the whole*. Since then every man is a part of the state, it is impossible that a man be good, unless he be well proportionate to the common good: nor can the whole be well consistent unless its parts be proportionate to it. Consequently the common good of the state cannot flourish, unless the citizens be virtuous, at least those whose business it is to govern. But it is enough for the good of the community, that the other citizens be so far virtuous that they obey the commands of their rulers....

Reply Obj. 4. A tyrannical law, through not being according to reason, is not a law, absolutely speaking, but rather a perversion of law....

Second Article

Whether the Acts of Law Are Suitably Assigned?

Objection 4. Further, the intention of a lawgiver is to make men good, as stated above (A. I). But he that obeys the law, merely through fear of being punished, is not good: because *although a good deed may be done through servile fear, i.e., fear of punishment, it is not done well,* as Augustine says (*Contra duas Epist. Pelag.* ii). Therefore punishment is not a proper effect of law.

On the contrary, Isidore says (*Etym.* v. 19): *Every law either permits something, as: "A brave man may demand his reward"*: or forbids something, as: "*No man may ask a consecrated virgin in marriage*": or punishes, as: "*Let him that commits a murder be put to death.*"

Reply Obj. 4. From becoming accustomed to avoid evil and fulfil what is good, through fear of punishment, one is sometimes led on to do so likewise, with delight and of one's own accord. Accordingly, law, even by punishing, leads men on to being good.

QUESTION 93

OF THE ETERNAL LAW

We must now consider each law by itself; and (1) The eternal law; (2) The natural law; (3) The human law; (4) The old law; (5) The new law, which is the law of the Gospel....

Second Article

Whether the Eternal Law Is Known to All?

Objection 1. It would seem that the eternal law is not known to all. Because, as the Apostle says (I Cor 2:11), *the things that are of God no man knoweth, but the Spirit of God.* But the eternal law is a type [ideal, model, plan] existing in the Divine mind. Therefore it is unknown to all save God alone....

On the contrary, Augustine says (*De Lib. Arb.* i. 6) that *knowledge of the eternal law is imprinted on us.*

I answer that, A thing may be known in two ways: first, in itself; secondly, in its effect, wherein some likeness of that thing is found: thus someone not seeing the sun in its substance, may know it by its rays. So then no one can know the eternal law, as it is in itself, except the blessed who see God in His Essence. But every rational creature knows it in its reflection, greater or less. For every knowledge of truth is a kind of reflection and participation of the eternal law, which is the unchangeable truth, as Augustine says (*De Vera Relig.* xxxi). Now all men know the truth to a certain extent, at least as to the common principles of the natural law: and as to the others, they partake of the knowledge of truth, some more, some less; and in this respect are more or less cognizant of the eternal law.

Reply Obj. 1. We cannot know the things that are of God, as they are in themselves; but they are made known to us in their effects, according to Romans 1:20: *The invisible things of God...are clearly seen, being understood by the things that are made....*

Third Article

Whether Every Law Is Derived from the Eternal Law?

Objection 2. Further, nothing unjust can be derived from the eternal law, because, as stated above (A. 2, Obj. 2), the eternal law is that, according to which it is right that all things should be most orderly. But some laws are unjust, according to Isaiah 10:1: *Woe to them that make wicked laws.* Therefore not every law is derived from the eternal law.

Objection 3. Further, Augustine says (*De Lib. Arb.* i. 5) that *the law which is framed for ruling the people, rightly permits many things which are punished by Divine providence.* But the type of Divine providence is the eternal law, as stated above (A. I). Therefore not even every good law is derived from the eternal law....

*I answer that,...*Since the eternal law is the plan of government in the Chief Governor, all the plans of government in the inferior governors must be derived from the eternal law. But these plans of inferior governors are all other laws besides the eternal law. Therefore all laws, in so far as they partake of right reason, are derived from the eternal law. Hence Augustine says (*De Lib. Arb.* i. 6) that *in temporal law there is nothing just and lawful, but what man has drawn from the eternal law....*

Reply Obj. 2. Human law has the nature of law in so far as it partakes of right reason; and it is clear that, in this respect, it is derived from the eternal law. But in so far as it deviates from reason, it is called an unjust law, and has the nature, not of law but of violence. Nevertheless even an unjust law, in so far as it retains some appearance of law, though being framed by one who is in power, is derived from the eternal law; since all power is from the Lord God, according to Romans 13:1.

Reply Obj. 3. Human law is said to permit certain things, not as approving of them, but as being unable to direct them. And many things are directed by the Divine law, which human law is unable to direct, because more things are subject to a higher than to a lower cause. Hence the very fact that human law does not meddle with matters it cannot direct, comes under the ordination of the eternal law. It would be different, were human law to sanction what the eternal law condemns. Consequently it does not follow that human law is not derived from the eternal law, but that it is not on a perfect equality with it....

QUESTION 94

OF THE NATURAL LAW

Second Article

Whether the Natural Law Contains Several Precepts, or One Only.

On the contrary, The precepts of the natural law in man stand in relation to practical matters, as the first principles to matters of demonstration. But there are several first indemonstrable principles. Therefore there are also several precepts of the natural law.

I answer that, As stated above (Q. 91, A. 3), the precepts of the natural law are to the practical reason, what the first principles of demonstrations are to the speculative reason; because both are self-evident principles. Now a thing is said to be self-evident in two ways: first, in itself; secondly, in relation to us. Any proposition is said to be self-evident in itself, if its predicate is contained in the notion of the subject: although, to one who knows not the definition of the subject, it happens that such a proposition is not self-evident. For instance, this proposition, *Man is a rational being*, is, in its very nature, self-evident, since who says *man*, says *a rational being*: and yet to one who knows not what a man is, this proposition is not self-evident. Hence it is that, as Boethius says (*De Hebdom.*), certain axioms or propositions are universally self-evident to all; and such are those propositions whose terms are known to all, as, *Every whole is greater than its part*, and, *Things equal to one and the same are equal to one another*. But some propositions are self-evident only to the wise, who understand the meaning of the terms of such propositions: thus to one who understands that an angel is not a body, it is self-evident that an angel is not circumscriptively in a place: but this is not evident to the unlearned, for they cannot grasp it.

Now a certain order is to be found in those things that are apprehended universally. For that which, before aught else, falls under apprehension, is *being*, the notion of which is included in all things whatsoever a man apprehends. Wherefore the first indemonstrable principle is that *the same thing cannot be affirmed and denied at the same time*, which is based on the notion of being and not-being: and on this principle all others are based, as is stated in *Metaph.* iv, text. 9. Now as *being* is the first thing that falls under the apprehension simply, so *good* is the first thing that falls under the apprehension of the practical reason, which is directed to action: since every agent acts for an end under the aspect of good. Consequently the first principle in the practical reason is one founded on the notion of good, viz., that *good is that which all things seek after*. Hence this is the first precept of law, that *good is to be done and pursued, and evil is to be avoided.* All other precepts of the natural law are based upon this: so that whatever the practical reason naturally apprehends as man's good (or evil) belongs to the precepts of the natural law as something to be done or avoided.

Since, however, good has the nature of an end, and evil, the nature of a contrary, hence it is that all those things to which man has a natural inclination, are naturally apprehended by reason as being good, and consequently as objects of pursuit, and their contraries as evil, and objects of avoidance. Wherefore according to the order of natural inclinations, is the order of the precepts of the natural law. Because in man there is first of all an inclination to good in accordance with the nature which he has in common with all substances: inasmuch as every substance seeks the preservation of its own being, according to its nature: and by reason of this inclination, whatever is a means of preserving human life, and of warding off its obstacles, belongs to the natural law. Secondly, there is in man an inclination to things that pertain to him more specially, according to that nature which he has in common with other animals: and in virtue of this inclination, those things are said to belong to the natural law, *which nature has taught to all animals* [*Pandect. Just.* I., tit. i], such as sexual intercourse, education of offspring and so forth. Thirdly, there is in man an inclination to good, according to the nature of his reason, which nature is proper to him: thus man has a natural inclination to know the truth about God, and to live in society: and in this respect, whatever pertains to this inclination belongs to the natural law; for instance, to shun ignorance, to avoid offending those among whom one has to live, and other such things regarding the above inclination.

Third Article

Whether All Acts of Virtue Are Prescribed by the Natural Law?

* * *

I answer that,...If...we speak of acts of virtue, considered as virtuous, thus all virtuous acts belong to the natural law. For it has been stated (A. 2) that to the natural law belongs everything to which a man is inclined according to his nature. Now each thing is inclined naturally to an operation that is suitable to it according to its form: thus fire is inclined to give heat. Wherefore, since the rational soul is the proper form of man, there is in every man a natural inclination to act according to reason: and this is to act according to virtue. Consequently, considered thus, all acts of virtue are prescribed by the natural law: since each one's reason naturally dictates to him to act virtuously....

* * *

Fourth Article

Whether the Natural Law Is the Same in All Men?

On the contrary, Isidore says (*Etym.* v. 4): *The natural law is common to all nations.*

I answer that, As stated above (AA. 2, 3), to the natural law belongs those things to which a man is inclined naturally: and among these it is proper to man to be inclined to act according to reason. Now the process of reason is from the common to the proper, as stated in *Phys.* i. The speculative reason, however, is differently stated in this matter, from the practical reason. For, since the speculative reason is busied chiefly with necessary things, which cannot be otherwise than they are, its proper conclusions, like the universal principles, contain the truth without fail. The practical reason, on the other hand, is busied with contingent matters, about which human actions are concerned: and consequently, although there is necessity in the general principles, the more we descent to matters of detail, the more frequently we encounter defects. Accordingly then in speculative matters truth is the same in all men, both as to principles and as to conclusions, but only as regards the principles which are called common notions. But in matters of action, truth or practical rectitude is not the same for all, as to matters of detail, but only as to the general principles: and where there is the same rectitude in matters of detail, it is not equally known to all.

It is therefore evident that, as regards the general principles whether of speculative or of practical reason, truth or rectitude is the same for all, and is equally known by all. As to the proper conclusions of the speculative reason, the truth is the same for all, but is not equally known to all: thus it is true for all that the three angles of a triangle are together equal to two right angles, although it is not known to all. But as to the proper conclusions of the practical reason, neither is the truth or rectitude the same for all, nor, where it is the same, is it equally known by all. Thus it is right and true for all to act according to reason: and from this principle it follows as a proper conclusion, that goods entrusted to another should be restored to their owner. Now this is true for the majority of cases: but it may happen in a particular case that it would be injurious, and therefore unreasonable, to restore goods held in trust; for instance if they were claimed for the purpose of fighting against one's country. And this principle will be found to fail the more, according as we descend further into detail, e.g., if one were to say that goods held in trust should be restored with such and such a guarantee, or in such and such a way; because the greater the number of conditions added, the greater the number of ways in which the principle may fail, so that it be not right to restore or not to restore.

Consequently we must say that the natural law, as to general principles, is the same for all, both as to rectitude and as to knowledge. But as to certain matters of detail, which are conclusions, as it were, of those general principles, it is the same for all in the majority of cases, both as to rectitude and as to knowledge; and yet in some few cases it may fail, both as to rectitude, by reason of certain obstacles (just as natures subject to generation and corruption fail in some few cases on account of some obstacle), and as to knowledge [cf. n. 272], since in some the reason is perverted by passion, or evil habit, or an evil disposition of nature; thus formerly, theft, although it is expressly contrary to the natural law, was not considered wrong among the Germans, as Julius Caesar relates (*De Bello Gall.* vi)....

* * *

QUESTION 95

Second Article

Whether Every Human Law Is Derived from the Natural Law?

Objection 3. Further, the law of nature is the same for all; since the Philosopher says (*Ethic* v. 7) that *the natural just is that which is equally valid everywhere.* If therefore human laws were derived from the natural law, it would follow that they too are the same for all: which is clearly false....

I answer that, As Augustine says (*De Lib. Arb.* i. 5), *that which is not just seems to be no law at all*: wherefore the force of a law depends on the extent of its justice. Now in human affairs a thing is said to be just, from being right, according to the rule of reason. But the first rule of reason is the law of nature, as is clear from what has been stated above (Q. 91, A. 2 *ad* 2). Consequently every human law has just so much of the nature of law, as it is derived from the law of nature. But if in any point it deflects from the law of nature, it is no longer a law but a perversion of law.

But it must be noted that something may be derived from the natural law in two ways: first, as a conclusion from premises, secondly, by way of determination of certain generalities. The first way is like to that by which, in sciences, demonstrated conclusions are drawn from the principles: while the second mode is likened to that whereby, in the arts, general forms are particularized as to details. Thus the craftsman needs to determine the general form of a house to some particular shape. Some things are therefore derived from the general principles of the natural law, by way of conclusions; *e.g.*, that *one must not kill* may be derived as a conclusion from the principle that *one should do harm to no man*:

while some are derived therefrom by way of determination; *e.g.*, the law of nature has it that the evil-doer should be punished; but that he be punished in this or that way, is a determination of the law of nature.

Accordingly both modes of derivation are found in the human law. But those things which are derived in the first way, are contained in human law not as emanating therefrom exclusively, but have some force from the natural law also. But those things which are derived in the second way, have no other force than that of human law....

Reply Obj. 3. The general principles of the natural law cannot be applied to all men in the same way on account of the great variety of human affairs: and hence arises the diversity of positive laws among various people....

QUESTION 96

OF THE POWER OF HUMAN LAW

* * *

Second Article

Whether It Belongs to the Human Law to Repress All Vices?

I answer that,...the same thing is not possible to one who has not a virtuous habit, as is possible to one who has. Thus the same is not possible to a child as to a full-grown man: for which reason the law for children is not the same as for adults, since many things are permitted to children, which in an adult are punished by law or at any rate are open to blame. In like manner many things are permissible to men not perfect in virtue, which would be intolerable in a virtuous man.

Now human law is framed for a number of human beings, the majority of whom are not perfect in virtue. Wherefore human laws do not forbid all vices, from which the virtuous abstain, but only the more grievous vices, from which it is possible for the majority to abstain; and chiefly those that are to the hurt of others, without the prohibition of which human society could not be maintained: thus human law prohibits murder, theft and suchlike.

Third Article

Whether Human Law Prescribes Acts of All the Virtues?

Objection 1. It would seem that human law does not prescribe acts of all the virtues. For vicious acts are contrary to acts of virtue. But human law does not prohibit all vices, as stated above (A. 2). Therefore neither does it prescribe all acts of virtue.

Objection 2. Further, a virtuous act proceeds from a virtue. But virtue is the end of law; so that whatever is from a virtue, cannot come under a precept of law. Therefore human law does not prescribe all acts of virtue.

Objection 3. Further, law is ordained to the common good, as stated above (Q. 90, A. 2). But some acts of virtue are ordained, not to the common good, but to private good. Therefore the law does not prescribe all acts of virtue.

On the contrary, The Philosopher says (*Ethic.* v. I) that the law *prescribes the performance of the acts of a brave man...and the acts of the temperate man...and the acts of the meek man: and in like manner as regards the other virtues and vices, prescribing the former, forbidding the latter.*

I answer that, The species of virtues are distinguished by their objects, as explained above (Q. 54, A. 2; Q. 60, A. I; Q. 62, A. 2). Now all the objects of virtues can be referred either to the private good of an individual, or to the common good of the multitude: thus matters of fortitude may be achieved either for the safety of the state, or for upholding the rights of a friend, and in like manner with the other virtues. But law, as stated above (Q. 90, A. 2), is ordained to the common good. Wherefore there is no virtue whose acts cannot be prescribed by the law. Nevertheless human law does not prescribe concerning all the acts of every virtue: but only in regard to those that are ordainable to the common good,—either immediately, as when certain things are done directly for the common good,—or mediately, as when a lawgiver prescribes certain things pertaining to good order, whereby the citizens are directed in the upholding of the common good of justice and peace.

Reply Obj. 1. Human law does not forbid all vicious acts, by the obligation of a precept, as neither does it prescribe all acts of virtue. But it forbids certain acts of each vice, just as it prescribes some acts of each virtue.

Reply Obj. 2. An act is said to be an act of virtue in two ways. First, from the fact that a man does something virtuous; thus the act of justice is to do what is right, and an act of fortitude is to do brave things: and in this way law prescribes certain acts of virtue.—Secondly an act of virtue is when a man does a virtuous thing in a way in which a virtuous man does it. Such an act always proceeds from virtue: and it does not come under a precept of law, but is the end at which every lawgiver aims.

Reply Obj. 3. There is no virtue whose act is not ordainable to the common good, as stated above, either mediately or immediately.

Questions

1. According to Aquinas, what is law?

2. What does Aquinas mean by reason? How does reason relate to law?

3. What is the purpose of law?

4. What four types of law does Aquinas identify? How does he define each?

5. Read Proverbs 2:1-9; 8:1-31; Romans 11:33-36. How do these passages on wisdom relate to the eternal law?

6. Can we know the eternal law?

7. Read Romans 1:18-20; 2:12-16; Proverbs 19:1-6. What do these passages teach about the existence of a natural law?

8. Are both natural law and divine law necessary?

9. According to Aquinas, what is the status of a human law that contradicts the natural law?

10. How would Aquinas assess the validity of the following laws:

    a. A state statute prohibiting coveting;

    b. A state statute prohibiting theft;

    c. A state statute prohibiting adultery;

    d. A city water conservation ordinance prohibiting the use of city water for watering lawns and washing cars;

    e. A federal constitutional amendment prohibiting parents from providing religious instruction to their children;

    f. A federal law funding the cloning of human beings for research purposes;

    g. A federal constitutional amendment (enacted to save Social Security and Medicare) providing the following:

    Medical providers may no longer provide medical treatment for a "serious illness" to anyone over seventy-five years of age. [A "serious illness" is defined as an illness or condition that would require medical procedures and treatments costing in excess of a certain dollar amount to cure or treat]. A patient denied treatment under this provision may either suffer with the illness untreated, may be assisted in committing suicide by a medical provider, or may be involuntarily euthanized at the request of two or more members of the patient's immediate family.

11. Aquinas argues that human laws should neither proscribe all vices nor prescribe all virtues. Why? Consider Matthew 19:3-9.

12. Do you agree that human laws should neither proscribe all vices nor prescribe all virtues? If so, should the following laws be enacted as human law?

    a. A law prohibiting coveting;

    b. A law prohibiting theft;

    c. A law prohibiting adultery;

    d. A law prohibiting same-sex marriage;

    e. A law requiring citizens to contribute 100 hours annually to serving the poor;

    f. A law prohibiting restaurants from serving food containing trans fat;

    g. A law prohibiting gambling;

    h. A law prohibiting the creation of human-animal hybrids for research purposes (in genetic research fertilizing animal eggs with human sperm and vice versa).

13. How does our fallen nature affect our ability to interpret and apply the natural law? Consider the following passages: Romans 1:18-32; Romans 3:9-18; Ephesians 2:1-10; I Corinthians 2:6-16; and John 16:7, 13-15.

C. Higher Law Thinking Displayed by the Common Law's Leading Commentators

1. Henrici de Bracton on Higher Law

Introduction

Together, the next three excerpts illustrate a very significant point. The common law at each stage of its development from the 1200s to the 1700s reflected a worldview that believed in and looked to a higher law as the basis for the common law. The excerpts are from three of the men who had the strongest influence on the development and systematization of the common law: Henrici de Bracton, Sir Edward Coke, and Sir William Blackstone.

Henrici de Bracton lived in England in the thirteenth century, dying in 1268. He was a learned man and, like many intellects of his day, held church office. He was well-versed in canon law, Roman law, and the common law. Bracton was also a judge. He was a Judge in Eyre (a representative of the king who rode from county to county holding court sessions) as well as a justice of the King's Bench (one of the three great common law courts along with Common Pleas and Exchequer).

Bracton is most remembered and revered for his treatise on the Common Law published in the 1250s—"the flower and crown of English Jurisprudence." The work, entitled *De Legibus et Consuetudinibus Angliae* (*The Laws and Customs of England*), was written during a crucial time at the very beginning of the systemization of the common law. Bracton more than anyone else gave the common law its form and structure. This work influenced the development of the common law for centuries to come.

In the following excerpt, Bracton describes the early common law view of the nature of law and justice.

Henrici de Bracton, *De Legibus et Consuetudinibus Angliae (The Laws and Customs of England)**

Chapter III

We must see now what is law; and it is to be known that law is the common precept of prudent men in council, the coercion of offenses, which are committed either voluntarily or through ignorance, and the common warrant of the body politic. Also God is the author of justice, for justice is in the Creator, and accordingly right and law have the same signification, and although in the widest sense of the term, everything which may be read is law, nevertheless, in the special sense, it signifies a rightful warrant, enjoining what is honest, forbidding the contrary.

Custom, also, is sometimes observed for law in parts, where it has been approved by habitual usage, and it fills the place of law, for the authority of long usage and custom is not slight.

Chapter IV

Since all rights arise out of justice, as out of a fountain, and what justice wills, right promotes the same; let us see, then, what is justice, and whence it is so termed; likewise, what is right, and whence it is so termed, and what are its precepts; likewise, what is law, and what is custom, without which a person cannot be just, so as to execute justice and a just judgment between man and man.

Justice, then, is a constant and perpetual will to award to each his right, the definition of which may be understood in two manners; in one manner as it is in the Creator, in another as it is the creature. And if it be understood as it is in the Creator, that is in God, all things are plain, since justice is the disposal of God, which orders rightly and disposes rightfully in all things.

For God himself awards to each according to his works. He himself is not variable, nor temporary in his disposition and will. His will is rather constant and perpetual, for he himself had no beginning, nor has, nor will have any end. It is understood in another manner according as it is in the creature, that is, in a just man. For a just man has the will of awarding to each his right, and so his will is termed justice, and it is said

* HENRICI DE BRACTON, DE LEGIBUS ET CONSUETUDINIBUS ANGLIAE (THE LAWS AND CUSTOMS OF ENGLAND) 13, 15, 17 (1990).

to be the will to award to each his right, not as regards the result, but as regards the intention; as an emperor is called August, not that he always augments his empire, but that he designs to augment it. As it is said of matrimony, that it is an inseparable union, for the parties are of a mind never to be separated, they are, however, separated afterwards when cause arises. Likewise, justice is termed constant, according to the definition, when justice is in the creature, that by the word "will" intention may be understood, and by the word "constant" good may be understood. For constancy is always taken in a good sense. Whence also the saints are termed constant, when it is said, "Oh! the constancy of the martyrs." Likewise, "Be ye constant," for constancy does not admit of variableness. By the phrase "perpetual" also is meant a habit, for justice is a good habit of mind, or the habit of a mind well constituted; or justice is a voluntary good, for it cannot be called good properly, unless the will intervenes, for take away the will, and every act will be indifferent; your agency, however, imposes a name upon your work. So a crime is not committed, unless the will to do harm intervenes. So the will and the purpose distinguish bad acts. But as regards the words "his right," the merit of a man is thereby intended, for a person is deprived of his right by means of an offense, or a breach of contract, or the like; but as regards the words "to each" that is, to himself, that he may live honestly; likewise to God, that he may love God; likewise to his neighbor, that he may not harm him; but as regards the words "his right," that is, of justice, and right is thus called justice, because all right is included in justice.

Questions

1. What is law in its "special sense?"

2. What is justice?

3. How does justice relate to: a) law; b) right?

4. How does God's justice differ from a just man's justice?

5. Can you think of anyone (historical or alive today) who meets Bracton's standard of a "just man?"

6. Read Psalm 9:7-8; Jeremiah 9:23-24; Job 34:17-19; and II Chronicles 19:5-7. How do these passages relate to Bracton's description of God's justice?

2. Sir Edward Coke on Higher Law

Introduction

Calvin's Case is a 1610 decision of the Court of Common Pleas, one of the common law courts. It was written by the Chief Justice of the Court of Common Pleas, Sir Edward Coke. The decision reveals that it was not only during medieval times that the common law looked to higher law principles. The same higher law thinking that motivated Bracton's work in the thirteenth century was still at the heart of the common law over 300 years later.

The case involved a claim by Calvin that Richard and Nicholas Smith had wrongly disseised (dispossessed) him from land that he had a right to occupy. One of their defenses was that Calvin, who was born in Scotland, was an alien and unable to bring an action regarding real property within England. An issue underlying this defense was whether Calvin owed *ligeance* (true and faithful obedience of a subject due his sovereign) to the King of England. Coke turned to higher law—what he calls the "law of nature"—to find that Calvin did owe *ligeance* and to reject the defense. Coke's discussion of the law of nature is contained in the following excerpt.

Sir Edward Coke was born in 1552. He attended Cambridge University (Trinity College) and then embarked on an extremely distinguished career in law and politics. In 1592 he became Solicitor General. In 1593 he became Speaker of the House of Commons. In 1594 he assumed the post of Attorney General. In 1606 he took the bench as Chief Justice of the Court of Common Pleas. In 1613 he was elevated to the position of Chief Justice of the King's Bench (another important common law court). King James I eventually viewed Coke as a political enemy and dismissed Coke from office in 1616. Coke spent several terms in Parliament in the remaining years before his death in 1634. In 1628, Coke was also one of the drafters of the Petition of Right, one of the most influential documents in English legal history.

Coke is significant in the development of the common law for several things. First, he preserved the continuity of the common law in the transition from medieval to modern times.

Second, he was devoted to the supremacy of the common law. During his time on the bench of the common law courts, Coke was a tireless supporter of the concept that the common law was supreme and that all men, including the King, were subject to it. He also championed the common law's supremacy over Chancery, the royal court that attempted to supplement the common law with equitable principles.

Finally, Coke is known for his reports of common law court decisions. His *Reports*, while no match for those of West Publishing Company, are outstanding records of common law decisions. Coke included in the report of a case a summary of all authority relating to the case from medieval times to his own day.

Calvin's Case[*]

* * *

Now followeth the Second Part, De Legibus, wherein these parts were considered: first that the ligeance or faith of the subject is due unto the King by the law of nature: secondly, that the law of nature is part of the law of England: thirdly, that the law of nature was before any judicial or municipal law: fourthly, that the law of nature is immutable.

The law of nature is that which God at the time of creation of the nature of man infused into his heart, for his preservation and direction; and this is *lex æterna*, the moral law, called also the law of nature. And by this law, written with the finger of God in the heart of man, were the people of God a long time governed, before the law was written by Moses, who was the first reporter or writer of law in the world. The Apostle in the second chapter to the Romans saith, *Cum enim gentes quæ legem non habent naturaliter ea quæ legissqunt faciunt* [When the Gentiles who have no law, do by nature what the law prescribes, those having no law are a law unto themselves]. And this is within the command of that moral law, *honora patrem* [honor your father], which doubtless doth extend to him that is *pater patriæ* [the father of Fatherland]. And that Apostle saith *Omnis anima potestatibus sublimioribus subdita sit* [Every soul should be subject to the higher authorities]. And these be the words of the Great Divine, *Hoc Deus in Sacris Scripturis jubet, hoc lex naturæ dictari, ut quilibet subditus obediat superior* [This God has ordered in the Sacred Scriptures, this the law of nature asserts repeatedly, such that anyone subjected obey the greater], and Aristotle, nature's secretary, lib. 5. Æthic. saith, that *jus naturale est, quod apud omnes homines eandem habet potentiam* [it is natural law that has the same authority for all men]. And herewith doth agree Bracton, lib. 1. cap. 5. and Fortescue, cap. 8. 12. 13. and 16. Doctor and Student, cap. 2. and 4. And the reason hereof is, for that God and nature is one to all, and therefore the law of God and nature is one to all. By this law of nature is the faith, ligeance, and obedience of the subject due to his Sovereign or superior.

[*] Calvin's Case, 7 Coke's Reports 1 (1610).

And Aristotle 1. Politicorum proveth, that to command and to obey is of nature, and that magistracy is of nature: for whatsoever is necessary and profitable for the preservation of the society of man is due by the law of nature: but magistracy and government are necessary and profitable for the preservation of the society of man; therefore magistracy and government are of nature. And herewith accordeth Tully, lib. 3. *De legibus, sine imperio nec domus ulla, nec civitas, nec gens, nec hominum universum genus stare, nec ipse denique mundus potest* [When it comes to laws, the whole of mankind is able to stand without command nor any home, nor city, nor nation, nor, in the end, the world itself]. This law of nature which indeed is the eternal law of the Creator, infused into the heart of the creature at the time of his creation, was two thousand years before any laws written, and before any judicial or municipal laws. And certain it is, that before judicial or municipal laws were made, Kings did decide causes according to natural equity, and were not tied to any rule or formality of law, but did *dare jura* [to give laws].

* * *

Now it appeareth by demonstrative reason, that ligeance, faith, and obedience of the subject to the Sovereign, was before any municipal or judicial laws. 1. For that government and subjection were long before any municipal or judicial laws. 2. For that it had been in vain to have prescribed laws to any but to such as owed obedience, faith, and ligeance before, in respect whereof they were bound to obey and observe them: *Frustra enim feruntur leges nisi subditis et obedientibus* [Indeed the laws are considered in vain unless you submit and obey them]. Seeing then that faith, obedience, and ligeance are due by the law of nature, it followeth that the same cannot be changed or taken away; for albeit judicial or municipal laws have inflicted and imposed in several places, or at several times, divers and several punishments and penalties, for breach or not observance of the law of nature, (for that law only consisted in commanding or prohibiting, without any certain punishment or penalty); yet the very law of nature itself never was nor could be altered or changed. And therefore it is certainly true, that *jura naturalia sunt immutabilia* [the natural laws are unchangeable].

Questions

1. How does Coke describe the law of nature?

2. Why did Coke believe the law of nature still applied to Englishmen in the 1600s?

3. Can human law change the law of nature?

3. William Blackstone on Higher Law

Introduction

William Blackstone was born in 1723. Both of his parents died by the time he was twelve, so he was raised by an uncle. As a boy, Blackstone was shy and studious. He attended Oxford (Pembroke College) where he studied and wrote on Shakespeare and architecture.

At age eighteen Blackstone changed his career plans and decided to study law. He graduated in 1745 with a bachelor's degree in Civil Law from Oxford. Civil law was a system based on Roman law that dominated on the continent. Even though England used the common law, civil law was the only system of law taught in English universities.

Blackstone practiced law for a while, but had little success. He apparently had a hard time attracting clients. Following the adage that "those who can't do, teach," he sought a professorship. Blackstone applied to, but was turned down by, Oxford. Although he was not on the Oxford faculty, Blackstone decided to give a series of lectures anyway. The lectures were on the common law and were popular and well-attended. Their success led to his appointment to an endowed chair at Oxford.

From 1765 to 1769, Blackstone decided to put these lectures in written form and produced them as a four-volume work entitled *Commentaries on the Laws of England.* This work was the most significant statement of the common law since Bracton's over 500 years earlier. Although the *Commentaries* were popular in England, they were most influential in the United States. They were the chief source of the knowledge of English common law in America's first century. Americans who studied the law prior to the Civil War learned it from Blackstone. He was foundational to America's legal development.

Blackstone's genius was not his original thought. He was not like Aquinas or Bracton in devising a new system. Instead, he was brilliant in categorizing and explaining the law as it already existed. He had a gift for taking very complex topics and making them accessible. His four-volume work is a brilliant summary and defense of the common law.

The following excerpt comes from Volume 1 of the *Commentaries.* In it, Blackstone discusses the nature and ultimate source of law.

William Blackstone, *Commentaries on the Laws of England, Vol I*[*]

Of The Nature Of Laws in General.

Law, in it's most general and comprehensive sense, signifies a rule of action; and is applied indiscriminately to all kinds of action, animate, or inanimate, rational or irrational. Thus we say, the laws of motion, of gravitation, of optics, or mechanics, as well as the laws of nature and of nations. And it is that rule of action, which is prescribed by some superior, and which the inferior is bound to obey.

Thus when the supreme being formed the universe, and created matter out of nothing, he impressed certain principles upon that matter, from which it can never depart, and without which it would cease to be. When he put that matter into motion, he established certain laws of motion, to which all moveable bodies must conform. And, to descend from the greatest operations to the smallest, when a workman forms a clock, or other piece of mechanism, he establishes at his own pleasure certain arbitrary laws for it's direction; as that the hand shall describe a given space in a given time; to which law as long as the work conforms, so long it continues in perfection, and answers the end of it's formation.

If we farther advance, from mere inactive matter to vegetable and animal life, we shall find them still governed by laws; more numerous indeed, but equally fixed and invariable. The whole progress of plants, from the seed to the root, and from thence to the seed again;—the method of animal nutrition, digestion, secretion, other branches of vital economy;—are not left to chance, or the will of the creature itself, but are performed in a wondrous involuntary manner, and guided by unerring rules laid down by the great creator.

This then is the general signification of law, a rule of action dictated by some superior being; and in those creatures that have neither the power to think, nor to will, such laws must be invariably obeyed, so long as the creature itself subsists, for it's existence depends on that obedience. But laws, in their more confined sense, and in which it is our present business to consider them, denote the rules, not of action in general, but of human action or conduct: that is, the precepts by which man, the noblest of all sublunary beings, a creature endowed with both reason and

[*] WILLIAM BLACKSTONE, COMMENTARIES ON THE LAWS OF ENGLAND, VOL I 38-46 (Univ. of Chicago Press 1979) (1765).

freewill, is commanded to make use of those faculties in the general regulation of his behaviour.

Man, considered as a creature, must necessarily be subject to the laws of his creator, for he is entirely a dependent being. A being, independent of any other, has no rule to pursue, but such as he prescribes to himself; but a state of dependence will inevitably oblige the inferior to take the will of him, on whom life depends, as the rule of his conduct: not indeed in every particular, but in all those points wherein his dependence consists. This principle therefore has more or less extent and effect, in proportion as the superiority of the one and the dependence of the other is greater or less, absolute or limited. And consequently as man depends absolutely upon his maker for everything, it is necessary that he should in all points conform to his maker's will.

This will of his maker is called the law of nature. For as God, when he created matter, and endued it with a principle of mobility, established certain rules for the perpetual direction of that motion; so, when he created man, and endued him with freewill to conduct himself in all parts of life, he laid down certain immutable laws of human nature, whereby that freewill is in some degree regulated and restrained, and gave him also the faculty of reason to discover the purport of those laws.

Considering the creator only as a being of infinite power, he was able unquestionably to have prescribed whatever laws he pleased to his creature, man, however unjust or severe. But as he is also a being of infinite wisdom, he has laid down only such laws as were founded in those relations of justice, that existed in the nature of things antecedent to any positive precept. These are the eternal, immutable laws of good and evil, to which the creator himself in all his dispensations conforms; and which he has enabled human reason to discover, so far as they are necessary for the conduct of human actions. Such among others are these principles: that we should live honestly, should hurt nobody, and should render to every one it's due; to which three general precepts Justinian has reduced the whole doctrine of law.

But if the discovery of these first principles of the law of nature depended only upon the due exertion of right reason, and could not otherwise be attained than by a chain of metaphysical disquisitions, mankind would have wanted some inducement to have quickened their inquiries, and the greater part of the world would have rested content in mental indolence, and ignorance it's inseparable companion. As therefore the creator is a being, not only of infinite power, and wisdom but also of infinite goodness, he has been pleased so to contrive the constitution and frame of humanity, that we should want no other prompter to enquire after and pursue the rule of right, but only our own self love, that universal principle of action. For he has so intimately connected, so inseparably interwoven the laws of eternal justice with the happiness of each individual, that the latter cannot be attained but by observing the former; and, if the former be punctually obeyed, it cannot but induce the latter. In consequence of which mutual connection of justice and human felicity, he has not perplexed the law of nature with a multitude of abstracted rules and precepts, referring merely to the fitness or unfitness of things, as some have vainly surmised; but has graciously reduced the rule of obedience to this one paternal precept, that man should "pursue his own happiness." This is the foundation of what we call ethics, or natural law. For the several articles into which it is branched in our systems, amount to no more than demonstrating, that this or that action tends to man's real happiness, and therefore very justly concluding that the performance of it is a part of the law of nature; or, on the other hand, that this or that action is destructive of man's real happiness, and therefore that the law of nature forbids it.

This law of nature, being co-eval with mankind and dictated by God himself, is of course superior in obligation to any other. It is binding over all the globe, in all countries, and at all times: no human laws are of any validity, if contrary to this; and such of them as are valid derive all their force, and all their authority, mediately or immediately, from this original.

But in order to apply this to the particular exigencies of each individual, it is still necessary to have recourse to reason; whose office it is to discover, as was before observed, what the law of nature directs in every circumstance of life; by considering, what method will tend the most effectually to our own substantial happiness. And if our reason were always, as in our first ancestor before his transgression, clear and perfect, unruffled by passions, unclouded by prejudice, unimpaired by disease or intemperance, the talk would be pleasant and easy; we should need no other guide but this. But every man now finds the contrary in his own experience; that his reason is corrupt, and his understanding full of ignorance and error.

This has given manifold occasion for the benign interposition of divine providence; which, in companion to the frailty, the imperfection, and the blindness of human reason, hath been pleased, at sundry times and in divers manners, to discover and enforce it's laws by an immediate and direct revelation. The doctrines thus delivered we call the revealed or divine law, and they are to be found only in the holy scriptures. These precepts, when revealed, are found upon comparison to be really a part of the original law of nature, as they tend in all their consequences to man's felicity. But we are not from thence to conclude that the knowledge of these truths was attainable by reason, in it's present corrupted state; since we find that, until they were revealed, they were hid from the wisdom of ages. As then the moral precepts of this law are indeed of the same original with these of the law of nature, so their intrinsic obligation is of equal strength and perpetuity. Yet undoubtedly the revealed law is (humanly speaking) of infinitely more authority than what we generally call the natural law. Because one is the law of nature, expressly declared so to be by God himself; the other is only what, by the assistance of human reason, we imagine to be that law. If we could be as certain of the latter as we are of the former, both would have an equal authority; but, till then, they can never be put in any competition together.

Upon these two foundations, the law of nature and the law of revelation, depend all human laws; that is to say, no human laws should be suffered to contradict these. There is, it is true, a great number of indifferent points, in which both the divine law and the natural leave a man at his own liberty; but which are found necessary for the benefit of society to be restrained within certain limits. And herein it is that human laws have their greatest force and efficacy; for, with regard to such points as are not indifferent, human laws are only declaratory of, and act in subordination to, the former. To instance in the case of murder: this is expressly forbidden by the divine, and demonstrably by the natural law; and from these prohibitions arises the true unlawfulness of this crime. Those human laws, that annex a punishment to it, do not at all increase it's moral guilt, or superadd any fresh obligation *in foro conscientiae* [in the court of justice of the conscience], to abstain from it's perpetration. Nay, if any human law should allow or injoin us to commit it, we are bound to transgress that human law, or else we must offend both the natural and the divine. But with regard to matters that are in themselves indifferent, and are not commanded or forbidden by those superior laws; such, for instance, as exporting of wool into foreign countries; here the inferior legislature has scope and opportunity to interpose, and to make that action unlawful which before was not so.

If man were to live in a state of nature, unconnected with other individuals, there would be no occasion for any other laws, than the law of nature, and the law of God. Neither could any other law possibly exist; for a law always supposes some superior who is to make it; and in a state of nature we are all equal, without any other superior but him who is the author of our being. But man was formed for society; and, as is demonstrated by the writers on this subject, is neither capable of living alone, nor indeed has the courage to do it. However, as it is impossible for the whole race of mankind to be united in one great society, they must necessarily divide into many; and form separate states, commonwealths, and nations; entirely independent of each other, and yet liable to a mutual intercourse. Hence arises a third kind of law to regulate this mutual intercourse, called "the law of nations;" which, as none of these states will acknowledge a superiority in the other, cannot be dictated by either; but depends entirely upon the rules of natural law, or upon mutual compacts, treaties, leagues, and agreements between these several communities: in the construction also of which compacts we have no other rule to report to, but the law of nature; being the only one to which both communities are equally subject: and therefore the civil law very justly observes, that *quod naturalis, ratio inter omnes homines constituit, vocatur jus gentium* [that which natural reason has established among all men is called the law of the nations].

Thus much I thought it necessary to premise concerning the law of nature, the revealed law, and the law of nations, before I proceeded to treat more fully of the principal subject of this section, municipal or civil law; that is, the rule by which particular districts, communities, or nations are governed; being thus defined by Justinian, "*jus civile est quod quisque sibi populus constituit*" [civil law is what each nation has established for itself]. I call it *municipal* law, in compliance with common speech; for, tho' strictly that expression denotes the particular customs of one single *municipium* or free town, yet it may with sufficient propriety be applied to any one state or nation, which is governed by the same laws and customs.

Municipal law, thus understood, is properly defined to be "a rule of civil conduct prescribed by the supreme power in a state, commanding what is right and prohibiting what is 'wrong'." Let us endeavour to explain it's several properties, as they arise out of this definition.

And, first, it is a rule; not a transient sudden order from a superior to or concerning a particular person; but something permanent, uniform, and universal. Therefore a particular act of the legislature to confiscate the goods of Titius, or to attaint him of high treason, does not enter into the idea of a municipal law: for the operation of this act is spent upon Titius only, and has no relation to the community in general; it is rather a sentence than a law. But an act to declare that the crime of which Titius is accused shall be deemed high treason; this has permanency, uniformity, and universality, and therefore is properly a rule. It is also called a rule, to distinguish it from advice or counsel, which we are at liberty to follow or not, as we see proper; and to judge upon the reasonableness or unreasonableness of the thing advised. Whereas our obedience to the law depends not upon our approbation, but upon the maker's will. Counsel is only matter of persuasion, law is matter of injunction; counsel acts only upon the willing, law upon the unwilling also. It is also called a rule, to distinguish it from a compact or agreement; for a compact is a promise proceeding from us, law is a command directed to us. The language of a compact is, "I will, or will not, do this;" that of a law is, "thou shalt, or shalt not, do it." It is true there is an obligation which a compact carries with it, equal in point of conscience to that of a law; but then the original of the obligation is different. In compacts, we ourselves determine and promise what shall be done, before we are obliged to do it; in laws, we are obliged to act, without ourselves determining or promising any thing at all. Upon these accounts law is defined to be "a rule."

Municipal law is also "a rule of civil conduct." This distinguishes municipal law from the natural, or revealed; the former of which is the rule of moral conduct, and the latter not only the rule of moral conduct, but also the rule of faith. These regard man as a creature, and point out his duty to God, to himself, and to his neighbour, considered in the light of an individual. But municipal or civil law regards him also as a citizen, and bound to other duties towards his neighbour, than those of mere nature and religion: duties, which he has engaged in by enjoying the benefits of the common union; and which amount to no more, than that he do contribute, on his part, to the subsistence and peace of the society.

It is likewise "a rule prescribed." Because a bare revolution, confined in the breast of the legislator, without manifesting itself by some external sign, can never be properly a law. It is requisite that this revolution be notified to the people who are to obey it. But the manner in which this notification is to be made, is matter of very great indifference. It may be notified by universal tradition and long practice, which supposes a previous publication, and is the case of the common law of England. It may be notified, *viva voce* [by word of mouth], by officers appointed for that purpose, as is done with regard to proclamations, and such acts of parliament as are appointed to be publicly read in churches and other assemblies. It may lastly be notified by writing, printing, or the like; which is the general course taken with all our acts of parliament. Yet, whatever way is made use of, it is incumbent on the promulgators to do it in the most public and perspicuous manner, not like Caligula, who (according to Dio Cassius) wrote his laws in a very small character, and hung them up upon high pillars, the more effectually to ensnare the people. There is still a more unreasonable method than this, which is called making of laws ex post facto; when *after* an action is committed, the legislator then for the first time declares it to have been a crime, and inflicts a punishment upon the person who has committed it; here it is impossible that the party could foresee that an action, innocent when it was done, should be afterwards converted to guilt by a subsequent law; he had therefore no cause to abstain from it; and all punishment for not abstaining must of consequence be cruel and unjust. All laws should be therefore made to commence *in futuro*, and be notified before their commencement; which is implied in the term "prescribed." But when this rule is in the usual manner notified, or prescribed, it is then the subject's business to be thoroughly acquainted therewith; for if ignorance, of what he *might* know, were admitted as a legitimate excuse, the laws would be of no effect, but might always be eluded with impunity.

But farther: municipal law is "a rule of civil conduct prescribed by the supreme power in a state." For legislature, as was before observed, is the greatest act of superiority that can be exercised by one being over another. Wherefore it is requisite to the very essence of a law, that it be made by the supreme power. Sovereignty and legislature are indeed convertible terms; one cannot subsist without the other.

Questions

1. According to Blackstone, what is law?
2. What is the difference between law in its comprehensive sense and its confined sense?
3. What is the law of nature?
4. According to Blackstone, what does the law of nature tell us about God? Consider the following passages: Isaiah 40:12-14; Job 28:20-28; Proverbs 2:1-6; and Psalm 145:3-10. Do the passages support Blackstone's view?
5. Is the law of nature the same as the natural law?
6. What is divine law and why do we need it?
7. Is natural law or divine law more important to Blackstone? Why? Again consider Romans 1:18-32; Romans 3:9-18; Ephesians 2:1-10; and I Corinthians 2:6-16.
8. How do Blackstone's views on natural law compare with Aquinas'?
9. What is the law of nations? Why is it needed?
10. What is municipal law?
11. How would Blackstone assess the validity of the following laws?

a. A state statute prohibiting coveting;

b. A state statute prohibiting theft;

c. A city water conservation ordinance prohibiting the use of city water for watering lawns and washing cars;

d. A federal constitutional amendment prohibiting parents from providing religious instruction to their children;

e. A federal law funding the cloning of human beings for research purposes;

f. A state statute prohibiting restaurants from serving foods containing trans fat;

g. A federal constitutional amendment (enacted to save Social Security and Medicare) providing the following:

> Medical providers may no longer provide medical treatment for a "serious illness" to anyone over seventy-five years of age. [A "serious illness" is defined as an illness or condition that would require medical procedures and treatments costing in excess of a certain dollar amount to cure or treat]. A patient denied treatment under this provision may either suffer with the illness untreated, may be assisted in committing suicide by a medical provider, or may be involuntarily euthanized at the request of two or more members of the patient's immediate family.

D. The Practical Impact of Higher Law Thinking on Citizens, Lawmakers, and Judges

Introduction

The previous pieces make lofty arguments about the nature of law and the higher law basis for law. The final pieces in this chapter take a step back and ask a very basic question: even if there is a higher law, does it matter in the real world? The authors of each of the next three pieces answer "yes."

The first piece is by Professor Charles Rice, Professor Emeritus of Law at Notre Dame University. He has taught jurisprudence at Notre Dame for over 30 years and has written extensively on the topic. For many years, he was the co-editor of the *American Journal of Jurispru-*

dence. Rice seeks to promote current consideration of the writings of Thomas Aquinas. In "Some Reasons for the Restoration of Natural Law Jurisprudence," Rice argues that natural law has important practical functions for citizens, legislators, judges, and the media.

The two pieces following Rice's discuss in more detail two ways the higher law has current relevance. The first, "Letter From Birmingham Jail," by Martin Luther King, Jr., discusses when citizens should engage in civil disobedience. The second, an excerpt from Professor Michael Paulsen's article "Accusing Justice," discusses how a judge should respond when asked to apply a law he or she believes violates the higher law.

Martin Luther King, Jr. was born on January 15, 1929 in Atlanta, Georgia. He attended Morehouse College, Crozer Theological Seminary, and Boston University School of Theology, where he earned his doctorate in 1955. By the time King was nineteen, he had been ordained and offered a pastoral position at the Dexter Avenue Baptist Church in Alabama.

King became involved in the civil rights movement after Rosa Parks was arrested for refusing to give up her bus seat to a white man, per the Jim Crow laws of Alabama. Following this event, King led a successful, peaceful boycott against the public bus system. King became known and respected as a nonviolent leader who opposed injustice against blacks. In order to continue the movement, King founded the Southern Christian Leadership Conference in 1957. Through this organization, King continued to encourage a nonviolent fight for civil rights, including safeguards for black voting rights, federal protection for blacks in the south, and integration of the public school system. King received the Nobel Peace Prize in 1964. He was assassinated on April 4, 1968 in Memphis, Tennessee.

King wrote "Letter from Birmingham Jail" on April 16, 1963 to defend himself from a statement printed in the newspaper by eight white Christian and Jewish clergymen who criticized a boycott King had organized against local merchants. King had come to Birmingham in February 1963 to lead a peaceful boycott against the merchants to urge the integration of public facilities.

On April 11, 1963, King was served with an injunction prohibiting him from leading civil rights demonstrations. King decided that he would, for the first time, violate an injunction. King knew this would lead to his arrest, but decided that his arrest, and the arrest of other leaders, might spur the black community to action. In addition, he saw the arrest as a physical and personal way to show his commitment to the civil rights movement. On April 13, 1963, Good Friday, King gave an address at Zion Hill Church. He then led volunteers downtown where they were arrested. King spent four days in jail under difficult conditions. On April 16, King's lawyers brought him a four-day-old newspaper where King found the clergymen's letter. King wrote his "Letter" in response.

Michael Paulsen, the author of the final piece in this chapter, is the McKnight Presidential Professor of Law and Public Policy and Briggs & Morgan Professor of Law at the University of Minnesota Law School. Paulsen received a B.A. from Northwestern University, a J.D. from Yale Law School, and an M.A.R. from Yale Divinity School. Paulsen joined the University of Minnesota faculty in 1991. He teaches and writes on civil procedure, criminal procedure, legal ethics, constitutional law, and law and religion.

Paulsen wrote *Accusing Justice* in part to flesh out themes set out in a book entitled, *Justice Accused*, written in 1975 by Robert Cover, Paulsen's professor and friend at Yale Law School. In *Justice Accused*, Cover explained what judges should do when asked to enforce an immoral law (the book used as its historical example the judicial enforcement of slavery laws in the years before the Civil War). In his article, Paulsen explores the same question, but uses judicial enforcement of modern abortion law as the context for his argument.

Charles Rice, *Some Reasons for a Restoration of Natural Law Jurisprudence*[*]

E. The Functions of the Natural Law

1. The constructive function

The natural law has two functions with respect to human law, which might be called the "constructive" and the "critical." In its "constructive" role, natural law serves as a guide for the enactment of laws to promote the common good. Natural law principles relating to economic, social and political justice ought to be a familiar part of public discussion on such issues as the family, employment relations and the prevention of racial and other discriminations. For example, the harmful effects of permissive divorce, especially on the children of the marriage, are widely noted. Legislators should therefore consider restrictions on divorce so as

[*] Charles Rice, *Some Reasons for a Restoration of Natural Law Jurisprudence*, 24 WAKE FOREST L. REV. 539, 566-71 (1989). Reprinted with the permission of Wake Forest Law Review.

to strengthen the family as a divinely ordained natural society entitled to the protection of the State.

This "constructive" role of the natural law includes Aquinas' limitation that the human law should not try to enforce every virtue or prohibit every vice. The natural law in this respect is a prescription for limited government. The "constructive" function of the natural law is at least as important as the "critical." In that "constructive" mode, the natural law argument can make a significant contribution as a guide for how things really ought to work according to the manufacturer's directions.

It would be a mistake, however, to suppose that natural law "pretends to be some sort of magic formula that furnishes handy answers for whatever practical legal questions may arise." Rather, in its "constructive" function the natural law provides, not a cookbook series of recipes but a reasonable guide to principles and general objectives. In the Catholic tradition, further specification of those principles and objectives is provided by the teaching Church, for example, on the "family wage," bioethics, in vitro fertilization, etc.

2. The critical function

The second function of the natural law is the critical function. In that critical function, the natural law, unlike positivism, provides a reason to draw a line and criticize an action of the state as unjust and even void. That is why Rosa Parks was right when she refused to step to the back of the bus in Montgomery, Alabama, on December 1, 1955. When the Nazis moved against the Jews, German lawyers were "disarmed," in Radbruch's phrase, by "positivism." It is interesting to speculate as to what might have been had the German legal profession responded to the early Nazi injustices with firm and principled denunciation.

The natural law principles advanced by George Mason, Blackstone, Aquinas and others are supra-constitutional. The question is not whether unconstitutional law-making power is assumed by a dictator, by a Supreme Court as constitutional interpreter, by a Congress, or by a majority of the people. The issue is whether there is a higher law which sets bounds to what the legal system, however it is structured, can do even through constitutional provisions. The natural law argument can serve, in the legislative process and the media, to forestall the enactment of unjust laws or constitutional amendments.

The first reaction to the assertion of a claimed right to kill innocent human beings should be to say that the recognition of such a right would be unjust as well as a violation of the fifth and fourteenth amendments to the Constitution. *Roe v. Wade*, however, in effect established the right to kill as a constitutional right. Assuming that the Supreme Court is correct in its claim that its decisions are the supreme law of the land, the issue remains whether the Constitution itself is subject to a higher law. If a constitutional amendment, for example, were adopted which required the confiscation without trial of the property of members of a particular race, would it be a valid law? A natural law adherent should respond in the negative:

> A law on citizenship in connection with the so-called Nuremberg anti-Semitic legislation of 1935 declared that German citizens of Jewish origin who lived at that time outside the country or in the future fled or emigrated would automatically lose their German citizenship and their property would be forfeited to the State. After the war many claimed the restoration of property thus illegitimately confiscated. The court recognized these claims and said: "These laws of confiscation, though clothed in the formal rules of the legality of a law, cannot be considered as a genuine *Rechts*-norm as to content.... This is an extremely grave *violation of the suprapositive principle of equality before the law* as well as of the suprapositive guarantee of property (Art. 153 Weimar Const.)"

The natural law, however, is not a hunting license empowering judges to impose their own morality to invalidate legislative decisions in genuinely debatable cases. Natural law theory would be especially limited in this respect in the United States where the Constitution itself incorporates some basic natural law principles, e.g., due process and equal protection, under which laws contrary to them could be violative of the supreme enacted law so that there would be no need for recourse to a supra-constitutional higher law. *Roe v. Wade*, for example, is wrong first, and sufficiently in legal terms, because it is a misinterpretation of the fourteenth amendment. One case, however, in which a supra-constitutional invocation of the natural law might have been arguably appropriate is *Brown v. Board of Education*. There is evidence to support the conclusion that the fourteenth amendment was intended to allow officially segregated public schools. If one accepted that conclusion and also found that public education today is sufficiently similar to that of 1868 to be governed by the intent of the fourteenth amendment on the subject, one could still argue that officially imposed racial segregation in schools (or elsewhere) is void because it is inherently unjust to an "intolerable degree," so as to violate the supra-constitutional standard of the natural law. A human law, according to Aquinas, may be unjust as "contrary to human good" when "burdens are imposed unequally on the community." A similar approach could have been appropriate in the *Dred Scott* case, in which the Supreme Court held that freed slaves and their free descendants could not be citizens and said that slaves were property rather than persons. Even if the Court there correctly interpreted the technical intent of the Constitution, the decision is insupportable because it attempts to break the inseparable connection that must exist, in any free and just society, between humanity and personhood. Although the Constitution is "the supreme law of the land," as a human law, it must itself be subject to the higher law. If a constitutional amendment were adopted to require the disenfranchisement of persons of a certain race or religion, there would seem little doubt that a judge would have the right and the duty to declare the amendment itself unlawful and void. Nevertheless, this responsibility offers no warrant for "non-interpretive" judges to roam at large over the constitutional landscape, acting as a "continuing constitutional convention" in disregard of the constitutional text and the evident intent of its framers. Only rarely would a judge be entitled or obliged to rely on supra-constitutional principles to refuse to uphold or enforce an enacted law. As the German courts indicated after World War II, judges should take this step only when the conflict between the law or precedent and justice is "intolerable" or "unendurable." Such a conflict could occur in the context of *Roe v. Wade*, since that ruling authorizes the execution of a certainly innocent human being. Unfortunately, however, to analyze the options open to a judge in a case involving supra-constitutional standards would require a separate article or book and would be beyond the limited scope of this article.

A wider recognition of the natural law as part of the law of God would serve as an incentive to the enactment of just laws as well as a brake on the enactment of unjust ones. However, arguments based on the natural law and the divine law will have little effect in a society that recognizes neither. It is not enough to argue the natural law case in academic terms. A restoration of societal respect for that law and for the divine law—a conversion—is needed before the natural law case will prevail in the public arena. We do appear to be in the early stages of a reaction to the positivistic jurisprudence which has deprived innocent life of any principled protection against extinction. This reaction, however, is less evident in the law schools than it is on the streets. One indication is the expansion of the abortion rescue movement. More than 30,000 persons have submitted to arrest in the past year as a result of their participation in non-violent efforts to close abortuaries and thereby to save the unborn children scheduled for abortion. The movement originated primarily as an initiative of Evangelical and other Bible Christians. It has since included large numbers of Catholics and others. Although the prudential justifications for the rescue movement are debatable, it is founded in explicit reliance on the natural law as an aspect of the law of God. "I am willing to be arrested for breaking a law," said one rescue participant, "because I'm obeying a higher law, the law of God. We are saving human lives." And Roman Catholic Bishop Austin Vaughan justified his involvement in rescues on the ground that, "The things that are decided by governments are not always right. We can't go along, passively accepting them.... The biggest threat to our country, faced with this, is complacency and toleration. The longer you live with something bad along side of you, you get used to it. I don't mean you accept it, but you no longer get excited. We can't afford to have that happen. That's an enormous disaster. Not just for the babies who are killed, not just for the people doing to [*sic*] killing, it's an enormous disaster for all of us. Our standards of what is important and vital wind up being eroded more and more as times goes on."

Conclusion

Every state has to have a God, an ultimate authority. It is increasingly obvious that the root issue posed by contemporary legal philosophy is religious: Who is God, the real One or the State? "Law, we must remember," said Rev. Rousas J. Rushdoony, "is a form of total war;... The modern state, by asserting its sovereignty, affirms that all things are under its jurisdiction, and it must therefore, like God, control all things." The main reason why so much has gone wrong with the law in the twentieth century is the reason given by Aleksandr Solzhenitsyn for the consequences of Soviet Communism:

> Over half a century ago, while I was still a child, I recall hearing a number of older people offer the following explanation for the great disasters that had befallen Russia: "*Men have forgotten God*; that's why all this has happened."
>
> And if I were called upon to identify the principal trait of the entire twentieth century, here too, I would be unable to find anything more precise and pithy than to repeat once again: *Men have forgotten God.*

It should give us pause when we reflect that, in numbers involved and in the degree of impact on the victim, legalized abortion is a worse evil than was slavery. God is merciful. But He is also just. We could with profit reflect on the remarks of George Mason, in the Constitutional

Convention of 1787, arguing against the continuation of the slave trade. "Every master of slaves," said Mason, "is born a petty tyrant. They bring the judgment of Heaven upon a country. As nations can not be rewarded or punished in the next world, they must be in this. By an inevitable chain of causes and effects providence punishes national sins, by national calamities."

Law students, unfortunately, are presented jurisprudential options mainly within the parameters of the Enlightenment, positivist view. They ought at least to have the opportunity to consider all the options, including the arguments for acceptance of "the laws of nature and of nature's God." This is so because the prevailing American legal theory is at a dead end. In its concept of law as merely an exercise of will and in its functional definition of personhood, it offers no prospect for restoration of the role of the law as guarantor of the inviolable rights of the innocent. It is hopeless because it has forgotten its roots and the Lawgiver. But there is a solution. It is simple. "What Moses brought down from Mount Sinai," said Ted Koppel at the 1987 Duke University commencement, "were not the Ten Suggestions; they are Commandments. Are, not were."

Martin Luther King, Jr., *Letter from Birmingham Jail*[*]

April 16, 1963
Birmingham, AL
My Dear Fellow Clergymen:

While confined here in the Birmingham City Jail, I came across your recent statement calling our present activities "unwise and untimely." Seldom, if ever, do I pause to answer criticism of my work and ideas. If I sought to answer all the criticisms that cross my desk, my secretaries would be engaged in little else in the course of the day, and I would have no time for constructive work. But since I feel that you are men of genuine goodwill and your criticisms are sincerely set forth, I would like to answer your statement in what I hope will be patient and reasonable terms.

* * *

[*] Martin Luther King, Jr., *Letter from Birmingham Jail*, THE CHRISTIAN CENTURY, June 12, 1963, at 767. Reprinted by arrangement with The Heirs to the Estate of Martin Luther King Jr., c/o Writers House as agent for the proprietor New York, NY. *Copyright 1963 Dr. Martin Luther King, Jr; copyright renewed Coretta Scott King 1991.*

You express a great deal of anxiety over our willingness to break laws. This is certainly a legitimate concern. Since we so diligently urge people to obey the Supreme Court's decision of 1954 outlawing segregation in the public schools, it is rather strange and paradoxical to find us consciously breaking laws. One may well ask: "How can you advocate breaking some laws and obeying others?" The answer is found in the fact that there are two types of laws: There are just and there are unjust laws. I would agree with Saint Augustine that "An unjust law is no law at all."

Now, what is the difference between the two? How does one determine when a law is just or unjust? A just law is a man-made code that squares with the moral law or the law of God. An unjust law is a code that is out of harmony with the moral law. To put it in the terms of Saint Thomas Aquinas, an unjust law is a human law that is not rooted in eternal and natural law. Any law that uplifts human personality is just. Any law that degrades human personality is unjust. All segregation statutes are unjust because segregation distorts the soul and damages the personality. It gives the segregator a false sense of superiority, and the segregated a false sense of inferiority. To use the words of Martin Buber, the Jewish philosopher, segregation substitutes an "I-it" relationship for an "I-thou" relationship, and ends up relegating persons to the status of things. So segregation is not only politically, economically and sociologically unsound, but it is morally wrong and sinful. Paul Tillich has said that sin is separation. Isn't segregation an existential expression of man's tragic separation, an expression of his awful estrangement, his terrible sinfulness? So I can urge men to disobey segregation ordinances because they are morally wrong.

Let us turn to a more concrete example of just and unjust laws. An unjust law is a code that a majority inflicts on a minority that is not binding on itself. This is difference made legal. On the other hand a just law is a code that a majority compels a minority to follow that it is willing to follow itself. This is sameness made legal.

Let me give another explanation. An unjust law is a code inflicted upon a minority which that minority had no part in enacting or creating because they did not have the unhampered right to vote. Who can say that the legislature of Alabama which set up the segregation laws was democratically elected? Throughout the state of Alabama all types of conniving methods are used to prevent Negroes from becoming registered voters and there are some counties without a single Negro registered to vote despite the fact that the Negro constitutes a majority of the population. Can any law set up in such a state be considered democratically structured?

These are just a few examples of unjust and just laws. There are some instances when a law is just on its face and unjust in its application. For instance, I was arrested Friday on a charge of parading without a permit. Now there is nothing wrong with an ordinance which requires a permit for a parade, but when the ordinance is used to preserve segregation and to deny citizens the First-Amendment privilege of peaceful assembly and peaceful protest, then it becomes unjust.

I hope you can see the distinction I am trying to point out. In no sense do I advocate evading or defying the law as the rabid segregationist would do. This would lead to anarchy. One who breaks an unjust law must do it *openly*, *lovingly*, (not hatefully as the white mothers did in New Orleans when they were seen on television screaming "nigger, nigger, nigger") and with a willingness to accept the penalty. I submit that an individual who breaks a law that conscience tells him is unjust, and willingly accepts the penalty by staying in jail to arouse the conscience of the community over its injustice, is in reality expressing the very highest respect for law.

Of course, there is nothing new about this kind of civil disobedience. It was seen sublimely in the refusal of Shadrach, Meshach and Abednego to obey the laws of Nebuchadnezzar because a higher moral law was involved. It was practiced superbly by the early Christians who were willing to face hungry lions and the excruciating pain of chopping blocks, before submitting to certain unjust laws of the Roman empire. To a degree academic freedom is a reality today because Socrates practiced civil disobedience.

We can never forget that everything Hitler did in Germany was "legal" and everything the Hungarian freedom fighters did in Hungary was "illegal." It was "illegal" to aid and comfort a Jew in Hitler's Germany. But I am sure that if I had lived in Germany during that time I would have aided and comforted my Jewish brothers even though it was illegal. If I lived in a Communist country today where certain principles dear to the Christian faith are suppressed, I believe I would openly advocate disobeying these anti-religious laws. I must make two honest confessions to you, my Christian and Jewish brothers. First, I must confess that over the last few years I have been gravely disappointed with the white moderate. I have almost reached the regrettable conclusion that the Negro's great stumbling block in the stride toward freedom is not the White Citizen's Counciler or the Ku Klux Klanner, but the white moderate who is more devoted to "order" than to justice; who prefers a negative peace which is the absence of tension to a positive peace which is the presence of justice; who constantly says "I agree with you in the goal you seek, but I can't agree with your methods of direct action;" who paternalistically feels he can set the timetable for another man's freedom; who lives by the myth of time and who constantly advises the Negro to wait until a "more convenient season." Shallow understanding from people of goodwill is more frustrating than absolute misunderstanding from people of ill will. Lukewarm acceptance is much more bewildering than outright rejection.

I had hoped that the white moderate would understand that law and order exist for the purpose of establishing justice, and that when they fail to do this they become dangerously structured dams that block the flow of social progress. I had hoped that the white moderate would understand that the present tension in the South is merely a necessary phase of the transition from an obnoxious negative peace, where the Negro passively accepted his unjust plight, to a substance-filled positive peace, where all men will respect the dignity and worth of human personality. Actually, we who engage in nonviolent direct action are not the creators of tension. We merely bring to the surface the hidden tension that is already alive. We bring it out in the open where it can be seen and dealt with. Like a boil that can never be cured as long as it is covered up but must be opened with all its pus-flowing ugliness to the natural medicines of air and light, injustice must likewise be exposed, with all of the tension its exposing creates, to the light of human conscience and the air of national opinion before it can be cured.

In your statement you asserted that our actions, even though peaceful, must be condemned because they precipitate violence. But can this assertion be logically made? Isn't this like condemning the robbed man because his possession of money precipitated the evil act of robbery? Isn't this like condemning Socrates because his unswerving commitment to truth and his philosophical delvings precipitated the misguided popular mind to make him drink the hemlock? Isn't this like condemning Jesus because His unique God-Consciousness and never-ceasing devotion to His will precipitated the evil act of crucifixion? We must come to see, as the federal courts have consistently affirmed, that it is immoral to urge an individual to withdraw his efforts to gain his basic constitutional rights because the quest precipitates violence. Society must protect the robbed and punish the robber.

* * *

You spoke of our activity in Birmingham as extreme. At first I was rather disappointed that fellow clergymen would see my nonviolent efforts as those of the extremist.

* * *

But as I continued to think about the matter I gradually gained a bit of satisfaction from being considered an extremist. Was not Jesus an extremist for love—"Love your enemies, bless them that curse you, pray for them that despitefully use you." Was not Amos an extremist for justice—"Let justice roll down like waters and righteousness like a mighty stream." Was not Paul an extremist for the gospel of Jesus Christ—"I bear in my body the marks of the Lord Jesus." Was not Martin Luther an extremist—"Here I stand; I can do none other so help me God." Was not John Bunyan an extremist—"I will stay in jail to the end of my days before I make a butchery of my conscience." Was not Abraham Lincoln an extremist—"This nation cannot survive half slave and half free." Was not Thomas Jefferson an extremist—"We hold these truths to be self-evident, that all men are created equal." So the question is not whether we will be extremist but what kind of extremist will we be. Will we be extremists for hate or will we be extremists for love? Will we be extremists for the preservation of injustice—or will we be extremists for the cause of justice? In that dramatic scene on Calvary's hill, three men were crucified. We must not forget that all three were crucified for the same crime—the crime of extremism. Two were extremists for immorality, and thusly fell below their environment. The other, Jesus Christ, was an extremist for love, truth and goodness, and thereby rose above his environment. So, after all, maybe the South, the nation and the world are in dire need of creative extremists.

* * *

Let me rush on to mention my other disappointment. I have been so greatly disappointed with the white church and its leadership. Of course, there are some notable exceptions. I am not unmindful of the fact that each of you has taken some significant stands on this issue. I commend you, Rev. Stallings, for your Christian stand on this past Sunday, in welcoming Negroes to your worship service on a non-segregated basis. I commend the Catholic leaders of this state for integrating Spring Hill College several years ago.

But despite these notable exceptions I must honestly reiterate that I have been disappointed with the church. I do not say that as one of those negative critics who can always find something wrong with the church. I say it as a minister of the gospel, who loves the church; who was nurtured in its bosom; who has been sustained by its spiritual blessings and who will remain true to it as long as the cord of life shall lengthen.

I had the strange feeling when I was suddenly catapulted into the leadership of the bus protest in Montgomery several years ago, that we would have the support of the white church. I felt that the white ministers, priests and rabbis of the South would be some of our strongest allies. Instead, some have been outright opponents, refusing to understand the freedom movement and misrepresenting its leaders; all too many others have been more cautious than courageous and have remained silent behind the anesthetizing security of the stained-glass windows.

In spite of my shattered dreams of the past, I came to Birmingham with the hope that the white religious leadership of this community would see the justice of our cause, and with deep moral concern, serve as the channel through which our just grievances would get to the power structure. I had hoped that each of you would understand. But again I have been disappointed. I have heard numerous religious leaders of the South call upon their worshippers to comply with a desegregation decision because it is the *law*, but I have longed to hear white ministers say, "Follow this decree because integration is morally *right* and the Negro is your brother." In the midst of blatant injustices inflicted upon the Negro, I have watched white churches stand on the sideline and merely mouth pious irrelevancies and sanctimonious trivialities. In the midst of a mighty struggle to rid our nation of racial and economic injustice, I have heard so many ministers say, "Those are social issues with which the gospel has no real concern." And I have watched so many churches commit themselves to a completely other-worldly religion which made a strange distinction between body and soul, the sacred and the secular.

So here we are moving toward the exit of the twentieth century with a religious community largely adjusted to the status quo, standing as a taillight behind other community agencies rather than a headlight leading men to higher levels of justice.

I have traveled the length and breadth of Alabama, Mississippi and all the other southern states. On sweltering summer days and crisp autumn mornings I have looked at her beautiful churches with their lofty spires pointing heavenward. I have beheld the impressive outlay of her massive religious education buildings. Over and over again I have found myself asking: "What kind of people worship here? Who is their God? Where were their voices when the lips of Governor Barnett dripped with words of interposition and nullification? Where were they when Governor Wallace gave the clarion call for defiance and hatred? Where were their voices of support when tired, bruised and weary Negro men and women decided to rise from the dark dungeons of complacency to the bright hills of creative protest?"

Yes, these questions are still in my mind. In deep disappointment, I have wept over the laxity of the church. But be assured that my tears have been tears of love. There can be no deep disappointment where there is not deep love. Yes, I love the church; I love her sacred walls. How could I do otherwise? I am in the rather unique position of being the son, the grandson and the great-grandson of preachers. Yes, I see the church as the body of Christ. But, oh! How we have blemished and scarred that body through social neglect and fear of being nonconformists.

There was a time when the church was very powerful. It was during that period when the early Christians rejoiced when they were deemed worthy to suffer for what they believed. In those days the church was not merely a thermometer that recorded the ideas and principles of popular opinion; it was a thermostat that transformed the mores of society. Whenever the early Christians entered a town the power structure got disturbed and immediately sought to convict them for being "disturbers of the peace" and "outside agitators." But they went on with the conviction that they were "a colony of heaven," and had to obey God rather than man. They were small in number but big in commitment. They were too God-intoxicated to be "astronomically intimidated." They brought an end to such ancient evils as infanticide and gladiatorial contest.

Things are different now. The contemporary church is often a weak, ineffectual voice with an uncertain sound. It is so often the arch supporter of the status quo. Far from being disturbed by the presence of the church, the power structure of the average community is consoled by the church's silent and often vocal sanction of things as they are.

But the judgement of God is upon the church as never before. If the church of today does not recapture the sacrificial spirit of the early church, it will lose its authentic ring, forfeit the loyalty of millions, and be dismissed as an irrelevant social club with no meaning for the twentieth century.

* * *

Never before have I written a letter this long, (or should I say a book?). I'm afraid it is much too long to take your precious time. I can assure you that it would have been much shorter if I had been writing from a comfortable desk, but what else is there to do when you are alone for days in the dull monotony of a narrow jail cell other than write long letters, think strange thoughts, and pray long prayers?

If I have said anything in this letter that is an overstatement of the truth and is indicative of an unreasonable impatience, I beg you to forgive me. If I have said anything in this letter that is an understatement of the truth and is indicative of my having a patience that makes me patient with anything less than brotherhood, I beg God to forgive me.

I hope this letter finds you strong in the faith. I also hope that circumstances will soon make it possible for me to meet each of you, not as an integrationist or a civil rights leader, but as a fellow clergyman and a Christian brother. Let us all hope that the dark clouds of racial prejudice will soon pass away and the deep fog of misunderstanding will be lifted from our fear-drenched communities and in some not too distant tomorrow the radiant stars of love and brotherhood will shine over our great nation with all their scintillating beauty.

Yours for the cause of Peace and Brotherhood,
Martin Luther King, Jr.

Michael Paulsen, *Accusing Justice: Some Variations on the Themes of Robert M. Cover's 'Justice Accused'*[*]

V. Justice Recused: A Principled Minimum Ethic for the Pro-life Judiciary

If natural law principles and natural law texts generally afford no legitimate interpretive escape from the moral-formal dilemma, and if "cheating" is rejected as a legitimate option, the choices available to the judge are reduced to three: follow law against conscience, follow conscience against law, or opt out of the dilemma by resigning. We are thus left with the central dilemma of *Justice Accused*: what is the conscientious judge to do, *qua judge*, when called upon to hand down a ruling based on unjust law? As noted above, Cover seems noticeably softer on the antislavery judges in *Justice Accused* than he was in his *Atrocious Judges*[¤] review. It is interesting to return to Cover's 1968 polemic for his earlier, harsher answer:

> The traditional answer to the dilemma is resignation—public and accompanied by a full justification for the act. Gandhi, accused of sedition, spoke to his judge's moral problem. He concluded that the judge must either "obey the law" and sentence him to the maximum sentence, or he must resign. Thoreau, in a similar vein, thought that a judge confronted with the "legal" question of whether one man is the slave of another ought to resign. Resignation enables the judge to abstain from becoming a cog in the machinery of state oppression while refraining from a willful

[*] Michael Paulsen, *Accusing Justice: Some Variations on the Themes of Robert M. Cover's 'Justice Accused,'* 7 J.L. & RELIGION 33, 73-88 (1990). Reprinted with the permission of Hamline University Journal of Law and Religion and the author.

[¤] In 1968, Cover wrote a review of R. Hildreth's book, ATROCIOUS JUDGES: LINES OF JUDGES INFAMOUS AS TOOLS OF TYRANTS AND INSTRUMENTS OF OPPRESSION (1956). Cover, *Book Review*, 68 COLUM. L. REV. 1003 (1968).

> violation of his oath to support and enforce the law as he believes the law to be.
>
> For many, however, resignation will appear to be an empty gesture. After all, other judges will be found to convict the [draft] resisters. For the judicial activist there are other alternatives.

But having narrowed the range of legitimate alternatives, we are left with the "traditional" answer that Cover thought inadequate—resignation. The standard criticism of this response is that it abandons the moral arena to judges who have no qualms about enforcing unjust law. The logic of the argument for resignation might have the practical effect of removing from eligibility for judicial appointments persons conscientiously opposed to abortion, and to *Roe*.

Moreover, taken to its logical extreme, would not the ethic of resignation tend to remove from *consideration* for judicial appointments *all* persons of strong moral conviction, regardless of viewpoint and regardless of the issue? And is it desirable to "sanitize" the judiciary from men and women of moral principle?

Despite these problems, the traditional answer of resignation can be seen as the best one, when applied in such a way as not to be an "empty gesture" or an emptying of the bench of persons of conviction. Judiciously applied, the resignation option can be a powerful, moral contribution to the law, faithful to the duty to law *and* the duty to conscience.

Again considering the case of abortion, I submit that the conscientious pro-life judge, consistent with recognition of a natural right to life for the unborn child, should pursue the following course. First, the judge should indulge every legitimate presumption in favor of the right to life. Abortion, like slavery, is an institution so odious that only the clearest of statements of positive law sanctioning it should be given binding effect. The natural right to life serves, interstitially, to supply the governing rule of law wherever positive law is not *expressly* to the contrary and as a choice of law principle in conflict-of-laws situations. In the case of decisional law, this does not mean ignoring or distorting *Roe v. Wade* and its progeny, but recognizing that the *Roe* decision, by its own terms, leaves a lot of leeway for ad hoc "balancing" of interests in a variety of contexts not literally controlled by the *Roe* holding, and that the Court's most recent decision in *Webster v. Reproductive Health Services* tilts that balance in favor of recognition of the "compelling" interest in protecting preborn human life *throughout* pregnancy. In the world after *Webster*, the presumption in favor of life should go far to provide a constitutional rule of decision that reaches to the very edges of *Roe v. Wade*, irrespective of the fact that the Court technically left *Roe* standing.

This approach is consonant with Cover's 1968 suggestion that judges, under the rubric of due process, insist upon the strictest of procedural safeguards for the draft resister within the selective service system. Similarly, the antislavery bar pressed for rulings recognizing the right of the fugitive slave to due process, including a jury trial in the rendering state (where juries would very likely be more libertarian than in the slaveholding state, and might even nullify the judge's legal instructions), and attempting to assign the burden of proof to the putative slaveholder.

The pro-life judge today should require that the party invoking the authority of the courts in an attempt to vindicate a right to abort (for example, against a restrictive state law or regulation) bear the burden of proof with respect to the question whether the unborn fetus is human life. *A fortiori*, a court should allow introduction of evidence that the unborn fetus *is* human life—in proceedings where it is relevant to a legal claim or defense advanced. This is not judicial obstructionism, but rather a sensible examination of legal theories not explicitly foreclosed by *Roe*, and quite possibly welcomed by *Webster*.

It should be noted that such questions will doubtless persist even if *Roe* is eventually overruled. For example, an increasingly common question presented by the growth of "Operation Rescue" and other civil disobedience at abortion businesses is that of the validity of a "necessity" or "choice of evils" defense. The defense, in a nutshell, is that trespass (or some other tort) is justified in order to prevent the death of another—the unborn child—and evidence is sought to be adduced and presented to a jury that the unborn child *is* human life. The defense has been raised and rejected numerous times by lower courts, frequently on the authority of *Roe* (even though *Roe* did not purport to decide such an issue). The standard counterargument to the "necessity" defense is that the law does not recognize the interest in saving the life of the unborn—that such a defense is foreclosed by positive law establishing a legal right to abortion. The same rejoinder might be made whether the positive law protecting abortion is *Roe v. Wade*, or state statutory or constitutional law accomplishing the same ends. I would argue, however, that allowing evidence of necessity (that is, evidence going to the life and humanity of the unborn) to go to the jury, perhaps even with instructions as to its availability as a valid defense if proven, is a legitimate use of the judicial role in implementing the presumptive natural right to life.

While the "rescue/necessity" argument may strike the uninitiated reader as strained, or even far-fetched, it will not so strike the reader of *Justice Accused*. For the arguments against judicial enforcement of slavery occured [*sic*] in almost *exactly* the same posture: typically, the argument was raised as a defense to a prosecution for trespass, kidnapping, violation of a warrant, or violation of the Fugitive Slave Act by someone accused of aiding or abetting a fugitive slave—from the viewpoint of history, a "rescuer". As Cover observes, "many of the cases under the [Fugitive Slave] Act of 1850 were not collateral proceedings directed to the capacity of the fugitive himself, but criminal or civil proceedings directed against the rescuer, aider, or abettor of the fugitive." Similarly, many direct challenges to *Roe* presenting the pro-life moral-formal dilemma are today arising not in cases challenging the validity of certain state abortion regulations but in cases seeking to invoke the necessity defense as a justification for trespass or some other property crime, committed in order to prevent the wrongful taking of human life. It is likely that, even if *Roe* is overruled, such challenges will continue to be made to the legitimacy of state laws protecting abortion.

Second, in doing the above, the judge should make explicit his premises and methods, engaging in public criticism of the *Roe* decision, and the incompatability of abortion with natural law. Cover compared the failure of judges to avail themselves "of the opportunity presented by a draft case to instruct the public on the moral issues of the war" to the "screaming silence of the German people" in response to the Nazi Holocaust. The analogy of abortion to the Holocaust is even more clear. (Estimates as of January 1990 range as high as twenty-five million deaths from the post-*Roe* abortion holocaust, a result as monstrous as the killing of more than six million Jews in Nazi concentration camps.) The moral acceptability of abortion in American culture is partially a function of the fact that the Supreme Court has for the past sixteen years legally authorized it. In a society where "*constitutional* rights" are placed on a rhetorical par with moral right, many regard *Roe* as a declaration that abortion is morally justified. Criticism of *Roe*'s result by the men and women of the judiciary is an important and necessary contribution to both moral reasoning and law; it undermines the moral legitimacy of an immoral holding.

Finally, where there is no honest, legitimate alternative for deciding the case but to follow positive law supporting the right to commit an abortion, the judge *should nonetheless refuse to do so*. This is true regardless of whether the legal rule is supplied by *Roe* or by a state statute or constitution. For purposes of illustration, I will consider chiefly the case of following or refusing to follow *Roe*, for two reasons. First, it presents the situation in which we now find ourselves. While *Webster* may portend the demise of *Roe*, it leaves *Roe* standing, leaving lower courts with the duty to confront it. Second, focusing on the judicial response to *Roe* illustrates all the points that are applicable to the situation of judges called upon to enforce unjust statutes, plus additional points unique to the situation of judges called upon to follow and apply erroneous and immoral *judicial precedent*. For in the case of the moral-formal conflict created by *Roe*, we reach an important fork in the road concerning the nature of judicial obligation—the terms under which the judge exercises authority. If the moral obligations of assuming the role of judge are thought to include the duty to follow even clearly wrong precedent of higher courts in the normal appellate hierarchy, one set of responses applies. However, if the judge's duty is solely to the *Constitution* and laws of the polity, and not necessarily to any precedents interpreting them, there are, to borrow Cover's phrase, "other alternatives."

Let us consider the former, more conventional, view first—that the "law" a judge is sworn to uphold includes precedents of courts to whom the judge must answer in the appellate hierarchy. The argument here is that precedent, where sufficiently clear and "settled," is part of the positive law that natural law cannot displace. (For reasons explained below, I believe there are some serious weaknesses in this position.) The pro-life lower federal court judge is then in a situation indistinguishable from that of antebellum lower court judges called upon to enforce proslavery law against conscience. The moral-formal conflict is inescapable.

The pro-life judge in such a situation must not enforce *Roe*, but also should not abuse the authority of the judicial role to say the law is something other than what he believes it to be. Instead, he should use the moral authority of his person (in a certain sense aided by his office) to say that he cannot enforce the law as it is. This does not necessarily mean resignation. Rather, it means *recusal*—removing himself from the case—*after* thorough legal investigation of the possibilities that the case may not in fact be controlled by *Roe*. And it means recusal accompanied by a full "judicial" opinion explaining (i) the natural right to life; (ii) why *Roe* is nonetheless the controlling positive law; *i.e.*, why the rule of *Roe* cannot be avoided in the case; (iii) why *Roe* is both lawless as a piece of judicial interpretation, and immoral as a work of raw judicial power contrary to natural right; and (iv) why the judge must therefore decline to enforce it, and must recuse himself from rendering a decision on the merits of the case before him.

The judge should not recuse himself in advance of the case, as one pro-life lower federal court judge is rumored to do in any case involving abortion. The case of conscientious scruple is different from the case of private bias. In the latter case, justice is enhanced by recusal. In the former, justice itself is recused—the ideals of natural right and justice are wrongly considered "biasing," and are regrettably absented from the proceedings. This is truly an empty gesture: the judge avoids personal complicity with evil in his judicial role, but the fact of evil and injustice is never spoken.

After-examination recusal shares the drawback of resignation: another judge simply may be found to enforce pro-abortion law in the particular case. But at least such a "focused recusal" has the advantage of keeping the pro-life judge on the court for another case, where the presumption in favor of life may be of greater use, not being contradicted by clear positive law. The focused recusal option is a classic dissonance-reducing maneuver, fully predictable under the "dissonance hypothesis" explained by Cover. It is an intermediate step. But the focused recusal strategy surely has risks beyond the possible disapprobation of professional colleagues and others. One can readily imagine the situation arising *after* a judge has engaged in the first two steps—indulging every presumption against *Roe* and in favor of life, and criticizing *Roe* while reaching a pro-life result distinguishing *Roe*—and has been reversed, *with directions*. In such a controversial, emotionally-charged context, the judge's self-recusal may be difficult to accomplish. The reversing court may not take "no" for an answer. The judge risks mandamus, administrative sanctions from judicial councils, or even impeachment, for refusal to follow the instructions of a higher court. (Indeed, sanctions or impeachment are possible based merely on the perception that conscientious criticism of unjust law, and consequent recusal, is improper judicial conduct.) At this point, resignation may be the only practical option. But it is better—more courageous, less an abandonment of principled morality, more likely tactically successful, more of a statement—for resignation to await such a point.

Indeed, a case can be made that the truly courageous, principled pro-life federal judge who is ordered to apply pro-abortion law contrary to conscience should take his case all the way to an impeachment trial on the Senate floor, if necessary. This would accord an important and highly visible public airing of the issue of abortion and moral conscience. It would probably be difficult for the Senate to muster the two-thirds majority to convict on an issue of conscience, as opposed to a matter of corruption. And if it did not convict, a strong signal would be sent to other judges that *Roe* is unenforceable except by the active concurrence of lower court judges. And even if the Senate did convict, the courageous judge would still have made a more important moral contribution to the law than he could have made any other way.

The hypothesized scenario has already been played out in one variation in the case of Michigan state court Judge Randall Hekman. Judge Hekman, sitting as a juvenile court judge, was called upon to order an abortion for a minor ward of the court, consistent with law but contrary to conscience. Judge Hekman declined to order the abortion on the alternative grounds (i) that it was not in the best interests of the girl; and (ii) that he would in any event feel compelled to reject the authority of *Roe* as a lawless and immoral decision. Hekman declined to remove himself from the case, on the ground that he satisfied none of the statutory or traditional grounds for disqualification. He further said that if ordered "to initiate procedures to kill innocent life for the expediency of others, that is a 'criminal order' which I cannot obey."[128]

Hekman was reversed on appeal, and the case reassigned to a different judge, by which time the girl changed her mind and decided not to abort her child. (Tragically, however, she suffered a miscarriage several months later.) Charges of judicial misconduct were filed against Hekman with the Michigan Supreme Court. Hekman eventually was cleared, though not before suffering much personal agony and public recrimination. Hekman's course of conduct seems *exactly* what is called for, but it also highlights the professional dangers of such open and candid criticism of *Roe*, even when actually deciding the case on available narrower grounds.

The "intermediate" step of recusal, as opposed to immediate resignation, appears justified with respect to abortion because the immorality of *Roe* does not infect the entire Constitution in quite the same way slavery did before the Civil War. The Garrisonian argument that the Constitution was a pro-slavery compact had considerable force: the Constitution did not merely decline to prohibit slavery; it sanctioned slavery and supported it with federal power. The fugitive rendition clauses of the Constitution were fundamentally supportive and protective of the institution of slavery in the South. While this may indeed have been the best deal that could have been struck at the time, the Constitution as written was still, in the Garrisonians' phrase, "a bargain with hell." For a judge to take an oath to enforce such a bargain, the terms of which committed the judge to enforcement of the fugitive slave clause, was, at some level, to take an oath to support slavery against the well established natural law rule of *Somersett's Case*. The Constitution was plainly contrary to natural law on this point.

The problem is less pronounced with abortion. *Roe* is an illegitimate interpretation of the Constitution. The document itself is not immoral with respect to abortion. Resignation, while an appropriate Garrisonian response to a pro-slavery Constitution, seems an overbroad remedy for

---

[128] Judge Hekman tells the story of the case and his ordeal in R. Hekman, JUSTICE FOR THE UNBORN (1984). Judge Hekman's opinion is reprinted as Appendix A to the book, at 151-165.

the problem of complicity with *Roe*. The conscientious judge can swear to uphold the Constitution and still refuse to enforce *Roe*.

But look where that conclusion leads. If a judge is not morally bound by his oath of office to enforce *Roe* because *Roe* is not "truly" part of the Constitution, why does not the stronger conclusion follow—that the judge is not bound by his oath of office to recognize *Roe* as valid precedent at all? This is the second branch of the fork: *lower court judges can, and should, disregard the authority of Roe*. And they may do so completely independent of any claim that the authority of *Roe* has been undermined by later decisions. The justification for defying *Roe* stems from the lawlessness and immorality of the decison itself. The judge may assume *Roe*'s validity *arguendo* for purposes of examining other ways of holding in favor of life in the particular case. But when push comes to shove, the judge may not only remove himself from the case, he may declare himself not to be bound as a judge by a lawless precedent. He may, in effect, "overrule" (or, perhaps a better term, given the relationship of the courts, "underrule") *Roe v. Wade*.

The argument for the power of lower court judges to "underrule" the Supreme Court is both straightforward and controversial: First, the judge's obligation, by oath, is to the Constitution, not to Supreme Court interpretations of the Constitution. There is nothing morally disingenuous in taking the oath and disobeying "controlling" precedent. As Andrew Jackson put it, "[e]ach public officer who takes an oath to support the Constitution swears that he will support it as he understands it, and not as it is understood by others." Second, there is nothing in the Constitution that requires lower courts to follow the constitutional decisions of the U.S. Supreme Court. There may be Supreme Court opinions that hold, or strongly suggest, that lower court judges are bound, by virtue of their oaths to uphold the *law*, to uphold also the precedents of higher courts. But that only begs the question of whether lower courts are bound to follow the holdings of the Supreme Court in all circumstances.

Third, the fact that not all decisions of "higher" federal courts are binding precedent, together with the strong Article III structural arguments for the equality of all federal judges, suggests that the obligation to follow controlling precedent is less a constitutional *duty* than an observed regularity attributable to the practical operating reality of a hierarchical system. Whether precedent is thought "controlling" is a function of the mechanisms Congress has provided for appellate review of lower federal and state courts, not a function of any inherent judicial hierarchy in the structure of the Constitution. Judges obey "controlling" precedent because they can be *reversed* if they do not. There is a reason why the U.S. District Court for the Southern District of New York considers the decisions of the Second Circuit "controlling," but not those of the First Circuit, but that reason does not derive from the Constitution. The fact that it does not is doubly significant. First, its [*sic*] suggests that precedents of higher courts, while worthy of respect, are not themselves law, but interpretations of law. They are secondary and derivative in nature. Second, whatever value inheres in following precedents within the chain-of-appeal can be vindicated by the chain-of-appeal itself.

My argument here owes much to Professor Akhil Amar's insightful contributions to the debate over interpretation of Article III of the Constitution. Amar argues that the "vesting" and "exceptions" clauses of Article III must be read in light of one another. For the mandatory categories of Article III (federal questions, ambassadors, admiralty), the judicial Power "*shall*" be vested in some federal court for "*all*" such cases. The exceptions that Congress may make to the Supreme Court's appellate jurisidiction in these cases are in favor of final decisions by some other federal court. In making this argument, Amar notes that if the Supreme Court's appellate jurisdiction over some class of cases is validly removed under the Exceptions Clause, there is no reason why the Supreme Court's *precedents* need any longer be considered binding by lower courts; the *decisions themselves* have no inherent constitutional status. If Amar is correct (and I believe he is), his arguments would appear to justify the further conclusion that lower courts are not "bound" by the Supreme Court's decisions even where the Supreme Court *does* have appellate jurisdiction: the decisions themselves have no constitutional status, and the Supreme Court may always choose to review the lower court decision and reverse.

So long as the lower court may still be reversed by the higher court, there is no interference with either the "supremacy" of the Supreme Court or with the idea of the rule of law. While lower courts may be "inferior" in the hierarchy—*i.e.*, their decisions can be *countermanded* by a higher tribunal—they are not constitutionally *subordinate* in terms of either their duties under the Constitution or their relationship to higher courts. Reviewing courts have no power to remove lower court judges from office, reduce their pay, or hold them in contempt, at least not in the federal system; only Congress may "fire" federal judges, by impeaching them. State court judges, while not institutionally equivalent to federal court judges, possess the same sworn obligation to uphold the Constitution. And while Article III requires that the decisions of state judges on federal questions be subject to review by some federal tribunal, the judges themselves are subject to no personal sanction by either federal courts or Congress. Thus, while it might be thought a breach of decorum for an inferior court to repudiate a precedent of a superior tribunal, such conduct is not constitutionally *insubordinate*, and is surely not categorically improper.

Neither can it be said that "underruling" actually undermines the rule of law, so long as the superior court is permitted to review and reverse. Indeed, quite to the contrary, such "underruling" may be an essential part of the process of judicial self-correction, and has occurred in the past to force Supreme Court reconsideration of questionable constitutional decisions. One of the most important, renowned examples of Supreme Court reconsideration of a constitutional holding—the flag salute cases—came about as a result of such "underruling" by a three-judge district court. In 1940, in *Minersville School District v. Gobitis*, "the Court upheld (8-1) a compulsory flag salute against a free exercise clause challenge. Just three years later, in *West Virginia State Board of Education v. Barnette*, the Court reversed itself (6-3). Importantly, the decision of the Supreme Court was an affirmance; the three-judge district court had "underruled" *Gobitis*. *Barnette* now stands as one of the Supreme Court's most famous defenses of religious liberty and freedom of conscience under the First Amendment.

Of course, were judges to choose such a course on *every* issue on which they disagreed with higher courts, the smooth functioning of the judicial system might rapidly break down. This is an important consideration for deciding *when* an issue is sufficiently important that the conscientious judge should flout controlling precedent. But it should be noted that this is a pure *process* value. There is far less *moral* content to this "formal" argument than there is to an argument against deliberate violation of the judicial oath. Disregarding clearly erroneous precedent subverting the meaning of the Constitution may be more faithful to the judicial oath—and to "process" notions of the rule of law—than following clearly erroneous precedent would be.

If there is any process value special to following higher court precedent above and beyond the usual values of *stare decisis* (which also apply when a court reconsiders its own decisions), it is that of the *costs* involved, in terms of delay, inconvenience, or expense, resulting from the necessity of appeal to re-establish in the particular case the rule of the Supreme Court. The asserted need for "uniformity" is not threatened, so long as the Supreme Court can review and reverse; only the costs of enforcing uniformity are new. I submit that those costs are justified by the benefit of forcing Supreme Court reconsideration of an issue when lower courts think the Supreme Court's decision clearly outside the range of allowable judicial interpretation of the Constitution—a standard that provides the full measure of judicial restraint in lower court "review" of Supreme Court decisions.

Roe v. Wade is such a case of clearly erroneous interpretation of the Constitution, a case of *ultra vires* exercise of judicial power. Lower courts should repudiate the holding of the Supreme Court in *Roe*, thus forcing its reconsideration. The case for "underruling" is especially strong where it is anticipated that the Supreme Court may be prepared to reconsider a constitutional holding, as with *Gobitis* in the 1940s and *Plessy* in the 1950s, and today with *Roe*, especially in light of *Webster*. But even if this did not appear likely (and the tides could well turn again), the conscientious, pro-life lower court judge legitimately may force the Supreme Court to reconsider *Roe* and reverse his or her decision. Such an approach was vigorously suggested by antislavery lawyers in the wake of *Dred Scott*. There is unmistakably something of a defiant quality to such action, but as long as the reviewing court is permitted review—as contrasted with the refusal of the Wisconsin Supreme Court to certify the appeal to the U.S. Supreme Court in the *Booth* case, with respect to the Fugitive Slave Act of 1850—the tactic is not lawless. It is faithful to the judge's oath. It merely requires the Supreme Court to do its own dirty work.

The conscientious lower court judge must not become an accomplice in such dirty work, however. It is possible, perhaps even likely, that a judge following this course will be reversed (and chastised) by a reviewing court, and directed to enter an order based on the unjust and unjustifiable precedent. At this point, the path of underruling links back up with that of criticism, recusal, and, if necessary, resignation, discussed above. But when the source of the judge's moral-formal dilemma is lawless judicial precedent rather than validly adopted positive law, the judge need not in the first instance follow the quasi-traditional path of criticism, recusal, and resignation, but should first undertake to underrule the lawless precedent.

Questions

1. According to Rice, what is the constructive function of the natural law?
2. You are a state legislator who believes in natural law. How could you use natural law constructively?
3. According to Rice, what is the critical function of the natural law? Who may use this function?
4. How does King explain his "willingness to break laws?"

5. According to King, how should one go about breaking an unjust law?

6. How does King view the church's role in the civil rights movement? Does this view of the church still hold true today regarding social issues? How should the church respond to social issues today?

7. At one point in his letter, King states that "segregation substitutes an 'I-it' relationship for the 'I-thou' relationship, and relegates persons to the status of things." What does he mean? How would this apply to abortion or embryonic stem cell research? Does King's letter provide guidance for how the pro-life movement should act?

8. According to Matthew 22:15-22; Romans 13:1-7; I Timothy 2:1-3; and I Peter 2:13-17, what is a Christian's duty to the civil government?

9. Read Exodus 1:15-21; Joshua 2:1-21; 6:17, 22-25; Hebrews 11:31; James 2:25; Daniel 3:8-18, 29-30; 6:4-11, 25-28; and Acts 4:13-20; 5:17-29. Based on these scriptures:

   a. Is civil disobedience ever appropriate?

   b. If so, when?

   c. If so, how?

10. Should the following individuals engage in civil disobedience?

    a. Parents confronting a law prohibiting them from giving religious instruction to their children;

    b. Taxpayers confronting a law providing that federal income tax revenue will be used to pay for abortions for low income women;

    c. A minister confronting a hate speech law that forbids public statements criticizing a homosexual lifestyle;

    d. A Chinese citizen forbidden to worship in a house church independent from government approved denominations;

    e. An individual forbidden to engage in public protests against his or her government when that government has abandoned the rule of law and has rigged elections in order to maintain power;

f. A United States soldier instructed by a superior officer to inflict what the soldier believes to be torture on an enemy detainee.

11. Were the following appropriate?

a. The American Revolution;

b. The French Revolution;

c. German citizens hiding Jews and homosexuals to prevent them from being sent to concentration camps for extermination;

d. Martin Luther King Jr. violating an injunction in order to lead a demonstration calling for the integration of public facilities in Birmingham, Alabama;

e. Pro-life activists trespassing on the private property of an abortion clinic in an effort to prevent abortions from taking place;

f. Paul Hill killing an abortionist.

12. According to Paulsen, what choices does a judge have when faced with handing down a decision based on an unjust law?

13. What does Paulsen believe the judge should do? Why are the other options inadequate?

14. A federal district court judge is faced with handing down a decision that would enforce the following laws. The judge is convinced that there is no argument based on positive law that would allow him or her to do anything other than enforce the laws. What would Charles Rice advise the judge to do? What would Michael Paulsen advise? What would you advise?

a. A constitutional amendment repealing the First Amendment and outlawing Christian worship and confiscating the property of all Christians;

b. A constitutional amendment requiring all states to recognize same-sex marriages;

c. A federal law providing that, to save costs, no lifesaving measures may be given to persons over eighty years old.

15. You are a Supreme Court justice. What would you say to a fellow justice who invokes natural law to strike down the following laws:

    a. A statute prohibiting the creation of human-animal hybrids (explaining that the law will interfere with research that may produce cures for diabetes, Parkinson's, and other diseases);

    b. A statute prohibiting same-sex marriage (explaining that the law discriminates against individuals who are born with a particular sexual orientation).

Chapter 2 The Influence of Higher Law Thinking on the Common Law

A. What is the Common Law?

Introduction

This chapter examines the impact that a belief in a higher law had on the development of the common law, particularly the common law's procedural system. It traces the influence of higher law thinking on such matters as common law decision-making, equity, and the rule of law.

The chapter's first two pieces introduce and define the common law. In the first piece, William Blackstone defines the common law and explains how common law decisions were made.

In the second piece, Russell Kirk compares the common law to other competing forms of law and describes some of the principles that are fundamental to the common law method. Russell Kirk has been described by both *Time* and *Newsweek* as one of America's leading thinkers. Born in 1918, Kirk received a masters degree from Duke University and a doctorate in literature from St. Andrews University in Scotland. At the time of his death in 1994, Kirk held twelve honorary doctorates. He was a visiting professor at various universities in the fields of history, political thought, humane letters, and journalism. Kirk was a prolific author. The piece included here is from his book entitled *The Roots Of American Order*, in which he reviews world history and describes the different civilizations, people, and ideas that most shaped America's legal system.

William Blackstone, *Commentaries on the Laws of England, Vol I*[*]

As to general customs, or the common law, properly so called; this is that law, by which proceedings and determinations in the king's ordinary courts of justice are guided and directed. This, for the most part, settles the course in which lands descend by inheritance; the manner and form of acquiring and transferring property; the solemnities and obligation of contracts; the rules of expounding wills, deeds, and acts of parliament; the respective remedies of civil injuries; the several species of temporal offences, with the manner and degree of punishment; and an infinite number of minute particulars, which diffuse themselves as extensively as the ordinary distribution of common justice requires. Thus, for example, that there shall be four superior courts of record, the chancery, the king's bench, the common pleas, and the exchequer;—that the eldest son alone is heir to his ancestor;—that property may be acquired and transferred by writing;—that a deed is of no validity unless sealed;—that wills shall be construed more favorably, and deeds more floridly;—that money lent upon bond is recoverable by action of debt;—that breaking the public peace is an offence, and punishable by fine and imprisonment;—all these are doctrines that are not set down in any written statute or ordinance, but depend merely upon immemorial usage, that is, upon common law, for their support.

Some have divided the common law into two principal grounds or foundations: 1. established customs; such as that where there are three brothers, the eldest brother shall be heir to the second, in exclusion of the youngest: and 2. established rules and maxims; as, "that the king can do no wrong, that no man shall be bound to accuse himself," and the like. But I take these to be one and the same thing. For the authority of these maxims rests entirely upon general reception and usage; and the only method of proving, that this or that maxim is a rule of the common law, is by showing that it has been always the custom to observe it.

But here a very natural, and very material, question arises: how are there customs or maxims to be known, and by whom is their validity to be determined? The answer is, by the judges in the several courts of justice. They are the depositary of the laws; the living oracles, who must decide in all cases of doubt, and who are bound by an oath to decide according to the law of the land. Their knowledge of that law is derived

[*] WILLIAM BLACKSTONE, COMMENTARIES ON THE LAWS OF ENGLAND, VOL I 68-71 (Univ. of Chicago Press 1979) (1765).

from experience and study; from the "*viginti annorum lucubrationes*" [working by night for twenty years], which Fortescue mentions; and from being long personally accustomed to the judicial decisions of their predecessors. And indeed these judicial decisions are the principal and most authoritative evidence, that can be given, of the existence of such a custom as shall form a part of the common law. The judgment itself, and all the proceedings previous thereto, are carefully registered and preserved, under the name of records, in public repositories set apart for that particular purpose; and to them frequent recourse is had, when any critical question arises, in the determination of which former precedents may give light or assistance. And therefore, even so early as the conquest, we find the "*praeteritorum memoria eventorum*" [remembrance of past events] reckoned up as one of the chief qualifications of those who were held to be "*legibus patriae optime instituti*" [best established by the laws of the country]. For it is an established rule to abide by former precedents, where the same points come again in litigation; as well to keep the scale of justice even and steady, and not liable to waver with every new judge's opinion; as also because the law in that case being solemnly declared and determined, what before was uncertain, and perhaps indifferent, is now become a permanent rule, which it is not in the breast of any subsequent judge to alter or vary from, according to his private sentiments: he being sworn to determine, not according to his own private judgment, but according to the known laws and customs of the land; not delegated to pronounce a new law, but to maintain and expound the old one. Yet this rule admits of exception, where the former determination is most evidently contrary to reason; much more if it be contrary to the divine law. But even in such cases the subsequent judges do not pretend to make a new law, but to vindicate the old one from misrepresentation. For if it be found that the former decision is manifestly absurd or unjust, it is declared, not that such a sentence was *bad law*, but that it was *not law*; that is, that it is not the established custom of the realm, as has been erroneously determined. And hence it is that our lawyers are with justice so copious in their encomiums on the reason of the common law; that they tell us, that the law is the perfection of reason, that it always intends to conform thereto, and that what is not reason is not law. Not that the particular reason of every rule in the law can at this distance of time be always precisely aligned; but it is sufficient that there be nothing in the rule flatly contradictory to reason, and then the law will presume it to be well founded. And it hath been an ancient observation in the laws of England, that whenever a standing rule of law, of which the reason perhaps could not be remembered or discerned, hath been wantonly broke in upon by statutes or new resolutions, the wisdom of the rule hath in the end appeared from the inconveniences that have followed the innovation.

The doctrine of the law then is this: that precedents and rules must be followed, unless flatly absurd or unjust for though their reason be not obvious at first view, yet we owe such a deference to former times as not to suppose they acted wholly without consideration. To illustrate this doctrine by examples. It has been determined, time out of mind, that a brother of the half blood (i.e. where they have only one parent the same, and the other different) shall never succeed as heir to the estate of his half brother, but it shall rather escheat to the king, or other superior lord. Now this is a positive law, fixed and established by custom, which custom is evidenced by judicial decisions; and therefore can never be departed from by any modern judge without a breach of his oath and the law. For herein there is nothing repugnant to natural justice; though the reason of it, drawn from the feudal law, may not be quite obvious to everybody. And therefore, on account of a supposed hardship upon the half brother, a modern judge might wish it had been otherwise settled; yet it is not in his power to alter it. But if any court were now to determine, that an elder brother of the half blood might enter upon and seise any lands that were purchased by his younger brother, no subsequent judges would scruple to declare that such prior determination was unjust, was unreasonable, and therefore was not *law*. So that *the law*, and the *opinion of the judge* are not always convertible terms, or one and the same thing; since it sometimes may happen that the judge may mistake the law. Upon the whole however, we may take it as a general rule, "that the decisions of courts of justice are the evidence of what is common law:" in the same manner as, in the civil law, what the emperor had once determined was to serve for a guide for the future.

Russell Kirk, *The Roots of American Order*[*]

The Reign of Law

The law, which is no respecter of persons, stands supreme: that is the essence of British legal theory and legal practice, and it passed into America from the first colonial settlements onward. The king himself is under the law; should he break it, his subjects would be absolved from

[*] RUSSELL KIRK, THE ROOTS OF AMERICAN ORDER 183-85 (1974). From the book The Roots of American Order by Russell Kirk.

their allegiance. And the law is not merely the creation of kings and parliaments, but rather the source of their authority. At heart, the law is the expression of natural justice and the ancient ways of a people.

From its Norman beginnings, English law had two aspects, and two systems of courts: common law, and equity. Both came to be administered by the king's judges. As the juridical structure developed, the common law was represented at its highest by the old courts of Common Pleas, King's Bench, and the Exchequer; equity by the court of Chancery, the lord chancellor's court (although Chancery, in one of its two tribunals, also was a court of common law). These distinctions endured in England from Norman times down to 1873. We turn first, and at greater length, to the common law.

The common law is quite different from statutory law—that is, different from the written statutes issued by the sovereign political authority. The common law is founded upon custom and precedent, although upon *national* customs and usages, rather than upon local. This common law is an "organic" development, arising out of centuries of judges' decisions upon the basis of what the people believed to be just. It is "prescriptive" law, derived from the man-to-man experience of people in community over a very long period of time; it is "customary" or "traditional" law. It is the fundamental body of law in England and in the countries that have received it from England: all other forms of law, in England and those other countries, have been developed later, in part to deal with cases for which the common law seemed inadequate.

The common law has been called "unwritten law," and so it probably was, in the very beginning. But soon the decisions of common-law judges began to be written down, and so there accumulated a mass of records of judgments, from which written precedents covering new cases of a similar character could be ascertained. Thus the common law is "case law," or a complex body of legal precedents upon which all judges are supposed to base their present and future decisions: to rule on a present case, they must consult the body of established precedents in earlier analogous cases. Or, to put this more accurately, the common-law judge is expected to hear the arguments of opposing litigants, both of whom will cite precedents favoring his own claim; and the judge is to decide in favor of the claimant whose lawyer has most convincingly demonstrated that precedent stands on his side.

Rather than "unwritten law," really, common law may be described as non-codified law. Formal statutes of a state ordinarily are embodied in a formal legal code; but common law is a different system, more complex, based on a multitude of precedents rather than upon a systematic compilation. To put matters in another fashion, the common law is not a corpus of acts passed by a legislature or a parliament, or of decrees issued by a sovereign; it is the "people's law," so to speak, for it has grown out of practical cases of actual contest at law, over centuries, and is sanctioned by popular assent to its fairness. There is no need for ratification of the common law by the Crown in Parliament or by some comparable political authority.

The central distinction of the common law, then, is the rule of *stare decisis*, "to stand by decided cases": all judges are supposed to be bound by previous decisions, that is (a principle which, in theory, still governs the judiciary in the United States, most of the time). The purpose of *stare decisis* is to ensure that evenhanded justice will be administered from one year to another, one decade to another, one century to another; that judges will not be permitted to create laws or to decide cases arbitrarily, or to favor particular persons in particular circumstances. They must abide by the accumulated experience of legal custom, so that the law will be no respecter of persons, and so that people may be able to act in the certitude that the law does not alter capriciously.

Questions

1. What is the common law?
2. How is it different from statutory law?
3. According to Blackstone, what is the source of the rules and doctrines that make up the common law?
4. What is stare decisis?
5. Why is stare decisis important?
6. Read Job 34:17-19; II Chronicles 19:4-7; Deuteronomy 17:8-13; and Leviticus 19:15. How do these passages support the doctrine of stare decisis?
7. Is it ever appropriate for a judge to depart from stare decisis and overturn a previous decision? If so, when?

B. Common Law and Equity

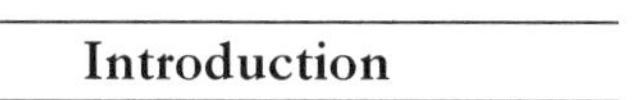

Introduction

Common law courts were not the only English courts that administered justice. The Harold Berman selection from Chapter 1 illustrated that common law courts competed with ecclesiastical courts that applied canon law. Later in their history, common law courts also competed somewhat with Chancery. Like the common law courts, Chancery was a royal court. Its power came from the King and it was headed by the Chancellor. Eventually, it became an alternative court for parties who felt that the common law did not provide an adequate remedy. Parties approached Chancery and sought equitable as opposed to legal relief.

The following two pieces describe the nature and function of equity and Chancery. The first is an excerpt from Arthur Hogue's *The Origins of the Common Law*. Arthur Hogue was born in Pittsburgh in 1906, the son of a Presbyterian minister. He received an A.B. from Oberlin College and an M.A. and a Ph.D. from Harvard University, all in history. Hogue then taught history at several universities, including Hanover College, the University of Illinois, and Indiana University. He was a member of the American Society of Legal History and wrote prominently in the field of legal history until his death in 1998.

In *The Origins of the Common Law*, Hogue sketches the development of the common law through its most formative period—the period between 1154 and 1307. In this excerpt, Hogue describes how all royal courts, including common law courts, were considered courts that dispensed equity. There was no strict distinction between law and equity at that time.

The second piece is an excerpt from Stephen Yeazell's *Civil Procedure*. Yeazell is a professor of law at the University of California, Los Angeles. He received a B.A. from Swarthmore College, an M.A. from Columbia University and a J.D. from Harvard Law School. Yeazell teaches civil procedure and legal history. He writes largely about the history and theory of procedure.

In this excerpt, Yeazell compares the jurisdiction and procedure of Chancery with that of the common law courts. He demonstrates that, while all royal courts were equitable early in their development, Chancery developed a very separate justice system over time.

Arthur Hogue, *Origins of the Common Law*[*]

The greater one's familiarity with the law of England, the more he will appreciate the long-range effects of the chancellor's acquiring an independent jurisdiction as judge of a court of equity. The English legal system has always shown a concern for what *ought* to be the results of a legal principle as well as a concern for the strict application of that principle. This distinction between *what is* and *what ought* to be may serve as a rough guide to the difference between common law and equity in the centuries after the fourteenth. Equity supplements the common law; its rules do not contradict the common law; rather, they aim at securing substantial justice when the strict rule of common law might work hardship.

The administration of equity did not begin with Chancery; the *Curia Regis* [king's senate] and the king's council were courts of equity long before Chancery began its judicial activity, and the king's council continued to act in this capacity after the Chancery court was clearly distinguished from the common-law courts. The equitable jurisdiction of the chancellor drained away none of the royal prerogative, none of the judicial power of the royal council; rather, the chancellor, after the fourteenth century, might be thought of as doing work which in an earlier time would have been handled by the council. He eventually carried into the court of Chancery the power to hear certain cases in much the same way as the itinerant justice carried into the county court the royal power to hear certain cases. In the county court itinerant justices dispensed justice as though in the presence of the king; persons seeking justice presented petitions, or plaints, to the justices-in-eyre in the thirteenth century in much the same fashion and in much the same words as persons later on in the fourteenth century presented petitions to Chancery. Whether or not the jurisdiction of the justices-in-eyre or the jurisdiction of the chancellor should be described as a delegated jurisdiction, one point is clear—the justices-in-eyre and the chancellor acted as judges in equity when they heard plaints and petitions.

A discussion of equity as a distinct body of procedures and legal principles can easily bog down in a swamp of definitions when it reaches backward into the Middle Ages. In theory, at least, all laws are equitable when they first come into use. With the passage of time laws become rigid and fixed in their application. Timid judges or unthinking officials

---

[*] ARTHUR HOGUE, ORIGINS OF THE COMMON LAW 175-77 (1985). Reprinted with the permission of David B. Hogue.

fail to grasp the principle or the intent embodied in a rule. They hesitate to widen its application. The social order constantly changes, but the laws all too frequently lag behind. It then becomes necessary to close in some fashion the gap between social change and the legal system. In the thirteenth century the English king and his council, including his judges and great officers, were able to exercise the royal duty and right to develop new remedies for new wrongs. Thus new forms of action, new writs such as Trespass, and new royal courts such as Common Pleas and King's Bench were all "equitable" in the thirteenth century. The emergence of Chancery as a court of "equity" in the fourteenth century is worth noting, because its procedures ultimately led to a widening distinction between what were later called the common-law courts and the equity courts. But we should not look for the sixteenth- or seventeenth-century distinctions between common law and equity in the court system of the thirteenth century. In the thirteenth century every institution concerned with the administration of justice was equitable in the sense that it was free to provide substantial justice by enlarging the existing remedies. The Crown, working through the chancellor's office, seems to have been prompt to invent new remedies, and the baronage, resenting the activity, sought at times to curb it. Nevertheless, the chancellor's office was so central for the administration of justice that it continued its equitable functions, particularly in the handling of petitions. Since the chancellor, better than any other official, knew the existing law, he was in an excellent position to make judgments about what the law ought to be.

Stephen Yeazell, *Civil Procedure**

Chancery has a rich and often misunderstood history. For the purposes of the student concerned solely with mastering modern American law, it is necessary to bear only a few points in mind. First, Chancery was like the courts of common law, a royal court, whose power came from the king. Chancery was headed by the Chancellor, a powerful royal official who, until well into the nineteenth century, had a number of other important political duties in addition to presiding over the Court of Chancery. (If one seeks a modern analogy, it would be as if the White House chief of staff also presided over a special court.) Second, everyone agreed that Chancery's job was to deal with cases that, for a variety of reasons, were not adequately handled by the ordinary royal courts.

---

* STEPHEN YEAZELL, CIVIL PROCEDURE 385-89 (4th ed. 1996). Reprinted with the permission of Aspen Publishers, Stephen Yeazell, Civil Procedure, 4th Edition, 385-89, 1996.

What were the cases that fell within Chancery jurisdiction? One makes a mistake by looking for an entirely coherent theory of Chancery power. Maitland once explained that one could comprehend Chancery jurisdiction only by listing all the claims the Chancellor would recognize and the remedies he would grant. Blackstone, writing in the eighteenth century, was more optimistic; after rejecting a number of fallacious distinctions, he summarized the distinction between Chancery and the common law as "principally consist[ing] in different modes of administering justice in each; in the mode of proof, the mode of trial, and the mode of relief." In other words, the distinctions were primarily procedural. One can understand this statement by seeing that Chancery's jurisdiction, even more than that of the common law, grew by happenstance: To the extent there is any common theme in this description of Chancery jurisdiction, it is that Chancery often acted when something about the common law seemed to result in unacceptable results. Frequently these unacceptable results flowed from an aspect of common law procedure.

For example, Chancery sometimes administered special *remedies* for claims as to which common law courts had jurisdiction. The best known examples of such remedies are decrees of specific performance for contracts and injunctions against torts. If one sought money damages, the common law courts could give the plaintiff what he wanted; if injunctive decrees were sought, the claim had to be brought in Chancery. In judging such cases, Chancery sometimes developed what eventually came to be seen as substantive rules. For example, in deciding cases seeking specific performance (a form of injunctive relief), Chancery developed the rule that the buyer of a parcel of land was entitled to a decree of specific performance—an order that the seller convey the land.

Another of Chancery's specialties was remedies for fraud. At common law—especially early common law—a formal, sealed written contract had enormous significance. If a debtor paid his debt but failed to get the physical contract canceled or destroyed, he could be sued again. Or, a contract arrived at by fraud could be enforced so long as it had actually been signed by the parties in question. Common law enforced these agreements, perhaps because it feared to turn such questions over to juries, perhaps because at early common law the parties could not themselves testify under oath, thus making it harder to get at the truth of the matter. Chancery, where parties could be forced to testify under oath, and where the Chancellors sat without juries, dared to make those judgments, which it enforced by rescinding contracts for fraud. That meant that a plaintiff alleging fraud would, before the eighteenth century, have had to seek relief in Chancery to get that remedy. In Adams's claim against

Jones, she might go to Chancery to have his "deed" *rescinded* for fraud, thus clarifying her title to the land.

A related form of relief—on a special form of contract, the mortgage—was also available in Chancery; its development shows equity behaving much like common law, by elaborating substantive rules around procedural forms. In their original forms, mortgages were quite severe instruments: a debtor who had made all but the final payment on time could lose his land. Chancery's answer was to grant a right of redemption to the late-paying debtor. At first redemption was available only in pressing circumstances—for example, the debtor had fallen into a ditch and broken his leg on the way to make the last payment—but it later became available to any debtor who, even very belatedly and without any real excuse, was willing to pay off the mortgage. This perhaps overgenerous relief led in turn to a remedy for the creditor: a right of foreclosure. In foreclosure, the debtor's right of redemption was "foreclosed," that is, cut off before its natural (and indefinite) expiration date. Mortgage lenders who wanted to seize and sell the property of defaulting debtors were well advised to use Chancery's foreclosure process, because only through it could they ensure clear title so that the debtor would not, years later, show up and redeem the mortgage. In foreclosure proceedings Chancery gave the debtor credit for any amount he had already paid—requiring that the lender give him that amount from the sale proceeds.

We still refer to such a debtor's interest as his "equity" in the property. We refer to it this way because the Court of Chancery came to be known as a court of equity, and its legal doctrines were known as doctrines of equity. "Equitable" in this context does not mean "fair" or "just" in the ordinary sense of that term—it refers instead to the body of law once administered by the Court of Chancery. To be sure, a number of Chancery's doctrines called for the application of discretion with an eye to fairness;[*] that does not mean, however, that all equitable doctrines are discretionary and vague.

Another large group of cases came to Chancery because they involved the administration of *trusts*—over which Chancery had jurisdiction. The trust is a device with its roots in a medieval tax evasion scheme that has given rise to a number of important modern institutions. The basic principle underlying a trust is that the trustee holds legal title and exercises control over property, but the benefits of that property go to the beneficiary. Chancery's jurisdiction over trusts, as with fraud, may have originated in the need to examine parties under oath. Because many

[*] One common example is the doctrine that an injunction will not be granted unless the applicant would, in its absence, suffer irreparable hardship.

wealthy families tied up their property in complex trusts, the beneficiaries of these trusts—and their creditors—spent a good deal of time in Chancery litigation. In administering the trust, Chancery developed new substantive law and a new remedy. The substantive law was the high standard of honesty and care to which trustees were held: the fiduciary obligation. The new remedy was the *constructive trust.* The constructive trust treated misused trust assets as if they were still held in trust. For example, if a trustee took trust assets and purchased land for himself, Chancery would impose a constructive trust on the land. The result would be that if the land were worth more than the original assets, the beneficiary would recover not just the original assets but a more valuable asset—here the land—into which those assets had been transformed.

Having argued that Chancery procedures were often the reason cases came to that court, we should sketch those processes. Like courts of common law, Chancery had its own procedures, many of which contrasted sharply with those of the common law. Some have already been mentioned. Chancery used no jury; judges—the Chancellor and a small number of lesser officials—deciding all the cases themselves.[**] Chancery's pleadings, instead of consisting of the formulas of common law, often went into enormous detail. Where common law insisted on live witnesses testifying in open court, Chancery depended instead on extensive written depositions, the ancestors of our modern discovery practice. Where common law forbade the parties from testifying under oath, Chancery insisted on it. Where common law depended on the parties' ability to persuade witnesses to testify, Chancery employed the subpoena, which compelled testimony, making it possible to compel reluctant witnesses. Where common law often sharply limited the number of parties who could participate in a suit, Chancery prided itself on including all those who were concerned—even to the point of refusing to act at all unless the optimum number of parties could be joined. As you examine modern American process more closely, you will see that at a number of points it has blended common law and Chancery procedures. A point sometimes disputed is whether we have chosen the most attractive features of the two systems.

Whatever their differences, common law and equity agreed on a point of pleading. As with an action at common law, a suit in equity required the pleader to state facts that brought him within the jurisdiction of Chancery. That allegation, in the case of Chancery, required that the

---

[**] Chancery judges would sometimes require that an issue of fact first be tried by a jury by bringing a common law action; then, aided by the jury's decision of the question of fact, Chancery would conduct further proceedings.

pleader state both that a claim was within royal power generally and that it was one for which the ordinary royal courts—the common law courts—afforded no adequate remedy. That requirement has persisted in modern pleading: a party seeking an injunction, for example, must allege that she has no adequate legal remedy. What did that—and what does that—mean? At the height of the system (say, the seventeenth century) it meant that the courts of common law could not grant an injunction (they simply lacked the power to give such a remedy), that the Court of Chancery had such power, and—this is the crucial point—that the case was one in which money damages (the ordinary legal remedy) would not be a sufficient remedy. Just what those circumstances are is the subject not only of part of Chapter V, but also of several substantive courses. For present purposes the point is that equity, like the common law, required pleadings that properly invoked its jurisdiction, and behind these invocations of jurisdiction lay the idea that power, even royal power, was limited and divided.

Questions

1. What is the difference between law and equity?

2. According to Hogue, why is it not possible to draw a strict line between law and equity in medieval times? How did common law courts dispense equity?

3. According to Yeazell, what are some of the most significant equitable doctrines? How did they develop?

4. In his book, *Fountain of Justice: A Study in the Natural Law*, Professor John Wu contrasts equity with law in this way: "Equity is to law what poetry is to prose. The beauty of 'law' consists in its clarity and orderliness. The beauty of equity lies in its flexibility and plasticity, in its untrammeled response to values and delicate sense of proportion." Wu argues that Luke 6:1-4 and I Samuel 21:1-6 reflect this understanding of equity. Is he right?

5. Read Matthew 23:1-4 and 16-24. How does this passage relate to the need for equity in the law?

6. Is there a danger with equity? The English Puritans of the seventeenth century thought so. Based upon their belief in man's fallen nature (and their unpleasant experience with discretionary non-common law courts like Star Chamber), the Puritans sought to severely limit Chancery's jurisdiction. Puritan lawyer and scholar

John Selden argued: "Equity in law is the same as the spirit is in religion, what everyone pleases to make it;" and "Equity is a roguish thing; equity is according to the conscience of him that is chancellor.... It is all one as if they should make the standard for the measure a chancellor's foot." Is this a legitimate concern? If so, how do you reconcile this with the passages above? Is there a balance?

C. Development of the Rule of Law and the Protection of Individual Liberty

Introduction

One of the hallmarks of the common law has been its commitment to the rule of law. The rule of law proclaims that law, and not individual rulers, is the ultimate authority in a state. The principle places significant limits on government officials. It requires them to rule by law (not arbitrarily) and under law (they are subject to the law, just as the citizens they govern are subject to the law).

A direct consequence of the common law's commitment to the rule of law has been the firm protection of individual liberties from government interference. Indeed, many of the most cherished personal liberties found in the United States Constitution were drawn directly from the common law.

What follows is a series of readings that focuses on the rule of law and protection of individual liberties from a philosophical, historical, and theological perspective.

The first piece is a famous excerpt from Bracton's *De Legibus et Consuetudinibus Angliae* (*The Laws and Customs of England*). In it, Bracton declares the principle that everyone, even the king, is bound by the law. This thirteenth century pronouncement set the standard by which the common law viewed royal power for the next half millenium.

Bracton's declaration had historical precedent. In 1215, English barons, led by Archbishop Stephen Langton, revolted against the tyrannical and arbitrary rule of King John. In exchange for the barons' financial support for his aggressive foreign policy, John was forced to sign Magna Carta, in which he agreed to be bound to certain fundamental limitations on royal authority that became part of the common law and the English Constitution. The second piece in this section contains several excerpts from this historic document.

The third piece is from Russell Kirk's *The Roots of American Order*. In it, Kirk traces specific liberties enjoyed by American citizens to the common law.

The fourth piece is an excerpt from a lecture given by theologian, philosopher, and statesman Abraham Kuyper. He gave the lecture at Princeton University in 1898 as part of the Stone Lecture series. In it, Kuyper lays out his view of the theological basis for both the authority of the state and for constitutional limits on that authority.

Kuyper was born in Holland in 1837. He received a doctorate in theology in 1862 and was called into the ministry. This was the first of many callings in his career. In 1872, Kuyper became the editor-in-chief of *The Standard*, a daily newspaper. Shortly after this he became editor of *The Herald*, a weekly Christian newspaper. He edited both papers for over forty-five years. In 1880, Kuyper established the Free University of Amsterdam, a school at which he served both as a teacher and an administrator. Kuyper was also heavily involved in politics as leader of the Anti-Revolutionary Party in the Netherlands. The party was formed to oppose the principles of the French Revolution (captured in the motto: "No God; No Master"). Kuyper believed in freedom from oppressive governments but opposed the eradication of religion from politics. He and the party sought to bring a Christian voice to political life. Kuyper served as Prime Minister of the Netherlands from 1901-1905. Kuyper also published numerous books in the areas of systematic theology, political theory, and devotional literature.

In 1897, Kuyper described what motivated him in each of these endeavors:

> One desire has been the ruling passion of my life. One high motive has acted like a spur upon my mind and soul. And sooner than that I should seek escape from the sacred necessity that is laid upon me, let the breath of life fail me. It is this: That in spite of worldly opposition, God's holy ordinances shall be established again in the home, in the school and in the State for the good of the people; to carve as it were into the conscience of the nation the ordinances of the Lord, to which the Bible and Creation bear witness, until the nation pays homage again to God.

The final piece is an excerpt from Craig Stern's 2004 article, "The Common Law and the Religious Foundations of the Rule of Law before *Casey*," published in the University of San Francisco Law Review. Stern is a law professor at Regent University School of Law. He received a B.A. *cum laude* from Yale University and a J.D. from the University of

Virginia. Stern joined the Regent faculty in 1990. He teaches federal courts, conflicts of law, jurisprudence, and criminal law. In this excerpt, Stern argues that four Christian doctrines significantly shaped the development of the rule of law in the common law tradition.

Henrici de Bracton, *De Legibus et Consuetudinibus Angliae (The Laws and Customs of England)*[*]

Chapter VIII

Before God there is no acceptance of men as free, nor of men as slaves, for God is not an acceptor of persons; for as regards the Lord, he who is greater becomes sometimes less, and he who precedes becomes, as it were, a servant. But there is a difference of persons before men, because some men are pre-excellent, and are preferred and take precedence of others. The Lord Pope, for instance, in spiritual matters, which pertain to the priesthood, and, under him, archbishops, bishops, and other prelates.

Likewise, in temporal matters, there are emperors, kings, and princes in those matters which pertain to the realm, and under them dukes, counts, barons, magnates, or vavasours, and knights; and also freemen and villeins, and different powers established under a king.

* * *

There are also under the king knights, that is, persons chosen to practice warfare, that they may make war in company with the king and those above mentioned, and may defend the country and the people of God. There are also under the king freemen and serfs subject to his power; and every person is under him, and he is under no person, but is only under God. He has no peer in his own kingdom, for so he would forfeit the precept since equal has no power over equal; also, much less has he any superior or more powerful person than himself [in his kingdom], for so he would be inferior to his own subjects, and inferiors cannot be equal to their superiors. But the king himself ought not to be subject to man, but subject to God and to the law, for the law makes the king. Let the king, then, attribute to the law what the law attributes to him, namely dominion and power, for there is no king where the will and not the law has dominion; and that he ought to be under the law, since he

[*] HENRICI DE BRACTON, DE LEGIBUS ET CONSUETUDINIBUS ANGLIAE (THE LAWS AND CUSTOMS OF ENGLAND) 37, 39, 41 (1990).

is the vicar of God, appears evidently after the likeness of Jesus Christ, whose place he fills on earth; for the true mercy of God, when many things were at his command to restore the human race in an ineffable manner, chose this way in preference to all others, as if to destroy the work of the devil he should use not the vigor of his power, but the reason of his justice, and so he was willing to be under the law, that he might redeem those who were under the law, for he was not willing to use his strength, but his reason and judgment. So likewise the Blessed Virgin Mary, the parent of God, the mother of our Lord, who by a singular privilege was above the law, nevertheless, in order to show an example of humility, she did not refuse to be subject to the institutions of law. So therefore the king, that his power should not be unrestrained; but there ought not to be a greater than he is in his own kingdom in the administration of justice, but he ought to be the least, or, as if it were so, if he is a petitioner to obtain judgment. But if a petition is made to him (since a writ does not run against him), there will be place for a supplication to him to correct and amend his own act, which indeed if he omits to do, it is sufficient for his punishment that he await the vengeance of the Lord. Let no one presume to dispute [before him] respecting his acts, much less to contravene his acts.

Magna Carta

John, by the grace of God King of England, Lord of Ireland, Duke of Normandy and Aquitaine, and Count of Anjou, to his archbishops, bishops, abbots, earls, barons, justices, foresters, sheriffs, stewards, servants, and to all his officials and loyal subjects, greeting.

Know that before God, for the health of our soul and those of our ancestors and heirs, to the honour of God, the exaltation of the holy Church, and the better ordering of our kingdom, at the advice of our reverend fathers Stephen, archbishop of Canterbury, primate of all England, and cardinal of the holy Roman Church, Henry archbishop of Dublin, William bishop of London, Peter bishop of Winchester, Jocelin bishop of Bath and Glastonbury, Hugh bishop of Lincoln, Walter bishop of Worcester, William bishop of Coventry, Benedict bishop of Rochester, Master Pandulf subdeacon and member of the papal household, Brother Aymeric master of the Knights of the Temple in England, William Marshal, earl of Pembroke, William earl of Salisbury, William earl of Warren, William earl of Arundel, Alan de Galloway constable of Scotland, Warin Fitz Gerald, Peter Fitz Herbert, Hubert de Burgh seneschal of Poitou, Hugh de Neville, Matthew Fitz Herbert, Thomas Basset, Alan Basset, Philip Daubeny, Robert de Roppeley, John Marshal, John Fitz Hugh, and other loyal subjects:

1. First, that we have granted to God, and by this present charter have confirmed for us and our heirs in perpetuity, that the English Church shall be free, and shall have its rights undiminished, and its liberties unimpaired. That we wish this so to be observed, appears from the fact that of our own free will, before the outbreak of the present dispute between us and our barons, we granted and confirmed by charter the freedom of the Church's elections—a right reckoned to be of the greatest necessity and importance to it—and caused this to be confirmed by Pope Innocent III. This freedom we shall observe ourselves, and desire to be observed in good faith by our heirs in perpetuity. We have also granted to all free men of our realm, for us and our heirs for ever, all the liberties written out below, to have and to keep for them and their heirs, of us and our heirs:

* * *

12. No 'scutage' or 'aid' may be levied in our kingdom without its general consent, unless it is for the ransom of our person, to make our eldest son a knight, and (once) to marry our eldest daughter. For these purposes only a reasonable 'aid' may be levied. 'Aids' from the city of London are to be treated similarly.

13. The city of London shall enjoy all its ancient liberties and free customs, both by land and by water. We also will and grant that all other cities, boroughs, towns, and ports shall enjoy all their liberties and free customs.

14. To obtain the general consent of the realm for the assessment of an 'aid'—except in the three cases specified above—or a 'scutage', we will cause the archbishops, bishops, abbots, earls, and greater barons to be summoned individually by letter. To those who hold lands directly of us we will cause a general summons to be issued, through the sheriffs and other officials, to come together on a fixed day (of which at least forty days notice shall be given) and at a fixed place. In all letters of summons, the cause of the summons will be stated. When a summons has been issued, the business appointed for the day shall go forward in accordance with the resolution of those present, even if not all those who were summoned have appeared.

15. In future we will allow no one to levy an 'aid' from his free men, except to ransom his person, to make his eldest son a knight, and (once) to marry his eldest daughter. For these purposes only a reasonable 'aid' may be levied.

16. No man shall be forced to perform more service for a knight's 'fee', or other free holding of land, than is due from it.

17. Ordinary lawsuits shall not follow the royal court around, but shall be held in a fixed place.

18. Inquests of *novel disseisin* [recent dispossession], *mort d'ancestor* [action to discover whether one's ancestor died in possession of land, thus validating his heir's succession], and *darrein presentment* [last presentment] shall be taken only in their proper county court. We ourselves, or in our absence abroad our chief justice, will send two justices to each county four times a year, and these justices, with four knights of the county elected by the county itself, shall hold the assizes in the county court, on the day and in the place where the court meets.

19. If any assizes cannot be taken on the day of the county court, as many knights and freeholders shall afterwards remain behind, of those who have attended the court, as will suffice for the administration of justice, having regard to the volume of business to be done.

20. For a trivial offence, a free man shall be fined only in proportion to the degree of his offence, and for a serious offence correspondingly, but not so heavily as to deprive him of his livelihood. In the same way, a merchant shall be spared his merchandise, and a husbandman the implements of his husbandry, if they fall upon the mercy of a royal court. None of these fines shall be imposed except by the assessment on oath of reputable men of the neighbourhood.

21. Earls and barons shall not be amerced save through their peers, and only according to the measure of the offence.

* * *

28. No constable or other bailiff of ours shall take the corn or other chattels of any one except he straightway give money for them, or can be allowed a respite in that regard by the will of the seller.

* * *

30. No sheriff nor bailiff of ours, nor any one else, shall take the horses or carts of any freeman for transport, unless by the will of that freeman.

31. Neither we nor our bailiffs shall take another's wood for castles or for other private uses, unless by the will of him to whom the wood belongs.

* * *

35. There shall be one measure of wine throughout our whole realm, and one measure of ale and one measure of corn—namely, the London quart;—and one width of dyed and russet and hauberk cloths—namely, two ells below the selvage. And with weights, moreover, it shall be as with measures.

* * *

38. No bailiff, on his own simple assertion, shall henceforth any one to his law, without producing faithful witnesses in evidence.

39. No freeman shall be taken, or imprisoned, or disseized, or outlawed, or exiled, or in any way harmed—nor will we go upon or send upon him—save by the lawful judgment of his peers or by the law of the land.

40. To none will we sell, to none deny or delay, right or justice.

41. All merchants may safely and securely go out of England, and come into England, and delay and pass through England, as well by land as by water, for the purpose of buying and selling, free from all evil taxes, subject to the ancient and right customs—save in time of war, and if they are of the land at war against us. And if such be found in our land at the beginning of the war, they shall be held, without harm to their bodies and goods, until it shall be known to us or our chief justice how the merchants of our land are to be treated who shall, at that time, be found in the land at war against us. And if ours shall be safe there, the others shall be safe in our land.

* * *

45. We will not make men justices, constables, sheriffs, or bailiffs unless they are such as know the law of the realm, and are minded to observe it rightly.

* * *

52. If any one shall have been disseized by us, or removed, without a legal sentence of his peers, from his lands, castles, liberties or lawful right, we shall straightway restore them to him. And if a dispute shall arise concerning this matter it shall be settled according to the judgment of the twenty-five barons who are mentioned below as sureties for the peace. But with regard to all those things of which any one was, by king Henry our father or king Richard our brother, disseized or dispossessed without legal judgment of his peers, which we have in our hand or which others hold, and for which we ought to give a guarantee: We shall have respite until the common term for crusaders. Except with regard to those concerning which a plea was moved, or an inquest made by our order, before we took the cross. But when we return from our pilgrimage, or if, by chance, we desist from our pilgrimage, we shall straightway then show full justice regarding them.

* * *

55. All fines imposed by us unjustly and contrary to the law of the land, and all amercements made unjustly and contrary to the law of the land, shall be altogether remitted, or it shall be done with regard to them according to the judgment of the twenty-five barons mentioned below as sureties for the peace, or according to the judgment of the majority of

them together with the aforesaid Stephen archbishop of Canterbury, if he can be present, and with others whom he may wish to associate with himself for this purpose. And if he can not be present, the affair shall nevertheless proceed without him; in such way that, if one or more of the said twenty-five barons shall be concerned in a similar complaint, they shall be removed as to this particular decision, and, in their place, for this purpose alone, others shall be substituted who shall be chosen and sworn by the remainder of those twenty-five.

* * *

61. Inasmuch as, for the sake of God, and for the bettering of our realm, and for the more ready healing of the discord which has arisen between us and our barons, we have made all these aforesaid concessions,—wishing them to enjoy forever entire and firm stability, we make and grant to them the following security: that the barons, namely, may elect at their pleasure twenty-five barons from the realm, who ought, with all their strength, to observe, maintain and cause to be observed, the peace and privileges which we have granted to them and confirmed by this our present charter. In such wise, namely, that if we, or our justice, or our bailiffs, or any one of our servants shall have transgressed against any one in any respect, or shall have broken one of the articles of peace or security, and our transgression shall have been shown to four barons of the aforesaid twenty-five: those four barons shall come to us, or, if we are abroad, to our justice, showing to us our error; and they shall ask us to cause that error to be amended without delay. And if we do not amend that error, or, we being abroad, if our justice do not amend it within a term of forty days from the time when it was shown to us or, we being abroad, to our justice: the aforesaid four barons shall refer the matter to the remainder of the twenty-five barons, and those twenty-five barons, with the whole land in common, shall distrain and oppress us in every way in their power,—namely, by taking our castles, lands and possessions, and in every other way that they can, until amends shall have been made according to their judgment, saving the persons of ourselves, our queen and our children. And when amends shall have been made they shall be in accord with us as they had been previously. And whoever of the land wishes to do so, shall swear that in carrying out all the aforesaid measures he will obey the mandates of the aforesaid twenty-five barons, and that, with them, he will oppress us to the extent of his power. And, to any one who wishes to do so, we publicly and freely give permission to swear; and we will never prevent any one from swearing. Moreover, all those in the land who shall be unwilling, themselves and of their own accord, to swear to the twenty-five barons as to distraining and oppressing us with them: such ones we shall make to wear by our mandate, as has

been said. And if any one of the twenty-five barons shall die, or leave the country, or in any other way be prevented from carrying out the aforesaid measures,—the remainder of the aforesaid twenty-five barons shall choose another in his place, according to their judgment, who shall be sworn in the same way as the others. Moreover, in all things entrusted to those twenty-five barons to be carried out, if those twenty-five shall be present and chance to disagree among themselves with regard to some matter, or if some of them, having been summoned, shall be unwilling or unable to be present: that which the majority of those present shall decide or decree shall be considered binding and valid, just as if all the twenty-five had consented to it. And the aforesaid twenty-five shall swear that they will faithfully observe all the foregoing, and will cause them to be observed to the extent of their power. And we shall obtain nothing from any one, either through ourselves or through another, by which any of those concessions and liberties may be revoked or diminished. And if any such thing shall have been obtained, it shall be vain and invalid, and we shall never make use of it either through ourselves or through another.

62. And we have fully remitted to all, and pardoned, all the ill-will, anger and rancor which have arisen between us and our subjects, clergy and laity, from the time of the struggle. Moreover we have fully remitted to all, clergy and laity, and—as far as pertains to us—have pardoned fully all the transgressions committed, on the occasion of that same struggle, from Easter of the sixteenth year of our reign until the re-establishment of peace. In witness of which, more-over, we have caused to be drawn up for them letters patent of lord Stephen, archbishop of Canterbury, lord Henry, archbishop of Dublin, the aforesaid bishops, and master Pandulf, regarding that surety and the aforesaid concessions.

63. Wherefore we will and firmly decree that the English church shall be free, and that the subjects of our realm shall have and hold all the aforesaid liberties, rights and concessions, duly and in peace, freely and quietly, fully and entirely, for themselves and their heirs from us and our heirs, in all matters and in all places, forever, as has been said. Moreover it has been sworn, on our part as well as on the part of the barons, that all these above mentioned provisions shall be observed with good faith and without evil intent. The witnesses being the above mentioned and many others. Given through our hand, in the plain called Runnymede between Windsor and Stanes, on the fifteenth day of June, in the seventeenth year of our reign.

Russell Kirk, *The Roots of American Order*[*]

Another distinguishing feature of the common law is its employment of a jury of twelve good men and true; for in general the decisions of other courts, operating on other juridical principles, are handed down by a judge or a panel of judges. This fact-finding jury is peculiar, in modern times, to England and those countries that have emulated the English common-law system. Guilt or innocence must be determined in open court, by free men whose determination the judge cannot reverse. Whatever the deficiencies of the jury method, serving on juries became a powerful instrument for instructing the public in the nature of law. Jury service, besides, is a form of popular representation in public affairs: one important reason, this, why representative government arose first in England, for participation in common-law juries taught free men to assert a share in public concerns.

The "adversary" method of legal proceedings also distinguished the common-law courts from the civil-law jurisprudence of those countries in which the Roman law had been revived. In Europe generally, as systems of law developed in early medieval times, the judge determined the issue to be settled in a case at law, and in such a European court, to this day, the accused person is presumed to be guilty unless he can prove himself innocent; the authorities hold him to inquire sternly into his behavior. But under the common law of England, the plaintiff and the defendant, or the prosecutor and the defendant, are regarded as adversaries, on an equal footing. Their lawyers define the issue to be settled, while the judge remains neutral. A defendant is presumed to be innocent unless the evidence proves him guilty beyond any reasonable doubt.

In this and many other matters, the common law gives those who come to it privileges unknown in "Roman" courts, where generally the interest of the state stands first. Under the common law, for instance, a defendant cannot be compelled to testify, if he chooses to stand silent: he is saved from self-incrimination. A complex system of writs, under common law, makes access to justice relatively easy for the individual. No man may be imprisoned without a warrant, and he must be tried speedily. Civil rights are protected by the jury, in the sense that a state-appointed judge cannot enforce the policies of the political establishment

[*] RUSSELL KIRK, THE ROOTS OF AMERICAN ORDER 185-92 (1974). From the book The Roots of American Order by Russell Kirk.

without the sanction of twelve independent citizens. Even the king's officers, if they interfere unlawfully with subjects' rights, may be sued for damages under common law, or perhaps charged in a common-law court with criminal actions. In all this, the "private law" called "common law" secures the private person against arbitrary actions by the possessors of power.

In the United States, many of the civil liberties originally guarded by the common law were incorporated into the "Bill of Rights," the first ten amendments to the federal Constitution. One reason for this was that Thomas Jefferson and his allies declared that the common law of England did not run in the new Republic. American advocates of the common law, on the other hand, generally opposed the first ten amendments, on the ground that the common law did and must prevail in America also, that the common law already extended such protections to citizens, and that to enumerate some civil liberties in the Constitution might endanger civil rights not there specified. However this may be, the Jeffersonian Bill of Rights amendments were simply a reassertion of common-law principles. In its origin, American personal liberty perhaps owes more to the common law than to any other single source.

Despite these virtues, the common law of medieval times presently tended to become inflexible and sometimes harsh, demanding the letter of the document rather than recognizing the spirit of fairness. In theory, the common law would not take into account extenuating circumstances or consequences of decisions that seemed contrary to natural justice; sometimes it was hidebound. Therefore the kings developed a remedy for this unyielding attachment to strict precedent: to "ease the king's conscience," they turned to "equity," or fairness, expressed through the lord chancellor's court. If the common law seemed not to cover some new sort of case, or if the common law as applied rigorously seemed to deny reasonable remedies to litigants, then the court of Chancery would take up a case, or a category of cases, as a matter of equity. For centuries, many litigants enjoyed a choice: cases might be tried either in a common-law court or in a court of equity, depending upon the remedy sought. Nowadays the same judges deal with both common law and equity.

In practice, the common-law courts often were not so utterly bound by precedent as they professed to be. Actually, judges might interpret precedents in the light of altered social circumstances, and so in effect establish fresh precedents more suited to a different era. But the general principle was maintained, and is maintained in common law today, that the common law is a continuity, opposed to innovation, adjudicating suits at law upon the basis of enduring norms that for a long while have been recognized as just and binding. The common law is empirical law: that is, it is based upon men's experience over many generations, a good test of practicality.

But can simple experience, no matter how far back in a people's history it extends, be a sufficient guide to justice? Must there not be some theological or philosophical sanction that gives meaning to collective experience? Did wisdom begin with the common-law judges? In medieval England, both courts of common law and courts of equity claimed that they derived their sanction from the established customs or the ethical beliefs of the realm, and not from Roman law; for a time, even the study of Roman law was forbidden in England. Hebrew law and Christian morals were recognized as part of the common law, but not so the Roman, or quasi-Roman, law that was revived in the Continent and in Scotland.

In reality, nevertheless, principles of Roman law formed an element in the common law, and more conspicuously in equity. The English first became acquainted with Roman ideas of law through the canon law, the law of the Church courts; and as more direct knowledge of Roman law was obtained at the Italian universities of Bologna, Padua, and Mantua, gradually that understanding filtered into medieval English jurisprudence, though never acknowledged formally. Natural-law concepts, owing much to Cicero, came to be a mainstay of both common law and equity. Besides, the opinions of the Roman jurisconsults, as collected in Justinian's code, increasingly served English judges as a basis for decision of puzzling cases. In theory, the common law offered a remedy for every complaint at law; privately, many common law judges seem to have found remedy and precedent by consulting Roman theory.

Sir Henry Maine, the most lively of English legal historians, declares that Henry de Bracton (often called "the father of English law"), in the reign of Henry III, borrowed from the Roman *Corpus Juris* the whole form of his own book on the common law, *De Legibus Angliae*, published about 1260; and a third of the contents of his book, too. Although later legal scholars have argued that Maine goes too far in this assertion, clearly Bracton and the other champions of the common law were much influenced by what they knew of Roman law. In the time of the Norman and Plantagenet kings, judges ordinarily were men in holy orders—some of them bishops; and naturally enough such judges' familiarity with canon law, rooted in Roman law, had its part in the early shaping of the common law. Anyone who had read the works of Gregory the Great and of Augustine of Hippo could not ignore the strength of natural-law doctrine and the whole Roman understanding of justice.

To have acknowledged being moved by Roman law would have made an English judge suspect both to his king and to the English people: that was something foreign, and possibly perilous to the "old laws" of England. For all that, the common law does combine English customary usage with some Roman principles—or rather, the Roman principles give order to English legal custom. Far from being subversive of English liberties, the Roman tinge to the common law helped to make possible the emergence of judges' independence and of representative government.

Why is the common law so important? In part, because it was the foundation of good order in England, so that upon it rose the whole fabric of a free society, the model of other free societies. For a body of law to be really enforceable, it must receive the willing assent of the mass of people, living under such a law. Stable government grows out of law, not law out of government. If the political power decrees positive laws without reference to general consent, those laws will be evaded or defied, and respect for law will diminish, so that force must be substituted for justice; precisely that resistance to statutory law occurred in some European countries, over the centuries.

Now the English people looked upon the common law as *their* law, the product of their historical experience; it was not something imposed upon them from above. That being so, most of them willingly abided by the law, and so down to our own time the English have been the most law-abiding people, generally, among the major nations. This voluntary obedience to law made it possible, despite intervals of civil strife, for the English to unite against foreign enemies, to reconcile old ways with prudent change, and to prosper materially. Not least among the benefits of general respect for common law was the regular enforcement of contracts, which mightily assisted the growth of English domestic and foreign commerce.

And if the common law was the foundation of order, also it was the foundation of freedom. The high claim of the old commentators on the common law was this: no man, not even the king, was above or beyond the law. "The king himself," Bracton wrote, "ought not to be under man but under God, and under the Law, because the Law makes the king. Therefore, let the king render back to the Law what the Law gives to him, namely, dominion and power; for there is no king where will, and not Law, wields dominion." The Law is a bridle upon the king. Though the king may not be sued, he may be petitioned; if he will not do justice upon receiving a reasonable petition, the king's own Great Council, or the barons and the people, then may restrain his power. Just that had been done to King John, less than half a century before Bracton wrote, and would be done to later kings who tried to set themselves above the Law. Here are the beginnings of the principle of a government of laws, not of men.

By the reign of Edward I, in the last quarter of the thirteenth century, the common law was so well entrenched that no king could defy it, whatever else he might aspire to. Edward I cast out corrupt or incompetent judges, but left the common law itself strong, and indeed extended its functions. Soon the Inns of Court, the lawyers' guilds of London, would take form, improving the practice of both common law and equity. The development and refinement of the common law, and the better education of its judges, would continue as the Middle Ages merged into what we call the Renaissance and the Reformation.

Even the Tudors, monarchs virtually absolute otherwise in the sixteenth century, would not think of tampering banefully with the common law; indeed, Henry VIII would profess himself the champion of the common law against Roman and canon law. By such jurists as Sir Edward Coke and Sir Matthew Hale, in the seventeenth century, the common law would be exalted still higher. And in the eighteenth century, Sir William Blackstone's *Commentaries on the Laws of England*, permeated with common-law doctrine, would exert a stronger attraction in America than in England.

As chastened and corrected by equity, the common law of medieval times was an instrument for social improvement, as well as for the conserving of old rights. It maintained the continuity of law, while itself amenable to correction by appeal to Chancery or to clarification by parliamentary statute. More than any juridical system on the Continent, it protected the subject from oppression by powerful individuals, through its writs, its court procedures, and its national enforcement. Its high value would not be seriously challenged until early in the nineteenth century, when Jeremy Bentham and his disciples would attempt to overthrow the common law for the sake of codified statutory law, on abstract principles of justice.

In America, common-law principles would work upon public affairs more powerfully than any other influences except Protestant Christianity and the colonial social experience itself. Into every colony, the common law would be introduced by colonial charter. The leading American public men of the last quarter of the eighteenth century—and especially the many practicing lawyers among them—and their successors in the first quarter of the nineteenth century, from Republicans like Jefferson and Madison to Federalists like Fisher Ames and Joseph Story, would be thoroughly read in the common-law exponents of medieval times and the Renaissance; they would know their Glanville, their Bracton, their Coke, and others. (John Adams was one of the few Americans to make a careful study also of canon law.) Best of all, the Americans knew their Blackstone's *Commentaries*—even though Blackstone himself strenuously opposed American independence.

With the Revolution, true, would come opposition to the common law, as to nearly everything else English; but the American advocates of the common law would win the struggle in the nineteenth century. It is difficult, for that matter, to conceive how American society could have cohered at all, in the early decades of the Republic, had not the common law been adapted to American circumstances: there had been no preparation in America for administration of justice by state or federal statutory codes, and President Madison rejected Bentham's offer to write a code for the infant United States.

In the twentieth century, the common law of England, of the United States, and indeed of every country that has adapted English common law to its needs, steadily gives ground before the advance of statutory law. Some legislators scarcely seem aware that the common law still exists, and they succeed in enacting statutes which deal in less satisfactory fashion with subjects already adequately covered by common law.

Yet had it not been for the work of the old common law, those representative assemblies which today pour out new statutes might never have come into existence. For the common law of medieval England did much to give stability first to one nation, and then to others; at the same time, the common law maintained the principle of the supremacy of law, and the practice of forms of self-government.

Abraham Kuyper, *Calvinism and Politics*[*]

My third lecture leaves the sanctuary of religion and enters upon the domain of the State—the first transition from the sacred circle to the secular field of human life. Only now therefore we proceed, summarily and in principle, to combat the unhistorical suggestion that Calvinism represents an exclusively ecclesiastical and dogmatic movement.

The religious momentum of Calvinism has placed also beneath political Society a fundamental conception, all its own, just because it not merely pruned the branches and cleaned the stem, but reached down to the very root of our human life.

That this had to be so becomes evident at once to everyone who is able to appreciate the fact that no political scheme has ever become

[*] ABRAHAM KUYPER, *Calvinism and Politics*, *in* LECTURES ON CALVINISM 78, 78-90 (Wm. B. Eerdmans Publ'g Co. 1999).

dominant which was not founded in a specific religious or anti-religious conception. And that this has been the fact, as regards Calvinism, may appear from the political changes which it has effected in those three historic lands of political freedom, the Netherlands, England and America.

Every competent historian will without exception confirm the words of Bancroft: "The fanatic for Calvinism was a fanatic for liberty, for in the moral warfare for freedom, his creed was a part of his army, and his most faithful ally in the battle." And Groen van Prinsterer has thus expressed it: "In Calvinism lies the origin and guarantee of our constitutional liberties." That Calvinism has led public law into new paths, first in Western Europe, then in two Continents, and today more and more among all civilized nations, is admitted by all scientific students, if not yet fully by public opinion.

But for the purpose I have in view, the mere statement of this important fact is insufficient.

In order that the influence of Calvinism on our political development may be felt, it must be shown for what fundamental political conceptions Calvinism has opened the door, and how these political conceptions sprang from its root principle.

This dominating principle was not, soteriologically, justification by faith, but, in the widest sense cosmologically, the Sovereignty of the Triune God over the whole Cosmos, in all its spheres and kingdoms, visible and invisible. A primordial Sovereignty which eradiates in mankind in a threefold deduced supremacy, viz., 1. The Sovereignty in the State; 2. The Sovereignty in Society; and 3. The Sovereignty in the Church.

Allow me to argue this matter in detail by pointing out to you how this threefold deduced Sovereignty was understood by Calvinism.

First then a deduced Sovereignty in that political sphere, which is defined as the State. And then we admit that the impulse to form states arises from man's social nature, which was expressed already by Aristotle, when he called man a zoon politikon. God might have created men as disconnected individuals, standing side by side and without genealogical coherence. Just as Adam was separately created, the second and third and every further man might have been individually called into existence; but this was not the case.

Man is created from man, and by virtue of his birth he is organically united with the whole race. Together we form one humanity, not only with those who are living now, but also with all the generations behind us and with all those who shall come after us pulverized into millions though we may be. All the human race is from one blood. The conception of States, however, which subdivide the earth into continents, and each continent into morsels, does not harmonize with this idea. Then only would the organic unity of our race be realized politically, if one State could embrace all the world, and if the whole of humanity were associated in one world empire. Had sin not intervened, no doubt this would actually have been so. If sin, as a disintegrating force, had not divided humanity into different sections, nothing would have marred or broken the organic unity of our race. And the mistake of the Alexanders, and of the Augusti, and of the Napoleons, was not that they were charmed with the thought of the One World Empire, but it was this—that they endeavored to realize this idea notwithstanding that the force of sin had dissolved our unity.

In like manner the international cosmopolitan endeavors of the Social-democracy present, in their conception of union, an ideal, which on this very account charms us, even when we are aware that they try to reach the unattainable, in endeavoring to realize this high and holy ideal, now and in a sinful world. Nay, even Anarchy, conceived as the attempt to undo all mechanical connections among men, together with the undoing of all human authority, and to encourage, in their stead, the growth of a new organic tie, arising from nature itself—I say, all this is nothing but a looking backward after a lost paradise.

For, indeed, without sin there would have been neither magistrate nor state-order; but political life, in its entirety, would have evolved itself, after a patriarchal fashion, from the life of the family. Neither bar of justice nor police, nor army, nor navy, is conceivable in a world without sin; and thus every rule and ordinance and law would drop away, even as all control and assertion of the power of the magistrate would disappear, were life to develop itself, normally and without hindrance, from its own organic impulse. Who binds up, where nothing is broken? Who uses crutches, where the limbs are sound?

Every State-formation, every assertion of the power of the magistrate, every mechanical means of compelling order and of guaranteeing a safe course of life is therefore always something unnatural; something against which the deeper aspirations of our nature rebel; and which, on this very account, may become the source both of a dreadful abuse of power, on the part of those who exercise it, and of a continuous revolt on the part of the multitude. Thus originated the battle of the ages between Authority and Liberty, and in this battle it was the very innate thirst for liberty which proved itself the God-ordained means to bridle the authority wheresoever it degenerated into despotism. And thus all true conception of the nature of the State and of the assumption of authority by the magistrate, and on the other hand all true conception of the right and duty of the people to defend liberty, depends on what Calvinism has here placed in the foreground, as the primordial truth—that God has instituted the magistrates, by reason of sin.

In this one thought are hidden both the light-side and the shady side of the life of the State. The shady-side for this multitude of states ought not to exist; there should be only one world-empire. These magistrates rule mechanically and do not harmonize with our nature. And this authority of government is exercised by sinful men, and is therefore subject to all manner of despotic ambitions. But the light-side also, for a sinful humanity, without division of states, without law and government, and without ruling authority, would be a veritable hell on earth; or at least a repetition of that which existed on earth when God drowned the first degenerate race in the deluge. Calvinism has, therefore, by its deep conception of sin laid bare the true root of state-life, and has taught us two things: first—that we have gratefully to receive, from the hand of God, the institution of the State with its magistrates, as a means of preservation, now indeed indispensable. And on the other hand also that, by virtue of our natural impulse, we must ever watch against the danger which lurks, for our personal liberty, in the power of the State.

But Calvinism has done more. In Politics also it taught us that the human element—here the people—may not be considered as the principal thing, so that God is only dragged in to help this people in the hour of its need; but on the contrary that God, in His Majesty, must flame before the eyes of every nation, and that all nations together are to be reckoned before Him as a drop in a bucket and as the small dust of the balances. From the ends of the earth God cites all nations and peoples before His high judgment seat. For God created the nations. They exist for Him. They are His own. And therefore all these nations, and in them humanity, must exist for His glory and consequently after his ordinances, in order that in their well-being, when they walk after His ordinances, His divine wisdom may shine forth.

When therefore humanity falls apart through sin, in a multiplicity of separate peoples; when sin, in the bosom of these nations, separates men and tears them apart, and when sin reveals itself in all manner of shame and unrighteousness—the glory of God demands that these horrors be bridled, that order return to this chaos, and that a compulsory force, from without, assert itself to make human society a possibility.

This right is possessed by God, and by Him alone.

No man has the right to rule over another man, otherwise such a right necessarily, and immediately becomes the right of the strongest. As the tiger in the jungle rules over the defenceless antelope, so on the banks of the Nile a Pharaoh ruled over the progenitors of the fellaheen of Egypt.

Nor can a group of men, by contract, from their own right, compel you to obey a fellow-man. What binding force is there for me in the allegation that ages ago one of my progenitors made a "Contrat Social," with other men of that time? As man I stand free and bold, over against the most powerful of my fellow-men.

I do not speak of the family, for here organic, natural ties rule; but in the sphere of the State I do not yield or bow down to anyone, who is man, as I am.

Authority over men cannot arise from men. Just as little from a majority over against a minority, for history shows, almost on every page, that very often the minority was right. And thus to the first Calvinistic thesis that sin alone has necessitated the institution of governments, this second and no less momentous thesis is added that: all authority of governments on earth originates from the Sovereignty of God alone. When God says to me, "obey," then I humbly bow my head, without compromising in the least my personal dignity, as a man. For, in like proportion as you degrade yourself, by bowing low to a child of man, whose breath is in his nostrils; so, on the other hand do you raise yourself, if you submit to the authority of the Lord of heaven and earth.

Thus the word of Scripture stands: "By Me kings reign," or as the apostle has elsewhere declared: "The powers, that be, are ordained of God. Therefore he that resisteth the power, withstandeth the ordinance of God." The magistrate is an instrument of "common grace," to thwart all license and outrage and to shield the good against the evil. But he is more. Besides all this he is instituted by God as His Servant, in order that he may preserve the glorious work of God, in the creation of humanity, from total destruction. Sin attacks God's handiwork, God's plan, God's justice, God's honor, as the supreme Artificer and Builder. Thus God, ordaining the powers that be, in order that, through their instrumentality, He might maintain His justice against the strivings of sin, has given to the magistrate the terrible right of life and death. Therefore all the powers that be, whether in empires or in republics, in cities or in states, rule "by the grace of God." For the same reason justice bears a holy character. And from the same motive every citizen is bound to obey, not only from dread of punishment, but for the sake of conscience.

Further Calvin has expressly stated that authority, as such, is in no way affected by the question how a government is instituted and in what form it reveals itself. It is well known that personally he preferred a republic, and that he cherished no predilection for a monarchy, as if this were the divine and ideal form of government. This indeed would have been the case in a sinless state. For had sin not entered, God would have remained the sole king of all men, and this condition will return, in the glory to come, when God once more will be all and in all. God's own direct government is absolutely monarchial; no monotheist will deny it. But Calvin considered a co-operation of many persons under mutual control, i.e., a republic, desirable, now that a mechanical institution of government is necessitated by reason of sin.

In his system, however, this could only amount to a gradual difference in practical excellency, but never to a fundamental difference, as regards the essence of authority. He considers a monarchy and an aristocracy, as well as a democracy, both possible and practicable forms of government; provided it be unchangeably maintained, that no one on earth can claim authority over his fellow-men, unless it be laid upon him "by the grace of God"; and therefore, the ultimate duty of obedience is imposed upon us not by man, but by God Himself.

The question how those persons, who by divine authority are to be clothed with power, are indicated, cannot, according to Calvin, be answered alike for all peoples and for all time. And yet he does not hesitate to state, in an ideal sense, that the most desirable conditions exist, where the people itself chooses its own magistrates.

Where such a condition exists he thinks that the people should gratefully recognize therein a favor of God, precisely as it has been expressed in the preamble of more than one of your constitutions;—"Grateful to almighty God that He gave us the power to choose our own magistrates." In his Commentary on Samuel, Calvin therefore admonishes such peoples:—"And ye, O peoples, to whom God gave the liberty to choose your own magistrates, see to it, that ye do not forfeit this favor, by electing to the positions of highest honor, rascals and enemies of God."

I may add that the popular choice gains the day, as a matter of course, where no other rule exists, or where the existing rule falls away. Wherever new States have been founded, except by conquest or force, the first government has always been founded by popular choice; and so also where the highest authority had fallen into disorder, either by want of a determination of the right of succession, or through the violence of revolution, it has always been the people who, through their representatives, claimed the right to restore it. But with equal decision, Calvin asserts that God has the sovereign power, in the way of His dispensing Providence, to take from a people this most desirable condition, or never to bestow it at all when a nation is unfit for it, or, by its sin, has utterly forfeited the blessing.

The historic development of a people shows, as a matter of course, in what other ways authority is bestowed. This bestowal may flow from the right of inheritance, as in a hereditary monarchy. It may result from a hard-fought war, even as Pilate had power over Jesus, "given him from above." It may proceed from electors, as it did in the old German empire. It may rest with the States of the country, as was the case in the old Dutch republic. In a word it may assume a variety of forms, because there is an endless difference in the development of nations. A form of government like your own could not exist one day in China. Even now, the people of Russia are unfit for any form of constitutional government. And among the Kaffirs and Hottentots of Africa, even a government, such as exists in Russia, would be wholly inconceivable. All this is determined and appointed by God, through the hidden counsel of His providence.

All this, however, is no theocracy. A theocracy was only found in Israel, because in Israel, God intervened immediately. For both by Urim and Thummim and by Prophecy; both by His saving miracles, and by His chastising judgments, He held in His own hand the jurisdiction and the leadership of His people. But the Calvinistic confession of the Sovereignty of God holds good for all the world, is true for all nations, and is of force in all authority, which man exercises over man; even in the authority which parents possess over their children. It is therefore a political faith which may be summarily expressed in these three theses: 1) God only—and never any creature—is possessed of sovereign rights, in the destiny of the nations, because God alone created them, maintains them by His Almighty power, and rules them by His ordinances. 2) Sin has, in the realm of politics, broken down the direct government of God, and therefore the exercise of authority for the purpose of government, has subsequently been invested in men, as a mechanical remedy. And 3) In whatever form this authority may reveal itself, man never possesses power over his fellow-man in any other way than by an authority which descends upon him from the majesty of God.

Directly opposed to this Calvinistic confession there are two other theories. That of the Popular-sovereignty, as it has been antitheistically proclaimed at Paris in 1789; and that of State-sovereignty, as it has of late been developed by the historico-pantheistic school of Germany. Both these theories are at heart identical, but for the sake of clearness they demand a separate treatment.

What was it that impelled and animated the spirits of men in the great French revolution? Indignation at abuses, which had crept in? A horror of a crowned despotism? A noble defense of the rights and liberties of the people? In part certainly, but in all this there is so little that is sinful, that even a Calvinist gratefully recognizes, in these three particulars, the divine judgment, which at that time was executed in Paris.

But the impelling force of the French Revolution did not lie in this hatred of abuses. When Edmund Burke compares the "glorious Revolution" of 1688 with the principle of the Revolution of 1789, he says: "Our revolution and that of France are just the reverse of each other, in almost every particular, and in the whole spirit of the transaction."

This same Edmund Burke, so bitter an antagonist of the French revolution, has manfully defended your own rebellion against England, as "arising from a principle of energy, showing itself in this good people the main cause of a free spirit, the most adverse to all implicit submission of mind and opinion."

The three great revolutions in the Calvinistic world left untouched the glory of God, nay, they even proceeded from the acknowledgement of His majesty. Every one will admit this of our rebellion against Spain, under William the Silent. Nor has it even been doubted of the "glorious Revolution," which was crowned by the arrival of William III of Orange and the overthrow of the Stuarts. But it is equally true of your own Revolution. It is expressed in so many words in the Declaration of Independence, by John Hancock, that the Americans asserted themselves by virtue—"of the law of nature and of nature's God"; that they acted—"as endowed by the Creator with certain unalienable rights"; that they appealed to "the Supreme Judge of the world for the rectitude of their intention"; and that they sent forth their "declaration of Independence"—"With a firm reliance on the protection of Divine Providence." In the "Articles of Confederation" it is confessed in the preamble,—"that it hath pleased the great Governor of the world to incline the hearts of the legislators." It is also declared in the preamble of the Constitution of many of the States:—"Grateful to Almighty God for the civil, political and religious liberty, which He has so long permitted us to enjoy and looking unto Him, for a blessing upon our endeavors." God is there honored as "the Sovereign Ruler," and the "Legislator of the Universe" and it is there specifically admitted, that from God alone the people received "the right to choose their own form of government." In one of the meetings of the Convention, Franklin proposed, in a moment of supreme anxiety, that they should ask wisdom from God in prayer. And if any one should still doubt whether or not the American revolution was homogeneous with that of Paris, this doubt is fully set at rest by the bitter fight in 1793 between Jefferson and Hamilton. Therefore it remains as the German historian Von Holtz stated it: "Es ware Thorheit zu sagen dass die Rousseauschen Schriften einen Einfluss auf die Entwicklung in America ausgeubt haben." ("Mere madness would it be to say that the American revolution borrowed its impelling energy from Rousseau and his writings.") Or as Hamilton himself expressed it, that he considered "the French Revolution to be no more akin to the American Revolution than the faithless wife in a French novel is like the Puritan matron in New England."

The French Revolution is in principle distinct from all these national revolutions, which were undertaken with praying lips and with trust in the help of God. The French Revolution ignores God. It opposes God. It refuses to recognize a deeper ground of political life than that which is found in nature, that is, in this instance, in man himself. Here the first article of the confession of the most absolute infidelity is "ni Dieu ni maitre." The sovereign God is dethroned and man with his free will is placed on the vacant seat. It is the will of man which determines all things. All power, all authority proceeds from man. Thus one comes from the individual man to the many men; and in those many men conceived as the people, there is thus hidden the deepest fountain of all sovereignty. There is no question, as in your Constitution, of a sovereignty derived from God, which He, under certain conditions, implants in the people. Here an original sovereignty asserts itself, which everywhere and in all states can only proceed from the people itself, having no deeper root than in the human will. It is a sovereignty of the people therefore, which is perfectly identical with atheism. And herein lies its self-abasement. In the sphere of Calvinism, as also in your Declaration, the knee is bowed to God, while over against man the head is proudly lifted up. But here, from the standpoint of the sovereignty of the people, the fist is defiantly clenched against God, while man grovels before his fellowmen, tinseling over this self-abasement by the ludicrous fiction that, thousands of years ago, men, of whom no one has any remembrance, concluded a political contract, or, as they called it, "Contrat Social." Now, do you ask for the result? Then, let History tell you how the rebellion of the Netherlands, the "glorious Revolution" of England and your own rebellion against the British Crown have brought liberty to honor; and answer for yourself the question: Has the French Revolution resulted in anything else but the shackling of liberty in the irons of State-omnipotence? Indeed, no country in our 19th century has had a sadder State history than France.

No wonder that scientific Germany has broken away from this fictitious sovereignty of the people, since the days of De Savigny and Niebuhr. The Historical school, founded by these eminent men, has pilloried the a-prioristic fiction of 1789. Every historical connoisseur now ridicules it. Only that which they recommended instead of it, bears no better stamp.

Now it was to be not the sovereignty of the people, but the Sovereignty of the State, a product of Germanic philosophical pantheism. Ideas are incarnated in the reality, and among these the idea of the State was the highest, the richest, the most perfect idea of the relation between man and man. Thus the State became a mystical conception. The State was considered as a mysterious being, with a hidden ego; with a State-consciousness, slowly developing; and with an increasing potent State-will, which by a slow process endeavored to blindly reach the highest State-aim. The people was not understood as with Rousseau, to be the sum total of the individuals. It was correctly seen that a people is no aggregate, but an organic whole. This organism must of necessity have its organic members. Slowly these organs arrived at their historic development. By these organs the will of the State operates, and everything must bow before this will. This sovereign State-will might reveal itself in a republic, in a monarchy, in a Caesar, in an Asiatic despot, in a tyrant as Philip of Spain, or in a dictator like Napoleon. All these were but forms, in which the one State-idea incorporated itself; the stages of development in a never-ending process. But in whatever form this mystical being of the State revealed itself, the idea remained supreme: the State shortly asserted its sovereignty and for every member of the State it remained the touchstone of wisdom to give way to this State-apotheosis.

Thus all transcendent right in God, to which the oppressed lifted up his face, fails away. There is no other right, but the immanent right which is written down in the law. The law is right, not because its contents are in harmony with the eternal principles of right, but because it is law. If on the morrow it fixes the very opposite, this also must be right. And the fruit of this deadening theory is, as a matter of course, that the consciousness of right is blunted, that all fixedness of right departs from our minds, and that all higher enthusiasm for right is extinguished. That which exists is good, because it exists; and it is no longer the will of God, of Him Who created us and knows us, but it becomes the ever-changing will of the State, which, having no one above itself, actually becomes God, and has to decide how our life and our existence shall be.

And when you further consider that this mystical State expresses and enforces its will only through men what further proof is demanded that this state-sovereignty, even as popular sovereignty, does not outgrow the abasing subjection of man to his fellow-man and never ascends to a duty of submission which finds its cogency in the conscience?

Therefore in opposition both to the atheistic popular-sovereignty of the Encyclopedians, and the pantheistic state-sovereignty of German philosophers, the Calvinist maintains the Sovereignty of God, as the source of all authority among men. The Calvinist upholds the highest and best in our aspirations by placing every man and every people before the face of our Father in heaven. He takes cognizance of the fact of sin, which erstwhile was juggled away in 1789, and which now, in pessimistic extravagance, is accounted the essence of our being. Calvinism points to the difference between the natural concatenation of our organic society and the mechanical tie, which the authority of the magistrate imposes. It makes it easy for us to obey authority, because, in all authority, it causes us to honor the demand of divine sovereignty. It lifts us from an obedience born of dread of the strong arm, into an obedience for conscience sake. It teaches us to look upward from the existing law to the source of the eternal Right in God, and it creates in us the indomitable courage incessantly to protest against the unrighteousness of the law in the name of this highest Right. And however powerfully the State may assert itself and oppress the free individual development, above that powerful State there is always glittering, before our soul's eye, as infinitely more powerful, the majesty of the King of kings, Whose righteous bar ever maintains the right of appeal for all the oppressed, and unto Whom the prayer of the people ever ascends, to bless our nation and, in that nation, us and our house!

Craig Stern, *The Common Law and the Religious Foundations of the Rule of Law before* Casey*

Four Christian ideas—doctrines, in fact—are both especially important to that religion and especially important to the rule of law in the common law tradition. The first of these is the doctrine of God himself, that is, his being and his work. Second is the doctrine of man, made in God's image. Third is the fall of man; fourth is the atonement of man. These doctrines are at the base of Christianity. They also happen to provide a base upon which the Anglo-American legal system could build a strong commitment to the rule of law. This section will explain the Christian doctrines and then show how different aspects of common law reflect and build upon these doctrines.

A. The Doctrine of God

1. The Being and Authority of God

The Christian faith holds that God is the "I AM," the uncreated creator of all that is, who is from everlasting to everlasting. He is also the God of Abraham, Isaac, and Jacob, a God of relationship, of covenant. In

* Craig Stern, *The Common Law and the Religious Foundations of the Rule of Law before* Casey, 38 U.S.F. L. REV. 499, 505-18 (2004). Reprinted with the permission of the author.

this way, he is both transcendent and immanent. According to the New Testament, he is love. His love is expressed, in part, in providing law for all his creation, understood both as rules describing what is, and as rules prescribing what ought to be. His law comes from his will, but his will expresses his eternal, unchanging nature. "The being of God is a kind of law to his working...." As Sir William Blackstone puts it, God is wise, and so his law is perfectly suited to his creation. God also keeps the covenants and the laws he makes. David declares of him, "thou hast magnified thy word above all thy name."

Within the Christian tradition, God holds all authority, but authorizes others to exercise portions of that authority as his ministers. Exercising authority for God does not make one a god. Caesar and God are distinct: "Render to Caesar the things that are Caesar's and to God the things that are God's." And yet Caesar is appointed by God to administer a share of God's justice. According to the Christian understanding, civil government is not divine; rather it is invested, like any human authority, with a limited commission from God. As such, civil government is under God and his law, and obliged to reflect God's justice.

The history of Anglo-American common law demonstrates a profound commitment to these truths. The common law proper operated among a diversity of authorities, civil and ecclesiastic. Its range was limited. For example, actions in the common law court began with a royal document called "the original writ...the source of the jurisdiction of the court:"

> The Court of Common Pleas was historically, and in legal theory, a court of delegates whose authority was not general, but derived from an ad hoc commission separately given for every individual case. Hence the court had no powers beyond those conferred by the original writ and could not go beyond the four corners of that document.

The king's writs, issued to bring cases before the English common law courts, applied only to specific cases; they supported no broad assertion of authority by the courts. And so "the rule of writs is the rule of law." Authority of the common law courts was limited by law.

The common law was but one of several competing legal systems. Professor Harold Berman largely ascribes the rise of the rule of law in the West to the diversity of legal authorities. This very diversity of legal authorities required rules limiting their respective operations. And beneath this diversity—perhaps most clearly in the diversity that embraced church as well as kingdom—lay the belief that ultimate authority rests with God, who has apportioned the ministerial exercise of authority to diverse human instruments.

A famous monument to this diversity of authority is the Magna Carta. There, King John pledged, "In the first place, we have granted to God, and by this our present charter confirmed, for us and for our heirs forever, that the English church shall be free, and shall hold its rights entire and its liberties uninjured...." Certainly, this pledge would have been idle had not the king been thought to have been bound to his words. Under God, and before God, a king must keep his pledge, like God himself who keeps his own pledge. Architect of the Magna Carta, Archbishop Stephen Langton of Canterbury, manifests in the charter not only his mastery of canon law, but also the familiarity with Holy Scriptures to be expected from the man who is credited with articulating the Bible into the chapter divisions we use to this day.

Thus, the Magna Carta stands for a kingship limited in its authority by law. The king is not God, but under God and God's law, and so obliged to keep his word. The king is limited in his power over the church. He exercises only a partial government. Beyond these things, however, the Magna Carta commits the crown to proceeding according to law: "No free man shall be taken or imprisoned or dispossessed, or outlawed, or banished, or in any way destroyed, nor will we go upon him, nor send upon him, except by the legal judgment of his peers or by the law of the land." If God himself is just and adheres to the law, so must his minister proceed according to the law. And proceeding according to law entails designating arbiters of judgment—courts—as separate from organs exercising will or force.

2. God the Lawgiver

The method of the common law itself manifests this rule of law notion that civil government should pursue judgment and not simply will or force. Consider the development of law by judges in deciding the cases before them. Common law judges were sworn to decide cases according to the law. They were directed not to innovate or to create law. They held no legislative power. Rather, judges were to declare and apply what was already law before that declaration. Law ruled, and judges were but its oracles.

This rule of law in the courts of the common law reflected the Christian doctrine of God in at least two distinct ways. First, civil justice mirrored God's justice in its commitment to law. The law established the standard, the breach of which supported a claim for redress. In turn, any redress was duly governed by law in its process and remedy. Justice was a matter of judgment in applying and vindicating the law. But, second, this method proceeded on the assumption that law existed before courts had occasion to declare and apply it. If judges were to discover the law and not make it, it must have been there to discover. To some degree, common law is the custom of the land—conventions from time immemorial. But to a great degree, common law is the law of nature, the law prescribed—as Christianity holds—by God himself for his creation.

As Blackstone explains, in the legal treatise standard in America at the Founding:

> This law of nature, being co-eval with mankind and dictated by God himself, is of course superior in obligation to any other. It is binding over all the globe, in all countries, and at all times: no human laws are of any validity, if contrary to this; and such of them as are valid derive all their force, and all their authority, mediately or immediately, from this original.

Men know the law of nature by reason and, more perfectly, by consulting divine law "to be found," Blackstone declared, "only in the holy scriptures." Municipal law, such as the common law of England, "is properly defined to be 'a rule of civil conduct prescribed by the supreme power in a state, commanding what is right and prohibiting what is wrong.'" Except where it reflects custom on matters indifferent, the common law reflects true right and true wrong, the law of nature.

It follows then, if a supposed rule of the common law derogated from the law of nature, it in fact was not law at all.

* * *

Customs, sifted and supplemented by God's own law of nature—revealed in the Bible and in reason—provided law for the courts to apply. Such a law of nature requires a legislator, and the Christian God—creator, lawgiver, and author of revelation—has supplied this necessary element to the common law.

3. God the Judge

Yet another aspect of the Christian doctrine of God supported the rule of law. God is the judge of all mankind. He holds men to his law, and to their oaths. When kings swore to uphold the law, and when judges swore to decide cases according to the law, they understood that God would vindicate his law, and would require them to keep their solemn word. This understanding cautioned those administering the law to submit to law, whatever opportunity they might have had to evade the penalties of merely human justice.

B. The Doctrine of Man

The Christian doctrine of God is most fundamental to the rule of law in the common law tradition. But a chief link between the doctrine of God and the rule of law is the doctrine of man that holds him to be created in God's image:...

Because man is made in God's image, he can enjoy a relationship with God that may encompass covenant; that may entail the human administration of God's authority and justice; that may require the exercise of judgment, applying God's law, or any law at all for that matter. Furthermore, because he is made in God's image, man may enjoy relationships with fellow man in enjoying these privileges and exercising these faculties. The support given the rule of law by the Christian doctrine of God would be incomplete without the Christian doctrine of man.

1. The Idea of Due Process

Beyond this aspect of man made in God's image and so enabled to act for and with God, lies the aspect of man made in God's image and therefore worthy of the respect due such a creature. That is, as a subject of the law, man's bearing God's image requires that he be given the benefit of the rule of law. From the very first biblical account of judgment, the rabbis derived the principle of due process, the principle that men deserve notice of charges of wrongdoing and the opportunity to answer them before their judge. Directly after the sin of Adam and Eve, God, though omniscient, asks Adam, "Hast thou eaten of the tree, whereof I commanded thee that thou shouldest not eat?" After listening to Adam's answer, he asks Eve, "What is this that thou hast done?" After listening to Eve's answer, but without speaking to the serpent at all, he declares his judgment upon all three offenders. Men, unlike the serpentine embodiment of the fallen angel, and although sinners, receive from God the respect due those made in his image. God charges, listens, and then judges, according to his previously declared law. He treats Adam and Eve much as King John would promise to treat his subjects in the Magna Carta.

2. The Idea of Legal Equality

Human dignity entails being treated according to law. As all humans equally bear the image of God, so all are to enjoy equality before the law: "Ye shall do no unrighteousness in judgment: thou shalt not respect the person of the poor, nor honour the person of the mighty: but in righteousness shalt thou judge thy neighbour." Adherence to this principle is one of the precepts that A.V. Dicey marks as components of the common law commitment to the rule of law:

> We mean...when we speak of the "rule of law" as a characteristic of our country, not only that with us no man is above the law, but (what is a different thing) that here every man, whatever be his rank or condition, is subject to the ordinary law of the realm and amenable to the jurisdiction of the ordinary tribunals.
> In England the idea of legal equality, or of the universal subjection of all classes to one law administered by the ordinary Courts, has been pushed to its utmost limit. With us every official, from the Prime Minister down to the constable or a collector of taxes, is under the same responsibility for every act done without legal justification as any other citizen. The Reports abound with cases in which officials have been brought before the Courts, and made, in their personal capacity, liable to punishment, or to the payment of damages, for acts done in their official character but in excess of their lawful authority.

Very different from other ancient near eastern legal codes, the Torah prescribes one law regarding civil matters. There is no grading of penalties based upon the status of the wrongdoer or upon the status of the victim. Instead, there is one law for all. Insofar as all equally bear God's image, all are to enjoy equality before the law.

C. The Doctrine of the Fall

Just as all men are made in the image of God, so the Christian faith teaches also that all men are sinners, fallen from their created state. Jesus Christ alone, the "God-Man," is without sin. Consequently, no ordinary man exercising a ministry from God exercises it exactly and without fail as God would have him exercise it. Imperfect men do not keep covenant, do not judge according to the law, do not treat other men as equals before the law. However divine their calling, or perhaps because their calling is divine, they fall short.

The common law acknowledges this third doctrine, the fall of man, in many of the principles we have already rehearsed. For example, recognizing the limits and diversity of human jurisdictions fits well with recognizing the sinful state of man. Unlimited authority is not for sinners, but for God alone. The method of the common law, requiring that judges decide only the cases before them, and that they give a reasoned opinion in support of that decision, combines epistemological modesty with the distrust of judgment without justification.

Another principle directly related to the fall of man is stare decisis, the principle that courts adhere to rules previously announced in judicial opinions....

Judges, as they discerned the customs and rules that composed the common law, had no discretion to alter the law, or even to depart from precedents unless clearly erroneous. This principle not only stabilized law, as Kent remarks, but also checked indulgence of any judicial impulse to pursue passion rather than law, as Aristotle might say. Dean Roscoe Pound attacked such constraints on judicial will as a product "'of men who believed in original sin,'" and predicted that "[m]any unhappy results" would follow:

> It is hardly too much to say that the ideal judge is conceived of as a pure machine. Being a human machine and in consequence tainted with original sin, he must be allowed no scope for free action. Hard and fast rules of evidence and strict review of every detail of practice by a series of reviewing tribunals are necessary to keep him in check. In many states he may not charge the jury in any effective manner; he must rule upon and submit or reject written requests for academically stated propositions of abstract law; he must not commit any error which might possibly prejudice a party—whether in fact there is prejudice or not. Dunning has pointed out that the Puritan in America was able to carry into effect what in England could only be speculative opinions. Hence in America, in addition to the ritual of justice, belonging to a past age of formalism that put gold lace and red coats on the skirmish line, we have a machinery of justice devised to keep down the judicial personality which has made legal procedure in some sort an end in itself.

Though not explicitly attacking stare decisis, Pound exposes the connection between a common law principle that holds judges to decisions previously announced and the Christian teaching that all men sin; they fall short of their calling.

D. The Doctrine of the Atonement

Sin finds its remedy under the fourth fundamental Christian doctrine, the atonement, worked by Jesus Christ. The orthodox understanding of the atonement sees Christ's death as satisfying the just wrath of God over man's sins. Desiring to save mankind from the full consequences of their sin, but unwilling to alter or to violate the law that condemned mankind to those consequences, God suffered those consequences in union with man. He did so by sending his only son, who was both human and God, to be punished as a man. In this way, God satisfied justice while working mercy. God himself adhered to the law. He did not alter it, or find some pragmatic remedy apart from it. Instead, Jesus Christ, the son of God, was sent to earth to live a perfect life under the law, and according to the Bible, Christ did so. He also was sent to die. God the Son, who is one with God the Father from eternity, would cry from the cross to his father, "My God, my God, why hast thou forsaken me?" When Christ died, the Trinity itself split, in order to fulfill the law while providing forgiveness to humans. The doctrine that God himself keeps the law—his own law—even at so a [sic] great a cost to himself, demonstrates his most profound commitment to the rule of law. Man cannot hope to achieve higher. Neither the magnitude of God's available authority, nor the magnitude of the result, nor the magnitude of the cost, justified the departure from the law. How much less, then, should man, bearing God's image, depart from the law? Henry Bracton, thirteenth century father of the common law, explained:

> The king must not be under man but under God and under the law, because law makes the king, Let him therefore bestow upon the law what the law bestows upon him, namely, rule and power. [F]or there is no rex where will rules rather than lex. Since he is the vicar of God, And that he ought to be under the law appears clearly in the analogy of Jesus Christ, whose vicegerent on earth he is, for though many ways were open to Him for his ineffable redemption of the human race, the true mercy of God chose this most powerful way to destroy the devil's work, he would use not the power of force but the reason of justice. Thus he willed himself to be under the law that he might redeem those who live under it. For He did not wish to use force but judgment.

The rule of law can receive no higher endorsement, in fact no greater sanctity, then it does from this distinctive doctrine of the Christian faith.

Whatever diverse sources give rise to the rule of law, whatever prudence and welfare enhancements support it, the rule of law scarcely could find more committed supporters than those who, like Bracton, view human government and law from a thoroughgoing and orthodox Christian worldview.

Here a corollary accompanying such a profound commitment to the rule of law should be noted. That is, if God himself adheres to the rule of law, so should civil government. This should be true, even to the extent that this adherence puts some matters beyond the authority of civil government. If parenting, or cultivation of the arts, or the provision of medical care, cannot be done properly within the rule of law, they ought not to be done by civil government, at least if its commission is to execute justice. The rule of law, then, is not only a precept for means, but also a precept for ends.

Questions

1. According to Bracton, the king is the most important person in the realm. Is the king subject to anyone or anything?
2. How was this demonstrated practically in Magna Carta?
3. Kirk argues that several liberties enjoyed in the United States are derived from the common law. What are some examples?
4. Why does Kirk believe the common law was the foundation of both order and freedom?
5. According to Kuyper, why do we have political states?
6. Consider the following passages: Genesis 1:24-28; 9:5-6; Deuteronomy 25:2-3; James 3:9; Isaiah 53:6; 64:6; Romans 3:10-18; and Ephesians 2:1-3. Based on these scriptures, what is man's nature? How does this relate to the creation of states?
7. According to Kuyper, from what source do human governments derive their authority? Is he right? Consider Romans 13:1-5; Matthew 22:21; Isaiah 40:17-24; Colossians 1:15-18; Daniel 4:28-37; and Acts 12:21-23.
8. Why does Kuyper reject both popular sovereignty and state sovereignty?
9. What is the rule of law?

10. Stern discusses four fundamental Christian doctrines. Why does he believe these doctrines support the rule of law?

11. What lesson does Stern draw from God's "trial" of Adam and Eve after the fall? See Genesis 3:8-19.

12. According to Stern, what do we learn about God from the atonement? What implications does the atonement have for human law? Consider Romans 3:21-26; and Philippians 2:5-11.

13. Is the rule of law part of the higher law? Consider the passages listed above as well as Leviticus 19:15; Deuteronomy 16:18-20; 19:15; and Job 34:17-19.

Chapter 3 The Shift from Higher Law Thinking to Legal Relativism

A. Legal Positivism

Introduction

This chapter examines the great shift in legal thought that has taken place since the late nineteenth century. One important development in legal thought has been the rise of legal positivism, a philosophy that rejects natural law and focuses on law as it is rather than as it ought to be. Positivists generally view law simply as imperatives emanating from government.

The following piece was written by Hans Kelsen, a prominent positivist scholar. Kelsen was born in 1881 in Prague. He studied in Heidelberg, Berlin, and Vienna and then taught law for many years at the University of Vienna. In 1920, while in Vienna, Kelsen drafted the Austrian Constitution. He later served as a member of the Constitutional Court of Austria. He then moved to Germany and was a professor of law in Cologne between 1929 and 1933. A Jew, Kelsen left Germany for Switzerland in 1933 as the Nazis were consolidating power in Germany. Kelsen eventually came to the United States. He taught briefly at Harvard and Wellesley before joining the faculty at the University of California at Berkeley where he spent the last nine years of his career. Kelsen retired in 1951 and died in 1973.

What follows are excerpts from an influential law review article that Kelsen published in two parts in 1934 and 1935. The article was written in German but was later translated into English and published in the Law Quarterly Review, a London law review. In the article, Kelsen sets forth his theory of positivism, what he calls the "pure theory of law." Kelsen explains why he opposes natural law theory and believes that the science of law ought to be freed from foreign elements such as the social sciences, morality, and theology.

Hans Kelsen, *The Pure Theory of Law Part I and II*[*]

1. The Pure Theory of Law is a theory of the positive law. As a theory it is exclusively concerned with the accurate definition of its subject-matter. It endeavours to answer the question, What is the law? but not the question, What ought it to be? It is a science and not a politics of law.

That all this is described as a 'pure' theory of law means that it is concerned solely with that part of knowledge which deals with law, excluding from such knowledge everything which does not strictly belong to the subject-matter law. That is, it endeavours to free the science of law from all foreign elements. This is its fundamental methodological principle. It would seem a self-evident one. Yet a glance at the traditional science of law in its nineteenth and twentieth century developments shows plainly how far removed from the requirement of purity that science was. Jurisprudence, in a wholly uncritical fashion, was mixed up with psychology and biology, with ethics and theology. There is to-day hardly a single social science into whose province jurisprudence feels itself unfitted to enter, even thinking, indeed, to enhance its scientific status by such conjunction with other disciplines. The real science of law, of course, is lost in such a process.

* * *

8. In delimiting law from nature, the Pure Theory of Law at the same time draws the line of demarcation between Nature and Idea. The science of law is a mental and not a natural science. It can be debated whether the opposition of nature and idea coincides with that of reality and value, of the Is and the Ought, of causal law and normative law; or whether the sphere of essence is broader than that of value, or than that of the norm. But it cannot be denied that the law, as norm, is an ideal and not a natural reality. And so emerges the necessity of distinguishing law, not only from nature, but also from other spiritual phenomena, particularly from other types of norms. What is here chiefly important is to liberate law from that association which has traditionally been made for it—its association with morals. This is not of course to question the requirement that law ought to be moral, that is, good. That requirement is self-evident. What is questioned is simply the view that law, as such, is a

[*] Hans Kelsen, *The Pure Theory of Law Part I and II*, 50 L.Q. REV. 474 (1934) and 51 L.Q. REV. 517 (1935), Sections 1, 8-10, 28-31, 47-50. Published by Sweet & Maxwell. Reprinted with the permission of Cengage Learning Services.

part of morals and that therefore every law, as law, is in some sense and in some measure moral. In looking on the law as a part-province of morals, while leaving obscure the issue as to whether this means that law ought to be constructed morally, or that it is as a matter of fact moral, the attempt is made to confer on law that absolute value which morals claims. As a moral category law meant the same as justice. This is the expression for the absolutely right social order. The word, however, is often used in the sense of positive accordance with the law, particularly accordance with statute law. In this sense, if a general norm is applied in one case and not in another identical case, the procedure is termed 'unjust' and this without reference to the value of the general norm itself. In this usage the just sentence expressed only the relative value of conformity to the norm. 'Just' is only another word for 'legal' or 'legitimate.' In its proper meaning, as distinct from that which it has in law, 'justice' connotes an absolute value. Its content cannot be ascertained by the Pure Theory of Law. Indeed it is not ascertainable by rational knowledge at all. The history of human speculation for centuries has been the history of a vain striving after a solution of the problem. That striving has hitherto led only to the emptiest of tautologies, such as the formula *suum cuique* or the categoric imperative. From the standpoint of rational knowledge there are only interests and conflicts of interests, the solution of which is arrived at by an arrangement which may either satisfy the one interest at the expense of the other, or institute an equivalence or compromise between them. To determine, however, whether this or that order has an absolute value, that is, is 'just,' is not possible by the methods of rational knowledge. Justice is an irrational ideal. However indispensable it may be for the willing and acting of human beings it is not viable by reason. Only positive law is known, or more correctly is revealed, to reason. If we refrain from distinguishing these two meanings of the term justice, if we do not repudiate the claim (of the legislating authority) that the law is just law, we are lending our support to that ideological tendency which was the specific characteristic of the classical, conservative theory of natural law. This latter was concerned not so much with the knowledge of the valid law but rather with its justification. It sought to demonstrate that the positive law was simply an emanation of a natural, divine or reasonable, absolutely just order. The revolutionary natural law school, on the other hand, which in the history of legal science plays a relatively minor role, was of the opposite opinion, questioning the validity of the positive law and maintaining that it contradicted a presupposed, absolute order. Thereby they brought the actual law for a time into a more unfavourable light than it truly deserved.

9. Even after the apparent defeat of the theory of natural law, these ideological tendencies, whose political intentions and effects are obvious, still hold sway over contemporary legal science. The Pure Theory of Law is directed against them. This theory is concerned to show the law as it is, without legitimizing it as just, or disqualifying it as unjust; it seeks the real, the positive law, not the right law. In this sense it is a radically realistic theory of law. It refuses to evaluate the positive law. As a science it considers itself bound only to comprehend the positive law according to its nature and to understand it by analysis of its structure. In particular it declines to serve any political interests by providing them with ideologies whereby to justify or disqualify the existing social order. In this point it finds itself in direct opposition to traditional legal science which, consciously or unconsciously, has always in some measure an ideological colouring. Precisely in this anti-ideological tendency the Pure Theory of Law reveals itself as a true science. For science, as a part of knowledge, is compelled, by an internal necessity, to lay bare its subject-matter. Ideology on the other hand covers up reality, by explaining it away if it wishes to defend it, by distorting it if it wishes to destroy it or replace it with a substitute. All ideology has its roots in willing and not in knowing; it springs from certain interests, or more correctly, from interests other than that of truth. In saying this, of course, nothing is implied as to the value or worth of these other interests. Knowledge must continue to tear down the veils which the will has laid about things. The authority which creates the law and is, therefore, anxious for its maintenance may well ask itself if such an unvarnished knowledge of its product is a useful thing. And the powers which desire to overthrow the existing order and replace it with one which they hold to be better may well not want to know much of such a science of law. But neither the one nor the other consideration can be allowed to prevent the emergence of a science of law such as the Pure Theory of Law desires to be.

II.

10. The ideological character of traditional legal theory is clearly revealed in the customary formulation of the concept of law. It stands still to-day under the influence of the conservative natural law school, which operates, as I have already shown, with a transcendental concept of law. This is in complete accordance with the basic metaphysical character of philosophy during the reign of natural right theories; a period which, politically, coincides with the development of the police state of absolute monarchy. With the victory of bourgeois liberalism in the nineteenth century an outspoken reaction against metaphysic and natural law theory set

in. The changeover of bourgeois legal science from natural law to positivism went hand in hand with the progress of the empirical natural sciences and with a critical analysis of religious ideology. Yet this changeover, however radical, was never a complete one. Law is, indeed, no longer presumed to be an eternal and absolute category; it is recognized that its content is subject to historical change and that as positive law it is a temporally and spatially conditioned phenomenon. The idea of an absolute legal value, however, is not quite lost but lives on in the ethical notion of justice to which positivist jurisprudence continues to cling. Even though the distinction between justice and law is firmly emphasized, the two are still bound together by more or less visible ties. If we are really to have 'law,' we are told, then the positive political order must participate in some measure in the idea of justice, must realize an ethical minimum and approximate to right 'law,' that is, to justice. Since, however, the legal character of the prevailing political order is presumed to be self-evident, its legitimization at the hands of this theory of the moral minimum (which is only a minimized theory of natural law) is an easy matter. And this minimum guarantee suffices alike for the comparatively peaceful periods of middle-class domination and for the periods of relative equilibrium of the social forces. The final consequences of the officially recognized positivist principle have not been clearly displayed. The science of law is not yet wholly positivistic, though predominantly so.

* * *

THE PURE THEORY OF LAW.

PART II.

IV.

28. The law, or the legal order, is a system of legal norms. The first question we have to answer, therefore, is this: What constitutes the unity in diversity of legal norms? Why does a particular legal norm belong to a particular legal order? A multiplicity of norms constitutes a unity, a system, an order, when validity can be traced back to its final source in a single norm. This basic norm constitutes the unity in diversity of all the norms which make up the system. That a norm belongs to a particular order is only to be determined by tracing back its validity to the basic norm constituting the order. According to the nature of the basic norm, *i.e.* the sovereign principle of validity, we may distinguish two different kinds of orders, or normative systems. In the first such system the norms are valid by virtue of their content, which has a directly evident quality

compelling recognition. This contentual quality the norms receive by descent from a basic norm to whose content their content is related as particular to universal. The norms of morals are of this character. Thus the norms: Thou shalt not lie, Thou shalt not deceive, Thou shalt keep thy promise, etc. derive from a basic norm of honesty. From the basic norm: Thou shalt love thy fellow-men, we can derive the norms: Thou shalt not injure thy fellow, Thou shalt accompany him in adversity, etc. The question as to what, in a particular system of morals, is the basic norm, is not here under consideration. What is important is to recognize that the many norms of a moral system are already contained in its basic norm, exactly as particulars in a universal, and that all the individual norms can be derived from the basic norm by an operation of thought, namely, by deduction from universal to particular.

29. With legal norms the case is different. These are not valid by virtue of their content. Any content whatsoever can be legal; there is no human behaviour which could not function as the content of a legal norm. A norm becomes a legal norm only because it has been constituted in a particular fashion, born of a definite procedure and a definite rule. Law is valid only as positive law, that is, statute (constituted) law. Therefore the basic norm of law can only be the fundamental rule, according to which the legal norms are to be produced; it is the fundamental condition of law-making. The individual norms of the legal system are not to be derived from the basic norm by a process of logical deduction. They must be constituted by an act of will, not deduced by an act of thought. If we trace back a single legal norm to its source in the basic norm, we do so by showing that the procedure by which it was set up conformed to the requirements of the basic norm. Thus, if we ask why a particular act of compulsion—the fact, for instance, that one man has deprived another of his freedom by imprisoning him—is an act of law and belongs to a particular legal order, the answer is, that this act was prescribed by a certain individual norm, a judicial decision. If we ask, further, why this individual norm is valid, the answer is, that it was constituted according to the penal statute book. If we inquire as to the validity of the penal statute book, we are confronted by the State's constitution, which has prescribed rules and procedure for the creation of the penal statute book by a competent authority. If, further, we ask as to the validity of the constitution, on which repose all the laws and the acts which they have sanctioned, we come probably to a still older constitution and finally to an historically original one, set up by some single usurper or by some kind of corporate body. It is the fundamental presupposition of our recognition of the legal order founded on this constitution that that which the original authors declared to be their will should be regarded as valid norm. Compulsion is

to be exercised according to the method and conditions prescribed by the first constitutional authority, or its delegated power. This is the schematic formulation of the basic norm of a legal order.

30. The Pure Theory of Law operates with this basic norm as with an hypothesis. Presupposed that it is valid, then the legal order which rests on it is valid also. Only under this presupposition can we systematize as law (*i.e.* arrange as a system of norms) the empirical material which presents itself for legal recognition. On the composition of this material (acts) will depend also the particular content of the basic norm. This norm is only an expression for the necessary presupposition of all positivistic constructions of legal material. In formulating the basic norm, the Pure Theory of Law in no way considers itself as inaugurating a new scientific method of jurisprudence. It is only trying to make conscious in the minds of jurists what they are doing when, in seeking to understand their subject, they reject a validity founded on natural law, yet affirm the positive law, not as a mere factual assembly of motives, but as a valid order, as Norm. With the theory of the basic norm, the Pure Theory of Law is only trying to elucidate, by an analysis of the actual procedure, the transcendental-logical conditions of the historic methods of positive legal knowledge.

31. Just as the nature of law, and of the community which it constitutes, stands most clearly revealed when its very existence is threatened, so the significance of the basic norm emerges most clearly when the legal order undergoes not legal change, but revolution or substitution. In an hitherto monarchic State a number of men attempt to overthrow by force the legitimate monarchic government and to set up a republican form in its place. If in this they are successful, if, that is, the old government ceases and the new begins to be effective, in that the behaviour of the men and women, for whom the order claims to be valid, conforms in the main no longer to the old but to the new order, then this latter is operated as a legal order, the acts which it performs are declared legal, the conditions which it proscribes, illegal. A new basic norm is presupposed—no longer that which delegated legislative authority to the monarch, but one which delegates such authority to the revolutionary government. Had the attempt been a failure, had the new order, that is, remained ineffective, in that behaviour did not conform to it, then the acts of the new government become not constitutional but criminal (high treason), not legislation but delict, and this on the ground of the validity of the old order, which presupposed a basic norm delegating legislative power to the monarch.

If we ask what, then, determines the content of the basic norm, we find, on analysing judicial decisions back to their first premise, the following answer: The content of the basic norm is determined by the condition of fact out of which the order emerges, given that to the order there corresponds, amongst the human beings to whom it refers, a substantial measure of actual behaviour.

This gives us the content of a positive legal norm. (It is not, of course, a norm of a State's legal order, but a norm of international law, which, as a legal order superior to that of the individual States, legally determines their sphere of jurisdiction.) This norm affirms (a) that a system of legal compulsion, which is directly subordinate to international law, should be regarded as legitimate, or the community constituted by that system valid as a State, within that area in which it has established an effective sovereignty, and (b) that, further, a government which has come to power by revolution or *coup d'etat* should equally be recognized as a valid government in the sense of international law, provided that it is in a position to secure a substantial observance of the norms which it has set up. Positive international law thus elevates the principle of efficacy to the rank of a legal principle. This principle it is which determines the basic norm of the individual State's legal order.

* * *

47. In the traditional distinction between public and private law there emerges clearly that powerful dualism which dominates modern legal science, the dualism of State and law. Traditional legal theory regards the State as something essentially different from the law and yet at the same time declares it to be a legal thing. It achieves this position by regarding the State as a person to whom it ascribes an existence independent of the legal order. Just as private law theory originally held it to be true of the legal personality of the individual that it was prior logically and in time to the objective law, so political theory holds it to be true of the State that, as a collective unity, as a being capable of willing and acting, it precedes and is independent of the law. But, we are told, the State fulfils its historic mission by making the law 'its' law, by creating the objective legal order only to subordinate itself to it, thus by its own law imposing obligations on and justifying itself. Thus the State is a 'metalegal' being, a kind of mighty macroanthropos or social organism, at once the presupposition of the law and its confirmation, since it itself is a legal subject with legal rights and duties. This is the celebrated theory of the auto-determinism of the State, which despite its demonstrable, and frequently demonstrated contradictions, persists with unexampled tenacity.

48. Traditional legal and political theory dare not renounce this doctrine, this dualism of State and law, for it performs an ideological function of a quite exceptional significance. The State must be presented as a

person different from the law, in order that the law may justify the at once creative and submissive State. And the law can only justify the State if it is presumed to be a right and just order fundamentally different from the State, whose original nature is force. Thus the State is transformed from a mere agent of force into a legal entity which is justified by its administration of law. According as the religious, metaphysical justification of the State became ineffective, this Legal State theory came to afford the only possible justification of the State. The effect of the 'theory' was not diminished by the contradictory nature of a State which was at once a juristic person, an object of legal knowledge, and a being, fundamentally different from the law, whose nature was force, that is, a being who could not be legally conceived at all.

49. The Pure Theory of Law views the State as a system of human behaviour, an order of social compulsion. This compulsive order is not different from the legal order for the reason that within one community only one and not two compulsive orders can be valid at the same time. Every expression of the life of a State, every act of State, is a legal act. A human act is only designated an act of State by virtue of a legal norm which qualifies it as such; on the basis of the norm the act is imputed to the State, is related to the unity of the legal order. The State as person is simply the personification of the law; as force, it is its efficacy. The dualism of State and law is one of those tautologies which double the object of knowledge—the mind first constitutes the object into a unity and then the unity itself is envisaged as a separate object. There is here an exact parallel, from an epistemological point of view, with the equally contradictory dualism of god and world. The legal dualism is simply a reflection of and substitute for the theological, with which it has substantial identity. When we have grasped, however, the unity of State and law, when we have seen that the law, the positive law (not justice), is precisely that compulsive order which is the State, we shall have acquired a realistic, nonpersonificative, non-anthropomorphous view, which will demonstrate clearly the impossibility of justifying the State by the law, just as it is impossible to justify the law by the law unless that term be used now in its positive sense, now in the sense of right law, justice. The attempt to justify the State by law is vain, since every State is necessarily a legal State. Law, says positivism, is nothing but an order of human compulsion. As to the justice or morality of that order, positivism itself has nothing to say. The State is neither more nor less than the law, an object of normative, juristic knowledge in its ideal aspect, that is, as a system of ideas, the subject-matter of social psychology or sociology in its material aspect, that is, as a motivated and motivating, physical act (force).

50. To resolve the dualism of State and law in this way, however, is also completely to destroy the present, very significant ideology of justification. Hence the passionate resistance offered by traditional theory to the Pure Theory of Law thesis as to the identity of law and the State.

In rejecting a justification of the State by the law, the Pure Theory of Law does not imply that no such justification is possible. It only denies that legal science can perform that office. Indeed, it denies that it can ever be the task of legal science to justify anything. Justification implies judgment of value, and judgment of value is an affair of ethics and of politics, not, however, of pure knowledge. To the service of that knowledge legal science is dedicated.

Questions

1. What does Kelsen mean by a "pure" theory of law?
2. What does Kelsen believe must be removed from law to purify it? Why?
3. What would Kelsen think of Aquinas' natural law theory? Why?
4. What is the "basic norm?"
5. When is a law valid according to Kelsen?
6. What is the relationship between the law and the state?
7. Recall Abraham Kuyper's criticism of both popular sovereignty and state sovereignty. How would he view Kelsen's pure theory of law?
8. To Kelsen, was the killing of Jews by the Nazis a legal act? A just act?
9. How would Kelsen assess the validity of the following laws?
    a. A federal statute prohibiting restaurants from serving foods containing trans fat;
    b. A federal statute prohibiting restaurants from serving foods containing trans fat where the statute was approved by the House of Representatives and signed by the President, but was never acted upon by the Senate;

c. A federal statute forbidding parents to give religious instruction to their children;

d. A federal constitutional amendment forbidding parents to give religious instruction to their children;

e. A federal law funding the cloning of human beings for research purposes;

f. A federal constitutional amendment (enacted to save Social Security and Medicare) providing the following:

> Medical providers may no longer provide medical treatment for a "serious illness" to anyone over seventy-five years of age. [A "serious illness" is defined as an illness or condition that would require medical procedures and treatments costing in excess of a certain dollar amount to cure or treat]. A patient denied treatment under this provision may either suffer with the illness untreated, may be assisted in committing suicide by a medical provider, or may be involuntarily euthanized at the request of two or more members of the patient's immediate family.

B. Legal Realism

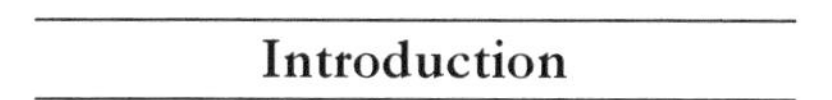

Introduction

We next turn to the intellectual movement that probably has had more impact on legal thinking and the law than any other in the last century: legal realism. Legal realism as a movement began in the 1920s and 1930s. The most current theories about law (law and economics, critical legal studies, feminist jurisprudence, and critical race theory) can all be said to be offshoots of legal realism. It has been said, "We are all realists now."

Realism began as a reaction to legal formalism, a philosophy that believed in the primacy of legal rules. As realists saw it, formalism insisted that results in individual cases could be derived through deductive reasoning from fixed fundamental principles and rules. Judges merely found the law, they did not make it.

Realists rejected these notions. While realists disagreed among themselves on many issues, they were united in a skepticism about existing legal rules and reasoning. Realists believed that the facts of cases were much more important than legal rules and that logical deduction could not explain legal decisions. They insisted, too, that judges made law, they did not find it.

What follows are three pieces that introduce legal realism. The first two pieces are by Oliver Wendell Holmes. Holmes is not technically a realist. He wrote both of these pieces at least a full generation before the rise of the realist movement. But Holmes was a precursor to realism. His thinking, demonstrated well in the excerpts that follow, significantly influenced the realist movement later. The first piece is an excerpt from a book by Oliver Wendell Holmes entitled *The Common Law*. The book came from a series of lectures Holmes gave in 1880. The second piece is an excerpt from Holmes' acclaimed 1897 Harvard Law Review article, "The Path of the Law."

Holmes was born in Boston in 1841. His father was a doctor and a professor of anatomy at Harvard University. Holmes himself graduated from Harvard in 1861. He immediately enlisted to fight in the Civil War. During his three-year commitment, Holmes was wounded three times. In 1864 he left the army and attended Harvard Law School. Holmes' legal career was quite distinguished. He both practiced law and taught at Harvard. In 1882 he was appointed as a justice on the Massachusetts Supreme Court. In 1902 President Theodore Roosevelt appointed Holmes as a justice on the United States Supreme Court where he served until 1932. He died in 1935.

The third piece is from a law review article written by Karl Llewellyn. Llewellyn, too, was a respected and influential legal scholar. He was born in West Seattle, Washington in 1893. While Llewellyn received some of his education abroad, he received his bachelor's and law degrees from Yale University. Llewellyn practiced law for two years at a prestigious New York firm and then became a law professor, teaching at Yale for three years and Columbia University for twenty-six years. He finished his career teaching eleven more years at the University of Chicago. Llewellyn died in 1962.

Llewellyn was a prolific writer, producing several books and over 125 articles. He was considered an expert in both commercial law and jurisprudence. He made major contributions in both areas. Llewellyn was one of the main architects of the Uniform Commercial Code. He was also one of the most influential members of the legal realism movement and was a driving force behind the movement.

The piece here is from a law review article Llewellyn wrote entitled: "Some Realism about Realism." Llewellyn wrote the article in response to Roscoe Pound, another famous and influential law professor, who had partially criticized realism. The piece is important because it is a realist defining and defending realism.

Oliver Wendell Holmes, Jr., *The Common Law*[*]

The object of this book is to present a general view of the Common Law. To accomplish the task, other tools are needed besides logic. It is something to show that the consistency of a system requires a particular result, but it is not all. The life of the law has not been logic: it has been experience. The felt necessities of the time, the prevalent moral and political theories, intuitions of public policy, avowed or unconscious, even the prejudices which judges share with their fellow-men, have had a good deal more to do than the syllogism in determining the rules by which men should be governed. The law embodies the story of a nation's development through many centuries, and it cannot be dealt with as if it contained only the axioms and corollaries of a book of mathematics. In order to know what it is, we must know what it has been, and what it tends to become. We must alternately consult history and existing theories of legislation. But the most difficult labor will be to understand the combination of the two into new products at every stage. The substance of the law at any given time pretty nearly corresponds, so far as it goes, with what is then understood to be convenient; but its form and machinery, and the degree to which it is able to work out desired results, depend very much upon its past.

In Massachusetts to-day, while, on the one hand, there are a great many rules which are quite sufficiently accounted for by their manifest good sense, on the other, there are some which can only be understood by reference to the infancy of procedure among the German tribes, or to the social condition of Rome under the Decemvirs.

I shall use the history of our law so far as it is necessary to explain a conception or to interpret a rule, but no further. In doing so there are two errors equally to be avoided both by writer and reader. One is that of supposing, because an idea seems very familiar and natural to us, that it has always been so. Many things which we take for granted have had to be laboriously fought out or thought out in past times. The other mistake is the opposite one of asking too much of history. We start with man full grown. It may be assumed that the earliest barbarian whose practices are to be considered, had a good many of the same feelings and passions as ourselves.

[*] OLIVER WENDELL HOLMES, JR., THE COMMON LAW 1-2 (1887).

Oliver Wendell Holmes, Jr., *The Path of the Law*[*]

When we study law we are not studying a mystery but a well-known profession. We are studying what we shall want in order to appear before judges, or to advise people in such a way as to keep them out of court. The reason why it is a profession, why people will pay lawyers to argue for them or to advise them, is that in societies like ours the command of the public force is intrusted to the judges in certain cases, and the whole power of the state will be put forth, if necessary, to carry out their judgments and decrees. People want to know under what circumstances and how far they will run the risk of coming against what is so much stronger than themselves, and hence it becomes a business to find out when this danger is to be feared. The object of our study, then, is prediction, the prediction of the incidence of the public force through the instrumentality of the courts.

The means of the study are a body of reports, of treatises, and of statutes, in this country and in England, extending back for six hundred years, and now increasing annually by hundreds. In these sibylline leaves are gathered the scattered prophecies of the past upon the cases in which the axe will fall. These are what properly have been called the oracles of the law. Far the most important and pretty nearly the whole meaning of every new effort of legal thought is to make these prophecies more precise, and to generalize them into a thoroughly connected system.... The primary rights and duties with which jurisprudence busies itself again are nothing but prophecies. One of the many evil effects of the confusion between legal and moral ideas, about which I shall have something to say in a moment, is that theory is apt to get the cart before the horse, and consider the right or the duty as something existing apart from and independent of the consequences of its breach, to which certain sanctions are added afterward. But, as I shall try to show, a legal duty so called is nothing but a prediction that if a man does or omits certain things he will be made to suffer in this or that way by judgment of the court; and so of a legal right.

* * *

I wish, if I can, to lay down some first principles for the study of this body of dogma or systematized prediction which we call the law, for men who want to use it as the instrument of their business to enable them

[*] Oliver Wendell Holmes, Jr., *The Path of the Law*, 10 HARV. L. REV. 457, 457-62, 464-67 (1897).

to prophesy in their turn, and, as bearing upon the study, I wish to point out an ideal which as yet our law has not attained.

The first thing for a businesslike understanding of the matter is to understand its limits, and therefore I think it desirable at once to point out and dispel a confusion between morality and law, which sometimes rises to the height of conscious theory, and more often and indeed constantly is making trouble in detail without reaching the point of consciousness. You can see very plainly that a bad man has as much reason as a good one for wishing to avoid an encounter with the public force, and therefore you can see the practical importance of the distinction between morality and law. A man who cares nothing for an ethical rule which is believed and practised by his neighbors is likely nevertheless to care a good deal to avoid being made to pay money, and will want to keep out of jail if he can.

I take it for granted that no hearer of mine will misinterpret what I have to say as the language of cynicism. The law is the witness and external deposit of our moral life. Its history is the history of the moral development of the race. The practice of it, in spite of popular jests, tends to make good citizens and good men. When I emphasize the difference between law and morals I do so with reference to a single end, that of learning and understanding the law. For that purpose you must definitely master its specific marks, and it is for that that I ask you for the moment to imagine yourselves indifferent to other and greater things.

I do not say that there is not a wider point of view from which the distinction between law and morals becomes of secondary or no importance, as all mathematical distinctions vanish in presence of the infinite. But I do say that that distinction is of the first importance for the object which we are here to consider—a right study and mastery of the law as a business with well understood limits, a body of dogma enclosed within definite lines. I have just shown the practical reason for saying so. If you want to know the law and nothing else, you must look at it as a bad man, who cares only for the material consequences which such knowledge enables him to predict, not as a good one, who finds his reasons for conduct, whether inside the law or outside of it, in the vaguer sanctions of conscience. The theoretical importance of the distinction is no less, if you would reason on your subject aright. The law is full of phraseology drawn from morals, and by the mere force of language continually invites us to pass from one domain to the other without perceiving it, as we are sure to do unless we have the boundary constantly before our minds. The law talks about rights, and duties, and malice, and intent, and negligence, and so forth, and nothing is easier, or, I may say, more common in legal reasoning, than to take these words in their moral sense, at some state of the argument, and so to drop into fallacy. For instance, when we speak of the rights of man in a moral sense, we mean to mark the limits of interference with individual freedom which we think are prescribed by conscience, or by our ideal, however reached. Yet it is certain that many laws have been enforced in the past, and it is likely that some are enforced now, which are condemned by the most enlightened opinion of the time, or which at all events pass the limit of interference, as many consciences would draw it. Manifestly, therefore, nothing but confusion of thought can result from assuming that the rights of man in a moral sense are equally rights in the sense of the Constitution and the law. No doubt simple and extreme cases can be put of imaginable laws which the statute-making power would not dare to enact, even in the absence of written constitutional prohibitions, because the community would rise in rebellion and fight; and this gives some plausibility to the proposition that the law, if not a part of morality, is limited by it. But this limit of power is not coextensive with any system of morals. For the most part it falls far within the lines of any such system, and in some cases may extend beyond them, for reasons drawn from the habits of a particular people at a particular time. I once heard the late Professor Agassiz say that a German population would rise if you added two cents to the price of a glass of beer. A statute in such a case would be empty words, not because it was wrong, but because it could not be enforced. No one will deny that wrong statutes can be and are enforced, and we would not all agree as to which were the wrong ones.

The confusion with which I am dealing besets confessedly legal conceptions. Take the fundamental question, What constitutes the law? You will find some text writers telling you that it is something different from what is decided by the courts of Massachusetts or England, that it is a system of reason, that it is a deduction from principles of ethics or admitted axioms or what not, which may or may not coincide with the decisions. But if we take the view of our friend the bad man we shall find that he does not care two straws for the axioms or deductions, but that he does want to know what the Massachusetts or English courts are likely to do in fact. I am much of this mind. The prophecies of what the courts will do in fact, and nothing more pretentious, are what I mean by the law.

Take again a notion which as popularly understood is the widest conception which the law contains—the notion of legal duty, to which already I have referred. We fill the word with all the content which we draw from morals. But what does it mean to a bad man? Mainly, and in the first place, a prophecy that if he does certain things he will be subjected to disagreeable consequences by way of imprisonment or compulsory payment of money....

Nowhere is the confusion between legal and moral ideas more manifest than in the law of contract. Among other things, here again the so-called primary rights and duties are invested with a mystic significance beyond what can be assigned and explained. The duty to keep a contract at common law means a prediction that you must pay damages if you do not keep it—and nothing else. If you commit a tort, you are liable to pay a compensatory sum. If you commit a contract, you are liable to pay a compensatory sum unless the promised event comes to pass, and that is all the difference. But such a mode of looking at the matter stinks in the nostrils of those who think it advantageous to get as much ethics into the law as they can.

* * *

For my own part, I often doubt whether it would not be a gain if every word of moral significance could be banished from the law altogether, and other words adopted which should convey legal ideas uncolored by anything outside the law. We should lose the fossil records of a good deal of history and the majesty got from ethical associations, but by ridding ourselves of an unnecessary confusion we should gain very much in the clearness of our thought.

So much for the limits of the law. The next thing which I wish to consider is what are the forces which determine its content and its growth. You may assume, with Hobbes and Bentham and Austin, that all law emanates from the sovereign, even when the first human beings to enunciate it are the judges, or you may think that law is the voice of the Zeitgeist, or what you like. It is all one to my present purpose. Even if every decision required the sanction of an emperor with despotic power and a whimsical turn of mind, we should be interested none the less, still with a view to prediction, in discovering some order, some rational explanation, and some principle of growth for the rules which he laid down. In every system there are such explanations and principles to be found. It is with regard to them that a second fallacy comes in, which I think it important to expose.

The fallacy to which I refer is the notion that the only force at work in the development of the law is logic. In the broadest sense, indeed, that notion would be true. The postulate on which we think about the universe is that there is a fixed quantitative relation between every phenomenon and its antecedents and consequents. If there is such a thing as a phenomenon without these fixed quantitative relations, it is a miracle. It is outside the law of cause and effect, and as such transcends our power of thought, or at least is something to or from which we cannot reason. The condition of our thinking about the universe is that it is capable of being thought about rationally, or, in other words, that every part of it is effect and cause in the same sense in which those parts are with which we are most familiar. So in the broadest sense it is true that the law is a logical development, like everything else. The danger of which I speak is not the admission that the principles governing other phenomena also govern the law, but the notion that a given system, ours, for instance, can be worked out like mathematics from some general axioms of conduct. This is the natural error of the schools, but it is not confined to them. I once heard a very eminent judge say that he never let a decision go until he was absolutely sure that it was right. So judicial dissent often is blamed, as if it meant simply that one side or the other were not doing their sums right, and if they would take more trouble, agreement inevitably would come.

This mode of thinking is entirely natural. The training of lawyers is a training in logic. The processes of analogy, discrimination, and deduction are those in which they are most at home. The language of judicial decision is mainly the language of logic. And the logical method and form flatter that longing for certainty and for repose which is in every human mind. But certainty generally is illusion, and repose is not the destiny of man. Behind the logical form lies a judgment as to the relative worth and importance of competing legislative grounds, often an inarticulate and unconscious judgment, it is true, and yet the very root and nerve of the whole proceeding. You can give any conclusion a logical form. You always can imply a condition in a contract. But why do you imply it? It is because of some belief as to the practice of the community or of a class, or because of some opinion as to policy, or, in short, because of some attitude of yours upon a matter not capable of exact quantitative measurement, and therefore not capable of founding exact logical conclusions. Such matters really are battle grounds where the means do not exist for the determinations that shall be good for all time, and where the decision can do no more than embody the preference of a given body in a given time and place. We do not realize how large a part of our law is open to reconsideration upon a slight change in the habit of the public mind. No concrete proposition is self evident, no matter how ready we may be to accept it, not even Mr. Herbert Spencer's "Every man has a right to do what he wills, provided he interferes not with a like right on the part of his neighbors."

Why is a false and injurious statement privileged, if it is made honestly in giving information about a servant? It is because it has been thought more important that information should be given freely, than that a man should be protected from what under other circumstances would be an actionable wrong. Why is a man at liberty to set up a business which he knows will ruin his neighborhood? It is because the public good is supposed to be best subserved by free competition. Obviously such judgments of relative importance may vary in different times and places. Why does a judge instruct a jury that an employer is not liable to an employee for an injury received in the course of his employment unless he is negligent, and why do the jury generally find for the plaintiff if the case is allowed to go to them? It is because the traditional policy of our law is to confine liability to cases where a prudent man might have foreseen the injury, or at least the danger, while the inclination of a very large part of the community is to make certain classes of persons insure the safety of those with whom they deal. Since the last words were written, I have seen the requirement of such insurance put forth as part of the programme of one of the best known labor organizations. There is a concealed, half conscious battle on the question of legislative policy, and if any one thinks that it can be settled deductively, or once for all, I only can say that I think he is theoretically wrong, and that I am certain that his conclusion will not be accepted in practice *semper ubique et ab omnibus* [always, everywhere, and by all].

Indeed, I think that even now our theory upon this matter is open to reconsideration, although I am not prepared to say how I should decide if a reconsideration were proposed. Our law of torts comes from the old days of isolated, ungeneralized wrongs, assaults, slanders, and the like, where the damages might be taken to lie where they fell by legal judgment. But the torts with which our courts are kept busy today are mainly the incidents of certain well known businesses. They are injuries to person or property by railroads, factories, and the like. The liability for them is estimated, and sooner or later goes into the price paid by the public. The public really pays the damages, and the question of liability, if pressed far enough, is really a question how far it is desirable that the public should insure the safety of one whose work it uses. It might be said that in such cases the chance of a jury finding for the defendant is merely a chance, once in a while rather arbitrarily interrupting the regular course of recovery, most likely in the case of an unusually conscientious plaintiff, and therefore better done away with. On the other hand, the economic value even of a life to the community can be estimated, and no recovery, it may be said, ought to go beyond that amount. It is conceivable that some day in certain cases we may find ourselves imitating, on a higher plane, the tariff for life and limb which we see in the Leges Barbarorum [the laws of the barbarians].

I think that the judges themselves have failed adequately to recognize their duty of weighing considerations of social advantage. The duty is inevitable, and the result of the often proclaimed judicial aversion to deal with such considerations is simply to leave the very ground and foundation of judgments inarticulate, and often unconscious, as I have said.

Karl Llewellyn, *Some Realism About Realism*[*]

Ferment is abroad in the law. The sphere of interest widens; men become interested again in the life that swirls around things legal. Before rules, were facts; in the beginning was not a Word, but a Doing. Behind decisions stand judges; judges are men; as men they have human backgrounds. Beyond rules, again, lie effects: beyond decisions stand people whom rules and decisions directly or indirectly touch. The field of Law reaches both forward and back from the Substantive Law of school and doctrine. The sphere of interest is widening; so, too, is the scope of doubt. *Beyond rules lie effects*—but do they? Are some rules mere paper? And if effects, what effects? Hearsay, unbuttressed guess, assumption or assertion unchecked by test—can such be trusted on this matter of what law is *doing*?

The ferment is proper to the time. The law of schools threatened at the close of the century to turn into words—placid, clear-seeming, lifeless, like some old canal. Practice rolled on, muddy, turbulent, vigorous. It is now spilling, flooding, into the canal of stagnant words. It brings ferment and trouble. So other fields of thought have spilled their waters in: the stress on behavior in the social sciences; their drive toward integration; the physicists' reëxamination of final-seeming premises; the challenge of war and revolution. These stir. They stir the law. Interests of practice claim attention. Methods of work unfamiliar to lawyers make their way in, beside traditional techniques. Traditional techniques themselves are reëxamined, checked against fact, stripped somewhat of confusion. And always there is this restless questing: what *difference* does statute, or rule, or court-decision, make?

Whether this ferment is one thing or twenty is a question; if one thing, it is twenty things in one. But it is with us. It spreads. It is no mere talk. It shows results, results enough through the past decade to demonstrate its value.

---

[*] Karl Llewellyn, *Some Realism About Realism—Responding to Dean Pound*, 44 HARV. L. REV. 1222, 1222-23, 1233-43 (1931). Used with permission of Harvard Law Review, from Harvard Law Review, Volume 44, 1931; permission conveyed through Copyright Clearance Center.

And those involved are folk of modest ideals. They want law to deal, they themselves want to deal, with things, with people, with tangibles, with *definite* tangibles, and *observable* relations between definite tangibles—not with words alone; when law deals with words, they want the words to represent tangibles which can be got at beneath the words, and observable relations between those tangibles. They want to check ideas, and rules, and formulas by facts, to keep them close to facts. They view rules, they view law, as means to ends; as only means to ends; as having meaning only insofar as they are means to ends. They suspect, with law moving slowly and the life around them moving fast, that some law may have gotten out of joint with life. This is a question in first instance of fact: what does law *do*, to people, or for people? In the second instance, it is a question of ends: what *ought* law to do to people, or for them? But there is no reaching a judgment as to whether any specific part of present law does what it ought, until you can first answer what it is doing now. To see this, and to be ignorant of the answer, is to start fermenting, is to start trying to find out.

All this is, we say, a simple-hearted point of view, and often philosophically naïve—though it has in it elements enough of intellectual sophistication. It denies very little, except the completeness of the teachings handed down. It knows too little to care about denying much. It affirms ignorance, pitched within and without. It affirms the need to know. Its call is for intelligent effort to dispel the ignorance. Intelligent effort to cut beneath old rules, old words, to get sight of current things. It is not a new point of view; it is as old as man. But its rediscovery in any age, by any man, in any discipline, is joyous.

* * *

II

Real Realists

What, then, are the characteristics of these new fermenters? One thing is clear. There is no school of realists. There is no likelihood that there will be such a school. There is no group with an official or accepted, or even with an emerging creed. There is no abnegation of independent striking out. We hope that there may never be. New recruits acquire tools and stimulus, not masters, nor over-mastering ideas. Old recruits diverge in interests from each other. They are related, says Frank, only in their negations, and in their skepticisms, and in their curiosity.

* * *

The common points of departure are several.

(1) The conception of law in flux, of moving law, and of judicial creation of law.

(2) The conception of law as a means to social ends and not as an end in itself; so that any part needs constantly to be examined for its purpose, and for its effect, and to be judged in the light of both and of their relation to each other.

(3) The conception of society in flux, and in flux typically faster than the law, so that the probability is always given that any portion of law needs reëxamination to determine how far it fits the society it purports to serve.

(4) The *temporary* divorce of Is and Ought for purposes of study. By this I mean that whereas value judgments must always be appealed to in order to set objectives for inquiry, yet during the inquiry itself into what Is, the observation, the description, and the establishment of relations between the things described are to remain *as largely as possible* uncontaminated by the desires of the observer or by what he wishes might be or thinks ought (ethically) to be. More particularly, this involves during the study of what courts are doing the effort to disregard the question what they ought to do. Such divorce of Is and Ought is, of course, not conceived as permanent. To men who begin with a suspicion that change is needed, a permanent divorce would be impossible. The argument is simply that no judgment of what Ought to be done in the future with respect to any part of law can be intelligently made without knowing objectively, as far as possible, what that part of law is now doing. And realists believe that experience shows the intrusion of Ought-spectacles *during the investigation of the facts* to make it very difficult to see what is being done. On the Ought side this means an insistence on informed evaluations instead of armchair speculations. Its full implications on the side of Is-investigation can be appreciated only when one follows the contributions to objective description in business law and practice made by realists whose social philosophy rejects many of the accepted foundations of the existing economic order. (*E.g.*, Handler *re* trade-marks and advertising; Klaus *re* marketing and banking; Llewellyn *re* sales; Moore *re* banking; Patterson *re* risk-bearing.)

(5) Distrust of traditional legal rules and concepts insofar as they purport to *describe* what either courts or people are actually doing. Hence the constant emphasis on rules as "generalized predictions of what courts will do." This is much more widespread as yet than its counterpart: the careful severance of rules *for* doing (precepts) from rules *of* doing (practices).

(6) Hand in hand with this distrust of traditional rules (on the descriptive side) goes a distrust of the theory that traditional prescriptive

rule-formulations are *the* heavily operative factor in producing court decisions. This involves the tentative adoption of the theory of rationalization for the study of opinions. It will be noted that "distrust" in this and the preceding point is not at all equivalent to "negation in any given instance."

(7) The belief in the worthwhileness of grouping cases and legal situations into narrower categories than has been the practice in the past. This is connected with the distrust of verbally simple rules—which so often cover dissimilar and non-simple fact situations (dissimilarity being tested partly by the way cases come out, and partly by the observer's judgment as to how they ought to come out; but a realist tries to indicate explicitly which criterion he is applying).

(8) An insistence on evaluation of any part of law in terms of its effects, and an insistence on the worthwhileness of trying to find these effects.

(9) Insistence on *sustained and programmatic attack* on the problems of law along any of these lines. None of the ideas set forth in this list is new. Each can be matched from somewhere; each can be matched from recent orthodox work in law. New twists and combinations do appear here and there. What is as novel as it is vital is for a goodly number of men to pick up ideas which have been expressed and dropped, used for an hour and dropped, played with from time to time and dropped—to pick up such ideas and set about *consistently, persistently, insistently to carry them through.* Grant that the idea or point of view is familiar—the results of steady, sustained, systematic work with it are not familiar. Not hit-or-miss stuff, not the insight which flashes and is forgotten, but sustained effort to force an old insight into its full bearing, to exploit it to the point where it laps over upon an apparently inconsistent insight, to explore their bearing on each other by the test of fact. This urge, in law, is quite new enough over the last decades to excuse a touch of frenzy among the locust-eaters.

The first, second, third and fifth of the above items, while common to the workers of the newer movement, are not peculiar to them. But the other items (4, 6, 7, 8 and 9) are to me the characteristic marks of the movement. Men or work fitting those specifications are to me "realistic" whatever label they may wear. Such, and none other, are the perfect fauna of this new land. Not all the work cited below fits my peculiar definition in all points. All such work fits most of the points.

Bound, as all "innovators" are, by prior thinking, these innovating "realists" brought their batteries to bear in first instance on the work of appellate courts. Still wholly within the tradition of our law, they strove to improve on that tradition.

(a) An early and fruitful line of attack borrowed from psychology the concept of *rationalization* already mentioned. To recanvass the opinions, viewing them no longer as mirroring the process of deciding cases, but rather as trained lawyers' arguments made by the judges (after the decision has been reached), intended to make the decision seem plausible, legally decent, legally right, to make it seem, indeed, legally inevitable—this was to open up new vision. It was assumed that the deductive logic of opinions need by no means be either a *description* of the process of decision, or an *explanation* of how the decision was reached. Indeed over-enthusiasm has at times assumed that the logic of the opinion *could* be neither; and similar over-enthusiasm, perceiving case after case in which the opinion is clearly almost valueless as an indication of how that case came to decision, has worked at times almost as if the opinion were equally valueless in predicting what a later court will do.

But the line of inquiry via rationalization has come close to demonstrating that in any case doubtful enough to make litigation respectable the available authoritative premises—*i.e.*, premises legitimate and impeccable under the traditional legal techniques—are at least two, and that the two are mutually contradictory as applied to the case in hand. Which opens the question of what made the court select the one available premise rather than the other. And which raises the greatest of doubts as to *how far* that supposed certainty in decision which derives merely from the presence of accepted rules really goes.

(b) A second line of attack has been to discriminate among rules with reference to their relative significance. Too much is written and thought about "law" and "rules," lump-wise. Which part of law? Which rule? Iron rules of policy, and rules "in the absence of agreement"; rules which keep a case from the jury, and rules as to the etiquette of instructions necessary to make a verdict stick—if one can get it; rules "of pure decision" for hospital cases, and rules which counsellors rely on in their counselling; rules which affect many (and which many, and how?) and rules which affect few. Such discriminations affect the traditional law curriculum, the traditional organization of law books and, above all, the orientation of study: to drive into the most important fields of ignorance.

(c) A further line of attack on the apparent conflict and uncertainty among the decisions in appellate courts has been to seek more understandable statement of them by grouping the facts in new—and typically but not always narrower—categories. The search is for correlations of fact-situation and outcome which (aided by common sense) may reveal *when* courts seize on one rather than another of the available competing premises. One may even stumble on the trail of *why* they do. Perhaps, *e.g.*, third party beneficiary difficulties simply fail to get applied to promises to make provision for dependents; perhaps the preexisting duty rule goes by the board when the agreement is one for a marriage-settlement. Perhaps, indeed, contracts in what we may broadly call family relations do not work out in general as they do in business. If so, the rules—viewed as statements of the course of judicial behavior—as *predictions* of what will happen—need to be restated. Sometimes it is a question of carving out hitherto unnoticed exceptions. But sometimes the results force the worker to reclassify an area altogether. Typically, as stated, the classes of situations which result are narrower, much narrower than the traditional classes. The process is in essence the orthodox technique of making distinctions, and reformulating—but undertaken systematically; exploited consciously, instead of being reserved until facts which refuse to be twisted by "interpretation" force action. The departure from orthodox procedure lies chiefly in distrust of, instead of search for, the widest sweep of generalization words permit. Not that such sweeping generalizations are not desired—*if they can be made so as to state what judges do.*

All of these three earliest lines of attack converge to a single conclusion: *there is less possibility of accurate prediction of what courts will do than the traditional rules would lead us to suppose* (and what possibility there is must be found in good measure outside these same traditional rules). The particular kind of certainty that men have thus far thought to find in law is in good measure an illusion.

Questions

1. According to Holmes, how much does logic explain legal rules and decisions? What does explain them?
2. In "The Path of the Law," Holmes asks this question: "What constitutes the law?" What is his answer?
3. Why is Holmes concerned about confusion between law and morals?
4. What would Holmes think of Aquinas' natural law theory? Why?
5. What does Llewellyn think of legal rules?
6. What does Llewellyn think explains legal decisions?
7. Llewellyn wrote his article to explain legal realism. What does legal realism mean to him?

8. What does Llewellyn believe is the purpose of law?

9. How is realism both similar to and different from positivism?

10. We saw in Chapter 2 that Blackstone believed that judges do not make law, they find it. Indeed, judicial decisions are merely "the evidence of what is common law." Even when judges overturn previous decisions, "the subsequent judges do not pretend to make a new law, but to vindicate the old one from misrepresentation." How would a legal realist evaluate Blackstone's position?

11. Legal realists applied their legal philosophy to legislation as well as judicial decision-making. Would a legal realist support the enactment of the following laws? How would he or she decide?

    a. A state law prohibiting theft;

    b. A state law prohibiting gambling;

    c. A federal law prohibiting the creation of human-animal hybrids for research purposes;

    d. A federal law funding the creation of human-animal hybrids for research purposes.

C. Legal Utilitarianism: Law and Economics

Introduction

People have long applied economic concepts to the law. But law and economics as a movement probably dates back to 1960 when Ronald Coase wrote an article entitled "The Problem of Social Cost." In it Coase set forth a principle that has since become known as the Coase Theorem: In a world without transaction costs, parties to a dispute will bargain toward efficient solutions regardless of their initial positions or the applicable rule of law.

The law and economics movement has developed significantly since the 1970s, due in large part to the work of the author of the next piece, Richard Posner. Posner is currently the Chief Judge of the United States Court of Appeals for the Seventh Circuit in Chicago. Prior to taking the bench, Posner was a law professor at the University of Chicago where law and economics scholarship has flourished. Posner is a prolific author of books and articles, and he continues to write and teach while serving as a judge.

The piece that follows contains two sections from Posner's book, *Economic Analysis of Law*. Posner first published the book in 1972; the excerpts come from the Third Edition published in 1986. In the first section, Posner describes law and economics and responds to some criticisms of the movement. In the second, Posner applies economic analysis to what most consider a non-economic issue, the legal protection of children. It is the use of economic principles in this and other areas that has led to some of the strongest criticism of the law and economics movement.

One piece of information may be helpful as background to what follows. As Posner makes clear, it is economic efficiency that motivates adherents to law and economics. One particular measure of efficiency is known as Kaldor-Hicks efficiency. A reallocation of resources is efficient under the Kaldor-Hicks standard if those who gain from the reallocation obtain enough to fully compensate those who lose from it. This does not mean there must be actual compensation, just that the gain is such that compensation is possible.

Richard Posner, *Economic Analysis of Law*[*]

---

§2.2 Normative and Positive Economic Analysis of Law

Subsequent chapters will show how the insights of Coase, Calabresi, Becker, and other pioneers have been generalized, empirically tested, and integrated with the insights of the "old" (and also rapidly evolving) law and economics to create an economic theory of law with growing explanative power and empirical support. The theory has normative as well as positive aspects. For example, although as noted in Chapter 1 the economist cannot tell society whether it should seek to limit theft, the economist can show that it would be inefficient to allow unlimited theft and can thus clarify a value conflict by showing how much of one value—efficiency—must be sacrificed to achieve another. Or, taking a goal of limiting theft as a given, the economist may be able to show that the means by which society has attempted to attain that goal are inefficient—that society could obtain more prevention, at lower cost, by using different methods. If the more efficient methods did not impair any other

---

[*] RICHARD POSNER, ECONOMIC ANALYSIS OF LAW 20-26, 137-41 (3rd ed. 1986). Reprinted with the permission of Aspen Publishers, Richard Posner, Economic Analysis of Law, 3rd Edition, 20-26, 105-08, 137-41, 1986.

values, they would be socially desirable even if efficiency were low on the totem pole of social values.

As for the positive role, which explains legal rules and outcomes as they are rather than changing them to make them better, we shall see in subsequent chapters that many areas of the law, especially but by no means only the great common law fields of property, torts, crimes, and contracts, bear the stamp of economic reasoning. Although few judicial opinions contain explicit references to economic concepts, often the true grounds of legal decision are concealed rather than illuminated by the characteristic rhetoric of opinions. Indeed, legal education consists primarily of learning to dig beneath the rhetorical surface to find those grounds, many of which may turn out to have an economic character. Remember how broadly economics was defined in Chapter 1. It would not be surprising to find that legal doctrines rest on inarticulate gropings toward efficiency, especially when we bear in mind that many of those doctrines date back to the late eighteenth and the nineteenth century, when a laissez faire ideology based on classical economics was the dominant ideology of the educated classes in society.

The efficiency theory of the common law is not that every common law doctrine and decision is efficient. That would be completely unlikely, given the difficulty of the questions that the law wrestles with and the nature of judges' incentives. The theory is that the common law is best (not perfectly) explained as a system for maximizing the wealth of society. Statutory or constitutional as distinct from common law fields are less likely to promote efficiency, yet even they as we shall see are permeated by economic concerns and illuminated by economic analysis.

But, it may be asked, do not the lawyer and the economist approach the same case in such different ways as to suggest a basic incompatibility between law and economics? X is shot by a careless hunter, Y. The only question in which the parties and their lawyers are interested and the only question decided by the judge and jury is whether the cost of the injury should be shifted from X to Y, whether it is "just" or "fair" that X should receive compensation. X's lawyer will argue that it is just that X be compensated since Y was at fault and X blameless. Y's lawyer may argue that X was also careless and hence that it would be just for the loss to remain on X. Not only are justice and fairness not economic terms, but the economist is not (one might think) interested in the one question that concerns the victim and his lawyer: Who should bear the costs of this accident? To the economist, the accident is a closed chapter. The costs that it inflicted are sunk. The economist is interested in methods of preventing future accidents (that are not cost-justified) and thus reducing the sum of accident and accident-prevention costs, but the parties to the litigation have no interest in the future. Their concern is limited to the financial consequences of a past accident.

This dichotomy, however, is overstated. The decision in the case will affect the future and so it should interest the economist, because it will establish or confirm a rule for the guidance of people engaged in dangerous activities. The decision is a warning that if one behaves in a certain way and an accident results, he will have to pay a judgment (or will be unable to obtain a judgment, if the victim). By thus altering the prices that confront people, the warning may affect their behavior and therefore accident costs.

Conversely, the judge (and hence the lawyers) cannot ignore the future. Since any ruling of law will constitute a precedent, the judge must consider the probable impact of alternative rulings on the future behavior of people engaged in activities that give rise to the kind of accident involved in the case before him. If, for example, judgment is awarded to the defendant on the ground that he is a "deserving," albeit careless fellow, the decision will encourage similar people to be careless, a type of costly behavior.

Once the frame of reference is thus expanded beyond the immediate parties to the case, justice and fairness assume broader meanings than what is just or fair as between this plaintiff and this defendant. The issue becomes what is a just and fair result for a class of activities, and it cannot be sensibly resolved without consideration of the impact of alternative rulings on the frequency of accidents and the cost of accident precautions. The legal and economic approaches are not so divergent after all.

§2.3 Criticisms of the Economic Approach

The economic approach to law, both in its normative and in its positive aspects, has aroused considerable antagonism, especially, but not only among academic lawyers who dislike the thought that the logic of the law might be economics. The major criticisms of the approach, as distinct from particular applications, will be discussed briefly here and should be kept in mind by the reader throughout the rest of this book.

The most frequent criticism is that the normative underpinnings of the economic approach are so repulsive that it is inconceivable that the legal system would (let alone should) embrace them. This criticism may appear to confound positive and normative analysis, but it does not. Law embodies and enforces fundamental social norms, and it would be surprising to find that those norms were inconsistent with the society's ethical system. But is the Kaldor-Hicks concept of efficiency really so at variance with that system? Besides what we said in the first chapter, we shall see in Chapter 8 that, provided only that this concept is a component, though not necessarily the only or most important one, of our ethical system, it may be the one that dominates the law as administered by the courts because of the courts' inability to promote other goals effectively. And so long as efficiency is any sort of value in our ethical system, two normative uses of economics mentioned earlier—to clarify value conflicts and to point the way toward reaching given social ends by the most efficient path—are untouched by the philosophical debate.

Even more clearly, the ability of economic analysis to enlarge our understanding of how the legal system actually operates is not undermined by philosophical attacks on efficiency, as distinct from attacks that deny that efficiency is a significant goal in fact in our society. If the participants in the legal process act as rational maximizers of their satisfactions—if the legal process itself has been shaped by a concern with maximizing economic efficiency—the economist has a rich field of study whether or not a society in which people behave in such a way, or institutions are shaped by such concerns, is a good society.

Another criticism of the economic approach to law, this one limited to the positive use of the approach, is that it doesn't explain every important rule, doctrine, institution, and outcome of the legal system. This criticism actually attacks a caricature of one component of the positive approach, the component being the hypothesis that the dominant—not exclusive—explanatory variable of the common law is wealth maximization. In any event, excessive emphasis on puzzles, anomalies, and contradictions is misplaced when speaking of so recent and yet so fruitful a field of scholarship. Bearing in mind the considerable explanatory power that the economic approach to law has managed to achieve by the efforts of a small number of scholars in a short space of years, it is too soon to write off the endeavor as a failure. The attempt to do so also ignores an important lesson from the history of scientific progress: A theory, unless quite hopeless, is overturned not by pointing out its defects or limitations but by proposing a more inclusive, more powerful, and above all more useful theory.

The economic theory of law is the most promising positive theory of law extant. While anthropologists, sociologists, psychologists, political scientists, and other social scientists besides economists also make positive analyses of the legal system, their work is thus far insufficiently rich in theoretical or empirical content to afford serious competition to the economists. (The reader is challenged to adduce evidence contradicting this presumptuous, sweeping, and perhaps uninformed judgment.)

A related but more powerful criticism of positive economic analysis of law is that it ought to give an economic reason why judges might be led to use efficiency to guide decision. Efforts to meet this criticism are made in Chapters 8 and 19. We shall also see that the idea of the common law as efficiency-promoting is just one aspect of a broader positive economic theory that says that law has been shaped by economic forces, not always in the direction of greater efficiency. For example, Chapter 11 will argue that modern labor law, although explicable in economic terms, is not a system for maximizing efficiency; its goal, which is an economic although not efficient one, is to increase the incomes of union members by cartelizing the labor supply.

Another common criticism of the "new" law and economics—although it is perhaps better described as a reason for the distaste with which the subject is regarded in some quarters—is that it manifests a conservative political bias. We shall see that its practitioners have found, for example, that capital punishment has a deterrent effect, legislation designed to protect consumers frequently ends up hurting them, no-fault automobile insurance is probably inefficient, and securities regulation may be a waste of time. Findings such as these indeed provide ammunition to the supporters of capital punishment and the opponents of the other policies mentioned. Yet economic research that provides support for liberal positions is rarely said to exhibit political bias. For example, the theory of public goods (see §16.4 *infra*) could be viewed as one of the ideological underpinnings of the welfare state but is not so viewed; once a viewpoint becomes dominant, it ceases to be perceived as having an ideological character. The criticism also overlooks a number of findings of economic analysts of law, discussed in subsequent chapters of this book—concerning right to counsel and standard of proof in criminal cases, bail, products liability, application of the First Amendment to broadcasting, social costs of monopoly, damages in personal-injury cases, and many others—that support liberal positions.

The economic approach to law is also criticized for ignoring "justice." In evaluating this criticism, one must distinguish between different meanings of the word. Sometimes it means distributive justice, which is the proper degree of economic equality. Although economists cannot tell society what that degree is, they have much to say that is highly relevant to the debate over inequality—about the actual amounts of inequality in different societies and in different periods, about the difference between real economic inequality and inequalities in pecuniary income that merely offset cost differences or reflect different positions in the life cycle, and about the costs of achieving greater equality. These matters are discussed in Chapter 16.

A second meaning of justice, perhaps the most common, is efficiency. We shall see, among many other examples, that when people describe as unjust convicting a person without a trial, taking property without just compensation, or failing to make a negligent automobile driver answer in damages to the victim of his negligence, this means nothing more pretentious than that the conduct wastes resources (see further §8.3 infra). Even the principle of unjust enrichment can be derived from the concept of efficiency (see §4.14 infra). And with a little reflection, it will come as no surprise that in a world of scarce resources waste should be regarded as immoral.

But there is more to notions of justice than a concern with efficiency. It is not obviously inefficient to allow suicide pacts; to allow private discrimination on racial, religious, or sexual grounds; to permit killing and eating the weakest passenger in the lifeboat in circumstances of genuine desperation; to force people to give self-incriminating testimony; to flog prisoners; to allow babies to be sold for adoption; to allow the use of deadly force in defense of a purely property interest; to legalize blackmail; or to give convicted felons a choice between imprisonment and participation in dangerous medical experiments. Yet all of these things offend the sense of justice of many (some almost all) modern Americans, and all are to a greater or lesser (usually greater) extent illegal. An effort will be made in this book to explain some of these prohibitions in economic terms, but most cannot be; there is more to justice than economics, a point the reader should keep in mind in evaluating normative statements in this book. There may well be definite although wide boundaries on both the explanative and reformative power of economic analysis of law. Always, however, economics can provide value clarification by showing the society what it must give up to achieve a noneconomic ideal of justice. The demand for justice is not independent of its price.

* * *

§5.4 The Legal Protection of Children

In considering the appropriate role of the state in relation to children, we may begin with the assumption congenial to economic analysis that the state desires to maximize the aggregate welfare of all of its citizens, including therefore children. To realize their potential as adults—in economic terms, to achieve a high level of lifetime utility—children require a considerable investment of both parental time and market inputs (food, clothing, tuition, etc.). Since costs as well as benefits must be considered in any investment decision, the optimal level of investment in a particular child is that which is expected to maximize the combined welfare of the child, his parents, and other family members. That level will vary from family to family depending on such factors as the child's aptitudes and the parents' wealth. It will also depend critically on how much the parents love the child; the more they love it, the higher will be the optimal investment, because the costs of the investment will be felt very lightly, even not at all, by the parents (can you see why?). Parents who make great "sacrifices" for their children are not worse off than those (of the same income) who make few or no sacrifices, any more than people who spend a large fraction of their income on housing are worse off than people who spend a smaller fraction of the same income on housing.

Even when parents love their children very much, there is a danger of underinvestment in children; and it is part of the explanation for free public education. Suppose a child is born to very poor parents. The child has enormous potential earning power if properly fed, clothed, housed, and educated, but his parents can't afford these things. This would not matter if the child or parents could borrow against the child's future earning capacity, but the costs of borrowing against a highly uncertain future stream of earnings, and also the difficulty (given the constitutional prohibition of involuntary servitude) of collateralizing a loan against a person's earning capacity (you cannot make him your slave if he defaults), make such loans an infeasible method of financing a promising child.

This problem, plus the fact that some parents love their children little or not at all and the existence of widespread altruism toward children in general (i.e., not just one's own children), may explain why legal duties are imposed on parents to provide care and support, including education, for their children. Child labor laws, as well as the already mentioned provision of free public education (discussed further in Chapter 16 of this book), are other social responses to the problem of underinvestment in children's human capital.

A serious practical problem with laws forbidding neglect is what to do with the child if the threat of fine or imprisonment fails to deter the parents from neglecting the child. The law's answer has been to place the neglected child either with foster parents or in a foster home. Both solutions are unsatisfactory because of the difficulty of monitoring the custodian's performance. The state can pay foster parents a subsidy sufficient to enable them to invest optimally in the care and upbringing of the child, but who is to know whether they have made that investment? The state cannot trust the foster parents: Because they have no property rights in the child's lifetime earnings, they have no incentive to make the investment that will maximize those earnings. Another solution to the problem of the neglected or unwanted child is, of course, to allow the parents (or mother, if the father is unknown or uninterested) to put up the child for adoption, preferably before they begin to neglect the child. Provided that the adoptive parents are screened to make sure they do not want the child for purposes of abusing it sexually or otherwise, adoption enables the child to be transferred from the custody of people unlikely to invest optimally in its upbringing to people much more likely to do so. But the universal availability of contraception, the decline in the stigma of being an unwed mother (can you think of an economic reason for this decline?), and the creation of a constitutional right to abortion have reduced to a trickle the supply of children for adoption, since most such children are produced as the unintended by-product of sexual intercourse. Recent advances in the treatment of fertility (perhaps spurred in part by the decline in the supply of babies for adoption) have reduced or at least controlled the demand for babies for adoption, but the demand remains high, and is much greater than the supply. The waiting period to obtain a baby from an adoption agency has lengthened to several years and sometimes the agencies have no babies for adoption. The baby shortage would be considered an intolerable example of market failure if the commodity were telephones rather than babies.

In fact the shortage appears to be an artifact of government regulation, in particular the state laws forbidding the sale of babies. The fact that there are many people who are capable of bearing children but who do not want to raise them and many other people who cannot produce their own children but want to raise children, and that the costs of production to natural parents are much lower than the value that many childless people attach to children, suggests the possibility of a market in babies. And as a matter of fact there is a black market in babies, with prices as high as $25,000 said to be common. Its necessarily clandestine mode of operation imposes heavy information costs on the market participants as well as expected punishment costs on the middlemen (typically lawyers and obstetricians). The result is higher prices and smaller quantities sold than would be likely in a legal market.

* * *

This analysis is oversimplified in assuming that all babies are adopted through the black market. That of course is not true. Adoption agencies—private, nonprofit organizations licensed by the state—use queuing and various nonmarket criteria (some highly intrusive and constitutionally questionable, such as requiring that the adoptive parents have the same religion as the natural parents) to ration the inadequate supply of babies that they control. The principal objection to the agencies is not, however, the criteria they use to ration the existing supply of babies but their monopoly of adoptions, which ensures (given their profit function) that the supply will remain inadequate.

Most states also permit (subject to various restrictions) independent adoption of babies, wherein the natural parents (normally the mother) arrange for the adoption without using the facilities of an adoption agency. This avoids the sometimes irrelevant and demeaning criteria of the agencies, but since the mother is not permitted to sell the child, independent adoption does not create a real baby market. The lawyer who arranges the adoption, however, is permitted to exact a fee for his services plus payment for the mother's hospital and related childbearing expenses, and since these charges are difficult to police, in practice they will often conceal a payment for the baby itself. And if the mother breaks a contract to give up her child for adoption, the adoptive parents may be able to recover damages measured by the lying-in expenses they had advanced to her. Also close to outright sale is the "family compact," wherein the mother agrees to give up the child to a close relative in exchange for financial consideration running to the child; such contracts have been enforced where the court was satisfied that the arrangement benefited the child.

Should the sale of babies be made legal? The idea strikes most people as bizarre and offensive; the usual proposal for getting rid of the black market in babies is not to decriminalize the sale of babies but to make the criminal penalties more severe. However, economists like to think about the unthinkable, so let us examine in a scientific spirit the objections to permitting the sale of babies for adoption.

There is, it is argued, no assurance that the adoptive parents who are willing to pay the most money for a child will provide it with the best home. But the parents who value a child the most are likely to give it the most care, and at the very least the sacrifice of a substantial sum of money to obtain a child attests to the seriousness of the purchaser's desire to have the child. The reply to this is that the high paying adoptive parents may value the child for the wrong reasons: to subject it to sexual abuse or otherwise to exploit it. But the laws forbidding child neglect and abuse would apply fully to the adoptive parents (as they do under present law, of course). Naturally one would want to screen adoptive parents carefully for possible criminal proclivities—just as is done today.

Questions

1. What is the positive or descriptive aspect of law and economics?
2. According to Posner, how can we explain the existence of most common law legal doctrines?

3. What is the normative aspect of law and economics?

4. How does law and economics relate to justice? Do efficiency and justice conflict?

5. How does Posner argue that principles of economics can help us even when our ultimate values and moral norms come from other sources?

6. Some people object to the use of economic analysis to evaluate a "non-economic" area like the legal custody of children. Do you agree?

7. According to Posner, what has caused the "baby shortage?"

8. Should the sale of babies be made legal? What would economic analysis say?

D. Legal Deconstructionism

1. Critical Legal Studies

Introduction

Law, like many disciplines, saw the rise of deconstructionist theory in the late 20th century. The broadest form of legal deconstructionism is known as critical legal studies (CLS). CLS began in the 1970s among law school professors who became concerned that law simply enforced existing power structures. Critical legal scholars believe that much existing legal argument is nonsensical and oppressive. Many CLS writings take existing arguments and point out inconsistencies. They strongly reject the idea that legal doctrines are objective, determinate, or politically neutral. They also generally promote a leftist political agenda.

Other deconstructionist theories have focused on particular groups of people or legal issues, such as feminist jurisprudence and critical race theory. These theories, too, object to inequalities created by legal doctrines and institutions and argue for the destruction of power structures that support those doctrines and institutions.

This section contains samples of writings from both CLS and critical race scholars. The author of the first piece, Professor Mark Kelman, is a critical legal scholar. Professor Kelman is the James C. Gaither Professor of Law and Vice Dean at Stanford University. He teaches and publishes in the fields of legal theory, criminal law, property, and taxation. The following piece is taken from "Trashing," an article Kelman published in the Stanford Law Review. "Trashing" is the term he uses to describe what critical legal scholars do. In the piece he defends CLS.

Mark Kelman, *Trashing*[*]

Here's one account of the technique that we in Critical Legal Studies often use in analyzing legal texts, a technique I call "Trashing": Take specific arguments very seriously in their own terms; discover they are actually foolish ([tragi]-comic); and then look for some (external observer's) order (not the germ of truth) in the internally contradictory, incoherent chaos we've exposed.

* * *

And here is one account of the most frequently recurring theme in the attacks on our own technique, the more-or-less hysterical counter-Revolution against Trashing: We take arguments too seriously; the arguments really aren't so bad after all; there is a germ of truth, a kernel of genuine wisdom, embedded in each of them even if they are, as are all human products, imperfect and therefore subject to smart-alecky mockery. Moreover, it is pointless or irresponsible or infuriating to trash if the ultimate task is political reconstruction; only by comparing Our State (our dad? our team?) with Their State can we (legitimately? as a purely tactical matter?) hope to prod people to a new political commitment. The attack on CLS trashing has a secondary aspect: When we're not "merely" trashing, we switch to uselessly general Utopian theorizing. That is, when we are both positive and constructive, we're so vague that it is impossible for anyone to know what concrete steps would satisfy our demands. Thus, we never fit into the "acceptable" category of being both constructive and concrete at the same time.

I'd like first, in Part I of this article, to look reasonably closely at this attack—to treat the typical argument that we are either destructive or vague as yet another text to be trashed. But I have a strong anti-trashing streak myself that I have never wanted or tried to hide. What strikes me as most distinctive about Critical Legal Studies, especially in comparison with left academic movements of the past is its focus on ambiguity, its resolute refusal to see a synthesis in every set of contradictions. We may well feel, at once, a need for agitated Utopian hope and more peaceful resignation to an inevitably tragic world; we may simultaneously seek

[*] Mark Kelman, *Trashing*, 36 STAN. L. REV. 293, 293, 295-303, 305, 318-26 (1984). Used with permission of Stanford Law Review, from Stanford Law Review, Volume 36, 1984; permission conveyed through Copyright Clearance Center.

solace in rational expertise/control and a mystical faith that is divorced from a need for exacting answers. Thus, no program satisfies all of our hopes for our work. Part II, then, is an internal account of the debates on trashing within CLS; while I will, once more, basically align myself with the trashers among us, I do so with more than a modicum of regret that trashing is, above all, simply the best available academic posture.

I. Trashing Anti-trashing

It is abundantly apparent that the vast preponderance of mainstream American legal academics were told (repeatedly) by their moms and dads, "If you don't have anything nice or constructive to say, say nothing at all." In the eyes of these academics, to violate this wholesome norm is an unquestionable disgrace, and they generally take for granted that we in CLS would bow our heads in deep shame if "all we'd done" was to make it impossible to wallow happily in the familiar ooze of traditional legal discourse, humming the same old tunes without embarrassment. Unless we've replaced traditional discourse with something that gives us better solutions to the problems we face, we've done bad. But what we've replaced it with, say the critics, is monumentally vague Utopian sloganeering with no discernible programmatic content.

Our answer to the accusation that we're some combination of worthless wreckers and hopelessly vague visionaries is hard to pin down, purposefully slithery and evasive (the lure of the guerrilla image, updated for those made too pessimistic by the Vietnamese, Cambodians, and Iranians to trust too many actual guerrillas), but it goes something like this: First, we don't do what you say we do or at least we don't do it all the time (we are often quite constructive and concrete); second, to the extent that we suffer from the problems you ascribe to us, you do too (although you don't trash arguments, you are generally quite vague and Utopian); and third, even if we do something you don't, it's a good thing that we do, for reasons you don't even begin to consider (trashing is good).

A. CLS Work Is By No Means as Invariably Destructive or Vague and Utopian as Its Critics Seem to Believe

It seems to me important to note what should be an obvious point: The academics and practitioners in CLS are role-restricted actors. Role restriction should certainly be a familiar concept. For instance, the work that "left" legal practitioners do as lawyers will often be quite hard to distinguish from the work of liberal reformers or social service providers. A National Lawyer's Guild lawyer may try to expand the scope of explicitly state-provided entitlements or work to increase the actual access to some program benefits of those already formally entitled. The Guild lawyer may also defend (generally poor) criminal defendants in much the same way any public defender would, probably taking a fairly expansive traditional civil libertarian position on police practices, or politically active defendants charged with either relatively traditional FBI "index" crimes, crimes that flow directly from their political activity, or crimes that combine the two aspects (such as assaults on officers during demonstrations). Finally, the Guild lawyer may attempt to expand (or, once again, increase the use of already formally existent) rights of workers or poor people to resist the domination or exploitation of other private citizens (as in suits against racially discriminatory employers or in consumer protection activity).

Just as the Guild lawyer may frequently act in a role that makes it hard to distinguish her work from that of a practitioner with very different political beliefs, so there will be times when a CLS scholar's work is fundamentally indistinguishable from that of colleagues with very different agendas. This confusion is most likely when the CLS academic addresses the "live" policy issues of the day. Of course, we can also adopt roles in which our work looks more "different," but this work is no less constructive or concrete. At times, for instance, we will, in a more radical mode, advocate particular legal reforms, hoping both to better the short-term position of the reform's beneficiaries and to expose the limits of legal reform. This second aim, political education, is perfectly concrete and constructive, even though it is far less relevant to those only interested in whether the reform ought to be enacted to help the beneficiaries. At other times, in our role as purely descriptive academics, hoping to explain the legal culture we all live in, we may simply deconstruct arguments in a way that is of no obvious immediate help whatsoever to those trying to pick and choose particular institutions they might find most desirable, except insofar as they are freed to evaluate their choices differently when their current cultural blinders are labeled, exposed, and, perhaps as a result, partly lifted.

With the preliminary points about role restriction in mind, let's take a quick survey of CLS work done in various roles. CLS academics often address the typical legal-political controversies between liberals and conservatives, generally, though not always, tending to argue for relatively traditional liberal positions, usually in reasonably traditional ways. For instance, academics who have associated themselves with the CLS have used traditional neoclassical economic analysis to question the a priori conservative assumption that housing code enforcement or compulsory (nonwaivable) warranties will either be of no moment to or detrimental to their purported beneficiaries, offered arguments against replacing the income tax with an almost inevitably less redistributive consumption tax; been wary of efforts to truncate the income tax base in ways that would contravene progressivity; defended affirmative action programs; urged the adoption of universalized clinical legal education programs so as to empower students to avoid traditional law firm jobs and to raise the issue of the validity of the model of the lawyer as advocate-as-agent for a presumed-to-be selfish will; argued against the Bar's attempts to solidify an unwarranted monopoly through unauthorized practice prosecutions; and pressed for state reforms of work rules and child care programs that would better permit working mothers to maintain their careers.

As "policy analysts" with a concern for redefining the proper scope of "live" legal and political issues, CLS people have been able to connect inevitably partial legal reform efforts with more radical consciousness-raising programs. Thus, some of our proposals have both met short-term meliorist goals and expanded our understanding that the meliorist programs are limited—that there are problems that the legal remedies will not address. Perhaps most notable among these efforts has been the work of feminist lawyers/academics in developing legal theories of sexual harassment, which were designed not only to reform practice so as to enable women to use state power to squelch one of the most extreme forms of exploitation (quid pro quo sex-for-advancement) but also to trigger collective exploration into the more general issue of sexual objectification as the form of the expropriation of female sexuality. Although it is obvious that few, if any, people associated with CLS believe that the use of civil suits for damages by every woman against every man is a feasible or desirable way to undo the general social practice of objectification, developing harassment as a legal claim serves two purposes. First, it helps women confirm their sense that they have a public/political concern, rather than merely a personal temperamental problem (oversensitivity to "flirting" is the typical smug dismissal) or a reasonable, but still private, anger with the particular, unpardonable behavior of some ungentlemanly, oversexed dastard. Second, and perhaps more central to my concerns here, figuring out what the actual injury is, something one must do in conceiving of a cause of action, is a politically developmental task. On one level—the traditional liberal one—harassment is tort-like, exceptional, disruptive of normal social relations, closely analogous to traditional rape except in that rather direct economic coercion replaces rather direct violent force. (This liberal vision is obviously meant to counter two traditional conservative conceptions: that the harassed must "ask for it" by being unvirtuous in reputation or seductive in manner and/or that harassment, though wrong, occurs too much in the intimate and private sphere to involve a properly limited state, so that redress, if any, should be nonlegal.) On a more critical level, though, we may see that the injury of harassment comes from its typicality: It is bound up in the inability of its victims fully to de-eroticize hierarchical domination or to "de-commodify" their own sexuality (that is, for the victim not to trade on men's perception of her "attractiveness" so as to gain other objects) or to be sure if it is ever the case that they are not predominantly sexual objects to the men around them.

CLS academics have proposed a number of other concrete "reform packages" that would serve both to bolster partially the positions of particular unnecessarily injured parties and to help focus attention on the structural deficiencies of legal/social relations as currently constituted. For instance, CLS writers have produced proposals to allow workers to operate the assets of would-be runaway factories; to alter the typical legal ethical supposition that a lawyer should simply presume that his client will act adversely to other parties; to expand the rights of workers to strike over midterm grievances, instead of relying on union stewardship of collective bargaining; to expand municipal powers so as to enable publicly established productive institutions to flourish; and to reformulate our ideas about the meaning of informed consent in the medical area. At other times, though, we abandon legal, state-focused reform without abandoning what we think of as politics. In this role, we naturally have little advice to give judges or legislators or administrators regarding the policy questions that might conceivably confront them. One may well believe, for instance, that the world would be a better place if The Boss did not expect The Secretary to make coffee, without believing either that anyone exercising public authority ought to sanction the misbehavior or that it will inexorably disappear through explicit public programs like nonsexist daycare centers or re-education camps for the recalcitrant. To counsel covert resistance (at least when you can get away with it), occasional expressions of terror-provoking rage ("make your own damn coffee"), or contained acts of counterviolence (a burn here or there is not the worst thing in the world) is meant to be neither "policy advice" nor a "program" that we need to detail. Still, these are perfectly concrete and, I believe, constructive political steps to take.

* * *

B. Mainstream Legal Thought Is Vague and Utopian, Not Concrete

To listen to the critics of CLS, one might forget oneself for a moment and imagine that the typical mainstream legal arguments to which we are routinely exposed are concrete, detailed, empirically grounded justifications for the social/legal system around us or for the particular alteration of a particular rule that the author is urging. How droll.

* * *

2. Strange interlude: formalism, legal process, and hunches.

I could, of course, discuss seriously the other noneconomic garden variety of legal academic "policy analysis": the residual formalism in nominally post-Realist legal thought. (I've even done it, at what some may consider ungodly length.) Or I could try, in a somber fashion, to find some argument worth destroying in the standard public law side of the Legal Process school, which posits (quite unfathomably) a strong relationship between certain more-or-less accidental and/or trivial American institutional developments (e.g., federalism, a "balance of powers" between the branches of government, a relatively aggressive court with the power to squelch legislative and executive actions) and more general liberal ideals of personal autonomy and the "Rule of Law" (political openness and experimentation coupled with stability and competent administration). The protection of certain significant processes is supposed to have some content or bite in preserving cultural virtues; attempts to trample over these processes lead to some variant or other of unpleasantness or social chaos. (Somber discussions of Legal Process abound, too.) I could even attempt to catalogue the out-of-thin-air empirical assertions routinely made by conventional law teachers in "justifying" some existing rule or institution or pet legal reform proposal. For example, I might subdivide these "empirical" hunches into (1) those that are arguably falsifiable, assuming that we can still imagine running some elaborate tests and experiments that we know perfectly well can never actually be run (e.g., hunches about the purported inability of jurors to properly weigh the probative value of hearsay evidence) and (2) those that, while sounding descriptive or empirical, refer fairly openly to concepts with no discernible external reference whatsoever (e.g., a contract may not be "mutually beneficial" to the contracting parties when there is "unequal bargaining power".)

I could take all this seriously (Tricky Dick, you were so right), but it would be wrong, that's for sure. Arguing that standard legal argument is vague, nonempirical, windbag rhetoric is just not worth it. For three years (I dimly recall, through a wall of repression so thick that my memories cannot be trusted half so far as they can be tossed), I was a model prisoner: I listened; I wrote (and later highlighted in yellow, pink, and on especially austere occasions, blue); I volunteered to play my supporting Socratic part; I took the whole business reasonably seriously. And for what? Well, how are these oldies but goodies for "arguments"?

(1) A hypothetical or moot case, without a self-interested party grumbling when his will is thwarted, paying the all-important lawyer's bill, and/or just inspiring the lawyer with his staggeringly concrete particularity (as IBM inspired the hordes at Cravath with its presence), will not be adequately litigated.

(2) A corporate defendant can't be sued just anywhere—that would expose it to undue prejudice (the well-known hatred of Minnesotans for Wisconsin-chartered corporations) and crushing expense (lugging its defense exhibits from the corporate defense exhibit vault?)—but can justly be sued wherever it maintains a bigger-than-a-breadbox branch.

(3) Because they constitute "social engines of destruction," conspiracies ought to be punished separately from the crimes that the parties agree to commit: As soon as two people agree to commit any crime, they will take advantage of the division of labor, probably to smuggle drugs that must pass through six cities in three nations, while bribed officials in at least four jurisdictions wink.

(4) Judicial review of the constitutionality of legislative pronouncements is particularly important in protecting liberties like freedom of speech because majorities may turn, at a moment's notice, against the unpopular. The fact that competing cultural and political ideas are occasionally voiced in, say, Sweden constitutes something of a miracle.

(5) If we allowed a second finder of lost property to maintain possession against a first finder who was not an owner, there would be a universal grab for property so that possession would henceforth be intolerably insecure, even though unconvincing "finders" would still be jailed as thieves and there are no discernible ways for these would-be finders to tell that any particular little object is in the possession of a nonowner.

Mercifully, I've burned the notebooks.

* * *

C. Trashing is Good

There are any number of reasons why CLS people might be right to debunk ordinary legal argument, even if they offered no well-grounded proposals for institutional change (as is not the case) while others routinely made detailed, concrete arguments for particular institutions (as is not the case).

* * *

1. Trashing as an anti-hierarchical strategy within the law schools.

Many of us (arguably influenced by Foucault) have been interested in understanding power in its most local manifestations ("micropractices"); for me, trashing is above all a technique of seeing (and undermining) illegitimate power in the most comprehensible and immediate institutions I see—the law schools where I've studied and worked.

Let me try to get at this point by starting with a list of typical left/idealist "CLS-style" propositions about the instrumental significance of coherent doctrine. The first proposition is the most localized, the second is more global, and the third is more global still.

(1) The first argument is that the elegance and coherence of legal argument is an issue primarily to its full-time producers—legal academics—and that attempts to discredit or trash these arguments are predominantly a threat to the producers' prestige. Most of the arguments that law professors make are not only nonsensical according to some obscure and unreachable criteria of Universal Validity but they are also patently unstable babble. The shakiness of the argumentative structure is, quite remarkably, readily elucidated. All the fundamental, rhetorically necessary distinctions collapse at a feather's touch—distinctions between substance and process, voluntary and involuntary action, public and private, legislative and adjudicative. Those who routinely use these distinctions "know" of their vulnerability, at least in the limited sense of being able to recognize it without being forced to look at the world in radically different ways. Law professors are, in fact, a kiss away from panic at every serious, self-conscious moment in which they don't have a bunch of overawed students to kick around.

At the same time, the prestige of law professors—for instance, their ability to inspire generally self-assured senior partners at ritzy law firms to tell remarkably heartfelt, awestruck rite-of-passage stories when these partners gather for reunions thirty years after the first shock—is intimately connected to their (purported) capacity to make arguments (both legal and social/political) that seem not only better than nonsensical but seem even downright wise.

This prestige, however, may be based on an illusory hierarchical legitimacy. The stability of hierarchical divisions—the social acceptance of inequality—is generally premised on purported distinctions in capacity to produce. Our well-honed ability to distinguish easily and objectively between two people in different status slots (teacher vs. student, elite professor vs. nonelite professor, lawyer vs. layman) will make hierarchies appear legitimate or inevitable, even when we are (or could be made to be) at least dimly aware that the distinctions, though clearly discernible, are irrelevant. (A "great" law professor may discuss affirmative action with an obvious elegance that most laymen clearly lack. But whether he has more insight into the substantive issues at stake or privileged access to the "right" answers is quite another question.)

(2) While the greatest desire of the producers of "good rhetoric" may be that people think their rhetoric good so that such producers can stay atop some pyramid, producers of apology also have a reasonably, perhaps unusually, strong belief that general status differentials are justified at a general level, and that legal arguments are, in essence, about desert, i.e., whether benefits are merited or punishments deserved. Thus, the acceptability of "good arguments" is significant to the professional producers of apology in justifying significant social institutions. Criminal law professors, for instance, typically believe it is important that those we label criminals are "blameworthy" and believe that they have "proven" this in a fairly elaborate and technical way. Other professional functionaries who hold positions in which they purvey civic myth—judges, teachers, editorial writers, clergymen—also find it reasonably important to believe that the legal system is well-grounded, that the particular legally-based disabilities and privileges they dimly perceive to frame one's social position are distributed according to an orderly scheme that has been honed in some high quality debate.

(3) Finally, relatively well-off citizens generally are more prone to be self-righteous and immune from crises of conscience because they sense that people are generally treated fairly—that, for both better or worse, people in this country pretty much get what they deserve. To a discernible degree, the idea that legal rules of the most general form are defensible and are being defended (somewhere) by experts bolsters this belief. (By general rules I mean the sort that, example, provide very broadly that, subject to more-or-less confiscatory taxation and some preclusion of impermissible bargaining tactics like industrial sabotage or holding a knife to an employer's throat, one is entitled to get paid whatever one can as a worker. This type of rule is rarely seen as explicitly involving expansions or restrictions on legally created bargaining capabilities. And once one gets paid what one deserves, the generally justified legal system tells us that one gets to buy "what one wants" and to keep what one "possesses"). Even citizens who are badly off are a bit more prone to accept rather passively their bad lot as reasonable if it seems to flow from a legal system that is not obviously personally focused on abusive [sic], since they've just gotten—for better and worse—what they were "entitled to" according to legitimate rules.

We in CLS are prone to defend our focus on debunking rhetoric against both mainstream "policy analysts" and traditional Marxists who believe in the vital significance of the material base (and the corresponding triviality of cultural artifacts like legal argument, if not bottom-line case results) by referring to the more global of these propositions. But my point here is that I am most willing to defend debunking at the local level, in part because I am decreasingly certain of each proposition as one goes down the list (from local to global): In fact, by the time one reaches the third proposition, I am currently agnostic as to the truth of the assertion and even as to how one could hope ever to have much of an opinion about its truth, although I feel certain it would be an important proposition if it were indeed valid. From my vantage point, which is the vantage of "micropractices," the primary thrust of the CLS enterprise at an academic level should be to explore, in a very concrete, particular setting, the vital general point that status hierarchies are founded, at least in significant part, on sham distinctions.

Here's a workplace: the law schools. One theory of division (the standard one) is that the intellectual cream rises, that ignorant initiates (students) must imitate their creamy masters (teachers), and especially creamy, elite intellectuals must set agendas for nonelite educators. Here's a different account: When the initiates begin, they already know virtually all the masters know. But this equality of knowledge is hidden by the masters' unwillingness to talk seriously about what they are really talking about (e.g., the dilemmas of stating legal pronouncements in rule-like or ad hoc form, the battle between deterministic and intentionalistic accounts of human behavior, the propriety of paternalism). Only by creating a technical fog to obscure the true concerns, concerns about which they have nothing much to say that would make them stand out, have the masters been able to make the initiates bow, scrape, and believe themselves to be deeply unfit and inferior. There are things to learn at law school. (And because they clearly have a head start, teachers should play a role in that. They also have presumably focused on the task of identifying and teaching learnable skills.) But the sense of awe that professors so often seek to inspire in the initiates, a sense similar to that one is supposed to get in the presence of keepers of great secrets or priests with access to privileged thought, would simply not be inspired if the students were told explicitly that people just need a little practice before they can engage in a subculture's discourse.

We are not just trying to "prove" an abstract or academic point about the phoniness of hierarchy. (Nor do we really believe that the debunking of technical rhetoric can fully and adequately demonstrate the contingent, potentially unstable position of rhetoric's producers and guardians.) For it is perfectly possible that the real Kingsfields of this world will still be sentimentally deified (perhaps for Oedipal reasons or perhaps because an unquenchable thirst for bigger-than-life heroes always exists) even after their arguments have been completely discredited. We are also engaged in an active, transformative anarcho-syndicalist political project, and it is only the project's success that serves as real proof of egalitarian possibilities: At the workplace level, debunking is one part of an explicit effort to level, to reintegrate the communities we live in along explicitly egalitarian lines rather than along the rationalized hierarchical lines that currently integrate them. We are saying: Here's what your teacher did (at you, to you) in contracts or torts. Here's what it was really about. Stripped of the mumbo-jumbo, here's a set of problems we all face, as equals in dealing with work, with politics, and with the world.

If there is a problem with this project, it is that the techniques of mystification have become so complex that we demystifiers may often end up sounding at least as highfalutin, technical, and ritzy as the people we critique. The fear is that there is a less-than-voluntary CLS elitism, parasitic on the dominant legal culture's elitism: Those who can deconstruct the most elaborate of the traditional arguments, those who resimplify and politicize the most obscured disputes, are lionized precisely like the original obscurantists. The problem is within as well as outside us; too few are immune to the charms of status and prestige.

Questions

1. What is "trashing?"
2. Why does Kelman think trashing is important?
3. What does Kelman think of most legal arguments, doctrines, and rules?
4. What does Kelman think of law schools and most law professors?
5. Is there a critical legal studies agenda? If so, what is it?
6. Kelman describes federalism and a "balance of powers" between the branches of government as "more-or-less accidental and/or trivial American institutional developments." Why? Do you agree?
7. While many in this country look to the Bill of Rights as foundational to our freedom, some critical legal scholars are less sure. Some believe that talk of rights is nothing more than "state-sponsored bone tossing." Consider this statement: "Belief in rights solidifies a belief in the inevitability and the correctness of the existing social and legal order." Why would critical legal scholars believe this? What do they mean?

2. Critical Race Theory

Introduction

While scholars have long adressed issues of race and law, Critical Race Theory (CRT) as a school of thought was formalized at a 1989 conference where the name "Critical Race Theory" was chosen. CRT writings vary greatly, but often focus on the struggle for racial justice and the existence of racial hierarchy within the legal system.

Two CRT pieces are included here. The first is a very short excerpt from a piece by Professor Athena Mutua in which she outlines the core beliefs and strategies of CRT. Professor Mutua is an associate professor of law at the University at Buffalo Law School of the State University of New York. She received a B.A. at Earlham College, a J.D. and an M.A. in International Affairs at American University, and an LL.M. at Harvard Law School. Professor Mutua teaches CRT, banking law, and corporations at Buffalo.

The second piece is from Professor Paul Butler's 1995 Yale Law Review article, "Racially Based Jury Nullification." Professor Butler is the Carville Dickinson Benson Research Professor of Law at the George Washington University Law School. He received a B.A. from Yale University and a J.D. from Harvard University. He teaches and writes in the areas of criminal law, civil rights, and jurisprudence. In this excerpt, Professor Butler argues that African-American jurors should refuse to convict guilty non-violent black criminal defendants in response to what he sees as pervasive racism in the criminal justice system. His goal is the "subversion of American criminal justice, at least as it now exists." In the piece he lays out why this strategy will lead to a more just criminal law and society.

Athena D. Mutua, *The Rise, Development and Future Directions of Critical Race Theory and Related Scholarship*[*]

IV. CRT Tenets and Methodology

The basic tenets of Critical Race Theory remain true to the original ideas discussed in the 1990 CRT workshop. With little modification, Critical Race Theory:

1. holds that racism is pervasive and endemic to, rather than a deviation from, American norms;
2. [rejects] dominant claims of meritocracy, neutrality, objectivity and color-blindness;
3. [rejects] ahistoricism, and insists on contextual, historical analysis of law;
4. challenges the presumptive legitimacy of social institutions;
5. insists on recognition of both the experiential knowledge and critical consciousness of people of color in understanding law and society;
6. is interdisciplinary and eclectic (drawing upon, *inter alia*, liberalism, poststructuralist [sic], feminism, Marxism, critical legal theory, postmodernism, and pragmatism) with the claim that the intersection of race and the law overruns disciplinary boundaries; and
7. works toward the liberation of people of color as it embraces the larger project of liberating all oppressed people.

The purpose of CRT, its *raison d'etre*, is twofold. First its purpose is to demonstrate the many ways in which white supremacy is endemic to American society by "exposing the facets of law and legal discourse that create racial categories and legitimate racial subordination." Second, its purpose is to destabilize and change this relationship, in part by challenging or proposing alternative laws, among other things, in order to contribute to the liberation of oppressed people. As Jerome Culp notes, Critical Race Theory may mean many different things to different people, but "there is a common belief in an opposition to oppression." And, CRT scholars such as Matsuda and Hutchinson, as well as LatCrit [Latino and Latina Critical Schools] and others have issued a clarion call

[*] Athena D. Mutua, *The Rise, Development and Future Directions of Critical Race Theory and Related Scholarship*, 84 DENV. U. L. REV. 329, 353-56 (2006). Reprinted with the permission of Denver University Law Review.

that *Antisubordination*, a stance against all forms of oppression and subordination, be both the commitment of race scholars and the *principle* upon which racial justice, particularly *equality*, be understood and practiced.

These tenets and the overall commitment to antisubordination that CRT scholars evidence also provide crucial insight into CRT methodological tendencies. CRT is said to have no single, unifying methodology. Rather it is eclectic, drawing from various schools, disciplines and approaches. Harris, in providing some examples of the different methodologies employed by Race Crits, notes that they include structuralism and historical, doctrinal (legal), empirical and economic analyses.

CRT approaches can, however, be said to possess some unifying themes or methodological tendencies. These include a particular focus on context and history. CRT suggests that a rule or principle may mean different things in different contexts and/or historical periods. So, for instance, they have argued that the idea of colorblindness, first expressed in Justice Harlan's 1896 dissent in *Plessy v. Ferguson*, can be understood at that time as a progressive idea in the context of a society in which law sanctioned the explicit and systematic oppression of blacks after slavery. However, a colorblind approach to race in the current era, when the subordination of blacks is no longer explicit but remains systematic, is no longer a progressive approach. Thus, as an abstract principle its meaning and progressive potential is neither universal nor trans-historical. CRT, therefore, pays particular attention to the specificity of context in order to understand the meanings of a particular concept or practice, to evaluate a particular position and to render additional information and ideas.

Further, CRT argues that as rules and principles mean different things in different contexts that they *should* mean different things in different contexts. So for instance, equality might mean symmetrical or "same treatment" in a society without vast racial, gender, and class inequalities but might mean and require affirmative practices to bring about equality for historically disadvantaged groups, treating them differently than the privileged, in a society with these alarming disparities.

In addition, CRT scholars listen to and scrutinize the voices, understandings and experiences of marginalized and oppressed peoples to situate, test, and inspire the examination of particular and/or novel approaches to law. The idea of distinctive minority voices recognizes, for example, that not every Native American critiques the American holiday "Columbus Day." But it does understand that, given Native American history, the conditions of oppression, and the cultural nature of their resistance, Native Americans might find the idea of Columbus discovering America problematic, and not exactly a cause for celebration. This understanding has led CRT scholars to excavate forgotten or overlooked histories, rules, and cases, as well as the cultural practices, stories, and perspectives of marginalized groups as sources for grounding their analysis.

Paul Butler, *Racially Based Jury Nullification*[*]

INTRODUCTION

I was a Special Assistant United States Attorney in the District of Columbia in 1990. I prosecuted people accused of misdemeanor crimes, mainly the drug and gun cases that overwhelm the local courts of most American cities. As a federal prosecutor, I represented the United States of America and used that power to put people, mainly African-American men, in prison. I am also an African-American man. While at the U.S. Attorney's office, I made two discoveries that profoundly changed the way I viewed my work as a prosecutor and my responsibilities as a black person.

The first discovery occurred during a training session for new Assistants conducted by experienced prosecutors. We rookies were informed that we would lose many of our cases, despite having persuaded a jury beyond a reasonable doubt that the defendant was guilty. We would lose because some black jurors would refuse to convict black defendants who they knew were guilty.

The second discovery was related to the first, but was even more unsettling. It occurred during the trial of Marion Barry, then the second-term mayor of the District of Columbia. Barry was being prosecuted by my office for drug possession and perjury. I learned, to my surprise, that some of my fellow African-American prosecutors hoped that the mayor would be acquitted, despite the fact that he was obviously guilty of at least one of the charges—he had smoked cocaine on FBI videotape. These black prosecutors wanted their office to lose its case because they believed that the prosecution of Barry was racist.

Federal prosecutors in the nation's capital hear many rumors about prominent officials engaging in illegal conduct, including drug use. Some African-American prosecutors wondered why, of all those people, the government chose to "set up" the most famous black politician in

[*] Paul Butler, *Racially Based Jury Nullification: Black Power in the Criminal Justice System*, 105 YALE L. J. 677, 678-80, 690-94, 700-01, 705-12, 715-18, 722-23 (1995). Reprinted with the permission of the author.

Washington, D.C. They also asked themselves why, if crack is so dangerous, the FBI had allowed the mayor to smoke it. Some members of the predominantly black jury must have had similar concerns: They convicted the mayor of only one count of a fourteen-count indictment, despite the trial judge's assessment that he had "'never seen a stronger government case.'" Some African-American prosecutors thought that the jury, in rendering its verdict, jabbed its black thumb in the face of a racist prosecution, and that idea made those prosecutors glad.

* * *

My thesis is that, for pragmatic and political reasons, the black community is better off when some nonviolent lawbreakers remain in the community rather than go to prison. The decision as to what kind of conduct by African-Americans ought to be punished is better made by African-Americans themselves, based on the costs and benefits to their community, than by the traditional criminal justice process, which is controlled by white lawmakers and white law enforcers. Legally, the doctrine of jury nullification gives the power to make this decision to African-American jurors who sit in judgment of African-American defendants. Considering the costs of law enforcement to the black community and the failure of white lawmakers to devise significant nonincarcerative responses to black antisocial conduct, it is the moral responsibility of black jurors to emancipate some guilty black outlaws.

* * *

My goal is the subversion of American criminal justice, at least as it now exists. Through jury nullification, I want to dismantle the master's house with the master's tools. My intent, however, is not purely destructive; this project is also constructive, because I hope that the destruction of the status quo will not lead to anarchy, but rather to the implementation of certain noncriminal ways of addressing antisocial conduct. Criminal conduct among African-Americans is often a predictable reaction to oppression. Sometimes black crime is a symptom of internalized white supremacy; other times it is a reasonable response to the racial and economic subordination every African-American faces every day. Punishing black people for the fruits of racism is wrong if that punishment is premised on the idea that it is the black criminal's "just deserts." Hence, the new paradigm of justice that I suggest in Part III rejects punishment for the sake of retribution and endorses it, with qualifications, for the ends of deterrence and incapacitation.

* * *

II. "JUSTICE OUTSIDE THE FORMAL RULES OF LAW"

Why would a black juror vote to let a guilty person go free? Assuming that the juror is a rational actor, she must believe that she and her community are, in some way, better off with the defendant out of prison than in prison. But how could any rational person believe that about a criminal?...

A. The Criminal Law and African-Americans: Justice or "Just us"?

Imagine a country in which more than half of the young male citizens are under the supervision of the criminal justice system, either awaiting trial, in prison, or on probation or parole.[73] Imagine a country in which two-thirds of the men can anticipate being arrested before they reach age thirty.[74] Imagine a country in which there are more young men in prison than in college.[75] Now give the citizens of the country the key to the prison. Should they use it?

Such a country bears some resemblance to a police state. When we criticize a police state, we think that the problem lies not with the citizens of the state, but rather with the form of government or law, or with the powerful elites and petty bureaucrats whose interests the state serves. Similarly, racial critics of American criminal justice locate the problem not so much with the black prisoners as with the state and its actors and beneficiaries. As evidence, they cite their own experiences and other people's stories, African-American history, understanding gained from social science research on the power and pervasiveness of white supremacy, and ugly statistics like those in the preceding paragraph.

For analytical purposes, I will create a false dichotomy among racial critics by dividing them into two camps: liberal critics and radical critics. Those are not names that the critics have given themselves or that they would necessarily accept, and there would undoubtedly be disagreement within each camp and theoretical overlap between the camps. Nonetheless, for the purposes of a brief explication of racial critiques, my oversimplification may be useful.

---

[73] One study found that, in Baltimore, Maryland, 56% of the African-American males between the ages of 18 and 35 were under criminal justice supervision on any given day in 1991....

[74] In California, nearly two-thirds of all black males are arrested at some point between the ages of 18 and 30....

[75] In 1991, 583,545 blacks were in local jails (188,300 people) or under the jurisdiction of state and federal correctional authorities (395,245 people).... The number of black men in college in the same year was approximately 517,000. STATISTICAL ABSTRACT 1994, *supra* note 13, at 178.

1. The Liberal Critique

According to this critique, American criminal justice is racist because it is controlled primarily by white people, who are unable to escape the culture's dominant message of white supremacy, and who are therefore inevitably, even if unintentionally, prejudiced. These white actors include legislators, police, prosecutors, judges, and jurors. They exercise their discretion to make and enforce the criminal law in a discriminatory fashion. Sometimes the discrimination is overt, as in the case of Mark Fuhrman, the police officer in the O.J. Simpson case who, in interviews, used racist language and boasted of his own brutality, and sometimes it is unintentional, as with a hypothetical white juror who invariably credits the testimony of a white witness over that of a black witness.

The problem with the liberal critique is that it does not adequately explain the extent of the difference between the incidence of black and white crime, especially violent crime. For example, in 1991, blacks constituted about fifty-five percent of the 18,096 people arrested for murder and non-negligent manslaughter in the United States (9924 people). One explanation the liberal critique offers for this unfortunate statistic is that the police pursue black murder suspects more aggressively than they do white murder suspects. In other words, but for discrimination, the percentage of blacks arrested for murder would be closer to their percentage of the population, roughly twelve percent. The liberal critique would attribute some portion of the additional forty-three percent of non-negligent homicide arrestees (in 1991, approximately 7781 people) to race prejudice. Ultimately, however, those assumptions strain credulity, not because many police officers are not racist, but because there is no evidence that there is a crisis of that magnitude in criminal justice. In fact, for all the faults of American law enforcement, catching the bad guys seems to be something it does rather well. The liberal critique fails to account convincingly for the incidence of black crime.

2. The Radical Critique

The radical critique does not discount the role of discrimination in accounting for some of the racial disparity in crime rates, but it also does not, in contrast to the liberal critique, attribute all or even most of the differential to police and prosecutor prejudice. The radical critique offers a more fundamental, structural explanation.

It suggests that criminal law is racist because, like other American law, it is an instrument of white supremacy. Law is made by white elites to protect their interests and, especially, to preserve the economic status quo, which benefits those elites at the expense of blacks, among others. Due to discrimination and segregation, the majority of African-Americans receive few meaningful educational and employment opportunities and, accordingly, are unable to succeed, at least in the terms of the capitalist ideal. Some property crimes committed by blacks may be understood as an inevitable result of the tension between the dominant societal message equating possession of material resources with success and happiness and the power of white supremacy to prevent most African-Americans from acquiring "enough" of those resources in a legal manner. "Black-on-black" violent crime, and even "victimless" crime like drug offenses, can be attributed to internalized racism, which causes some African-Americans to devalue black lives—either those of others or their own. The political process does not allow for the creation or implementation of effective "legal" solutions to this plight, and the criminal law punishes predictable reactions to it.

I am persuaded by the radical critique when I wonder about the roots of the ugly truth that blacks commit many crimes at substantially higher rates than whites. Most white Americans, especially liberals, would publicly offer an environmental, as opposed to genetic, explanation for this fact. They would probably concede that racism, historical and current, plays a major role in creating an environment that breeds criminal conduct. From this premise, the radical critic deduces that but for the (racist) environment, the African-American criminal would not be a criminal. In other words, racism creates and sustains the criminal breeding ground, which produces the black criminal. Thus, when many African-Americans are locked up, it is because of a situation that white supremacy created.

* * *

B. Jury Nullification

* * *

1. What Is Jury Nullification?

Jury nullification occurs when a jury acquits a defendant who it believes is guilty of the crime with which he is charged. In finding the defendant not guilty, the jury refuses to be bound by the facts of the case or the judge's instructions regarding the law. Instead, the jury votes its conscience.

In the United States, the doctrine of jury nullification originally was based on the common law idea that the function of a jury was, broadly, to decide justice, which included judging the law as well as the facts. If jurors believed that applying a law would lead to an unjust conviction, they were not compelled to convict someone who had broken that law. Although most American courts now disapprove of a jury's deciding anything other than the "facts," the Double Jeopardy Clause of the Fifth Amendment prohibits appellate reversal of a jury's decision to acquit, regardless of the reason for the acquittal. Thus, even when a trial judge thinks that a jury's acquittal directly contradicts the evidence, the jury's verdict must be accepted as final. The jurors, in judging the law, function as an important and necessary check on government power.

* * *

C. The Moral Case for Jury Nullification by African-Americans

Any juror legally may vote for nullification in any case, but, certainly, jurors should not do so without some principled basis. The reason that some historical examples of nullification are viewed approvingly is that most of us now believe that the jurors in those cases did the morally right thing; it would have been unconscionable, for example, to punish those slaves who committed the crime of escaping to the North for their freedom. It is true that nullification later would be used as a means of racial subordination by some Southern jurors, but that does not mean that nullification in the approved cases was wrong. It only means that those Southern jurors erred in their calculus of justice. I distinguish racially based nullification by African-Americans from recent right-wing proposals for jury nullification on the ground that the former is sometimes morally right and the latter is not.

The question of how to assign the power of moral choice is a difficult one. Yet we should not allow that difficulty to obscure the fact that legal resolutions involve moral decisions, judgments of right and wrong. The fullness of time permits us to judge the fugitive slave case differently than the Southern pro-white-violence case. One day we will be able to distinguish between racially based nullification and that proposed by certain right-wing activist groups. We should remember that the morality of the historically approved cases was not so clear when those brave jurors acted. After all, the fugitive slave law was enacted through the democratic process, and those jurors who disregarded it subverted the rule of law. Presumably, they were harshly criticized by those whose interests the slave law protected. Then, as now, it is difficult to see the picture when you are inside the frame.

In this section, I explain why African-Americans have the moral right to practice nullification in particular cases. I do so by responding to the traditional moral critiques of jury nullification.

1. African-Americans and the "Betrayal" of Democracy

There is no question that jury nullification is subversive of the rule of law. It appears to be the antithesis of the view that courts apply settled, standing laws and do not "dispense justice in some ad hoc, case-by-case basis." To borrow a phrase from the D.C. Circuit, jury nullification "betrays rather than furthers the assumptions of viable democracy." Because the Double Jeopardy Clause makes this power part-and-parcel of the jury system, the issue becomes whether black jurors have any moral right to "betray democracy" in this sense. I believe that they do for two reasons that I borrow from the jurisprudence of legal realism and critical race theory: First, the idea of "the rule of law" is more mythological than real, and second, "democracy," as practiced in the United States, has betrayed African-Americans far more than they could ever betray it....

2. The Rule of Law as Myth

The idea that "any result can be derived from the preexisting legal doctrine" either in every case or many cases, is a fundamental principle of legal realism (and, now, critical legal theory). The argument, in brief, is that law is indeterminate and incapable of neutral interpretation. When judges "decide" cases, they "choose" legal principles to determine particular outcomes. Even if a judge wants to be neutral, she cannot, because, ultimately, she is vulnerable to an array of personal and cultural biases and influences; she is only human. In an implicit endorsement of the doctrine of jury nullification, legal realists also suggest that, even if neutrality were possible, it would not be desirable, because no general principle of law can lead to justice in every case.

It is difficult for an African-American knowledgeable of the history of her people in the United States not to profess, at minimum, sympathy for legal realism. Most blacks are aware of countless historical examples in which African-Americans were not afforded the benefit of the rule of law: Think, for example, of the existence of slavery in a republic purportedly dedicated to the proposition that all men are created equal, or the law's support of state-sponsored segregation even after the Fourteenth Amendment guaranteed blacks equal protection. That the rule of law ultimately corrected some of the large holes in the American fabric is evidence more of its malleability than of its virtue; the rule of law had, in the first instance, justified the holes.

* * *

If the rule of law is a myth, or at least is not applicable to African-Americans, the criticism that jury nullification undermines it loses force. The black juror is simply another actor in the system, using her power to fashion a particular outcome; the juror's act of nullification—like the act of the citizen who dials 911 to report Ricky but not Bob, or the police officer who arrests Lisa but not Mary, or the prosecutor who charges Kwame but not Brad, or the judge who finds that Nancy was illegally entrapped but Verna was not—exposes the indeterminacy of law, but does not create it.

3. The Moral Obligation to Disobey Unjust Laws

For the reader who is unwilling to concede the mythology of the rule of law, I offer another response to the concern about violating it. Assuming, for the purposes of argument, that the rule of law exists, there still is no moral obligation to follow an unjust law. This principle is familiar to many African-Americans who practiced civil disobedience during the civil rights protests of the 1950s and 1960s. Indeed, Martin Luther King suggested that morality requires that unjust laws not be obeyed. As I state above, the difficulty of determining which laws are unjust should not obscure the need to make that determination.

Radical critics believe that the criminal law is unjust when applied to some antisocial conduct by African-Americans: The law uses punishment to treat social problems that are the result of racism and that should be addressed by other means such as medical care or the redistribution of wealth. Later, I suggest a utilitarian justification for why African-Americans should obey most criminal law: It protects them. I concede, however, that this limitation is not morally required if one accepts the radical critique, which applies to all criminal law.

4. Democratic Domination

Related to the "undermining the law" critique is the charge that jury nullification is antidemocratic. The trial judge in the Barry case, for example, in remarks made after the conclusion of the trial, expressed this criticism of the jury's verdict: "'The jury is not a mini-democracy, or a mini-legislature.... They are not to go back and do right as they see fit. That's anarchy. They are supposed to follow the law.'" A jury that nullifies "betrays rather than furthers the assumptions of viable democracy."

In a sense, the argument suggests that the jurors are not playing fair: The citizenry made the rules, so the jurors, as citizens, ought to follow them.

What does "viable democracy" assume about the power of an unpopular minority group to make the laws that affect them? It assumes that the group has the power to influence legislation. The American majority-rule electoral system is premised on the hope that the majority will not tyrannize the minority, but rather represent the minority's interests. Indeed, in creating the Constitution, the Framers attempted to guard against the oppression of the minority by the majority. Unfortunately, these attempts were expressed more in theory than in actual constitutional guarantees, a point made by some legal scholars, particularly critical race theorists.

* * *

Democratic domination undermines the basis of political stability, which depends on the inducement of "losers to continue to play the political game, to continue to work within the system rather than to try to overthrow it." Resistance by minorities to the operation of majority rule may take several forms, including "overt compliance and secret rejection of the legitimacy of the political order." I suggest that another form of this resistance is racially based jury nullification.

If African-Americans believe that democratic domination exists..., they should not back away from lawful self-help measures, like jury nullification, on the ground that the self-help is antidemocratic. African-Americans are not a numerical majority in any of the fifty states, which are the primary sources of criminal law. In addition, they are not even proportionally represented in the U.S. House of Representatives or in the Senate. As a result, African-Americans wield little influence over criminal law, state or federal. African-Americans should embrace the antidemocratic nature of jury nullification because it provides them with the power to determine justice in a way that majority rule does not.

* * *

III. A PROPOSAL FOR RACIALLY BASED JURY NULLIFICATION

To allow African-American jurors to exercise their responsibility in a principled way, I make the following proposal: African-American jurors should approach their work cognizant of its political nature and their prerogative to exercise their power in the best interests of the black community. In every case, the juror should be guided by her view of what is "just." For the reasons stated in the preceding parts of this Essay, I have more faith in the average black juror's idea of justice than I do in the idea that is embodied in the "rule of law."

A. A Framework for Criminal Justice in the Black Community

In cases involving violent malum in se crimes like murder, rape, and assault, jurors should consider the case strictly on the evidence presented, and, if they have no reasonable doubt that the defendant is guilty, they should convict. For nonviolent malum in se crimes such as theft or perjury, nullification is an option that the juror should consider, although there should be no presumption in favor of it. A juror might vote for acquittal, for example, when a poor woman steals from Tiffany's, but not when the same woman steals from her next-door neighbor. Finally, in cases involving nonviolent, malum prohibitum offenses, including "victimless" crimes like narcotics offenses, there should be a presumption in favor of nullification.

This approach seeks to incorporate the most persuasive arguments of both the racial critics and the law enforcement enthusiasts. If my model is faithfully executed, the result would be that fewer black people would go to prison; to that extent, the proposal ameliorates one of the most severe consequences of law enforcement in the African-American community. At the same time, the proposal, by punishing violent offenses and certain others, preserves any protection against harmful conduct that the law may offer potential victims. If the experienced prosecutors at the U.S. Attorney's Office are correct, some violent offenders currently receive the benefit of jury nullification, doubtless from a misguided, if well-intentioned, attempt by racial critics to make a political point. Under my proposal, violent lawbreakers would go to prison.

In the language of criminal law, the proposal adopts utilitarian justifications for punishment: deterrence and isolation. To that extent, it accepts the law enforcement enthusiasts' faith in the possibility that law can prevent crime. The proposal does not, however, judge the lawbreakers as harshly as the enthusiasts would judge them. Rather, the proposal assumes that, regardless of the reasons for their antisocial conduct, people who are violent should be separated from the community, for the sake of the nonviolent. The proposal's justifications for the separation are that the community is protected from the offender for the duration of the sentence and that the threat of punishment may discourage future offenses and offenders. I am confident that balancing the social costs and benefits of incarceration would not lead black jurors to release violent criminals simply because of race. While I confess agnosticism about whether the law can deter antisocial conduct, I am unwilling to experiment by abandoning any punishment premised on deterrence.

Of the remaining traditional justifications for punishment, the proposal eschews the retributive or "just deserts" theory for two reasons. First, I am persuaded by racial and other critiques of the unfairness of punishing people for "negative" reactions to racist, oppressive conditions. In fact, I sympathize with people who react "negatively" to the countless manifestations of white supremacy that black people experience daily. While my proposal does not "excuse" all antisocial conduct, it will not punish such conduct on the premise that the intent to engage in it is "evil." The antisocial conduct is no more evil than the conditions that cause it, and, accordingly, the "just deserts" of a black offender are impossible to know. And even if just deserts were susceptible to accurate measure, I would reject the idea of punishment for retribution's sake.

My argument here is that the consequences are too severe: African-Americans cannot afford to lock up other African-Americans simply on account of anger. There is too little bang for the buck. Black people have a community that needs building, and children who need rescuing, and as long as a person will not hurt anyone, the community needs him there to help. Assuming that he actually will help is a gamble, but not a reckless one, for the "just" African-American community will not leave the lawbreaker be: It will, for example, encourage his education and provide his health care (including narcotics dependency treatment) and, if necessary, sue him for child support. In other words, the proposal demands of African-Americans responsible self-help outside of the criminal courtroom as well as inside it. When the community is richer, perhaps then it can afford anger.

* * *

C. Some Political and Procedural Concerns

1. What if White People Start Nullifying Too?

One concern is that whites will nullify in cases of white-on-black crime. The best response to this concern is that often white people do nullify in those cases. The white jurors who acquitted the police officers who beat up Rodney King are a good example. There is no reason why my proposal should cause white jurors to acquit white defendants who are guilty of violence against blacks any more frequently. My model assumes that black violence against whites would be punished by black jurors; I hope that white jurors would do the same in cases involving white defendants.

If white jurors were to begin applying my proposal to cases with white defendants, then they, like the black jurors, would be choosing to opt out of the criminal justice system. For pragmatic political purposes, that would be excellent. Attention would then be focused on alternative methods of correcting antisocial conduct much sooner than it would if only African-Americans raised the issue.

2. How Do You Control Anarchy?

Why would a juror who is willing to ignore a law created through the democratic process be inclined to follow my proposal? There is no guarantee that she would. But when we consider that black jurors are already nullifying on the basis of race because they do not want to send another black man to prison, we recognize that these jurors are willing to use their power in a politically conscious manner. Many black people have concerns about their participation in the criminal justice system as jurors and might be willing to engage in some organized political conduct, not unlike the civil disobedience that African-Americans practiced in the South in the 1950s and 1960s. It appears that some black jurors now excuse some conduct—like murder—that they should not excuse. My proposal, however, provides a principled structure for the exercise of the black juror's vote. I am not encouraging anarchy. Instead, I am reminding black jurors of their privilege to serve a higher calling than law: justice. I am suggesting a framework for what justice means in the African-American community.

Questions

1. According to Mutua, what are the basic tenets of critical race theory?
2. What are the purposes of critical race theory?
3. How does Butler assess the current criminal justice system?
4. How does he explain racism in the criminal law?
5. What is jury nullification?
6. In what situations does Butler believe African-American jurors should practice jury nullification?
7. Why does he believe African-American jurors have a moral right to practice jury nullification in such situations?

8. Butler believes that jury nullification would be a constructive, and not a purely destructive, act. Why?

9. Butler concedes that jury nullification is "subversive to the rule of law." Why does he believe that it is nonetheless appropriate? Do you agree?

Part B The Clash Over Legal Thinking in Contemporary Legal Issues

Part A of the book explored many of the most influential legal philosophies that have arisen during the last millennium. It also illustrated the fundamental shift in legal thinking away from a belief in a higher law that has occurred in the last 150 years. Part B takes a step back and asks how these legal philosophies—and often the clash between competing philosophies—have shaped and are shaping our legal doctrines and institutions today.

The readings in Part B span a wide range of legal issues. Some illustrate the battle over legal thinking in subjects that were traditionally covered by the common law, such as criminal law, civil and criminal procedure, and contracts. Others address contemporary claims to abortion rights and special legal protections for transgendered individuals. Still other readings discuss the controversial topic of the legitimacy of preemptive war under international law.

The readings that follow show the influence of higher law thinking on each of the issues addressed as well as the clash between higher law thinking and competing schools of thought.

Chapter 4 Criminal Law

A. Goals of the Criminal Justice System

1. Retribution

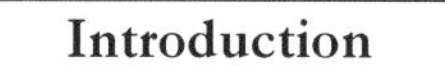

Introduction

Why do we punish criminals? This question is at the heart of any criminal justice system. It is foundational to how society promotes obedience to the law and treats those who break the law. The justification for punishment also determines many other important issues, such as what justifications and excuses are recognized in defense of criminal charges.

The justification for punishment is not only foundational, it is controversial. People have justified punishment variously as promoting safety, deterring crime, rehabilitating the criminal, giving the criminal his or her just desert, vindicating the law, or restoring the relationship between victim and offender. State and federal penal codes have at times based punishments on each of these justifications—and often on multiple justifications at the same time.

This book cannot cover punishment theory exhaustively. Instead, it will focus on two justifications for punishment: retribution and restorative justice. Both have ancient roots, but have gained new prominence in the late 20th and early 21st centuries.

Retributivism is a theory of just desert. It maintains that punishment is justified when it is deserved. Retributivism requires punishment for a defendant who voluntarily commits a crime. It does not concern itself with the future implications of punishment (such as whether it will deter others or rehabilitate the offender). It concerns itself with this defendant and this act.

Retributivism is one of the most controversial justifications for punishment. For much of the 20th century, retribution was criticized as an inhumane response to crime. Accordingly, most states focused on deterrence and rehabilitation. Since the 1970s, however, perhaps because of the perceived failure of the other justifications, there has been a resurgence in support for retribution.

The next four pieces examine whether retribution is an appropriate basis for punishment. The first is by William Blackstone from Volume 4 of his *Commentaries*. Blackstone's views reveal that retribution has been controversial for centuries.

The second and third pieces are excerpts from a debate between Judge Richard Nygaard and Professor Jeffrey Tuomala that was published in the Spring 1995 issue of the *Regent University Law Review*. Judge Nygaard is a judge on the United States Court of Appeals for the Third Circuit. He is a graduate of the University of Southern California and the University of Michigan Law School. He was appointed to the bench by President Ronald Reagan in 1988. In "The Myth of Punishment," Judge Nygaard argues that retribution has no place in our judicial system. Instead he urges that the judicial system should focus on safety and correction.

Professor Tuomala is the Associate Dean for Academic Affairs at Liberty University School of Law. He received a B.S. from Ohio State University, a J.D. from Capital University, and an LL.M. from George Washington University. He teaches a number of subjects including administrative law, civil procedure, constitutional law, jurisprudence, and legal history. In "The Value of Punishment," Professor Tuomala argues that retribution is not only an appropriate basis but is also the most just basis for punishment.

The fourth piece is by C. S. Lewis. Clive Staples Lewis was born in 1898 in Belfast, Northern Ireland. Lewis became a classical English scholar, theologian, philosopher, and author. While Lewis is renowned as a Christian apologist, he was cynical about Christianity in his youth, believing that Christianity was a myth. In 1924, Lewis read some classical literature that set him on a path to validate his cynicism. Instead, Lewis became a Christian. He wrote an autobiography of his conversion and the path he followed to arrive at faith in Christ in his book *Surprised by Joy* (1955).

Lewis was a professor of medieval and renaissance literature at Oxford and Cambridge universities and was a prolific scholar and writer. His works spanned the fields of the classics, apologetics, theology, science fiction, and children's literature. He died on November 22, 1963, the same day President John F. Kennedy was assassinated.

The piece from Lewis is an excerpt from his work, *God in the Dock*. In it, Lewis critiques the "Humanitarian Theory" of punishment, which rejects retribution as "barbarous and immoral." Lewis counters that retribution is really the only just basis for the punishment of crime.

William Blackstone, *Commentaries on the Laws of England, Vol IV*[*]

As to the *end*, or final cause of human punishments. This is not by way of atonement or expiation for the crime committed; for that must be left to the just determination of the supreme being: but as a precaution against future offences of the same kind. This is effected three ways: either by the amendment of the offender himself; for which purpose all corporal punishments, fines, and temporary exile or imprisonments are inflicted: or, by deterring others by the dread of his example from offending in the like way, "*ut poena* (as Tully expresses it) *ad paucos, metus ad omnes perveniat*;" which gives rise to all ignominious punishments, and to such executions of justice as are open and public: or, lastly, by depriving the party injuring of the power to do future mischief; which is effected by either putting him to death, or condemning him to perpetual confinement, slavery, or exile. The same one end, of preventing future crimes, is endeavoured to be answered by each of these three species of punishment. The public gains equal security, whether the offender himself be amended by wholesome correction; or whether he be disabled from doing any farther harm: and if the penalty fails of both these effects, as it may do, still the terror of his example remains as a warning to other citizens. The method however of inflicting punishment ought always to be proportioned to the particular purpose it is meant to serve, and by no means to exceed it: therefore the pains of death, and perpetual disability by exile, slavery, or imprisonment, ought never to be inflicted, but when the offender appears *incorrigible*: which may be collected either from a repetition of minuter offenses; or from the perpetration of some one crime of deep malignity, which of itself demonstrates a disposition without hope or probability of amendment, and in such cases it would be cruelty to the public, to defer the punishment of such a criminal, till he had an opportunity of repeating perhaps the world of villanies.

---

[*] WILLIAM BLACKSTONE, COMMENTARIES ON THE LAWS OF ENGLAND, VOL IV 11-12 (Univ. of Chicago Press 1979) (1769).

Judge Richard Nygaard, *The Myth of Punishment: Is American Penology Ready for the 21st Century?*[*]

Citizens increasingly feel that America has a gun to its head and someone has a finger on the trigger. Crime in America has grown significantly and grows steadily more serious. Our theories of criminal law are not necessarily at fault. Our trial mechanism, prosecutors, attorneys and judges, although overburdened and underfunded, systemically work well. Our prison system does what government intends it to do. American penology, however, is in shambles. It is critically important in any omnibus approach to crime control that we examine and reconsider the theoretical underpinnings of American penology which is now guided by a philosophy that has been parodied and condemned by writers, penologists and philosophers since the time of Aeschylus, and it simply does not work well.[16] The entire belief in punishment as the sole response to crime is a myth. The simple truth is that punishment alone does not and will not control crime.

* * *

When the court sentences a person to a term of years in prison, it is making a statement that this is what it believes is necessary to punish him for his transgression. Its intention is offense-based punishment, and really no more. My point, however, is that we should also be able to say something more. We should be able to say that the sentence imposed is sufficient in both its duration and its demands upon the malefactor to protect society. This latter half, unfortunately, has no place in our sentencing calculus. It exists, if at all, only as a coincidental by-product of the first. Safety is only a myth of punishment.

I submit that punishment, for one whose behavior is not improved by it, has no utilitarian value except as reinforcement for the law-abiding.[19]

---

[*] Judge Richard Nygaard, *The Myth of Punishment: Is American Penology Ready for the 21st Century?*, 5 REGENT L. REV. 1, 3-4, 6-10 (1995). Reprinted with the permission of Regent University Law Review.

[16] There are really only four principal penological or philosophical bases for sentencing: Retribution, Containment, Deterrence, and Rehabilitation. For two centuries America has followed the theories of Locke, Hume, Kant, Hegel and others—retribution. But justice is not a Kantian or Hegelian balance sheet, and the role of retribution, or "just deserts," is legitimate solely as an outer limit of punishment, not its raison d'etre. A "get tough," retributivist sentencing system does not correct man; it tends to harden him and render him more cruel. If one is punished beyond just deserts, the sentence merely becomes a part of the spiral of violence as recrimination between our laws and the rebellious escalates.

[19] Punishment performed as a part of a social vendetta against criminals does not work, because while retribution assuages the punisher's need for revenge—it does nothing for the punished. Retri-

The system can punish, but then what? What follows? Only treatment aimed at modifying behavior, a correction-based system of sentencing has any enduring functional value. From the point of view of public safety, most sentences we now impose cannot be substantiated philosophically, psychologically, or practically. The theory of "lock 'em up and throw away the key" is fine, I suppose, if we truly do throw away the key. But if the person sentenced will ever be returned to society, and if safety is truly our product, logic dictates that correction must be the primary goal.[20] Any other goal defies reason.

* * *

When we lock people up for periods of time, what do we really accomplish? Are we making that person any less criminal? Quite the contrary,...[t]hey become meaner. They become more dangerous. They become more antisocial. They become better schooled criminals. Are we making society any safer? I think not—unless you count the period of time that the person is actually behind bars.

The law predetermines to hold responsible and punish any should they transgress the law. For most, the punishment is prison. Few question why. Society seems somehow to think collectively that we must only imprison. It is a seemingly fitting epilogue to a criminal trial. The system is simply following the myth.[24] But that is not the real world. Prison is

---

bution only provides a fertile bed for the malignant growth of hatred. The public has said that the sinner must suffer, but an odious punishment imposed upon a person who has committed a vile act, while cathartic to a victimized society, has short-lived effects. A sentencing system must answer real needs, and not pander to the immediate passions of society.

[20] Retribution, vengeance lives wholly in the past. It has no future. It is an expression of society's anger and a revulsion from the past in spite of the future. There is, however, nothing so futile as regret. I suggest that our system cannot really call itself enlightened or productive unless all sentences take a view towards the future, towards change, towards correction.

[24] We simply give malefactors too much credit or credit them with too much analysis if we delude ourselves into thinking that the duration of jail time is any consideration whatsoever. Crime has more an emotive genesis than intellective. Deterrence by punishment, I am afraid, accounts for little.

Moreover, our philosophy of sentencing fails to make an adequate adjustment for the free will of ordinary, mainstream American culture and the determinism one finds on the fringes. Our penology is libertarian, which maintains that the only circumstantial equality to which all are entitled is equality of opportunity. Equality of opportunity, however, is insufficient in our social republic to provide a stable economy, a stable workforce, or a stable political equilibrium. So too, it is an inadequate basis to determine appropriate treatment of criminals and the socially maladjusted.

Penology is based upon a theory that presumes a free will: that each person, regardless of whether a resident of the ghetto or tree-shaded suburbia, is equally free to choose between right and wrong—free to do acts which are legal or illegal—free to abide by the law or disregard it—and hence, free to change. This theory is almost totally inapplicable to sentencing as we approach the 21st Century.

Since punishment only modifies to the extent of one's perceived free will to change, the fact of the matter is that the freer one sees himself able to choose, the more effective punishment is as a deterrent. The more one's acts are perceived determined by forces external and exclusive of one's will, the less effective punishment will be and the more critical a correction-based sentencing structure becomes.

systemically unsuccessful except as a temporary human warehouse, a social bandaid. Beyond that, unless and until prisons are turned loose and turned on to correct, they cannot, and will not, provide an incentive for a significant and growing portion of society to abide by the law.

Is it not time we recognize the hard fact that our system is not correcting significant numbers of malefactors? Not preventing crimes? Not deterring criminals? Not assuring anyone's safety? If your doctor followed eighteenth century theory and if your hospital followed nineteenth century practices, would you not seek change? If your educational system had a 60-70% failure rate, would you not require that something else be done? The American penitentiary system has advanced little in the 200 years since it was conceived and some American prisons have an 80% failure rate. Our penological system stumbles uncertainly in darkness, clinging to antiquated and ineffective notions. The American prison is like a cathedral to a false god. Our response—build more of them.

Few in our legislatures seem to know how to cure the socially destructive malaise of crime. One thing, however, is sure: we cannot effect cures unless we discover causes. Until now, little effort has been made in the institutional sense to research and discover the causes of crime, which are, I am sure, as legion as viruses. But I am equally sure that if the behavioral sciences had the resources and applied them with a vigor equal to the physical and medical sciences, breakthroughs would begin. Behavior can be studied scientifically. Antisocial behavior can be modified.

I suggest that criminals be treated like dreaded diseases and examined just as closely to see what caused them to err. We must "discover" why one commits crimes before we set about in any deliberate fashion to develop appropriate remedies.[25] Getting "tough" on crime sounds good, but standing alone as it does now, it is an empty slogan that does not work. I have nothing against tough remedies. I do not make a plea of mercy for the criminal, but for society. Let us be practical. It is time to also get "smart" on crime. We must study the motives that produced the offense, with an eye towards the future and prevention, not towards the

---

[25] Traditionally one committed a crime predominantly for one of two reasons—greed or passion. But now we have to contend with another. It has arisen in the last two decades from a lesser statistic to the point where it now predominates. Indeed, it has been described as the number one health problem in the county. It is a third reason which has come to dominate all other reasons—need.

In *The Politics*, Aristotle also described the need-driven criminal. He is the one who steals of necessity—to eat. Today, however, there are few crimes in the United States motivated by the need to eat. We, nevertheless, have a close analog—drugs. Drugs too create crimes driven by need—not the need of an empty belly, but the need born of an addiction.

past and punishment. As Thomas Fuller said centuries ago, "To punish and not prevent is to labor at the pump and leave open the leak."

Do not misunderstand me: no one wants to be punished. So any punishment has corrective value for some. But it is painfully obvious that punishment, as now administered by the American penal system, is not enough. Beyond punishment, we must discover what inside this individual makes him socially tick so that we can design a system that will effect change.

I believe we should move towards a system of correction that is organized along the same lines as our triage system for treating the wartime wounded. I believe we must segregate our thinking, our treatment, and our sentencing into at least three discrete groups: the benign for whom nothing need be done, the truly dangerous for whom nothing can be done, and those for whom the expenditure of some effort may effect change.

As Michel Foucault said, "Even the shallowest emotions and the weakest intellects can meet and master punishment; few can confront change." Rehabilitation? Perhaps we should dust this concept off and try it again. I am not talking about the goody-goody rehabilitation of the fifties and sixties. I do not bleed for the criminal. I bleed for the society which must reassimilate him after he has served his time. What I propose is real, honest-to-goodness, sincere, no nonsense, severe if necessary, attempts to say to this person in a way he cannot ignore, "You are all screwed up and we are going to change your mind. You must convince us you are capable of living in society, or you are here until you do." The sentenced individual must be made to realize that he must change in such a way that society remains safe, or know that he will not be reinculturated at all. The key to behavioral change lies with the individual—whether we are treating alcoholism, drug addiction or antisocial behavior.

Jeffrey C. Tuomala, *The Value of Punishment: A Response to Judge Richard L. Nygaard*[*]

A. The Value of Punishment

Let me suggest that the desire to see criminals punished is a legitimate value, just as the desire for public safety is a legitimate value. As values they cannot be scientifically "proven" to be right or wrong. However, this does not mean that they are simply matters of preference or that they cannot be validated and supported in a satisfactory manner. It is important to remember that just because values may be misconstrued does not mean they have been invalidated. For example, punishment is often excessive or imposed with improper motives or for improper ends, but that does not mean punishment is not a legitimate value. Likewise, the desire for public safety may improperly lead to a loss of freedom or be used to summarily rid society of undesirables, but that does not mean public safety is not a legitimate value.

If punishment is a legitimate value, and if it is applied fairly, then we should expect it to promote public safety. However, punishment is not legitimized just because it promotes safety. Nor is punishment necessarily a subordinate value which we promote as a means to the greater value and end of public safety. Instead we should expect that all values are interrelated and foster one another. We should also expect in a society where proper values are applied, to find supportive evidence of their effectiveness, although not necessarily in the nature of "empirical proof."

The problem then is to establish the legitimacy of particular values. Few people are willing, and none are able, to live consistently with the relativistic view that all values are equally legitimate. At the same time, few people, if any, are willing to accept the views of the most powerful, or the brightest and best, or even the majority as necessarily right. However, people inevitably founder on the rocks and shoals of relativism if they are unwilling to recognize that it is God who reveals truth and establishes legitimate values. In fact, the surest guide to securing genuine public and self-interest is to value what God values and to act accordingly. Because God knows everything and reveals some things to man, man can know some truths without knowing everything. He is spared the empiricist's dilemma of having to know everything in order to know anything.

---

[*] Jeffrey C. Tuomala, *The Value of Punishment: A Response to Judge Richard L. Nygaard*, 5 REGENT L. REV. 13, 18-27 (1995). Reprinted with the permission of Regent University Law Review.

The critical importance of Christian theology in the development of Western criminal law is well-documented.[27] Legal doctrines are justified by, and maintain coherence as part of, a particular worldview. In Christian theology, the supreme demonstration of the principles of justice is found in the doctrine of atonement.[29] The Christian doctrine of atonement is of singular importance for theories of punishment, as it is the judicial archetype of the way in which God deals with sin and crime. The civil magistrate, as God's agent and minister of justice, should deal with crime and civil wrongs according to the same principles by which God deals with sin through the atonement.

Christian Scripture teaches that all men have sinned and are therefore deserving of death.[32] Sin is a personal offense against God, and his disposition toward sin is one of wrath and determination to exact justice.[33] Because punishment is a necessary component of atonement, men must be punished, or Christ must vicariously suffer the punishment that they deserve.[34] The essence of the atonement doctrine is that Christ died a substitutionary death as both a punishment and a payment for man's sins. God could not simply remit man's punishment nor accept less than full satisfaction without himself acting unjustly.[35] The reason for this is that God's very character is just. Consequently, all his laws and ways reflect his just character. Justice is therefore not the product simply of God's will, but rather of his unchanging nature.[36]

---

[27] *See* Harold J. Berman, LAW AND REVOLUTION (1983), and sources cited therein.

[29] "God presented him as a sacrifice of atonement, through faith in his blood, He did this to demonstrate his justice, because in his forbearance he had left the sins committed beforehand unpunished—he did it to demonstrate his justice at the present time, so as to be just and the one who justifies the man who has faith in Jesus." *Romans* 3:25-26. Hugo Grotius notes that "[n]othing is more influential with men than examples of justice." Quoting Valerius Maximus in A DEFENSE OF THE CATHOLIC FAITH CONCERNING THE SATISFACTION OF CHRIST AGAINST FAUSTUS SOCINUS 98 (Frank Foster trans., 1889). Conversely, few things are so demoralizing as demonstrations of injustice. *II Corinthians* 2:13.

[32] *Romans* 1:32.

[33] *Psalm* 51:3-4; *Romans* 1:18.

[34] *Romans* 5:9-11; *Ephesians* 2:4-5; *Colossians* 1:21; *I John* 4:7-12.

[35] Christ's death as a punishment is reflected in the following passages: *Isaiah* 53:5 ("But he was pierced for our transgressions, he was crushed for our iniquities; the punishment that brought us peace was upon him, and by his wounds we are healed."). *I Peter* 2:24 ("He himself bore our sins in his body on the tree, so that we might die to sins and live for righteousness; by his wounds have you been healed."). Similarly Christ's death was a payment for our debts. *Psalm* 49:7-9 ("No man can redeem the life of another or give to God a ransom for him—the ransom for a life is costly, no payment is ever enough—that he should live on forever and not see decay."); *I Peter* 1:18-19 ("For you know that it was not with perishable things such as silver or gold that you were redeemed from the empty way of life handed down to you from your forefathers, but with the precious blood of Christ, a lamb without blemish or defect.").

[36] *Deuteronomy* 32:4; *Psalm* 92:15; *Matthew* 5:48; *Revelation* 4:8.

The primary effect of Christ's death was to change God's judicial disposition toward man, not man's disposition toward God. But Christ's death also establishes an objective basis for man's reconciliation to God.[37] However, it is the peculiar work of the Holy Spirit which makes reconciliation a reality by revealing the truth to men and thereby transforming their lives.[38]

God has established civil authority; it does not come into existence simply as a matter of social contract.[39] He has called judges to serve as his "agent[s] of wrath to bring punishment on the wrongdoer."[40] As an agent exercising delegated authority, the judge must administer civil justice according to the same principles by which God dealt with all sin through Christ's atonement. Our justice system should reflect two key principles: that an offender deserves to be punished (retribution), and that he owes payment (restitution) to the offended party. It is true that vengeance is the Lord's, but vengeance also belongs to God's human agents of wrath and ministers of justice.[42] The desire to see criminals punished need not be irrational or vindictive. In fact, we should be reluctant to call a man good who does not respond with indignation toward the wickedness he sees in the world. We should respond with satisfaction in seeing wickedness punished,[43] not out of vengeance, but out of respect for justice.

Punishment of sin is a necessary condition of Christian salvation. If that requirement is rooted in the very nature of a righteous, just and holy God, punishment should be viewed as a positive moral value.

B. Punishment is Valuable

Judge Nygaard finds a system of justice that focuses on punishment to be faulty because it is backward-looking. Instead, he believes our focus should be on rehabilitation because it is valuable in securing our future safety. However, I believe the biblical atonement model teaches that we should focus on satisfying the demands of justice. Restitution restores victims, and retribution expiates the guilt of offenders, thereby establishing a sound basis for reconciliation of the offender to his victim, the

---

[37] *Romans* 3:25; *Hebrews* 2:17; *I John* 2:1-2, 4:10.

[38] *John* 3:1-21; *Romans* 8; *Ephesians* 2:1, *Titus* 3:5-7.

[39] *Romans* 13:1.

[40] *Romans* 13:4.

[42] *Romans* 13:4 "For he [the civil magistrate] is God's servant to do you good. But if you do wrong, be afraid, for he does not bear the sword for nothing. He is God's servant, an agent of wrath to bring punishment on the wrongdoer."

[43] *Psalm* 45:7 "You love righteousness and hate wickedness; therefore God, your God, has set you above your companions by anointing you with the oil of joy."

community and himself. When the system focuses on changing the criminal's behavior through deterrence, or on changing the criminal's character through rehabilitation, the victim is left with a sense of injustice and the offender is left with the burden of guilt. The opportunity for reconciliation and restoration is then lost. Just as Christ's death establishes the objective basis for reconciliation, retribution and restitution establish the basis for rehabilitation.

Although the state is appointed to serve as God's agent of justice, is it similarly appointed to serve as his agent of reconciliation and rehabilitation? Judge Nygaard assumes the answer is yes. Therefore, it becomes the state's role to tax and spend for the purpose of finding the causes and cures for crime and administering rehabilitation programs. However, I believe on this point that Scripture gives quite a different answer. It is the Church, not the state, that has been primarily entrusted with the ministry of reconciliation.[46] While the state exercises the ministry of justice through the sword of steel,[47] the Church performs the ministry of reconciliation through the power and sword of the Holy Spirit.[48] The modern state is notorious for neglecting justice and appropriating for itself the role of the Church under the guise of "social justice." But it is a role for which the state is neither entrusted, empowered nor competent.

I believe that acceptance of a criminal justice system which focuses on state-imposed rehabilitation entails a massive threat to liberty. This is especially true if the medical model of detection and treatment forms the basis of penology. Logically, criminals could be indeterminately incarcerated until cured. Procedural protections, such as trial by jury, proof beyond a reasonable doubt, and a right to remain silent, impede detection of illness. These procedures should then be eliminated since they hamper diagnosis and treatment. Criminals and potential criminals would be dealt with on the basis of what they might do rather than what they have done.

Judge Nygaard quite properly believes that the key to rehabilitation lies within the individual. But what if social scientists "discover" that the real problem lies with unjust social and economic systems? A rational policy might then include a comprehensive preventive program of social hygiene that would encompass all potential offenders. Eventually, reha-

---

[46] *II Corinthians* 5:18-19 "All this is from God, who reconciled us to himself through Christ and gave us the ministry of reconciliation: that God was reconciling the world to himself in Christ, not counting men's sins against them. And he has committed to us the message of reconciliation."

[47] *Romans* 13:1-7.

[48] *Acts* 2:8 "Take the helmet of salvation and the sword of the Spirit which is the word of God."; *Ephesians* 6:17 "But you will receive power when the Holy Spirit comes on you; and you will be my witnesses in Jerusalem, and in all Judea and Samaria, and to the ends of the earth."

bilitation would become indistinguishable from theories of social justice which focus on a statist reordering of social structures and control of the entire population. After all, preventive medicine is always more effective than curative or remedial treatment.

Rather than using the adjudication of particular wrongs as an occasion to promote some vision of the public good by means of deterrence or rehabilitation, the state would then engage in an increasingly comprehensive, continuous and purposive intervention in all human affairs. This perspective demands that regardless of the source of a problem the state must take corrective action. If the "causes" of crime are illiteracy, poverty, inadequate housing, unemployment, malnutrition, substance abuse, or broken homes, the state must act. The state then ends up usurping the role of individuals, families, voluntary associations and churches. Individuals and other institutions in turn default on their responsibilities with the ready excuse that only the state has the adequate professional skills and resources to deal with the problems.

Rehabilitation, like punishment and public safety, is a legitimate value, but it is not the immediate goal of a justice system. Punishment establishes a basis for rehabilitation, and it may incidentally deter, but its primary purpose is to satisfy justice. The state's role should be limited to punishing criminals and requiring restitution.

Although the empirical method is unable to prove the causes of crime or to legitimatize values, certainly evidentiary considerations have a role to play in supporting a theory of penology. The facts that the penal system is such a failure and that the crime rate is so high are good indications that we are doing something wrong. Judge Nygaard does us a great service in stressing the importance of penal theory. Without a theory there is no direction to look for evidence nor a framework to order and explain the meaning of our observations.

A criminology based on scriptural principles recognizes that the causes of crime are linked to the sin nature of man.[54] Social conditions may influence people for good or for bad,[55] but the heart of the problem is the human heart.[56] Do social theorists factor this into their theories? If they do not, and if Scripture is true, they will look forever and never identify the problem. Likewise, do their theories, as they relate to cure, take into consideration the power of God's word and of the Holy Spirit to

---

[54] *Mark* 7:15 "Nothing outside a man can make him 'unclean' by going into him. Rather, it is what comes out of a man that makes him 'unclean.'"

[55] *I Corinthians* 15:33 "Do not be misled: 'Bad company corrupts good character.'"

[56] *Mark* 7:21-22 "For from within, out of men's hearts, come evil thoughts, sexual immorality, theft, murder, adultery, greed, malice, deceit, lewdness, envy, slander, arrogance and folly."

change lives? Most likely they begin with the assumption that these claims are false, or at best irrelevant. As a result, studies do not focus on these religious factors.

Scripture repeatedly links obedience to God's blessing and disobedience to his curse.[58] Part of his blessing is to live in safety.[59] This applies to nations as well as to individuals. Perhaps the number one assumption that criminologists share is that the state can and must go beyond punishment and compensation to rehabilitate criminals and establish vast social programs designed to control human behavior. That these programs seem to be such a failure is a good indication that they are unlawful. That we have such a crime problem should give us cause to examine how we do criminal justice and how we order ourselves socially. We must interpret events and "facts" in light of God's word, because it gives them meaning.

Perhaps an example would be helpful. Compulsory state school attendance was offered as the first panacea for the crime problem. Even to this day it is promoted as the surest solution to a plethora of social problems, including crime. But consider the facts. Most criminals are young, most have had six to twelve years of compulsory schooling. The state spends ever-increasing amounts of money on schooling, yet crime increases, even within the schools.

One of the primary conditions of God's blessing is to train our children in God's truth and law.[61] But we have rejected this as a society in a massive way and are reaping the results. Just as jails become a training ground for criminals, state schools have become the spawning pond. In part, the celebrated cure for crime has become a cause. This is not to suggest that religious instruction be added to a state school curriculum. Instead, it is a call to examine the legitimacy of state schools. Has God commissioned the state to serve as society's broker of truth and molder

---

[58] *Deuteronomy* 28:1-2 "If you fully obey the LORD your God and carefully follow all his commands I give you today, the Lord your God will set you high above all the nations on earth. All these blessings will come upon you and accompany you if you obey the LORD your God."; *Deuteronomy* 28:15 "However, if you do not obey the LORD your God and do not carefully follow all his commands and decrees I am giving you today, all these curses will come upon you and overtake you."

[59] *Jeremiah* 32:37b-39 "I will bring them back to this place and let them live in safety. They will be my people, and I will be their God. I will give then [sic] singleness of heart and action, so that they will always fear me for their own good and the good of their children after them."

[61] *Deuteronomy* 6:6-7 "These commandments that I give you today are to be upon your hearts. Impress them on your children. Talk about them when you sit at home and when you walk along the road, when you lie down and when you get up." This kind of education certainly provides a sharp contrast to that provided in public schools where the Ten Commandments, Bible reading, and prayer are curtailed. *See* Stone v. Graham, 449 U.S. 39 (1980); Abington Sch. Dist. v. Schempp, 374 U.S. 203 (1963); Engel v. Vitale, 370 U.S. 421 (1962).

of character? Other government programs and laws have weakened the family. The breakdown of the American family is perhaps an even greater cause in the rise of crime.

Scripture makes it clear that punishment is valuable and that it contributes to rehabilitation and public safety. When law-abiding people see justice done they should rejoice, and the wicked should be terrified. Criminals realize they deserve punishment because their consciences bear witness to that fact.[65] Civil punishment reflects God's justice and expiates that burden of guilt. It also reminds men of their own sin and accountability ultimately to God and their own need to be reconciled to Him.[66] For this reason punishment, including capital punishment, has a rehabilitative effect where it counts most—for eternity.

C. S. Lewis, *God in the Dock*[*]

The Humanitarian Theory of Punishment

In England we have lately had a controversy about Capital Punishment. I do not know whether a murderer is more likely to repent and make a good end on the gallows a few weeks after his trial or in the prison infirmary thirty years later. I do not know whether the fear of death is an indispensable deterrent. I need not, for the purpose of this article, decide whether it is a morally permissible deterrent. Those are questions which I propose to leave untouched. My subject is not Capital Punishment in particular, but that theory of punishment in general which the controversy showed to be almost universal among my fellow-countrymen. It may be called the Humanitarian theory. Those who hold it think that it is mild and merciful. In this I believe that they are seriously mistaken. I believe that the 'Humanity' which it claims is a dangerous illusion and disguises the possibility of cruelty and injustice without end. I urge a return to the traditional or Retributive theory not solely, not even primarily, in the interests of society, but in the interests of the criminal.

---

[65] *Romans* 13:3 "For rulers hold no terror for those who do right, but for those who do wrong."; *Romans* 2:15 "[T]hey show that the requirements of the law are written on their hearts, their consciences also bearing witness, and their thoughts now accusing, now even defending them."

[66] In fact, All Soul's Day was instituted to remind Christians that all men will stand before God in judgment. It is a guard against spiritual arrogance as all men reflect upon their own sin as well as the promise of forgiveness. Berman, *supra* note 27, at 170-71.

[*] CLIVE STAPLES LEWIS, GOD IN THE DOCK 287-294 (1970). Humanitarian Theory of Punishment from GOD IN THE DOCK by C.S. Lewis copyright © C.S. Lewis Pte. Ltd. 1970. Extract reprinted by permission.

According to the Humanitarian theory, to punish a man because he deserves it, and as much as he deserves, is mere revenge, and, therefore, barbarous and immoral. It is maintained that the only legitimate motives for punishing are the desire to deter others by example or to mend the criminal. When this theory is combined, as frequently happens, with the belief that all crime is more or less pathological, the idea of mending tails off into that of healing or curing and punishment becomes therapeutic. Thus it appears at first sight that we have passed from the harsh and self-righteous notion of giving the wicked their deserts to the charitable and enlightened one of tending the psychologically sick. What could be more amiable? One little point which is taken for granted in this theory needs, however, to be made explicit. The things done to the criminal, even if they are called cures, will be just as compulsory as they were in the old days when we called them punishments. If a tendency to steal can be cured by psychotherapy, the thief will no doubt be forced to undergo the treatment. Otherwise, society cannot continue.

My contention is that this doctrine, merciful though it appears, really means that each one of us, from the moment he breaks the law, is deprived of the rights of a human being.

The reason is this. The Humanitarian theory removes from Punishment the concept of Desert. But the concept of Desert is the only connecting link between punishment and justice. It is only as deserved or undeserved that a sentence can be just or unjust. I do not here contend that the question 'Is it deserved?' is the only one we can reasonably ask about a punishment. We may very properly ask whether it is likely to deter others and to reform the criminal. But neither of these two last questions is a question about justice. There is no sense in talking about a 'just deterrent' or a 'just cure'. We demand of a deterrent not whether it is just but whether it will deter. We demand of a cure not whether it is just but whether it succeeds. Thus when we cease to consider what the criminal deserves and consider only what will cure him or deter others, we have tacitly removed him from the sphere of justice altogether; instead of a person, a subject of rights, we now have a mere object, a patient, a case.

The distinction will become clearer if we ask who will be qualified to determine sentences when sentences are no longer held to derive their propriety from the criminal's deservings. On the old view the problem of fixing the right sentence was a moral problem. Accordingly, the judge who did it was a person trained in jurisprudence; trained, that is, in a science which deals with rights and duties, and which, in origin at least, was consciously accepting guidance from the Law of Nature, and from Scripture. We must admit that in the actual penal code of most countries at most times these high originals were so much modified by local custom, class interests, and utilitarian concessions, as to be very imperfectly recognizable. But the code was never in principle, and not always in fact, beyond the control of the conscience of the society. And when (say, in eighteenth-century England) actual punishments conflicted too violently with the moral sense of the community, juries refused to convict and reform was finally brought about. This was possible because, so long as we are thinking in terms of Desert, the propriety of the penal code, being a moral question, is a question on which every man has the right to an opinion, not because he follows this or that profession, but because he is simply a man, a rational animal enjoying the Natural Light. But all this is changed when we drop the concept of Desert. The only two questions we may now ask about a punishment are whether it deters and whether it cures. But these are not questions on which anyone is entitled to have an opinion simply because he is a man. He is not entitled to an opinion even if, in addition to being a man, he should happen also to be a jurist, a Christian, and a moral theologian. For they are not questions about principle but about matter of fact; and for such *cuiquam in sua arte credendum.*[1] Only the expert 'penologist' (let barbarous things have barbarous names), in the light of previous experiment, can tell us what is likely to deter: only the psychotherapist can tell us what is likely to cure. It will be in vain for the rest of us, speaking simply as men, to say, 'but this punishment is hideously unjust, hideously disproportionate to the criminal's deserts'. The experts with perfect logic will reply, 'but nobody was talking about deserts. No one was talking about *punishment* in your archaic vindictive sense of the word. Here are the statistics proving that this treatment deters. Here are the statistics proving that this other treatment cures. What is your trouble?'

The Humanitarian theory, then, removes sentences from the hands of jurists whom the public conscience is entitled to criticize and places them in the hands of technical experts whose special sciences do not even employ such categories as rights or justice. It might be argued that since this transference results from an abandonment of the old idea of punishment, and, therefore, of all vindictive motives, it will be safe to leave our criminals in such hands. I will not pause to comment on the simple-minded view of fallen human nature which such a belief implies. Let us rather remember that the 'cure' of criminals is to be compulsory; and let us then watch how the theory actually works in the mind of the Humanitarian. The immediate starting point of this article was a letter I read in one of our Leftist weeklies. The author was pleading that a cer-

---

[1] 'We must believe the expert in his own field.'

tain sin, now treated by our laws as a crime, should henceforward be treated as a disease. And he complained that under the present system the offender, after a term in gaol, was simply let out to return to his original environment where he would probably relapse. What he complained of was not the shutting up but the letting out. On his remedial view of punishment the offender should, of course, be detained until he was cured. And of course the official straighteners are the only people who can say when that is. The first result of the Humanitarian theory is, therefore, to substitute for a definite sentence (reflecting to some extent the community's moral judgment on the degree of ill-desert involved) an indefinite sentence terminable only by the word of those experts—and they are not experts in moral theology nor even in the Law of Nature—who inflict it. Which of us, if he stood in the dock, would not prefer to be tried by the old system?

It may be said that by the continued use of the word punishment and the use of the verb 'inflict' I am misrepresenting Humanitarians. They are not punishing, not inflicting, only healing. But do not let us be deceived by a name. To be taken without consent from my home and friends; to lose my liberty; to undergo all those assaults on my personality which modern psychotherapy knows how to deliver; to be re-made after some pattern of 'normality' hatched in a Viennese laboratory to which I never professed allegiance; to know that this process will never end until either my captors have succeeded or I grown wise enough to cheat them with apparent success—who cares whether this is called Punishment or not? That it includes most of the elements for which any punishment is feared—shame, exile, bondage, and years eaten by the locust—is obvious. Only enormous ill-desert could justify it; but ill-desert is the very conception which the Humanitarian theory has thrown overboard.

If we turn from the curative to the deterrent justification of punishment we shall find the new theory even more alarming. When you punish a man *in terrorem*,[2] make of him an 'example' to others, you are admittedly using him as a means to an end; someone else's end. This, in itself, would be a very wicked thing to do. On the classical theory of Punishment it was of course justified on the ground that the man deserved it. That was assumed to be established before any question of 'making him an example' arose. You then, as the saying is, killed two birds with one stone; in the process of giving him what he deserved you set an example to others. But take away desert and the whole morality of the punishment

[2] 'to cause terror'.

disappears. Why, in Heaven's name, am I to be sacrificed to the good of society in this way?—unless, of course, I deserve it.

But that is not the worst. If the justification of exemplary punishment is not to be based on desert but solely on its efficacy as a deterrent, it is not absolutely necessary that the man we punish should even have committed the crime. The deterrent effect demands that the public should draw the moral, 'If we do such an act we shall suffer like that man.' The punishment of a man actually guilty whom the public think innocent will not have the desired effect; the punishment of a man actually innocent will, provided the public think him guilty. But every modern State has powers which make it easy to fake a trial. When a victim is urgently needed for exemplary purposes and a guilty victim cannot be found, all the purposes of deterrence will be equally served by the punishment (call it 'cure' if you prefer) of an innocent victim, provided that the public can be cheated into thinking him guilty. It is no use to ask me why I assume that our rulers will be so wicked. The punishment of an innocent, that is, an undeserving, man is wicked only if we grant the traditional view that righteous punishment means deserved punishment. Once we have abandoned that criterion, all punishments have to be justified, if at all, on other grounds that have nothing to do with desert. Where the punishment of the innocent can be justified on those grounds (and it could in some cases be justified as a deterrent) it will be no less moral than any other punishment. Any distaste for it on the part of a Humanitarian will be merely a hang-over from the Retributive theory.

It is, indeed, important to notice that my argument so far supposes no evil intentions on the part of the Humanitarian and considers only what is involved in the logic of his position. My contention is that good men (not bad men) consistently acting upon that position would act as cruelly and unjustly as the greatest tyrants. They might in some respects act even worse. Of all tyrannies a tyranny sincerely exercised for the good of its victims may be the most oppressive. It may be better to live under robber barons than under omnipotent moral busybodies. The robber baron's cruelty may sometimes sleep, his cupidity may at some point be satiated; but those who torment us for our own good will torment us without end for they do so with the approval of their own conscience. They may be more likely to go to Heaven yet at the same time likelier to make a Hell of earth. Their very kindness stings with intolerable insult. To be 'cured' against one's will and cured of states which we may not regard as disease is to be put on a level with those who have not yet reached the age of reason or those who never will; to be classed with infants, imbeciles, and domestic animals. But to be punished, however severely, because we have deserved it, because we 'ought to have known better', is to be treated as a human person made in God's image.

In reality, however, we must face the possibility of bad rulers armed with a Humanitarian theory of punishment. A great many popular blue prints for a Christian society are merely what the Elizabethans called 'eggs in moonshine' because they assume that the whole society is Christian or that the Christians are in control. This is not so in most contemporary States. Even if it were, our rulers would still be fallen men, and, therefore, neither very wise nor very good. As it is, they will usually be unbelievers. And since wisdom and virtue are not the only or the commonest qualifications for a place in the government, they will not often be even the best unbelievers.

The practical problem of Christian politics is not that of drawing up schemes for a Christian society, but that of living as innocently as we can with unbelieving fellow-subjects under unbelieving rulers who will never be perfectly wise and good and who will sometimes be very wicked and very foolish. And when they are wicked the Humanitarian theory of punishment will put in their hands a finer instrument of tyranny than wickedness ever had before. For if crime and disease are to be regarded as the same thing, it follows that any state of mind our masters choose to call 'disease' can be treated as crime; and compulsorily cured. It will be vain to plead that states of mind which displease government need not always involve moral turpitude and do not therefore always deserve forfeiture of liberty. For our masters will not be using the concepts of Desert and Punishment but those of disease and cure. We know that one school of psychology already regards religion as a neurosis. When this particular neurosis becomes inconvenient to government, what is to hinder government from proceeding to 'cure' it? Such 'cure' will, of course, be compulsory; but under the Humanitarian theory it will not be called by the shocking name of Persecution. No one will blame us for being Christians, no one will hate us, no one will revile us. The new Nero will approach us with the silky manners of a doctor, and though all will be in fact as compulsory as the *tunica molesta* or Smithfield or Tyburn, all will go on within the unemotional therapeutic sphere where words like 'right' and 'wrong' or 'freedom' and 'slavery' are never heard. And thus when the command is given, every prominent Christian in the land may vanish overnight into Institutions for the Treatment of the Ideologically Unsound, and it will rest with the expert gaolers to say when (if ever) they are to re-emerge. But it will not be persecution. Even if the treatment is painful, even if it is life-long, even if it is fatal, that will be only a regrettable accident; the intention was purely therapeutic. In ordinary medicine there were painful operations and fatal operations; so in this. But because they are 'treatment', not punishment, they can be criticized only by fellow-experts and on technical grounds, never by men as men and on grounds of justice.

This is why I think it essential to oppose the Humanitarian theory of punishment, root and branch, wherever we encounter it. It carries on its front a semblance of mercy which is wholly false. That is how it can deceive men of good will. The error began, perhaps, with Shelley's statement that the distinction between mercy and justice was invented in the courts of tyrants. It sounds noble, and was indeed the error of a noble mind. But the distinction is essential. The older view was that mercy 'tempered' justice, or (on the highest level of all) that mercy and justice had met and kissed. The essential act of mercy was to pardon; and pardon in its very essence involves the recognition of guilt and ill-desert in the recipient. If crime is only a disease which needs cure, not sin which deserves punishment, it cannot be pardoned. How can you pardon a man for having a gumboil or a club foot? But the Humanitarian theory wants simply to abolish Justice and substitute Mercy for it. This means that you start being 'kind' to people before you have considered their rights, and then force upon them supposed kindnesses which no one but you will recognize as kindnesses and which the recipient will feel as abominable cruelties. You have overshot the mark. Mercy, detached from Justice, grows unmerciful. That is the important paradox. As there are plants which will flourish only in mountain soil, so it appears that Mercy will flower only when it grows in the crannies of the rock of Justice: transplanted to the marshlands of mere Humanitarianism, it becomes a man-eating weed, all the more dangerous because it is still called by the same name as the mountain variety. But we ought long ago to have learned our lesson. We should be too old now to be deceived by those humane pretensions which have served to usher in every cruelty of the revolutionary period in which we live. These are the 'precious balms' which will 'break our heads'.[3]

---

[3] Psalm cxli.6.

There is a fine sentence in Bunyan: 'It came burning hot into my mind, whatever he said, and however he flattered, when he got me home to his House, he would sell me for a Slave.'[4] There is a fine couplet, too, in John Ball:

Be war or ye be wo;
Knoweth your frend from your foo.[5]

Questions

1. Why do Blackstone and Nygaard reject retribution as the proper basis for punishment? Does Romans 12:17-21 support their position?

2. Consider footnotes 19 and 20 in Nygaard's article. Why does he strongly object to the backward looking nature of retribution?

3. What do Blackstone and Nygaard propose in place of retribution?

4. Why do Tuomala and Lewis accept retribution as a proper basis for punishment?

5. Consider the following passages relating to the atonement: Romans 3:21-26; Isaiah 53:5; I Peter 1:18-19; 2:24; and II Corinthians 5:17-21. According to Tuomala, how does the atonement relate to whether retribution is an appropriate basis for punishment?

6. Why does Tuomala reject Nygaard's proposed solution to our crime problem? Consider: Mark 7:14-21; Matthew 15:10-20; and James 3:13-4:10.

7. Why does Lewis insist that, of retribution, deterrence, and correction, only retribution has anything to do with justice?

8. Two aspects of human nature (made in God's image yet fallen) cause Lewis to reject what he calls the humanitarian theory. Why?

9. With which author on this subject do you most agree? What is (are) the appropriate basis (bases) for criminal punishment? Consider the passages listed above as well as: Genesis 9:5-6; Exodus

[4] THE PILGRIM'S PROGRESS, ed. James Blanton Wharey, second edition revised by Roger Sharrock, Oxford English Texts (Oxford, 1960), Part I. p. 70.
[5] 'John Ball's Letter to the Peasants of Essex, 1381', lines 11-12, found in FOURTEENTH CENTURY VERSE AND PROSE, ed. Kenneth Sisam (Oxford, 1921), p. 161.

22:1-5; Leviticus 6:1-7; 24:17-21; Numbers 35:33-34; Deuteronomy 13:6-11; 17:8-13; 19:16-21; 21:18-21; 25:1-3; Ecclesiastes 8:11; Joel 2:12-14; Jonah 3:3-10; Romans 12:17-13:7; and I Timothy 5:20.

10. Is it possible to devise a system that combines retribution with correction or deterrence? Is it desireable?

11. In 1998, Texas executed convicted murderer Carla Faye Tucker, over strong objections, including many from the Christian community. Tucker reportedly had put her faith in Christ, had repented of her crime, and to all observers appeared to be a new person. On that basis, many Christians argued that punishment would serve no purpose. Under these circumstances, should Tucker have been executed? Should she have been punished at all?

12. In 1994, South Africa formed the Truth and Reconciliation Commission to deal with human rights violations committed both by defenders of apartheid and the African National Congress. The Commission was empowered to grant amnesty to anyone who fully confessed to having committed a crime involving a political objective from 1960 to 1993 where the act committed was proportional to the political objective being sought. In a speech in the United States, Nobel Peace Prize winner Archbishop Desmond Tutu declared: "Your concept of what constitutes justice is retributive justice, but we believe in restorative justice." He praised South Africa's system for bringing about forgiveness and healing.

    a. Was the amnesty program a proper way of dealing with human rights violations in South Africa?

    b. Should this sort of "restorative justice" be used to deal with all human rights violations or war crimes?

    c. Should it be used in our criminal justice system?

2. Restorative Justice

Introduction

Restorative justice, as its name indicates, seeks to bring restoration after criminal acts have been committed. It seeks to restore victims and involve them in the criminal justice process. It seeks to restore the relationship between offenders and society—and, if possible, between offenders and victims. It seeks to restore order and peace to the community. Proponents of restorative justice believe victims are often ignored in the criminal justice system and that other approaches to punishment simply deepen wounds and fail to bring healing to the community.

The next four pieces examine whether restorative justice is an appropriate basis for punishment. The first is an excerpt from a law review article by Charles Colson and Pat Nolan entitled, "Prescription for Safer Communities." In it Colson and Nolan argue that our current criminal justice system is broken. It spends ever increasing resources and yet fails to help victims, offenders, or society. They propose that the United States turn instead to restorative justice as an alternative that would make a real difference in the lives of those impacted by crime.

Charles Colson served as special counsel to President Nixon from 1969 to 1973. He was later sentenced to prison for his part in the Watergate break-in and cover-up. It was in prison that Colson became a Christian and began to devote his life to the service of God. In 1976 he founded Prison Fellowship Ministries, an organization that seeks to reach out "to prisoners, ex-prisoners, and their families both as an act of service to Jesus Christ and as a contribution to restoring peace to our cities and communities endangered by crime."

Pat Nolan is the President of Justice Fellowship, an arm of Prison Fellowship that works to reform the criminal justice system through application of restorative justice principles. Nolan received a B.A. and a J.D from the University of Southern California. He served for 15 years in the California State Assembly before being caught in an FBI sting operation relating to a campaign contribution and pleading guilty to racketeering. He spent 25 months in federal prison.

In the second piece, Professor Mary Ellen Reimund follows up on the themes begun by Colson and Nolan. She explains in more depth what restorative justice is and describes concrete restorative justice models that have been implemented around the world. Reimund is the chair of the Law and Justice Department at Central Washington University-Des Moines. She received a B.S at Bowling Green State University, a J.D.

and an M.A. from Drake University, and an LL.M. from the University of Missouri-Columbia.

The third piece analyzes statistically the attempts by one community, Philadephia, to implement a component of restorative justice: restitution to victims (it also looks at fines paid by offenders to the state). Professor R. Barry Ruback conducted the study based on data from 1994 to 2000. Ruback is a professor of crime, law, and justice and the chair of the Center for Research on Crime and Justice at Pennsylvania State University. Ruback received a J.D. from the University of Texas and a Ph.D. from the University of Pittsburgh.

The fourth piece is an excerpt from Professor Stephen Garvey's article, "Punishment as Atonement." In it, Garvey criticizes restorative justice as doomed to fail because it does not take seriously the need to punish offenders. Garvey teaches criminal law at Cornell University. He received a B.A. from Colgate University, an M.Phil. from Oxford University, and a J.D. from Yale University.

Charles Colson and Pat Nolan, *Prescription for Safer Communities*[*]

II. The Growing Crisis in Our Criminal Justice System

To understand the immensity of the crisis in our criminal justice system, a few facts are in order. One out of every 142 Americans is behind bars today—over two million people. That is triple the rate of just twenty years ago. In addition, another 4.7 million Americans are on probation or parole, meaning that one in about every forty-four adults is either in custody or on supervised release.

The annual cost of this imprisonment and supervision exceeds $40 billion. Government at all levels spent $147 billion on crime related expenses: police protection, corrections, and judicial and legal activities in 1999. Each prison cell costs $100,000 to build, plus we spend at least $20,000 annually to house, feed, and guard each inmate. Prisons have become one of the fastest growing items in state budgets, siphoning off dollars that might otherwise be available for schools, roads, or hospitals.

Offenders are often sentenced for years to overcrowded prisons where they are exposed to the horrors of violence including homosexual rape, isolation from family and friends, and despair. Instead of working

[*] Charles Colson & Pat Nolan, *Prescription for Safer Communities*, 18 NOTRE DAME J.L. ETHICS & PUB. POL'Y 387, 388-92 (2004). Reprinted with permission of Prison Fellowship, www.breakpoint.org, and Pat Nolan.

on the outside to repay their victims and support their families, many non-dangerous offenders are idle in prison; warehoused with little preparation to make better choices when they return to the free world. Upon leaving prison they will have great difficulty finding employment. The odds are great that their first incarceration will not be their last.

Our large investment in our prisons might be justified if the inmates released from them were reformed in hearts as well as habits. However, most inmates do not leave prison transformed into law-abiding citizens. In fact, the very skills inmates develop to survive inside prison make them anti-social when they are released. Prisons are, indeed, graduate schools of crime.

The statistics tell the story. A recent study by the Department of Justice Bureau of Statistics found that two out of three released inmates were rearrested within three years, victimizing more innocents in the process.

Over the last thirty years, the rate of rearrest has hovered stubbornly around sixty-seven percent as both the liberals and conservatives tried their solutions. Both approaches have failed to break the cycle of crime. Whether the therapeutic model or the tough-on-crime philosophy was guiding crime policy, the results have remained the same: more crime, more victims, and more prisons. If two-thirds of the patients leaving a hospital had to be readmitted soon thereafter, the public would quickly find a new place to be treated.

III. Why Does the Current System Fail Us?

Even more disturbing than our failing prisons is the fact that our criminal justice system marginalizes victims. Rather than focusing on the injured victim, the current system focuses on the broken law. The legal dimension of crime is certainly important. However, by focusing solely on the legal side of crime, we have missed the more important reality of crime—it injures people. The system should hold offenders accountable to repair the injuries they have caused. While our usual response of locking offenders in prison for a long sentence may limit their ability to harm other people, it does nothing to help the victim. Crime is more than law breaking and justice is more than punishment.

The reason that offenders are not held accountable to repay their victims is because our criminal justice system defines crime as an offense against the state, not against the victim. You can see this in the way criminal cases are titled: State v. Defendant.

Because crime has come to be defined as "law breaking" rather than "victim harming," the purpose of criminal justice has come to be "maintaining order" by (1) punishing the offender for breaking the law and (2) ensuring that the offender does not break the law again. Where does that leave the victim? Out in the cold.

In most criminal proceedings, victims have no opportunity to confront the offender or work out a restitution agreement. The victim's only role in most criminal proceedings is as a witness in the state's case against the accused—a "prop" for the prosecution.

Confession and acceptance of responsibility by the offender are often punished by the system rather than rewarded, and any money collected from the offender usually goes to the state rather than the victim. In addition, the process ignores the long-term damage to the families of both the victim and the offender, as well as the crime's ongoing impact on the community.

We must ask ourselves why we continue to expand a system that ignores the needs of victims, releases prisoners that are more dangerous than before they entered prison, fails to make our communities safer, and consumes an ever-increasing portion of our tax dollars. Einstein has been quoted as saying that repeating a process and expecting the results to be different is insanity. According to that definition, our current criminal policies are insane. Getting "tough" on crime has not worked. Neither has being "understanding" of criminal behavior. It is time to get smart on crime.

IV. Restorative Justice: A Better Way

Fortunately, a smarter way to deal with crime exists. It is called *Restorative Justice*. Restorative Justice focuses on the injured victim as well as the broken law, and seeks to heal those injuries and restore the right order for the community, rather than solely offering retribution.

Victims are involved and given a voice in every stage of the Restorative Justice process. Offenders are held accountable to make things right with their victims through restitution and victim-offender mediation. Restorative Justice recognizes that communities are also hurt by crime, and involves members of the community in determining the appropriate sanctions to be imposed, and in restoring offenders back into the community when they have paid the price for their crime. By working to repair the damage they have caused to their victims, families, and communities, offenders develop the sense of responsibility that is essential to leading a productive life upon their eventual return to society. Through these processes, Restorative Justice seeks to reintegrate both victim and offender as productive members of a safe community.

Restorative Justice has its foundation in the Old and New Testament principles emphasizing the peace of the community, the needs and rights of victims, and the potential of every offender to experience redemption. Crime is seen as a rift in the *shalom* of a community—a breach in the right relationships among individuals, the community, and God. Under Restorative Justice the legal process seeks to mend those broken relationships, and thereby to restore the *shalom*, the right order, to the community.

Restorative Justice is not exclusively a Christian concept. Restorative practices are integral to many indigenous cultures around the world, among the Maoris in New Zealand, the Inuits in Canada, Native Americans in the United States, and tribal cultures throughout Africa. Restorative principles are the foundation of the Truth and Reconciliation Commission that has helped restore peace after decades of bloody conflict in South Africa.

Restorative Justice is not merely a program; rather, it is a completely different paradigm for doing justice. In previous centuries, paradigm shifts have brought great human progress. When astronomers discovered that the sun, not the earth, was the center of the universe, the orbits of the planets were finally predictable. When scholars realized that the earth was round rather than flat, travel around the globe became possible without fear of falling off the edge of the earth. So, also, a paradigm shift in our criminal justice system will allow us to reverse the destructive cycle of crime and make our communities safer.

The U.S. Catholic Bishops summarized Restorative Justice beautifully in their recent letter on Justice: "We are convinced that our tradition and our faith offer better alternatives that can hold offenders accountable and challenge them to change their lives; reach out to victims and reject vengeance; restore a sense of community and resist the violence that has engulfed so much of our culture."

Mary Ellen Reimund, *The Law and Restorative Justice: Friend or Foe? A Systemic Look at the Legal Issues in Restorative Justice*[*]

II. Principles and Definition of Restorative Justice

When a crime has been committed, there is a need to right the wrong. Restorative justice looks at "[c]rime [as] a violation of people and of interpersonal relationships." With the violation, there is an obligation to right the wrong and repair the damaged relationship. Before William the Conqueror, crimes were viewed as wrongs against individual victims. That changed in the twelfth century, when the focus shifted from crime as a conflict between victim and offender, to crime becoming a violation of the king's peace. The state stole conflicts away from the parties; restorative justice moves toward giving them back.

"Restorative justice requires, at minimum, that we address victims' harms and needs, hold offenders accountable to put right those harms, and involve victims, offenders, and communities in this process." While those principles are being examined at an academic level, they are "also being practiced by countless individuals who have given little thought to its definition, but simply find that a particular process 'works.'" Moving beyond the principles of restorative justice to a generally accepted definition is a difficult task. Although some suggest that "[i]t is critically important to develop definitions of restorative justice philosophy, practice and programs that are consistent," others embrace the flexibility.

III. Restorative Justice and the Criminal Justice System

Is restorative justice a complement to the existing court system or a candidate to replace it? "Redeem or divert out?" These questions reflect two views regarding the role of restorative justice within the criminal justice system. One view shows a paradigm shift where restorative philosophy is the predominant way of handling criminal cases—a transformation for criminal jurisprudence. "Restorative justice advocates dream of a day when justice is fully restorative, but whether this is realistic is debatable, at least in the immediate future."

---

[*] Mary Ellen Reimund, *The Law and Restorative Justice: Friend or Foe? A Systemic Look at the Legal Issues in Restorative Justice*, 53 DRAKE L. REV. 667, 670-87 (2005). Reprinted with the permission of Drake Law Review.

The second approach to restorative justice in the criminal justice system offers it as another tool in the toolbox of options—a complement to the existing system. "[F]ocus[ing] on repairing harm and not on what should be done to the offender is the key to understanding restorative justice and is what distinguishes it from punitive and rehabilitative justice approaches." "Crime is defined by the harm it causes and not by its transgression of a legal order."

In his widely cited book, *Changing Lenses*, Howard Zehr contrasts the retributive approach in the traditional criminal justice system with a restorative view of the justice system. However, in his new book, *The Little Book of Restorative Justice*, Zehr expressed concern about the polarization that results from framing the issues as either restorative or retributive because it may mislead by "hid[ing] important similarities and areas of collaboration." His current analysis is likely more representative of present perceptions regarding restorative justice in the criminal justice system today. Not a single jurisdiction in the United States has "fully embraced restorative/community values and practices." There are, however, numerous programs operating as complements to the criminal justice system.

Positioning restorative justice as a complement to the traditional criminal justice system is a starting point for gaining greater systemic acceptance. No one has a magic wand to wave that will instantly transform the criminal justice system into a restorative one. Showing individual program successes within the system helps lay the groundwork for the infiltration of restorative attitudes and approaches within the criminal justice system.

IV. Types of Restorative Justice Processes and Outcomes

Restorative justice programs can be divided into two categories: "those providing restorative processes, and those providing restorative outcomes." Victim-offender mediation, family group conferencing, sentencing circles, and reparative boards fit within the processes category. Understanding the basic models of restorative justice and seeing system applications in adult restorative justice programs aids in our later discussion of legal issues. Although these models help in understanding what happens in these restorative processes, there are variations and hybrids of these models in practice. "It is important to view restorative justice processes along a continuum, from fully restorative to not restorative, with several points or categories in between."

A. Models of Restorative Justice Processes

1. Victim-Offender Mediation

Of all the restorative justice processes, victim-offender mediation (VOM) has been in operation the longest—over twenty years. It is the most utilized model in the United States, accounting for almost 400 programs. There are variations in terminology for VOM programs; examples include victim-offender reconciliation, victim-offender conferencing, victim-offender dialogue, victim-offender meeting, or community conferencing. Despite the variation in names, most follow a similar process by "provid[ing] a safe place for dialogue among the involved parties," usually facilitated by a trained community member. The steps in a VOM meeting are as follows:

1. Introductory opening statement by mediator[;]

2. Storytelling by victim and offender[;]

3. Clarification of facts and sharing of feelings[;]

4. Reviewing victim losses and options for compensation[;]

5. Developing a written restitution agreement[; and]

6. Closing statement by mediator[.]

VOM gives victims an opportunity to meet offenders, discuss how the crime has impacted their lives, discuss the physical, emotional, and financial impact of the crime, and "receive answers to lingering questions about the crime and the offender." The offender is able to explain what happened, take responsibility for his behavior, and make amends to both the victim and the community. Although the majority of victim-offender meetings reach a restitution agreement, this is "seen as secondary to emotional healing and growth."

The Milwaukee County District Attorney's Office operates a Community Conferencing Program similar to this model. Milwaukee is unique because it is one of two counties in Wisconsin where the state legislature has funded an assistant district attorney position in the prosecutor's office to serve as a restorative justice coordinator. According to Assistant District Attorney David Lerman, who coordinates the community conferencing program in Milwaukee County, referrals to the program come from prosecutors, defense attorneys, victim-witness advocates, judges, law enforcement, probation officers, or victims who wish to speak directly with an offender. The program works with adult offenders in nonviolent cases where the offender admits wrongdoing. According to a legislative audit, only 8.8 percent of offenders who participated in a Milwaukee County Community Conferencing program in 2002 were rearrested for a crime within one year, as compared to 27.6 percent of nonparticipating offenders in a control group.

Victim-offender reconciliation has saturated the adult criminal justice system in Polk County, Des Moines, Iowa. According to Assistant Polk County Attorney Fred Gay, sending cases to victim-offender reconciliation is a consideration for Polk County prosecutors in the following situations: when reviewing cases during initial intake, during pre-plea at the defense attorney's request, and during felony presentence investigations. "It is just part of the way we do business," Gay explains. All types of cases are eligible to go through victim-offender reconciliation except domestic violence cases. Liaisons in the Polk County Attorney's Office coordinate the conferences between victims and offenders and community members conduct the meetings. Victim satisfaction with victim-offender reconciliation is what has gained the political support for funding.

While the Milwaukee and Des Moines programs handle adult offenders, the majority of cases across the country referred to VOM involve misdemeanors, property crimes, and minor assaults—all committed by youthful offenders. As programs have matured and greater trust is gained from the referring justice system agencies, there has developed a push to work with victims and offenders involved in serious crimes, such as sexual assault, attempted homicide, and murder. As programs handle more cases involving serious crimes, concerns about the legal implications of restorative processes will be greater due to heightened concerns about offenders' rights.

2. Family Group Conferencing

Family group conferencing (FGC) is similar to VOM, but FGC involves a broader group of people—such as family, friends, coworkers, and teachers—to resolve the criminal incident. The origin of family group conferencing comes from the Maori in New Zealand "where it is used...for most juvenile offenses." In 1989, New Zealand became the first country to adopt a fully restorative juvenile justice system using FGC. With the New Zealand model, "all but the most serious and violent youthful offenders are diverted from the court [system]."

A second model of FGC is used in Australia, but it is based on ideas borrowed from the New Zealand model. This approach utilizes a "standardized, scripted model of facilitation, "and is used by police and school officials to "facilitate meetings between the parties and their families." Estimates in 2001 showed ninety-four active FGC programs in the United States. The vast majority of FGC programs are limited to juvenile offenders and thus fall outside the parameters of this Article.

3. Circles

Circles—referred to as sentencing circles, peacemaking circles, and community circles—are derived from First Nation's community practices in Canada. They were first used in the Canadian criminal justice system "as an alternative way of sentencing that involves all stakeholders." The use of circles in the United States began in 1995 with a pilot project in Minnesota. They are now used in both juvenile and adult cases to determine sentences and decide offenders' terms of accountability. Circles also "help families and communities take responsibility for mending broken relations and creating new lives, [and] give criminal justice professionals a chance to work with victims and offenders in new ways."

"In a circle process, participants arrange themselves in a circle." A "talking piece" is passed around the circle to allow each person to speak, one at a time, in the order they are seated in the circle. This process emphasizes respect, valuing what each participant has to say, and "the importance of speaking from the heart." Participants in the sentencing circles may include the victim, supporters of the victim, the offender, supporters of the offender, judges, court personnel, prosecutors, defense counsel, police, and interested community members. Sentencing circles typically have four stages: (1) determination of suitability; (2) preparation; (3) the peacemaking circle meeting; and (4) follow-up and maintenance of accountability. When cases are referred from the court for sentencing, the agreement reached in a circle can be the sentencing recommendation that is presented to the court. "Using circles to respond to crime…[is] an ongoing process with stages that can extend over weeks, months, or years, depending on the case and the needs involved."

Several communities in Minnesota use circles for sentencing recommendations. Minnesota is unique because there is legislative authority for restorative justice programs, including circles, to "assign an appropriate sanction to [an] offender." Minnesota's restorative justice statute withstood a challenge before the Minnesota Supreme Court in *State v. Pearson*. The Washington County circle handles misdemeanor case referrals from city attorneys. Prior to *Pearson*, the Washington County prosecutor sent felony cases to sentencing circles, but after that decision, the county attorney discontinued participation.

One of the older operating circles in the United States is the South Saint Paul Restorative Justice Council. This group utilizes circles for a variety of purposes, including sentencing. A study of that program exposed disagreement between the community, prosecutors, judges, and corrections as to what cases would be appropriate for a circle. Despite disagreement as to appropriate referrals,

> Judge Barry Stuart, the pioneer of circle sentencing in the Yukon...[who has] work[ed] primarily with quite serious cases involving multiple recidivists, suggest[ed] that the extensive time and resources required for peacemaking circles are primarily warranted in [recidivist] cases...rather than the very minor cases involving first time offenders that are diverted from the justice system.

A circle is the most restorative process available because it encompasses more of the restorative justice values than other processes. Community members have direct involvement in determining which cases come to the circle. Circles address the needs of both victims and offenders. Members of the circle have a role in making sentencing recommendations.

4. Reparative Boards

Reparative boards are usually composed of citizens in the community who conduct face-to-face meetings with offenders who have been ordered by a court to participate. Board members and the offender discuss the nature and impact of the offense and draw up a contract. These boards have been implemented statewide through the Department of Corrections in Vermont, where persons sentenced to probation go through this process to work out the conditions of probation. By legislative mandate, restorative justice became the law and official policy in Vermont, and the reparative boards are used in cases where offenders commit nonviolent crimes and do not require significant intervention.

B. Outcomes

The outcomes of these processes "include restitution, community service, victim support services, victim compensation programs, and rehabilitation programs for offenders." Similar outcomes emerge from the traditional criminal justice system, so there are some restorative outcomes that do not flow from restorative processes. An example would be community service, which is considered "an alternative form of punishment, not restorative justice." Restitution, however, has the potential for being restorative if it is "seen as repayment to or a contribution to the community, mutually agreed upon by all parties." Although these judicially imposed obligations can have an explicit restorative meaning, their restorative impact will be reduced. Between the fully restorative processes and the partially restorative reactions, degrees of restorativeness exist. "A fully restorative system would be characterized by both restorative processes and outcomes."

Howard Zehr raises several issues that point out the dangers in defining categories for what is and is not restorative justice. For example, he has asked: "[I]s it primarily a process?...[Y]ou can do the process and you can come up with some pretty awful things.... Can you come to a good restorative healing outcome in a bad way?" Familiarity with the restorative processes and outcomes as well as understanding that there are degrees of restorativeness helps when assessing the legal protections, processes, and role of attorneys in restorative justice.

V. Law and Restorative Justice

The foundations of law may be impeding the wider adoption of restorative justice within the criminal justice system.

* * *

Critics of restorative justice have noted concerns about due process protection and procedural safeguards that exist in more formal processes. "[R]ights can be trampled because of the inferior articulation of procedural safeguards in restorative justice processes compared to [the] courts." When "the values are similar between restorative [justice] and conventional processes, such as offender rehabilitation and accountability," tension is low. However, when the rights of offenders are involved, "a value less compatible with restorative justice theory" emerges, and the divide becomes greater.

If restorative justice is fully embraced through a paradigm shift, then a different way of looking at legal issues should be considered. "Due process, legality, equality, right of defen[s]e, presumption of innocence and proportionality may be irrelevant or may need to be experienced in a different form. Maybe other legal principles need to be constructed in a manner more appropriate for the restorative perspective." One author has even explored what a restorative constitution might look like.

Since that shift has not taken place, restorative justice is practiced today within existing constitutional parameters and procedures in the criminal justice system. A closer examination of the pertinent legal concerns as they relate to restorative justice reveals that the issues may be of greater magnitude in theoretical discussions than in practice. Most restorative theorists and practitioners recognize that the rights of offenders cannot be ignored and responsibility for their protection falls on the professionals.

A. Constitutional Implications

Our Constitution guarantees the criminally accused certain rights, including due process and the right to avoid self-incrimination. The system relies on procedural rules to determine legal guilt or innocence, with lawyers and judges as the keepers of procedural expertise. Although constitutional rights are a vital part of the United States criminal justice system and have to be protected in restorative processes, how that process looks may be different under a restorative justice model because restoration of violated relationships is key. Expertise in substantive law becomes less necessary because crime is not viewed as breaking a state law, but rather as violating community norms. With direct participation by the victim, offender, and community, fewer specialized roles are needed. Restorative justice simplifies procedure by putting parties in control of a conflict's resolution.

1. Due Process

As guardians of due process, public defenders want to make sure that restorative justice programs protect the rights of offenders. Although there are concerns about the erosion of rights in restorative processes, it is a misnomer to believe that restorative justice requires abandonment of due process and procedural safeguards or that the two concepts are incompatible. There are times when the full array of procedural protections afforded by formal court processes are desired, especially if guilt is in dispute. "Conferences should never proceed in cases where the defendant sees him, or herself as innocent or blameless...." "Courts of law are designed to be 'truth machines'—forums for sorting out disputed facts" in those types of situations. But this machinery is unnecessary and can be "counterproductive in cases where significant facts are not in dispute." Concerns regarding due process are lessened in many restorative programs when the offender participates after pleading guilty. In those cases, the question becomes whether due process was infringed upon in any greater degree in a restorative process than through plea bargaining. Plea bargaining "circumvents…'rigorous standards of due process and proof imposed during trials.'"

If an offender is compelled to participate in restorative processes, the concerns about due process are greater. When VOM was endorsed by the American Bar Association in 1994, the number one item on its list of program requirements was that participation by both the offender and the victim be voluntary. Although coerciveness has been a criticism of restorative justice, the same could be said regarding plea bargaining, which occurs in ninety percent of felony prosecutions. Voluntariness can remedy coercive elements of restorative practices that have a tendency to impede due process.

An example of how voluntariness can be achieved within a restorative program is the Milwaukee Community Conferencing Program. Offenders are given two options: (1) what the penalty will be with restorative conferencing; and (2) what the penalty will be without conference participation. Coercion is lessened because the offender has the option of whether to participate, and thus an option to choose the corresponding penalty.

Another way to protect due process rights is to give an offender the opportunity to opt out of the restorative process at any time to pursue her case in the traditional criminal justice system with its full panoply of rights. In contrast would be restorative programs where offenders are ordered to engage in a restorative process as part of their sentence. Not only does the system take away the ability of the offender to be a voluntary participant in restorative justice, it softens the voice of victims since the options regarding the terms of an agreement reached during a VOM would be reduced.

2. Right Against Self-Incrimination and of Confidentiality

There is the potential that an offender participating in a restorative justice process could trigger her Fifth Amendment privilege against self-incrimination. The constitutional rights of a person accused of a crime and directed into a restorative process could be violated if she was not given any warning about rights against self-incrimination and then revealed information which later could be used against her in court. Most restorative justice programs "do not legally guarantee the American Bar Association's…guideline that 'statements made by victims and offenders and documents and other material produced during the mediation/dialogue process [should be] inadmissible in criminal or civil court proceedings.'"

Legislation is not providing the solution to this concern in most states, because it is unclear whether restorative justice programs are covered by statutory confidentiality provisions in existence for other types of mediation, and there are few states with statutes specific to restorative processes. The Uniform Mediation Act, which has extensive provisions pertaining to confidentiality in mediation, has been adopted by several states and is being considered by others, but that Act does not provide the protections addressed in the American Bar Association Guidelines.

This issue is minimized if the person pleads guilty prior to participation in the restorative process. However, there have been instances where the offender has admitted committing crimes outside of the offense at issue during the restorative process. As a consequence, such information could potentially be used against the person in a subsequent prosecution.

Although disclosure of other crimes is not a frequent occurrence, it does occur. In the Polk County program, Assistant Polk County Attorney Fred Gay confirms there have been a few instances where the issue has arisen and the facilitator has stopped the conference in order to avoid a potential incriminatory comment. He also explained that facilitators are trained to avoid probing into matters outside of the current case.

In the Milwaukee program, the Consent to Participate form contains information that may be revealed outside of the conference in the following situations: "Someone is being physically harmed. Someone is in danger of being physically harmed. Someone has committed a felony, or a sexual assault of any type. [There exists e]vidence that tends to prove an accused innocent of the charges leveled against him or her."

Confidentiality in sentencing circles is different "because the law requires sentencing to be a public process." As with VOM, confidentiality should be discussed up front. Unreported crimes could come into the circle through the offender, victim, or participants and is addressed on a case-by-case basis, depending on what is the most appropriate community response. An obvious exception to confidentiality in circles "involves personal or public safety, such as when a victim seeks additional formal sanctions or when a child or anyone else is in danger of further harm." The better practice, from a legal perspective in VOM and in sentencing circles, is to be clear about what will and will not be confidential prior to participation.

If these precautions are taken, it is less likely that legal conflicts will exist. Also, the potential to infringe on participants' rights in restorative processes would be greatly reduced.

R. Barry Ruback, *The Imposition of Economic Sanctions in Philadelphia: Costs, Fines, and Restitution*[*]

Other than traffic offenses, economic sanctions have been used relatively infrequently in the United States, in large part because of the country's heavy reliance on incarceration. Moreover, financial penalties are considered to have no effect on wealthy defendants, for whom the amounts are assumed to be inconsequential, and to be unfair to poor defendants, for whom the additional monetary burdens are assumed to be overwhelming.

Despite these arguments for not using economic sanctions, there are three reasons why they are being imposed more frequently than in the past. First, the costs of criminal justice operations are becoming so high that offenders are now expected to pay at least part of those costs. Second, concern for victims has increased and will continue to increase, causing restitution to be awarded more frequently. Third, there are pressures for alternatives to prison because of the high cost of incarceration, the limited number of spaces available in some prison systems, and the belief of some people that long periods of incarceration are unjustifiable on grounds of just deserts and are ineffective in deterring future crime.

Purpose, Imposition, and Payment of Economic Sanctions

This study uses data from Philadelphia during the period 1994–2000 to examine the imposition of three types of economic sanctions: fines, costs, and restitution. Although research typically focuses on only one of these economic sanctions, in actual cases they are usually not used in isolation. That is, sentencing often involves multiple economic sanctions used in conjunction with probation and sometimes incarceration.

Fines. Fines are monetary penalties paid by the offender to the state. Fines have several advantages over other types of penalties (Hillsman,1990). They are obviously punitive. They can be tailored to the seriousness of the particular crime and to the specific individual's criminal history and resources. They are also flexible, since they can serve as sole penalties or can be combined with other sanctions, ranging from treatment to incarceration. Moreover, they allow the offender to remain in the

---

[*] R. Barry Ruback, *The Imposition of Economic Sanctions in Philadelphia: Costs, Fines, and Restitution*, 68 FED. PROBATION 21, 21-22, 24-25 (2004). Reprinted with the permission of the author.

community, work, and avoid the stigma and social costs of incarceration (Gordon & Glaser, 1991).

* * *

Costs. Costs refer to money paid by the offender to the state to partially cover the expenses of prosecution, confinement, and community supervision. In some cases, these funds also support expenditures such as victim/witness assistance and victim compensation. Generally, the amount of costs imposed is a standard rate for each count. Thus, the only question in these courts is whether to impose costs, not how much.

* * *

Restitution. Restitution refers to a convicted offender's court-ordered obligation to compensate victims for their losses resulting from the crime. Most often, restitution involves an offender making monthly payments to cover the costs of damaged or stolen property, although these monies may also be ordered to cover medical expenses and lost wages (Harland, 1981). Restitution is widely supported because it both addresses victims' needs for compensation and meets the criminal justice system goals of punishment and rehabilitation. Today, every state has a law addressing restitution, and 29 states mandate restitution unless the judge gives compelling reasons for not doing so (Office for Victims of Crime, 1998, p. 356), consistent with the call made by the President's Task Force on Victims of Crime (1982).

In one study of restitution, Outlaw and Ruback (1999) examined adult probation cases from Allegheny County (Pittsburgh), Pennsylvania in which restitution was or could have been a condition of probation. Results indicated that judges ordered restitution most often when damages were easy to quantify and that offenders were most likely to pay the restitution when they were able to pay and when the victim was a business. Restitution payment was negatively related to rearrest, and this effect was especially strong among married persons, who were more integrated into the community. This finding is consistent with an experimental study in which juveniles randomly assigned to formal restitution programs had lower recidivism than juveniles randomly assigned to other dispositions (Ervin & Schneider, 1990).

Restitution programs have generally not been seen as successful because 1) there is a reluctance to impose restitution on offenders who are assumed not to be able to pay it, 2) payment on restitution orders typically follows other financial obligations (e.g., costs, fines), and 3) there is often ambiguity about who is responsible for monitoring, collecting, disbursing, and enforcing restitution payments (Office for Victims of Crime, 1998, p. 358). Thus, it is not surprising that collection rates of restitution are low, ranging in two national studies from 45 percent (Smith, Davis, & Hillenbrand, 1989) to 54 percent (Cohen, 1995).

* * *

Statutory Changes in Pennsylvania

Aside from looking at the relationship among three types of economic sanctions, we were also interested in looking at the effect of the 1995 statutory change making restitution mandatory. In 1995 Pennsylvania made mandatory the paying of restitution to victims whose property was stolen or damaged or who suffered personal injury as a direct result of a crime (18 Pa. C.S.A. §1106). Moreover, judges were to impose full restitution regardless of the offender's financial resources. Consistent with results in four medium-sized urban counties in the state, we expected an increase in the imposition of restitution after the statutory change and either no effect or a decrease in the imposition of fines and costs. In 1998, Pennsylvania enacted a second statutory change regarding restitution. Under this law, 50 percent of all payments by an offender had to be directed to restitution for victims. We expected this change to result in slightly higher rates of imposition of restitution, as judges would be more likely to believe that ordered restitution would reach victims.

* * *

Summary of the Findings

Overall we found that restitution was more likely to be imposed for property crime whereas fines and costs were more likely to be imposed for nonproperty crimes (most of which were violent). One of the clear findings from this study was that the 1995 statute making restitution mandatory had an effect: both restitution imposition rates and restitution amounts ordered were higher after the statute than before. Contrary to our expectation, restitution was awarded to the State at a higher rate than to private victims, and this difference was even more pronounced after the statutory change making restitution mandatory.

The increase in imposition rates for crimes against private individuals and businesses after the statute was probably not greater for three reasons. First, despite the mandatory nature of the statute, it may be that in practice restitution is ordered only if the victims request it. It is likely that victims are not aware that they must make this request. Second, most of the offenders are probably poor and the odds are low that they would be able to make payments. Third, the amounts of money involved are relatively small, and judges, prosecutors, and probation officers may not believe that the money that could be recovered is worth their involvement.

In contrast to private victims, offenders of most crimes in which the State is the victim were ordered to pay restitution, and the increase after the statutory change was even more dramatic. This effect of greater benefit to the State than to private individuals and businesses probably represents an unintended consequence, in which the State was simply better able to meet the legal and practical requirements of receiving restitution. Specifically, with the State, there was no possibility of victim precipitation or victim responsibility, the state agencies involved asked for restitution, the exact amounts of loss were known and easily quantified (see Outlaw and Ruback 1999), the offenders in the non-welfare fraud cases probably did have money (since they were relatively more likely to have private attorneys) and therefore there was a greater probability of payment, and the average amounts of money involved were relatively large.

This study also found no simple relationship among the three different types of economic sanctions examined here. On the one hand, judges appeared to make tradeoffs between restitution and fines for both individual/business victims and the State as victim. Thus, when the statute required higher rates of restitution, judges appeared to balance that increase with a decrease in the imposition of fines. On the other hand, however, the relationship between fines and costs was positive for both individual/business victims and the State as victim. That is, if judges imposed fines, they were also likely to impose costs.

Taken together, these patterns suggest that judges might be looking at offenders' ability to pay these sanctions. When the choice lies between restitution to victims and fines paid to the government, judges follow the mandatory law and impose restitution. However, when payments are due to the State and County governments through fines and fees, judges impose both or do not impose either.

This explanation is consistent with results from an anonymous statewide survey concerning the imposition of restitution, which was sent to all criminal court judges in the State in September 2001. Of the 147 judges responding, 17 identified their county as Philadelphia. Typical of these judges' views of restitution was the statement of one: "Except in fraud and theft/burglary cases, we rarely see requests for restitution. Most of our offenders are too poor to pay anything substantial." Another judge wrote, "You can't get blood out of a stone. When you have rapes, aggravated assaults, gun-point robberies of those with no skills who have never held a job, what good is restitution? They will be in jail for five to ten years and have no assets. It's the exception, not the rule, in the major cases in a large city."

More quantitative responses were also consistent with the view that most offenders in Philadelphia could not afford to pay restitution. A set of *t*-tests comparing the responses of these 17 judges from Philadelphia to the remaining judges indicated several significant differences. Compared to the judges in the rest of the state, Philadelphia judges were more likely to take type of offense into account, more likely to lower fines in order to reduce the total economic sanctions, less likely to say they impose restitution for violent victims, more likely to say collecting restitution is a problem, more likely to impose indirect criminal contempt charges for failing to pay, more likely to believe that too much time elapses before payment is made, more likely to believe that there is inadequate contact with offenders, more likely to believe that inadequate priority is given to warrants, and more likely to believe that offenders think nothing serious will happen to them.

These responses suggest that judges in large cities impose economic sanctions differently than do judges in suburban and rural areas.

Stephen P. Garvey, *Punishment as Atonement*[*]

Imagine your ideal community. Whatever community you want. Maybe it's the community of your coworkers or fellow union members. Maybe your bowling team or a group of friends. Maybe your church or synagogue. Maybe your family. Now ask yourself: Do its members do wrong? If so, how do you deal with them? Do you punish them? If so, what do you understand yourself to be doing when you punish them? In other words, what model of punishment, if any, operates in an ideal community?

* * *

That's the question I want to answer here. My aim is to develop an account of punishment—what it is, how it works, and what it means—in an ideal community. Punishment in such a community would, I suggest, be a form of secular penance aimed at the expiation of the wrongdoer's guilt and his reconciliation with the victim and the community. I use this model of punishment to display the shortcomings of other models, in-

[*] Stephen P. Garvey, *Punishment as Atonement*, 46 UCLA L. REV. 1801, 1802, 1819-23, 1829, 1840-44 (1999). Reprinted with the permission of the author.

cluding the mainstays of deterrence and retribution, that have for so long guided how we think about punishment.

* * *

[Garvey's model of "secular atonement" has two stages: expiation and reconciliation. The expiation stage requires four things: repentance, apology, reparation, and penance.]

Penance is the final, critical piece of the expiation half of the atonement process. Ideally, penance is a self-imposed punishment, i.e., self-imposed hardship or suffering, which completes the process of expiation and finally rids the wrongdoer of his guilt. The pressing question is: Why? Once he repents, apologizes, and makes reparation, why must a wrongdoer endure penance too?

We can look at this question from both the victim's perspective and the wrongdoer's. Consider it first from the victim's perspective. What does the victim get out of the suffering or hardship the wrongdoer suffers through penance?

In order to answer that question, we need first to appreciate that crime is not simply a matter of action—of taking something that doesn't belong to you, or of hurting someone. Nor is punishment simply a matter of imposed hardship or suffering. Crime and punishment do things in the physical world, but they also do things in the world of meaning. Crime and punishment are expressive. They alter the material world, but the material world is also the medium through which they "speak." When we commit a crime or inflict a punishment, we not only do something but also say something.

What, then, do crime and punishment say? What do they mean? Crime speaks the language of dishonor and disrespect, while punishment speaks the language of condemnation, censure, and vindication. On this view, when an offender commits a crime, he not only imposes a material loss on his victim but also sends a message. In effect, he says: "I'm better than you. I don't need to respect you or your rights." His crime changes not only the material relationship between himself and his victim, but also their moral relationship. Crime degrades, demeans, diminishes, and dishonors the victim, in addition to whatever material damage it may cause.

One way of marking this distinction is to say that most of the acts we call crimes are both harms and wrongs. The harm of a crime is the material loss it causes, for which reparation makes amends. The wrong of a crime is the message of disrespect or dishonor it conveys. Of course, this demeaning message is loudest and clearest in the traditional mala in se crimes, such as murder, assault, and rape, but it's also present in lesser crimes. When someone slips into a parking spot reserved for the handicapped, for example, she doesn't diminish the standing of anyone in particular, but she does convey disrespect for limitations by which the rest of us abide, which in turn broadcasts her own sense of superiority.

Of course, this message of disrespect is morally false. It just isn't true that the victim of a crime has lower moral standing than the perpetrator. That's where punishment comes in. Punishment, in contrast to crime, speaks the truth. It sends a countermessage to annul the false message sent by the offender's wrongdoing. When the state punishes, it therefore says two things. First, it says to the offender: "We condemn what you did. We will not tolerate it here. You are no better than the rest of us, including the one you wronged." Second, it says to the victim: "We stand by you. You are a prized member of the community. We know that, and we want you to know that too." Punishment is thus our way of censuring or condemning the wrongdoer's wrong, of annulling the false message he implicitly conveys through his wrongdoing, and of vindicating the moral value and standing of his victim.

But the atonement model insists that punishment should do more: It should restore the offender to full standing in the community, which raises the critical question: How does suffering manage to effect this restoration? Now, in order to answer this question, you need to shift perspectives. You need to look at punishment not from the victim's perspective, but from the wrongdoer's, and you need to begin where the process of atonement itself begins—with guilt.

Guilt has "a logic whose guidelines we often unthinkingly and unconsciously follow, a logic that certainly appears to connect guilt in some intimate way with pain and suffering." But what is that connection? Recall once again that the wrongness of a crime is the affront it makes to the victim's moral standing and dignity. It is an insult that justifiably makes the victim resentful and angry. The victim's impulse to punish represents, among other things, a legitimate urge to strike back, not vindictively, but as a way of reaffirming his own moral worth. The retributive instinct is to that extent a healthy sign of self-respect.

However—and here's the critical move—in an ideal community the wrongdoer identifies with the victim. Why? Because identifying with one's fellows is in large measure what makes a community a community. It follows that the wrongdoer, because he identifies with the victim whom he has insulted and diminished, will himself feel insulted and diminished. And just as his victim will feel legitimate anger and its accompanying urge to strike back, so too will the wrongdoer feel legitimate anger and the urge to strike back—only at himself. This self-directed anger is guilt.

Guilt is thus a product of empathic self-identification that manifests itself as a form of self-directed anger. If a wrongdoer identifies with the victim of his wrongdoing, he will experience all that his victim experiences as a consequence of that wrong. He will feel smaller than before, just as he has made his victim feel smaller. He will experience anger and resentment toward himself, just as his victim feels resentment and anger toward him. Moreover, just as his victim's moral worth cannot be restored unless the wrongdoer is punished, so too the wrongdoer cannot restore his own moral standing unless he submits to punishment.

We now have an answer to the question with which we began. Repentance, apology, and reparation are necessary but not sufficient steps in the process of atonement. We need penance too, because insofar as the wrongdoer identifies with the victim and insofar as punishment is necessary (albeit conventionally so) to vindicate the victim's moral worth, so too is penance a necessary part of the process of expiation and atonement.

* * *

II. How Does Atonement Compare?

Having described what atonement is and how it's supposed to work, I now want to compare it to what I see as its primary competitors.

* * *

1. Restorativism

Restorativism is part theory of punishment, part "global social movement." By and large, however, you won't find this movement in law reviews. You'll find it instead among members of corrections departments, advocates of alternative dispute resolution, religious figures, and criminologists and sociologists....

Restorativism goes by many names—"reconciliation," "redress," "peacemaking"—and, like retributivism, it's hard to pin down exactly what it stands for. Probably the best statement—a manifesto really—of restorativism, or what he calls "restorative justice," comes from criminologist John Braithwaite. As Braithwaite describes it, restorative justice embraces a far-reaching and ambitious agenda, asking the criminal justice system to achieve restoration along multiple fronts.

According to Braithwaite, restorative justice first means restoring victims, which entails restoring their property loss, personal injury, sense of security, dignity, sense of empowerment, deliberative democracy, harmony, and social support. It also means restoring offenders, which includes not only restoring the loss of dignity offenders suffer from the "shame associated with arrest" but also recognizing that criminal offenders are often "victims of racism" whose "sense of security and empowerment" needs restoring too. Last but not least, restorative justice means restoring community through a "proliferation of restorative justice rituals in which social support around specific victims and offenders is restored." In sum, the "overall purpose" of restorative justice "is the restoration into safe communities of victims and offenders who have resolved their conflicts."

How, though, is all this restoring supposed to happen (whether or not it actually does)? Again, it's difficult to say, since "no single version of the restorative paradigm has yet established itself in either theory or practice." Still, most restorativists seem to agree that the basic mechanism includes a sanction of restitution or community service assessed through mediation or some similar process, which together advance the broader aim of getting the criminal process out of the hands of the state and putting it back where it belongs, in the hands of the "community" and "civil society." Restorativists encourage (others say coerce) wrongdoers and their victims to forego adversarial criminal trials in favor of victim-offender mediation, in which the wrongdoer and victim talk face-to-face and reach a "settlement." The process is ideally not so much about punishment as it is about "dialogue" and "conflict resolution."

Now, you'd think an approach to punishment that placed such heavy emphasis on the idea of restoration would be right at home with an approach that emphasized the idea of atonement. In fact, however, restoration and atonement are farther apart than you might think. Why? Because they differ over the importance of and need for punishment—which is no small difference.

Put bluntly, restorativists really don't much care for punishment. For example, in an extended treatment of restorativism in which he discusses the "sorts of sentences" restorativism favors, Braithwaite gives first priority to voluntary victim restitution or compensation, followed by mandatory victim restitution or compensation, followed finally by a fine used to fund a state-administered victim compensation fund. If the offender cannot or will not pay, community service is in order. Prison is a "last resort," used only as a way to incapacitate the violent and incorrigible. Missing from the restorativist agenda, however, is the idea of punishment as moral condemnation. Of course, restitution, compensation, community service, and the like can function as condemnation, but that's typically not how restorativists see them as functioning. Nor, perhaps, is it how they actually do function.

If that's true, however, then restorativism—gentle and inspiring as it may be—is ultimately self-defeating. Restorativism cannot achieve the victim's restoration if it refuses to vindicate the victim's worth through punishment. Nor can it restore the offender, who can only atone for his wrong if he willingly submits to punishment. And if neither the victim nor the wrongdoer is restored, then neither is the community of which they are a part. In short, restorativism longs for atonement without punishment, but punishment—tragically—is for us an inescapable part of atonement.

Questions

1. What do Colson and Nolan think is wrong with our current criminal justice system?
2. What do they propose as a substitute? Why?
3. What is restorative justice?
4. How do the following passages relate to the concept of restorative justice? Exodus 21:18-19; 21:33-22:15; Leviticus 6:1-7; 24:17-21; and Luke 19:1-10.
5. According to Reimund, what restorative justice processes are being used around the world today? In what types of cases are these processes being used?
6. According to Reimund, what are restorative outcomes?
7. Are the constitutional concerns discussed by Reimund a serious barrier to a more widespread use of restorative justice processes?
8. What lessons does Ruback draw from Philadelphia's experience with restitution and other economic sanctions from 1994-2000?
9. Would Reimund consider Philadelphia's program to be a restorative justice program?
10. Does Philadelphia's experience have any implications for implementing restorative justice principles elsewhere?
11. Why does Garvey reject restorative justice as "ultimately self-defeating?"

12. Should restorative justice processes and outcomes be used more widely in the United States today? If so, how?

B. Human Responsibility and Criminal Guilt

1. The Common Law View

Introduction

Every legal system must determine under what circumstances a person may be held responsible for committing wrongful acts. As the next two pieces show, the common law held human beings to a very high standard of responsibility under the criminal law. In the first piece, William Blackstone discusses what is required before a person may be found guilty of a crime under the common law. He then applies those requirements to a host of situations that arose at common law, many of which still arise today. Indeed, the requirements for criminal guilt laid out by Blackstone in this piece continue to inform American criminal law today.

The second piece is an excerpt from a famous and controversial common law decision: *The Queen v. Dudley and Stephens*. The case involved cannibalism on the high seas, and the opinion squarely confronts these issues: 1) Is it proper to hold individuals responsible for criminal acts that they commit while in dire straits and under extraordinary pressure?; and 2) under what circumstances does necessity justify breaking the law?

William Blackstone, *Commentaries on the Laws of England, Vol IV**

Chapter the Second.

Of the Persons Capable of Committing Crimes.

Having, in the preceding chapter, considered in general the nature of crimes, and punishments, we are next led, in the order of our distribution, to enquire what persons are, or are not, *capable* of committing

* WILLIAM BLACKSTONE, COMMENTARIES ON THE LAWS OF ENGLAND, VOL IV 20-33 (Univ. of Chicago Press 1979) (1769).

crimes; or, which is all one, who are exempted from the censures of the law upon the commission of those acts, which in other persons would be severely punished. In the process of which enquiry, we must have recourse to particular and special exceptions: for the general rule is, that no person shall be excused from punishment for disobedience to the laws of his country, excepting such as are expressly defined and exempted by the laws themselves.

All the several pleas and excuses, which protect the committer of a forbidden act from the punishment which is otherwise annexed thereto, may be reduced to this finale consideration, the want or defect of *will*. An involuntary act, as it has no claim to merit, so neither can it induce any guilt: the concurrence of the will, when it has it's choice either to do or to avoid the fact in question, being the only thing that renders human actions either praiseworthy or culpable. Indeed, to make a complete crime, cognizable by human laws, there must be both a will and an act. For though, *in foro conscientiae* [in the court of justice of the conscience], a fixed design or will to do an unlawful act is almost as heinous as the commission of it, yet, as no temporal tribunal can search the heart, or fathom the intentions of the mind, otherwise than as they are demonstrated by outward actions, it therefore cannot punish for what it cannot know. For which reason in all temporal jurisdictions an overt act, or some open evidence of an intended crime, is necessary, in order to demonstrate the depravity of the will, before the man is liable to punishment. And, as a vitious will without a vitious act is no civil crime, so, on the other hand, an unwarrantable act without a vitious will is no crime at all. So that to constitute a crime against human laws, there must be, first, a vitious will; and, secondly, an unlawful act consequent upon such vitious will.

Now there are three cases, in which the will does not join with the act: 1. Where there is a defect of understanding. For where there is no discernment, there is no choice; and where there is no choice, there can be no act of the will, which is nothing else but a determination of one's choice, to do or to abstain from a particular action: he therefore, that has no understanding, can have no will to guide his conduct. 2. Where there is understanding and will sufficient, residing in the party; but not called forth and exerted at the time of the action done: which is the case of all offences committed by chance or ignorance. Here the will fits neuter; and neither concurs with the act, nor disagrees to it. 3. Where the action is constrained by some outward force and violence. Here the will counteracts the deed; and is so far from concurring with, that it loaths and disagrees to, what the man is obliged to perform. It will be the business of the present chapter briefly to consider all the several species of defect in will, as they fall under some one or other of these general heads: as infancy, idiocy, lunacy, and intoxication, which fall under the first class; misfortune, and ignorance, which may be referred to the second; and compulsion or necessity, which may properly rank in the third.

I. First, we will consider the case of infancy, or nonage; which is a defect of the understanding. Infants, under the age of discretion, ought not to be punished by any criminal prosecution whatever. What the age of discretion is, in various nations is matter of some variety. The civil law distinguished the age of minors, or those under twenty five years old, into three stages: *infantia*, from the birth till seven years of age; *pueritia*, from seven to fourteen; and *pubertas* from fourteen upwards. The period of *pueritia*, or childhood, was again subdivided into two equal parts; from seven to ten and an half was *aetas infantiae proxima* [the nearest age to infancy]; from ten and an half to fourteen was *aetas pubertati proxima* [the nearest age to puberty]. During the first stage of infancy, and the next half stage of childhood, *infantiae proxima* [nearest to infancy], they were not punishable for any crime. During the other half stage of childhood, approaching to puberty, from ten and an half to fourteen, they were indeed punishable, if found to be *doli capaces*, or capable of mischief; but with many mitigations, and not with the utmost rigor of the law. During the last stage (at the age of puberty, and afterwards) minors were liable to be punished, as well capitally, as otherwise.

The law of England does in some cases privilege an infant, under the age of twenty one, as to common misdemeanors; so as to escape fine, imprisonment, and the like: and particularly in cases of omission, as not repairing a bridge, or a highway, and other similar offences: for, not having the command of his fortune till twenty one, he wants the capacity to do those things, which the law requires. But where there is any notorious breach of the peace, a riot, battery, or the like, (which infants, when full grown, are at least as liable as others to commit) for these an infant above the age of fourteen, is equally liable to suffer, as a person of the full age of twenty one.

With regard to capital crimes, the law is still more minute and circumspect; distinguishing with greater nicety the several degrees of age and discretion. By the ancient Saxon law, the age of twelve years was established for the age of possible discretion, when first the understanding might open: and from thence till the offender was fourteen, it was *aetas pubertati proxima* [the nearest age to puberty], in which he might, or might not, be guilty of a crime, according to his natural capacity or incapacity. This was the dubious stage of discretion: but, under twelve, it was held that he could not be guilty in will, neither after fourteen could he be supposed innocent, of any capital crime which he in fact committed. But by the law, as it now stands, and has stood at least ever since the time of Edward the third, the capacity of doing ill, or contracting guilt, is not so much measured by years and days, as by the strength of the delinquent's understanding and judgment. For one lad of eleven years old may have as much cunning as another of fourteen; and in these cases our maxim is, that "*malitia supplet aetatem*" [ill will supplies the age]. Under seven years of age indeed an infant cannot be guilty of felony; for then a felonious discretion is almost an impossibility in nature: but at eight years old he may be guilty of felony. Also, under fourteen, though an infant shall be *prima facie* adjudged to be *doli incapax* [incapable of mischief]; yet if it appear to the court and jury, that he was *doli incapax*, and could discern between good and evil, he may be convicted and suffer death. Thus a girl of thirteen has been burnt for killing her mistress: and one boy of ten, and another of nine years old, who had killed their companions, have been sentenced to death, and he of ten years actually hanged; because it appeared upon their trials, that the one hid himself, and the other hid the body he had killed; which hiding manifested a consciousness of guilt, and a discretion to discern between good and evil. And there was an instance in the last century, where a boy of eight years old was tried at Abingdon for firing two barns; and, it appearing that he had malice, revenge, and cunning, he was found guilty, condemned, and hanged accordingly. Thus also, in very modern times, a boy of ten years old was convicted on his own confession of murdering his bedfellow; there appearing in his whole behaviour plain tokens of a mischievous discretion: and, as the sparing this boy merely on account of his tender years might be of dangerous consequence to the public, by propagating a notion that children might commit such atrocious crimes with impunity, it was unanimously agreed by all the judges that he was a proper subject of capital punishment. But, in all such cases, the evidence of that malice, which is to supply age, ought to be strong and clear beyond all doubt or contradiction.

II. The second case of a deficiency in will, which excuses from the guilt of crimes, arises also from a defective or vitiated understanding, viz. in an *idiot* or a *lunatic*. For the rule of law as to the latter, which may easily be adapted also to the former, is, that "*furiosus furore solum punitur*" [a madman is punished only by his own madness]. In criminal cases therefore idiots and lunatics are not chargeable for their own acts, if committed when under these incapacities: no, not even for treason itself. Also, if a man in his found memory commits a capital offence, and before arraignment for it, he becomes mad, he ought not to be arraigned for it; because he is not able to plead to it with that advice and caution that he ought. And if, after he has pleaded, the prisoner become mad, he shall not be tried; for how can he make his defence? If, after he be tried and found guilty, he loses his senses before judgment, judgment shall not be pronounced; and if, after judgment, he becomes of nonsane memory, execution shall be stayed: for peradventure, says the humanity of the English law, had the prisoner been of sound memory, he might have alleged something in stay of judgment or execution. Indeed, in the bloody reign of Henry the eighth, a statute was made, which enacted, that if a person, being *compos mentis* [having a sound mind], should commit high treason, and after fall into madness, he might be tried in his absence, and should suffer death, as if he were of perfect memory. But this savage and inhuman law was repealed by the statute 1 & 2 Ph. & M. c. 10. "For, as is observed by sir Edward Coke, the execution of an offender is for example, *ut poena ad paucos, metus ad omnes perveniat* [that few may suffer, but all may dread punishment]: but so it is not when a madman is executed; but should be a miserable spectacle, both against law, and of extreme inhumanity and cruelty, and can be no example to others." But if there be any doubt, whether the party be *compos* [in control] or not, this shall be tried by a jury. And if he be so found, a total idiocy, or absolute insanity, excuses from the guilt, and of course from the punishment, of any criminal action committed under such deprivation of the senses: but, if a lunatic hath lucid intervals of understanding, he shall answer for what he does in those intervals, as if he had no deficiency. Yet, in the case of absolute madmen, as they are not answerable for their actions, they should not be permitted the liberty of acting unless under proper control; and, in particular, they ought not to be suffered to go loose, to the terror of the king's subjects. It was the doctrine of our ancient law, that persons deprived of their reason might be confined till they recovered their senses, without waiting for the forms of a commission or other special authority from the crown: and now, by the vagrant acts, a method is chalked out for imprisoning, chaining, and sending them to their proper homes.

III. Thirdly; as to artificial, voluntarily contracted madness, by *drunkenness* or intoxication, which, depriving men of their reason, puts them in a temporary phrenzy; our law looks upon this as an aggravation of the offence, rather than as an excuse for any criminal misbehaviour. A drunkard, says sir Edward Coke, who is *voluntarius daemon* [voluntarily mad], hath no privilege thereby; but what hurt or ill soever he doth, his drunkenness doth aggravate it: *nam omne crimen ebrietas, et incendit, et detegit* [for drunkenness aggravates, and also discovers every crime]. It hath been observed, that the real use of strong liquors, and the abuse of them by drinking to excess, depend much upon the temperature of the climate in which we live. The same indulgence, which may be necessary to make the blood move in Norway, would make an Italian mad. A German therefore, says the resident Montesquieu, drinks through custom, founded upon constitutional necessity; a Spaniard drinks through choice, or out of the mere wantonness of luxury: and drunkenness, he adds, ought to be more severely punished, where it makes men mischievous and mad, as in Spain and Italy, than where it only renders them stupid and heavy, as in Germany and more northern countries. And accordingly, in the warmer climate of Greece, a law of Pittacus enacted, "that he who committed a crime, when drunk, should receive a double punishment;" one for the crime itself, and the other for the ebriety which prompted him to commit it. The Roman law indeed made great allowances for this vice: "*per vinum delapsis capitalis poena remittitur*" [the capital punishment is remitted to those overcome by wine]. But the law of England, considering how easy it is to counterfeit this excuse, and how weak an excuse it is, (though real) will not suffer any man thus to privilege one crime by another.

IV. A fourth deficiency of will, is where a man commits an unlawful act by *misfortune* or *chance*, and not by design. Here the will observes a total neutrality, and does not co-operate with the deed; which therefore wants one main ingredient of a crime. Of this, when it affects the life of another, we shall find more occasion to speak hereafter; at present only observing, that if any accidental mischief happens to follow from the performance of a *lawful* act, the party stands excused from guilt: but if a man be doing anything *unlawful*, and a consequence ensues which he did not foresee or intend, as the death of a man or the like, his want of foresight shall be no excuse; for, being guilty of one offence, in doing antecedently what is in itself unlawful, he is criminally guilty of whatever consequence may follow the first misbehaviour.

V. Fifthly, *ignorance* or *mistake* is another defect of will; when a man, intending to do a lawful act, does that which is unlawful. For here the deed and the will acting separately, there is not that conjunction between them, which is necessary to form a criminal act. But this must be an ignorance or mistake of fact, and not an error in point of law. As if a man, intending to kill a thief or housebreaker in his own house, by mistake kills one of his own family, this is no criminal action: but if a man thinks he has a right to kill a person excommunicated or outlawed, wherever he meets him, and does so; this is wilful murder. For a mistake in point of law, which every person of discretion not only may, but is bound and presumed to know, is in criminal cases no sort of defence. *Ignorantia juris, quod quisque tenetur scire, neminem excusat* [ignorance of the law, which every man is presumed to know, does not afford excuse], is as well the maxim of our own law, as it was of the Roman.

VI. A sixth species of defect of will is that arising from *compulsion* and inevitable *necessity*. These are a constraint upon the will, whereby a man is urged to do that which his judgment disapproves; and which, it is to be presumed, his will (if left to itself) would reject. As punishments are therefore only inflicted for the abuse of that free-will, which God has given to man, it is highly just and equitable that a man should be excused for those acts, which are done through unavoidable force and compulsion.

1. Of this nature, in the first place, is the obligation of *civil subjection*, whereby the inferior is constrained by the superior to act contrary to what his own reason and inclination would suggest: as when a legislator establishes iniquity by a law, and commands the subject to do an act contrary to religion or found morality. How far this excuse will be admitted *in foro conscientiae* [in the court of justice of the conscience], or whether the inferior in this case is not bound to obey the divine, rather than the human law, it is not my business to decide; though the question I believe, among the casuists, will hardly bear a doubt. But, however that may be, obedience to the laws in being is undoubtedly a sufficient extenuation of civil guilt before the municipal tribunal. The sheriff, who burnt Latimer and Ridley, in the bigotted days of queen Mary, was not liable to punishment from Elizabeth, for executing so horrid an office; being justified by the commands of that magistracy, which endeavoured to restore superstition under the holy auspices of it's merciless sister, persecution.

As to persons in private relations; the principal case, where constraint of a superior is allowed as an excuse for criminal mis-conduct, is with regard to the matrimonial subjection of the wife to her husband: for neither a son or a servant are excused for the commission of any crime, whether capital or otherwise, by the command or coercion of the parent or master; though in some cases the command or authority of the husband, either express or implied, will privilege the wife from punishment, even for capital offences. And therefore if a woman commit theft, burglary, or other civil offences against the laws of society, by the coercion of her husband; or merely by his command, which the law construes a coercion; or even in his company, his example being equivalent to a command; she is not guilty of any crime: being considered as acting by compulsion and not of her own will. Which doctrine is at least a thousand years old in this kingdom, being to be found among the laws of king Ina the West Saxon. And it appears that, among the northern nations on the continent, this privilege extended to any man transgressing in concert with a man, and to any servant that committed a joint offence with a freeman: the male or freeman only was punished, the female or slave dismissed; "*proculdubio quad alterum libertas, alterum necessitas impelleret*" [without a doubt wherein the one urges freedom, the other, fate]. But (besides that in our law, which is a stranger to slavery, no impunity is given to servants, who are as much free agents as their masters) even with regard to wives, this rule admits of an exception in crimes that are *mala in se* [evil in itself], and prohibited by the law of nature, as murder and the like: not only because these are of a deeper dye; but also, since in a state of nature no one is in subjection to another, it would be unreasonable to screen an offender from the punishment due to natural crimes, by the refinements and subordinations of civil society. In treason also, (the highest crime which a member of society can, as such, be guilty of) no plea of coverture shall excuse the wife; no presumption of the husband's coercion shall extenuate her guilt as well because of the odiousness and dangerous consequence of the crime itself, as because the husband, having broken through the most sacred tie of social community by rebellion against the state, has no right to that obedience from a wife, which he himself as a subject has forgotten to pay. In inferior misdemeanors also, we may remark another exception; that a wife may be indicted and set in the pillory *with* her husband, for keeping a brothel: for this is an offence touching the domestic economy or government of the house, in which the wife has principal share; and is also such an offence as the law presumes to be generally concluded by the intrigues of the female sex. And in all cases, where the wife offends alone, without the company or command of her husband, she is responsible for her offence, as much as any feme-sole.

2. Another species of compulsion or necessity is what our law calls *duress per minas*; or threats and menaces, which induce a fear of death or other bodily harm, and which take away for that reason the guilt of any crimes and misdemeanors; at least before the human tribunal. But then that fear, which compels a man to do an unwarrantable action, ought to be just and grounded; such, "*qui cadere possit in virum: constantem non timidum et meticulosum*" [which fear might fall on a resolute man; not on one who is timid and cowardly], as Bracton expresses it, in the words of the civil law. Therefore, in time of war or rebellion, a man may be justified in doing many treasonable acts by compulsion of the enemy or rebels, which would admit of no excuse in the time of peace. This however seems only, or at least principally, to hold as to positive crimes, so created by the laws of society; and which therefore society may excuse; but not as to natural offences, so declared by the law of God, wherein human magistrates are only the executioners of divine punishment. And therefore though a man be violently assaulted, and hath no other possible means of escaping death, but by killing an innocent person; this fear and force shall not acquit him of murder; for he ought

rather to die himself, than escape by the murder of an innocent. But in such a case he is permitted to kill the assailant; for there the law of nature, and self-defence it's primary canon, have made him his own protector.

3. There is a third species of necessity, which may be distinguished from the actual compulsion of external force or fear; being the result of reason and reflection, which act upon and constrain a man's will, and oblige him to do an action, which without such obligation would be criminal. And that is, when a man has his choice of two evils set before him, and, being under a necessity of choosing one, he chooses the least pernicious of the two. Here the will cannot be said freely to exert itself, being rather passive, than active; or, if active, it is rather in rejecting the greater evil than in choosing the less. Of this sort is that necessity, where a man by the commandment of the law is bound to arrest another for any capital offence, or to disperse a riot, and resistance is made to his authority: it is here justifiable and even necessary to beat, to wound, or perhaps to kill the offenders, rather than permit the murderer to escape, or the riot to continue. For the preservation of the peace of the kingdom, and the apprehending of notorious malefactors, are of the utmost consequence to the public; and therefore excuse the felony, which the killing would otherwise amount to.

4. There is yet another case of necessity, which has occasioned great speculation among the writers upon general law; viz. whether a man in extreme want of food or clothing may justify stealing either, to relieve his present necessities. And this both Grotius and Puffendorf, together with many other of the foreign jurists, hold in the affirmative; maintaining by many ingenious, humane, and plausible reasons, that in such cases the community of goods by a kind of tacit concession of society is revived. And some even of our own lawyers have held the same; though it seems to be an unwarranted doctrine, borrowed from the notions of some civilians: at least it is now antiquated, the law of England admitting no such excuse at present. And this it's doctrine is agreeable not only to the sentiments of many of the wisest ancients, particularly Cicero, who holds that "*Suum cuique incommodum ferendum est, potius quam de alterius commodis detrahendum*" [every man should bear his own inconvenience rather than diminish the comforts of another]; but also to the Jewish law, as certified by king Solomon himself: "if a thief steal to satisfy his soul when he is hungry, he shall restore sevenfold, and shall give all the substance of his house:" which was the ordinary punishment for theft in that kingdom. And this is founded upon the highest reason: for men's properties would be under a strange insecurity, if liable to be invaded according to the wants of others; of which wants no man can possibly be an ade-

quate judge, but the party himself who pleads them. In this country especially, there would be a peculiar impropriety in admitting so dubious an excuse: for by our laws such sufficient provision is made for the poor by the power of the civil magistrate, that it is impossible that the most needy stranger should ever be reduced to the necessity of thieving to support nature. This case of a stranger is, by the way, the strongest instance put by baron Puffendorf, and whereon he builds his principal arguments: which, however they may hold upon the continent, where the parsimonious industry of the natives orders every one to work or starve, yet must lose all their weight and efficacy in England, where charity is reduced to a system, and interwoven in our very constitution. Therefore our laws ought by no means to be taxed with being unmerciful, for denying this privilege to the necessitous; especially when we consider, that the king, on the representation of his ministers of justice, hath a power to soften the law, and to extend mercy in cases of peculiar hardship. An advantage which is wanting in many states, particularly those which are democratical: and these have in it's stead introduced and adopted, in the body of the law itself, a multitude of circumstances tending to alleviate it's rigour. But the founders of our constitution thought it better to vest in the crown the power of pardoning particular objects of compassion, than to countenance and establish theft by one general undistinguishing law.

VII. In the several cases before-mentioned, the incapacity of committing crimes arises from a deficiency of the will. To these we may add one more, in which the law supposes an incapacity of doing wrong from the excellence and perfection of the person; which extend as well to the will as to the other qualities of his mind. I mean the case of the king: who, by virtue of his royal prerogative, is not under the coercive power of the law; which will not suppose him capable of committing a folly, much less a crime. We are therefore, out of reverence and decency, to forbear any idle enquiries, of what would be the consequence if the king were to act thus and thus: since the law deems so highly of his wisdom and virtue, as not even to presume it possible for him to do any thing inconsistent with his station and dignity; and therefore has made no provision to remedy such a grievance. But of this sufficient was said in a former volume, to which I must refer the reader.

The Queen v. Dudley & Stephens[*]

Dec. 4 and 9, 1884.

(Before Lord COLERIDGE, C.J., GROVE and DENMAN, JJ., POLLOCK and HUDDLESTON, BB.)

REG. v. DUDLEY AND STEPHENS[a]

The two prisoners were indicted for the wilful murder of Richard Parker on the 25th July 1884 on the high seas, within the jurisdiction of the Admiralty of England.

* * *

The record, after setting out the commission and the indictment against the prisoners, concluded with the following special verdict:

> The jurors, upon their oath, say and find that, on the 5th July 1884, the prisoners, with one Brooks, all able-bodied English seamen, and the deceased, also an English boy, between seventeen and eighteen years of age, the crew of an English yacht [a registered English vessel], were cast away in a storm on the high seas, 1600 miles from the Cape of Good Hope, and were compelled to put into an open boat [belonging to the said yacht]. That in this boat they had no supply of water and no supply of food, except two 1 lb. tins of turnips, and for three days they had nothing else to subsist upon. That on the fourth day they caught a small turtle, upon which they subsisted for a few days, and this was the only food they had up to the twentieth day, when the act now in question was committed. That on the twelfth day the remains of the turtle were entirely consumed, and for the next eight days they had nothing to eat. That they had no fresh water, except such rain as they from time to time caught in their oilskin capes. That the boat was drifting on the ocean, and it was probably more than a thousand miles away from land. That on the eighteenth day, when they had been seven days without food and five without water, the prisoners spoke to Brooks as to what should be done if no succour came, and suggested that someone should be sacrificed to save the rest, but Brooks dissented, and the boy to whom they were understood to refer was not consulted. That on the 24th July, the day before the act now in question, the prisoner Dudley proposed to Stephens and to Brooks that lots should be cast who should be put to death to save the

[*] The Queen v. Dudley & Stephens, 14 Q.B. 273 (1884).

[a] The words in brackets were by consent struck during the argument.

rest, but Brooks refused to consent, and it was not put to the boy, and in point of fact there was no drawing of lots. That on that day the prisoners spoke of their having families, and suggested that it would be better to kill the boy that their lives should be saved, and the prisoner Dudley proposed that if there was no vessel in sight by the morrow morning the boy should be killed. That next day, the 25th July, no vessel appearing, Dudley told Brooks that he had better go and have a sleep, and made signs to Stephens and Brooks that the boy had better be killed. The prisoner Stephens agreed to the act, but Brooks dissented from it. That the boy was then lying at the bottom of the boat quite helpless and extremely weakened by famine and by drinking sea water, and unable to make any resistance, nor did he ever assent to his being killed. The prisoner, Captain Dudley, offered a prayer, asking forgiveness for them all if either of them should be tempted to commit a rash act, and that their souls might be saved. That the prisoner Dudley, with the assent of the prisoner Stephens, went to the boy, and telling him that his time was come, put a knife into his throat and killed him then and there. That the three men fed upon the body and blood of the boy for four days. That, on the fourth day after the act had been committed, the boat was picked up by a passing vessel, and the prisoners were rescued still alive, but in the lowest state of prostration. That they were carried to the port of Falmouth, and committed for trial at Exeter. That, if the men had not fed upon the body of the boy, they would probably not have survived to be so picked up and rescued, but would within the four days have died of famine. That the boy, being in a much weaker condition, was likely to have died before them. That at the time of the act in question there was no sail in sight, nor any reasonable prospect of relief. That under the circumstances there appeared to the prisoners every probability that, unless they then fed, or very soon fed, upon the boy or one of themselves, they would die of starvation. That there was no appreciable chance of saving life except by killing someone for the others to eat. That, assuming any necessity to kill anybody, there was no greater necessity for killing the boy than any of the other three men.

But whether upon the whole matter aforesaid by the said jurors in form aforesaid found the killing of the said Richard Parker by the said Thomas Dudley and Edwin Stephens done and committed in manner aforesaid be felony and murder or not the said jurors so as aforesaid chosen, tried, and sworn, are ignorant, and pray the advice of the court thereupon. And if upon the whole matter aforesaid by the said jurors in form aforesaid found the court shall be of opinion that the aforesaid killing of the said Richard Parker in manner aforesaid done and committed be felony and murder, then the said jurors on their oath say that the said Thomas Dudley and Edwin Stephens are each guilty of the felony and murder aforesaid in manner and form as in and by the indictment aforesaid above specified is against them alleged.

* * *

Dec. 9.—The judgment of the court was delivered by

Lord COLERIDGE, C.J.—The two prisoners, Thomas Dudley and Edwin Stephens, were indicted for the murder of Richard Parker on the high seas on the 25th July in the present year. They were tried before my brother Huddleston at Exeter on the 6th Nov., and, under the direction of my learned brother, the jury returned a special verdict, the legal effect of which has been argued before us, and on which we are now to pronounce judgment. The special verdict is as follows: [The learned Judge read the special verdict as set out above.] From these facts, stated with the cold precision of a special verdict, it appears sufficiently that the prisoners were subject to terrible temptation and to sufferings which might break down the bodily power of the strongest man, and try the conscience of the best. Other details yet more harrowing, facts still more loathsome and appalling, were presented to the jury, and are to be found recorded in my learned brother's notes. But nevertheless this is clear, that the prisoners put to death a weak and unoffending boy, upon the chance of preserving their own lives by feeding upon his flesh and blood after he was killed, and with a certainty of depriving him of any possible chance of survival. The verdict finds in terms that, "if the men had not fed upon the body of the boy, they would probably not have survived," and that "the boy, being in a much weaker condition, was likely to have died before them." They might possibly have been picked up next day by a passing ship; they might possibly not have been picked up at all, in either case it is obvious that the killing of the boy would have been an unnecessary and profitless act. It is found by the verdict that the boy was incapable of resistance, and, in fact, made none; and it is not even suggested that his death was due to any violence on his part attempted against, or even so much as feared by, them who killed him. Under these circumstances the jury say they are ignorant whether those who killed him were guilty of murder, and have referred it to this court to say what is the legal consequence which follows from the facts which they have found.

* * *

There remains to be considered the real question in the case, whether killing under the circumstances set forth in the verdict, be or be not murder. The contention that it could be anything else was to the minds of us all both new and strange, and we stopped the Attorney-General in his negative argument that we might hear what could be said in support of a proposition which appeared to us to be at once dangerous, immoral, and opposed to all legal principle and analogy. All, no doubt, that can be said has been urged before us, and we are now to consider and determine what it amounts to. First, it is said that it follows from various definitions of murder in books of authority—which definitions imply, if they do not state, the doctrine—that, in order to save your own life you may lawfully take away the life of another, when that other is neither attempting nor threatening yours, nor is guilty of any illegal act whatever towards you or anyone else. But, if these definitions be looked at, they will not be found to sustain the contention. The earliest in point of date is the passage cited to us from Bracton, who wrote in the reign of Henry III. It was at one time the fashion to discredit Bracton, as Mr. Reeves tells us, because he was supposed to mingle too much of the canonist and civilian with the common lawyer. There is now no such feeling, but the passage upon homicide on which reliance is placed, is a remarkable example of the kind of writing which may explain it. Sin and crime are spoken of as apparently equally illegal; and the crime of murder, it is expressly declared, may be committed *lingua vel facto* [even with the tongue]; so that a man, like Hero, "done to death by slanderous tongues," would, it seems, in the opinion of Bracton, be a person in respect of whom might be grounded a legal indictment for murder. But in the very passage as to necessity, on which reliance has been placed, it is clear that Bracton is speaking of necessity in the ordinary sense the repelling by violence—violence justified so far as it was necessary for the object—any illegal violence used towards oneself. If, says Bracton (Lib. iii., Art. De Corona, cap. 4, fol. 120), the necessity be "*evitabilis et evadere posset absque occisione, tunc erit reus homicidii*" [avoidable and evadable without murder, then it is culprit homicide]; words which show clearly that he is thinking of physical danger, from which escape may be possible, and that "*inevitabilis necessitas*" [the unavoidable need], of which he speaks as justifying homicide, is a necessity of the same nature. It is, if possible, yet clearer that the doctrine contended for receives no support from the great authority of Lord Hale. It is plain that in his view the necessity which justifies homicide is that only which has always been, and is now, considered a justification. "In all these cases of homicide by necessity," says he, "as in pursuit of a felon, in killing him that assaults to rob, or comes to burn or break a house, or the like, which are in themselves no felony:" (1 Hale P. C. 491.) Again, he says that the necessity which justifies homicide is of two kinds: "(1) That necessity which is of a private nature; (2) That necessity which relates to the public justice and safety. The former is that necessity which obligeth a man to his own defence and safeguard; and this takes in these inquiries: 1. What may be done for the safeguard of a man's own life;" and then follow three other heads not necessary to pursue. Then Lord Hale proceeds: "1. As touching the first of these, viz., homicide in defence of a man's own life, which is usually styled *se defendendo*" [defending himself]: (1 Hale P. C. 478.) It is not possible to use words more clear to show that Lord Hale regarded the private necessity which justified, and alone justified, the taking the life of another for the safeguard of one's own to be what is commonly called self-defence. But if this could be even doubtful upon Lord Hale's words, Lord Hale himself has made it clear, for, in the chapter in which he deals with the exemption created by compulsion or necessity, he thus expresses himself: "If a man be desperately assaulted, and in peril of death, and cannot otherwise escape, unless to satisfy his assailant's fury he will kill an innocent person then present, the fear and actual force will not acquit him of the crime and punishment of murder if he commit the fact, for he ought rather to die himself than to kill an innocent; but if he cannot otherwise save his own life, the law permits him in his own defence to kill the assailant, for, by the violence of the assault and the offence committed upon him by the assailant himself, the law of nature and necessity hath made him his own *protector cum debito moderamine inculpatæ tutelæ*" [a protector with indebted governing of blameless management]: (1 Hale P. C. 51.) But, further still, Lord Hale, in the following chapter, deals with the position asserted by the casuists, and sanctioned, as he says, by Grotius and Puffendorf, that in a case of extreme necessity either of hunger or clothing, "theft is no theft or at least not punishable as theft," and some even of our own lawyers have asserted the same, "but," says Lord Hale, "I take it that here in England that rule, at least by the laws of England, is false and, therefore, if a person, being under necessity for want of victuals or clothes, shall upon that account clandestinely and *animo furundi* [with a raving intellect] steal another man's goods, it is a felony and a crime by the laws of England punishable with death." (1 Hale P. C. 54.) If, therefore, Lord Hale is clear, as he is, that extreme necessity of hunger does not justify larceny, what would he have said to the doctrine that it justified murder?

* * *

Is there, then, any authority for the proposition which has been presented to us? Decided cases there are none. The case of the seven English sailors referred to by the commentator on Grotius and by Puffendorf has been discovered by a gentleman of the bar, who communicated with my brother Huddleston, to convey the authority, if it conveys so much, of a single judge of the island of St. Kitts, when that island was possessed partly by France and partly by this country, somewhere about the year 1641. It is mentioned in a medical treatise published at Amsterdam, and is altogether, as authority in an English court, as unsatisfactory as possible. The American case cited by my brother Stephen in his Digest from Wharton on Homicide, p. 237, in which it was decided, correctly indeed, that sailors had no right to throw passengers overboard to save themselves, but, on the somewhat strange ground that the proper mode of determining who was to be sacrificed was to vote upon the subject by ballot, can hardly, as my brother Stephen says, be an authority satisfactory to a court in this country.

* * *

The one real authority of former time is Lord Bacon, who in his Commentary on the maxim, "*Necessitas inducit privilegium quoad jura private*" [with respect to private rights necessity induces privilege], lays down the law as follows: "Necessity carrieth a privilege in itself. Necessity is of three sorts: Necessity of conservation of life, necessity of obedience, and necessity of the act of God or of a stranger. First, of conservation of life. If a man steal viands to satisfy his present hunger, this is no felony nor larceny. So if divers be in danger of drowning by the casting away of some boat or barge, and one of them get to some plank, or on the boat's side, to keep himself above water, and another to save his life thrust him from it, whereby he is drowned this is neither *se defendendo* [defending himself] nor by misadventure, but justifiable." On this it is to be observed that Lord Bacon's proposition that stealing to satisfy hunger is no larceny is hardly supported by Staundforde, whom he cites for it, and is expressly contradicted by Lord Hale in the passage already cited. And for the proposition as to the plank or boat it is said to be derived from the canonists; at any rate, he cites no authority for it, and it must stand upon his own. Lord Bacon was great even as a lawyer, but it is permissible to much smaller men, relying upon principle and on the authority of others the equals and even the superiors of Lord Bacon as lawyers, to question the soundness of his dictum. There are many conceivable states of things in which it might possibly be true: but, if Lord Bacon meant to lay down the broad proposition that a man may save his life by killing, if necessary, an innocent and unoffending neighbour, it certainly is not law at the present day.

* * *

Now except for the purpose of testing how far the conservation of a man's own life is in all cases and under all circumstances an absolute, unqualified, and paramount duty, we exclude from our consideration all the incidents of war. We are dealing with a case of private homicide, not one imposed upon men in the service of their Sovereign or in the defence of their country. Now, it is admitted that the deliberate killing of this unoffending and unresisting boy was clearly murder, unless the killing can be justified by some well-recognised excuse admitted by the law. It is further admitted that there was in this case no such excuse, unless the killing was justified by what has been called necessity. But the temptation to the act which existed here was not what the law has ever called necessity. Nor is this to be regretted. Though law and morality are not the same, and though many things may be immoral which are not necessarily illegal, yet the absolute divorce of law from morality would be of fatal consequence, and such divorce would follow if the temptation to murder in this case were to be held by law an absolute defence of it. It is not so. To preserve one's life is generally speaking, a duty, but it may be the plainest and the highest duty to sacrifice it. War is full of instances in which it is a man's duty not to live but to die. The duty, in case of shipwreck, of a captain to his crew, of the crew to the passengers, of soldiers to women and children, as in the noble case of the *Birkenhead*—these duties impose on men the moral necessity, not of the preservation, but of the sacrifice, of their lives for others from which in no country—least of all it is to be hoped in England—will men ever shrink, as indeed they have not shrunk. It is not correct, therefore, to say that there is any absolute and unqualified necessity to preserve one's life. "*Necesse est ut eam, non ut vivam*" [it needs that I go, it is not necessary I should live], is a saying of a Roman officer quoted by Lord Bacon himself with high eulogy in the very chapter on Necessity, to which so much reference has been made. It would be a very easy and cheap display of common-place learning to quote from Greek and Latin authors—from Horace, from Juvenal, from Cicero, from Euripides—passage after passage in which the duty of dying for others has been laid down in glowing and emphatic language as resulting from the principles of heathen ethics. It is enough in a Christian country to remind ourselves of the Great Example which we profess to follow. It is not needful to point out the awful danger of admitting the principle which has been contended for. Who is to be the judge of this sort of necessity? By what measure is the comparative value of lives to be measured? Is it to be strength, or intellect, or what? It is plain that the principle leaves to him who is to profit by it to determine the necessity which will justify him in deliberately taking another's life to save his own. In this case the weakest, the youngest, the most unresisting was chosen. Was it more necessary to kill him than one of the grown men? The answer must be, No.

> So spake the Fiend and with necessity,
> The tyrant's, plea, excused his devilish deeds.

It is not suggested that in this particular case the "deeds" were "devilish;" but it is quite plain that such a principle, once admitted, might be made the legal cloke for unbridled passion and atrocious crime. There is no path safe for judges to tread but to ascertain the law to the best of their ability, and to declare it according to their judgment, and if in any case the law appears to be too severe on individuals, to leave it to the Sovereign to exercise that prerogative of mercy which the Constitution has intrusted to the hands fittest to dispense it. It must not be supposed that in refusing to admit temptation to be an excuse for crime, it is forgotten how terrible the temptation was, how awful the suffering, how hard in such trials to keep the judgment straight and the conduct pure. We are often compelled to set up standards we cannot reach ourselves, and to lay down rules which we could not ourselves satisfy. But a man has no right to declare temptation to be an excuse, though he might himself have yielded to it, nor allow compassion for the criminal to change or weaken in any manner the legal definition of the crime. It is therefore our duty to declare that the prisoners' act in this case was wilful murder; that the facts as stated in the verdict are no legal justification of the homicide; and to say that, in our unanimous opinion, they are, upon this special verdict, guilty of murder.[a]

Sir *Henry James*, (A.G.) prayed the sentence of the court.

The LORD CHIEF JUSTICE thereupon passed sentence of death in the usual form.[b]

Judgment for the Crown.

---

[a] My brother Grove has furnished me with the following suggestion, too late to be embodied in the judgment, but well worth preserving "If the two excused men were justified in killing Parker, then, if not rescued in time, two of the three survivors would be justified in killing the third: and, of the two who remained, the stronger would be justified in killing the weaker, so that three men might be justifiably killed to give the fourth a chance of surviving."—C.

[b] The prisoners were afterwards respited and their sentence commuted to one of six months' imprisonment without hard labour.

Questions

1. What did the common law require before it held someone responsible for a crime?

2. Read Matthew 15:10-20; Mark 7:14-23; and James 3:13-4:10. Where does evil come from?

3. Read Exodus 21:12-14; Deuteronomy 19:4-13; Joshua 20:1-9; I Samuel 16:7; and Revelation 2:23. Does our intent matter when we do a bad act?

4. Suppose we know (through a mind-reading device) that a man intends to kill his wife, but he has not yet acted on his murderous intention. Should he be guilty of a crime?

5. What is Dudley's and Stephens' defense to the charge of murder?

6. Does one have the right to preserve his life at all costs?

7. How does Lord Coleridge find scripture helpful on this point?

8. What is Lord Coleridge's response to the argument that to find Dudley and Stephens guilty is to hold them to an impossible standard?

9. Was it proper to hold Dudley and Stephens responsible despite the tremendous pressure they were under? Consider Genesis 3:1-19; 4:1-7; II Thessalonians 1:6-10; John 3:18; and I Corinthians 15:33-34.

10. What is Coleridge's view of the nature of human beings?

11. How would you decide the case if the facts were changed in the following ways:

    a. All four of the seamen agreed that one needed to die to save the others. Together they accepted Dudley's suggestion to draw lots. Richard Parker was selected and killed;

    b. The seamen knew to a certainty that Parker was going to die no matter what they did. They also knew that if they killed Parker and ate his flesh the remaining three would survive; if they did not, all four would die.

2. Current Issues: Environmental Influence as an Excuse

Introduction

Today's criminal law is still based in large part upon the common law and its requirements for criminal guilt. The criminal law continues for the most part to condition criminal guilt on a finding that the defendant both had the required mental state and committed a voluntary act.

Over the past several decades, however, the law has been changing within this overall framework. To some degree there has been a challenge to the level of personal responsibility the criminal law required at common law. Defendants have sought to raise new and creative defenses to argue that they ought not to be held criminally responsible for acts they have committed because of influences from their environment or genetic makeup.

The following pieces discuss this development. The first piece is taken from a 2007 law review article by Professor Henry Fradella. Fradella is a Professor of Law and Criminal Justice at California State University, Long Beach. He received a B.A. from Clark University, a J.D. and an M.F.S. in forensic science from George Washington University, and a Ph.D. from Arizona State University. In the article, Fradella outlines a number of the new environmental defenses raised by defendants. Some have been accepted as legal excuses; some have not.

The second piece is a very short excerpt from a 1996 law review article by Professor Patricia Falk. Falk is a law professor at Cleveland-Marshall College of Law at Cleveland State University. She has both a J.D and a Ph.D. in Psychology from the University of Nebraska. Most of Falk's article, like Fradella's, discusses recent trends in criminal law to excuse criminal defendants based upon their exposure to certain environmental factors. The excerpt included here is her conclusion about why courts should embrace the new theories of criminal defense that take this exposure into account.

The third piece is an essay by Phillip Johnson that appeared in a recent book from Yale University Press, *Christian Perspectives on Legal Thought*. Johnson is the Jefferson E. Peyser Professor of Law, Emeritus at the Boalt Hall School of Law at the University of California-Berkeley. Johnson received an A.B. from Harvard University and a J.D. from the University of Chicago Law School. His specialty is criminal law, an area in which he has published numerous articles and a casebook. In recent years, Johnson has done a great deal of writing and speaking regarding the impact of evolutionary theory and naturalistic philosophy on science, education, and law. He is the author of a number of influential works in this area, including *Darwin on Trial* and *Reason in the Balance.*

In the essay reproduced here, Johnson discusses the influence that evolutionary theory and naturalistic philosophy had on the development of insanity law in the 20th century. He concludes that the criminal law ultimately—and correctly—rejected an evolutionary view of human nature and responsibility in favor of a more biblical view.

Henry Fradella, *From Insanity to Beyond Diminished Capacity: Mental Illness and Criminal Excuse in the Post-Clark Era*[*]

The insanity defense is one way the law operates to relieve criminal responsibility from those who, as a result of mental illness, do not act with true moral culpability. But there are significant restrictions on the availability of the insanity defense. Consider people who are mentally ill, but not "severely" enough to qualify as legally insane under IDRA [Insanity Defense Reform Act of 1984] and its progeny. Alternatively, consider people who are severely mentally ill, but still knew both the nature and quality of their acts and the difference between right and wrong. Although the law generally does not recognize such conditions as qualifying for a total excuse defense, defendants with such impairments may not be as culpable as those who are not mentally ill. For such persons, the doctrine of diminished capacity might be available to mitigate their criminal responsibility, their sentence, or in some circumstances, even excuse their criminal responsibility altogether.

A. Attempting a Definition of Diminished Capacity

Unfortunately, there is no standard definition for the doctrine of diminished capacity. The doctrine exists, either statutorily or in case law, in more than half of all U.S. jurisdictions. Although diminished capacity is often referred to as a defense, doing so is somewhat inappropriate. As commentators have often pointed out, it is not a defense at all, but rather deals with the admissibility of evidence concerning the accused's mental state.

* * *

---

[*] Henry Fradella, *From Insanity to Beyond Diminished Capacity: Mental Illness and Criminal Excuse in the Post-Clark Era*, 18 U. FLA. J.L. & PUB. POL'Y 7, 47-48, 52-70 (2007). Excerpts printed with permission from the *University of Florida Journal of Law & Public Policy* © 2007.

IV. Beyond Diminished Capacity

The rationale underlying diminished capacity has been extended to a variety of situations. By its use, defendants share the common goal to reduce criminal liability "due to some extenuating circumstance that allegedly rendered the defendant unable to form the requisite mens rea of a crime or led to it being formed defectively—as a result of some mental condition rather than out of 'normal' criminal intent." Accordingly, these "defenses" are really just extensions of diminished capacity.

A. Posttraumatic Stress Disorder Defense

Extreme cases of Posttraumatic Stress Disorder (PTSD) may serve as the qualifying "mental disease or defect" for an insanity defense. Of course, to do so effectively in the overwhelming majority of courts in the United States, the disorder would have to render the defendant unable to substantially appreciate the wrongfulness or criminality of his or her actions. But if the level of impairment does not rise to the level of insanity, the disorder may still be used as the predicate for a finding of diminished capacity.

PTSD was first noted in America after the Civil War, though little was known about it then. Subsequent wars, especially the two World Wars (during which time it was often referred to as "shell shock" and "combat fatigue") and the Vietnam War, led to study of the condition. PTSD was recognized as a mental disorder in 1980 by the American Psychiatric Association. The condition originally applied only to veterans of wars who experienced intense "flashbacks" to times of combat. During these flashbacks, individuals were known to have violent outbreaks, but PTSD evolved to encompass almost any individual who experienced extreme trauma or violence. Such exposure remains a "necessary, but not sufficient, condition for the development of PTSD." Because PTSD can affect one's perception of reality, including the circumstances in which one finds oneself even in "normal" situations, PTSD can interfere with the formation of mens rea and therefore serve as a predicate for introducing diminished capacity evidence.

Since its acceptance as a bona fide medical condition, courts have been more accepting of the PTSD defense than other excuse defenses since it appears to be the very type of disorder diminished capacity is designed to encompass. For example, in *State v. Phipps*, the defendant was a Gulf War veteran who was on trial for murder. On the day in question, Phipps went to his wife's home, where upon he got into an argument with his wife's lover who threatened Phipps with a stick. Phipps took the stick and hit the wife's lover repeatedly with it, eventually killing him. At trial, the defense presented expert testimony that Phipps suffered from depression and posttraumatic stress disorder. Even the prosecution's expert testified that his impairment was "'of a sufficient level to significantly affect his thinking, reasoning, judgment, and emotional well-being.'" Moreover, his PTSD "'may have lessened his threshold or made him more sensitive to defending himself and protecting himself and increased the likelihood of him overreacting to a real or perceived threat.'"

The trial court judge refused to give a jury instruction which would have allowed the jury to consider the evidence of mental disorders in relation to whether Phipps possessed the required mens rea for first-degree murder. The appeals court reversed the decision, holding that evidence of the defendant's mental state at the time of the offense is admissible to refute elements of specific intent in first-degree murder cases.

But the acceptance of PTSD as a form of diminished capacity has not been universal, in spite of the generally accepted proposition that PTSD impairs an individual's mental functioning. Some critics have challenged the diagnosis of the disorder as being overly subjective, largely due to the fact that a PTSD diagnosis is based on patient testimonials and personal observations. These critics fear that the disorder is often contrived just for the purposes of criminal defense. Efforts are underway to provide a physiological basis for PTSD diagnosis, rather than relying on the patient's subjective assertions. As of yet, no physiological evidence has been presented to a court. For now, in those jurisdictions that allow the use of diminished capacity evidence, mental health professionals are generally allowed to testify not only as to whether the defendant has PTSD, but also whether the disorder influenced the defendant's capacity to form the requisite criminal intent at the time of the offense.

B. Battered Women's Syndrome Defense

1. Battered Women's Syndrome Defense

Dr. Lenore Walker first coined the term "Battered Women's Syndrome" (BWS) in her 1979 book, *The Battered Woman*. In it, Walker put forth a theory that attempted to explain why abused women stayed in abusive relationships, and what finally triggers them to strike back. Walker's research has been criticized as "little more than a patchwork of pseudo-scientific methods employed to confirm a hypothesis that its author and participating researchers never seriously doubted." Such criticisms aside, there can be no doubt that Walker's work had a significant impact on the law, even if not on psychology. Her theory of BWS has been accepted in many U.S. courts and continues to enjoy widespread acceptance.

As conceptualized by Walker, BWS develops as a result of exposure to a three-phase cycle of violence that typifies abusive relationships. The first phase is called the "tension-building phase," which is characterized by arguments and ever increasing tensions and may include minor acts of violence, such as slapping. Eventually, however, there is an event that triggers the second phase, which Walker calls the "acute battering incident." During this phase, the abuser explodes in a fit of rage and batters the victim. Walker hypothesized that the acute battering incident causes the abuser to feel and express remorse, apologize profusely, and engage in loving, caring, and helpful behaviors to promote reconciliation. In spite of the abuser's promises that it will "never happen again," the cycle inevitably repeats itself.

* * *

Walker used the theory of learned helplessness to explain why battered women do not leave abusive relationships.... According to Walker, a woman stays for a number of psycho-social reasons. She may have old-fashioned notions that "a woman's proper place is in the home." She may be economically dependent on the abuser. They may have children and the woman may not want to separate them from their father. The stigma that attaches to a woman who leaves the family without her children undoubtedly also acts as a further deterrent to moving out. Some women may even perceive the battering cycle as normal, especially if they grew up in a violent household. And even when battered women want to leave, they are typically unwilling to reach out and confide in their friends, family, or the police, either out of shame and humiliation, fear of reprisal by their husband, or the feeling they will not be believed. But one of the most important factors for Walker in a woman's decision to stay with her abuser is the loving and caring behavior the batterer exhibits during the reconciliation phase. For Walker, the abuser's contrite behavior acts as a "positive reinforcement for [the victim] remaining in the relationship."

The combination of the above factors leads a victim of abuse to feel powerless to leave. Moreover, as she stays and tries to prevent the cycle of violence from repeating, she learns that it is not really within her power to control the abuser's feelings and temper. Her repeated failures to prevent tension from building up to an acute battering incident mirrors the learning of the dogs in Seligman's research. The repeated, failed attempts "to control the violence would, over time, produce learned helplessness and depression as the repeated batterings, like electrical shocks, [would] diminish the woman's motivation to respond."

The cycle of violence tends to worsen as time passes. Not only may acute battering incidents become more frequent, but also they may become more severe. Eventually, however, the woman endures "so much frustration, despair, and isolation that her perceptions of violence are altered. The woman may violently strike back against the batterer in an effort to free herself from the cycle of abuse that she may believe ultimately will lead to her death." When the woman's strike-back leads to the filing of criminal charges against her for aggravated assault or homicide because the elements of the traditional defense of self-defense appear to be missing, BWS evidence will normally become the foundation of the woman's defense.

2. Emergence of a Battered Women's Syndrome Defense

Whether there is actually a Battered Women's Syndrome Defense (BWSD) is a matter of some controversy. "The defense of battered women who kill their mates is slowly developing a distinct style or technique called the abused spouse defense," which is a hybrid of "the more familiar and established defenses of self-defense and diminished capacity." Others insist it is not a defense in and of itself, but rather a psychological theory offered in support of the traditional defense of self-defense.

The purpose of offering evidence of BWS is to fill a gap left by the law of self-defense and by the PTSD. BWSD is most frequently used in courts to explain the behavior of women who turn on their abusers and, in turn, to reduce their criminal responsibility. BWSD is similar to PTSD in that the defendant's prior history or experience triggers a violent response. Battered women were frequently unable to assert PTSD, however, because they could not fulfill all of the diagnostic requirements of PTSD.

The traditional self-defense doctrine recognizes the legitimacy of the use of force only when necessary to prevent an imminent attack from unlawful force. As such, when a battered woman uses force to defend herself from such an unlawful, imminent attack, there is no problem in using the defense of self-defense. But in many cases, battered women act against their abusers when they are not in "imminent danger" and, therefore, are not acting within the technical requirements of the law of self-defense. Alternatively, battered women may use deadly force when they were confronted only with physical force, another requirement of the law of self-defense. BWS evidence can help to explain why a woman might reasonably believe, in light of her history of abuse, her life was in danger, even though to the lay person she was not facing what objectively looked like a threat of imminent, unlawful force.

* * *

3. Validity of the BWS Defense

As noted above, Walker's research suffered from serious methodological flaws. In fact, the research fails to demonstrate that abused women experience the cycle of violence as explained by Walker or that abused women learn they are helpless to prevent it. Consequently, some courts have excluded BWS evidence as unreliable. However, in spite of these shortcomings, many courts continue to embrace BWS testimony in BWS cases. Some believe this is driven by political motivation (i.e., not wanting to seem unsympathetic to the plight of the battered woman), while others see it as blind adherence to precedent established in the wake of Walker's initial research without critically examining the questionable reliability and validity of the BWS as elucidated by contemporary research. Regardless of the reasons underlying its continued acceptance, it is clear that many states continue to allow BWS evidence. The presentation of psychological evidence concerning both the syndrome itself and the application of it to the facts of any particular case, therefore, remains an important function of forensic psychologists and psychiatrists.

C. Black Rage defense

The Black Rage defense is arguably the most controversial extension of the diminished capacity doctrine. Although discussed in the literature from time to time, the defense was brought into the spotlight during the trial of Colin Ferguson. Ferguson had opened fire on a Long Island railroad car full of passengers, killing six people and injuring nineteen more. After his arrest for the 1994 shooting, police discovered writings in which Ferguson wrote of his hatred for "whites, Asians and Uncle Tom Negroes," which led his lawyer, the late, celebrated civil rights attorney William Kunstler, to formulate a variant of the PTSD defense predicated upon "black rage." Before trial, however, Ferguson fired Kunstler and was granted permission to represent himself pro se. When acting as his own attorney (his competence to do so being highly questionable), Ferguson did not argue Black Rage. Instead, and in spite of a train car full of eyewitnesses, he argued that he had fallen asleep on the train and someone else stole his gun from his bag and committed the shootings. The

Black Rage defense, therefore, was never tested in court. It did, however, provoke national debate over the legitimacy of such a defense.

* * *

The theoretical underpinning of the Black Rage defense is clearly the diminished capacity doctrine. Psychiatrists William H. Grier and Price M. Cobbs first advanced the notion of Black Rage in 1969 when they asserted that African-Americans, as an insular racial minority in the United States, have endured years of discrimination starting in colonial days with slavery and continuing to the present. This discrimination resulted in inadequate educational and employment opportunities for African-Americans as a group, and thus disproportionate suffering from poverty and high unemployment. As a result of this significant inequality, African-Americans suffer both "pent-up frustration" and "'cultural paranoia' in which every member of the white race is a possible enemy." The frustration and the paranoia eventually builds to a point of "blind rage, hatred, and ultimately, lethal violence" when someone suffering from Black Rage retaliates against one or more of the perceived oppressors, namely members of the white race.

The notion of building frustration leading to violence embodied in the concept of Black Rage is referred to as frustration-aggression. The Black Rage defense does not seek to excuse conduct along the lines of the insanity defense. Rather, it seeks to explain the evolution of anger so intense that it can impair someone's capacity to form mens rea in a normal way.

The Black Rage defense has been criticized as an invalid extension of other forms of diminished capacity. PTSD, for example, seeks to explain the conduct of a single person which arose in connection with an identifiable, traumatic event that is generally outside the range of usual human experience, such as "military combat, violent personal assault, being kidnapped, being taken hostage, terrorist attack, torture, [and] incarceration as a prisoner of war or in a concentration camp." Although there is no doubt that African-Americans have endured invidious discrimination, it is highly questionable whether discrimination in the post-civil rights era would qualify as a trauma of such magnitude that it could cause something akin to PTSD. Moreover, to the extent that it might qualify, even harsh discrimination is quite different from a traumatic occurrence. For example, if one witnessed a family member as the victim of a racially motivated lynching, such an experience would be well within the diagnostic predicate for PTSD and its associated defense based on diminished capacity. However, blanket assertions of racism over one's lifetime do not demonstrate the same clear requisite trauma. Other groups have faced intense forms of racism and oppression, including women, Jews, homosexuals, and certain ethnicities at various points in history. Yet, there has been no significant movement to classify any such groups as candidates for a variant of PTSD sufficient to diminish the capacity to form mens rea.

Some might argue that Black Rage is more similar to the development of BWS, since a cycle of mistreatment over time is allegedly responsible for both, and the victim feels helpless to overcome or escape from that which inflicts the suffering. Copp pointed out, however, that when a battered woman strikes back, she does so at her abuser. In doing so, she insulates herself from future abuse at his hands. In contrast, someone with Black Rage has no readily identifiable person at the root of his or her oppression, nor will striking out against someone eliminate racism or discrimination.

To date, the debate about the propriety of using Black Rage as a criminal defense has been mostly academic. It is feasible that forensic mental health professionals might be called upon to assess someone suffering from Black Rage. But in light of the fact that it is not recognized as a mental disorder in the DSM-IV-TR, it is questionable whether it would be accepted in court as a bona fide defense....

D. The PMS Defense

* * *

2. The PMS Defense

PMS was first used to mitigate criminal culpability in England where it was first recognized as a variant of diminished responsibility. Defendants in the United States, however, have attempted to use PMS as a type of diminished capacity defense to wholly excuse their conduct. In *People v. Santos*, one of [sic] first cases to attempt such a use of the PMS defense, the legitimacy of the defense was not tested at trial since the parties negotiated a plea bargain after the defendant gave notice of her intent to use the defense. Other cases attempting to use PMS as a defense were rejected in the years following Santos.

In 1991, however, the first successful PMS defense in the United States was used in a Virginia trial in *Commonwealth v. Richter*. The defendant was a physician who was stopped for erratic driving. She had her children in the car with her. The state trooper who pulled her over noticed a strong smell of alcohol on her breath. The defendant refused to take field sobriety tests, tried to kick the officer in the groin, used offensive language, and threatened the officer by saying, "You son of a [expletive]; you [expletive] can't do this to me; I'm a doctor. I hope you [expletive] get shot and come to my hospital so I can refuse to treat you...."

At her trial for driving under the influence, the defendant's attorney successfully used a dual line of defense. First, the defense argued the results of the breathalyzer test, which yielded a 0.13% blood alcohol concentration, were invalid. The defense then attempted to explain her hostile conduct was due to PMS, not intoxication. The defendant was found not guilty. Given the unique facts of this case, it is important to note that the PMS defense was not specifically accepted or rejected in *Richter*. Rather, it was used to explain the defendant's hostile and combative behavior, thereby assisting in the creation of reasonable doubt with respect to whether she had been driving while intoxicated.

In the years since *Richter*, PMDD [Premenstrual Dysmorphic Disorder] was officially recognized in the DSM-IV. Whether it will be accepted as a qualifying mental disease or defect for insanity or for diminished capacity purposes has not yet been determined. Critics argue that medical disagreement about its cause, symptoms, and treatment makes it very difficult for PMS to gain legal recognition as a complete defense. Even if allowed, using the defense successfully might prove very difficult in light of the fact that the diagnosis is almost completely dependent on self-reported data from an obviously interested party (i.e., a criminal defendant) and other biased witnesses who are close to her.

Other critics of the PMS defense argue that it is a dangerous precedent that can be used to encroach upon women's rights. Its use could lead to the societal labeling of women as "deficient" or being "mentally and physically unstable." Such arguments, if accepted, could be used to justify keeping women out of certain executive and military roles and could even be used against women in divorce or custody proceedings. In spite of these concerns, supporters of the defense feel it should be used as a tool to mitigate punishment and to provide for therapeutic sentencing. Whatever its future, it is clear that forensic behavioral scientists will play an important role in the evolution of the PMS defense.

E. Media Intoxication

A number of cases have asserted claims of insanity based on "media intoxication" from television, movies, pornography, and music. These cases have all been unsuccessful in their quests to do so. For example, in the case of *Florida v. Zamora*, a fifteen-year-old boy was accused of killing an eighty-two-year-old woman after breaking into her house and stealing a gun and money. Zamora's attorney pled insanity on his behalf. In support of the insanity claim, the defense offered evidence that

Zamora acted under a state of pseudo-intoxication resulting from watching hours of violent television programs which, in turn, drove the boy to kill the woman. The trial court refused to allow testimony on television intoxication, finding it to be irrelevant to the question of Zamora's insanity.

Media intoxication, however, could meet with more success in the diminished capacity realm, although to date, such attempts have been generally unsuccessful. In a provocative article, Patricia Falk reviewed the extensive body of literature addressing the nature and effects of media intoxication and addiction. She noted: "[t]he primary, and almost unanimous, finding common to this extensive body of research is that a positive correlation exists between viewing violent television programs and subsequent aggressive behavior." Similar research findings have linked violence against women to the viewing of pornography. Serial killer Bobby Joe Long asserted in the sentencing phase of his murder trial that his addiction to violent pornography should have constituted a mitigating factor against the death penalty. This argument was rejected by the jury and he was sentenced him [sic] to death.

In *Schiro v. Clark*, the defendant "argued that he was a sexual sadist and that his extensive viewing of rape pornography and snuff films rendered him unable to distinguish right from wrong." The defendant produced the testimony of two leading experts on the link between violence and pornography and sought to have it used as evidence of insanity and as a type of intoxication which the applicable state law recognized as a mitigating factor. The defendant was convicted and his subsequent appeals were all denied on the rationale that allowing a criminal defense based on exposure to materials protected by the First Amendment would be incongruous. Similar reasoning resulted in the unsuccessful assertion of an analogous argument using music lyrics in the case of Ronald Ray Howard. The nineteen-year-old defendant killed a police officer and sought to avoid the death penalty by arguing that his addiction to "gangsta rap" was a mitigating factor. The argument was rejected by the jury who sentenced Howard to death.

The link between violence depicted in different media forms and actual violence will continue to be an important part of expert testimony in both civil and criminal cases. Whether media intoxication is eventually is [sic] accepted as a form or [sic] either diminished capacity or diminished responsibility remains to be seen. Either way, defense attorneys will undoubtedly call upon forensic mental health clinicians to assess defendants who assert the defense in guilt and sentencing phases of criminal trials.

F. Summary of Diminished Capacity Evidence

Part III should make clear that criminal defendants have attempted to expand the notion of diminished capacity into a multitude of defenses with varying degrees of success. Diminished capacity arguments based on bona fide mental illnesses that interfere with sensation, perception, and cognition tend to fare well. In contrast, attempts to cast defendants as less culpable because they were victims of abuse or neglect generally do not succeed. This ever-increasing trend towards disease-based explanations for criminal behavior has clearly taken a toll on public attitudes towards excuse defenses based on mental illness. While defendants and their lawyers who seek to avoid punishment are partially to blame, behavioral scientists also share in the responsibility for this trend.

"The abuse excuse," "battered woman syndrome," "child sexual abuse accommodation syndrome," "false memory syndrome," "television intoxication," "urban survival syndrome," "XYY chromosome abnormality"—"these are just a few of the colorful appellations used to describe claims that mental health professionals have bolstered with their testimony over the years." "From reading the popular press, one could easily come to the conclusion that such testimony is spurious 'psychobabble' that will eventually swallow up our justice system."

An overwhelming number of psychologists and psychiatrists do not take part in sensational trials that attempt to extend diminished capacity into the realm of questionable scientific practice. Media attention on the few cases that are the exception to this rule, however, has had real and palpable effects on the jurisprudence of defenses of excuse. The perception that these defenses undermine legal notions of autonomy, free-will, and personal responsibility has led legislatures, judges, and juries to "define the grounds of excuse too narrowly." The abolition of the insanity defense in favor of the mens rea approach is one of the best examples of the efforts to narrow legitimate criminal excuse. Other examples include the move towards "guilty except insane" formulations of the insanity defense and the elimination of diminished capacity evidence altogether, even when offered to challenge the defendant's alleged formation of mens rea.

Patricia Falk, *Novel Theories of Criminal Defense Based Upon the Toxicity of the Social Environment: Urban Psychosis, Television Intoxication and Black Rage*[*]

We cannot rationally decry crime and brutality and racial animosity without at the same time struggling to enhance the fairness and integrity of the criminal justice system. That system has first-line responsibility for probing and coping with these complex problems.

Acid rain, ozone depletion, the greenhouse effect—environmentalists are warning us that our physical milieu is becoming increasingly polluted and toxic. But the physical environment is not the only one suffering from degradation. Social scientists are beginning to document that our social environment is also becoming increasingly toxic to members of our society. Three of the most pervasive and noxious components of this social toxicity are real-life violence, media violence, and racism.

The consequences of the increasing toxicity of our social environment are less noticeable than rivers on fire, the results of acid rain, or the clouds of smog hanging over major industrial cities. The effects of social toxins are reflected in the human component of our society, taking the form of developmental impairment and psychological, psychiatric, and medical damage to the citizenry. As one author wrote about the devastating effects of real-life violence but with equal applicability to other social toxins: "Chronic violence in the community permeates every aspect of these children's lives, affecting their families, their education and their sense of self, hence also affecting what type of citizen they will mature into."

The criminal justice system, in the guise of defendants' presentation of new theories of defense such as urban psychosis, television intoxication, and black rage, and those that are sure to follow, will be asked to accommodate increasing knowledge about the toxicity of the social environment and its psychological sequelae within the context of established criminal law doctrine. These theories of defense demand thoughtful, reasoned consideration commensurate with the importance and complexity of the challenges which they pose for the evolution of criminal law.

---

[*] Patricia Falk, *Novel Theories of Criminal Defense Based Upon the Toxicity of the Social Environment: Urban Psychosis, Television Intoxication and Black Rage*, 74 N.C. L. REV. 731, 810-11 (1996). Reprinted with the permission of the North Carolina Law Review.

Law is not a static entity, numbly frozen in time and divorced from the current realities of modern life. Law must continue to evolve in response to the changing world in which it functions. As Holmes commented, "The life of the law has not been logic: it has been experience." Legal evolution requires the integration of information coming from other bodies of knowledge, including the social sciences. As Justice Murphy observed fifty years ago in *United States v. Fisher*: "[T]hese claims, whatever their merit, afford a rare opportunity to explore some of the frontiers of criminal law, frontiers that are slowly but undeniably expanding under the impact of our increasing knowledge of psychology and psychiatry." The defense theories of urban psychosis, television intoxication, and black rage are on the current frontiers of the criminal law. Recognition of their importance and their fit within the existing doctrinal structure is recognition of a changing society and its sometimes deleterious effects on the human psyche.

Phillip E. Johnson, *Human Nature and Criminal Responsibility: The Biblical View Restored*[*]

At the beginning of *The Selfish Gene*, Richard Dawkins poses the question "What is man?" and in answer quotes with approval George Gaylord Simpson's comment that "all attempts to answer that question before 1859 are worthless and that we will be better off if we ignore them completely." Eighteen fifty-nine was the year of publication of Darwin's *Origin of Species*, and what Dawkins and Simpson meant was that Darwin did not just say that humans descended from monkeys. What Darwinian theory came to mean is that human beings, like other animals, are a part of nature and hence can in principle be completely comprehended in terms of material causes that are accessible to scientific investigation. In the words of the evolutionary geneticist Richard Lewontin, "We exist as material beings in a material world, all of whose phenomena are the consequences of material relations among material entities." To put the same point in the negative, scientific materialists see no need to invoke a mysterious "soul" or spiritual dimension to understand human nature. Scientists comprehend living organisms in terms of their chemistry, particularly their genes, and the environmental influences

[*] Phillip E. Johnson, *Human Nature and Criminal Responsibility: The Biblical View Restored*, *in* CHRISTIAN PERSPECTIVES ON LEGAL THOUGHT 426, 426-34 (Michael W. McConnell, Robert F. Cochran, Jr., & Agnela C. Carmella eds., 2001). Reprinted with the permission of the author.

(also material) to which they are subject. Scientific explanations of human nature and behavior thus are framed in terms of some combination of heredity and environment, because the ruling assumption is that these factors exhaust the possibilities.

In short, human behavior, like all other natural phenomena, is caused. From a scientific materialist point of view, it is virtually meaningless to say that a person "chose" to commit a particular action. What is important is to understand what combination of genetic or environmental circumstances caused him to commit this action rather than a different one. In the more logically rigorous versions of this model, the human subject itself—the "I" in "I choose"—is taken to be merely a placeholder for causative factors that we do not yet understand. It follows that the rational approach for a discipline of criminology is to discover the "root causes" of crime, whether genetic, psychological, or sociological—and having discovered them, to ameliorate them. Blame and retributive punishment are seen as relics of prescientific superstition, premised on a view of human nature that science has discarded.

This scientific materialist view is often qualified in important ways, indeed in ways that may seem to contradict its central point. I will get to the qualifications in due course, but for now I want to inquire into the influence of the basic premise of scientific causation upon criminal law. How did the scientific revolution that occurred after 1859 change our notions of criminal responsibility, and was the change a success or a flop?

The inquiry is important because the criminal law handed down to us by pre-Darwinian legal authorities has traditionally been based on quite different assumptions. Perhaps the clearest example is the classic *M'Naghten* definition of the insanity defense, which takes its name from an English decision in 1843, just sixteen years before the publication of *Origin of Species*. According to the *M'Naghten* rule, an accused is excused from criminal punishment (but usually remitted to civil commitment) only if "at the time of committing the act, the party accused was laboring under such a defect of reason, from disease of the mind, as not to know the nature and quality of the act he was doing, or if he did know it, that he did not know he was doing what was wrong."

The concept of human responsibility assumed by that legalistic formula finds its metaphysical support in biblical theism, not scientific materialism. First, there is no reference to free will, or to the opposing concept of compulsion, because the law conclusively presumed that human adults have freedom to choose between good and evil. What the test puts in issue is not the defendant's freedom but his knowledge of the wrongfulness of his act. Second, the knowledge in question is not of legal wrongfulness but of moral wrongfulness. As the old maxim says, ignorance of the law is no excuse. What responsible persons are deemed to know is not that the law forbids murder, theft, perjury, and adultery (as it once did) but that such deeds are wrongful and would be so even if the law permitted them. If God is the ultimate source of morality, then the concept of a moral order independent of positive law makes sense. Matter by itself has no morality; nor does Darwinian evolution. When there is no transcendent authority, morality can be constructed only by human choice, which is why variations on the theme of a social contract have come to have such importance in contemporary moral theory.

When a person does know right from wrong, the *M'Naghten* standard holds him responsible for his choice. There is no concept of an irresistible compulsion to commit evil deeds because the defense is based solely on cognitive factors. Persons who do not know the nature and moral quality of their acts are analogous to small children, who may say "Bang! Bang!" and point a loaded pistol at a playmate without grasping the consequences of what they are doing. This is a very narrow exception to the general rules of responsibility, and successful insanity defenses are consequently rare. Successful defendants under *M'Naghten* are also generally so incapable of living in normal circumstances that there is no question of granting them freedom. Liberal reformers have often thought that a broader defense would more adequately take account of the irrationality of much criminal behavior, but they never had a clear idea what to do with nearly normal people who commit crimes and are not convicted. The problem became particularly acute when public policy turned to deinstitutionalizing the mentally ill. If insanity acquittees were treated like other mentally ill people, they would be speedily released to the streets. It they were confined in an institution because they had committed a crime, then in what sense could they be said to have been acquitted?

Be that as it may, Darwinism at its flood tide certainly did influence our ideas of criminal responsibility, but only temporarily. The main point of entry was through the insanity defense, as reformulated by the Model Penal Code of the American Law Institute (hereafter ALI), which represents the elite of the legal profession. At its high-water mark around 1980, the ALI test was the law in every federal circuit court and in about half of the states. The ALI version of the insanity defense proposed that "a person is not responsible for criminal conduct if at the time of such conduct as a result of mental disease or defect he lacks substantial capacity either to appreciate the wrongfulness of his conduct or to conform his conduct to the requirements of law." Superficially, this formulation may seem no more than a modest expansion of the *M'Naghten* rule. It retains the concept of knowledge of wrongfulness, only broadening the defense to excuse one who "knows" that his conduct is wrongful but lacks substantial capacity to "appreciate" this very point. The radical difference is in the introduction of a new excuse for a defendant who lacks "substantial capacity...to conform his conduct to the requirements of law." This new element reflected a philosophical position called "soft determinism," which is best described as an uneasy halfway house between the scientific model (behavior is caused) and the common-law model (behavior is chosen). For soft determinists the question is one of degree, rather than either/or, and criminal acts represent a continuum between freely chosen at one pole and totally compelled at the other. The jury, guided by expert testimony, was expected to locate the particular defendant's act on the continuum and somehow to decide whether that location fell inside or outside the imaginary boundary of "substantial capacity to conform."

Other tests of mental incapacity that flourished during the same period (around 1960) reflected the same soft determinist philosophy and the same logical quagmire over where to draw the boundary between free will and compulsion. The District of Columbia's *Durham* formula, judicially enacted in 1954 and replaced by the ALI formula in 1972, said that an accused should be found not guilty by reason of insanity if his act was the "product of a mental disease or defect." The California Supreme Court grafted a mental-illness defense onto its definition of "malice aforethought" so that a killer who could not control his conduct would be convicted of manslaughter rather than murder.[6] All these tests came to grief once they were tested in practice, for reasons I will explain presently, and so they are best understood as reflecting a cultural and ideological moment rather than a permanent trend in the law.

In my opinion the vogue for these soft determinist defenses, which aimed to split the difference between scientific and traditional understandings of human action, is best explained by two circumstances. First, the defenses flourished (in the sense of being approved by scholars and appellate judges) during a period in which the death penalty was being vigorously attacked, and eventual abolition of capital punishment seemed probable. Allowing expert witnesses the greatest leeway to present mitigating circumstances as scientific knowledge seemed an effec-

---

[6] *See People v. Gorshen*, 51 Cal.2d 716 (1959). The California defense of "diminished mental capacity" was eventually abolished by a combination of legislation and a ballot initiative in the early 1980s. There was bipartisan reaction against the diminished-capacity defense after a notorious case in which a disappointed politician named Dan White assassinated two popular public officials in San Francisco and was convicted only of manslaughter. Because one element in the psychiatric defense involved an assertion that White behaved impulsively after gorging himself on high-sugar foods, the lenient verdict was popularly attributed to "the Twinkie defense."

tive way of reducing the number of death penalty verdicts during the period while the abolition movement was gathering support. Progress (if that is the correct term) in this direction was halted in 1976 by the Supreme Court's decision in *Gregg v. Georgia*. The Supreme Court decision probably reflected the fact that the death penalty opponents by then had lost their case decisively in the court of public opinion.

Second, the mid-twentieth century was a period of scientific hubris sparked by such genuine triumphs of technology as radar, nuclear bombs, antibiotics, insecticides, the polio vaccine, and space travel. It seemed that science, accompanied by the scientific materialist ideology, provided the most promising way to deal with previously intractable social problems such as crime. Soft determinism could be justified as an illogical but practical compromise between the traditional and scientific models for the time being, with the expectation that the scientific model would eventually triumph. Progress (again, if that is the correct term) in this direction was set back in 1968 by the Supreme Court's decision in *Powell v. Texas*, in which the very liberal Justice Thurgood Marshall's opinion held that a chronic alcoholic may be punished for public intoxication notwithstanding an apparent scientific consensus that "alcoholism is a disease."

The ALI insanity defense outlived its historical moment, mainly because juries ignored it. All it took was for the defense to have tangible consequences in a highly publicized case, and immediately a bipartisan consensus appeared in support of a return to the *M'Naghten* rule.

The seminal event was the attempted assassination of President Ronald Reagan by John Hinckley, who hoped to attract the attention of a movie star he was stalking by this daring act of self-sacrifice. By traditional standards Hinckley was dead-bang guilty of attempted murder and related crimes. But he came to trial in a federal court in the District of Columbia, in a legal culture that by this time had absorbed not only the letter of the ALI defense but also its spirit. Hinckley, whose parents were both wealthy and devoted to him, had the benefit not only of the ALI standard, and of the testimony of expert witnesses with sterling scientific qualifications, but also of the general principle of evidence that the burden of proof rests on the prosecution, not the defense. Thus the federal rule required the prosecutor to prove beyond a reasonable doubt that a demented man, who had attempted to assassinate a president for utterly bizarre reasons, was not insane. Ordinarily one can rely upon a jury to ignore unrealistic legal standards, but the Hinckley jury surprised everyone by taking the judge's instructions seriously and returning a verdict of not guilty.

Hinckley himself gained little or nothing by the verdict. The courts remitted him to civil custody in a secure mental hospital, and there he remains to this day, though most civil committees are released after a few months of treatment. But the prospect of his release convinced the public that it was the legal standard that was insane, and that a standard as loose as that of the ALI insanity defense could permit rich people to buy a verdict. The resulting counterrevolution led Congress to take the issue away from the judges by enacting a modernized version of the *M'Naghten* rule, omitting the defense for a defendant who "lacks substantial capacity to conform his conduct to the requirements of law" and placing the burden of proof squarely on the defense. The federal Insanity Defense Reform Act of 1984 now provides as follows:

> (a) Affirmative defense. It is an affirmative defense to a prosecution under any federal statute that, at the time of the commission of the acts constituting the defense, the defendant, as a result of a severe mental disease or defect, was unable to appreciate the nature and quality or the wrongfulness of his acts. Mental disease or defect does not otherwise constitute a defense.
>
> (b) Burden of Proof. The defendant has the burden of proving the defense of insanity by clear and convincing evidence.

Superficially, one might have interpreted the public reaction to the Hinckley verdict as a victory of popular opinion over the experts. The trouble with this interpretation is that the American Psychiatric Association (APA), the official voice of the psychiatric profession, enthusiastically agreed with the popular decision. The APA's 1982 *Statement on the Insanity Defense* was clear in its conclusion but confused in its reasoning. It started by assuming that the basis of criminal punishment is moral culpability and that there must therefore logically be a defense for defendants who do not possess free will and therefore cannot be said to have "chosen to do wrong." Despite this soft-determinist rationale for the insanity defense, the APA recommended that the law drop the concept of lack of free will and go back to the *M'Naghten* formula. Why? The APA statement explained that psychiatric testimony about whether a defendant understood the wrongfulness of his act "is more reliable and has a stronger scientific basis" than does psychiatric testimony about whether a defendant could control his behavior. The APA acknowledged that "psychiatry is a deterministic discipline that views all human behavior as, to a good extent, 'caused.'" On the other hand, the APA admitted that psychiatrists disagree about how these deterministic presuppositions should affect the moral and philosophical question of whether a person is responsible for his conduct. Expert testimony about volitional capacity (free will) is therefore likely to be confusing to the jury, and psychiatrists like other people are therefore content to restrict psychiatric testimony to the old standard of "knowledge of wrongfulness."

I do not take this mishmash seriously. If scientific psychiatry views all behavior as caused, then psychiatrists never should have undertaken to draw a line between behavior that is caused and behavior that is chosen in the first place. Yet eminent psychiatrists were involved in drafting the ALI standard, and the legal experts thought that the psychiatrists were pleased with it. Why did psychiatrists not object from the beginning that the crucial dividing line between caused behavior and chosen behavior does not exist? Why does the APA continue to say that there should be a defense for those defendants who lack free will if nobody has free will? And what scientific content does the concept of "wrongfulness" have? One reason the federal courts rapidly adopted the ALI test was that the psychiatrists had told them that the old *M'Naghten* formula was so unsatisfactory that expert witnesses even found it necessary to commit "professional perjury" to couch their testimony in terms of right and wrong when they really wanted to testify that the defendant lacked free will.

A better explanation for the APA's changed attitude was that the psychiatric profession had changed drastically between the 1950s and the 1980s. The experts who had supported the broadened insanity and diminished-mental-capacity defenses were mainly Freudian in orientation and had ambitions for political and social reform that far outstripped the modest therapeutic value of their "talking cure." The result was that they promised a great deal more than they could deliver, in terms both of a scientific understanding of why people commit crimes and of a practical knowledge of what to do about it. The subjectiveness of Freudian explanations led to the notorious courtroom "battle of the experts" and consequent public ridicule of the psychiatric profession as witch doctors or "headshrinkers." By 1982 psychiatric medicine had turned away from psychoanalysis in favor of innovative drug therapies that were genuinely effective in mitigating psychotic behavior. Greater knowledge led to greater modesty, and most psychiatrists now found the pretentious claims of the Freudians absurd. In short, psychiatry wanted to escape from an embarrassing situation, and going back to a much narrower test offered a way out.

By the end of the twentieth century, the idea of replacing retributive justice with a scientific search for the "root causes" of criminal behavior was virtually dead. There has been some confusion about this in the public mind because of a few high-profile cases in which a fashionable "abuse excuse" has seemed to be successful. The leading example was the first trial in the notorious Menendez brothers case in Los Angeles County, California. The brothers, who had cold-bloodedly murdered their wealthy parents, claimed that they acted in self-defense because the parents were planning to kill them to cover up a history of sexual abuse. The defense managed to muddy the waters enough with this preposterous story that the jurors could not agree on a verdict. That was embarrassing for the criminal justice system, but it did not do the defendants any good. On retrial the judge ran a tighter ship, and the jury had no difficulty convicting both brothers of first-degree murder, with resulting sentences of life imprisonment without possibility of parole. The anomalous outcome of the first Menendez trial, like the highly publicized acquittal of O.J. Simpson shortly afterward in the same court system, probably owed more to postmodernist relativism and its "victim perspective" than to anything even distantly related to science.

The failure of the scientific materialists to change the criminal law permanently stems from the inherent shortcomings of the attempt to understand human nature and the human predicament in exclusively scientific categories. Even the most dedicated scientific materialists tend to be ambivalent about applying their theories to the mind, and especially to the problem of moral choice. At the beginning of *The Selfish Gene*, for example, Richard Dawkins asserts that "we, like other animals, are machines created by our genes" solely for the purpose of reproducing their own genetic kind. Although there are special circumstances under which genes might encourage a limited form of altruism (mainly for the benefit of close relatives), ruthless selfishness must be the norm because our genes have survived by emulating "successful Chicago gangsters." Dawkins's bleak conclusion is that "much as we might wish to believe otherwise, universal love and the welfare of the species as a whole are concepts that simply do not make evolutionary sense."

On the very next page (and without a shred of scientific justification), Dawkins tosses this vision of a gangster world overboard, calling on his readers to rebel against their genetic creators in the name of the very concepts that simply do not make evolutionary sense. "Be warned that if you wish, as I do, to build a society in which individuals cooperate generously and unselfishly towards a common good, you can expect little help from biological nature. Let us try to *teach* generosity and altruism, because we are born selfish. Let us understand what our own selfish genes are up to, because we may then at least have a chance to upset their designs, something that no other species has ever aspired to." But where did those ideals come from, and how can they be anything but nonsense in a world ruled by gangster genes? Dawkins the moral prophet winds up endorsing something very much like the biblical view of human nature that generated the *M'Naghten* rule. Man may be born in sin, but he has the capacity to know good from evil and to choose the good. Indeed, Dawkins in his moralizing vein seems to agree with Pope John Paul II, who is the farthest thing from a scientific materialist. The pope's 1996 statement granted approval to a vaguely defined principle of evolution, with the very significant qualification that "theories of evolution which, in accordance with the philosophies inspiring them, consider the spirit as emerging from the forces of living matter or as a mere epiphenomenon of this matter, are incompatible with the truth about man. Nor are they able to ground the dignity of the person." That is why concepts that simply do not make evolutionary sense may be the most important concepts of all.

Questions

1. Fradella's article describes certain environmental or physiological conditions that may affect one's thinking or behavior. Why might these conditions be relevant to criminal guilt?

2. Which of the defenses described by Fradella have been most embraced by legislatures and courts? Which have been least embraced? Why?

3. What challenges confront defendants who seek to use the disorders described by Fradella as a legal defense?

4. As Fradella notes, traditionally, a defendant could only succeed on a claim of self-defense if he or she used deadly force when it was necessary to prevent an imminent attack from deadly force. Why have some states modified these requirements for victims of Battered Woman Syndrome? Should states do so?

5. Why does Patricia Falk argue that the law should embrace legal defenses based on environmental or physiological conditions?

6. Falk's comments most reflect what legal philosophy?

7. What is the difference between the M'Naghten and ALI tests for legal insanity?

8. According to Johnson, how do the different insanity tests reflect different views of human nature?

9. How does Johnson explain the following two 20th century trends regarding the insanity defense:

   a. A shift away from the M'Naghten rule to what Johnson calls the "soft-determinism" of the ALI rule;

   b. A shift back toward the M'Naghten rule since the 1980's.

10. Consider I Corinthians 15:33; Proverbs 22:24-25; 30:7-9; Matthew 19:23-24; Mark 7:14-23; Ephesians 4:31-32; Colossians 3:5-14; and James 3:13-4:10. Do environmental factors influence our behavior? Do they cause it?

11. If so, to what extent should those factors excuse wrongful acts? Should they be considered in sentencing? In addition to the passages referenced in Question #10, consider Genesis 3:1-19; 4:1-7; I Corinthians 15:34; John 3:18; and II Thessalonians 1:6-10.

Chapter 5 Civil and Criminal Procedure: Jury Trial

A. Blackstone and the Jury at Common Law

Introduction

One of the defining features of the common law system was—and is—the right to a jury trial. William Blackstone expressed the common lawyer's admiration for the jury system in two places in his *Commentaries*. Accordingly, two excerpts follow. The first is taken from Volume 3 and discusses the right to a jury in civil cases. The second is taken from Volume 4 and discusses the right to a jury in criminal cases. Throughout, Blackstone eloquently defends the jury system.

William Blackstone, *Commentaries on the Laws of England, Vol III*[*]

Upon these accounts the trial by jury ever has been, and I trust ever will be, looked upon as the glory of the English law. And, if it has so great an advantage over others in regulating civil property, how much more that advantage be heightened, when it is applied to criminal cases! But this we must refer to the ensuing book of these commentaries: only observing for the present, that it is the most transcendent privilege which any subject can enjoy, or wish for, that he cannot be affected either in his property, his liberty, or his person, but by the unanimous consent of twelve of his neighbours and equals. A constitution, that I may venture to affirm has, under providence, secured the just liberties of this nation for a long succession of ages. And therefore a celebrated French writer, who

[*] William Blackstone, Commentaries on the Laws of England, Vol III 379-81 (Univ. of Chicago Press 1979) (1768).

concludes, that because Rome, Sparta, and Carthage have left their liberties, therefore those of England in time must perish, should have recollected that Rome, Sparta, and Carthage, were strangers to the trial by jury.

Great as this eulogium may seem, it is no more than this admirable constitution, when traced to it's principles, will be found in sober reason to deserve. The impartial administration of justice, which secures both our persons and our properties, is the great end of civil society. But if that be entirely entrusted to the magistracy, a select body of men, and those generally selected by the prince or such as enjoy the highest offices in the state, their decisions, in sight of their own natural integrity, will have frequently an involuntary bias towards those of their own rank and dignity: it is not to be expected from human nature, that the few would be always attentive to the interests and good of the many. On the other hand, if the power of judicature were placed at random in the hands of the multitude, their decisions would be wild and capricious, and a new rule of action would be every day in our courts. It is wisely therefore ordered, that the principles and axioms of law, which are general propositions, flowing from abstracted reason, and not accommodated to times or to men, should be deposited in the breasts of the judges, to be occasionally applied to such facts as come properly ascertained before them. For here partiality can have little scope: the law is well known, and is the same for all ranks and degrees; it follows as a regular conclusion from the premises of fact pre-established. But in settling and adjusting a question of fact, when intrusted to any single magistrate, partiality and injustice have an ample field to range in; either by boldly asserting that to be proved which is not so, or more artfully by suppressing some circumstances, stretching and warping others, and distinguishing away the remainder. Here therefore a competent number of sensible and upright jurymen, chosen by lot from among those of the middle rank, will be found the best investigators of truth, and the surest guardians of public justice. For the most powerful individual in the state will be cautious of committing any flagrant invasion of another's right, when he knows that the fact of his oppression must be examined and decided by twelve indifferent men, not appointed till the hour of trial; and that, when once the fact is ascertained, the law must of course redress it. This therefore preserves in the hands of the people that share which they ought to have in the administration of public justice, and prevents the encroachments of the more powerful and wealthy citizens. Every new tribunal, erected for the decision of facts, without the intervention of a jury, (whether composed of justices of the peace, commissioners of the revenue, judges of a court of conscience, or any other standing magistrates) is a step towards establishing aristocracy, the most oppressive of absolute governments. The feudal system, which, for the sake of military subordination, pursued an aristocratical plan in all it's arrangements of property, had been intolerable in times of peace, had it not been wisely counterpoised by that privilege, so universally diffused through even part of it, the trial by the feudal peers. And in every country on the continent, trial by the peers has been gradually disused, so the nobles have increased in power, till the state has been torn to pieces by rival factions, and oligarchy in effect has been established, though under the shadow of regal government; unless where the miserable commons have taken shelter under absolute monarchy, as the lighter evil of the two. And, particularly, it is a circumstance well worthy an Englishman's observation, that in Sweden the trial by jury, that bulwark of northern liberty, which continued in it's full vigor so lately as the middle of last century, is now fallen into disuse: and that these, though the regal power is in no country so closely limited, yet the liberties of the commons are extinguished, and the government is degenerated into a mere aristocracy. It is therefore, upon the whole, a duty which every man owes to his country, his friends, his posterity, and himself, to maintain to the utmost of his power this valuable constitution in all it's rights; to restore it to it's ancient dignity, if at all impaired by the different value of property, or otherwise deviated from it's first institution; to amend it, wherever it is defective; and, above all, to guard with the most jealous circumspection against the introduction of new and arbitrary methods of trial, which, under a variety of plausible pretenses, may in time imperceptibly undermine this best preservative of English liberty.

William Blackstone, *Commentaries on the Laws of England, Vol IV*[*]

The several methods of trial and conviction of offenders, established by the laws of England, were formerly more numerous than at present, through the superstition of our Saxon ancestors: who, like other northern nations, were extremely addicted to divination; a character, which Tacitus observes of the ancient Germans. They therefore invented a considerable number of methods of purgation or trial, to preserve innocence from the danger of false witnesses, and in consequence of a notion that God would always interpose miraculously, to vindicate the guiltless.

[*] WILLIAM BLACKSTONE, COMMENTARIES ON THE LAWS OF ENGLAND, VOL IV 336-44 (Univ. of Chicago Press 1979) (1769).

I. The most ancient species of trial was that by ordeal; which was peculiarly distinguished by the appellation of *judicium Dei* [the judgment of God]; and sometimes *vulgaris purgation* [common purification], to distinguish it from the canonical purgation, which was by the oath of the party. This was of two sorts, either *fire*-ordeal, or *water*-ordeal; the former being confined to persons of higher rank, the latter to the common people. Both these might be performed by deputy: but the principal was to answer for the success of the trial; the deputy only venturing some corporal pain, for hire, or perhaps for friendship. Fire-ordeal was performed either by taking up in the hand, unhurt, a piece of red hot iron, of one, two, or three pounds weight; or else by walking, barefoot, and blindfold, over nine redhot plowshares, laid lengthwise at unequal distances: and if the party escaped being hurt, he was adjudged innocent; but if it happened otherwise, as without collusion it usually did, he was then condemned as guilty. However, by this latter method queen Emma, the mother of Edward the confessor, is mentioned to have cleared her character, when suspected of familiarity with Alwyn bishop of Winchester.

Water-ordeal was performed, either by plunging the bare arm up to the elbow in boiling water, and escaping unhurt thereby: or by casting the person suspected into a river or pond of cold water: and, if he floated therein without any action of swimming, it was deemed an evidence of his guilt; but, if he sunk, he was acquitted. It is easy to trace out the traditional relics of this water-ordeal, in the ignorant barbarity still practiced in many countries to discover witches, by casting them into a pool of water, and drowning them to prove their innocence. And in the Eastern empire the fire-ordeal was used to the same purport by the emperor Theodore Lascaris; who, attributing his sickness to magic, caused all those whom he suspected to handle the hot iron: thus joining (as has been well remarked) to the most dubious crime in the world, the most dubious proof of innocence.

And indeed this purgation by ordeal seems to have been very ancient, and very universal, in the times of superstitious barbarity. It was known to the ancient Greeks: for in the Antigone of Sophocles, a person, suspected by Creon of a misdemeanor, declares himself ready "to handle hot iron and to walk over fire," in order to manifest his innocence; which, the scholiast tells us, was then a very usual purgation. And Grotius gives us many instances of water-ordeal in Bithynia, Sardinia, and other places. There is also a very peculiar species of water-ordeal, said to prevail among the Indians on the coast of Malabar; where a person accused of any enormous crime is obliged to swim over a large river abounding with crocodiles, and, if he escapes unhurt, he is reputed innocent. As in Siam, besides the usual methods of fire and water ordeal, both parties are sometimes exposed to the fury of a tiger let loose for that purpose: and, if the beast spares either, that person is accounted innocent; if neither, both are held to be guilty; but if he spares both, the trial is incomplete, and they proceed to a more certain criterion.

One cannot but be astonished at the folly and impiety of pronouncing a man guilty, unless he was cleared by a miracle; and of expecting that all the powers of nature should be suspended, by an immediate interposition of providence to save the innocent, whenever it was presumptuously required. And yet in England, so late as king John's time, we find grants to the bishops and clergy to use the *judicium ferri, aquae, et ignis* [judgment of the sword, of water, and of fire]. And, both in England and Sweden, the clergy presided at this trial, and it was only performed in the churches or in other consecrated ground: for which Stiernhook gives the reason; "*non desuit illis operae et laboris pretium; semper enim ab ejus modi judicio aliquid lucri sacerdotibus obveniebat*" [the value of work and labor does not fall to them; for always, from a trial of this kind, anything of gain fell to the lot of the priests]. But, to give it it's due praise, we find the canon law very early declaring against trial by ordeal, or *vulgaris purgatio*, as being the fabric of the devil, "*cum sit contra praeceptum Domini, non tentabis Dominum Deum tuum*" [when it is against a precept of the Lord, you will not tempt the Lord your God]. Upon this authority, though the canons themselves were of no validity in England, it was thought proper (as had been done in Denmark above a century before) to disuse and abolish this trial entirely in our courts of justice, by an act of parliament in 3 Hen. III. according to Sir Edward Coke, or rather by an order of the king in council.

II. Another species of purgation, somewhat similar to the former, but probably sprung from a presumptuous abuse of revelation in the ages of dark superstition, was the *corsned*, or morsel of execration: being a piece of cheese or bread, of about an ounce in weight, which was consecrated with a form of exorcism; desiring of the Almighty that it might cause convulsions and paleness, and find no passage, if the man was really guilty; but might turn to health and nourishment, if he was innocent: as the water of jealousy among the Jews was, by God's especial appointment, to cause the belly to swell and the thigh to rot, if the woman was guilty of adultery. This corsned was then given to the suspected person; who at the same time also received the holy sacrament: if indeed the corsned was not, as some have suspected, the sacramental bread itself; till the subsequent invention of transubstantiation preserved it from profane uses with a more profound respect than formerly. Our historians assure us, that Godwyn, earl of Kent in the reign of king Edward the confessor, abjuring the death of the king's brother, at last appealed to his corsned, "*per buccellam deglutiendam abjuravit*" [he abjured it by swallowing the morsel of execration], which stuck in his throat and killed him. This custom has been long since gradually abolished, though the remembrance of it still subsists in certain phrases of abjuration retained among the common people.

However, we cannot but remark, that though in European countries this custom most probably arose from an abuse of revealed religion, yet credulity and superstition will, in all ages and in all climates, produce the same or similar effects. And therefore we shall not be surprised to find, that in the kingdom of Pegu there still subsists a trial by the corsned, very similar to that of our ancestors, only substituting raw rice instead of bread. And, in the kingdom of Monomopata, they have a method of deciding lawsuits equally whimsical and uncertain. The witness for the plaintiff chews the bark of a tree, endued with an emetic quality, which, being sufficiently masticated, is then infused in water, which is given the defendant to drink. If his stomach rejects it, he is condemned: if it stays with him, he is absolved, unless the plaintiff will drink some of the same water; and, if it stays with him also, the suit is left undetermined.

These two antiquated methods of trial were principally in use among our Saxon ancestors. The next, which still remains in force, though very rarely in use, owes it's introduction among us to the princes of the Norman line. And that is

III. The trial by *battel*, duel, or single combat: which was another species of presumptuous appeals to providence, under an expectation that heaven would unquestionably give the victory to the innocent or injured party. The nature of this trial in cases of civil injury, upon issue joined in a writ of right, was fully discussed in the preceding book: to which I have only to add, that the trial by battel may be demanded at the election of the appellee, in either an appeal or an approvement; and that it is carried on with equal solemnity as that on a writ of right: but with this difference, that there each party might hire a champion, but here they must fight in their proper persons. And therefore if the appellant or approver be a woman, a priest, an infant, or of the age of fifty, lame, or blind, he or she may counterplead and refuse the wager of battel; and compel the appellee to put himself upon the country. Also peers of the realm, bringing an appeal, shall not be challenged to wage battel, on account of the dignity of their persons; nor the citizens of London, by special charter, because fighting seems foreign to their education and employment. So likewise if the crime be notorious; as if the thief be taken with the *mainour* [in the act; red-handed], or the murderer in the room with a bloody knife, the appellant may refuse the tender of battel from the appellee; for it is unreasonable that an innocent man should stake his life against one who is already half-convicted.

The form and manner of waging battel upon appeals are much the same as upon a writ of right; only the oaths of the two combatants are vastly more striking and solemn. The appellee, when appealed of felony, pleads *not guilty*, and throws down his glove, and declares he will defend the same by his body: the appellant takes up the glove, and replies that he is ready to make good the appeal, body for body. And thereupon the appellee, taking the book in his right hand, and in his left the right hand of his antagonist, swears to this effect. "*Hoc audi, homo, quem per manum teneo*," & *c*: "hear this, O man whom I hold by the hand, who callest thyself John by the name of baptism, that I, who call myself Thomas by the name of baptism, did not feloniously murder thy father, William by name, nor am any way guilty of the said felony. So help me God, and the saints; and this I will defend against thee by my body, as this court shall award." To which the appellant replies, holding the bible and his antagonist's hand in the same manner as the other: "hear this, O man whom I hold by the hand, who called thyself Thomas by the name of baptism, that thou art perjured; and therefore perjured, because that thou feloniously did murder my father, William by name. So help me God and the saints; and this I will prove against thee by my body, as this court shall award." The battel is then to be fought with the same weapons, viz. batons, the same solemnity, and the same oath against amulets and sorcery, that are used in the civil combat: and if the appellee be so far vanquished, that he cannot or will not fight any longer, he shall be adjudged to be hanged immediately; and then, as well as if he be killed in battel, providence is deemed to have determined in favour of the truth, and his blood shall be attainted. But if he kills the appellant, or can maintain the fight from sunrising till the stars appear in the evening, he shall be acquitted. So also if the appellant becomes recreant, and pronounces the horrible word of *craven*, he shall lose his *liberam legem* [legal freedom], and become infamous; and the appellee shall recover his damages, and also be for ever quit, not only of the appeal, but of all indictments likewise for the same offence.

IV. The fourth method of trial used in criminal cases is that by the peers of Great Britain, in the court of parliament, or the court of the lord high steward, when a peer is capitally indicted. Of this enough has been said in a former chapter; to which I shall now only add, that, in the method and regulations of it's proceedings, it differs little from the trial *per patriam*, or by jury: except that the peers need not all agree in their verdict; but the greater number, confiding of twelve at the least, will conclude, and bind the minority.

V. The trial by jury, or the country, *per patriam*, is also that trial by the peers of every Englishman, which, as the grand bulwark of his liberties, is secured to him by the great charter, "*nullus liber homo capiatur, vel imprisonetur, aut exulet, aut aliquo alio modo destruatur, nisi per legale judicium parium fuorum, vel per legem terrae*" [no free man may be captured or imprisoned or banished in a destructive manner unless through the legal judgment of his equals or the law of the land].

The antiquity and excellence of this trial, for the settling of civil property, has before been explained at large. And it will hold much stronger in criminal cases; since, in times of difficulty and danger, more is to be apprehended from the violence and partiality of judges appointed by the crown, in suits between the king and the subject, than in disputes between one individual and another, to settle the metes and boundaries of private property. Our law has therefore wisely placed this strong and twofold barrier, of a presentment and a trial by jury, between the liberties of the people, and the prerogative of the crown. It was necessary, for preserving the admirable balance of our Constitution, to vest the executive power of the laws in the prince: and yet this power might be dangerous and destructive to that very constitution, if exerted without check or control, by justices of *oyer* and *terminer* [to hear and determine] occasionally named by the crown; who might then, as in France or Turkey, imprison, dispatch, or exile any man that was obnoxious to the government, by an instant declaration, that such is their will and pleasure. But the founders of the English laws have with excellent forecast contrived, that no man should be called to answer to the king for any capital crime, unless upon the preparatory accusation of twelve or more of his fellow subjects, the grand jury: and that the truth of every accusation, whether preferred in the shape of indictment, information, or appeal, should afterwards be confirmed by the unanimous suffrage of twelve of his equals and neighbours, indifferently chosen, and superior to all suspicion. So that the liberties of England cannot but subsist, so long as this palladium remains sacred and inviolate, not only from all open attacks, (which none will be so hardy as to make) but also from all secret machinations, which may sap and undermine it; by introducing new and arbitrary methods of trial, by justices of the commissioners of the revenue, and courts of conscience. And however convenient there may appear at first, (as doubtless all arbitrary powers, well executed, are the most convenient) yet let it be again remembered, that delays, and little inconveniences in the forms of justice, are the price that all free nations must pay for their liberty in more substantial matters; that these inroads upon this sacred bulwark of the nation are fundamentally opposite to the spirit of our constitution; and that, though begun in trifles, the precedent may gradually increase and spread, to the utter disuse of juries in questions of the most momentous concern.

Questions

1. How important to Blackstone is the right to a jury trial?

2. What is Blackstone's view of human nature? Is it biblical? Consider Isaiah 64:6; Romans 3:9-18; and Ephesians 2:1-3.

3. How does Blackstone's view of human nature affect his view of juries?

4. Is a jury more important in civil or criminal cases? Why?

5. How does the jury trial compare with earlier methods of resolving disputes at common law?

6. Why does Blackstone reject trial by ordeal?

B. The Jury Trial Today

Introduction

Few today are as excited about the jury system as Blackstone was two and a half centuries ago. Several prominent jury verdicts in the last two decades, such as those acquitting O.J. Simpson and Robert Blake, have fueled a debate over whether juries should continue to decide cases.

The debate is not new. Critics of the jury system have long argued that jury trials should be limited (to criminal cases or to non-complex civil cases), significantly altered, or abolished altogether. The three pieces that follow address many of the main points of contention in the debate over juries.

The first is by Jerome Frank from his 1949 book *Courts on Trial*. Frank was born in 1889. He studied political science and then law at the University of Chicago. He graduated from law school in 1912 with the highest average any student had yet achieved at Chicago. Frank practiced law with firms in Chicago and New York. He also was a visiting lecturer at Yale Law School, being appointed a Sterling Fellow at Yale in 1932.

Frank was a legal realist. Like many realists, Frank sought to use law as a tool for social reform. He was committed to Roosevelt's New Deal. In private practice he represented the Department of the Interior and the Public Works Administration against lawsuits challenging the federal government's authority to intervene in the economy. During the 1930s and 1940s he also served in various capacities in the federal government, including as general counsel for the Agricultural Adjustment Administration; special counsel to the Reconstruction Finance Corporation; and chairman of the Securities and Exchange Commission. Frank was very interested in psychology, particularly Freudian psychology, and this interest deeply influenced his legal writing—especially *Law and the Modern Mind* (1930), probably Frank's most influential book.

Frank was appointed in 1941 as a judge on the United States Court of Appeals for the Second Circuit. He served on the court until his death in 1957.

Frank's attack on juries is the attack of legal realism. In classic realist fashion he demands that we look at what actually goes on in a jury trial. He concludes that when we do, we find a system that works much differently than the ideal trumpeted by Blackstone. While Frank wrote the piece in the 1940s, his criticism of juries sounds modern. He raises many of the same concerns about juries that critics point to today.

The second piece summarizes the status of jury reform efforts in various states. While some jury critics, like Frank, have advocated abolishing the jury system, most have advocated reform instead. Their advocacy has borne fruit. Since the early 1990's many states have modified their jury systems believing that, with these changes, the jury can still serve justice effectively today. The piece reproduced here is a report generated by the Center for Jury Studies of the National Center for State Courts (NCSC). The NCSC's mission is to "improve the administration of justice through leadership and service to state courts, and courts around the world." It seeks to accomplish this mission through research, conferences, publications, and consulting services.

The third piece is an excerpt from a law review article by Benjamin Madison, who is a law professor at Regent University School of Law. Madison received a B.A. from Randolph-Macon College and an M.A. and a J.D. from the College of William & Mary. Madison is well-acquainted with juries. For over 17 years he served as a top litigator with the firm of Hunton & Williams where he obtained the largest jury verdict in Virginia history. He now teaches civil procedure, Virginia procedure, appellate advocacy, and Christian foundations of law. In the piece reproduced here, Madison defends the continuing viability of the jury system based on transcendent principles of justice.

Jerome Frank, *Courts on Trial*[*]

The Jury System

As you know, sometimes a case is tried before a trial judge, sometimes before a judge and jury. I shall for the time being treat principally of jury trials.

Blackstone called the jury "the glory of the English law." Jefferson, who detested Blackstone as a Tory, agreed with him at least on that one subject. Judge Knox, chief federal district judge in the Southern District of New York, said a few years ago, "In my opinion, the jury system is one of the really great achievements of English and American jurisprudence."

As you'll see, I dissent from those views. When I hear the jury praised as the "palladium of our liberties," I keep thinking that, while a palladium (a word derived from the ancient use of the image of Pallas Athena) means something on which the safety of a nation or an institution depends, it also is the name of a chemical element which, in the spongy state "has the remarkable quality of absorbing, up to nearly 1,000 times its own volume in hydrogen gas."

* * *

In the United States, the jury still retains much of its glamour. True, there has been something of an increase in the number of civil (i.e., non-criminal) suits in which jury trials have been waived. But in criminal cases the jury still largely keeps its hold. Except in this country, however, trial by jury fell into disfavor in the 20th century. In some Swiss cantons it was abolished. In pre-Hitler Germany and France, its use was more and more limited. This unpopularity cannot be explained as a symptom of decreased interest in liberty and democracy. For Scotland, surely a land of liberty-loving individuals, having virtually rejected the non-criminal jury in the 16th century, readopted it in 1815, and subsequently all but gave it up. In England, even before World War II, it was seldom employed in civil suits, was abandoned in criminal prosecutions except for major crimes, and even there was, and is, used decreasingly. Surely that attitude in England, the birthplace of the modern jury, should give us pause. Especially should it do so, when it is recalled that American defenders of the jury have often asserted that the major ills of our jury system would vanish if only we adopted the English way of using it. If, as

[*] JEROME FRANK, COURTS ON TRIAL 109-23 (1949). Frank, Jerome; *COURTS ON TRIAL*.

Judge Knox says, the jury system "is one of the really great achievements of English and American jurisprudence," why has it all but gone into the discard in England, except in a decreasing percentage of major criminal prosecutions? And why has Congress never granted the privilege of trial by jury in a suit against the United States?

It will not do then to make Fourth-of-July speeches about the glorious jury system, to conceal its grave defects, or merely to palliate them with superficial, cosmetic-like, remedies. We need to have our public comprehend what the jury actually is like in order to arouse public interest to the point where steps will be taken to eradicate its most glaring deficiencies.

I have said that, supposedly, the task of our courts is this: To make reasoned applications of legal rules to the carefully ascertained facts of particular law-suits. You will recall my crude schematization of the alleged nature of the process—$R \; x \; F = D$—i.e., the Rules times the Facts equals the Decision. Where, in that scheme, does the jury fit in?

In most jury trials, the jury renders what is called a "general verdict." Suppose that Williams sues Allen claiming (1) that Allen falsely told him there was oil on some land Williams bought from Allen, but (2) that in fact there was no oil there, so that Williams was defrauded. The jury listens to the witnesses. Then the judge tells the jurors, "If you find Allen lied, and Williams relied on that lie, a legal rule requires that you hold for the plaintiff Williams, and you must compute the damages according to another rule," which the judge explains. "But if you find that Allen did not lie, then the legal rule requires you to hold for the defendant Allen." The jury deliberately deliberates in the jury-room and reports either, "We find for the plaintiff in the sum of $5,000," or "We find for the defendant." In other words, the jury does not report what facts it found. Such an undetailed, unexplained, jury report is called a "general verdict."

There are three theories of the jury's function:

(1) The naive theory is that the jury merely finds the facts; that it must not, and does not, concern itself with the legal rules, but faithfully accepts the rules as stated to them by the trial judge.

(2) A more sophisticated theory has it that the jury not only finds the facts but, in its deliberation in the jury-room, uses legal reasoning to apply to those facts the legal rules it learned from the judge. A much respected judge said in 1944 that a jury's verdict should be regarded as "the reasoned and logical result of the concrete application of the law [i.e., the rules] to the facts."

On the basis of this sophisticated theory, the jury system has been criticized. It is said that juries often do not find the facts in accordance with the evidence, but distort—or "fudge"—the facts, and find them in such a manner that (by applying the legal rules laid down by the judge to the facts thus deliberately misfound) the jury is able to produce the result which it desires, in favor of one party or the other. "The facts," we are told, "are found in order to reach the result."

This theory ascribes to jurors a serpentine wisdom. It assumes that they thoroughly understand what the judge tells them about the rules, and that they circumvent the rules by falsely contriving—with consummate skill and cunning—the exact findings of fact which, correlated with those rules, will logically compel the result they desire.

(3) We come now to a third theory which may be called the "realistic" theory. It is based on what anyone can discover by questioning the average person who has served as a juror—namely that often the jury are neither able to, nor do they attempt to, apply the instructions of the court. The jury are more brutally direct. They determine that they want Jones to collect $5,000 from the railroad company, or that they don't want pretty Nellie Brown to go to jail for killing her husband; and they bring in their general verdict accordingly. Often, to all practical intents and purposes, the judge's statement of the legal rules might just as well never have been expressed. "Nor can we," writes Clementson, "cut away the mantle of mystery in which the general verdict is enveloped, to see how the principal facts were determined, and whether the law was applied under the judge's instructions.... It is a matter of common knowledge that the general verdict may be the result of anything but the calm deliberation, exchange of impressions and opinions, resolution of doubts, and final intelligent concurrence which, theoretically, produced it. It comes into court unexplained and impenetrable."

The "realistic" theory, then, is that, in many cases, the jury, often without heeding the legal rules, determine, not the "facts", but the respective legal rights and duties of the parties to the suit. For the judgment of the court usually follows the general verdict of the jury, so that the verdict results in a decision which determines those rights and duties.

Some lawyers indignantly repudiate this "realistic" theory. They deny that juries can disregard the judicial instructions concerning the legal rules. The history of that denial is enlightening. In this country, during the latter part of the 18th century and the early part of the 19th, judges told juries, especially in criminal cases, that it was for the jury to decide not only the facts but also the "law"—i.e., what legal rules were applicable—and that the jury was not bound to accept the judge's instructions concerning the rules. In the federal courts and in most states, that practice was later repudiated. The judges and lawyers who then denounced that earlier practice declared that, if juries had the right to ignore the judge's charge as to the applicable rules, horrible consequences would ensue.

Here are some sample statements of what those consequences would be: The "law" would "become as variable as the prejudices, the inclinations, and the passions of men." "The parties would suffer from an arbitrary decision." "Decisions would depend entirely on juries uncontrolled by any settled, fixed legal principle," and would be "according to what the jury in their own opinion suppose the law is or ought to be." "Jurymen, untrained in the law, would determine questions affecting life, liberty or property, according to such legal principles as in their judgment were applicable in the particular case." Our government "would cease to be a government of laws and become a government of men." "Jurors would become not only judges but legislators as well." The "law" would "be as fluctuating and uncertain as the diverse opinions of different juries in regard to it." Jurors would be "superior to the national legislature, and its laws...subject to their control," so that "a law of Congress" would "be in operation in one state and not in another."

Now the truth is, as every lawyer knows, that, in many criminal cases, the jury does have an "uncontrollable power" to disregard rules laid down in the judge's instructions. For if, in a criminal case, the jury brings in a verdict for the defendant, the judge (because of constitutional provisions) must follow that verdict, even if he is convinced that the jury ignored his legal instructions. In other words, such a verdict is final and conclusive.

At first blush, the situation may seem very different in non-criminal suits. In such a suit, if the evidence is insufficient to justify a verdict for one side, the judge may and should "direct a verdict" for the other side; that is, in effect, he dispenses with the jury and himself decides the case for that side. But [sic] the conflicting oral testimony is such that it would justify a verdict for either side, then, if the judge behaves correctly, he lets the jury return a verdict. Unless he knows—as he seldom does—that the jury ignored the *R*'s of which he told them, he should let that verdict stand. True, the judge can grant a new trial. But he is not supposed to do so, in such a case, if it was properly tried. And, if nevertheless, he does order another trial, he is merely exercising a veto which may be overruled. For another jury will then decide the case; and it may again, unknown to the judge, ignore the *R*'s. Moreover, if two juries, in successive trials of that case, bring in the same verdict, then, in many states (with exceptions that need not here concern us) that concludes the matter. So you see, even in non-criminal cases, many juries do have the power to make decisions regardless of the legal rules.

Those who point to what, they say, would be the dire results of allowing the jury to disregard the rules, have deluded themselves with words. "It is true," said Judge Thompson, typically, "the jury may disregard the instructions of the court, and in some cases there may be no remedy; but it is still the right of the court to instruct the jury on the law and the duty of the jury to obey the instructions." Sometimes there is a verbal play on the distinction between the jury's "power" and the jury's "right": The jury, it is said, has the power but cannot "rightfully exercise it." Chamberlayne states that most American courts in this connection "very properly distinguish between a *right* and an incorrectible *abuse* of power."

I think the reader will agree, however, that, to the litigant interested in a jury's verdict, it makes no practical difference, when the jury uses its "incorrectible power," whether their exercise of that power is called a "right," a defiance of its "duty," or an "abuse." The important fact is that juries have that incorrectible power and frequently use it.

Practically, then, we do have the very conditions which we were warned would exist if juries had the right to ignore the judge's instructions as to the correct rules: Cases *are* often decided "according to what the jury supposes the law is or ought to be"; the "law" *is* "as fluctuating and uncertain as the diverse opinions in regard to it"; often juries *are* "not only judges but legislators as well"; jurors do become "superior to the national legislature," and its laws *are* "subject to their control" so that "a law of Congress" *is* "in operation in one state and not in another."

This truth the general verdict conceals. "Whether," says Sunderland, "the jurors deliberately threw the law into the discard, and rendered a verdict out of their own heads, or whether they applied the law correctly as instructed by the court, or whether they tried to apply it properly but failed for lack of understanding—these are questions respecting which the verdict discloses nothing.... The general verdict serves as the great procedural opiate...draws the curtain upon human errors, and soothes us with the assurance that we have attained the unattainable."

Now what does bring about verdicts? Longenecker, in a book written by a practical trial lawyer for practical trial lawyers, says: "In talking to a man who had recently served for two weeks on juries, he stated that in one case after they had retired to consider the verdict, the foreman made a speech to them somewhat like this: 'Now boys, you know there was lying on both sides. Which one did the most lying? The plaintiff is a poor man and the defendant is rich and can afford to pay the plaintiff something. Of course the dog did not hurt the plaintiff much, but I think we ought to give him something, don't you?' There were several 'sures'; we thought the plaintiff might have to split with his lawyers, so we gave him a big verdict." A case is reported in which the jurors explained their verdict thus: "We couldn't make head or tail of the case, or follow all the messing around the lawyers did. None of us believed the witnesses on either side, anyway, so we made up our minds to disregard the evidence on both sides and decide the case on its merits." "Competent observers," says Judge Rossman, "who have interviewed the jurors in scores of jury trials, declare that in many cases...principal issues received no consideration from the jury." Bear that in mind, when considering these remarks by Ram: "And to what a fearful extent may a verdict affect a person! It may pronounce a man sane or insane; it may establish character, or take it away; it may give liberty to the captive, or turn liberty into slavery: it may continue life to a prisoner, or consign him to death."

Again and again, it has been disclosed that juries have arrived at their verdicts by one of the following methods: (1) Each juror, in a civil case, writes down the amount he wants to award; the total is added and the average taken as the verdict. (2) The jurors, by agreement decide for one side or the other according to the flip of a coin. (3) A related method, reported in a case where a man was convicted of manslaughter and sentenced to life imprisonment, is as follows: The "jury at first stood six for assault and battery, and, as a compromise, the six agreed to vote for manslaughter, and the vote then stood six for manslaughter, and six for murder in the second degree; it was then agreed to prepare 24 ballots—12 for manslaughter and 12 for murder in the second degree—place all of them in a hat, and each juror draw one ballot therefrom, and render a verdict either for manslaughter or murder in the second degree, as the majority should appear; the first drawing was a tie, but the second one resulted in eight ballots for murder in the second degree and four for manslaughter, and thereupon, according to the agreement, a verdict was rendered for murder in the second degree."

How do the courts react to such a disclosure? When it is made known before the jury is discharged, a court will usually reject the verdict. But, frequently, the revelation occurs after the jury's discharge. In most states, and in the federal system, the courts then refuse to disturb the verdict. They say that any other result would mean that jurors would be subjected to pressures, after a case is over, to induce them to falsify what had occurred in the jury-room, so that all verdicts would be imperilled.

One may doubt whether there is much danger of such falsifications. I surmise that the underlying reason for that judicial attitude is this: The judges feel that, were they obliged to learn the methods used by jurors, the actual workings of the jury-system would be shown up, devastatingly. From my point of view, such a consequence would be desirable: The public would soon discover this skeleton in the judicial closet.

My surmise as to the basic reason for judicial unwillingness to examine jury operations closely is perhaps borne out by the following:

In 1947, two enterprising, able, and earnest law-school students sought to study at first-hand how jurors decide cases. They wanted to have a trial judge, after a jury trial had concluded, present to the jurors a carefully worded questionnaire, with the suggestion that they answer it in writing if they wished, and with the further suggestion that, if they cared to, they should allow themselves to be interviewed by these students. This proposal was made without success to nine judges of several different jurisdictions. One federal judge said he did not approve "a holier-than-thou attitude toward juries," and that the project could serve "no worthy end," but would only increase differences among federal judges concerning the value of the jury system. Another federal judge, in refusing his cooperation, remarked that he had never made such a study when he was in law-school. Still another federal judge, unwilling to have jurors interrogated, said, "How they decide is their business." Two state-court judges deemed the undertaking "improper." One highly intelligent state-court judge, enthusiastic about the study, submitted the questionnaire to the jurors in one case and gave the written answers to the students. He also granted them permission to conduct informal interviews, but withdrew that permission because he had received adverse criticism from some of his colleagues.

Are jurors to blame when they decide cases in the ways I've described? I think not. In the first place, often they cannot understand what the judge tells them about the legal rules. To comprehend the meaning of many a legal rule requires special training. It is inconceivable that a body of twelve ordinary men, casually gathered together for a few days, could, merely from listening to the instructions of the judge, gain the knowledge necessary to grasp the true import of the judge's words. For these words have often acquired their meaning as the result of hundreds of years of professional disputation in the courts. The jurors usually are as unlikely to get the meaning of those words as if they were spoken in Chinese, Sanskrit, or Choctaw. "Can anything be more fatuous," queries Sunderland, "than the expectation that the law which the judge so carefully, learnedly and laboriously expounds to the laymen in the jury box becomes operative in their minds in true form?" Judge Rossman pointedly asks whether it "is right to demand that a juror swear that he will obey the instructions (which the lawyers frequently say they are not sure of until they have been transcribed) and return a general verdict in obedience thereto." Judge Bok says that "juries have the disadvantage...of being treated like children while the testimony is going on, but then being doused with a kettleful of law, during the charge, that would make a third-year law student blanch."

Under our system, however, the courts are obligated to make the unrealistic assumption that the often incomprehensible words, uttered in the physical presence of the jurors, have some real effect on their thought processes. As a logical deduction from that unfounded assumption, the trial judge is required to state the applicable rule to the jury with such nicety that some lawyers do not thoroughly comprehend it. If the judge omits any of those niceties, the upper court will reverse a judgment based on the jury's verdict. For, theoretically, the jury actually worked in accordance with the $R \times F = D$ formula, applying the R they received from the judge, so that, if he gave them the wrong R, then, in theory, the D—their verdict—must logically be wrong. Lawyers thus set traps for trial judges. Decisions, in cases which have taken weeks to try, are reversed on appeal because a phrase, or a sentence, meaningless to the jury, has been included in or omitted from the charge.

When a decision is reversed on such a ground, it results, at best, in a new trial at which the trial judge will intone a more meticulously worded R to another uncomprehending jury. This leads to an enormous waste of time and money. And note that the prospect of a prolonged expensive new trial often induces a litigant who won in the first trial, and who has only modest means, to accept an unfair settlement.

Many of the precise legal rules on which, according to the conventional theory, men in their daily affairs have a right to and supposedly do rely, are found solely in upper-court opinions admonishing trial judges to use, in charges to juries, words and phrases stating those rules. But if jurors do not understand those words and phrases, and consequently do not apply those rules, then reliance on the rules is unreliable: Men who act in reliance on that purported right to rely are deceived. I cannot, therefore, agree with Dickinson when he says that, although no precedents emerge from the verdicts of successive juries "so long as the application of a rule is left to the jury under no other guidance than the statement of the rule as such by the court," yet "the moment of elaboration of a rule is definitely isolated and registered as that at which a court for the first time instructs a jury that a rule does or does not apply to a particular state of facts, and this instruction is tested and approved on appeal," and that "this is an important and powerful aid in minting new law into stable and recognizable form, and offers one of the cogent arguments for the preservation of the jury system."

Suppose, however, that the jurors always did understand the R's. Nevertheless, often they would face amazing obstacles to ascertaining the *F*'s. For the evidence is not presented all at once or in an orderly fashion. The very mode of its presentation is confusing. The jurors are supposed to keep their minds in suspense until all of the evidence is in.

Can a jury perform such a task? Has it the means and capacity? Are the conditions of a jury trial such as to make for the required calm deliberation by the jurors? Wigmore, who defends the jury system, himself tells us that the court-room is "a place of surging emotions, distracting episodes, and sensational surprises. The parties are keyed up to the contest; and the topics are often calculated to stir up the sympathy, or prejudice, or ridicule of the tribunal." Dean Green remarks: "The longer the trial lasts, the larger the scanning crowds, the more intensely counsel draw the lines of conflict, the more solemn the judge, the harder it becomes for the jury to restrain their reason from somersault."

We may, therefore, seriously question the statement of Professors Michael and Adler that, unlike the witnesses, the jury "observes the things and events exhibited to its senses under conditions designed to make the observation reliable and accurate. In the case of what (the jury) observes directly the factor of memory is negligible." As shown by Wigmore, Green, and Burrill, the first of those comments surely does not square with observable courtroom realities. As to the second—that the factor of the jurors' memory is negligible—consider the following: Theoretically, as we saw, the jury, in its process of fact-finding, applies to the evidence the legal rules it learns from the judge. If the jury actually did conduct itself according to this theory, it would be unable to comprehend the evidence intelligently until it received those instructions about the rules. But those instructions are given, not before the jury hears the evidence, but only after all the witnesses have left the stand. Then, for the first time, are the jurors asked to consider the testimony in the light of the rules. In other words, if jurors are to do their duty, they must now recollect and assemble the separate fragments of the evidence (including the demeanor of the several witnesses) and fit them into the rules. If the trial has lasted for many days or weeks, the required feat of memory is prodigious. As Burrill says: "The theory of judicial investigation requires that the juror keep his mind wholly free from impressions until all facts are before him in evidence, and that he should then frame his conclusion. The difficulty attending this mode of dealing with the elements of evidence (especially in important cases requiring protracted investigation) is that the facts thus surveyed in a mass, and at one view, are apt to confuse, distract, and oppress the mind by their very number and variety.... They are, moreover, necessarily mixed up with remembrance of the mere machinery of their introduction, and the contests (often close and obstinate) attending their proof; in the course of which attempts are sometimes made to suppress or distort the truth, in the very act of presentation."

In a discussion I recently had with Professor Michael, he maintained that, since jurymen, in their daily out-of-court living, conduct most of their affairs on the basis of conclusions reached after listening to other men, they are adequately equipped as fact-finders in the court-room. One answer to this argument is that often the issues in trials are of a complicated kind with which most jurymen are unfamiliar. But let us ignore that answer. A more telling criticism of Michael's assertion is this: The surroundings of inquiry during a jury trial differ extraordinarily from those in which the juryman conducts his ordinary affairs. At a trial, the jurors hear the evidence in a public place, under conditions of a kind to which they are unaccustomed: No juror is able to withdraw to his own room, or office, for private individual reflection. And, at the close of the trial, the jurors are pressed for time in reaching their joint decision. Even twelve experienced judges, deliberating together, would probably not function well under the conditions we impose on the twelve inexperienced laymen.

In 1930, I pointed out that what might be called "jury-made law," as compared with "judge-made law," is peculiar in form. It does not, I said, issue in general pronouncements. You will not find it set forth in the law reports or in text-books. It does not become embodied in a series of precedents. It is nowhere codified. For each jury makes its own "law" in each case with little or no knowledge of, or reference to, what has been done before, or regard to what will be done thereafter, in similar cases.

Three years later, in 1933, Judge Ulman, with long experience in a trial court, confirmed my statement. He told in his book how, in case after case relating to traffic accidents, "the jury has made the law...in...direct conflict with the law as laid down by the highest law-making authority of the state" and told to them by the trial judge. "The jury has substituted its own notion of law for that which the law-books say is the law." Noting that, in his court, generally, juries refuse to accept the law-book doctrine of contributory negligence, he said, "The strange part of it is that in the classical law-books you will not find a single word even hinting that the law of contributory negligence is what it has become by this habitual action of juries. This is because the men who write the law-books have not troubled to look at the law as...it actually works in the courtroom. They, like other members of the legal profession, have riveted their eyes...upon the printed page...The jury gets in the way of their neat formulae, and messes up their rules and doctrines."

Judge Ulman, however, implied that all juries uniformly reject the legal rule about contributory negligence. This involves an untenable belief that the verdict in any specific jury case would be the same, regardless of the particular men or women who composed the jury. Were such a belief well-founded, practicing lawyers would be fools for spending much time in selecting jurors.

But they do indeed spend time on that project. Typically, in his book for practicing trial lawyers, Longenecker writes: "No more important matter presents itself in the trial of a case than that of selecting a jury.... Do not take a chance (in this matter) because you have no right to gamble with your client's interests."

Do the lawyers strive to pick impartial jurors? Do they want jurymen whose training will best enable them to understand the facts of the case? Of course not. If you think they usually do, watch the trial lawyers at work in a court-room. Or read the books written for trial lawyers by seasoned trial lawyers.

Here are a few excerpts from such a book, Goldstein's *Trial Techniques*, a book commended for its accuracy by Professor Morgan of Harvard. Always demand a jury, says Goldstein, if you represent a plaintiff who is a "woman, child, an old man or an old woman, or an ignorant, illiterate or foreign-born person unable to read or write or speak English who would naturally excite the jury's sympathies," especially if the defendant is a large corporation, a prominent or wealthy person, an insurance company, railroad or bank. Then, he advises, seek the type of juror who "will most naturally respond to an emotional appeal." Make every effort, this author counsels, to exclude from the jury anyone "who is particularly experienced in the field of endeavor which is the basis of the law suit." As such a person is likely, says Goldstein, to have too much influence with the other jurors, it is always better to submit the issues "to a jury who have no knowledge of the particular subject."

In that book much is made of the fact that "the jury tries the lawyers rather than the clients," that, "without realizing it, the jurors allow their opinions of the evidence to be swayed in favor of the side represented by the lawyer they like." That notion is repeated in some of the pamphlets, written by eminent trial lawyers, published in 1946 under the auspices of the American Bar Association. They advise the lawyer to "ingratiate himself" with the jury. One of these pamphlets says that the jurors' reaction to the trial lawyer "may be more important than the reaction to the client, for the client appears on the stand only during a relatively brief period, while the lawyer is before the jury all the time." Harris, in his well-known book on "advocacy," says, "It may be that judgment is more easily deceived when the passions are aroused, but if so, you [the lawyers] are not responsible. Human nature was, I presume, intended to be what it is, and when it gets into the jury-box, it is the duty of the advocate to make the best use of it he fairly can in the interests of his client." The Supreme Court of Tennessee has solemnly decided that "tears have always been considered legitimate arguments before a jury," that such use of tears is "one of the natural rights of counsel which no court or constitution could take away," and that "indeed, if counsel has them at command, it may be seriously questioned whether it is not his professional duty to shed them whenever proper occasion arises...."

This is no laughing matter. For prejudice has been called the thirteenth juror, and it has been said that "Mr. Prejudice and Miss Sympathy are the names of witnesses whose testimony is never recorded, but must nevertheless be reckoned with in trials by jury." The foregoing tends to justify Balzac's definition of a jury as "twelve men chosen to decide who has the better lawyer."

In any law-suit, success or defeat for one of the parties may turn on his lawyer's abilities. But, in the light of the fact that juries "try the lawyers," it is peculiarly true, in many a jury trial, that a man's life, livelihood or property often depends on his lawyer's skill or lack of it in ingratiating himself with the jury rather than on the evidence. Not that lawyers, trying to protect their clients, should be censured for exploiting jurors' weaknesses—as long as we retain the general-verdict jury system.

Since, as every handbook on trial practice discloses, and as visits to a few jury trials will teach anyone, the lawyers are allowed—more, are expected—to appeal to the crudest emotions and prejudices of the jurors, and jurors are known often to respond to such appeals, I confess that it disturbs me not a little that we require trial judges to perform the futile ritual of saying to each jury something like this: "The law will not permit jurors to be governed by mere sentiment, sympathy, passion or prejudice, and you will reach a verdict that will be just to both sides, regardless of what the consequences may be." We tell jurors to do—have them take an oath to do—what we do not at all expect them to do.

As I said in a previous chapter, the search for the facts in a courtroom must necessarily be limited by lack of time; also, for important reasons of public policy, some ways of obtaining evidence are precluded—by the rule against self-incrimination, for instance, or by the rule against any unreasonable search and seizure.

But there are other rules of exclusion which, no matter what their origin, have been perpetuated primarily because of the admitted incompetence of jurors. Notable is the rule excluding hearsay evidence. Hearsay may be roughly (and somewhat inaccurately) described as the report in court by a witness of a statement made by another person, out of court, who is not subject to cross-examination at the trial, when the report of that statement is offered as evidence to prove the truth of a fact asserted in that statement. It is, so to speak, second-hand evidence. Now doubtless hearsay should often be accepted with caution. But 90% of the evidence on which men act out of court, most of the data on which business and industry daily rely, consists of the equivalent of hearsay. Yet, because of distrust of juries—a belief that jurors lack the competence to make allowance for the second-hand character of hearsay—such evidence, although accepted by administrative agencies, juvenile courts and legislative committees, is (subject, to be sure, to numerous exceptions) barred in jury trials. As a consequence, frequently the jury cannot learn of matters which would lead an intelligent person to a more correct knowledge of the facts.

So, too, of many other exclusionary rules. They limit, absurdly, the court-room quest for the truth. The result, often, is a gravely false picture of the actual facts. Thus trial by jury seriously interferes with correct—and, therefore, just—decisions. Even if the juries could understand what the trial judges tell them of the *R*'s, the juries would often be unable to apply these rules to anything like the real *F*'s, because of the exclusion of relevant evidence.

But, even apart from that difficulty, since jurors frequently cannot understand the *R*'s, the general-verdict jury trial renders absurd the conventional description of the decisional process—the $R \times F = D$. To my mind a better instrument than the usual jury trial could scarcely be imagined for achieving uncertainty, capriciousness, lack of uniformity, disregard of the *R*'s, and unpredictability of decisions.

National Center for State Courts, Center for Jury Studies, *The State-of-the-States Survey of Jury Improvement Efforts, Executive Summary*[*]

Beginning in the early 1990s, debates between supporters and detractors of the jury system prompted renewed efforts by judges, lawyers, and scholars to examine jury performance and to implement various improvement initiatives through changes to court rules and case law, and through judicial and legal education. While these policy changes are easy to track on a statewide level, the details about local practices vary from court to court. It is also difficult to determine what occurs during trials

[*] NATIONAL CENTER FOR STATE COURTS, CENTER FOR JURY STUDIES, THE STATE-OF-THE-STATES SURVEY OF JURY IMPROVEMENT EFFORTS, EXECUTIVE SUMMARY (2007). Reprinted with the permission of National Center for State Courts.

themselves, as most jury trial techniques are permitted "in the sound discretion of the trial court." Until now, we have had little idea how often judges exercise that discretion.

This executive summary sets forth key findings derived from the first-ever State-of-the-States Survey of Jury Improvement Efforts.

* * *

National Jury Trial Rate

* * *

The State-of-the-States Survey provided an opportunity to estimate the number of jury trials that take place in state courts. Annually, state courts conduct an estimated 148,558 jury trials. An additional 5,940 jury trials (estimated) are conducted annually in federal courts. California has the largest volume of jury trials – approximately 16,000 per year. Vermont and Wyoming had the lowest volume (126 trials annually). Jury trial rates also varied substantially from a low of 15 per 100,000 population in Alabama to a high of 177 per 100,000 population in Alaska.

* * *

Trial Practices

Once the jury has been impaneled, the evidentiary portion of the trial begins. This aspect of trial practice has perhaps undergone the most dramatic changes in recent years. In particular, a change has occurred in the way judges and attorneys view the jury's role during trial. The traditional view is that jurors are passive receptacles of evidence and law who are capable of suspending judgment about the evidence until final deliberations, of remembering all of the evidence presented at trial, and of considering the evidence without reference to preexisting experiences or attitudes. This view has rapidly given way to a contemporary understanding of how adults process information, which posits that jurors actively filter evidence according to preexisting attitudes, making preliminary judgments throughout the trial. This view of juror decision-making has spurred a great deal of support for trial procedures designed to provide jurors with common-sense tools to facilitate juror recall and comprehension of evidence. The Judge and Lawyer Survey asked trial practitioners to report their experiences with these types of techniques in their most recent trial.

Permitting jurors to take notes is a widely accepted practice in most states. Judges in more than two-thirds of trials in both state and federal courts permitted juror note taking. Other practices, such as providing at least one written copy of instructions and providing guidance on conducting deliberations, are also common in state courts.

A more controversial technique involves permitting jurors to submit written questions to witnesses. A substantial and growing body of empirical research has found that this practice, if properly controlled by the trial judge, improves juror comprehension without prejudicing litigants' rights to a fair trial. The crux of the controversy stems from philosophical arguments about the role of the jury in the context of an adversarial system of justice. Given the ongoing controversy in many jurisdictions, what is most surprising from the data is that jurors were allowed to submit written questions in 15.1 percent of all trials.

Again, states vary to the extent that these types of trial practices are encouraged or discouraged through state statutes, court rules, and case law. There was a surprising degree of judicial non-compliance with established rules on trial practices, especially where those rules prohibited innovative techniques. For example, Pennsylvania and South Carolina prohibit jurors to take notes in criminal trials, yet more than one-fourth of juries were permitted to do so in those states and, in most instances, jurors were even given writing materials with which to do so! Non-compliance with other rules governing jury trial practices was widespread, although generally not to the extent of non-compliance with prohibitions on juror note taking.

To gauge the extent to which statewide initiatives had an effect on judges' willingness to use jury innovations, we constructed an index of key jury techniques consisting of juror note taking, juror questions, juror discussions, pre-instructions, instructions before closing arguments, and written instructions. We then measured the impact of various statewide initiatives to determine which, if any, resulted in increased use of these techniques. We found that educational efforts and efforts to test and evaluate these techniques resulted in increased use of innovative techniques.

Jury Trial Innovations: Percent of Trial Practitioners reporting...

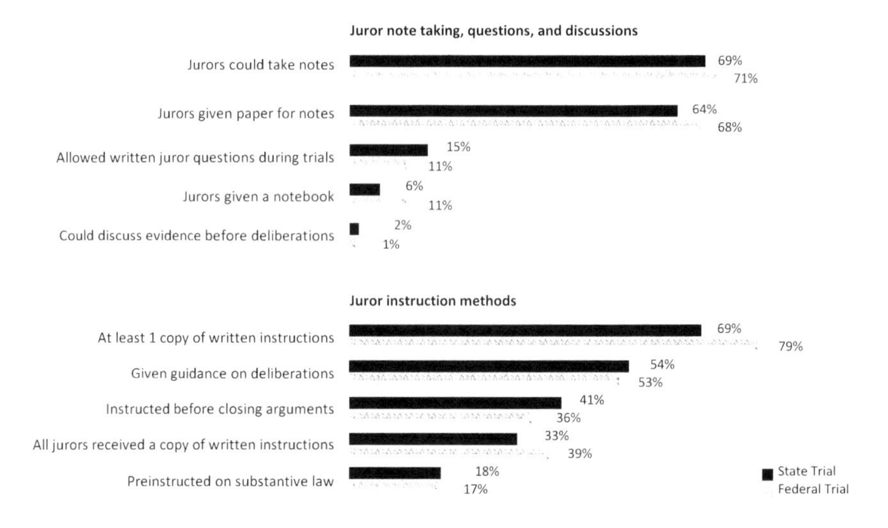

Benjamin Madison, *Trial by Jury or by Military Tribunal for Accused Terrorist Detainees Facing the Death Penalty? An Examination of Principles that Transcend the U.S. Constitution*[*]

A. Transcendent Principles Underlying the Right to a Jury Trial

1. The Jury as Part of Governmental Checks and Balances

The Founding Fathers undoubtedly were familiar with the historical roots of the jury in the English legal system. They would have known that the genesis of the Magna Carta in 1215 was a controversy involving the king's power. English barons led by Archbishop Stephen Langton forced King John to sign the famous document by which he recognized limits on the king's powers. Chief among these limits was the right of the barons to be free from imprisonment without a judgment of their peers....

[*] Benjamin V. Madison III, *Trial by Jury or by Military Tribunal for Accused Terrorist Detainees Facing the Death Penalty? An Examination of Principles that Transcend the U.S. Constitution*, 17 U. FLA. J.L. & PUB. POL'Y 347, 391-97 (2006). Reprinted with the permission of the author.

Likewise, many of the Framers of the U.S. Constitution would have studied Sir William Blackstone's Commentaries on the Laws of England and thereby learned that the right to jury, with its genesis in Magna Carta, developed in the common law as a right of each person regardless of social station. Blackstone placed the right to a jury trial among the chief protections of free persons....

Juries served as a buffer between the king and the people. Blackstone [wrote]:

> [I]n times of difficulty and danger, more is to be apprehended from the violence and partiality of judges appointed by the crown, in suits between the king and the subject, than in disputes between one individual and another, to settle the metes and boundaries of private property. Our law has therefore wisely placed this strong and two-fold barrier, of a presentment and a trial by jury, between the liberties of the people, and the prerogative of the crown.

The Framers' enthusiasm for the jury system resulted in part from the trial in 1735 of John Peter Zenger, an editor and printer of a New York newspaper. Zenger had criticized the Royal Governor of New York for removing a chief justice. Zenger was charged with seditious libel. Three grand juries refused to indict. The Attorney General of New York then charged Zenger by information and thus bypassed the grand jury. Andrew Hamilton, Zenger's defense counsel at trial, argued that the jury had a right to challenge both law and fact. A jury acquitted Zenger and his trial became a symbol of the power of the jury to protect individuals from the power of the king and his agents. To circumvent similar verdicts, the British extended the jurisdiction of the admiralty courts—which lacked juries—to enforce English revenue laws. Such executive manipulation is precisely what the Declaration of Independence decried in complaining that King George III was "depriving us...of the benefits of trial by jury."

From the genesis of the U.S. system, the jury has served as the primary means of protecting individuals from being unjustly imprisoned or executed. The Federal Farmer, Anti-Federalist writings published at the time of The Federalist Papers, asserted that the people secured through the jury "their just and rightful control in the judicial department." The Federal Farmer also asserted that the jury "enables them [the jurors] to acquire information and knowledge in the affairs and government of the society; and to come forward, in turn, as sentinels and guardians of each other." Another Anti-Federalist writing called the jury the "democratic lower branch of the judiciary power." A recent decision by the U.S. Supreme Court echoed the words of the Federal Farmer and reiterated that the jury serves as an important check on the government.

In the Anglo-American tradition, therefore, persons of all political stripes have agreed on at least one thing: the jury system serves justice by allowing average citizens to serve as a check within the broader scheme of governmental checks and balances. This broad support—based on the intuitive awareness that the jury serves a crucial role in administering justice—derives from the fact that the jury system is actually tapping into a number of transcendent principles. A deeper exploration of those principles is thus in order.

2. Principles Underlying the Jury as Part of Governmental Checks and Balances

The Framers were not only well versed in English law—they knew both the truths revealed in Scripture and their own experience of human nature. In this respect, John Calvin significantly influenced the Framers' perspective. Likewise, the political theorist who most influenced the Framers—Baron de Montesquieu—shared a keen awareness of the vulnerabilities of human nature. In the opening to *The Spirit of Laws*, Montesquieu states:

> Man, as a physical being…incessessantly transgresses the laws established by God, and changes those of his own instituting. He is left to his private direction, though a limited being, like all finite intelligences, to ignorance and error; even his imperfect knowledge he loses; and a sensible creature he is hurried away by a thousand impetuous passions.

Although Calvin and Montesquieu held a stark view of human nature, the two thinkers shared the hope that properly devised institutions could offset the effects of the vulnerability of human nature to bias, prejudice, and self-interest. At the Philadelphia Convention, the Founding Fathers examined each institution with the assumption that it could be corrupted, but carried a "steadfast, if wary, optimism that they might craft a governmental structure that would preserve liberty." They knew the weaknesses of a monarchy, having experienced them first-hand under King George III. They also, however, knew all too well the limitations of a democracy lacking institutional leadership, such as that which existed under the Articles of Confederation. Hence, the Framers developed a republican form of government, with defined institutional limits and delegated powers, and an intricate series of checks and balances designed to minimize the effects of human frailties and self-interest.

The institutions most often identified as providing constitutional checks are the Judiciary, the Congress, and the President. Yet the People represent another important check within the system. The People may, of course, serve as a check by speaking at the polls, by exercising their right to free speech, and by other means. A more subtle way in which the People may actually become part of the governmental system is through service on a jury. The jury represents one of the checks on the judicial power in which average laypersons can actively participate.

The jury is the favored Anglo-American procedural mechanism for limiting the vulnerabilities of human nature to bias, prejudice, and self-interest in the judicial system. In other words, it is the mechanism traditionally favored in England and America to promote impartial decision-making. This root desire for impartiality in the judicial process is universal. It is a central tenet of Christianity. In Leviticus, for instance, the Torah states: "Do not pervert justice, do not show partiality to the poor or favoritism to the great, but judge your neighbor fairly." And in Deuteronomy we again hear the same injunction: "And I charged your judges at that time: Hear the disputes between your brothers and judge fairly, whether the case is between brother Israelites or between one of them and an alien. Do not show partiality in judging: hear both small and great alike." Scripture elsewhere explains that human judges, in doing their job, are emulating the divine judge:

> Consider carefully what you do, because you are not judging for man but for the Lord, who is with you whenever you give a verdict. Now let the fear of the Lord be upon you. Judge carefully, for with the Lord our God there is no injustice or partiality or bribery.

This insistence of impartiality as the sine qua non of a judicial system is a tenet not only of Christianity but also of other leading world religions.

As Calvin, Montesquieu, and the Framers recognized, the problem in achieving the principle of impartial decision-making arises from the nature of mankind. Human nature is imperfect and, as a result, we must have checks on individual decision-makers to avoid the bias and prejudice that impede justice. James Madison, the architect of the intricate system of checks and balances in the Constitution, put it best in *Federalist No. 51*:

> But what is government itself but the greatest of all reflections on human nature? If men were angels, no government would be necessary. If angels were to govern men, neither external nor internal controuls on government would be necessary. In framing a government which is to be administered by men over men, the great difficulty lies in this: You must first enable the government to controul the governed; and in the next place, oblige it to controul itself....

One could argue that adding together a number of individuals carries the risk of multiplying human frailties as opposed to limiting them. Such an argument is unpersuasive, however, because it rests on an overly pessimistic view of human nature. Every person has flaws, but their moral compass helps in sorting out right and wrong. Aristotle conceived of a sense of natural justice within each person that, though imperfect, helped the person toward virtue. The natural law tradition, perhaps best stated by Thomas Aquinas, contemplates this inherent ability to move toward truth as "right reason." Great legal minds like Coke and Blackstone reiterated the principal that all persons, though limited by human vulnerabilities, have the inherent capacity through "right reason" (conscience) to get to the true or just answer to a human situation. By bringing together a number of moral compasses, one in each jury member, a jury is more likely to get to a correct or just result by having several moral compasses at work on a problem (the case). If one person's moral compass is weak due to greater human vulnerability (or perhaps even a life crisis distracting that person), the other jury members' moral compasses may work to offset that individual's weakness.

Nevertheless, no one should hold out the jury as a perfect means of limiting the biases and prejudices of human beings. At the least, the jury serves as one means of seeking the goal of providing a check within the judicial system on such prejudices. Madison refers not only to "dependence on the People," but also to "auxiliary precautions" as being essential to controlling government. He then explains more fully the rationale behind such auxiliary precautions:

> This policy of supplying, by opposite and rival interests, the defect of better motives, might be traced through the whole system of human affairs, private as well as public. We see it particularly displayed in all the subordinate distributions of power; where the constant aim is to divide and arrange the several offices in such a manner as that each may be a check on the other; that the private

interest of every individual, may be a Sentinel over the public rights.

The jury certainly fits within this concept of a check on other branches of government, especially on judges (appointed by the executive in the federal system) in criminal matters. The lesson of centuries of English experience was that the jury filled this role well. Thus, whether a jury as a whole checks the vulnerabilities of the individual members of the jury, experience suggests that the jury at least serves as a check on judges.

Questions

1. What is Frank's "realistic" theory of the jury's function?

2. Frank uses a rough calculation to reflect how the facts and legal rules are supposed to generate a decision: $R \times F = D$ (the Rules times the Facts equals the Decision). The traditional view is that juries determine the F, but merely follow the judge's instructions about the R. Why does Frank reject the traditional view?

3. According to Frank, how effective is the jury at determining the F? Why?

4. Whose view of juries is more accurate, Blackstone's or Frank's? Is the truth somewhere in the middle?

5. According to the National Center for State Courts, what are some recent innovations in the way juries operate?

6. Do the recent jury innovations adequately respond to Frank's concerns?

7. According to Madison, what explains the enthusiasm of the Constitution's framers for the jury trial?

8. Madison argues that both scripture and "their own experience of human nature" shaped the framer's view of juries. How?

9. Is trial by jury consistent with biblical principles? Is it compelled by biblical principles? Consider Deuteronomy 1:16-17; II Chronicles 19:4-7; Job 34:17-19; Isaiah 64:6; Ephesians 2:1-3; Genesis 1:26-30; and Romans 2:14-15.

10. If you were the Jury Czar and could create any jury system you wanted (such as abolishing jury trials, preserving the system as is, or reforming it) what would you do?

Chapter 6 Contracts: The Efficient Breach Theory

Introduction

A controversial issue in the law of contracts surrounds what is known as the efficient breach of contract. An efficient breach occurs where a party to a contract breaches it because he or she is economically better off breaching the contract and compensating the other party than in performing the contract, often because the breach enables him or her to enter into a contract even more lucrative than the first one.

How should the law address such breaches? At common law, the breaching party merely had to pay compensatory damages to the aggrieved party, even in the case of an efficient yet willful breach. In some cases this rule provides an incentive to breach a contract. The author of our first piece, Judge Richard Posner, applying economic analysis, defends this rule as efficient and appropriate. This piece, like the one appearing in Chapter 3 Section C, comes from Posner's book, *Economic Analysis of Law*.

The author of the second piece, Peter Linzer, a law professor at the University of Houston Law Center, argues that the existing common law rule should not be applied in all cases. He insists that in many cases, the law should take into account moral considerations and award specific performance (require the breaching party to fulfill the contract rather than simply pay damages). Linzer received an A.B. from Cornell University and a J.D from Columbia University. He is a noted contracts scholar. In addition to publishing numerous articles in the field, he has published two editions of his *A Contracts Anthology* and he served as the editorial adviser for the *Restatement (Second) of Contracts*. The piece reproduced here is an excerpt from an article Linzer published in the *Columbia Law Review* in 1981.

Richard Posner, *Economic Analysis of Law**

§4.8 Fundamental Principles of Contract Damages

When a breach of contract is established, the issue becomes one of the proper remedy. There are, in theory anyway, a bewildering variety of possibilities, which in very rough order of increasing severity can be arrayed as follows:

(1) the promisee's reliance loss (the costs he incurred in reasonable reliance on the promisor's performing the contract);

(2) the expectation loss (loss of the anticipated profit of the contract);

(3) liquidated damages (damages actually specified in the contract as the money remedy for a breach);

(4) consequential damages (ripple effects on the promisee's business from the breach);

(5) restitution (to the promisee of the promisor's profits from the breach);

(6) specific performance (ordering the promisor to perform on penalty of being found in contempt of court);

(7) a money penalty specified in the contract, or other punitive damages; and

(8) criminal sanctions.

We shall examine all of these possible sanctions—plus self-help—in this and succeeding sections.

It will help to frame the discussion to come back to the fundamental distinction between opportunistic and other breaches of contract. If a promisor breaks his promise merely to take advantage of the vulnerability of the promisee in a setting (the normal contract setting) where performance is sequential rather than simultaneous, then we might as well "throw the book" at the promisor. An example would be where A pays B in advance for goods and instead of delivering them B simply pockets A's money. Such conduct has no economic justification and ought to be heavily punished to deter such conduct in the future. However, as we shall see in Chapter 7, severe sanctions are costly to impose, so that, in general anyway, the lightest sanction that will do the trick is the most efficient. In the case of the opportunistic breach, that sanction is restitu-

* RICHARD POSNER, ECONOMIC ANALYSIS OF LAW 105-08 (3rd ed. 1986). Reprinted with the permission of Aspen Publishers, Richard Posner, Economic Analysis of Law, 3rd Edition, 20-26, 105-08, 137-41, 1986.

tion. The promisor broke his promise in order to make money—there can be no other reason in the case of such a breach. We can deter this kind of behavior by making it worthless to the promisor, which we do by making him hand over all his profits from the breach to the promisee; no lighter sanction would deter.

Most breaches of contract, however, are not opportunistic. Many are involuntary (performance is impossible at a reasonable cost); others are voluntary but (as we are about to see) efficient—which from an economic standpoint is the same case as that of an involuntary breach. These observations both explain the centrality of remedies to the law of contracts (can you see why?) and give point to Holmes's dictum, overbroad though it is, as we shall see, that it is not the policy of the law to compel adherence to contracts but only to require each party to choose between performing in accordance with the contract and compensating the other party for any injury resulting from a failure to perform. This view contains an important economic insight. In many cases it is uneconomical to induce completion of performance of a contract after it has been broken. I agree to purchase 100,000 widgets custom-ground for use as components in a machine that I manufacture. After I have taken delivery of 10,000, the market for my machine collapses. I promptly notify my supplier that I am terminating the contract, and admit that my termination is a breach of the contract. When notified of the termination he has not yet begun the custom grinding of the other 90,000 widgets, but he informs me that he intends to complete his performance under the contract and bill me accordingly. The custom-ground widgets have no use other than in my machine, and a negligible scrap value. To give the supplier any remedy that induced him to complete the contract after the breach would result in a waste of resources. The law is alert to this danger and, under the doctrine of mitigation of damages, would not give the supplier damages for any costs he incurred in continuing production after my notice of termination.

But isn't the danger unreal, if the Coase Theorem[¤] is true? There are only two parties, and there is a price for the supplier's forbearing to enforce his contract rights—indeed a range of prices—that will make both parties better off. But of course this is just another example of bilateral monopoly; transaction costs will be high even though (in a sense, because) there are only two parties.

Now suppose the contract is broken by the seller rather than the buyer. I need 100,000 custom-ground widgets for my machine but the

---

[¤] In a world without transaction costs, parties to a dispute will bargain toward efficient solutions regardless of their initial positions or the applicable rule of law.

supplier, after producing 50,000, is forced to suspend production because of a mechanical failure. Other suppliers are in a position to supply the remaining widgets that I need but I insist that the original supplier complete his performance of the contract. If the law compels completion (specific performance), the supplier will have to make arrangements with other producers to complete his contract with me. Not only may it be more costly for him to procure an alternative supplier than for me to do so directly (after all, I know my own needs best); it probably *is* more costly; otherwise the original supplier would have done it voluntarily, to minimize his liability for the breach of contract. To compel completion of the contract (or costly negotiations to discharge the promisor) would again result in a waste of resources, and again the law does not compel completion but confines the victim to simple damages.

But what are simple contract damages? Usually the objective of giving the promisor an incentive to fulfill his promise unless the result would be an inefficient use of resources (the production of the unwanted widgets in the first example, the roundabout procurement of a substitute supplier in the second) can be achieved by giving the promisee his expected profit on the transaction. If the supplier in the first example receives his expected profit from making 10,000 widgets, he will have no incentive to make the unwanted 90,000. We do not want him to make them; no one wants them. In the second example, if I receive my expected profit from dealing with the original supplier, I become indifferent to whether he completes his performance.

In these examples the breach was in a sense involuntary. It was committed only to avert a larger loss. The promisor would have been happier had there been no occasion to commit a breach. But in some cases a party would be tempted to break the contract simply because his profit from breach would exceed his expected profit from completion of the contract. If his profit from breach would also exceed the expected profit to the other party from completion of the contract, and if damages are limited to the loss of that expected profit, there will be an incentive to commit a breach. But there should be, as an example will show. I sign a contract to deliver 100,000 custom-ground widgets at 10¢ apiece to A, for use in his boiler factory. After I have delivered 10,000, B comes to me, explains that he desperately needs 25,000 custom-ground widgets at once since otherwise he will be forced to close his pianola factory at great cost, and offers me 15¢ apiece for 25,000 widgets. I sell him the widgets and as a result do not complete timely delivery to A, causing him to lose $1,000 in profits. Having obtained an additional profit of $1,250 on the sale to B, I am better off even after reimbursing A for his loss, and B is no worse off. The breach is Pareto superior, assuming that

A is fully compensated and no one else is hurt by the breach. True, if I had refused to sell to B, he could have gone to A and negotiated an assignment to him of part of A's contract with me. But this would have introduced an additional step, with additional transaction costs. Notice how careful the law must be not to exceed compensatory damages if it doesn't want to deter efficient breaches. This raises the question of whether the problem of overdeterring breaches of contract by heavy penalties could not be solved more easily by redefining the legal concept of breach of contract so that only inefficient terminations count as breaches. It could not be. Remember that an important function of contracts is to assign risks to superior risk bearers. If the risk materializes, the party to whom it was assigned must pay. It is no more important that he could not have prevented the risk from occurring at a reasonable, perhaps at any, cost than it is important that an insurance company could not have prevented the fire that destroyed the building it insured. The breach of contract corresponds to the occurrence of the event that is insured against.

Is the expectation loss, the loss of the expected profit of the contract, always the correct measure of compensatory damages for breach of contract? What if it exceeds the reliance loss? Suppose a manufacturer agrees to sell a machine for $100,000, delivery to be made in six months; and the day after the contract is signed the manufacturer defaults, realizing that he will lose $5,000 at the agreed-on price. The buyer's reliance loss—the sum of the costs he has irretrievably incurred as a result of the contract—is, let us say, zero, but it would cost him $112,000 to obtain a substitute machine. Why should he be allowed to use a measure of damages that gives him more (by $12,000) than he has actually lost? Isn't the $12,000, the money he would have saved if the contract had not been broken, a windfall? Whether it is or not, the reliance measure would encourage inefficient breaches. In the example, the net gain to the buyer from contractual performance is greater (by $7,000, the difference between $12,000 and $5,000) than the net loss ($5,000) to the seller, and we make that net gain a cost of breach to the seller, by giving the buyer his profit on the deal if the seller breaks the contract, in order to discourage an inefficient breach.

Peter Linzer, *On the Amorality of Contract Remedies*[*]

It seems right that people who make fair bargains should be held to them. Absent unconscionability, incapacity, or a like excuse, it should be wrong to break a contract. But the very notion of contracts is tied to remedies, and the law of contracts, unlike tort, has traditionally been sparing, if not niggardly, with them. It has emphasized an approach that excludes considerations of morality and is said to advance the objective of economic efficiency. This approach is evident in the introduction to contract remedies presented by the Restatement (Second) of Contracts:

> The traditional goal of the law of contract remedies has not been compulsion of the promisor to perform his promise but compensation of the promisee for the loss resulting from breach. "Willful" breaches have not been distinguished from other breaches, punitive damages have not been awarded for breach of contract, and specific performance has not been granted where compensation in damages is an adequate substitute for the injured party. In general, therefore, a party may find it advantageous to refuse to perform a contract if he will still have a net gain after he has fully compensated the injured party for the resulting loss.

This Article examines both the amoral stance reflected in the language of the second Restatement and the theory of economic efficiency that is used to defend it. It will be shown that in many cases the alleged necessary connection between efficiency and amorality is mythical. Especially in noncommercial transactions, where the exclusion of idiosyncratic values from efficiency analysis distorts that analysis, an accurate use of efficiency theory supports a moral approach to contracts.

* * *

I. Morality, Efficiency, and Breach

A. Breach in the Commercial Setting

In this Article, "morality" stands for the idea that it is both fair and appropriate to hold people to promises that they freely made. This view

[*] Peter Linzer, *On the Amorality of Contract Remedies*, 81 COLUM. L. REV. 111, 111-17, 131-32, 138-39 (1981). This article originally appeared at 81 COLUM. L. REV. 111 (1981). Reprinted by permission.

is inspired both by a desire to protect the promisee's reasonable expectations and by a sense that personal liberty requires that people be able to bind themselves in a manner that will be enforced by the courts. Notions of liberty of contract have changed over the years, and courts will not enforce promises that are induced unfairly or that contain unfair terms. Assuming a fair bargain, however defined, the law ought to hold the parties to their agreement. This notion, however, has never been universally accepted. In a famous passage in *The Path of the Law*, Holmes wrote:

> Nowhere is the confusion between legal and moral ideas more manifest than in the law of contract.... The duty to keep a contract at common law means a prediction that you must pay damages if you do not keep it—and nothing else. If you commit a tort, you are liable to pay a compensatory sum. If you commit a contract, you are liable to pay a compensatory sum unless the promised event comes to pass, and that is all the difference. But such a mode of looking at the matter stinks in the nostrils of those who think it advantageous to get as much ethics into the law as they can.

Holmes's amorality is reflected today in economic rationales of contract. The essential theory, labeled efficiency, seeks to maximize net social welfare by encouraging actions that benefit some without harming others. Efficiency seeks to approach Pareto optimality, the position from which it is impossible to move to benefit one individual without harming another. A corollary to Pareto optimality is the so-called Kaldor-Hicks Compensation Principle, which posits that a benefit to one individual, even if it carries with it a loss to another, increases society's welfare so long as the benefited party is able fully to compensate the losing party and to remain better off than before.

In the context of contracts, efficiency theory suggests that promisors who breach increase society's welfare if their benefit exceeds the losses of their promisees. Such failure to perform, the so-called efficient breach of contract, is illustrated by the following. Assume that Athos owns a woodworking factory capable of taking on one more major project. He contracts to supply Porthos with 100,000 chairs at $10 per chair, which will bring Athos a net profit of $2 per chair, or $200,000 on the contract. Before any work takes place, Aramis, who sells tables, approaches Athos. Although there are several chair factories in the area, only Atho's factory can make tables. If Athos will supply Aramis with 50,000 tables, Aramis will pay him $40 per table. Athos can produce the tables for $25, so he can make a net profit of $750,000 if he uses his factory for

Aramis's tables. But to do so, he must breach his contract with Porthos. There are other chair factories, and Porthos will be able to get the chairs from one of them—for example, from D'Artagnan's. Let us assume that because of his distress situation Porthos will have to pay D'Artagnan 20% more than Athos's price for comparable chairs, and that Porthos will sustain $100,000 in incidental administrative costs and consequential costs such as damages for delay to his customers. Even with these costs, Porthos will lose only $300,000 because of Athos's breach, and Athos can reimburse him in full and still make $450,000 profit, over twice the profit from his contract with Porthos.

As one might expect, efficiency theorists applaud the Athoses of the world for breaching their contracts. Thus, Richard Posner sets up a similar illustration and notes that "if damages are limited to loss of expected profit, there will be an incentive to commit a breach. There should be....The expectation rule thus assures that the product ends up where it is most valuable." Robert Birmingham reaches similar conclusions about a labor contract when the employee is offered a better job.

Although these positions conflict with the notion of *pacta sunt servanda* [pacts must be respected] and with the moral view developed above, they do make some sense. People generally enter into commercial contracts and routine labor contracts for purely economic reasons and can therefore be fully compensated with damages for injuries caused by breach. If we prevent Athos from building tables for Aramis, we force him to waste his resources, with no economic benefit to Porthos. Therefore, while it would be possible to restrain Athos by making his breach of contract a crime, by imposing punitive damages or penalties on him, or by ordering specific performance, the law does not do this. Instead, section 2-712 of the Uniform Commercial Code compensates the aggrieved buyer for exactly the loss that Porthos suffered: the difference between the cost of cover and the contract price, together with incidental and consequential damages. Thus, despite our concern for holding parties to their word, at least in the conventional market situation that we have illustrated, law, economics, and arguably common sense all condone the deliberate and willful breach.

B. Breach in the Noncommercial Setting

While the amoral approach may be justified in the commercial setting, where fungible substitutes are available, it is not necessarily justified in other surroundings. Efficiency theory requires valuing all costs and benefits of breach; consequently, much of the scholarship in law and economics has been devoted to measuring values for which there is no conventional market. Economists have attempted to discern some of these values by inquiring how much someone would relinquish for them. The problem with this approach, however, is that it is hypothetical—there is no actual auction going on. The economist can only speculate about what is important to the parties, and is likely to ignore or denigrate those values that only the parties can accurately assess. Thus, in attempting to apply his theories to the right of privacy, Posner stated his economic assumption that privacy is an "intermediate" rather than "final" good: "people are assumed not to desire or value privacy or prying in themselves but to use these goods as inputs into the production of income or some other broad measure of utility or welfare." Posner did this, of course, to avoid the deeply felt idiosyncratic values that cause people to value privacy in its own right, values that he had no way to assess.

When people enter into contracts, they also may be motivated by nonmonetary considerations. The end to be achieved by performance may be desired in and of itself, not as a means to an increase in wealth measured by conventional methods of valuation. Consider the well-known case of *Peevyhouse v. Garland Coal & Mining Co.*,[23] in which a strip-mining company breached its promise to restore a couple's farmland. If the land was important to them as a home as well as a source of income, the loss caused them by the breach could not be measured solely by a reduction in market value. Any economic analysis that assigns no value to their love of their home or treats the promise to restore the land as merely instrumental to protecting its market value is incapable of measuring the true costs and benefits of breach.

* * *

III. Morality, Efficiency, and Specific Performance

A. A Proposed Approach

Economic efficiency and the moral value in enforcing promises, far from being in conflict, together challenge the traditional primacy of money damages favored by the second *Restatement*. In place of the second *Restatement*'s requirement that money damages be inadequate, courts should adopt a two-step test for determining whether specific performance should be decreed. First, they should compare the efficacy of money damages with that of specific performance in giving the promisee what he bargained for, paying attention especially to his idiosyncratic in-

[23] 382 P.2d 109 (Okla. 1962), cert. denied, 375 U.S. 906 (1963).

terests. In the typical commercial transaction involving fungible goods, this comparison will often favor money damages; if so, the analysis is complete and only damages should be awarded. In the noncommercial transaction, however, because of the promisee's idiosyncratic values, the comparison will often find money damages less efficacious than specific performance.

In such a case, the court should then balance the cost to the promisee of receiving money damages in the place of performance against costs of judicial supervision, unusual hardships caused the promisor by threatened or actual punishment, and costs to a society that holds itself above imprisonment for debt or for matters of conscience. These burdens, which are often overstated in the abstract, will often prove avoidable through careful tailoring of remedies. Only when these burdens are insurmountable in the particular case, and justify the costs to the promisee, should the court deny him specific relief and remit him to money damages.

This cost-benefit analysis, which the second *Restatement* adopts with respect to the problem of judicial administration, is illustrated by the celebrated case of *City Stores Co. v. Ammerman*.[137] The defendants, developers of a suburban shopping center, promised the owner of a Washington, D.C., department store, Lansburgh's, that it would be given the "opportunity to accept a lease on terms at least equal to those offered to other major department stores in the [shopping] center." Defendants breached, because a lease to Lansburgh's would have precluded renting to Sears, a potentially more profitable tenant, and plaintiff sued for specific performance. Declaring that contracts requiring extensive court supervision should be enforced "unless the difficulties of supervision outweigh the importance of specific performance to the plaintiff," Judge Gasch of the District of Columbia District Court balanced these two considerations. Despite the absence of substantial terms of the lease, including details of design, construction, and price of the building, which, with other factors, could have caused the court substantial supervisory problems, Judge Gasch deemphasized the enforcement problems, finding that rival department stores' leases provided such standards "as to make design and approval of plaintiff's store a fairly simple matter, if the parties deal with each other in good faith and expeditiously, as I shall hereafter order." In addition, he provided that a master would be appointed to resolve disputes if the parties were unable to agree on terms. On the other side of the scale, Judge Gasch found three reasons the plaintiff needed

---

[137] 266 F. Supp. 766 (D.D.C. 1967), aff'd, 394 F.2d 950 (D.C. Cir. 1968).

equitable relief: damages for breach of a long-term contract would be impossible to compute; the plaintiff could not build the store itself and seek damages, since it needed defendants' permission to go on the land in question; and the shopping center was the plaintiff's only remaining way effectively to expand into the Washington suburbs. Since the plaintiff's need for specific relief outweighed the supervisory burden on the court, Judge Gasch granted the plaintiff's plea for specific performance.

* * *

Conclusion

The general use of specific performance will produce truer economic efficiency than a system that counts the money cost of performance to the promisor but not the unquantifiable emotional and other costs of nonperformance to the promisee. Money damages lend themselves to the selective valuation so often used by economists, discounting things that are important to some people but that do not easily translate into money. By holding the parties to their bargain, but permitting them to negotiate out, specific performance lets no outsiders substitute their values for those of the parties. Except in the most fungible of commercial transactions, courts should encourage this self-regulating and thus more efficient method of valuation and dispute resolution.

More important, it is simply right that one get what he was promised. This is not the place to figure out why we enforce promises, but surely there is a reason beyond efficient allocation of resources. The origins of enforcement may be religious, or religion may have been used to achieve utility, but I think that today most people believe that one should stand by one's word. This is as it should be, for when a person bargains for a promise he puts trust in the promisor. This is especially true in noncommercial transactions and in transactions involving idiosyncratic values, yet often these are the situations where courts are most likely to remit the victim to inadequate money damages, rather than to compel the promisor to carry out his bargain.

Predictability is an important value in law, as should be the promotion of economic efficiency. But most important are fairness and justice. If courts take the amoral approach of Holmes or the second *Restatement*, defaulting promisors will often be able to shift costs ignored by the law to promisees, parties who trusted their promisors and who must now take second best through money damages. If, instead, the courts regularly order specific performance and hold promisors to their promises rather than to a diluted substitute in money damages, predictability, economic efficiency, and fairness all will be achieved.

Questions

1. Both Posner and Linzer refer to Holmes. What was Holmes' view on the purpose of contract law? Is it to enforce contracts?

2. Do Posner and Linzer agree with Holmes?

3. What does Posner believe is the appropriate remedy for an efficient breach of contract? Why doesn't he want to deter efficient breaches?

4. Why does Linzer believe morality should affect the choice of remedies for breach of contract?

5. Does Linzer agree with Posner about how an efficient breach should be handled?

6. According to Linzer, why aren't compensatory damages always enough?

7. With which author do you most agree? Are the following passages relevant? Ecclesiastes 5:4-5; Proverbs 20:25; and Psalm 15:1-5.

Chapter 7 Constitutional and Human Rights

A. Abortion Rights

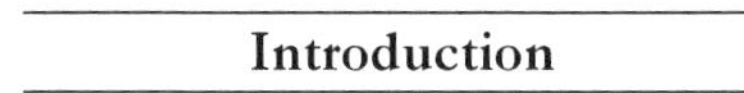

Introduction

In the last 60 years or so, many of the most significant and controversial legal issues have involved rights claims by individuals or groups. In the United States, claimants have increasingly requested legal protection for constitutional rights based on the Bill of Rights or the Fourteenth Amendment. Around the world, individuals have increasingly sought enforcement of human rights enumerated in international conventions ratified since the end of World War II. This chapter examines the way courts have responded to both sets of rights claims.

Section A addresses the claim that the Fourteenth Amendment to the constitution protects a woman's right to obtain an abortion. The Supreme Court first concluded that the Fourteenth Amendment protects such a right in its 1973 decision, *Roe v. Wade*, 410 U.S. 113 (1973). In later decisions, the Court considered the extent to which states could put limitations on that right. The next piece is an excerpt from one of those decisions, *Planned Parenthood of Southeastern Pennsylvania v. Casey*, 505 U.S. 833 (1992). In it, the Supreme Court considered whether certain restrictions placed by Pennsylvania on abortion violated the Due Process clause of the Fourteenth Amendment.

The case is included here for the legal philosophy seen in the decision, not for the details of the constitutional analysis. Nonetheless, the following may be helpful as background. The Fourteenth Amendment states in relevant part: "nor shall any state deprive any person of life, liberty, or property without due process of law." The readings in Chapter 2 reveal that this amendment comes from the common law, which protected citizens' life, liberty, and property from government oppression by requiring the government to follow just procedures before interfering with any of the three rights. In the United States, due *process* has been interpreted to enable courts to strike down certain laws based on their *substance*, even if the procedure by which those laws were enacted and enforced was just.

Following *Casey* is another excerpt from Michael Paulsen's article, "Accusing Justice." In it, Paulsen makes a natural law argument against abortion. As you read, compare the worldview expressed in the article with the worldview expressed in *Casey*.

Planned Parenthood v. Casey[*]

Justice O'CONNOR, Justice KENNEDY, and Justice SOUTER announced the judgment of the Court and delivered the opinion of the Court with respect to Parts I, II, III, V-A, V-C, and VI, an opinion with respect to Part V-E, in which Justice STEVENS joins, and an opinion with respect to Parts IV, V-B, and V-D.

I

Liberty finds no refuge in a jurisprudence of doubt. Yet 19 years after our holding that the Constitution protects a woman's right to terminate her pregnancy in its early stages, *Roe v. Wade*, 410 U.S. 113, 93 S.Ct. 705, 35 L.Ed.2d 147 (1973), that definition of liberty is still questioned. Joining the respondents as *amicus curiae*, the United States, as it has done in five other cases in the last decade, again asks us to overrule *Roe*. See Brief for Respondents 104-117; Brief for United States as *Amicus Curiae* 8.

At issue in these cases are five provisions of the Pennsylvania Abortion Control Act of 1982, as amended in 1988 and 1989. 18 Pa. Cons. Stat. §§ 3203-3220 (1990). Relevant portions of the Act are set forth in the Appendix. *Infra*, at 2833. The Act requires that a woman seeking an abortion give her informed consent prior to the abortion procedure, and specifies that she be provided with certain information at least 24 hours before the abortion is performed. § 3205. For a minor to obtain an abortion, the Act requires the informed consent of one of her parents, but provides for a judicial bypass option if the minor does not wish to or cannot obtain a parent's consent. § 3206. Another provision of the Act requires that, unless certain exceptions apply, a married woman seeking an abortion must sign a statement indicating that she has notified her husband of her intended abortion. § 3209. The Act exempts compliance

[*] Planned Parenthood of Se. Pa. v. Casey, 505 U.S. 833 (1992).

with these three requirements in the event of a "medical emergency," which is defined in § 3203 of the Act. See §§ 3203, 3205(a), 3206(a), 3209(c). In addition to the above provisions regulating the performance of abortions, the Act imposes certain reporting requirements on facilities that provide abortion services. §§ 3207(b), 3214(a), 3214(f).

Before any of these provisions took effect, the petitioners, who are five abortion clinics and one physician representing himself as well as a class of physicians who provide abortion services, brought this suit seeking declaratory and injunctive relief. Each provision was challenged as unconstitutional on its face. The District Court entered a preliminary injunction against the enforcement of the regulations, and, after a 3-day bench trial, held all the provisions at issue here unconstitutional, entering a permanent injunction against Pennsylvania's enforcement of them. 744 F.Supp. 1323 (ED Pa.1990). The Court of Appeals for the Third Circuit affirmed in part and reversed in part, upholding all of the regulations except for the husband notification requirement. 947 F.2d 682 (1991). We granted certiorari. 502 U.S. 1056, 112 S.Ct. 931, 117 L.Ed.2d 104 (1992).

The Court of Appeals found it necessary to follow an elaborate course of reasoning even to identify the first premise to use to determine whether the statute enacted by Pennsylvania meets constitutional standards. See 947 F.2d, at 687-698. And at oral argument in this Court, the attorney for the parties challenging the statute took the position that none of the enactments can be upheld without overruling *Roe v. Wade*. Tr. of Oral Arg. 5-6. We disagree with that analysis; but we acknowledge that our decisions after *Roe* cast doubt upon the meaning and reach of its holding. Further, THE CHIEF JUSTICE admits that he would overrule the central holding of *Roe* and adopt the rational relationship test as the sole criterion of constitutionality. See *post*, at 2855, 2867. State and federal courts as well as legislatures throughout the Union must have guidance as they seek to address this subject in conformance with the Constitution. Given these premises, we find it imperative to review once more the principles that define the rights of the woman and the legitimate authority of the State respecting the termination of pregnancies by abortion procedures.

After considering the fundamental constitutional questions resolved by *Roe*, principles of institutional integrity, and the rule of *stare decisis*, we are led to conclude this: the essential holding of *Roe v. Wade* should be retained and once again reaffirmed.

It must be stated at the outset and with clarity that *Roe*'s essential holding, the holding we reaffirm, has three parts. First is a recognition of the right of the woman to choose to have an abortion before viability and to obtain it without undue interference from the State. Before viability, the State's interests are not strong enough to support a prohibition of abortion or the imposition of a substantial obstacle to the woman's effective right to elect the procedure. Second is a confirmation of the State's power to restrict abortions after fetal viability, if the law contains exceptions for pregnancies which endanger the woman's life or health. And third is the principle that the State has legitimate interests from the outset of the pregnancy in protecting the health of the woman and the life of the fetus that may become a child. These principles do not contradict one another; and we adhere to each.

II

Constitutional protection of the woman's decision to terminate her pregnancy derives from the Due Process Clause of the Fourteenth Amendment. It declares that no State shall "deprive any person of life, liberty, or property, without due process of law." The controlling word in the cases before us is "liberty." Although a literal reading of the Clause might suggest that it governs only the procedures by which a State may deprive persons of liberty, for at least 105 years, since *Mugler v. Kansas*, 123 U.S. 623, 660-661, 8 S.Ct. 273, 291, 31 L.Ed. 205 (1887), the Clause has been understood to contain a substantive component as well, one "barring certain government actions regardless of the fairness of the procedures used to implement them." *Daniels v. Williams*, 474 U.S. 327, 331, 106 S.Ct. 662, 665, 88 L.Ed.2d 662 (1986). As Justice Brandeis (joined by Justice Holmes) observed, "[d]espite arguments to the contrary which had seemed to me persuasive, it is settled that the due process clause of the Fourteenth Amendment applies to matters of substantive law as well as to matters of procedure. Thus all fundamental rights comprised within the term liberty are protected by the Federal Constitution from invasion by the States." *Whitney v. California*, 274 U.S. 357, 373, 47 S.Ct. 641, 647, 71 L.Ed. 1095 (1927) (concurring opinion). "[T]he guaranties of due process, though having their roots in Magna Carta's '*per legem terrae*' [by the law of the land] and considered as procedural safeguards 'against executive usurpation and tyranny,' have in this country 'become bulwarks also against arbitrary legislation.'" *Poe v. Ullman*, 367 U.S. 497, 541, 81 S.Ct. 1752, 1776, 6 L.Ed.2d 989 (1961) (Harlan, J., dissenting from dismissal on jurisdictional grounds) (quoting *Hurtado v. California*, 110 U.S. 516, 532, 4 S.Ct. 111, 119, 28 L.Ed. 232 (1884)).

The most familiar of the substantive liberties protected by the Fourteenth Amendment are those recognized by the Bill of Rights. We have held that the Due Process Clause of the Fourteenth Amendment incorporates most of the Bill of Rights against the States. See, *e.g.*, *Duncan v. Louisiana*, 391 U.S. 145, 147-148, 88 S.Ct. 1444, 1446, 20 L.Ed.2d 491 (1968). It is tempting, as a means of curbing the discretion of federal judges, to suppose that liberty encompasses no more than those rights already guaranteed to the individual against federal interference by the express provisions of the first eight Amendments to the Constitution. See *Adamson v. California*, 332 U.S. 46, 68-92, 67 S.Ct. 1672, 1683-1697, 91 L.Ed. 1903 (1947) (Black, J., dissenting). But of course this Court has never accepted that view.

It is also tempting, for the same reason, to suppose that the Due Process Clause protects only those practices, defined at the most specific level, that were protected against government interference by other rules of law when the Fourteenth Amendment was ratified. See *Michael H. v. Gerald D.*, 491 U.S. 110, 127-128, n. 6, 109 S.Ct. 2333, 2344-2345, n. 6, 105 L.Ed.2d 91 (1989) (opinion of SCALIA, J.). But such a view would be inconsistent with our law. It is a promise of the Constitution that there is a realm of personal liberty which the government may not enter. We have vindicated this principle before. Marriage is mentioned nowhere in the Bill of Rights and interracial marriage was illegal in most States in the 19th century, but the Court was no doubt correct in finding it to be an aspect of liberty protected against state interference by the substantive component of the Due Process Clause in *Loving v. Virginia*, 388 U.S. 1, 12, 87 S.Ct. 1817, 1824, 18 L.Ed.2d 1010 (1967) (relying, in an opinion for eight Justices, on the Due Process Clause). Similar examples may be found in *Turner v. Safley*, 482 U.S. 78, 94-99, 107 S.Ct. 2254, 2265-2267, 96 L.Ed.2d 64 (1987); in *Carey v. Population Services International*, 431 U.S. 678, 684-686, 97 S.Ct. 2010, 2015-2017, 52 L.Ed.2d 675 (1977); in *Griswold v. Connecticut*, 381 U.S. 479, 481-482, 85 S.Ct. 1678, 1680-1681, 14 L.Ed.2d 510 (1965), as well as in the separate opinions of a majority of the Members of the Court in that case, *id.*, at 486-488, 85 S.Ct., at 1682-1683 (Goldberg, J., joined by Warren, C.J., and Brennan, J., concurring) (expressly relying on due process), *id.*, at 500-502, 85 S.Ct., at 1690-1691 (Harlan, J., concurring in judgment) (same), *id.*, at 502-507, 85 S.Ct., at 1691-1694 (WHITE, J., concurring in judgment) (same); in *Pierce v. Society of Sisters*, 268 U.S. 510, 534-535, 45 S.Ct. 571, 573, 69 L.Ed. 1070 (1925); and in *Meyer v. Nebraska*, 262 U.S. 390, 399-403, 43 S.Ct. 625, 627, 67 L.Ed. 1042 (1923).

Neither the Bill of Rights nor the specific practices of States at the time of the adoption of the Fourteenth Amendment marks the outer limits of the substantive sphere of liberty which the Fourteenth Amendment protects. See U.S. Const., Amdt. 9. As the second Justice Harlan recognized:

> "[T]he full scope of the liberty guaranteed by the Due Process Clause cannot be found in or limited by the precise terms of the specific guarantees elsewhere provided in the Constitution. This 'liberty' is not a series of isolated points pricked out in terms of the taking of property; the freedom of speech, press, and religion; the right to keep and bear arms; the freedom from unreasonable searches and seizures; and so on. It is a rational continuum which, broadly speaking, includes a freedom from all substantial arbitrary impositions and purposeless restraints,...and which also recognizes, what a reasonable and sensitive judgment must, that certain interests require particularly careful scrutiny of the state needs asserted to justify their abridgment." *Poe v. Ullman*, supra, 367 U.S., at 543, 81 S.Ct., at 1777 (opinion dissenting from dismissal on jurisdictional grounds).

Justice Harlan wrote these words in addressing an issue the full Court did not reach in *Poe v. Ullman*, but the Court adopted his position four Terms later in *Griswold v. Connecticut, supra*. In *Griswold*, we held that the Constitution does not permit a State to forbid a married couple to use contraceptives. That same freedom was later guaranteed, under the Equal Protection Clause, for unmarried couples. See *Eisenstadt v. Baird*, 405 U.S. 438, 92 S.Ct. 1029, 31 L.Ed.2d 349 (1972). Constitutional protection was extended to the sale and distribution of contraceptives in *Carey v. Population Services International, supra*. It is settled now, as it was when the Court heard arguments in *Roe v. Wade*, that the Constitution places limits on a State's right to interfere with a person's most basic decisions about family and parenthood, see *Carey v. Population Services International, supra*; *Moore v. East Cleveland*, 431 U.S. 494, 97 S.Ct. 1932, 52 L.Ed.2d 531 (1977); *Eisenstadt v. Baird, supra*; *Loving v. Virginia, supra*; *Griswold v. Connecticut, supra*; *Skinner v. Oklahoma ex rel. Williamson*, 316 U.S. 535, 62 S.Ct. 1110, 86 L.Ed. 1655 (1942); *Pierce v. Society of Sisters, supra*; *Meyer v. Nebraska, supra*, as well as bodily integrity, see, *e.g.*, *Washington v. Harper*, 494 U.S. 210, 221-222, 110 S.Ct. 1028, 1036-1037, 108 L.Ed.2d 178 (1990); *Winston v. Lee*, 470 U.S. 753, 105 S.Ct. 1611, 84 L.Ed.2d 662 (1985); *Rochin v. California*, 342 U.S. 165, 72 S.Ct. 205, 96 L.Ed. 183 (1952).

The inescapable fact is that adjudication of substantive due process claims may call upon the Court in interpreting the Constitution to exercise that same capacity which by tradition courts always have exercised:

reasoned judgment. Its boundaries are not susceptible of expression as a simple rule. That does not mean we are free to invalidate state policy choices with which we disagree; yet neither does it permit us to shrink from the duties of our office. As Justice Harlan observed:

> "Due process has not been reduced to any formula; its content cannot be determined by reference to any code. The best that can be said is that through the course of this Court's decisions it has represented the balance which our Nation, built upon postulates of respect for the liberty of the individual, has struck between that liberty and the demands of organized society. If the supplying of content to this Constitutional concept has of necessity been a rational process, it certainly has not been one where judges have felt free to roam where unguided speculation might take them. The balance of which I speak is the balance struck by this country, having regard to what history teaches are the traditions from which it developed as well as the traditions from which it broke. That tradition is a living thing. A decision of this Court which radically departs from it could not long survive, while a decision which builds on what has survived is likely to be sound. No formula could serve as a substitute, in this area, for judgment and restraint." *Poe v. Ullman*, 367 U.S., at 542, 81 S.Ct., at 1776 (opinion dissenting from dismissal on jurisdictional grounds).

See also *Rochin v. California*, *supra*, 342 U.S., at 171-172, 72 S.Ct., at 209 (Frankfurter, J., writing for the Court) ("To believe that this judicial exercise of judgment could be avoided by freezing 'due process of law' at some fixed stage of time or thought is to suggest that the most important aspect of constitutional adjudication is a function for inanimate machines and not for judges").

Men and women of good conscience can disagree, and we suppose some always shall disagree, about the profound moral and spiritual implications of terminating a pregnancy, even in its earliest stage. Some of us as individuals find abortion offensive to our most basic principles of morality, but that cannot control our decision. Our obligation is to define the liberty of all, not to mandate our own moral code. The underlying constitutional issue is whether the State can resolve these philosophic questions in such a definitive way that a woman lacks all choice in the matter, except perhaps in those rare circumstances in which the pregnancy is itself a danger to her own life or health or is the result of rape or incest.

It is conventional constitutional doctrine that where reasonable people disagree the government can adopt one position or the other. See, *e.g.*, *Ferguson v. Skrupa*, 372 U.S. 726, 83 S.Ct. 1028, 10 L.Ed.2d 93 (1963); *Williamson v. Lee Optical of Okla., Inc.*, 348 U.S. 483, 75 S.Ct. 461, 99 L.Ed. 563 (1955). That theorem, however, assumes a state of affairs in which the choice does not intrude upon a protected liberty. Thus, while some people might disagree about whether or not the flag should be saluted, or disagree about the proposition that it may not be defiled, we have ruled that a State may not compel or enforce one view or the other. See *West Virginia Bd. of Ed. v. Barnette*, 319 U.S. 624, 63 S.Ct. 1178, 87 L.Ed. 1628 (1943); *Texas v. Johnson*, 491 U.S. 397, 109 S.Ct. 2533, 105 L.Ed.2d 342 (1989).

Our law affords constitutional protection to personal decisions relating to marriage, procreation, contraception, family relationships, child rearing, and education. *Carey v. Population Services International*, 431 U.S., at 685, 97 S.Ct., at 2016. Our cases recognize "the right of the *individual*, married or single, to be free from unwarranted governmental intrusion into matters so fundamentally affecting a person as the decision whether to bear or beget a child." *Eisenstadt v. Baird*, *supra*, 405 U.S., at 453, 92 S.Ct., at 1038 (emphasis in original). Our precedents "have respected the private realm of family life which the state cannot enter." *Prince v. Massachusetts*, 321 U.S. 158, 166, 64 S.Ct. 438, 442, 88 L.Ed. 645 (1944). These matters, involving the most intimate and personal choices a person may make in a lifetime, choices central to personal dignity and autonomy, are central to the liberty protected by the Fourteenth Amendment. At the heart of liberty is the right to define one's own concept of existence, of meaning, of the universe, and of the mystery of human life. Beliefs about these matters could not define the attributes of personhood were they formed under compulsion of the State.

These considerations begin our analysis of the woman's interest in terminating her pregnancy but cannot end it, for this reason: though the abortion decision may originate within the zone of conscience and belief, it is more than a philosophic exercise. Abortion is a unique act. It is an act fraught with consequences for others: for the woman who must live with the implications of her decision; for the persons who perform and assist in the procedure; for the spouse, family, and society which must confront the knowledge that these procedures exist, procedures some deem nothing short of an act of violence against innocent human life; and, depending on one's beliefs, for the life or potential life that is aborted. Though abortion is conduct, it does not follow that the State is entitled to proscribe it in all instances. That is because the liberty of the woman is at stake in a sense unique to the human condition and so unique to the law. The mother who carries a child to full term is subject to anxieties, to physical constraints, to pain that only she must bear. That these sacrifices have from the beginning of the human race been endured by woman with a pride that ennobles her in the eyes of others and gives to the infant a bond of love cannot alone be grounds for the State to insist she make the sacrifice. Her suffering is too intimate and personal for the State to insist, without more, upon its own vision of the woman's role, however dominant that vision has been in the course of our history and our culture. The destiny of the woman must be shaped to a large extent on her own conception of her spiritual imperatives and her place in society.

It should be recognized, moreover, that in some critical respects the abortion decision is of the same character as the decision to use contraception, to which *Griswold v. Connecticut*, *Eisenstadt v. Baird*, and *Carey v. Population Services International* afford constitutional protection. We have no doubt as to the correctness of those decisions. They support the reasoning in *Roe* relating to the woman's liberty because they involve personal decisions concerning not only the meaning of procreation but also human responsibility and respect for it. As with abortion, reasonable people will have differences of opinion about these matters. One view is based on such reverence for the wonder of creation that any pregnancy ought to be welcomed and carried to full term no matter how difficult it will be to provide for the child and ensure its well-being. Another is that the inability to provide for the nurture and care of the infant is a cruelty to the child and an anguish to the parent. These are intimate views with infinite variations, and their deep, personal character underlay our decisions in *Griswold*, *Eisenstadt*, and *Carey*. The same concerns are present when the woman confronts the reality that, perhaps despite her attempts to avoid it, she has become pregnant.

It was this dimension of personal liberty that *Roe* sought to protect, and its holding invoked the reasoning and the tradition of the precedents we have discussed, granting protection to substantive liberties of the person. *Roe* was, of course, an extension of those cases and, as the decision itself indicated, the separate States could act in some degree to further their own legitimate interests in protecting prenatal life. The extent to which the legislatures of the States might act to outweigh the interests of the woman in choosing to terminate her pregnancy was a subject of debate both in *Roe* itself and in decisions following it.

While we appreciate the weight of the arguments made on behalf of the State in the cases before us, arguments which in their ultimate formulation conclude that *Roe* should be overruled, the reservations any of us may have in reaffirming the central holding of *Roe* are outweighed by the explication of individual liberty we have given combined with the force of stare decisis.

* * *

[The Court struck down the husband notification provision of the Pennsylvania law but upheld its informed consent, parental notification, 24-hour waiting period, and record-keeping and reporting requirements.]

* * *

Justice SCALIA, with whom THE CHIEF JUSTICE, Justice WHITE, and Justice THOMAS join, concurring in the judgment in part and dissenting in part.

My views on this matter are unchanged from those I set forth in my separate opinions in *Webster v. Reproductive Health Services*, 492 U.S. 490, 532, 109 S.Ct. 3040, 3064, 106 L.Ed.2d 410 (1989) (opinion concurring in part and concurring in judgment), and *Ohio v. Akron Center for Reproductive Health*, 497 U.S. 502, 520, 110 S.Ct. 2972, 2984, 111 L.Ed.2d 405 (1990) (*Akron II*) (concurring opinion). The States may, if they wish, permit abortion on demand, but the Constitution does not require them to do so. The permissibility of abortion, and the limitations upon it, are to be resolved like most important questions in our democracy: by citizens trying to persuade one another and then voting. As the Court acknowledges, "where reasonable people disagree the government can adopt one position or the other." *Ante*, at 2806. The Court is correct in adding the qualification that this "assumes a state of affairs in which the choice does not intrude upon a protected liberty," *ante*, at 2807—but the crucial part of that qualification is the penultimate word. A State's choice between two positions on which reasonable people can disagree is constitutional even when (as is often the case) it intrudes upon a "liberty" in the absolute sense. Laws against bigamy, for example—with which entire societies of reasonable people disagree—intrude upon men and women's liberty to marry and live with one another. But bigamy happens not to be a liberty specially "protected" by the Constitution.

That is, quite simply, the issue in these cases: not whether the power of a woman to abort her unborn child is a "liberty" in the absolute sense; or even whether it is a liberty of great importance to many women. Of course it is both. The issue is whether it is a liberty protected by the Constitution of the United States. I am sure it is not. I reach that conclusion not because of anything so exalted as my views concerning the "concept of existence, of meaning, of the universe, and of the mystery of human life." *Ibid*. Rather, I reach it for the same reason I reach the conclusion that bigamy is not constitutionally protected—because of two simple facts: (1) the Constitution says absolutely nothing about it, and (2) the longstanding traditions of American society have permitted it to be legally proscribed. *Akron II, supra*, at 520, 110 S.Ct., at 2984 (SCALIA, J., concurring).

There is, of course, no comparable tradition barring recognition of a "liberty interest" in carrying one's child to term free from state efforts to kill it. For that reason, it does not follow that the Constitution does not protect childbirth simply because it does not protect abortion. The Court's contention, *ante*, at 2811, that the only way to protect childbirth is to protect abortion shows the utter bankruptcy of constitutional analysis deprived of tradition as a validating factor. It drives one to say that the only way to protect the right to eat is to acknowledge the constitutional right to starve oneself to death.

The Court destroys the proposition, evidently meant to represent my position, that "liberty" includes "only those practices, defined at the most specific level, that were protected against government interference by other rules of law when the Fourteenth Amendment was ratified," *ante*, at 2805 (citing *Michael H. v. Gerald D.*, 491 U.S. 110, 127, n. 6, 109 S.Ct. 2333, 2344, n. 6, 105 L.Ed.2d 91 (1989) (opinion of SCALIA, J.)). That is not, however, what *Michael H.* says; it merely observes that, in defining "liberty," we may not disregard a specific, "relevant tradition protecting, or denying protection to, the asserted right," *ibid.* But the Court does not wish to be fettered by any such limitations on its preferences. The Court's statement that it is "tempting" to acknowledge the authoritativeness of tradition in order to "cur[b] the discretion of federal judges," *ante*, at 2804, is of course rhetoric rather than reality; no government official is "tempted" to place restraints upon his own freedom of action, which is why Lord Acton did not say "Power tends to purify." The Court's temptation is in the quite opposite and more natural direction—towards systematically eliminating checks upon its own power; and it succumbs.

Beyond that brief summary of the essence of my position, I will not swell the United States Reports with repetition of what I have said before; and applying the rational basis test, I would uphold the Pennsylvania statute in its entirety. I must, however, respond to a few of the more outrageous arguments in today's opinion, which it is beyond human nature to leave unanswered. I shall discuss each of them under a quotation from the Court's opinion to which they pertain.

"The inescapable fact is that adjudication of substantive due process claims may call upon the Court in interpreting the Constitution to exercise that same capacity which by tradition courts always have exercised reasoned judgment." *Ante*, at 2806.

Assuming that the question before us is to be resolved at such a level of philosophical abstraction, in such isolation from the traditions of

American society, as by simply applying "reasoned judgment," I do not see how that could possibly have produced the answer the Court arrived at in *Roe v. Wade*, 410 U.S. 113, 93 S.Ct. 705, 35 L.Ed.2d 147 (1973). Today's opinion describes the methodology of *Roe*, quite accurately, as weighing against the woman's interest the State's "important and legitimate interest in protecting the potentiality of human life." *Ante*, at 2817 (quoting *Roe*, *supra*, at 162, 93 S.Ct., at 731). But "reasoned judgment" does not begin by begging the question, as *Roe* and subsequent cases unquestionably did by assuming that what the State is protecting is the mere "potentiality of human life."...The whole argument of abortion opponents is that what the Court calls the fetus and what others call the unborn child *is a human life*. Thus, whatever answer *Roe* came up with after conducting its "balancing" is bound to be wrong, unless it is correct that the human fetus is in some critical sense merely potentially human. There is of course no way to determine that as a legal matter; it is in fact a value judgment. Some societies have considered newborn children not yet human, or the incompetent elderly no longer so.

The authors of the joint opinion, of course, do not squarely contend that *Roe v. Wade* was a correct application of "reasoned judgment"; merely that it must be followed, because of stare decisis. *Ante*, at 2808, 2812, 2817. But in their exhaustive discussion of all the factors that go into the determination of when stare decisis should be observed and when disregarded, they never mention "how wrong was the decision on its face?" Surely, if "[t]he Court's power lies...in its legitimacy, a product of substance and perception," *ante*, at 2814, the "substance" part of the equation demands that plain error be acknowledged and eliminated. *Roe* was plainly wrong—even on the Court's methodology of "reasoned judgment," and even more so (of course) if the proper criteria of text and tradition are applied.

The emptiness of the "reasoned judgment" that produced *Roe* is displayed in plain view by the fact that, after more than 19 years of effort by some of the brightest (and most determined) legal minds in the country, after more than 10 cases upholding abortion rights in this Court, and after dozens upon dozens of amicus briefs submitted in these and other cases, the best the Court can do to explain how it is that the word "liberty" must be thought to include the right to destroy human fetuses is to rattle off a collection of adjectives that simply decorate a value judgment and conceal a political choice. The right to abort, we are told, inheres in "liberty" because it is among "a person's most basic decisions," ante, at 2806; it involves a "most intimate and personal choic[e]," *ante*, at 2807; it is "central to personal dignity and autonomy," *ibid.*; it "originate[s] within the zone of conscience and belief," *ibid.*; it is "too intimate and personal" for state interference, *ante*, at 2807; it reflects "intimate views" of a "deep, personal character," *ante*, at 2808; it involves "intimate relationships" and notions of "personal autonomy and bodily integrity," *ante*, at 2810; and it concerns a particularly "'important decisio[n],'" *ante*, at 2811 (citation omitted). But it is obvious to anyone applying "reasoned judgment" that the same adjectives can be applied to many forms of conduct that this Court (including one of the Justices in today's majority, see *Bowers v. Hardwick*, 478 U.S. 186, 106 S.Ct. 2841, 92 L.Ed.2d 140 (1986)) has held are not entitled to constitutional protection—because, like abortion, they are forms of conduct that have long been criminalized in American society. Those adjectives might be applied, for example, to homosexual sodomy, polygamy, adult incest, and suicide, all of which are equally "intimate" and "deep[ly] personal" decisions involving "personal autonomy and bodily integrity," and all of which can constitutionally be proscribed because it is our unquestionable constitutional tradition that they are proscribable. It is not reasoned judgment that supports the Court's decision; only personal predilection. Justice Curtis's warning is as timely today as it was 135 years ago:

> "[W]hen a strict interpretation of the Constitution, according to the fixed rules which govern the interpretation of laws, is abandoned, and the theoretical opinions of individuals are allowed to control its meaning, we have no longer a Constitution; we are under the government of individual men, who for the time being have power to declare what the Constitution is, according to their own views of what it ought to mean." *Dred Scott v. Sandford*, 19 How. 393, 621, 15 L.Ed. 691 (1857) (dissenting opinion).

Michael Paulsen, *Accusing Justice: Some Variations on the Themes of Robert M. Cover's 'Justice Accused'**

III. The Natural Right to Life

The conclusion that abortion is murder is a classic instance of natural law moral reasoning. The structure—and in many respects the substance—of the moral argument from natural law is the same for abortion as for slavery, and supports the conclusion that there is a *natural right to life*, firmly grounded in natural law reasoning.

"Abortion is murder" is a classic natural law norm. It is a "legal" inference (in the sense not that it is itself positive law, but that it states a controlling rule that must be, [sic] interpreted, applied, and obeyed), derived from a *combination* of divine revelation and human reason and conscience, informed by secular as well as religious sources. As with antislavery, the religious arguments do not devolve *directly* from the Bible (there is no commandment "Thou Shalt Not Commit Abortion"), but are conscientious applications of broader scriptural principles affirming the value and inherent dignity of all human life—including life before birth—as being made in the image of God, and affirming the sovereignty of God over the life and death of His special creation.[42]

But the application of these religious principles specifically to the unborn is buttressed by heavy reliance on medical, scientific evidence—findings of biological and genetic research, embryological studies, ultrasound pictures, medical texts, examination of fetal remains—for the conclusion that the unborn fetus is *life*, and *human* life. Indeed, for many, the scientific and medical evidence and arguments are sufficient by themselves to compel the moral insight that abortion is the deliberate killing of innocent human life, without resort to any religious arguments. As with slavery, the argument here is a sort of *res ipsa loquitur* intuition—the thing speaks for itself. To see, with unprejudiced eyes, what is being done is, for the morally aware individual, to witness horrendous injustice.

---

* Michael Paulsen, *Accusing Justice: Some Variations on the Themes of Robert M. Cover's Justice Accused*, 7 J.L. & RELIGION 33, 46-49 (1990). Reprinted with the permission of Hamline University Journal of Law and Religion and the author.

[42] *See, eg.*, Psalm 139:13-16; Luke 1:41-44; Exodus 20:13; Jeremiah 1:5. For an excellent short compendium of the religious moral arguments against abortion, made by the major world religious faiths, *see* Rabbi Aryeh Spero, *Therefore Choose Life: How the Great Faiths View Abortion*, 48 POLICY REVIEW 38-44 (Spring 1989).

The argument from science and Nature is so straightforward and obvious that it can be avoided only by willful resistance. From a biological standpoint, the full genetic makeup of a unique human being is present at the moment of conception. The being is unquestionably alive. And the form of life involved is unquestionably human, though not yet recognizable as such. (The life form is not that of a cow, or an amoeba, or a cancer cell.) If implanted in the wall of the uterus and allowed to develop naturally thereafter (and absent a medical problem), this human life will very quickly—within a matter of weeks—grow into the recognizable form of a human baby. After conception and implantation, the process is one of human development along a continuum, greater in degree but little different in principle from human development that continues in the infant after birth. There is no principled line to be drawn between conception and birth, in terms of the question whether the biological being is *human life* (as opposed to the question whether that being is capable of survival independent of his or her mother). Biologically speaking, the human fetus is not "potential" human life, but *actual* human life whose potential for growth and development has not yet been realized. At some point along this continuum, before birth, few will dispute that the being in question is human life. Yet, there are many who will not follow this reasoning back along the line of development, who will not follow the principles of natural law as informed by science where they logically lead—to the conclusion that the preborn are living human beings at all stages of development—but who instead pick an arbitrary point at which to define away legal status for preborn human life.

Once it is determined (whether on the basis of religious inspiration or biological evidence and logic) that the conceived, preborn human is a living, growing human life, religiously-based natural law moral norms again take over the argument. These moral norms generally refute asserted "justifications" for fetal homicide. This is an important stage in the argument from natural law. The pro-abortion argument usually comes to rest on one of two points—(i) denial that the fetus at all stages is human life morally worthy of protection from arbitrary destruction (which has just been discussed); and/or (ii) assertion that, even if the fetus may be human life, the prerogatives of the mother may, in a range of circumstances, justify the destruction of this life. But the circumstances in which such killing might be thought morally justified must be affected by the determination that the fetus is a human being. "Thou shalt not kill" is, as applied to human beings, a nearly universally accepted rule of natural law, even outside the Judeo-Christian tradition. Even if not taken as an absolute, this natural law ordinance drastically curtails the circumstances in which taking the life of another is permissible, and forecloses justifications based on mere convenience, economics, social stigma, arbitrary "choice," or malice. The manner in which the law should treat "hard cases"—exceptions to any ban on abortions, based on claims of "self-defense" spanning a range of cogency (life of the mother, rape, incest, health of the mother, emotional distress)—will be affected by the breadth accorded the natural law principle by the process of interpretation. (The range of acceptable justifications may be affected by religious natural law principles concerning abnegation of self and caring for others, even at personal expense, risk, burden, or anguish.) In short, the accommodations reached by the law in this area should, and inevitably must, reflect a process of "legal" interpretation of sometimes competing and sometimes complementary principles of natural law.

Finally, the pro-life movement, like the abolitionist movement, points to traditional natural law documents like the Declaration of Independence as a source of authority. The Declaration's language concerning "inalienable rights" to "*life*, *liberty*, and the pursuit of happiness" is a source for, and an implicit hierarchy of, natural rights, with human liberty ranking higher than property rights, and with the right to life ranking higher than competing claims to liberty.

If the pro-life natural law argument is correct, the moral stakes of the abortion controversy are at least as high as they were with respect to slavery, and perhaps higher. Abortion is literally a matter of life and death.

Questions

1. According to the Court, how do we know if something is a constitutionally protected liberty?
2. Does the Court believe we can turn to biblical principles of morality in defining "liberty?"
3. What types of things have been found to be protected liberties?
4. Is abortion a protected liberty? Why?
5. What legal philosophies are reflected in the joint opinion?
6. Is there any sense in which the authors of the joint opinion make a natural law argument?
7. Why does Scalia reject the joint opinion?

8. What is Paulsen's natural law argument against abortion? Are you persuaded by his argument?

9. Is scripture alone enough to justify Paulsen's conclusion? Consider the following passages: Genesis 1:26-27; 9:5-6; Exodus 20:13; 21:22-25; Psalm 139:13-16; Isaiah 49:1-6; Jeremiah 1:4-5; Luke 1:44-45; and I Corinthians 7:4.

10. What role does reason play in the natural law argument against abortion?

11. What are the implications of Paulsen's argument for issues like human cloning and embryonic stem cell research?

B. Rights of Transgendered Individuals

Introduction

Since the end of World War II, there has been tremendous growth in the number of rights claims asserted around the world. These claims have not only been claims by citizens for the protection of constitutional rights within their own nations. Often, they have been human rights claims brought by individuals to international bodies and tribunals against their own nations.

The birth of the modern international human rights movement was one of the most significant results of World War II. Leaders of the movement were motivated by revulsion at the genocide and other atrocities committed by Germany and its allies, in some cases committed by nations against their own citizens. Shortly after the end of the war, the United Nations was created. One of its core missions was to protect international human rights. The United Nations continues to have a major role in this area.

Also in the aftermath of World War II, nations created regional bodies devoted to the protection of human rights, such as the Council of Europe and the Organization of American States. Both of these regional bodies created key documents enumerating human rights to be protected. They also established mechanisms to enforce those rights.

Today, the European human rights system is the most powerful human rights enforcement system in the world. The 46 member states of the Council of Europe have entered into an important human rights treaty: the European Convention for the Protection of Human Rights and Fundamental Freedoms (The European Convention). The European Convention sets forth a number of basic human rights such as life, liberty and freedom of expression. Under this convention, the member states created a powerful human rights enforcement organ, the European Court of Human Rights (ECHR). They have agreed that individuals (including their own citizens) may bring claims against them to the ECHR alleging violations of human rights. In the years since the ECHR was created, claims brought to the ECHR have grown exponentially.

Compared with other international bodies, the ECHR has a high compliance rate with its decisions. Nations throughout Europe regularly pay penalties assessed by the ECHR or adjust domestic laws to comply with ECHR decisions. In addition, the United States Supreme Court has cited decisions by the ECHR in a number of high profile cases. It is no exaggeration to say that the ECHR is one of the most powerful and influential courts in the world.

The first piece in this section is an excerpt from a 2002 ECHR decision, *Goodwin v United Kingdom.*[¤] The case involves an individual who underwent an operation to change her[+] sex from male to female. She claimed that the United Kingdom violated her right to "respect" for "private and family life" under Article 8 of the European Convention because it would not allow her to change her birth certificate to reflect her new sexual identity.

As with *Casey,* the *Goodwin* case is not included here so that readers will understand the details of the ECHR's human rights jurisprudence. Instead, it is here to illustrate the legal philosophy underlying that jurisprudence.

Nonetheless, the following may be helpful as background. The ECHR regularly uses a key doctrine in its cases: the margin of appreciation. The margin of appreciation is not mentioned in the European Convention. Rather, the ECHR created the doctrine to help it interpret the convention. The ECHR applies the margin of appreciation to decide how much deference it should give to national governments when interpreting specific clauses of the convention known as limitation clauses. A limitation clause is one that allows nations to restrict individuals' exercise of substantive human rights. One such limitation clause is found in Article 8, the provision relied upon by Goodwin.

Paragraph one of Article 8 strongly affirms protections for private and family life: "Everyone has the right to the respect for his private and family life, his home and his correspondence." Paragraph two of this ar-

---

[¤] Goodwin v. United Kingdom [GC], no. 28957/95, ECHR 2002-VI.

[+] This book uses a feminine pronoun when referring to Goodwin, following the terminology used by the ECHR in its opinion.

ticle, however, contains very important and potentially broad limitations on that right:

> There shall be no interference by a public authority with the exercise of this right except as is in accordance with the law and is necessary in a democratic society in the interests of national security, public safety or the economic well-being of the country, for the prevention of disorder or crime, for the protection of health and morals, or for the protection of the rights and freedoms of others.

In a series of cases from 1986 (*Rees v. United Kingdom*[¤]) until 1998 (*Sheffield and Horsham v. United Kingdom*[+]), the ECHR had resolved cases like Goodwin's in favor of the United Kingdom, ruling that the United Kingdom had a wide margin of appreciation to determine what was necessary in structuring its birth certificate system to protect morals. In *Goodwin*, the ECHR reached the opposite conclusion.

The second piece in this section is an excerpt from an article written by the author of this book, Jeffrey Brauch, in the *Columbia Journal of European Law* entitled, "The Margin of Appreciation and the Jurisprudence of the European Court of Human Rights: Threat to the Rule of Law." The article criticizes the both the ECHR's decision in *Goodwin* and more fundamentally the ECHR's jurisprudence illustrated in the decision. Specifically, the article objects to the ECHR determining the scope of the margin of appreciation—and thereby the scope of fundamental human rights—based upon a "European consensus."

Goodwin v. United Kingdom[*]

THE FACTS

I. THE CIRCUMSTANCES OF THE CASE

12. The applicant is a United Kingdom citizen born in 1937 and is a post-operative male to female transsexual.

13. The applicant had a tendency to dress as a woman from early childhood and underwent aversion therapy in 1963-64. In the mid-1960s, she was diagnosed as a transsexual. Though she married a woman and

[¤] Rees v. United Kingdom, no. 9532/81, ECHR 1986.

[+] Sheffield and Horsham v. United Kingdom [GC], no. 22985/93; 23390/94, ECHR 1998-V.

[*] Goodwin v. United Kingdom [GC], no. 28957/95, ECHR 2002-VI.

they had four children, her conviction was that her "brain sex" did not fit her body. From that time until 1984 she dressed as a man for work but as a woman in her free time. In January 1985, the applicant began treatment in earnest, attending appointments once every three months at the Gender Identity Clinic at the Charing Cross Hospital, which included regular consultations with a psychiatrist as well as on occasion a psychologist. She was prescribed hormone therapy, began attending grooming classes and voice training. Since this time, she has lived fully as a woman. In October 1986, she underwent surgery to shorten her vocal chords. In August 1987, she was accepted on the waiting list for gender re-assignment surgery. In 1990, she underwent gender re-assignment surgery at a National Health Service hospital. Her treatment and surgery was provided for and paid for by the National Health Service.

14. The applicant divorced from her former wife on a date unspecified but continued to enjoy the love and support of her children.

15. The applicant claims that between 1990 and 1992 she was sexually harassed by colleagues at work. She attempted to pursue a case of sexual harassment in the Industrial Tribunal but claimed that she was unsuccessful because she was considered in law to be a man. She did not challenge this decision by appealing to the Employment Appeal Tribunal. The applicant was subsequently dismissed from her employment for reasons connected with her health, but alleges that the real reason was that she was a transsexual.

16. In 1996, the applicant started work with a new employer and was required to provide her National Insurance ("NI") number. She was concerned that the new employer would be in a position to trace her details as once in the possession of the number it would have been possible to find out about her previous employers and obtain information from them. Although she requested the allocation of a new NI number from the Department of Social Security ("DSS"), this was rejected and she eventually gave the new employer her NI number. The applicant claims that the new employer has now traced back her identity as she began experiencing problems at work. Colleagues stopped speaking to her and she was told that everyone was talking about her behind her back.

17. The DSS Contributions Agency informed the applicant that she would be ineligible for a State pension at the age of 60, the age of entitlement for women in the United Kingdom. In April 1997, the DSS informed the applicant that her pension contributions would have to be continued until the date at which she reached the age of 65, being the age of entitlement for men, namely April 2002. On 23 April 1997, she therefore entered into an undertaking with the DSS to pay direct the NI contributions which would otherwise be deducted by her employer as for all

male employees. In the light of this undertaking, on 2 May 1997, the DSS Contributions Agency issued the applicant with a Form CF 384 Age Exemption Certificate (see Relevant domestic law and practice below).

18. The applicant's files at the DSS were marked "sensitive" to ensure that only an employee of a particular grade had access to her files. This meant in practice that the applicant had to make special appointments for even the most trivial matters and could not deal directly with the local office or deal with queries over the telephone. Her record continues to state her sex as male and despite the "special procedures" she has received letters from the DSS addressed to the male name which she was given at birth.

19. In a number of instances, the applicant stated that she has had to choose between revealing her birth certificate and foregoing certain advantages which were conditional upon her producing her birth certificate. In particular, she has not followed through a loan conditional upon life insurance, a re-mortgage offer and an entitlement to winter fuel allowance from the DSS. Similarly, the applicant remains obliged to pay the higher motor insurance premiums applicable to men. Nor did she feel able to report a theft of 200 pounds sterling to the police, for fear that the investigation would require her to reveal her identity.

* * *

THE LAW

I. ALLEGED VIOLATION OF ARTICLE 8 OF THE CONVENTION

59. The applicant claims a violation of Article 8 of the Convention, the relevant part of which provides as follows:

> "1. Everyone has the right to respect for his private...life...
>
> 2. There shall be no interference by a public authority with the exercise of this right except such as is in accordance with the law and is necessary in a democratic society in the interests of national security, public safety or the economic well-being of the country, for the prevention of disorder or crime, for the protection of health or morals, or for the protection of the rights and freedoms of others."

* * *

B. The Court's assessment

1. Preliminary considerations

71. This case raises the issue whether or not the respondent State has failed to comply with a positive obligation to ensure the right of the applicant, a post-operative male to female transsexual, to respect for her private life, in particular through the lack of legal recognition given to her gender re-assignment.

72. The Court recalls that the notion of "respect" as understood in Article 8 is not clear cut, especially as far as the positive obligations inherent in that concept are concerned: having regard to the diversity of practices followed and the situations obtaining in the Contracting States, the notion's requirements will vary considerably from case to case and the margin of appreciation to be accorded to the authorities may be wider than that applied in other areas under the Convention. In determining whether or not a positive obligation exists, regard must also be had to the fair balance that has to be struck between the general interest of the community and the interests of the individual, the search for which balance is inherent in the whole of the Convention (Cossey v. the United Kingdom judgment of 27 September 1990, Series A no. 184, p. 15, § 37).

73. The Court recalls that it has already examined complaints about the position of transsexuals in the United Kingdom (see the Rees v. the United Kingdom judgment of 17 October 1986, Series A no. 106, the Cossey v. the United Kingdom judgment, cited above; the X., Y. and Z. v. the United Kingdom judgment of 22 April 1997, *Reports of Judgments and Decisions* 1997-II, and the Sheffield and Horsham v. the United Kingdom judgment of 30 July 1998, *Reports* 1998-V, p. 2011). In those cases, it held that the refusal of the United Kingdom Government to alter the register of births or to issue birth certificates whose contents and nature differed from those of the original entries concerning the recorded gender of the individual could not be considered as an interference with the right to respect for private life (the above-mentioned Rees judgment, p. 14, § 35, and Cossey judgment, p. 15, § 36). It also held that there was no positive obligation on the Government to alter their existing system for the registration of births by establishing a new system or type of documentation to provide proof of current civil status. Similarly, there was no duty on the Government to permit annotations to the existing register of births, or to keep any such annotation secret from third parties (the above-mentioned Rees judgment, p. 17, § 42, and Cossey judgment, p. 15, §§ 38-39). It was found in those cases that the authorities had taken steps to minimise intrusive enquiries (for example, by allowing

transsexuals to be issued with driving licences, passports and other types of documents in their new name and gender). Nor had it been shown that the failure to accord general legal recognition of the change of gender had given rise in the applicants' own case histories to detriment of sufficient seriousness to override the respondent State's margin of appreciation in this area (the Sheffield and Horsham judgment cited above, p. 2028-29, § 59).

74. While the Court is not formally bound to follow its previous judgments, it is in the interests of legal certainty, foreseeability and equality before the law that it should not depart, without good reason, from precedents laid down in previous cases (see, for example, *Chapman v. the United Kingdom* [GC], no. 27238/95, ECHR 2001-I, § 70). However, since the Convention is first and foremost a system for the protection of human rights, the Court must have regard to the changing conditions within the respondent State and within Contracting States generally and respond, for example, to any evolving convergence as to the standards to be achieved (see, amongst other authorities, the Cossey judgment, p. 14, § 35, and *Stafford v. the United Kingdom* [GC], no. 46295/99, judgment of 28 May 2002, to be published in ECHR 2002-, §§ 67-68). It is of crucial importance that the Convention is interpreted and applied in a manner which renders its rights practical and effective, not theoretical and illusory. A failure by the Court to maintain a dynamic and evolutive approach would indeed risk rendering it a bar to reform or improvement (see the above-cited *Stafford v. the United Kingdom* judgment, § 68). In the present context the Court has, on several occasions since 1986, signalled its consciousness of the serious problems facing transsexuals and stressed the importance of keeping the need for appropriate legal measures in this area under review (see the Rees judgment, § 47; the Cossey judgment, § 42; the Sheffield and Horsham judgment, § 60).

75. The Court proposes therefore to look at the situation within and outside the Contracting State to assess "in the light of present-day conditions" what is now the appropriate interpretation and application of the Convention (see the *Tyrer v. the United Kingdom* judgment of 25 April 1978, Series A no. 26, § 31, and subsequent case-law).

2. The applicant's situation as a transsexual

76. The Court observes that the applicant, registered at birth as male, has undergone gender re-assignment surgery and lives in society as a female. Nonetheless, the applicant remains, for legal purposes, a male. This has had, and continues to have, effects on the applicant's life where

sex is of legal relevance and distinctions are made between men and women, as, *inter alia*, in the area of pensions and retirement age. For example, the applicant must continue to pay national insurance contributions until the age of 65 due to her legal status as male. However as she is employed in her gender identity as a female, she has had to obtain an exemption certificate which allows the payments from her employer to stop while she continues to make such payments herself. Though the Government submitted that this made due allowance for the difficulties of her position, the Court would note that she nonetheless has to make use of a special procedure that might in itself call attention to her status.

77. It must also be recognised that serious interference with private life can arise where the state of domestic law conflicts with an important aspect of personal identity (see, *mutatis mutandis*, Dudgeon v. the United Kingdom judgment of 22 October 1981, Series A no. 45, § 41). The stress and alienation arising from a discordance between the position in society assumed by a post-operative transsexual and the status imposed by law which refuses to recognise the change of gender cannot, in the Court's view, be regarded as a minor inconvenience arising from a formality. A conflict between social reality and law arises which places the transsexual in an anomalous position, in which he or she may experience feelings of vulnerability, humiliation and anxiety.

78. In this case, as in many others, the applicant's gender re-assignment was carried out by the national health service, which recognises the condition of gender dysphoria and provides, *inter alia*, re-assignment by surgery, with a view to achieving as one of its principal purposes as close an assimilation as possible to the gender in which the transsexual perceives that he or she properly belongs. The Court is struck by the fact that nonetheless the gender re-assignment which is lawfully provided is not met with full recognition in law, which might be regarded as the final and culminating step in the long and difficult process of transformation which the transsexual has undergone. The coherence of the administrative and legal practices within the domestic system must be regarded as an important factor in the assessment carried out under Article 8 of the Convention. Where a State has authorised the treatment and surgery alleviating the condition of a transsexual, financed or assisted in financing the operations and indeed permits the artificial insemination of a woman living with a female to-male transsexual (as demonstrated in the case of X., Y. and Z. v. the United Kingdom, cited above), it appears illogical to refuse to recognise the legal implications of the result to which the treatment leads.

79. The Court notes that the unsatisfactory nature of the current position and plight of transsexuals in the United Kingdom has been ac-

knowledged in the domestic courts (see *Bellinger v. Bellinger*, cited above, paragraph 52) and by the Interdepartmental Working Group which surveyed the situation in the United Kingdom and concluded that, notwithstanding the accommodations reached in practice, transsexual people were conscious of certain problems which did not have to be faced by the majority of the population (paragraph 50 above).

80. Against these considerations, the Court has examined the countervailing arguments of a public interest nature put forward as justifying the continuation of the present situation. It observes that in the previous United Kingdom cases weight was given to medical and scientific considerations, the state of any European and international consensus and the impact of any changes to the current birth register system.

3. Medical and scientific considerations

81. It remains the case that there are no conclusive findings as to the cause of transsexualism and, in particular, whether it is wholly psychological or associated with physical differentiation in the brain.

* * *

83. The Court is not persuaded therefore that the state of medical science or scientific knowledge provides any determining argument as regards the legal recognition of transsexuals.

4. The state of any European and international consensus

84. Already at the time of the Sheffield and Horsham case, there was an emerging consensus within Contracting States in the Council of Europe on providing legal recognition following gender re-assignment (see § 35 of that judgment). The latest survey submitted by Liberty in the present case shows a continuing international trend towards legal recognition (see paragraphs 55-56 above). In Australia and New Zealand, it appears that the courts are moving away from the biological birth view of sex (as set out in the United Kingdom case of *Corbett v. Corbett*) and taking the view that sex, in the context of a transsexual wishing to marry, should depend on a multitude of factors to be assessed at the time of the marriage.

85. The Court observes that in the case of Rees in 1986 it had noted that little common ground existed between States, some of which did permit change of gender and some of which did not and that generally speaking the law seemed to be in a state of transition (see § 37). In the later case of Sheffield and Horsham, the Court's judgment laid emphasis on the lack of a common European approach as to how to address the re-

percussions which the legal recognition of a change of sex may entail for other areas of law such as marriage, filiation, privacy or data protection. While this would appear to remain the case, the lack of such a common approach among forty-three Contracting States with widely diverse legal systems and traditions is hardly surprising. In accordance with the principle of subsidiarity, it is indeed primarily for the Contracting States to decide on the measures necessary to secure Convention rights within their jurisdiction and, in resolving within their domestic legal systems the practical problems created by the legal recognition of post-operative gender status, the Contracting States must enjoy a wide margin of appreciation. The Court accordingly attaches less importance to the lack of evidence of a common European approach to the resolution of the legal and practical problems posed, than to the clear and uncontested evidence of a continuing international trend in favour not only of increased social acceptance of transsexuals but of legal recognition of the new sexual identity of post-operative transsexuals.

* * *

92. In the previous cases from the United Kingdom, this Court has since 1986 emphasised the importance of keeping the need for appropriate legal measures under review having regard to scientific and societal developments (see references at paragraph 73). Most recently in the Sheffield and Horsham case in 1998, it observed that the respondent State had not yet taken any steps to do so despite an increase in the social acceptance of the phenomenon of transsexualism and a growing recognition of the problems with which transsexuals are confronted (cited above, paragraph 60). Even though it found no violation in that case, the need to keep this area under review was expressly re-iterated. Since then, a report has been issued in April 2000 by the Interdepartmental Working Group which set out a survey of the current position of transsexuals in *inter alia* criminal law, family and employment matters and identified various options for reform. Nothing has effectively been done to further these proposals and in July 2001 the Court of Appeal noted that there were no plans to do so (see paragraphs 52-53). It may be observed that the only legislative reform of note, applying certain non-discrimination provisions to transsexuals, flowed from a decision of the European Court of Justice of 30 April 1996 which held that discrimination based on a change of gender was equivalent to discrimination on grounds of sex (see paragraphs 43-45 above).

93. Having regard to the above considerations, the Court finds that the respondent Government can no longer claim that the matter falls within their margin of appreciation, save as regards the appropriate means of achieving recognition of the right protected under the Conven-

tion. Since there are no significant factors of public interest to weigh against the interest of this individual applicant in obtaining legal recognition of her gender re-assignment, it reaches the conclusion that the fair balance that is inherent in the Convention now tilts decisively in favour of the applicant. There has, accordingly, been a failure to respect her right to private life in breach of Article 8 of the Convention.

Jeffrey A. Brauch, *The Margin of Appreciation and the Jurisprudence of the European Court of Human Rights: Threat to the Rule of Law*[*]

This line of cases [the line of cases from *Rees* to *Goodwin* addressing the right of transsexuals to change their birth certificate] reveals deep problems with the Court relying on European consensus as a key and sometimes dispositive factor in applying the margin of appreciation. They reveal a doctrine that fails to satisfy the most basic requirements of the rule of law.

First, a "European consensus" provides no predictability for decisions. "European consensus" is not a legal standard. It does not tell individuals or governments when a state action becomes a Convention violation. In these cases, the Court essentially told the United Kingdom: "You may rely on your birth certificate record system for now, but at some undetermined time in the future, there will be a consensus. And then you must stop." Yet the United Kingdom had no guidance on when that would be or how such a consensus would be reached—or even identified.

Even worse, in the end, the United Kingdom was waiting for the wrong thing. When the Court finally arrived at the *I.* and *Goodwin* decisions, finding the United Kingdom's system to violate Article 8, it did so upon a totally different basis. Not a consensus. A "trend." And not even a European trend, but an "international trend." Apparently, the United Kingdom and other countries within the Council of Europe should have been monitoring legal trends in Australia and New Zealand to determine their obligations under the European Convention.

A legal standard this is not. And the problem is more than just applying the consensus standard in a fair, predictable way. We do not know

[*] Jeffrey A. Brauch, *The Margin of Appreciation and the Jurisprudence of the European Court of Human Rights: Threat to the Rule of Law*, 11 COLUM. J. EUR. L. 113, 145-47 (2004). Reprinted with the permission of the author.

what the "consensus" standard is. There are several vital but unanswered questions: 1) what is needed to satisfy the consensus requirement—a trend or a consensus? 2) where must that trend or consensus be found, in Europe or in the world as a whole?; and 3) how will anyone, individuals or member States, know when a trend or consensus exists? Is the consensus or trend identified by [sic] number of member States adopting a particular law?; percentage of states adopting it?; pace of change toward adoption? Scholar Aileen McHarg among others has properly noted the "unsystematic and unscientific approach to ascertaining whether, and in respect of what, a consensus exists."

Ironically, the Court in *I.* (and *Goodwin*) identified three hallmarks of proper decision-making (all basic to the rule of law): "legal certainty, foreseeability and equality." Yet its arbitrary "consensus" standard violates each. There is no legal certainty because no one really knows what the standard is. Lack of forseeability flows directly from this. Neither an applicant nor a member State can know whether their actions comply with the Convention without knowing just what a "consensus" is or when it is reached. They do not know whether they must monitor legal and cultural changes in Europe alone or worldwide. Even equality is compromised by this standard. The Court treats the standard very differently from case to case. A clear social and legal trend in the treatment of transsexuals narrows the margin of appreciation. A similar trend regarding legal advertising does not. In failing to provide certainty, predictability, and equality, the margin of appreciation, relying on this deeply flawed consensus standard, violates the rule of law.

Another danger exists in relying on the consensus standard. Ironically, in the name of protecting human rights, the Court adopts a standard that actually threatens human rights. "[I]ts tendency to rely on the presence or absence of a European consensus provides a flimsy basis on which to assert human rights standards." When the modern human rights movement began, the term "human rights" meant fundamental rights that are universal and basic to the human person at any time at any place. It does not matter if a particular government, or majority, or consensus chooses not to protect such rights; they are human rights nonetheless. But rights are fragile if they are tied to a consensus at a particular time and place.

Despite protestations to the contrary, there is no compelling reason why the protection of human rights will not diminish if consensus is the primary determiner of whether a right exists. Consider the current struggle with global terrorism. As the world grows smaller and technology advances, terrorism poses a greater and more imminent threat. Nations are responding more forcefully and aggressively to that threat. As they do, tomorrow's "consensus" on what is needed to counter international terrorism may embrace stronger measures and more infringements on individual privacy—perhaps those measures and infringements we consider to be human rights violations today. But under a consensus standard they may not be violations tomorrow.

This concern is not mere speculation. In 1978, in *Klass v. Germany*, the Court upheld a German law allowing thoroughgoing surveillance of certain individuals against claims that this violated Convention Articles 6, 8, and 13. The German law allowed the government to open and inspect mail and telegraph messages and to listen to and record telephone conversations in order to "protect against 'imminent dangers' threatening the 'free democratic constitutional order', 'the existence or the security of the Federation or of a *Land*,'" or of the armed forces. The Court found that the law interfered with the rights protected under Article 8. But it found that this interference was necessary in order to protect national security. The Court gave Germany greater leeway in implementing the law in light of

> the development of terrorism in Europe in recent years. Democratic societies nowadays find themselves threatened by highly sophisticated forms of espionage and by terrorism, with the result that the State must be able, in order effectively to counter such threats, to undertake the secret surveillance of subversive elements operating within its jurisdiction.

Undoubtedly this is true. States must be able to respond appropriately to terrorism threats. But there is also a real danger that states could overreact to threats of terrorism, even that the majority—or a consensus—of states could so overreact. If that consensus is the standard for protecting rights, it is no protection at all.

This potential inspired one commentator to conclude, "The Convention's ability to protect human rights is seriously threatened...by the doctrine of margin of appreciation." Indeed, the Court could circumvent express requirements of the Convention (determined by the Court to be a living document) in order to follow a consensus that has developed to the contrary.

Questions

1. How does Goodwin claim that the United Kingdom has failed to protect the right to respect for her private and family life under Article 8 of the European Convention?

2. Does the ECHR follow the common law's doctrine of stare decisis? What is the ECHR's policy with regard to precedents laid down in previous cases?

3. What is the ECHR's approach to interpreting and applying the European Convention?

4. Why does the ECHR deviate from its previous decisions (*Rees* and *Sheffield and Horsham*) and rule against the United Kingdom in this case?

5. What legal philosophy is reflected in the ECHR's opinion?

6. Why does Brauch argue that the ECHR's use of the "European consensus" standard threatens the rule of law?

7. Why does Brauch argue that the "European consensus" standard undermines the protection of fundamental human rights?

8. Is it appropriate for the ECHR to determine the scope and content of human rights based on societal consensus?

9. Is the ability to change one's sexual identification on official records a right that is universal and basic to being human?

10. How should one determine the content and scope of fundamental human rights?

Chapter 8 Preemptive War

Introduction

In the aftermath of the attacks on September 11, 2001, United States President George W. Bush set forth a doctrine of preemptive war. Established against the backdrop of a rise in global terrorism and the proliferation of weapons of mass destruction (WMD), the doctrine justifies military action against nations viewed as a threat or potential threat to the United States before they have taken action to harm the United States. As the White House stated in a 2006 National Security Strategy document: "[U]nder long-standing principles of self-defense, we do not rule out use of force before attacks occur, even if uncertainty remains as to the time and place of the enemy's attack. When the consequences of an attack with WMD are potentially so devastating, we cannot afford to stand idly by as grave dangers materialize."[¤] Bush relied upon the doctrine to invade Iraq in 2003. The doctrine, like the Iraq war, has been widely criticized both at home and abroad.

This chapter is devoted to the topic of preemptive war. It specifically addresses this question: Is it just—and legal under international law—to engage in preemptive warfare? The pieces that follow offer varying answers to this question.

The first piece contains excerpts from the United Nations Charter. Chapter 7 noted that the protection of human rights is a key goal of the United Nations (U.N.). Perhaps the U.N.'s preeminent goal is the peaceful resolution of international disputes. As seen in Charter Articles 2 and 51, the nations founding the U.N. greatly restricted the circumstances under which one nation may go to war with another under international law.

The second piece is an excerpt from Professor John Coverdale's article, "An Introduction to the Just War Tradition." In it, Coverdale gives a

[¤] The National Security Strategy of the United States of America 23 (2006).

brief overview of just war theory. Just war theory arose initially out of Christian thinking about when it is morally justified for a nation to go to war with another. He sets forth the main outlines of just war theory, including its application to preemptive war. Coverdale is a professor of law at Seton Hall University School of Law. He received a B.A. from the Lateran University, an M.A. from the University of Navarre, a Ph.D. from the University of Wisconsin, and a J.D. from the University of Chicago. Before teaching law at Seton Hall, Coverdale taught history at Northwestern and Princeton universities.

The third and fourth pieces debate the appropriateness of preemptive war as it has been waged in the first decade of the 21st century. The third piece is an article by Michael J. Glennon that appeared in *The Weekly Standard*. Glennon defends preemptive war as necessary today given the failure of the U.N. to prevent armed conflict, the existence of WMD and organizations committed to terror on a global scale, and advances in intelligence capabilities. Glennon is a professor of international law at Tufts University and the Director of Tufts' LL.M. Program. He received a B.A. from the College of St. Thomas and a J.D. from University of Minnesota. Glennon consults for the United States Department of State and the International Atomic Energy Agency.

The fourth piece is an article by Charles Kegley and Gregory Raymond that appeared in *USA TODAY*. Kegley and Raymond oppose the doctrine of preemptive war as currently articulated by the United States. In the article they lay out their conviction that tremendous international instability would result from world-wide acceptance of the doctrine of preemptive war.

Kegley is a Professor Emeritus at the University of South Carolina, where he starting teaching in 1972, and has been the Pearce Professor of International Relations since 1984. He received a B.A. from American University and a Ph.D. from Syracuse University. Kegley has been a Visiting Scholar in Geneva and a Visiting Professor at the People's University of China in Beijing. Raymond is the Frank Church Professor of International Relations at Boise State University. He received a B.A. from Park College and an M.A. and a Ph.D. from University of South Carolina. Raymond and Kegley have coauthored eight books and numerous articles.

United Nations Charter*

Article 2

The Organization and its Members, in pursuit of the Purposes stated in Article 1, shall act in accordance with the following Principles.

* * *

3. All Members shall settle their international disputes by peaceful means in such a manner that international peace and security, and justice, are not endangered.

4. All Members shall refrain in their international relations from the threat or use of force against the territorial integrity or political independence of any state, or in any other manner inconsistent with the Purposes of the United Nations.

* * *

Article 51

Nothing in the present Charter shall impair the inherent right of individual or collective self-defence if an armed attack occurs against a Member of the United Nations, until the Security Council has taken measures necessary to maintain international peace and security. Measures taken by Members in the exercise of this right of self-defence shall be immediately reported to the Security Council and shall not in any way affect the authority and responsibility of the Security Council under the present Charter to take at any time such action as it deems necessary in order to maintain or restore international peace and security.

* U.N. Charter art. 2, 51.

John F. Coverdale, *An Introduction to the Just War Tradition*[*]

II. The Justification for Killing Enemy Combatants

Many just war theorists simply assume that the deliberate killing of enemy combatants can be morally justified provided that the *ius ad bellum* and *ius in bello* conditions are met. There are two reasons, however, why we need to explore the moral justification for the deliberate killing of enemy combatants: first, if it cannot be justified, there can be no just war, and second, an understanding of why deliberate killing of enemy combatants is permissible is essential to understanding one of the principal aspects of the *ius in bello*, the immunity of non-combatants from direct attack.

Virtually every ethical system reflects the basic principle that deliberately taking the life of an innocent human being is wrong. Classical just war theory requires "the habitual and mutual recognition" of "the fundamental unity and moral equality of the belligerents." In a just war, "the state of war in which [the belligerents] find themselves is not allowed to obscure the common humanity of the belligerents." Just war theory requires, therefore, even more than other positions, a justification for killing enemy combatants.

Many just war theorists simply translate the moral principle that intentionally killing innocent human beings is wrong, into the principle that intentionally killing noncombatants is wrong, with the implication that killing combatants is not wrong. It is not, however, immediately obvious that noncombatants are innocent and combatants are not, and therefore it is not immediately obvious that one may kill combatants with moral impunity.

If we take the term "innocent" to mean "free from moral wrong, sin or guilt," some noncombatants, for example a newspaper editor who deliberately stirs up an unjust war, may be guilty with respect to the war. Many enemy soldiers, on the other hand, may be entirely guilt-free with respect to the war. They may have been conscripted against their will, and may scrupulously avoid violating the legal and moral rules of war. Whatever the moral character of their individual private lives, there may be nothing about their status as combatants that stains them with any

[*] John F. Coverdale, *An Introduction to the Just War Tradition*, 16 PACE INT'L L. REV. 221, 224-32, 242-44, 248 (2004).

moral guilt. They may be equally innocent from the legal point of view, having broken no laws that would expose them to punishment, much less to capital punishment.

If the principle that it is always wrong to directly kill the innocent absolutely forbade killing those who are not morally or legally guilty, there could be no just war. It is essential, therefore, to ask in what sense enemy combatants should be considered guilty, or at least non-innocent, and therefore subject to being deliberately killed in war.

One of the earliest and most influential formulators of a just war theory, Augustine, analogizes a just war to an individual's defense of another person who is being attacked. Just as an individual who witnesses an unjust attack on another may use force to defend the person being attacked, so too public authorities may defend the common good and society with violence, even lethal violence. This analogy throws light on the meaning of innocence because, in the case of defense of an individual, we do not require the defender to inquire into the personal moral guilt of the attacker before repelling his attack. Provided that the attack does not seem to be objectively justified, the mere fact of attacking another renders the attacker liable to being repulsed by force, even if the aggressor is suffering from a psychological condition that deprives him of freedom and consequently of moral and legal responsibility. What is significant in self-defense is not the personal moral guilt or innocence of the attacker but his use of force against another without objective moral justification. This is also true of an enemy combatant.

Thomas Aquinas does not directly address the justification for killing individual enemy combatants, but the answer he would have given had he posed the question can be clearly discerned from what he says about closely related topics. In the internal affairs of a community, Aquinas says, public authorities may lawfully kill someone who has become "dangerous and infectious to the community." In fact, according to Aquinas, "it is praiseworthy and advantageous that he be killed in order to safeguard the common good." Aquinas' stress here is on the defense of the common good.

Similarly, in order to safeguard the common good of the community against external enemies, public authorities may use lethal force. It is important to note that Aquinas is not talking here only about indirect or unintended killing of enemy combatants. In a justified war, according to Aquinas, direct, i.e., intentional, killing of enemy combatants is permissible as a means of defending the community against injustice.

Individual enemy soldiers may be killed because being a combatant in an army which is waging an unjust war makes a man dangerous and harmful to the community against which he is fighting, and therefore "non-innocent" in the relevant sense, independent of personal moral guilt or innocence. As Regan puts it, "It is the wrong that enemy personnel are committing, not their individual moral responsibility for it, that justifies the victim nation's use of killing force against them."

Modern just war theorists follow Augustine and Aquinas in focusing on the defense of the common good and the analogy to self-defense to justify the deliberate killing of enemy combatants. Potter, for instance, argues:

> We live by the presumption that men must do no harm to their neighbors. That presumption can be overridden when it is necessary to restrain wrongdoers from inflicting harm. Only the necessity can grant to anyone an excuse to kill.... Only those immediately and actively engaged in the bearing of hostile force in an unjust cause are properly subject to direct attack.

Murphy puts it as follows:

> If one believes (as I do) that the only even remotely plausible justification for war is self-defense, then one must in waging war confine one's hostility to those against whom one is defending oneself, i.e. those in the (both causal and logical) chain of command or responsibility or agency all those who can reasonably be regarded as engaged in an attempt to destroy you.

This moral justification of killing enemy combatants depends on the fulfillment of the *ad bellum* conditions. It is only in a war in which one is justified and the enemy objectively unjustified that one may rightly kill enemy combatants. Only the defense of the community against unjust danger provides the moral justification for the direct killing of enemy combatants.

According, then, to those just war theorists who stop to answer the question, deliberate killing of enemy combatants in a just war is morally acceptable because their participation in an unjust attack on others means that they are not innocent human beings whose killing would be immoral. They may not be personally guilty from a moral or legal point of view, but their role in an unjust attack deprives them of the kind of innocence that would make targeting them immoral.

III. *Ius ad bellum.* When is Recourse to War Justified?

Just war theory establishes four conditions which must be met in order for a war to be considered justified: A) There must be a just cause; B) The war must be declared by a lawful authority; C) There must be an appropriate proportion between the goals sought and the costs, both physical and moral; and D) War must be the last resort. The following four subsections will explore each of these conditions.

* * *

1. What Causes Are Sufficient to Justify War?

Medieval just war theory generally recognized three goals that could justify recourse to war: defense against attack, recovery of something wrongfully taken, and punishment of evil. The goal of punishing evil loomed large in medieval theory, to the point that, for Thomas Aquinas, it was the principal justification of war. Modern theorists have abandoned punishment for moral guilt as a justification of war, stressing instead the righting of objective wrongs, including the defense of human rights.

In the nineteenth century, the great European powers (and the United States in the Caribbean) frequently resorted to war to protect the economic interests of their citizens or to resolve territorial disputes, especially in their dealings with what we now call developing countries. Although injury to the economic interests of nationals and territorial disputes may give one nation a just claim against another, the contemporary consensus is that the enormously destructive character of modern warfare, even when carried out only with conventional weapons, makes war an inappropriate instrument for resolving such questions. In one sense, this is a question of "proportionality" rather than just cause, but because the conclusion is that the means are *always* disproportional to the end, it seems clearer, as well as briefer, to say that neither economic injury to the interests of nationals nor claims to lost territory constitute just cause for war. This is not to say that the claims themselves are not grounded in justice, but only that they are not sufficient to justify resort to war.

Many contemporary just war theorists limit just cause exclusively to defense. This approach began in the nineteenth century, in response to the growing destructiveness of war caused by technical developments such as the repeating rifle and machine gun, and by the vastly increased size of armies made possible by the *levee en mass* [mass conscription], which in turn reflected the spread of nationalism and revolutionary fervor. The horrific experience of World War I lent new strength to the movement to eliminate war altogether, or at least to limit the justifiable causes of war to defense against armed aggression. Immediately after World War I, the Covenant of the League of Nations expressed the signatories' desire "to promote international co-operation and to achieve international peace and security by the acceptance of obligations not to resort to war." Members of the League took on obligations to submit various types of disputes to arbitration, judicial settlement, or enquiry by the League Council, and renounced the right to go to war against any state that accepted the outcome of those processes.

In 1928, the signatories of the Kellogg Briand Pact "condemn[ed] recourse to war for the solution of international controversies, and renounce[d] it, as an instrument of national policy in the relations [of the parties] with one another." They "agree[d] that the settlement or solution of all disputes or conflicts of whatever nature or of whatever origin they may be, which may arise among them, shall never be sought except by pacific means." Neither the League Covenant nor the Kellogg Briand Pact included any effective enforcement mechanism, but each reflected a growing international consensus against war as a legitimate instrument of national policy.

The enormous carnage of World War II further increased revulsion toward war. As a result, the drafters of the United Nations Charter limited the circumstances in which recourse to war would be legal to defense against active aggression.

* * *

3. Preemption

Treating defense as the only just cause for war and equating first use of force with aggression, closes the door on preemptive use of force. By contrast, since the time of Augustine, the just war tradition has accepted, at least implicitly, the use of force to preempt an imminent unjust attack.

The Dutch legal scholar Hugo Grotius (1583-1645), who played a pivotal role in the development of just war theory, explicitly approved preemptive strikes, finding justification for war in "an injury not yet inflicted, which menaces either persons or property." He was quick, however, to clarify that the "danger [of being attacked] must be immediate," and criticized as "much mistaken" those who hold that "any degree of fear ought to be a ground for killing another, to prevent his supposed intention."

According to Grotius, preemptive attacks are justified only when it is certain that the other party will attack. He rejects as sufficient grounds for war "fear with respect to a neighboring power...for in order that a self-defence may be lawful it must be necessary; and it is not necessary unless we are certain, not only regarding the power of our neighbor, but also regarding his intention; the degree of certainty required is that which is accepted in morals." Grotius criticizes as "repugnant to every principle of justice" the doctrine that "the bare possibility that violence may be some day turned on us gives us the right to inflict violence on others." It is not permissible, he urges, "to take up arms in order to weaken a rising power, which, if it grew too strong, might do us harm."

Later authors within the just war tradition, building on Grotius' insights, distinguished between *preempting* an attack which was certain and imminent, and launching a *preventive* attack to head off a danger, which was feared might develop in the future if measures were not taken now. A preventive attack, they said, could not be justified, because "the danger to which it alludes is not only distant but speculative, whereas the costs of a preventive war are near, certain, and usually terrible." But a genuinely preemptive attack could be justified in the "rare circumstances…when an unavoidable attack is likely to be imminent and the threat is grave." Walzer, for instance, asserts that a preemptive strike may be justified when there is

> a manifest intent to injure, a degree of active preparation that makes the intent a positive danger, and a general situation in which waiting, or doing anything other than fighting, greatly magnifies the risk.... Instead of previous signs of rapacity and ambition, current and particular signs are required; instead of an "augmentation of power," actual preparation for war; instead of the refusal of future securities, the intensification of present danger.

Regan agrees, "it is as much an act of self-defense to initiate hostilities to prevent imminent attack as it is to respond to hostilities already initiated by an aggressor." He argues that it [sic] not necessary to wait until the would-be aggressor is immediately poised to attack or has stockpiled nuclear or chemical weapons, but he requires "practical certainty, no reasonable doubt (better than 90% probability)" that aggression will take place if not preempted.

* * *

The question of preemption is a troubling one and unlikely to be definitively resolved. It has always involved prudential judgments about how imminent is imminent enough, but the pressure on answering those questions correctly has been vastly increased by the availability of weapons of mass destruction.

Michael J. Glennon, *Preemptive Terrorism: The Case for Anticipatory Self-Defense*[*]

The Bush Doctrine, as promulgated by President Bush following the events of September 11, contemplates preemptive use of force against terrorists as well as the states that harbor them. If the United Nations Charter is to be believed, however, carrying out that doctrine would be unlawful: The Charter permits use of force by states only in response to an armed attack. In 1945, when the Charter was framed, this prohibition against anticipatory self-defense may have seemed realistic. Today, it is not. Indeed, it is no longer binding law.

Since time immemorial, the use of force has been permitted in self-defense in the international as well as all domestic legal systems, and for much the same reason: With states as with individuals, the most elemental right is survival. So powerful has been its claim that the right of self-defense was considered implicit in earlier treaties limiting use of force by states; the Kellogg-Briand Peace Pact of 1928, like the 1919 Covenant of the League of Nations, made no mention of it.

In 1945, the right was made explicit. Article 51 of the United Nations Charter states expressly: "Nothing in the present Charter shall impair the inherent right of individual or collective self-defense if an armed attack occurs against a Member of the United Nations...." Self-defense thus emerged as the sole purpose under the Charter for which states may use force without Security Council approval.

While the Charter professes not to "impair" the inherent right to self-defense, it does precisely that. Prior to 1945, states used defensive force before an attack had occurred, to forestall an attack. The plain language of Article 51 permits defensive use of force only if an armed attack occurs. If none has occurred, defensive force—"anticipatory self-defense"—is not permitted.

This new impairment of the right of self-defense was widely seen as sensible when the Charter was adopted. States had often used the claim of self-defense as a pretext for aggression. (The Nazi defendants at Nuremberg argued that Germany had attacked the Soviet Union, Norway, and Denmark in self-defense, fearing that Germany was about to be attacked.) If profligate use of force was ever to be reined in, narrower limits had to be imposed. And those limits had to be set out with a bright

---

[*] Michael J. Glennon, *Preemptive Terrorism: The Case for Anticipatory Self-Defense*, THE WEEKLY STANDARD, Jan. 28, 2002, at 24, 24-27. Reprinted with the permission of The Weekly Standard.

line; qualifying defensive rights with words like "reasonable," "imminent," or even "necessary" would leave states too much discretion and too much room for abuse. The occurrence of an actual armed attack was thus set up as an essential predicate for the use of force. The new requirement narrowed significantly the circumstances in which force could be used. And it set out a readily identifiable and, it was thought, objectively verifiable event to trigger defensive rights. Phony defensive justifications would be less plausible and war would be less frequent, thereby vindicating the first great purpose of the Charter—"to maintain international peace and security."

The impairment was realistic, it was further thought, because the need for anticipatory defense would diminish. The reason was that the Security Council would pick up where individual states were now compelled by the Charter to leave off. The Council, to be equipped with its own standing or standby forces, was authorized to use force in response to any "threat to the peace"—authority far broader than that accorded individual states. Coupled with the requirement that states report to the Security Council when using defensive force, this new institution—this "constabulary power before which barbaric and atavistic forces will stand in awe," as Churchill described it—would make anticipatory self-help a thing of the past.

All know that it didn't work out that way. Throughout the Cold War the Security Council deadlocked repeatedly on security issues. States never gave the Council the peace enforcement troops contemplated by the Charter's framers. The Council authorized (rather than used) force only haphazardly "to maintain or restore international peace and security." And, as discussed later, states continued to use force often, obviously not in response to armed attacks.

Still, like most states, the United States never formally claimed a right to anticipatory self-defense—i.e., to use armed force absent an armed attack, so as to prevent one from occurring. During the 1962 Cuban Missile Crisis, the United States declined to rely upon Article 51, claiming instead that the "quarantine" of Cuba was authorized by the Organization of American States (and implicitly by the Security Council). When Israel seemed to assert a right to use defensive force to prevent an imminent Arab attack in June 1967, and even when Israel squarely claimed that right in attacking an Iraqi nuclear reactor in 1981, the United States steered clear of the issue of anticipatory self-defense. In 1986, however, the United States finally did claim the right to use "preemptive" force against Libya following the bombing of a Berlin night club that killed two Americans.

This last incident is worth considering closely: The Libyan bombing highlights the doctrinal confusion surrounding self-defense and also marks a proverbial "paradigm shift" in American thinking on the question. Why insist upon an actual armed attack as a precondition for the use of force? The axiomatic answer, under long-standing dogma, is of course that force is necessary to protect against the attack. But by acknowledging that its use of force against Libya was preemptive, the United States in effect moved beyond the conventional justification. The Berlin bombing was obviously over and finished; no use of force was, or conceivably could have been, instrumental in "defending" Americans killed at the Berlin club. The United States was not, in this sense, responding defensively. It was engaged in a forward-looking action, an action directed at future, not past, attacks on Americans. Its use of force against Libya was triggered by the Berlin attack only in the sense that that attack was evidence of the threat of future attacks. Evidence of Libyan capabilities and intentions sufficient to warrant preemptive force might well have taken (and, in fact, also did take) the form of intelligence reports. From a purely epistemological standpoint, no actual armed attack was necessary.

Although the United States did not spell out its thinking this explicitly, in later incidents it acted on precisely this future-looking rationale. True, the United States was in each instance able to argue that actual armed attacks had occurred. But in each of those subsequent incidents, the United States was responding to evidence of future intent and capability, not defending against past action. Its objective was to avert future attacks through preemption and deterrence.

In 1993, for example, the United States fired cruise missiles at the Iraqi intelligence headquarters in Baghdad following an alleged effort by Iraq to assassinate President Bush. But the assassination attempt was long since over; the United States used force not to defend against illicit force already deployed, but to discourage such force from being deployed in the future. In 1998, the United States fired cruise missiles at a terrorist training camp in Afghanistan and a pharmaceutical plant in Sudan following attacks on U.S. embassies in Kenya and Tanzania. Again, the provocation had ended; in no way can the United States be seen as having defended itself against the specific armed attack to which its embassies had been subject.

So, too, with the use of force against Afghanistan following September 11. The armed attack against the World Trade Center and the Pentagon was over, and no defensive action could have ameliorated its effects. The U.S. use of force was prompted by the threat of future attacks. And it was evidence of that threat—gleaned from multiple intelligence sources, not simply from the September 11 attack—to which the United

States responded with its action against Afghanistan. That action could well have been warranted even if September 11 had never occurred. The problem lay in the future, not the past.

In each of these incidents, the United States justified its action under Article 51 of the Charter, claiming to be engaged in the defensive use of force. But in fact something different was going on. In each incident, the United States was—as it acknowledged forthrightly following the 1986 bombing of Libya—engaged in the use of preemptive force. The two are not the same. The justification for genuine defensive force was set forth by U.S. Secretary of State Daniel Webster in the famous Caroline case of 1837. To use it, he wrote, a state must "show a necessity of self-defense, instant, overwhelming, leaving no choice of means, and no moment of deliberation." (This formula continues to be widely cited by states, tribunals, and commentators as part and parcel of the law of the Charter.) Obviously, in none of the incidents canvassed above can the American use of force be said to meet the Caroline standard. None of the American armed responses needed to be, or was, instant. In each the United States deliberated for weeks or months before responding, carefully choosing its means. Those means were directed not at defending against an attack that had already begun, but at preempting, or deterring, an attack that could begin at some point in the future.

In fact, the United States had long ago accepted the logic of using armed force without waiting to be attacked. In the early 1960s, President Kennedy seriously considered launching a preemptive strike against the People's Republic of China to prevent it from developing nuclear weapons. In 1994, President Clinton contemplated a preemptive attack against North Korea for the same reason. During the Cold War, the United States retained the option of launching its nuclear weapons upon warning that a nuclear attack was about to occur—before the United States actually had been attacked—so as to protect command and control systems that were vulnerable to a Soviet first strike.

It thus came as no dramatic policy change when, in the Bush Doctrine, the United States publicly formalized its rejection of the armed attack requirement and officially announced its acceptance of preemption as a legitimate rationale for the use of force. "Every nation now knows," President Bush said on December 11, "that we cannot accept—and we will not accept—states that harbor, finance, train, or equip the agents of terror."

That formalization was overdue. Twenty-first-century security needs are different from those imagined in San Francisco in 1945.

First, as noted above, the intended safeguard against unlawful threats of force—a vigilant and muscular Security Council—never materialized. Self-help is the only realistic alternative.

Second, modern methods of intelligence collection, such as satellite imagery and communications intercepts, now make it unnecessary to sit out an actual armed attack to await convincing proof of a state's hostile intent.

Third, with the advent of weapons of mass destruction and their availability to international terrorists, the first blow can be devastating—far more devastating than the pinprick attacks on which the old rules were premised.

Fourth, terrorist organizations "of global reach" were unknown when Article 51 was drafted. To flourish, they need to conduct training, raise money, and develop and stockpile weaponry—which in turn requires communications equipment, camps, technology, staffing, and offices. All this requires a sanctuary, which only states can provide—and which only states can take away.

Fifth, the danger of catalytic war erupting from the use of preemptive force has lessened with the end of the Cold War. It made sense to hew to Article 51 during the Cuban Missile Crisis, when two nuclear superpowers confronted each other toe-to-toe. It makes less sense today, when safe-haven states and terrorist organizations are not themselves possessed of preemptive capabilities.

Still, it must be acknowledged that, at least in the short term, wider use of preemptive force could be destabilizing. The danger exists that some states threatened with preemptive action (consider India and Pakistan) will be all too ready to preempt probable preemptors. This is another variant of the quandary confronted when states, in taking steps to enhance their security, unintentionally threaten the security of adversaries—and thus find their own security diminished as adversaries take compensatory action.

But the way out of the dilemma, here as elsewhere, is not underreaction and concession. The way out lies in the adoption of prudent defensive strategies calculated to meet reasonably foreseeable security threats that pose a common danger. Such strategies generate community support and cause adversaries to adapt perceptions and, ultimately, to recalibrate their intentions and capabilities. That process can take time, during which the risk of greater systemic instability must be weighed against the risk of worldwide terrorist attacks of increased frequency and magnitude.

The greater danger is not long-term instability but the possibility that use of preemptive force could prove incomplete or ineffective. It is not always possible to locate all maleficent weapons or facilities, thereby posing the risk that some will survive a preemptive strike and be used in retaliation. Similarly, if a rogue state such as Iraq considers itself the likely target of preemptive force, its leaders may have an incentive to defend with weapons of mass destruction—weapons they would not otherwise use—in the belief that they have nothing to lose. A reliable assessment of likely costs is an essential precondition to any preemptive action.

These are the sorts of considerations that policymakers must weigh in deciding whether to use preemptive force. Preemption obviously is a complement, not a stand-alone alternative, to non-coercive policy options. When available, those options normally are preferable. The point here is simply that preemption is a legitimate option, and that—the language of the Charter notwithstanding—preemption is lawful. States can no longer be said to regard the Charter's rules concerning anticipatory self-defense—or concerning the use of force in general, for that matter—as binding. The question—the sole question, in the consent-based international legal system—is whether states have in fact agreed to be bound by the Charter's use-of-force rules. If states had truly intended to make those rules obligatory, they would have made the cost of violation greater than the perceived benefits.

They have not. The Charter's use-of-force rules have been widely and regularly disregarded. Since 1945, two-thirds of the members of the United Nations—126 states out of 189—have fought 291 interstate conflicts in which over 22 million people have been killed. In every one of those conflicts, at least one belligerent necessarily violated the Charter. In most of those conflicts, most of the belligerents claimed to act in self-defense. States' earlier intent, expressed in words, has been superseded by their later intent, expressed in deeds.

Rather, therefore, than split legal hairs about whether a given use of force is an armed reprisal, intervention, armed attack, aggression, forcible countermeasure, or something else in international law's over-schematized catalogue of misdeeds, American policymakers are well advised to attend directly to protecting the safety and well-being of the American people. For fifty years, despite repeated efforts, the international community has been unable to agree on when the use of force is lawful and when it is not. There will be plenty of time to resume that discussion when the war on terrorism is won. If the "barbaric and atavistic" forces succeed, however, there will be no point in any such discussion, for the law of the jungle will prevail. Completing that victory is the task at hand. And winning may require the use of preemptive force against terrorist forces as well as against the states that harbor them.

Charles W. Kegley, Jr. and Gregory A. Raymond, *Preemptive War: A Prelude to Global Peril?*[*]

In the immediate aftermath of the terrorist attacks on Sept. 11, 2001, the U.S. began a war against global terrorism. Soon thereafter, America abandoned its Cold War strategy of containment, embracing the doctrine of preemptive warfare aimed at attacking suspected aggressors before they could strike first. This, in turn, led to the invasion of Iraq in March, 2003.

The Bush Administration's doctrine of preempting terrorists and rogue states, in what is called alternatively "forward deterrence" or "anticipatory self-defense," raises anew timeless moral and legal issues about the conditions under which, and purposes for which, a just war for self-defense is permissible to counter a threat to national security. What it has advanced as a new national security strategy is nothing less than an amputation of the normative pillar on which global society has been based at least since 1928, when the Kellogg-Briand pact outlawed war as an instrument of foreign policy. This radical revision of customary international law is leading the world into uncharted waters. If it becomes permissible to attack other international actors who do not pose an *imminent* threat, then, without a moral principle to guide international conduct, war is likely to increase.

Pres. Bush first signaled the policy change he was initiating on June 1, 2002, at West Point. To his way of thinking, 9/11 created unprecedented "new deadly challenges" that necessitated new approaches and rules for statecraft. Chastising tyrants like Iraq's Saddam Hussein as international outlaws, the President announced that "We must be prepared to stop rogue states and their terrorist clients before they are able to threaten or use weapons of mass destruction against the United States and our allies and friends.... Traditional concepts of deterrence will not work against a terrorist enemy whose avowed tactics are wanton destruction and the targeting of innocents, whose so-called soldiers seek martyrdom in death.... The greater the threat, the greater the risk of inaction—and the more compelling the case for taking anticipatory action to defend ourselves, even if uncertainty remains as to the time and place of the enemy's attack. To forestall or *prevent* such hostile acts by our adver-

[*] Charles W. Kegley, Jr. & Gregory A. Raymond, *Preemptive War: A Prelude to Global Peril?*, USA TODAY, May 2003, at 14, 14-16. Reprinted with permission from USA Today Magazine, May 2003.

saries, the United States will, if necessary, act preemptively." (Emphasis added.)

This reasoning soon thereafter became the cornerstone of The National Security Strategy of the United States of America (NSS), released on Sept. 17. It reiterated Bush's West Point declaration that the era of deterrence was over and preemption was an idea whose time had come. It then proceeded to assert that, "Given the goals of rogue states and terrorists, the United States can no longer solely rely on a reactive posture as we have in the past.... We cannot let our enemies strike first." The NSS added, "Nations need not suffer an attack before they can lawfully take action to defend themselves against forces that present an imminent danger of attack."

The extreme revisionism of the Bush doctrine undercuts a key preemptory norm in international law that underpins all others—the use of force cannot be justified merely on account of an adversary's capabilities, but solely in defense against its aggressive actions. Preemption represents a frontal rejection of Articles 2(4) and 51 of the United Nations Charter that condones war only in self-defense. It opens the door to military first strikes against adversaries, under the claim that their motives are evil and that they are building the military capabilities to inflict mass destruction.

It is not difficult to appreciate the grave dangers that have prompted this watershed in U.S. national strategy. The threats which provoked the President's extreme strategic response are real. *Raison d'etat* dictates that actions be taken for the preservation of the state, and, in these threatening circumstances, many find reasonable the claim that the national interest makes such countermeasures imperative. The temptation to attack first an adversary who might attack you is, of course, often overwhelming. Why stand by in the face of a potential threat? "An ounce of prevention is worth a pound of cure," a popular cliche advises. Better to hit an enemy before it attacks, than to be left prostrate. The thinking underlying the rationale is expressed well in Umberto Eco's *Baudolino*, where the protagonist argues, "Better to be rid at once of someone who does not yet threaten you, than leave him alive so that he may threaten you one day. Let us strike first."

That realpolitik logic was at the root of the NSS proposition that the "best defense is a good offense," and the premise behind the President's explanation in an Oct. 7, 2002, speech in Cincinnati that "We have every reason to assume the worst, and we have an urgent duty to prevent the worst from happening." A proactive policy through preemption is defined as necessary because it was argued that America "cannot wait for the final proof—the smoking gun—that could come in the form of a mushroom cloud."

Fear is a great motivator. There are ample reasons to fear terrorists like Osama bin Laden and tyrants like Saddam. The threats are real in this age of globalization in which boundaries are no longer barriers to external threats, a suitcase nuclear bomb or a chemical/biological weapon can obliterate any American city, and a terrorist can strike anywhere and anytime. The U.S. is vulnerable, so there is an understandable compulsion to eliminate threats by any means available, including preemptive strikes.

Preemption is advocated as a policy, but what must be understood is that this strategy goes beyond that goal to a whole other level—to *preventive* war. The Bush doctrine transcends the established limitations of the use of armed force in self-defense against a prior armed attack. "The President is not 'reserving a right' to respond to imminent threats," wrote Duke University professor of international relations Michael Byers in the July 25, 2002, issue of *The London Review of Books*, "he is seeking an extension of the fight of self-defense to include action against potential future dangers."

As the wording of the Bush NSS illuminates, the line between preemption and prevention is blurry. How does one distinguish intentions from capabilities? Because an adversary amasses arsenals of weapons, does that necessarily mean that those weapons are for aggression instead of defense? Without knowledge of motives, prudence dictates worst-case assumptions. This invites the so-called "security dilemma" that results when one country's arms acquisitions provokes corresponding actions by alarmed adversaries, with the result that all participants in the arms race experience reduced security as their weaponry increases. Preemption addresses the danger by attacking first and asking questions about intentions later.

The quest to redefine international rules to permit preemptive strikes has deeper philosophical, ethical, and legal consequences for the long term, beyond its unforeseen immediate impact. Does it threaten to weaken international security and, paradoxically, U.S. national security as well? To probe this questions, let us look briefly at some historical precedents to preemptive practices in order to put the current policy into perspective. Consider some salient illustrations that precede Bush's rationale:

• In the third Punic War fought between the Roman and Carthaginian empires (264-147 B.C.), after a 50-year hiatus, the Romans bought the advice of the 81-year-old Cato the Elder. Consumed with the fear that renewed Punic power would culminate eventually in Roman defeat unless drastic military measures were taken, he ended every speech to the Roman Senate by proclaiming "*Carthaginian esse delendum*" (Carthage must be destroyed). Heeding Cato's advice, Rome launched a preventive war of annihilation and, in 146 B.C., some 500,000 Carthaginian citizens were destroyed in an act of mass genocide, and an entire civilization was obliterated. The foreign threat *had* been met; thereafter, no challenges to Roman hegemony existed—but at what cost? The Roman historian Polybius prophetically lamented, "I feel a terror and dread lest someone someday should give the same order about my own native city." Perhaps this led him to conclude that "it is not the object of war to annihilate those who have given provocation to it, but to cause them to mend their ways." Worse still, this preventive war can be said to have destroyed the soul of Rome. After it, Rome suffered a prolonged period of revolutionary strife, and much later found itself victim of the same savage preemptive measures by invaders it had once inflicted on Carthage. "*Val victis*" (Woe betide the defeated), the Romans cried after the city was sacked by the Gauls in 390 A.D. Is there an object lesson here? Read on.

• Dec. 7, 1941, was "a day that will live in infamy," as Pres. Franklin D. Roosevelt declared in reaction to Japan's sneak attack on Pearl Harbor. That strike removed most of the U.S. Pacific fleet and thereby redressed the Japanese-American military balance of power. The attack was premeditated, for arguably preventive purposes—to hit the U.S. before it could use its superior military capabilities to smother Japanese imperialism and Japan's Asian Co-Prosperity Sphere in its cradle. However, preventive action hardly proved practical. It backfired, provoking the sleeping American giant from isolationistic neutrality into an angry wrath without restraint, leading to the annihilating atomic bombing of Hiroshima on Aug. 6, 1945.

• In June, 1981, Iraq was making rapid headway, with French assistance, toward building a nuclear reactor. Israeli warplanes destroyed that facility in a strike that prevented Iraq from acquiring nuclear weapons. The attack was planned, and, with pinpoint accuracy and effectiveness, the potential threat (that Prime Minister Menachem Begin regarded as the most-serious challenge to Israeli self-preservation) was removed. Begin, a former terrorist, undertook terrorism against a proven terrorist and tyrant, thus practicing the same strategy he sought to contain. As G. John Ikenberry, the Peter F. Krogh Professor of Geopolitics and Global Justice at Georgetown University, notes, this attack broke normative barriers, "and the world condemned it as an act of aggression"—as unjustifiable and shortsighted. The Reagan Administration condemned the strike; France pronounced it "unacceptable"; and Great Britain berated it as "a grave breach of international law." The strategy worked, however, in the short run, as Iraqi plans for cross-border attacks on Kuwait, Iran, and, in all likelihood, Israel were averted. In the long run, though, the preventive attack strengthened Saddam's grip on power at home and animated his military ambitions to try harder—in the name of defense.

History is thus replete with examples of states that have rationalized preemptive surgical attacks against a rival for preventive purposes. In fact, it is hard to find many cases of states that did not claim that, in initiating war, they were merely acting prudently in self-defense. Nearly all wars have been justified by that claim. This record suggests that preventive war is a problem, not a solution.

Bush asserts that, "If we wait for threats to fully materialize, we will have waited too long." That justification has been voiced by many before as an excuse for war. As *New York Times* columnist Bill Keller observes, historians cite as U.S. examples of preemptive interventions "Woodrow Wilson's occupation of Haiti in 1915, Lyndon Johnson's dispatch of U.S. Marines to the Dominican Republic in 1965, and Ronald Reagan's invasion of Grenada in 1983. [But] while preemption has been an occasional fact of life, [until George W. Bush] no president has so explicitly elevated the practice to a doctrine. Previous American leaders preferred to fabricate pretexts [such as] the sinking of the *Maine*...rather than admit they were going in 'unprovoked.'"

If a permissive climate of opinion on the acceptability of preemptive and preventive warfare takes root, will the U.S. and the world at large be safer and more secure? The normative barriers to the first-strike initiation of war vanish in a world in which preemption for prevention is accepted. Let us examine the blaring downside of the U.S. advocacy of preemptive warfare.

Preemption and its extension to preventive war is a direct challenge to prevailing norms. To encapsulate the international legal consensus prior to 9/11, before U.S. doctrine began to challenge it, one might say that international law over time had gravitated toward increasingly restrictive sets of rules for justified war making. Aggressive war was illegal, but defensive war was not. International law, therefore, did not break down whenever war broke out, for there are specified conditions under which states were permitted to wage a war. Those criteria were highly restrictive, though, confining war to serve as a penal method for punishing a prior attack by an aggressor.

How the U.S. chooses to act—its code of conduct—will be a powerful determinant of the rules followed throughout the international arena. Global leaders lead in creating the system's rules. When the reigning hegemon abandons an established rule and endorses a substitute one, the rules change for everyone. What the strongest do eventually defines what everybody should do, and when a practice becomes common it tends to be seen as obligatory. As Harvard University professor of international relations Stanley Hoffmann puts it, rules *of* behavior become rules *for* behavior.

Changing circumstances call for changes in policy, and extreme times of trouble invite extreme responses. However, policies engineered in crises have rarely proven wise. In judging the ethics of a proposed standard of action, it is enlightening to recall German philosopher Immanuel Kant's insight into the situation. In his famous principle, the "categorical imperative," Kant asked humanity to consider, when contemplating an action or a policy, what the consequences would be if everyone practiced that same conduct. In evaluating the probity and prudential value of an action, he counseled that the sole ethical international activity is one that would be advantageous for humanity if it were to become a universal law practiced by all. Would that activity make for a better world? If all behave accordingly, as the practice becomes customary, would humanity benefit or suffer?

Kant preached an ethic that springs from the question "What if everybody did that?" and applied it to international relations. He believed, that the best reason for abiding by the ethics of Jesus Christ as propounded in the Sermon on the Mount was that those nonviolent principles would make for a better, more-rewarding life for all, and that killing creates a hell on Earth. We should treat others as we ourselves would wish to be treated, because those actions will, reciprocally, provoke others to treat us as we treat them. Nonaggression thus serves not only our best ideals, but benefits our self-interest, as reciprocity in altruism creates better relationships and a better world in which to live. This is the realism of idealism.

Taking this a short step forward, other questions can be asked about the moral responsibilities of the strong and mighty. What are the obligations of the powerful? How should they react to threats from weaker states? In asymmetrical contests of will, where the playing field is strongly slanted to the advantage of a superpower such as the U.S., should it play according to the same rules as its enemies? Lowering itself to the modus operandi of the likes of Saddam can reduce the U.S. superpower to the standards of those it opposes. Flexing military muscles without an international mandate and without convincing justification can prostitute traditional and honorable American principles, erode the U.S.'s reputation, and undermine its capacity to lead. To practice what is not right is to sacrifice respect for a country's most-valuable asset—its reputation for virtue, the most-important factor in what is known as "soft power" in the exercise of global influence.

Can smashing perceived threats serve justice efficiently? Recall moral philosopher John Rawls' simple test of justice—"Would the best off accept the arrangements if they believed at any moment they might find themselves in the same place of the worst off?" Historian Christopher Dawson provided a partial answer when he noted that, "As soon as men decide that all means are permitted to fight an evil, then their good becomes indistinguishable from the evil they set out to destroy."

Applying this reasoning, what is likely to result if global norms are redefined to permit all states to defend themselves against potential threats in advance, before an enemy undertakes an attack or inflicts an injury? What if the U.S. doctrine becomes every state's and every terrorist movement's policy?

What the big powers do sets the standards that others follow. If other states act on the same rationale the U.S. has promulgated and take preventive military action against any enemy they claim is threatening them, the right to use force will be legitimized. The danger is that every country could conclude that preemption for preventive purposes is an acceptable practice. This doctrine of preemption would invite any state to attack any adversary that it perceived was threatening it.

A bottomless legal pit

Perhaps unwittingly, the Bush Administration appears not to have taken into consideration the probability that its doctrine will encourage most others to accept that same doctrine, or that a bottomless legal pit will be created. "The specific doctrine of preemptive action," argues Ikenberry, "poses a problem: once the United States feels it can take such a course of action, nothing will stop other countries from doing the same." Indeed, that prophecy has already been fulfilled as others have emulated the American position by taking "up preemption as a way of dealing with these problems. The Bush doctrine—or at best the rhetoric—has already been appropriated by Russia against Georgia, by India against Pakistan. The dominoes can be expected to fall if the strategy of preemption continues to spread, as surely it will if the United States pursues its new policy." Or, as Keller opines, "If everyone embraces [the U.S.] new doctrine, a messy world would become a lot messier. Caveat pre-emptor."

If a permissive climate of opinion on the acceptability of preemptive and preventive warfare takes root, will the U.S. and the world at large be safer and more secure? That is doubtful. It has taken a long time for an international consensus to build behind the view that a preemptive attack to prevent an enemy's potential attack is outside the boundaries of justified warfare. In earlier epochs, states believed that they could attack another country for any reason deemed in the attacker's national interests. That climate of normative opinion has evaporated, and, partially as a consequence, the frequency of interstate war has steadily declined and almost vanished since the Cold War ended. Now, however, the U.S. has justified preemptive war under the claim that the benefits of preemption exceed the costs of acting only on retaliation for prior attacks for defense.

This shift is not a cure; it is a curse. In pleading for preservation of the restrictive norms that prohibit preemptive strikes, historian Paul Schraeder, writing in *The American Conservative*, warns that the universal values "are changeable, fragile, gained only by great effort and through bitter lessons of history, and are easily destroyed, set aside, or changed for the worse for the sake of monetary gain or individual interest. And the fate of these norms and standards depends above all on what great powers, especially hegemons and superpowers do with them and to them.... The American example and standard for preemptive war, if carried out, would invite imitation and emulation, and get it.... A more dangerous, illegitimate norm and example can hardly be imagined. As could easily be shown by history, it completely subverts previous standards for judging the legitimacy of resorts to war, justifying any number of wars hitherto considered unjust and aggressive. [And] one can easily imagine plausible scenarios in which India could justly attack Pakistan or vice versa, or Israel or any one of its neighbors, or China Taiwan, or South Korea North Korea, under this rule that suspicion of what a hostile regime might do justifies launching preventive wars to overthrow it."

The Bush Administration has been vocal about the urgent need it perceives to do something about the dangers that confront U.S. security, but silent about the consequences that are likely to follow from that doctrinal shift to preemptive warfare. Do we really want to remove the normative handcuffs on the use of force? Do we really want to return to the freewheeling unrestricted sovereign right of any and all rulers to define for themselves when they are threatened, so as to license anticipatory preemptive warfare? Europe experimented with that Machiavellian basis for international statecraft in the 17th century during the deadly Thirty Years' War, which reduced its population by a third. Autonomy makes for global anarchy. Is severing normative anchors on permissible warfare that demonstrably have reduced its incidence really an idea that serves American and global interests and ideals? This radical departure in radical times looks increasingly like a path to peril and a road to ruin.

Questions

1. Under the United Nations Charter, when is it appropriate for one nation to go to war with another? Is preemptive war permitted?

2. According to Coverdale, under just war theory when is it appropriate to kill an enemy combatant? What is the moral justification for such killing?

3. Is war ever appropriate? Consider the following passages: Deuteronomy 5:17; Matthew 5:38-47; 7:12; 5:3-12; Proverbs 20:22; Romans 12:17-21; I Thessalonians 5:15; I Peter 3:9; Matthew 26:50-52; I Peter 2:13-14; Romans 13:1-6; Ecclesiastes 3:1, 8; Matthew 24:6-7; I Samuel 14:6-23; 15:1-3; Revelation 19:11-21; Hebrews 11:32-34; Matthew 8:5-10; and Acts 10:1-5.

4. Is preemptive war ever permitted under just war theory? If so, under what circumstances?

5. Does the Bush doctrine of preemptive war violate the UN Charter? Does it violate the principles of just war theory?

6. According to Glennon, why does the UN Charter improperly impair nations' abilities to defend themselves?

7. What has occurred since the UN Charter was created in 1945 that leads Glennon to conclude that the United States must—despite the Charter's language to the contrary—employ preemptive warfare?

8. What lessons do Kegley and Raymond draw from history regarding the legitimacy and wisdom of employing preemptive warfare?

9. What do they believe will be the consequences of the United States' advocacy of preemptive warfare?

10. Were the following appropriate acts?

    a. The United States bombing of Hiroshima and Nagasaki in World War II;

    b. Israel's bombing of Iraq's Osirak nuclear facilities in 1981;

    c. The 1991 United States invasion of Iraq;

    d. The 2003 United States invasion of Iraq.

Part C Current Thinking on How Higher Law Should Affect Human Law

Does the higher law matter today? Parts A and B traced the development of higher law thinking over the last millennium. They also described the shift away from a belief in a higher law over the past 150 years. Despite this shift, many still believe that a higher law exists. If it does, does it matter? The continuing relevance of the higher law is the subject of Part C.

Part C explores the relevance of the higher law by asking two questions. First, what is the role of Old Testament law today? Second, to what extent should higher law principles be applied to modern society? Both of these questions are important. Both are extremely controversial, even among those who believe in a higher law.

Chapter 9 deals with the role of Old Testament law. Blackstone argued that scripture provides the surest guide to the content of the higher law: "[U]ndoubtedly the revealed law is (humanly speaking) of infinitely more authority than what we generally call the natural law" because it "is the law of nature, expressly declared so to be by God himself." Many of the "legal" texts of scripture are found in the law of the Old Testament. Thus, to understand the "revealed law," we must understand the place of Old Testament law. The readings in chapter 9 explore whether and to what extent the Old Testament law has relevance for Christians and society today.

Chapter 10 deals with the extent to which the higher law should be applied in modern society. Even if one knows the content of the higher law, that knowledge does not determine how much of the higher law should be enacted as part of human law. Recall that Aquinas argued:

> Now human law is framed for a number of human beings, the majority of whom are not perfect in virtue. Wherefore human

> laws do not forbid all vices, from which the virtuous abstain, but only the more grievous vices, from which it is possible for the majority to abstain; and chiefly those that are to the hurt of others, without the prohibition of which human society could not be maintained: thus human law prohibits murder, theft and suchlike.

The readings in chapter 10 explore what higher law principles should be applied to 21st century America.

Chapter 9 What is the Role of Old Testament Law Today?

Introduction

Christians have debated the continuing role of Old Testament law since the very beginning of the church. Acts 15 records the story of early church leaders gathering in Jerusalem for a council to determine whether gentile believers were required to be circumcised and to obey other aspects of Old Testament law. The council ruled that gentile believers need not be circumcised and should be instructed only "to abstain from food sacrificed to idols, from blood, from the meat of strangled animals and from sexual immorality."[¤] While the council settled the issue of circumcision, it left open many other issues relating to Old Testament law.

Complicating matters is that the rest of the New Testament does not set forth a simple answer to whether other parts of the Old Testament law have continuing relevance. On the one hand, some passages describe the Christian as free from the Old Testament law. For example, Romans 7:6 states: "[B]y dying to what once bound us, we have been released from the law so that we serve in the new way of the Spirit, and not in the old way of the written code." And Galatians 3:25 states: "Now that faith has come, we are no longer under the supervision of the law."

On the other hand, some passages suggest a continuing role for Old Testament law even after the coming of Jesus Christ. For example, in Matthew 5:17, Jesus states: "Do not think that I have come to abolish the law or the prophets; I have not come to abolish them but to fulfill them." Romans 8:4 states that Jesus Christ died for our sins "in order that the righteous requirements of the law might be fully met in us, who do not live according to the sinful nature but according to the Spirit."

[¤] *Acts* 15:24 (NIV).

Theologians have studied these and similar passages and reached very different views as to whether Old Testament law applies today. On one end of the spectrum are Christian reconstructionists or theonomists. They believe that the Old Testament sets forth God's unchanging standard of righteousness that applies to both the church and society as a whole. Leading reconstructionists include the late R. J. Rushdoony, Greg Bahnsen, and Gary North. They acknowledge that the ceremonial aspects of Old Testament law (circumcision, animal sacrifices, food regulations) were fulfilled in Christ and no longer apply. But they believe that all other aspects of the law do apply, including the moral law (the ten commandments) and the judicial law (specific applications of the ten commandments given to Israel, such as the Old Testament law's system of punishments). The Old Testament law governs Christians except in those instances where the New Testament explicitly abolishes a particular rule or practice.

To a reconstructionist, the Old Testament law does not simply apply to Christians. It applies to modern society. Why? Reconstructionists argue that law is inherently religious. A society must either adopt God's law as set out in scripture (including the Old Testament) or the law of another god (such as human reason). Further, reconstructionists argue that the dominion mandate of Genesis 1:28 ("Be fruitful and increase in number; fill the earth and subdue it") still applies and requires human beings to subdue the earth and exercise dominion over it in God's authority through God's law.

On the other end of the spectrum regarding the application of Old Testament are dispensationalists. Like reconstructionists, dispensationalists believe in the authority of scripture. But they differ on major presuppositions about how scripture should be interpreted. The most significant difference is over the relationship between Israel and the church. Where reconstructionists see great continuity between Israel and the church—and thus great application of Old Testament law to the church, dispensationalists see great discontinuity—and thus a limited application of Old Testament law to the church. Dispensationalists believe God's program for the church is distinctly different from God's plan for Israel. While Israel was governed by law, the church is governed by the principle of grace. Dispensationalists highlight verses such as Romans 7:6 and Galatians 3:25, quoted above, that emphasize the passing away of the Old Testament law.

Leading dispensationalists have included the late C. I. Scofield, J. I. Pentecost, and Norman Geisler. Some dispensationalists go so far as to argue that no aspect of Old Testament law applies today, including the ten commandments. Instead, they argue Christians are bound only by the moral principles taught in the New Testament (many of which parallel those given to Israel in the law).

The four pieces included in this chapter articulate something of a middle ground position between reconstructionism and dispensationalism. The first piece is an excerpt from Chapter 19 of the Westminster Confession of Faith. The Westminster Confession is a doctrinal statement drawn up in 1646 at the behest of the English Parliament. Parliament summoned "learned, godly and judicious Divines" to meet at Westminster Abbey to provide guidance regarding doctrine, worship, and government in the Church of England. The confession is one of the most influential doctrinal statements in the world. It has been adopted by many churches coming out of the reformed or Calvinistic tradition as setting forth their standard of doctrine, subordinate to scripture. It has likewise influenced some churches within the Congregationalist and Baptist traditions.

Chapter 19 of the Westminster Confession is entitled "Of the Law of God." It sets forth the view that the ten commandments still apply today, but that the ceremonial law and the judicial law applied only to Israel and do not apply today—except as "the general equity" of the judicial law "may require."

The second piece contains excerpts from an essay by Tremper Longman III. Longman is the Robert H. Gundry Professor of Biblical Studies at Westmont College. Longman received a B.A. from Ohio Wesleyan University, an M.Div. from Westminster Theological Seminary, and an M.Phil. and a Ph.D. from Yale University. He teaches a variety of Old Testament courses.

Longman shares some presuppositions with reconstructionists. Like reconstructionists, he believes that there is a continuity between Israel and the church and that the law has relevance today. However, he believes that the question of how the law should be applied—particularly to the modern state—is much more complex than reconstructionists acknowledge. In his essay he argues that reconstructionists fail to take into account important differences between Old Testament Israel and both the church and modern society.

The third piece contains excerpts from Professor Vern Poythress' book, *The Shadow of Christ in the Law of Moses.* Poythress is a professor of New Testament interpretation at Westminster Theological Seminary. He received a B.S. from the California Institute of Technology, a Ph.D. from Harvard University, an M.Div. from Westminster Theological Seminary, an M.Litt. from Cambridge University, and a D.Th. from the University of Stellenbosch, South Africa.

Poythress agrees in many points with Longman. In the excerpt reprinted here, he argues that while the Old Testament law applies today, we must use care in deciding what aspects of the law express universal principles as opposed to specialized rules that applied to Israel in its unique situation. In addition, Poythress insists we must take into account the way in which the law points to and is fulfilled in Jesus Christ. In the first half of the piece, Poythress lays out general principles of interpretation. In the second half, Poythress applies these principles to concrete issues of criminal law.

The fourth piece is an excerpt from Pope John Paul II's 1993 encyclical letter, *Veritatis Splendor (The Splendor of Truth)*. Born in Poland as Karol Jozef Wojtyla, Pope John Paul II served as the 264th Pope of the Roman Catholic Church. He served from October 1978 to April 2005. Pope John Paul II was one of the world's most influential leaders and perhaps its most powerful moral voice. He had a superb ability to relate to people all over the world. He traveled to over 100 nations and spoke fluently Polish, Italian, English, Spanish, French, German, Dutch, Croatian, Portuguese, Russian, and Latin. He spoke powerfully against communism, materialism, and war, and was a passionate defender of the right to life.

In *Veritatis Spendor*, Pope John Paul II sets forth the Catholic Church's position on key questions of moral theology, including asserting the existence of unchanging moral truth against the challenge of relativism. In the excerpts contained here, he describes the relationship between natural law and revealed law (including Old Testament law). He also insists that moral truth should affect all of life, including political life.

Westminster Confession of Faith*

Chapter XIX

Of the Law of God

I. God gave to Adam a law, as a covenant of works, by which He bound him and all his posterity, to personal, entire, exact, and perpetual obedience, promised life upon the fulfilling, and threatened death upon the breach of it, and endued him with power and ability to keep it.

* Westminster Confession of Faith, Chapter 19.

II. This law, after his fall, continued to be a perfect rule of righteousness; and, as such, was delivered by God upon Mount Sinai, in ten commandments, and written in two tables: the first four commandments containing our duty towards God; and the other six, our duty to man.

III. Besides this law, commonly called moral, God was pleased to give to the people of Israel, as a church under age, ceremonial laws, containing several typical ordinances, partly of worship, prefiguring Christ, His graces, actions, sufferings, and benefits; and partly, holding forth divers instructions of moral duties. All which ceremonial laws are now abrogated, under the New Testament.

IV. To them also, as a body politic, He gave sundry judicial laws, which expired together with the State of that people; not obliging under any now, further than the general equity thereof may require.

V. The moral law does forever bind all, as well justified persons as others, to the obedience thereof; and that, not only in regard of the matter contained in it, but also in respect of the authority of God the Creator, who gave it. Neither does Christ, in the Gospel, any way dissolve, but much strengthen this obligation.

VI. Although true believers be not under the law, as a covenant of works, to be thereby justified, or condemned; yet is it of great use to them, as well as to others; in that, as a rule of life informing them of the will of God, and their duty, it directs and binds them to walk accordingly; discovering also the sinful pollutions of their nature, hearts and lives; so as, examining themselves thereby, they may come to further conviction of, humiliation for, and hatred against sin, together with a clearer sight of the need they have of Christ, and the perfection of His obedience. It is likewise of use to the regenerate, to restrain their corruptions, in that it forbids sin: and the threatenings of it serve to show what even their sins deserve; and what afflictions, in this life, they may expect for them, although freed from the curse thereof threatened in the law. The promises of it, in like manner, show them God's approbation of obedience, and what blessings they may expect upon the performance thereof: although not as due to them by the law as a covenant of works. So as a man's doing good, and refraining from evil, because the law encourages to the one and deters from the other, is no evidence of his being under the law: and not under grace.

VII. Neither are the forementioned uses of the law contrary to the grace of the Gospel, but do sweetly comply with it; the Spirit of Christ subduing and enabling the will of man to do that freely, and cheerfully, which the will of God, revealed in the law, requires to be done.

Tremper Longman, *God's Law and Mosaic Punishments Today* in *Theonomy: A Reformed Critique*[*]

God's law (theonomy) or man's law (autonomy)? This is the choice that the classic texts of theonomy place before the Christian public. Divine revelation or human subjectivity? Which do Christians want to guide them in their civic life? With the question put in these terms, Christians do not hesitate to give an answer. Of course, we want God's law and divine revelation to direct us in all aspects of our lives.

The extensive literature of theonomy, however, proclaims that God's law for society is the Mosaic law in its entirety (except in those rare instances where the New Testament explicitly discontinues its observance). Most disturbing to those who are introduced to theonomy for the first time, it seems, is its advocacy, not only of the Mosaic case law, but also of its system of punishments. The death penalty for murder is one thing to the contemporary Christian; death for homosexuality, intercourse with one's wife during her period, adultery, and blasphemy is another.

Theonomists, however, challenge Christians to reconsider their reaction. "Remember," they say, "these are God's laws and God's punishments. Don't let your 'Christian' feelings let you get soft in the heart. God commanded them; therefore they are just."

However, before giving in to the logic of this argument we need to take a close look both at theonomy's position on penology as well as the teaching of Scripture. Perhaps there is something to the typical Christian "gut reaction" to theonomy. Although often not thought through, Christians' ideas are shaped by principles that may at least in part be defensible, since they are gained through study of the Bible. But first, what is a theonomic penology?

Theonomic Penology

As is pointed out in this book, theonomy is no longer a monolithic movement. There are many points of disagreement among people who use the term to describe their position. This chapter analyzes the views found in the seminal works of Greg Bahnsen and Rousas Rushdoony. Even these men do not always agree in detail, and their own views have

[*] TREMPER LONGMAN III, *God's Law and Mosaic Punishments Today*, *in* THEONOMY: A REFORMED CRITIQUE 41, 41-54 (William S. Barker & W. Robert Godfrey eds., 1990). Taken from Theonomy: A Reformed Critique by William S. Barker and W. Robert Godfrey.

progressed since they completed these works. However, their books are the most systematic expositions of a theonomic position in general and on penology in particular and are arguably the best known and most widely used books written from a theonomic perspective.

On the surface, a theonomic penology is quite clear-cut: We must return to a Mosaic system of punishments, and the Old Testament gives us the just penalty for all punishable offenses. To depart from God's law on this point is to introduce human, sinful subjectivity into the process. This will result in either a lenient penal code that will produce a rampant criminal society or a rigid penal code and its attendant tyranny.

What would the penology advocated by theonomy look like?

Restitution

In today's society, it is often the case that crime does pay and the victim suffers the penalty. In the Bible the principle of restitution counteracts both of these evils. For instance, a thief must restore to the victim what he stole and pay a penalty (Ex 22:1, 4). In this way, the criminal does not profit (provided he is caught), and the victim is compensated for his loss. In contemporary society, the criminal may pay a fine (in addition to a jail term), but that money is paid to the state. Victims must have recourse to the costly civil court system if they are to recover their losses. A further evil of contemporary practice is the large insurance premiums we pay to protect ourselves against theft. This protection, according to Bahnsen and Rushdoony, should come from the principle of restitution.

What happens if the criminal can't make restitution? The Bible again provides the answer: "A thief must certainly make restitution, but if he has nothing, he must be sold to pay for his theft" (Ex 22:3). Rushdoony comments, "This means today some kind of custody whereby the full income of the convicted thief is so ordered that full restitution is provided for." Elsewhere he doesn't mince words: "A man who abuses his freedom to steal can be sold into slavery in order to work out his restitution; if he cannot use his freedom for its true purpose, godly dominion, reconstruction, and restoration, he must then work towards restitution in his bondage."

In the modern setting, one might wonder how cooperative a teenager who has been stealing to support his crack habit might be with such a program. Once again the answer of theonomy is simple: habitual criminals, particularly those who rebel against the restitution principle, must be put to death. Quoting Deuteronomy 21:18-21, Rushdoony asserts, "A criminal community cannot be allowed to exist. In terms of Biblical law, the habitual criminal must be executed, as well as the incorrigible delinquent. The community of the atonement cannot tolerate habitual criminals."

The Prison System

Rushdoony finds no place for a prison system in a biblically based penology. After all, prison terms are never sanctioned by biblical law. According to Rushdoony, prisons support criminals and hurt honest taxpayers. Our prisons are overcrowded with men and women who should be executed for their crimes, working to pay off their victims, or physically punished.

Death Penalty

Certainly the most controversial aspect of a theonomic penology is its advocacy of the death penalty for a variety of crimes. Most Christians agree that the death penalty is still in effect for murder, but Bahnsen and Rushdoony extend the list of capital offenses in line with the Mosaic law.

Bahnsen lists the following crimes as worthy of the death penalty: "murder, adultery and unchastity, sodomy and bestiality, homosexuality, rape, incest, incorrigibility in children, sabbath breaking, kidnapping, apostasy, witchcraft, sorcery, and false pretension to prophecy, and blasphemy." Rushdoony adds offering human sacrifice, propagating false doctrines, sacrificing to false gods, rejecting a decision of the court, and failing to restore bail. He believes that the death penalty for sabbath breaking is no longer in effect.

Rushdoony argues that a consistent use of the death penalty will radically reduce crime by eliminating the criminal element from our society and also by providing a deterrent. In order to heighten the deterrent value of capital punishment, he would like to have public executions. In addition, minors, the insane, and the mentally deficient all are treated like anyone else in the courtroom and are eligible for the death penalty if convicted of a capital crime.

Motivation for Penology

Modern liberals often speak of rehabilitation as a primary motivation for penology. In the past twenty years many have been disillusioned by the poor results achieved by such "enlightened attitudes." Rehabilitation doesn't work. Rushdoony and Bahnsen argue that rehabilitation never motivates biblical penology. The guiding principles are "retribution, restitution and compensation," not rehabilitation.

Assessment

There simply isn't space to treat the following points fully. My object in this section is to demonstrate the problems of a theonomic penology. The approach sounds clear and simple enough—just apply the laws and penalties of the Old Testament—but in practice such a procedure is very difficult. Even though Bahnsen and Rushdoony oversimplify the biblical data, we can observe the difficulty even in their own writings.

Fundamental Tension

My first point has to do with the approach of adherents of theonomy to law in general. Of course, their approach to the law is integrally connected with their approach to penology. Many of the chapters in this volume critique theonomy's application of the Mosaic law to today's society. These arguments are also telling against its application of Old Testament penalties as well. In this context, however, I wish to point out what I believe is a fundamental tension in the writings of Bahnsen and Rushdoony. At many points they make it clear that they believe that our modern civil law should simply be the Mosaic code in its entirety. At times they remind their readers that they do not mean only the Ten Commandments, but the Old Testament law in its entirety. For instance, Bahnsen inveighs against those "who balk before the *extent* of God's law and decide to recognize only the decalogue as applicable" (emphasis his).

However, what is the Mosaic case law but the application of the Ten Commandments to the nation of Israel? None of the civil or moral laws is independent of the Ten Commandments; they are all summarized in them. The case laws are specifications of the general principles of the Ten Commandments.

As we then seek to apply the Old Testament case laws and penalties to our own situation, we need to ask, In what ways are we like Israel and in what ways are we different? How does this affect our application of the law and its penalties?

Bahnsen understands this occasionally, and the result is the tension to which I refer. For example, in his discussion of Deuteronomy 22:8 (concerning the law to build a parapet around the roof of a house), Bahnsen correctly identifies a cultural gap between ancient Israel and modern America. The Israelite law was an extension of the principle of the sixth commandment. Since the roof of a house was used as living space in ancient Israel, the law was given in order to protect life. Most houses in America don't utilize the roof as a living area. Bahnsen correctly applies the principle of the law by saying that it mandates fences around swimming pools. By making this move, however, he is doing precisely what he appears to forbid others to do. He has really applied the sixth commandment to contemporary society, using the contextualization of that commandment in Deuteronomy 22 as a guide, and no more.

But a further step must be taken: we must recognize that there is more than a cultural difference between Israel and America; there is also a difference in their respective places in redemptive history.

Israel: God's Chosen Nation

There is apparently little problem with the fact of cultural differences. In applying the law and penalties of the Old Testament to modern societies, Bahnsen and Rushdoony recognize the need to bridge the cultural distance between Israel and modern times. Deuteronomy 22:8 does not require modern home-builders to construct a parapet around their roofs, but it does mean that a swimming pool must be bordered by a fence. In the area of penology, I don't think that either of the two theonomists would object to replacing stoning with the electric chair, a firing squad, or some modern equivalent in order to carry out an execution. It's the principle that counts, and these principles are summarized in the Ten Commandments. As we apply the law and the penalties to contemporary society we must first inquire into the cultural differences between ancient Israel and modern America.

However, once we accept this point (and Bahnsen and Rushdoony write as if they do), we must ask why we shouldn't take into account an even more fundamental difference between Israel and any modern nation. Israel as a nation was chosen by God "out of all the peoples on the face of the earth to be his people, his treasured possession" (Dt 7:6). No other nation of the ancient or modern world is like Israel in its place in redemptive history. Even if a majority of American citizens were sincere Christians—or even if everyone were—America would not be like Israel in terms of God's redemptive history.

It would seem to follow that there is at least the possibility that Israel's civil law might undergo some adaptation as it is applied to contemporary society. Rushdoony recognizes this fact in connection with the death penalty for Sabbath breaking (a view not shared with Bahnsen) when he writes:

> Does this mean that, in the modern world, Sabbath-breaking is punishable by death, or should be? The answer is, very clearly and emphatically no. The modern state is not in covenant with God but is an enemy of God. Sabbath-breaking has no specific penalty of death, just as there is no death penalty for adultery

> (Hos. 4:14), because the nations are not in covenant with God and are therefore under sentence of death. Because of this general and central indictment, the lesser offenses have no place. Covenant offenses are one thing, enemy offense another.

In another place Rushdoony gives a more theoretical expression to this idea when he says, "The covenant people are *doubly* God's property: *first*, by virtue of His creation, and, *second*, by virtue of His redemption. For this reason, sin is more personal and more than man-centered. It is a theological offense" (emphasis his).

Before applying a case law from the Old Testament today, therefore, we must consider not only cultural adaptations but also discontinuities that result because of the difference in redemptive status between Israel and any modern society. How, for instance, would the difference in redemptive status between Israel and America change the laws that concern the divine-human relationship? Since God chose Israel as a nation to be his elect people, it was intolerable that a blasphemer or idolater or witch could be allowed to live. God caused his special presence to rest in the midst of Israel; his holiness would not allow such blatant rebellion to continue. However, God has not chosen America as a nation. He does not dwell on the banks of the Potomac as he did on Mount Zion. It seems strange to seek legislation by which witches, idolaters, apostates, heretics, or blasphemers would be executed in the United States or even to hope for a time when such legislation would be enacted.

As has been traditionally recognized, the proper analogue to the nation of Israel is the Christian church. God chooses to make his special presence known in the assembly of the saints. He will tolerate no blasphemy, heresy, or idolatry in the midst of his priestly people. God has given spiritual weapons to his spiritual people to fight a spiritual enemy. The church does not seek the death of blasphemers who are in the church but their excommunication.

It is not a simple thing to apply the Old Testament law and its penalties to the New Testament period. We must take into account not only cultural differences, but also redemptive-historical differences. The latter will have a definite impact on how Old Testament civil laws, which have to do with the relationship between God and Israel, will be brought over into modern society. Each law and each penalty needs to be studied in the light of the changes between Israel and America, the old covenant and the new covenant. Theonomy tends to grossly overemphasize continuity to the point of being virtually blind to discontinuity.

Subjectivity in Penology

Theonomy fears subjectivity in lawmaking and in the administration of penalties. Human autonomy is something to be feared because of man's sinfulness, and in the area of law it can be downright dangerous. The results of human autonomy are either leniency and a criminal society or tyranny and a criminal state. According to Bahnsen and Rushdoony, the only way to avoid autonomy and achieve theonomy is to simply apply the entire Old Testament law and its penalties to modern society. If there is no penalty in the Bible for a given act, then modern societies have no right to impose one. Such an act may be sinful, but it is not criminal. Further, human governments may not lessen or increase a biblical penalty.

While I too fear human autonomy and subjectivity and while I recognize that lawmaking has produced chaotic and tyrannical societies throughout history and today, the claim that theonomy would alleviate this problem is simply misleading. What is especially frightening about such an attitude is that the subjectivity of the theonomic interpreter is pressed upon us as the Word of God. Rushdoony in particular seems unaware of the enormity of the subjective side of theonomic interpretation and quite often presents his exegetical results as if they are without doubt the Word of God for today. Perhaps this in part explains the rather dogmatic and condescending style that characterizes his writing.

It has been correctly observed that the application of the Old Testament law to contemporary society would necessitate a new scribal caste that would produce a new Mishnah. Why is this the case?

In the first place, Old Testament law does not always provide a set penalty, but requires the human judges to decide the severity of the punishment. An instance of this is found in Deuteronomy 25:1-3:

> When men have a dispute, they are to take it to court and the judges will decide the case, acquitting the innocent and condemning the guilty. If the guilty man deserves to be beaten, the judge shall make him lie down and have him flogged in his presence with the number of lashes his crime deserves, but he must not give him more than forty lashes. If he is flogged more than that, your brother will be degraded in your eyes.

This passage illustrates the complexity and difficulty involved in applying Old Testament penology to the present situation. In the first place, we are left in the dark concerning the type of dispute under consideration here. It would have been clear to the original audience of this legal code, but it is not clear to us. This type of interpretive ambiguity is not infrequent and renders the theonomic application more difficult than either Bahnsen or Rushdoony is willing to admit. But the main reason I have cited this passage is to illustrate the responsibility placed on the human judge to determine the extent of the punishment. There is a significant difference between receiving two and receiving forty lashes with a rod, and the decision was the responsibility of the *human* judge with all the subjectivity that would involve. Surely, according to the biblical ideal (as opposed to historical reality), the judges of Israel would be men who showed themselves blessed by godly wisdom, but this fact does not entail infallibility. In any case, Bahnsen and Rushdoony make it clear that they fear permitting anyone, Christian or not, to make such a decision.

However, even when there is a clear Old Testament penalty for a crime, the subjectivity of the human interpreter comes into play. A prime example of this is Sabbath breaking. Bahnsen believes the death penalty still holds; Rushdoony believes there is clear biblical evidence against such a view.

A further illustration comes from the law of restitution in case of a theft. I, for one, agree that restitution is a basic biblical principle of justice. But theonomists are very careful to apply the details of the penalties in the modern period. Now, according to Exodus 22:1, a thief must restore four sheep for one he has stolen and disposed of but five oxen for an ox. Why the difference? The Bible never says. How do we apply this principle today? If a thief steals my car, do I get four cars in return, or five? Rushdoony provides a wonderful example of modern midrash to argue that the victim gets fewer sheep because they reproduce so fast but how does this apply to my car? Going further, what if I don't want four or five cars, can I receive the cash equivalent? If so, who will determine the present value of the car?

I would not be surprised if Bahnsen and Rushdoony would agree that the human interpreter is heavily involved in these decisions. However, the impression they give in their writings is that it is possible to avoid human subjectivity (which they refer to with the emotive word *autonomy*) by simply applying the laws and penalties of the Old Testament to the New Testament period.

It is my opinion that Bahnsen, Rushdoony, and their followers are more frightened than they have a right to be about Christians making legal and moral judgments guided by the principles of Scripture rather than by the explicit statements of the Old Testament. There is no doubt that the judgments of the law of the Old Testament were perfectly just in their Old Testament context. But God has given Christians the spirit of wisdom, not to make infallible judgments, but responsible ones. Indeed, he requires Christians to make judgments of this sort:

> I tell you the truth, whatever you bind on earth will be bound in heaven, and whatever you loose on earth will be loosed in heaven (Mt 18:18). Do you not know that we will judge angels? How much more the things of this life! (1Co 6:3)

Flexibility in Old Testament Law

In reading the standard works of theonomy, one can easily get the impression that Old Testament laws are simple and clear-cut. We have already seen evidence to dispute this, at least from the perspective of the modern interpreter. In the same vein, one also gets the impression that there is one and only one just penalty for a crime. A closer look at the Old Testament, however, exposes flexibility in the application of penalties.

A clear example of such flexibility is in the law of the goring ox (Ex 21:28-32). According to this law, if an ox gores and kills a second time after a warning, the owner is to be put to death. However, there is the possibility that he can pay a ransom if it is demanded of him. Thus this law at least is flexible. Two further points may be made from these verses. Once again, we witness the difficulty of interpretive ambiguity. Ransom is a possibility, it appears, if "payment is demanded of him" (v. 30). But demanded by whom? The judge? The victim's family? We don't know, and if we apply this law to the present day, who is going to make the decision? The second point to bring out is the difference in severity between the two alternatives. No matter how high the ransom is, I doubt that anyone ever turned it down in favor of the death penalty. Rushdoony, in particular, insists that a biblical penalty is always perfectly proportionate in severity to the crime. The principle is always, in his opinion, "an eye for an eye" (the *ius talionis*). However, here we have a law that envisions two possible penalties of vastly different levels of severity. The flexibility of this law plus an examination of other penalties in the Old Testament lead me to believe that the *ius talionis* (Ex 21:23-24) is setting a limit to the severity of the punishment allowed, not mandating in every case the maximum allowed.

This insight leads us to another interesting passage, one that was suggested to me by an article written by James Jordan. "Do not accept a ransom for the life of a murderer, who deserves to die. He must surely be put to death. Do not accept a ransom for anyone who has fled to a city of refuge and so allow him to go back and live on his own land before the death of the high priest" (Nu 35:31-32). It appears from these passages that ransoms were a possibility for many other crimes. Rushdoony, I believe, would argue that this law specifically appeals to the goring-ox law, which we have just studied and which explicitly provides the possibility of a ransom. However, this approach seems very unlikely because the law in Numbers 35 implies that there are a number of exceptions. If the goring-ox law were the only exception, who would need Numbers 35:31-32 to clear up any possible misunderstanding?

Conclusion

Many other texts and examples could be cited to support the points I have made. Further, there are other arguments that could be brought forward to critique the form of penology advocated by Bahnsen and Rushdoony. For instance, we could demonstrate that they have not successfully countered John Murray's interpretation that the New Testament does not recognize the death penalty for adultery. Jesus speaks of divorce rather than the death penalty in cases of adultery (Mt 5:31-32). Bahnsen is so blinded by his idiosyncratic translation and interpretation of Matthew 5:17 that he can't see that Jesus, as the Son of God, does indeed introduce adaptations of the Old Testament law for a new redemptive situation. In the same vein, James Jordan has also cited the fact that Joseph was going to quietly divorce Mary when he believed that she had committed fornication. Significantly, while narrating Joseph's plan, Matthew calls him a righteous man (Mt 1:19).

But let's conclude on a positive note and an agenda for the future. The above criticisms should not be taken as a complete rejection of theonomy's insight into the law and its penalties. The distortions produced by theonomy result from its advocates' strong concern about Christians who overemphasize the situational and personal aspects of biblical ethics and also the discontinuity of the covenants. However, they have swung the pendulum too far in the direction of the normative character of the law and the continuity of the covenants. Nonetheless, some very helpful and important themes are presented by Rushdoony and Bahnsen, if one can see through the bombast. For instance, the time is ripe for a reconsideration of the use of imprisonment as the primary punishment for crime. Further, restitution and the needs of victims must be taken into account in a just system of penalties.

Perhaps the most significant contribution of theonomists, however, is simply their pointing to the Bible as crucial to the whole issue of just punishments. Although it is not the clearcut blueprint that theonomic rhetoric makes it out to be, there is deep wisdom and necessary guidance to be found in the principles of law and punishment contained in the Old Testament. Old Testament laws must be studied individually and sensitively to see precisely how they should be applied to our modern societies. Such studies are presently underway, but they are only a beginning to a much needed and long-neglected study of God's law. We can be grateful to theonomy for forcing the church to take these issues seriously.

Vern S. Poythress, *The Shadow of Christ in the Law of Moses*[*]

Interpreting Old Testament Law

The Relation of This Book to Theonomy

In this book I disagree with theonomy on some significant matters of detail, but I affirm much of its principle concern regarding the value of the Old Testament. Let us first be more specific about the disagreements. I repudiate the view that state penalties for false worship are ever just or appropriate within this age. But I do so on the basis of my understanding of the Mosaic law and of the penalties for false worship in Deuteronomy 13:1-18 and 17:2-7 in particular. Hence, I affirm what is often regarded as the essence of the theonomic view, i.e., the abiding value of the law. I affirm with great vigor the continuing value and relevance of the whole Old Testament, on the basis of the fact that it reveals our Lord Jesus Christ. Its law and its tabernacle imagery express the righteousness and holiness of Christ.

Thus the most significant disputes between myself and theonomy concern not the question of whether the law is binding but what the law means. The law is indeed binding on Christians. For example, we should obey the principles articulated in Deuteronomy 13 and 17 and other Old Testament passages. But to obey them properly we must understand what they mean and how they foreshadow the fullness of righteousness and holiness found in Jesus Christ. Once we have that understanding, we can see that keeping the law means following Christ.

We are thus saying what all Christians know in their hearts: Jesus is Lord. We are to follow Him, reflect His character, and praise His beauty and holiness. We are to know Him, to use the language of Philippians 3:10. Knowing Him in a full and deep way includes knowing "the power of His resurrection and the fellowship of sharing in his sufferings." The Old Testament law helps us in this process because it reveals Him (Luke

---

[*] VERN S. POYTHRESS, THE SHADOW OF CHRIST IN THE LAW OF MOSES 159-63, 165-68, 335-43 (1991). Reprinted with the permission of the Presbyterian & Reformed Publishing Company.

24:25-27, 44-48). The challenging task remaining for us is to appreciate just how the law reveals Christ.

When I phrase things in this way I may appear to differ from theonomists mainly in emphasis. But such differences may be far-reaching in practice. If the law is related in a comprehensive fashion to the death and resurrection of Christ, and if it is full of typological correspondences to Christ, we must expect radical transformation of the texture of the law and radical reinterpretation in the light of the accomplishments of Christ. Such transfiguration is just as significant as the truth that the deepest principles of God's righteousness are unchangeable. I would therefore urge readers to be just as much at home with Paul's affirmations about the passing away of the Mosaic law as they are at home with Matthew's affirmation about its continuing force (Ephesians 2:15; Galatians 3:25; 2 Corinthians 4:3-11; Romans 6:15-7:6).

One function of the law is to reveal general principles of justice, that is, universal standards of Christ's righteous character and His rule. But here also there is a difficulty: how do we find general principles of justice in the law? Some laws are adapted in obvious ways to unique cultural and redemptive-historical circumstances in Israel, as both Bahnsen and I would agree. Other laws, such as "Love the LORD your God with all your heart and with all your soul and with all your strength" (Deuteronomy 6:5) and "Love your neighbor as yourself" (Leviticus 19:18), are completely universal moral principles. But every law, even the most specialized adaptations to Israel, expresses God's character and reveals something of Christ; thus every law somehow expresses universal principles. In fact, every law illustrates the principles of loving God and loving neighbor. Obviously, the principles of loving God and loving neighbor are binding and applicable now. Jesus and the apostles affirm so. Hence, the whole law, *as an illustration* of these two principles, is applicable.

But other principles besides these two basic ones are also universal. How do we determine what they are? More precisely, how do we discern the universal principles in what is more specialized, and how do we discern in what is more universal a special focus on God's care for Israel? One major difficulty in interpreting the Old Testament and in applying it lies precisely here.

Suppose that in our hermeneutics we want to "play it safe." We decide only to extract the most obviously universal principles from each particular law. Then we are left only with the two general principles of loving God and loving neighbor. Or perhaps we look for slightly less general principles than those and end up with the Ten Commandments as our summary of the law. Every law is seen as a particularization of one or more of the Ten Commandments. Such a result is valid enough as far as it goes, but it still does not go far enough. We miss the rich instruction from the details of the law.

On the other hand, suppose that we want to "play it safe" in the other direction. We fear that we will miss something by overgeneralizing. So we cling fanatically to each detail. We argue, perhaps, that we must follow all the details literally today, except those specifically abolished in the New Testament. The law regarding sowing with two kinds of seeds would have to be included, the law about making tassels on one's cloaks (Deuteronomy 22:12), and many other particulars. If we follow this route, we inevitably miss the true generalizations and carry over many unnecessary features of the Israelite situation. Worse, we run a risk of missing or underestimating the heart of the matter, namely, the Old Testament's revelation of Christ. We destroy the liberty of Christian people with unnecessary extra rules. We obscure the fact that Christians are betrothed to Christ, not to the law, and that their love of the law arises from its revelation of Christ, not from some innate property of self-sufficient rules.

In actual fact, the level of generality that we happen to find in a particular passage depends a great deal on our point of view. Inferring a very general principle from a passage is a little like looking at a meadow from the top of a mountain. We may not see the details very well, but we see one way in which the meadow fits into a whole mountain range. On the other hand, when we come down to the foot of the mountain and stand right in the meadow, we see many details. But these details may so overwhelm us that we have little idea how the meadow is related to the whole mountain range. Likewise, when we look at a passage, we may infer from it either a very general principle or a very specific teaching that may not have obvious broad implications.

* * *

We may illustrate these issues using the passage Deuteronomy 13:1-18. What general principles of morality and justice are expressed in this passage? Let us start at the most general level.... The rejection of idolatry in Deuteronomy 13:1-18 expresses the principles of loving God. Loving your neighbor is expressed by preventing the false prophet from staying around to tempt other people. Hence, at the level of greatest generality, Deuteronomy 13:1-18 expresses the two general principles of morality, loving God and loving your neighbor.

Let us descend to a slightly lower level of generality. Deuteronomy 13:1-18 expresses the principles of some of the Ten Commandments, in particular the first commandment. Having no other gods before the Lord is expressed in rejecting temptations from a false prophet or seducer.

Other kinds of general principle are also illustrated and embodied in the text. The purity of the people of God and their separation from overt unbelief is expressed by the rejection of the false prophet. "Be holy because I, the Lord your God, am holy" is embodied. As I have argued in chapter 10, the retributive principle, "as you have done it will be done to you" is expressed, as is the principle of restoring what is damaged (in this case, restoring the damaged purity of Israel).

The instructions concerning holy war that are particular to Israel are also embodied in the language of "condemned things" (Deuteronomy 13:17). As we saw in chapter 10, the whole process of holy war contains principles of destruction of sin and purification through divine power and through divinely ordained sacrifice. Such principles are still operative in the New Testament, though the particulars of our spiritual holy war are transformed in a way suitable to the circumstances of the New Testament and the reign of the resurrected Christ.

At a lower level of generality the language of Deuteronomy 13 applies only to the circumstances of Israel while in the land. The formula, "physically kill proven false prophets and seducers to false worship," represents this level of generality. Most theonomists agree that this formula does not represent an absolutely general principle, since they would want to qualify it in the form, "Kill convicted false prophets and seducers to false worship in a nation that has become largely Christian and in which such laws have been adopted as the law of the land." (However, I do not agree with theonomists even when they make their special restriction.) We can also put forward even more particular formulas, such as "stone to death the seducer, the hand of the witness being first in throwing a stone, and all the people also doing the stoning." This formula is even closer than the others to the exact specifications of Deuteronomy 13:9-10. Are the new particulars that we have added here part of a general principle that we dare not ignore in any circumstance? Or are they specialized to Israel? Are they part of the "meadow" of Israel's specific circumstances, but not characteristic of the whole "mountain range" of universal moral principle? How do we tell? Must execution be by stoning? Must the witness throw the first stone? Must all the people participate in stoning?

We can raise similar questions concerning the passage in Deuteronomy 13:12-18 on an idolatrous town. We can compose a whole succession of formulas that include more and more detail.

1. Destroy any idolatrous town.
2. Destroy any idolatrous town proven to be idolatrous by further investigation.
3. Destroy any idolatrous town within a nation dedicated to God.

4. Destroy any idolatrous town within Israel.
5. Destroy any idolatrous town completely.
6. Destroy any idolatrous town completely, including animals.
7. Destroy any idolatrous town completely, including animals and all goods ("plunder" in Deuteronomy 13:16).
8. Destroy any idolatrous town completely, with the sword.
9. Burn it in addition to the above.
10. Gather the plunder into the public square and then burn it.
11. Never rebuild it in addition to the above.
12. Make the town a burnt offering in addition to the above.

Thus we can summarize the teaching and the implications of Deuteronomy 13 either with a very general summary ("love God") or with a very specific description including many of the details. All the details were relevant to the Israelites to whom the commandments were originally given. All the details are in a sense relevant to us, since we must try to understand what God spoke through Moses to the Israelites. But not all details are relevant in the same way. To learn lessons for our own situation and to apply the law to our own situation, we must have some grasp of its purpose. (We must see how the meadow is related to the whole mountain range.) Such a grasp is obtained in the light of the context.

Which contexts, then, throw light on the purpose? The context of the Mosaic law is certainly relevant, and so are the Ten Commandments as the heart of the law. The context of the tabernacle is also relevant because the tabernacle and the law are closely related. The context of the exodus from Egypt is relevant too, not only because it is mentioned in Deuteronomy 13:5, 10, and elsewhere, but because for Moses and the Israelites, the Exodus was the immediate background experience of the revelation of God that would have qualified everything that God said in the revelation at Mount Sinai and subsequent revelation through Moses. The context of the whole Bible is also important because the Bible is the whole story of which God's story in Deuteronomy 13 is a part. Finally, the context of Christ's life and death is important, because it is the preeminent revelation to which the whole Old Testament points forward. All in all, interpreting Deuteronomy 13:1-18 involves a large number of factors.

Let us return now from the particular example of Deuteronomy 13 to the general issues. Understanding the law involves discerning its general principles in order that it may be properly applied in changed circumstances. Everyone must engage in this process, because everyone must decide when details of Israelite context are tangential to general principle and when they are part of it or influence it.

The advice that we should presume that the Old Testament law continues to bind us does not really help much. The advice really means that the *general principles* of the law bind us. But to say this much is a truism. By definition general principles continue to be the same, because to be general or to be principle is to be applicable to all times and places. Of course the principles continue! We do not need to *presume* that they continue; we *know* that they continue because it is so by definition of the word *principle*.

Do we need continuity of other things *besides* the general principles? The only other things besides principles are details that are not principial, that is, details that in themselves need not be continued.

The basic issue, then, is not whether there is continuity but what are the general principles embedded in each Old Testament law. At precisely what level of generality...will we find a universal principle, either in Deuteronomy 13 or in some other passage? To answer that question is simultaneously to answer what carries over to today.

On this issue no simple formula will do. No formula will automatically guarantee that principles of just the right amount of generality will automatically pop out of each law of Moses. There is no substitute for careful study and meditation. Disagreements exist between Bahnsen and me, not over whether the Old Testament law applies but what are the general principles embodied in penal law. I think that there are such principles. Bahnsen thinks that there are such principles. Neither of us wants to abandon valid general principles, and neither wants blindly to carry over details whose significance has altered in our time.

Bahnsen wrote as he did to encourage respect for the Old Testament and careful meditation on its precepts. The language in his books about presuming continuity between Old Testament and New was part of this effort. In this respect his work is valuable. But his language can be misused to prejudge the meaning of the Old Testament. Suppose that we have listed before us a whole series of increasingly particular formulations of a supposedly general principle, such as the formulations I have provided above for Deuteronomy 13. "Presuming continuity" can easily mean, "Stop at the lowest level of generality that you can, subject to not being too absurd, not carrying over what look to you like real trivia, and not coming into direct tension with any New Testament pronouncement." Such a recipe gives us quick answers, but there is no particular reason to believe that we will always obtain the right answers. In addition, the desire for quick answers short-circuits the process of meditating on the unfathomable wisdom of God in the riches of His word, riches that come to their fulfillment in the full treasure of wisdom and knowledge hidden in

Christ (Colossians 2:3). Such a short-circuiting is the opposite of what Bahnsen and his books intend.

Moreover, when we look for general principles in the Bible, there is always a danger that we conceive of such principles as abstract, impersonal absolutes. But in the Bible all general moral principles are deeply personal. They are expressions of God's character, implications of who He is in His righteousness and holiness. The Bible never gives us naked principles, but reveals Jesus Christ, who in His righteousness, justice, and mercy is the same yesterday, today, and forever (Hebrews 13:8). Principles always exist "incarnated" in the particulars of Israel and the particulars of God's ways with His people, leading up to the great particular of the incarnation of Jesus Christ. Hence, in looking for principles in the Old Testament, we must never imagine that such principles constitute something different from or unrelated to the foreshadowing of the New Testament kingdom of God, which is summed up in Christ our King.

A dispute about state punishments can be settled only by studying the Bible as a whole, studying the Old Testament, studying its penology in particular, studying its fulfillment in Christ, and endeavoring ever more capably to discern principles expressed in the law. Our discernment grows only as we know Christ more and more deeply (Ephesians 3:17-19), for His law reflects His just character. Such is the purpose of my book. In my view, it represents an advance in our understanding of Old Testament law. Others may write books in turn that will advance our understanding still further. I hope that they do. But let us not unfairly understand Bahnsen's books. Comparatively speaking, his books are at the beginning of this process rather than at its end. If they are understood as dogmatically closing down our options for interpreting the Old Testament, they are understood in less than the best light.

* * *

Principles for Just State Punishments

What penalties are just for the state? In this area also we meet much disagreement. Christians have agreed in large measure over what things are sins, but over the ages there has been much diversity of opinion over what sins warranted official punishments and over what the punishments should be. Again we must be cautious.

Our best course is to start with the principles of justice that we have already derived from the Old Testament, and to supplement our insights by delving into both the Old Testament and the New Testament in greater detail. We must also keep before us three complementary principles with respect to the state.

First, the state derives its authority from God, is answerable to God for its actions, and must endeavor to embody in its laws and its punishments the standards of God's justice.

Second, the state has a limited authority, an authority over a limited territory on earth. It cannot release criminals or pardon them on the basis of Christ's sacrifice, because access to Christ is by way of faith in Christ and spiritual union with Him.

Third, the state deals with injuries against other human beings, not injuries against God. Such a limitation arises from the differences between the role of God and the role of human beings in executing punishment. As we have seen in chapter 9, distinct punishments correspond to the two types of offense. Injuries against God are redressed by God, both in a final form in hell and in a preliminary form through disasters brought by God. Injuries against human beings are redressed by the victim or a representative of the victim. Typically, redress takes place by repayment to the injured party. The state can never be responsible to make sure that people give redress to God, either by compelling them to faith, or by consigning them to hell. It does have responsibility to see that human injuries are redressed, but such redress is often imperfect.

In fulfilling its responsibilities, the state must not insist on attaining divine perfection. It cannot wait until all the facts are in before judgment is pronounced; it must rely on a looser principle like "guilty beyond reasonable doubt." Moreover, it cannot hope to redress all wrongs. It must be content with partial redress in many cases. The very imperfections of human justice are one way, as we have observed, that such justice continues to provide a pointer to the ultimacy of God's justice.

In particular, the limitations of the state require that due legal process must be used. No penalty ought to be executed until guilt has been established. Evidence given against accused persons must be adequate to convince human judges of their guilt. Moses indicates that two witnesses are necessary for conviction (Numbers 35:30; Deuteronomy 17:6; 19:15). This provision appears to be a matter of general principle, so general in fact that it can be invoked even in the case of divine testimony (John 8:17-19; 1 John 5:8-9). But this provision also embodies common sense. Human judges would be unable to render a confident decision if they have only the witness of one person against the witness of the offender. In practice, this provision also protects people against malicious witnesses (Deuteronomy 19:16-21).

If I am correct in thinking that independent corroborating evidence is the important issue, material evidence such as fingerprints might also be used as a substitute at times for a human witness (such appears to be the case in 1 John 5:8-9; Deuteronomy 22:13-17). On a more general level, the practice of weighing evidence and counting a person innocent until proven guilty is so clearly wise that it has deeply embedded itself in Western justice. Such practice fully conforms to God's justice and the principles of state responsibility.

Next, the state is obliged to act only when disputes and injuries are not settled privately. For example, if a thief repents and restores to the owner what he has stolen, as in Leviticus 6:1-7, the case would never come to court. Similarly, if one man hits another and knocks out a tooth, the offender and the injured person can negotiate a monetary payment. Only if the injured person was not satisfied with what the offender offered would he bring the case to court, and then the judges would inflict the specified reciprocal penalty (Leviticus 24:19-20). Thus in many cases the penalties in the Old Testament represent not a penalty used every time, but a maximum penalty. They fix a limit on the requirements of restitution and a limit on the demands for vengeance. In the case of certain serious violations, however, the penalty must be enforced as is and cannot be diminished (Numbers 35:31; Deuteronomy 13:5, 8-9; possibly 19:21).

In my judgment, the same principles apply now. Generally speaking, the state should take a hand in actual punishment only when the offender and victim are unable to negotiate a suitable solution more privately. Sometimes the privately negotiated solution might include the offender's apology and spiritual reconciliation as well as monetary restitution. Because of its potential spiritual dimensions, such a path is clearly superior. Judges or other official mediators would of course aid the negotiation and take care to protect the victim. However, murder and crimes involving usurpation of state authority cannot be dealt with privately, because of their extreme seriousness (cf. Numbers 35:31) and the lack of the authority on the part of the state to pronounce pardon.

The earthly character of the state and the imperfect, shadowy character of its justice resemble the situation of Israel in many ways. There is something to be learned from Israelite law about ways in which God's justice can be concretely embodied and practiced by imperfect agents in an imperfect world. But as we examine the Old Testament we must constantly be aware as well of the way in which Israel and its institutions foreshadow the great work of Christ. Only in such a way will we learn deeply about God's justice. Only so will we also avoid certain mistakes in interpreting the implications of Mosaic law. As we have seen from chapter 10, the passage in Deuteronomy 13 about false worship, when properly understood, points forward to Christ's victory over demons and the church's activity in excommunication, not to a holy war conducted by a modern state. Generalizing from this example, we may say that we need special circumspection when we deal with Old Testament penalties that express the special holiness of Israel and punish profanation of her holiness.

In all the cases that we undertake to analyze, we will focus on the twin features of restoration and punishment, sometimes called "retribution." Each crime deserves a penalty that justly fits it, a penalty that restores damage and brings balanced punishment on the offender. When cases come before the state, the state is responsible before God to ensure that just retribution takes place. In some cases, fit punishment may also achieve subsidiary results in terms of deterrence and rehabilitation. That is, the threat of punishment for a particular crime may motivate some people not to engage in the crime—it may deter them. The type of punishment may also on occasion prove to be a means of reintegrating the offender into society in a positive way. The thief who is forced to repay may learn the value of honest work in the process (cf. Ephesians 4:28). Deterrence and rehabilitation are thus extra secondary benefits flowing from just practices on the part of the state.

* * *

In the arguments that follow I do not claim to have infallible answers. But I would ask you to keep an open mind and to consider not only my arguments in favor of certain punishments, but also my arguments in Chapter 14 against the present-day preference for punishment in the form of imprisonment ("doing time").

Just Penalties for Many Crimes

We may now proceed to analyze laws and penalties with regard to particular types of crimes. Mosaic laws with regard to crimes may conveniently be grouped together on the basis of the general nature of the crime. Crimes of theft and cases of accident both involve damage to the property, and so they relate most directly to the eighth commandment, "You shall not steal." Similarly, crimes involving damage to or destruction of human life are most closely related to the sixth commandment, "You shall not murder." We shall consider separately the crimes related to each of these commandments.

Penalties for Theft and Accident

Let us begin with the matters concerning theft and accident, related to the eighth commandment. As we saw in chapter 9, the penalty for theft and for accidental destruction of property embodies a clear-cut reciprocity and balance. Accidental destruction must be balanced by restoration of a substitute (Exodus 22:5-6; 21:36; Leviticus 24:18). If an animal engages in a destructive act, the owner is normally responsible in only a diminished way, and hence the penalty is correspondingly diminished (Exodus 21:28-36). A monetary payment given to the person damaged is the fit penalty. But if the animal has previously had a history of goring, and the owner does not keep it in, he is fully responsible (Exodus 21:29, 36). This type of case is obviously generalizable into a principle of full responsibility when there has been a previous problem.

Thievery must be balanced by double payment, restoration plus punishment, because there was evil intent. The thief restores the original item as a borrower would, and then gives a second item so that the thief suffers the same penalty that he inflicted on the owner. Both restoration and punishment are involved.

The sacrifice of Jesus Christ fulfills the principles of restoration and punishment in the fullest possible way. Full punishment for all the sins of the redeemed and full restoration of the cosmos to God are implied. His sacrifice is even construed in Scripture as like a monetary payment or ransom. "For you know that it was not with perishable things such as silver or gold that you were redeemed from the empty way of life handed down to you from your forefathers, but with the precious blood of Christ, a lamb without blemish or defect" (1 Peter 1:18-19). But Christ's sacrifice does not eliminate the responsibility of the state to redress wrongs on its limited human plane. In fact, if the state properly executes its responsibility, it produces on earth little pictures or shadows of Christ's great work. It will be a positive but limited aid to the process of bringing the nations to Christ and causing God's will to be done on earth as it is in heaven. Since theft and accident still injure the owner in the same way that they did in the Old Testament, there is every reason to think that the human penalties should be the same now.

If my interpretation of Exodus 22:1 is correct, thieves who have destroyed or sold what they stole are required to pay fourfold to the owner. The general principle of balanced recompense, rather than some special situation in Israel, appears to lead to this result. If so, the same general principle applied today leads to the same result. The same penalties would be appropriate, specifically, fourfold restitution for items that the thief has disposed of. A thief who steals the most expensive and useful item in the culture that is subject to being easily stolen, i.e., an automobile or truck, is required to pay fivefold if the item has been sold or destroyed. But because of the uncertainties surrounding the intent of Exodus 22:1, it might also be argued that a general policy of double payment is best.

But other considerations weigh in favor of a lesser amount of restitution. In typical cases in modern postindustrial societies, stolen items are resold to a "fence" at greatly reduced prices, partly because used goods typically bring a much reduced value even on the open market, partly because disposing of stolen items is not easy. Hence, a thief who is required to repay double the market value will actually end up paying the victim many times what he gained through the sale of stolen items. Moreover, since the market resale value of used items is on the average something like half the price of a new item, payment of double the value of a new item already represents virtually fourfold compensation. Such factors regarding the differences between new and used manufactured products were not typically present in the Israelite situation. But the Old Testament law does recognize the general principle that the value of an item can be depreciated on the basis of its remaining useful life (e.g., Leviticus 25:15-16, 50-52). On this basis, as well as because of the uncertainties in understanding the rationale for fourfold and fivefold payment in Exodus 22:1, I think that a general rule of double repayment is best.

According to Mosaic law, thieves who cannot pay the penalty for their crimes are to be sold into servitude for their theft (Exodus 22:3). The same logic of justice is operative here. The thief must be forced to pay even if such action involves selling the price of his future work. The time in which the thief would be in servitude should be just enough to pay for the damage done. We must beware of importing into this practice the modern connotations of slavery. In the Old Testament context the period of servitude is limited. The offender can always be rescued from servitude by a relative or friend who is willing to pay the value of the remaining period of labor. The offender can even rescue himself from servitude if he earns enough money through a second spare-time job (Leviticus 25:49). The situation is somewhat similar to our modern system of parole, except that a private citizen buys the labor of the offender and simultaneously becomes the parole officer. The buyer receives authority to supervise the offender during the time of parole and also receives responsibility to care for the offender. The system is in fact probably more workable as well as more just than the present parole system, since the employer remains in much more regular contact with the offender and can discipline him immediately for transgressions of duty.

This last case concerning the thief who cannot pay is of course more difficult than the previous cases. But the principles of justice and balanced recompense suggest that the same solution is as valid in our day as in Israelite times. Variations are possible in which the state would more directly supervise the parole and the schedule of repayments. We may debate what arrangements in detail are most workable, and whether some variation on the parole system can be made into a suitable vehicle for supervision. But the general idea is clearly useful as well as just. Besides being a true execution of just recompense, such a penalty has practical value. When the thief loses what he hoped to gain, he is made to experience the other person's point of view. When a greater value of goods is involved, the thief must come to realize the greater value. Moreover, in being forced to serve other people for a time, he unwillingly receives an illustration in his own body of the principle that the person who has been a thief must learn to work hard and honestly (Ephesians 4:28). If all goes well, the thief may at the end have found a useful vocation. The process far exceeds in its wisdom the present criminal system, which bottles thieves up in prison in a situation of frustration, groups them together with others of like mind, and frequently intensifies the inclinations to criminality.

Nowadays some criminals are allowed to "pay a debt to society" by doing meaningful work for the state or for some charitable cause. But such a course is still wrongheaded. The thief's debt is not to the state or to society but to the injured person. We help the thief understand better the nature of his crime as well as conform to Biblical principles of restoration and punishment when we follow the Old Testament practice more directly.

Pope John Paul II, *Veritatis Splendor*[*]

44. The Church has often made reference to the Thomistic doctrine of natural law, including it in her own teaching on morality. Thus my Venerable Predecessor Leo XIII emphasized *the essential subordination of reason and human law to the Wisdom of God and to his law.* After stating that "the *natural law* is written and engraved in the heart of each and every man, since it is none other than human reason itself which commands us to do good and counsels us not to sin," Leo XIII appealed to the "higher reason" of the divine Lawgiver: "But this prescription of human reason could not have the force of law unless it were the voice and the interpreter of some higher reason to which our spirit and our freedom must be subject." Indeed, the force of law consists in its authority to impose duties, to confer rights and to sanction certain behaviour: "Now all of this, clearly, could not exist in man if, as his own supreme legislator, he gave himself the rule of his own actions." And he con-

[*] POPE JOHN PAUL II, VERITATIS SPLENDOR 59-62, 118-23 (1993).

cluded: "It follows that the natural law is *itself the eternal law,* implanted in beings endowed with reason, and inclining them *towards their right action and end*; it is none other than the eternal reason of the Creator and Ruler of the universe."

Man is able to recognize good and evil thanks to that discernment of good from evil which he himself carries out by his *reason, in particular by his reason enlightened by Divine Revelation and by faith,* through the law which God gave to the Chosen People, beginning with the commandments on Sinai. Israel was called to accept and to live out *God's law* as *a particular gift and sign of its election and of the divine Covenant,* and also as a pledge of God's blessing. Thus Moses could address the children of Israel and ask them: "What great nation is that that has a god so near to it as the Lord our God is to us, whenever we call upon him? And what great nation is there that has statutes and ordinances so righteous as all this law which I set before you this day?" (Dt 4:7-8). In the Psalms we encounter the sentiments of praise, gratitude and veneration which the Chosen People is called to show towards God's law, together with an exhortation to know it, ponder it and translate it into life. "Blessed is the man who walks not in the counsel of the wicked, nor stands in the way of sinners, nor sits in the seat of scoffers, but his delight is in the law of the Lord and on his law he meditates day and night" (Ps 1:1-2). "The law of the Lord is perfect, reviving the soul; the testimony of the Lord is sure, making wise the simple; the precepts of the Lord are right, rejoicing the heart; the commandment of the Lord is pure, enlightening the eyes" (Ps 18/19:8-9).

45. The Church gratefully accepts and lovingly preserves the entire deposit of Revelation, treating it with religious respect and fulfilling her mission of authentically interpreting God's law in the light of the Gospel. In addition, the Church receives the gift of the New Law, which is the "fulfilment" of God's law in Jesus Christ and in his Spirit. This is an "interior" law (cf. Jer 31:31-33), "written not with ink but with the Spirit of the living God, not on tablets of stone but on tablets of human hearts" (2 Cor 3:3); a law of perfection and of freedom (cf. 2 Cor 3:17); "the law of the Spirit of life in Christ Jesus" (Rom 8:2). Saint Thomas writes that this law "can be called law in two ways. First, the law of the spirit is the Holy Spirit...who, dwelling in the soul, not only teaches what it is necessary to do by enlightening the intellect on the things to be done, but also inclines the affections to act with uprightness.... Second, the law of the spirit can be called the proper effect of the Holy Spirit, and thus faith working through love (cf. Gal 5:6), which teaches inwardly about the things to be done...and inclines the affections to act."

Even if moral-theological reflection usually distinguishes between the positive or revealed law of God and the natural law, and, within the economy of salvation, between the "old" and the "new" law, it must not be forgotten that these and other useful distinctions always refer to that law whose author is the one and the same God and which is always meant for man. The different ways in which God, acting in history, cares for the world and for mankind are not mutually exclusive; on the contrary, they support each other and intersect. They have their origin and goal in the eternal, wise and loving counsel whereby God predestines men and women "to be conformed to the image of his Son" (Rom 8:29). God's plan poses no threat to man's genuine freedom; on the contrary, the acceptance of God's plan is the only way to affirm that freedom.

* * *

96. The Church's firmness in defending the universal and unchanging moral norms is not demeaning at all. Its only purpose is to serve man's true freedom. Because there can be no freedom apart from or in opposition to the truth, the categorical—unyielding and uncompromising—defence of the absolutely essential demands of man's personal dignity must be considered the way and the condition for the very existence of freedom.

This service is directed to *every man,* considered in the uniqueness and singularity of his being and existence: only by obedience to universal moral norms does man find full confirmation of his personal uniqueness and the possibility of authentic moral growth. For this very reason, this service is also directed to *all mankind:* it is not only for individuals but also for the community, for society as such. These norms in fact represent the unshakable foundation and solid guarantee of a just and peaceful human coexistence, and hence of genuine democracy, which can come into being and develop only on the basis of the equality of all its members, who possess common rights and duties. *When it is a matter of the moral norms prohibiting intrinsic evil, there are no privileges or exceptions for anyone.* It makes no difference whether one is the master of the world or the "poorest of the poor" on the face of the earth. Before the demands of morality we are all absolutely equal.

97. In this way, moral norms, and primarily the negative ones, those prohibiting evil, manifest their *meaning and force, both personal and social.* By protecting the inviolable personal dignity of every human being they help to preserve the human social fabric and its proper and fruitful development. The commandments of the second table of the Decalogue in particular—those which Jesus quoted to the young man of the Gospel (cf. Mt 19:19)—constitute the indispensable rules of all social life.

These commandments are formulated in general terms. But the very fact that "the origin, the subject and the purpose of all social institutions is and should be the human person" allows for them to be specified and made more explicit in a detailed code of behaviour. The fundamental moral rules of social life thus entail *specific demands* to which both public authorities and citizens are required to pay heed. Even though intentions may sometimes be good, and circumstances frequently difficult, civil authorities and particular individuals never have authority to violate the fundamental and inalienable rights of the human person. In the end, only a morality which acknowledges certain norms as valid always and for everyone, with no exception, can guarantee the ethical foundation of social coexistence, both on the national and international levels.

Morality and the renewal of social and political life

98. In the face of serious forms of social and economic injustice and political corruption affecting entire peoples and nations, there is a growing reaction of indignation on the part of very many people whose fundamental human rights have been trampled upon and held in contempt, as well as an ever more widespread and acute sense of *the need for a radical* personal and social *renewal* capable of ensuring justice, solidarity, honesty and openness.

Certainly there is a long and difficult road ahead; bringing about such a renewal will require enormous effort, especially on account of the number and the gravity of the causes giving rise to and aggravating the situations of injustice present in the world today. But, as history and personal experience show, it is not difficult to discover at the bottom of these situations causes which are properly "cultural," linked to particular ways of looking at man, society and the world. Indeed, at the heart of the issue of culture we find the *moral sense,* which is in turn rooted and fulfilled in the *religious sense.*

99. Only God, the Supreme Good, constitutes the unshakable foundation and essential condition of morality, and thus of the commandments, particularly those negative commandments which always and in every case prohibit behaviour and actions incompatible with the personal dignity of every man. The Supreme Good and the moral good meet in *truth:* the truth of God, the Creator and Redeemer, and the truth of man, created and redeemed by him. Only upon this truth is it possible to construct a renewed society and to solve the complex and weighty problems affecting it, above all the problem of overcoming the various forms of totalitarianism, so as to make way for the authentic *freedom* of the person. "Totalitarianism arises out of a denial of truth in the objective sense. If there is no transcendent truth, in obedience to which man achieves his

full identity, then there is no sure principle for guaranteeing just relations between people. Their self-interest as a class, group or nation would inevitably set them in opposition to one another. If one does not acknowledge transcendent truth, then the force of power takes over, and each person tends to make full use of the means at his disposal in order to impose his own interests or his own opinion, with no regard for the rights of others.... Thus, the root of modern totalitarianism is to be found in the denial of the transcendent dignity of the human person who, as the visible image of the invisible God, is therefore by his very nature the subject of rights which no one may violate—no individual, group, class, nation or State. Not even the majority of a social body may violate these rights, by going against the minority, by isolating, oppressing, or exploiting it, or by attempting to annihilate it."

Consequently, the inseparable connection between truth and freedom—which expresses the essential bond between God's wisdom and will—is extremely significant for the life of persons in the socio-economic and socio-political sphere. This is clearly seen in the Church's social teaching—which "belongs to the field...of theology and particularly of moral theology"—and from her presentation of commandments governing social, economic and political life, not only with regard to general attitudes but also to precise and specific kinds of behaviour and concrete acts.

100. The *Catechism of the Catholic Church* affirms that "in economic matters, respect for human dignity requires the practice of the virtue of *temperance,* to moderate our attachment to the goods of this world; of the virtue of *justice,* to preserve our neighbour's rights and to render what is his or her due; and of *solidarity,* following the Golden Rule and in keeping with the generosity of the Lord, who 'though he was rich, yet for your sake...became poor, so that by his poverty you might become rich' (2 Cor 8:9)." The Catechism goes on to present a series of kinds of behaviour and actions contrary to human dignity: theft, deliberate retention of goods lent or objects lost, business fraud (cf. Dt 25:13-16), unjust wages (cf. Dt 24:14-15), forcing up prices by trading on the ignorance or hardship of another (cf. Am 8:4-6), the misappropriation and private use of the corporate property of an enterprise, work badly done, tax fraud, forgery of cheques and invoices, excessive expenses, waste, etc. It continues: "The seventh commandment prohibits actions or enterprises which for any reason—selfish or ideological, commercial or totalitarian—lead to the *enslavement of human beings,* disregard for their personal dignity, buying or selling or exchanging them like merchandise. Reducing persons by violence to use-value or a source of profit is a sin against their dignity as persons and their fundamental rights. Saint Paul

set a Christian master right about treating his Christian slave 'no longer as a slave but...as a brother...in the Lord' (Philem 16)."

101. In the political sphere, it must be noted that truthfulness in the relations between those governing and those governed, openness in public administration, impartiality in the service of the body politic, respect for the rights of political adversaries, safeguarding the rights of the accused against summary trials and convictions, the just and honest use of public funds, the rejection of equivocal or illicit means in order to gain, preserve or increase power at any cost—all these are principles which are primarily rooted in, and in fact derive their singular urgency from, the transcendent value of the person and the objective moral demands of the functioning of States. When these principles are not observed, the very basis of political coexistence is weakened and the life of society itself is gradually jeopardized, threatened and doomed to decay (cf. Ps 14:3-4; Rev 18:2-3, 9-24). Today, when many countries have seen the fall of ideologies which bound politics to a totalitarian conception of the world—Marxism being the foremost of these—there is no less grave a danger that the fundamental rights of the human person will be denied and that the religious yearnings which arise in the heart of every human being will be absorbed once again into politics. This is *the risk of an alliance between democracy and ethical relativism,* which would remove any sure moral reference point from political and social life, and on a deeper level make the acknowledgement of truth impossible. Indeed, "if there is no ultimate truth to guide and direct political activity, then ideas and convictions can easily be manipulated for reasons of power. As history demonstrates, a democracy without values easily turns into open or thinly disguised totalitarianism."

Thus, in every sphere of personal, family, social and political life, morality—founded upon truth and open in truth to authentic freedom—renders a primordial, indispensable and immensely valuable service not only for the individual person and his growth in the good, but also for society and its genuine development.

Questions

1. According to Chapter 19 of the Westminster Confession of Faith, on whom is Old Testament law binding today? In what respect(s)?

2. How, according to Chapter 19 of the Westminster Confession of Faith, is the law of God compatible with the "grace of the Gospel?"

3. What significant differences does Longman see between Old Testament Israel and modern society?

4. What impact do these differences have on whether and how to apply Old Testament law to modern society?

5. Why does Poythress believe that the life and death of Jesus Christ affect the way in which Old Testament law should be applied today?

6. Poythress argues that a modern state should impose the punishments below. Are the punishments appropriate? Are they workable? Do they represent a proper application of the Old Testament law to modern society?

   a. A thief who has disposed of the item(s) taken must reimburse the owner double the market value of the item(s);

   b. An offender who cannot immediately repay the victim should be forced into involuntary servitude.

7. A Christian reconstructionist (see the introduction to Chapter 9) would likely argue that Poythress' choices of which laws to apply and at what level of generality are arbitrary. Do you agree?

8. According to Pope John Paul II, how should the church view Old Testament Law?

9. What role does Pope John Paul II believe "universal and unchanging moral norms" should play in contemporary society?

10. Read Exodus 20:13, 14; Leviticus 19:5-8, 15, 19; 20:10; Deuteronomy 19:15; 22:8. Should any of these laws be applied today? If so, how?

Chapter 10 To What Extent Should Higher Law Be Applied to Modern Society?

A. Encouragements Toward the Use of Higher Law

Introduction

Even if we could know with certainty each principle of the higher law, we would be faced with challenging questions: What higher law principles should be implemented as part of human law today? How should Christians go about seeking to implement those principles?

The authors in this section believe the higher law can and should play an important role in today's political and legal systems. Each encourages Christians as to how they should apply the higher law to human law in the 21st century.

The first piece is an excerpt from Michael Schutt's book, *Redeeeming Law*. Schutt is an associate professor at Regent University School of Law. He is also the director of the Institute for Christian Legal Studies (ICLS), a joint ministry of Regent Law School and the Christian Legal Society. The ICLS mission is:

> [T]o train and encourage Christian law students, law professors, and practicing lawyers to seek and study Biblical truth, including the natural law tradition, as it relates to law and legal institutions, and to encourage them toward spiritual growth, compassionate outreach to the poor and needy, and the integration of faith with learning, teaching, and legal practice.

Schutt received a B.A. from Stephen F. Austin State University and a J.D. from the University of Texas School of Law. He has taught torts, legal ethics, and business associations. His writings have focused on the relationship of lawyers, faith, and culture. In the excerpt from *Redeeming*

Law reprinted here, Schutt contends that Christian lawyers must submit all aspects of their lives to the lordship of Christ—their work life as well as their devotional life. He calls on Christian lawyers to "work with God in his redemption of culture," including law and politics.

The second piece is an excerpt from Charles Colson's book, *Kingdoms in Conflict*. Colson points to both history and scripture to argue that the church must be a moral influence in society. He looks to William Wilberforce (the statesman whose tenacity and moral courage brought about the end of the slave trade in England) as a model of how a Christian leader should apply higher law principles to public policy. Even as he encourages Christians to use moral influence, he warns that the church must be careful to not be seduced by political power. He insists that institutionally there must be a balance between two kingdoms: the kingdom of God and the kingdom of man.

The final piece is an excerpt from C. Scott Pryor's article, "Consideration in the Common Law of Contracts: A Biblical-Theological Critique." Pryor is a professor at Regent University School of Law. He received a B.A. from Dordt College, a J.D. from the University of Wisconsin, and an M.A. from Reformed Theological Seminary. Pryor teaches contracts, commercial law, bankruptcy, and international business transactions.

Pryor is widely published and his publications reveal a deep and thoughtful integration of faith and law. "Consideration in the Common Law of Contracts" is an excellent example. In the excerpt reproduced here, Pryor sets forth a framework for how a Christian can apply biblical principles to a particular legal issue or doctrine—here consideration in contract law—in a scholarly and biblically sound way.

Michael P. Schutt, *Redeeming Law*[*]

Sacred and Secular: False Disjunctions and Compartments

I have a friend who likes to say that "all we really need to know is John 3:16." There is a sense, of course, in which this is true: knowledge of God's love revealed in the redemption of sinners by Christ forms an umbrella that covers all of our daily lives and decisions. But there is a sense in which this claim is dangerous. What of our specific duties on earth? What about work, marriage, and the created world? How do we fit

[*] MICHAEL P. SCHUTT, REDEEMING LAW 102, 104-109 (2007). Reprinted with the permission of the author.

into God's plan for redeeming his creation and what role do we play in relation to his kingdom?

My friend's approach is in a way emblematic of American Christianity. Having been birthed out of revivalism, evangelicalism tends to keep the question of personal salvation uppermost, even at the expense of engaging cultural and social institutions we encounter every day, even—believe it or not—over and above ordinary legal work.

* * *

The Kingdom of God

Jesus came to seek and save that which was lost (Luke 19:10). He died in order that we might spend eternity with him in heaven, but his death also works to redeem all that was corrupted by the Fall: he died to restore God's reign over *all* creation. And while that will not be fully accomplished until his ultimate return, his kingdom is in operation wherever he is king. Jesus came to inaugurate the kingdom in which God will fix all that is broken. This means that God is at work, right now, to bring all that he has made under his kingship. This view of God's kingdom rejects any dualism between the sacred and secular in our approach to mission. Indeed we are called to work with God in his redemption of culture. "If the good news that Jesus proclaimed was that God was beginning to reclaim a lost creation and restore it to his creational intentions, does it not call us to live for and seek the love, truth and justice of God *in whatever way it is being challenged in our world?*" Our devotional activities and our religious duties are but part of the larger call of the gospel: faithfulness to Christ at work, at home, at church, and on the golf course.

Some view the kingdom as coextensive with the church or religious activities, or perhaps even the life of the world to come. Yet the kingdom of God is at hand; it is among us (Luke 11:20; 17:21). God has rescued us from the kingdom of darkness and brought us into the kingdom of the Son he loves (Colossians 1:13). And a war wages over the territory of creation, where nothing is neutral:

> The chief protagonists are two kings, one legitimate and the other usurper, each having his own sovereignty and army, each waging war for the possession of the same territory. The kingship of the rightful sovereign is what the Bible calls "the kingdom of God" while that of his rival is called "the world" or the kingdom of darkness. The Scriptures call one of the armies "the people of God" ("the church" in the New Testament) and the

other "those outside"—that is, all of mankind outside Christ and in bondage to Satan.

We live in the tension of the kingdom "already here" and "not yet" at the same time. We live in the old age but already participate in the age to come, which is not yet here in its fullness. A commitment to unity—to the reality of one world—recognizes that while the kingdom of God and the kingdom of this world are both here at the same time, there can be only one ruler at a time over any one part of any contested territory. The implications for our call to integrity in the law are all-encompassing:

> Yes, we are to seek the salvation of men and women of all nations. No, that does not necessarily take precedence over feeding the poor, seeking justice for the oppressed or dismantling racism and corruption in society. As we individuals interact with our world, we need to consider how God's reign would be seen in all of our encounters and relationships.

Our call as lawyers is to minister God's truth, beauty, goodness, justice, mercy, compassion, or love wherever it is lacking, whether it be in our law office, our law school, the county courthouse, the adversary system, our client's family, our partner's life, or at the coffee shop.

* * *

Boldness. [O]ur commitment to unity will *embolden* us to rise to the challenge of those who would build a materialist mansion out of stolen, reprimed, repainted metaphysical lumber. In short, we'll stand up and shout when someone claims that there are no universal truths and then argues the point by relying on some universal truth. "However rude it may be to say so these days," remarks J. Budziszewski, "there are some moral truths that we all really know—truths which a normal human being is unable not to know." Like the child who knew the emperor was naked and simply said so, we ought to speak the truth as well, though it appears to be rude.

Spiritual apathy—sloth—with regard to first things is an enemy of the Christian lawyer in this area (see chap. 2). Simple intentionality or "caring" about the religious truths at the heart of law and legal institutions is the necessary first response in resuscitating the Christian lawyer. Our teaching, scholarship, and practice will become more expressly religious once we wake up to the fact that religious assumptions—albeit false ones—already dominate the legal academy and courthouse. At the very least we should be able to mention that the emperor is naked as we face the parade of legal instrumentalism and those who pretend that metaphysical realities are irrelevant to the lawyer's task. In the first place, we ought to be able to engage such jurisprudence as if we are human beings with souls. In addition, and more specifically, we should be bold enough to confront that devious grandchild of the Enlightenment, the myth of the secular society, which flows directly from the modern materialist assumptions that rule the legal academy today.

Again, fundamental notions of the nature of humanity and its place in the universe, the nature of law, and the obligations of the state all flow from moral and religious convictions. For example, Judge Posner's defense of philosophical pragmatism as the best foundation for legal theory is based on his religious views on human nature, the end and limits of human knowledge, and the value of seeking the mystery at the heart of existence (see chap. 2). We should be invigorated by Judge Posner's approach. It is refreshing to read, for a change, an honest articulation of the importance of moral anthropology, epistemology, and theology as a foundation for legal theory! What a strong testimony to the metaphysical nature of our inquiry into the true purpose of the law. What a great invitation to discuss the nature of persons and our ability to grasp metaphysical problems and bring reason and faith to the law. What better example of the necessity of religious commitments to legal inquiry? This sort of legal scholarship should embolden our own scholarship to state and explore the metaphysical foundations of our work. It should embolden our study, causing us to dig deeper into the biblical implications of torts, contracts, or corporations. And it should embolden our practice, encouraging us to love our clients as eternal beings with temporal needs.

Yet many Christian law students I meet are convinced that religious language and convictions are inappropriate in the public discussion of law and politics. How many times have we heard, even from Christians, that religion and politics don't mix? After all, we live in a pluralistic society. Their error of course is that *pluralism* is not the equivalent of a *secular* society, where religious neutrality reigns. As Lesslie Newbigin eloquently established in his 1989 classic, *The Gospel in a Pluralist Society*, the idea of a secular society is a myth, and the pluralistic ideal is misunderstood. To begin with, the very nature of society renders impossible any meaningful separation of the private and public human being (see chap. 4). Public policies accepted by any given society, argues Newbigin, are "a function of the commitments the members of society have, the values they cherish, and—ultimately—the beliefs they hold about the world and their place in it."

A faithful life in the legal profession starts with recognizing and rejecting the secularizing impulse to privatize virtue and faith commitments. The call into discipleship with Jesus Christ cannot mean "that one accepts the lordship of Christ as governing personal and domestic life and the life of the Church, while another sovereignty is acknowledged for the public life of society." In rejecting the myth of the secular society, we emphatically reject the false compartmentalization between the public lawyer and the private person, and to do so, we must awake to the fact that we live not in a secular society without religious faith but in a religious society that has faith in other things—in "gods that are not God."

In the law office the rejection of this secularizing myth might embolden us to treat clients as if they have souls and their problems as if they are not simply legal puzzles to be solved but moral and spiritual issues that need to be addressed in community. It may mean that we commit to certain financial boundaries or particular ways of organizing our law practices. It might mean that we pray with our clients and our secretaries, or that we take a public stand on legal or political issues about which we have some expertise.

Charles Colson, *Kingdoms in Conflict*[*]

Kingdoms in Conflict

Men never do evil so completely and cheerfully as when they do it from religious conviction.
—Blaise Pascal

Without Christian culture and Christian hope, the modern world would come to resemble a half-derelict fun-fair, gone nasty and poverty-racked, one enormous Atlantic City.
—Russell Kirk

* * *

On one side are those who believe that religion provides the details for a political agenda. On the other are those who see any religious involvement in the public arena as dangerous. Not since the Crusades have religious passions and prejudices posed such a worldwide threat—if not through a religious zealot or confused idealist whose finger is on the nuclear trigger, then certainly by destroying the tolerance and trust essential for maintaining peace and concord among peoples.

---

[*] CHARLES COLSON, KINGDOMS IN CONFLICT 43-44, 46-48, 109-13, 115-21 (1987). From *Kingdoms in Conflict*, reprinted with permission of Prison Fellowship, P.O. Box 1550, Merrifield, VA 22116, www.pfm.org.

Middle East terrorists, many religiously motivated, have spread panic throughout Europe and the United States. Ireland, Sri Lanka, India, and Indonesia are grim examples of nations deeply torn by sectarian strife. Jews, Muslims, and Christians alike endure horrendous persecution under oppressive Marxist regimes. In the West, church-state confrontations are multiplying. As one prominent sociologist observed, this strife "has little to do with whether the state espouses a leftist or rightist political philosophy"; the fires rage amid a variety of political systems.

Diverse as they may seem, these tensions all arise from one basic cause: confusion and conflict over the respective spheres of the religious and the political. What Augustine called the City of God and the city of man are locked in a worldwide, frequently bitter struggle for influence and power.

Nowhere has this conflict been more hotly debated than in America.

* * *

On one side are certain segments of the Christian church, religious conservatives who are determined to regain lost ground and restore traditional values. "America needs a president who will speak for God," proclaimed one leader. Whether out of frustration or sincere theological conviction, the Christian New Right has become politicized, attempting to take dominion over culture through legislation and court decisions.

Those on the other side are no less militant. Believing Christian political activists will cram religious values down the nation's unwilling throat, they heatedly assert that faith is a private matter and has no bearing on public life. The *New York Times,* for example, accused Ronald Reagan of being "primitive" when he publicly referred to his faith: "You don't have to be a secular humanist to take offense at that display of what, in America, should be private piety."

The real tragedy is that both sides are so deeply entrenched that neither can listen to the other. Invective and name calling have replaced dialogue. Nothing less than obliteration of the enemy will suffice; either Christianize or secularize America. Many citizens feel that they must choose sides; either enlist with Norman Lear and People of the American Way, or join up with the Moral Majority (now the Liberty Federation) and the Christian New Right.

No matter how we got to this point, the fact is that both extremes—those who want to eliminate religion from political life as well as those who want religion to dominate politics—have overreacted and overreached. Theologian Richard John Neuhaus does not overstate the case when he argues that this confrontation can be "severely damaging, if not fatal, to the American democratic experiment." Furthermore, both exclusivist arguments are wrong.

There is another way, however. It's a path of reason and civility that recognizes the proper and necessary roles of both the political and the religious. Each respective role is, as I hope this book will demonstrate, indispensable to the health of society.

Wise men and women have long recognized the need for the transcendent authority of religion to give society its legitimacy and essential cohesion. One of the most vigorous arguments was made by Cicero, who maintained that religion is "indispensable to private morals and public order...and no man of sense will attack it." Augustine argued that the essence of public harmony could be found only in justice, the source of which is divine. "In the absence of justice," he asked, "what is sovereignty but organized brigandage?"

In the West the primary civilizing force was Christianity. According to historian Christopher Dawson, Christianity provided a transcendent spiritual end which gave Western culture its dynamic purpose. It furnished the soul for Western civilization and provided its moral legitimization; or, as was stated somewhat wistfully in the *London Times* recently, "The firm principles which could mediate between the individual and society to provide both with a sense of proportion and responsibility in order to inform behavior."

The American experiment in limited government was founded on this essential premise; its success depended on a transcendent reference point and a religious consensus. John Adams wrote, "Our constitution was made only for a moral and religious people. It is wholly inadequate for the government of any other." Tocqueville credited much of America's remarkable success to its religious nature; it was later called a nation with "the soul of a church."

Today, increasing numbers of thinkers, even those who reject orthodox faith, agree that a religious-value consensus is essential for justice and concord. Polish dissident Adam Michnik, who describes himself as a "pagan," applauds the church for resisting tyranny. Religion, he says, is "the key source of encouragement for those who seek to broaden civil liberties." To disregard the historic Western consensus about the role of religion in culture is to ignore the foundation of our civilization.

But men and women need more than a religious value system. They need civic structures to prevent chaos and provide order. Religion is not intended or equipped to do this; when it has tried, it has brought grief on itself and the political institutions it has attempted to control. An independent state is crucial to the commonweal. Both the City of God and the city of man are vital to society—and they must remain in delicate balance. "All human history and culture," one historian observed, "may be viewed as the interplay of the competing values of these...two cities"; and wherever they are out of balance, the public good suffers.

This is why today's conflict is so dangerous. It would be a Pyrrhic victory indeed should either side win unconditionally. Victory for either would mean defeat for both.

* * *

The Cross and the Crown

I die the king's good servant, but God's first.
—Sir Thomas More

If I am faced with the choice between religion and my country...I will choose my fatherland.
—Father Miguel d'Escoto, Nicaraguan Foreign Minister

Wilberforce's dogged campaign to rid the British empire of the slave trade shows what can happen when a citizen of the Kingdom of God challenges corrupt structures within the kingdoms of man. One excellent Wilberforce biography is aptly titled God's Politician, and truly he was, holding his country to God's standard of moral accountability.

The kind of conflict that Wilberforce and other activist Christians experience—between their Christian conscience and their political mandates—is unavoidable. Both church and state assert standards and values in society; both seek authority; both compete for allegiance. As members of both the religious and the political spheres, the Christian is bound to face conflict.

The conflict is particularly apparent in the Judeo-Christian tradition because of the assertion that the God of both the Old and New Testament Scriptures is King. That has been an offense to the proud and powerful since the beginning—and the reason Jews and Christians alike have been systematically persecuted.

The tension between the Kingdom of God and the kingdoms of man runs like an unbroken thread through the history of the past two thousand years. It began not long after Christ's birth. Herod, the Roman-appointed king over the Jews and as vicious a tyrant as ever lived, was gripped with fear when the Magi arrived from the East seeking the "King of the Jews." Though not a believer, Herod knew the ancient Jewish prophecies that a child would be born to reign over them, ushering in a Kingdom of peace and might.

Herod called the Magi to his ornate throne room. In what has become common practice in the centuries since, he tried to manipulate the religious leaders for political advantage. He told them to go find this King in Bethlehem so he too could worship Him.

The rest of the story is familiar. The Magi found Jesus but were warned in a dream to avoid Herod and return to the East. Jesus' parents, similarly warned, escaped with their son to Egypt—just ahead of Herod's marauding soldiers who massacred all the male children of Jesus' age in and near Bethlehem.

Herod didn't fear Jesus because he thought He would become a religious or political leader. He had suppressed such opponents before. Herod feared Christ because He represented a Kingdom greater than his own.

Jesus was later executed for this same reason. Though He told Pilate His Kingdom was not of this world, the sign over His cross read "INRE"—King of the Jews. The executioner's sarcasm was double-edged.

His followers' faithfulness to Christ's announcement of His Kingdom led to their persecution as well. An enraged mob in Thessalonica threatened Paul and Silas, shouting, "These men who have caused trouble all over the world...are all defying Caesar's decrees, saying that there is another king, one called Jesus." During the early centuries Christians were martyred not for religious reasons—Rome, after all, was a land of many gods—but because they refused to worship the emperor. Because they would not say, "We have no king but Caesar," the Roman government saw them as political subversives.

Christians who refused to offer incense before the statue of the emperor were flogged, stoned, imprisoned, condemned to the mines. Later, when Christianity was officially outlawed, they were tortured mercilessly and fed to the lions, to the delight of bloodthirsty crowds.*

With the conversion of Constantine, however, Christianity was legalized in A.D. 313. This marked the end of persecution and ushered in a

---

* In the second half of the second century, Christians were systematically persecuted. This account of a massacre in the Rhone Valley is not atypical: "Many Christians were tortured in the stocks or in cells. Sanctus, a deacon from Vienna, had red-hot plates applied to his testicles—his poor body was one whole wound and bruise having lost the outward form of a man. Christians who were Roman citizens were beheaded. Others were forced through a gauntlet of whips into the amphitheater and then...given to the beasts. Severed heads and limbs of Christians were displayed, guarded for six days, then burned, the ashes being thrown into the Rhone.... One lady, Blandina, was the worst treated of all, tortured from dawn until evening till her torturers were exhausted and marveled that the breath was still in her body. She was then scourged, roasted in the frying pan and finally put in the basket to be tossed to death by wild bulls." Paul Johnson, HISTORY OF CHRISTIANITY (New York: Atheneum, 1979) 72-73.

Many Christians went to their death praising their King, and such martyrdom became the church's most potent witness. Pagan Romans were convinced that Christ had taken away their pains. As has often been said, the church was built on the martyrs' blood.

second phase in church-state relations. In A.D. 381 Christianity became the official religion of Rome, and in an ironic turnabout, church leaders began exploiting their new-found power. As historian F. F. Bruce has written: "Christian leaders...exploit[ed] the influential favor they enjoyed even when it meant subordinating the cause of justice to the apparent interest of their religion...they were inclined to allow the secular power too much control in church affairs.... Where church leaders were able to exercise political as well as spiritual authority, they did not enjoy any marked immunity from the universally corrupting tendency of power."

Even Augustine, the great church father who provided the classic definition of the roles of the City of God and the city of man, was beguiled by the lure of temporal power; after a wrenching internal struggle he endorsed the suppression of heretics by the state.

Through succeeding centuries the church relied increasingly on the state to punish heresy. By the time of the Byzantine empire in the East, the state had become a theocracy with the church serving as its department of spiritual affairs. In the West both church and state jockeyed for control in an uneasy alliance. In the thirteenth century, for example, Frederick II, king of Sicily, was first excommunicated for not going on a crusade, then excommunicated for going on one without the Pope's permission. The state conquered territory, but the Pope distributed the land to the more faithful crusaders.

The consequences of this alliance were mixed. Certainly Christianity provided a civilizing influence on Western culture through art, music, literature, morality, and ultimately in government. One eminent historian concluded that "society developed only so fast as religion enlarged its sphere." On the darker side, however, the excesses of the politicized church created horrors Augustine could not have imagined.

The church turned to military conquest through a series of "holy wars" that became more racial than religious. Jews, Muslims, and dark-skinned Christians were massacred alike. The goal was not to convert the populace, but to conquer it.

In the twelfth and thirteenth centuries a system was organized for adjudicating heresy. Like many well-intentioned reforms, however, the Inquisition simply produced a new set of horrors. Unrepentant heretics were cast out by a church tribunal, which regularly used torture, and were executed by the state.

The spiritual corruption of the church led to the Reformation of the sixteenth century, which produced several streams of church-state relations. One, believing the state to be essentially coercive and violent, rejected participation in any form of government. A second strand of Reformation thought dictated that the religion of a resident king or prince would be the church of the state. Thus, many kings became their own pope. A third principle encouraged church independence. Scottish church leaders like Samuel Rutherford revived the biblical view that God's law reigns over man and his kingdoms. This profoundly influenced the experiment in constitutional government then beginning in the New World.

A new phase of hostility between church and state began in the eighteenth century when waves of skepticism washed over the continent of Europe. Voltaire, one of the most influential philosophers of the day, was vehemently dedicated to the extirpation of what he called "this infamous superstition."

Religions had been assaulted before but always in the name of other religions. With the French Revolution, Tocqueville noted, "Passionate and persistent efforts were made to wean men away from the faith of their fathers.... Irreligion became an all-prevailing passion, fierce, intolerant and predatory." For a time this all-prevailing passion was successful. Wrote Tocqueville: "The total rejection of any religious belief, so contrary to man's natural instincts and so destructive of his peace of mind, came to be regarded by the masses as desirable." The French Revolution was a conscious effort to replace the Kingdom of God with the kingdoms of man.

But the state must have some moral justification for its authority. Thus France's irreligion was soon replaced by a new faith—man's worship of man.

Against this backdrop Wilberforce and other heirs of John Wesley's Great Awakening in England brought the Christian conscience to bear on a society that was nominally Christian but engaged in vile practices. Their stand strengthened the church in England at the very moment it was under its most vicious assault.

Meanwhile, in the New World a radical experiment opened another chapter in church-state relations. There a group of gentlemen farmers, who were neither naive about human nature nor pretentious about human society, were drawing up the American Constitution. By refusing to assign redemptive powers to the state or to allow coercive power to the church, the American experiment separated these two institutions for the first time since Constantine.

What might be considered the modern phase in church-state history has emerged in our century. It is an amalgam of elements from the previous eras. The rise of totalitarian regimes has brought back the kind of persecution the church experienced in early Rome; like Herod, modern dictators tolerate no other kings. In the West secularism has aggressively spread irreligion, turning Europe into a post-Christian culture and America into a battleground with orthodox religion in retreat.

Can we conclude from this cursory overview that the church and the state must inevitably be in conflict? To some extent the answer is yes. Dual allegiances always create tension. And in a sinful world the struggle for power, which inevitably corrupts, is unavoidable. When the church isn't being persecuted, it is being corrupted. So as much as anything else, it is man's own nature that has created centuries of conflict.

But every generation has an obligation to seek anew a healthy relationship between church and state. Both are reflections of man's nature; both have a role to play. Christ's teaching clearly delineates these roles.

* * *

[T]he church, whose principal function is to proclaim the Good News and witness the values of the Kingdom of God, must resist the tempting illusion that it can usher in that Kingdom through political means.* Jesus provided the best example for the church in His wilderness confrontation with Satan when the Devil tempted Jesus to worship him and thus take dominion over the kingdoms of this world.

No small temptation. With that kind of power, Christ could enforce the Sermon on the Mount; love and justice could reign. He might have reasoned that if He didn't accept, someone else would. This rationalization is popular today, right up through the highest councils of government: compromise to stay in power because there you can do more for the common good.

And think of the popularity Jesus could have gained. After all, the people wanted a Messiah who would vanquish their oppressors. But Jesus understood His mission, and it could not be accomplished by taking over the kingdoms of the world in a political coup.

Yet the most consistent heresy of the church has been to succumb to the very temptation Christ explicitly denied. In the Middle Ages this produced bloody crusades and inquisitions; in modern times it has fostered a type of utopianism expressed in a stanza from one of William Blake's most famous poems:

> I will not cease from mental flight,
> Nor shall my sword sleep in my hand,
> Till we have built Jerusalem,

* James Schall reminds us that "if there is any constant temptation of the history of Christianity, from reaction to Christ's rejection of Jewish zealotism on to current debates about the relation of Marxism to the Kingdom of God, it is the pressure to make religion a formula for refashioning political and economic structures." James Schall, *The Altar as the Throne*, in CHURCHES ON THE WRONG ROAD (Chicago: Regnery/Gateway, 1986), 227.

In England's green and pleasant land.[†]

This century's social-gospel movement echoed Blake's sentiments, dissolving Christian orthodoxy into a campaign to eliminate every social injustice through governmental means. Objectives became political and economic to the detriment of the spiritual. The reformers' well-intentioned efforts were shattered as social programs failed to produce the promised utopia, leaving observers to conclude, "Things are no better. Where is your God now?"

Utopianism is often articulated today in contemporary Christian circles; it crosses political lines, from the liberation theologians to the New Right and to the mainline church leaders. As one bishop confided to Richard Neuhaus, "The mission of the church is to build the kingdom of God on earth, and the means of the mission is politics."

Such preoccupation with the political diverts the church from its primary mission. This was evident in the comment of an American lay missionary who described liberation theology as "a concern for man and the world as opposed to the concern of the traditional church for the salvation of man's soul." All Christian political movements run this risk.

They run another risk too, particularly those on the political right where many want to impose Christian values on society by force of law. Some, such as those in the theonomist movement, even want to reinstate Old Testament civil codes, ignoring Christ's teaching in the parable of the wheat and the tares in which He warns that we live with both good (the wheat) and evil (the tares), and cannot root out the tares. Only God is able to do that and He will—when the Kingdom comes in its final glory.

It is on this point that the church most frequently has stumbled in its understanding of the Kingdom of God. Oscar Cullman writes: "In the course of history the church has always assumed a false attitude toward the state when it has forgotten that the present time is already fulfillment, but not yet consummation."[*] Even if Christians advocating dominion

---

[†] The problem is, as historian Christopher Dawson observed, "There are quite a number of different Jerusalems.... There is the Muscovite Jerusalem which has no temple, there is Herr Hitler's Jerusalem which has no Jews, and there is the Jerusalem of the social reformers which is all suburbs. But none of these are Blake's Jerusalem, still less [the Kingdom of God]." Christopher Dawson, *Religion and Politics*, CATHOLICISM IN CRISIS (June 1985), 8.

All these New Jerusalems are earthly cities established by the will and power of man. And if we believe that the Kingdom of Heaven can be established by political or economic measures, then we can hardly object to the claims of such a state to embrace the whole of life and to demand the total submission of the individual will and conscience.

[*] Cullman amplifies his point: "The church's task with regard to the state which is posed for all time is thus clear. First, it must loyally give the state everything necessary to its existence. It has to op-

gained power, they would be doomed to failure. As Martin Luther once wrote, "It is out of the question that there should be a Christian government even over one land...since the wicked always outnumber the good. Hence a man who would venture to govern...with the gospel would be like a shepherd who should place in one fold wolves, lions, eagles and sheep together and let them freely mingle."

It was perhaps because he realized this truth—that the world cannot be ruled by spiritual structures and that the church has long abused power—that John Paul I at his inauguration in 1978 refused to be crowned with the papal tiara, the vestigial symbol of the claim to temporal power. John Paul II followed his example. These dramatic gestures renounced a centuries-old tradition that has contributed to the darkest moments for the church.

But while the church must avoid utopianism and diversion from its transcendent mission, it is not to ignore the political scene. To the contrary, as will be explored in later chapters, its members, who are also citizens of the world, have a duty, as Carl Henry puts it, "to work through civil authority for the advancement of justice and human good." They may provide "critical illumination, personal example and vocational leadership." Wilberforce is a prime example. There are proper ways as well for the institutional church to provide society with its moral vision and hold government to moral account.[†]

Through the individual Christian's involvement in politics, as we will discuss later, the standards of civic righteousness can be influenced by the standards of righteousness of the Kingdom of God. Such an influence is what theologians call common grace (as distinguished from God's special grace that offers citizenship in the Kingdom of God to all who desire admission). Common grace is God's provision for the welfare of all His created beings, both those who believe in Him and those who don't.

---

pose anarchy and all zealotism within its own ranks. Second, it has to fulfill the office of watchmen over the state. That means it must remain in principle critical towards every state and be ready to warn it against transgression of its legitimate limits. Third, it must deny to the state which exceeds its limits, whatever such a state demands that lies within the province of religio-ideological excess; and in its preaching, the church must courageously describe this excess as opposition to God." Cullman, THE STATE IN THE NEW TESTAMENT, 90-91.

[†] Some Christian traditions similarly believe that they can best model Kingdom values not by involvement in politics but by the establishment of alternative communities in which they live out the teachings of the Kingdom. In its proper form, this is not a withdrawal from the world or abandonment of Christian responsibility; nor is it a privatization of Christian values as with those who profess to believe but live as if they do not. It is instead a different strategy to the same end of providing a witness in the kingdoms of man of the values of the Kingdom of God. While I do not agree with the generally negative view of government held by such groups, I respect the faithfulness by which they live their convictions.

The critical dynamic in the church-state tension is separation of institutional authority. Religion and politics can't be separated—they inevitably overlap—but the institutions of church and state must preserve their separate and distinct roles. In this regard, the American experiment merits closer examination.

America is not the New Jerusalem or a "city upon a hill," though some of its founders harbored that vision. Nor are Americans God's chosen people. The Kingdom of God is universal, bound by neither race nor nation. But Abraham Lincoln used an interesting phrase; Americans, he said, were the "almost chosen people." If there is any justification for that term—not theologically but historically—it is because in the hammering out of a new republic, the combination of wisdom, reason, and providence produced a church-state relationship that uniquely respected the differing roles of each.

The basis of this radical idea came from the partial convergence of at least two conflicting ideologies: confidence in the eighteenth-century Enlightenment belief that both public and private virtue were possible without religion; and a reaction against the excesses of the state church in Europe. The first view was held by the Deists among America's founders, while the second particularly motivated the avowed Christians among them.

These men and women believed that Christ had given the church its own structures and charter, and the state, ordained in God's providence for the maintenance of public order, was not to tamper with it. The church was ordained principally for the conversion of men and women—conversion grounded in individual conscience wrought by the supernatural work of a sovereign God upon the soul. So the state could neither successfully establish nor destroy the church, since it could not rule conscience nor transform people's hearts and souls.

Thus two typically mortal enemies, the Enlightenment and the Christian faith, found a patch of common ground on American soil. Both agreed (for different reasons) that the new government should neither establish nor interfere with the church.[†] It was this reasoning that led to the adoption of the First Amendment, expressly to protect the individual's

---

[†] One phrase in James Madison's *Memorial and Remonstrance*, presented to the Commonwealth of Virginia in 1785, succinctly sums up the thinking of our Founding Fathers: "...that Religion or the duty which we owe to our Creator and the manner of discharging it, can be directed only by reason and conviction, not by force or violence. The Religion then of every man must be left to the conviction and conscience of every man; and it is the right of every man to exercise it as these may dictate." *James Madison's Memorial and Remonstrance, 1785*, in Gaustad, ed., A DOCUMENTARY HISTORY OF RELIGION IN AMERICA: VOL. 1, 262.

right to freedom of conscience and expression, and to prevent the establishment of a state church.

John Adams eloquently acknowledged the understanding of our constitutional framers when in 1798 he wrote: "We have no government armed in power capable of contending with human passions unbridled by morality and religion.... Our constitution was made only for a moral and religious people. It is wholly inadequate for the government of any other."

Many of these original American visionaries believed that Christian citizens would actively bring their religious values to the public forum. George Washington faintly echoed Augustine when he asserted, "Of all the dispositions and habits which lead to a political prosperity, religion and morality are indispensable supports. In vain would that man claim that tribute of patriotism, who should labor to subvert these great pillars of human happiness."

Thus, when laws were passed reflecting the consensus of Christian values in the land, no one panicked supposing that the Christian religion was being "established" or that a sectarian morality was being imposed on an unwilling people. The point of the First Amendment was that such convictions could only become the law of the land if a majority of citizens could be persuaded (without coercion), whether they shared the religious foundation or not, of the merits of a particular proposition.

Today's widespread relegation of religion to merely something people do only in the privacy of their homes or churches would have been unimaginable to the founders of the republic—even those who personally repudiated orthodox Christian faith. Though America has drifted far from the vision of its founders, this system continues to offer one of the world's most hopeful models in an otherwise contentious history of conflict.

The record of the centuries should not cause despair, however. Tension between church and state is inherent and inevitable. Indeed, it is perhaps the outworking of one of God's great mysteries, part of the dynamic by which He governs His universe. For from the constant tension—the chafing back and forth—a certain equilibrium is achieved.

To maintain this balance the church and the state must fulfill their respective roles. One cannot survive without the other; yet neither can do the work of the other. Both operate under God's rule, each in a different relationship to that rule.

Certainly one thing is clear. When they fail in their appointed tasks—that is, when the church fails to be the visible manifestation of the Kingdom of God and the state fails to maintain justice and concord—civic order collapses.

C. Scott Pryor, *Consideration in the Common Law of Contracts: A Biblical Theological Critique*[*]

This article will discuss one aspect of contracts law—consideration—in light of biblical criteria. Such a move requires some preliminary groundwork. Application of biblical teachings requires more than citing a series of proof-texts. And application of biblical doctrine includes more than the Bible. I will thus begin by describing three Christian doctrines that are particularly relevant to legal analysis. I will then follow with three perspectives that demonstrate how to apply the doctrines as tools for legal criticism. With these foundations, I will then move on to address consideration in two parts: What purpose does it serve? And how should courts draw its boundaries?

* * *

I. BIBLICAL-THEOLOGICAL FOUNDATIONS

A. The Three Doctrines

1. The Creator-Creature Distinction

"God is God, and we're not," is an oft-quoted refrain. But what does it mean? Like many slogans, this one leaves out a great deal of important information: What is "God?" How do we know if God "is"? Even if God is, what difference does it make? What does it mean to say, "we're not" God? And so on. Biblically elaborated, this catch phrase suggests that it is God (through His Word) who sets the standards for what is true and just, not our experience or rationality. In theological parlance, God possesses aseity. "Aseity" describes God's self-existence: "He has the ground of His existence in Himself." Or, in plain English, God is *independent*: "[He] does not need us or the rest of creation for anything...." As the Apostle Paul proclaimed to the skeptical Greek philosophers on Mars Hill:

> The God who made the world and all things in it, since He is Lord of heaven and earth, does not dwell in temples made with

---

[*] C. Scott Pryor, *Consideration in the Common Law of Contracts: A Biblical Theological Critique*, 18 REGENT U. L. REV. 1, 2-11, 19-20, 30-38, 42-48 (2005). Reprinted with the permission of the author.

hands; neither is He served by human hands, as though He needed anything, since He Himself gives to all life and breath and all things....

If God the creator is *in*dependent, it follows that all creation, including human beings, are [sic] *dependent*. We are dependent regardless of whether we like it or acknowledge it. Our dependence is not only physical, it is cognitive. Human beings ultimately rely on God for their ability to know as well as for the contents of their knowledge. Human perception, cognition, and reason are equally as dependent on God as are the number of the hairs on our heads. In other words, what we believe we know about justice in general and the law of contracts in particular is dependent on what God thinks about justice and contracts. Anything we say about these topics is subject to what God says about them.

The dependent character of knowing is entailed by the biblical account of creation *ex nihilo* (creation "from nothing"). If God originally created and now maintains all that exists, then creation and providence include human object qualities such as perception, cognition, and reasoning as well as the subjects of human investigation like the law (of contracts). Divine aseity and human dependence account for Scripture's reference to "knowledge" in a lengthy list of ethical categories. Neither reason nor experience has ever ultimately justified human ethical knowledge (although both are means by which ethical knowledge is acquired). Dependence on divine revelation characterized the prelapsarian ethical injunction not to eat of the fruit of a particular tree. God through His Word provides the rule for all aspects of human life, not merely worship, evangelism, and personal ethics: "Whether, then, you eat or drink or whatever you do, do all to the glory of God."

Atheism in Scripture is not described as an abstract concept; it is the practical matter of ignoring God in connection with daily life (including academic studies). To think and act as if the law of contracts were unrelated to God denies His aseity, asserts our independence, and amounts to a practical atheism. Our insights into the structures of created reality are not neutral; they are obedient or disobedient, righteous or unrighteous. As the Apostle Paul notes, "[W]e are taking every thought captive to the obedience of Christ...."

We must seek knowledge in an obedient way. In the quest to know the law—including the law of contracts—we must acknowledge our dependence and recognize that all knowledge is under authority. Our search for the correct rules and their accurate applications is not *autonomous* but rather is subject to the God whose will is revealed in Scripture (*heteronomous*).

The Scriptures not only reveal God as the creator and sustainer of all that exists, they also disclose God as the absolute personality. God is not some impersonal force pervading the universe or a set of abstract rules of logic suspended above the world. God exists in an absolutely personal relationship as Trinity. As creatures made in God's image, human beings cannot help but be personal and relational as well. Our relationships to God and to each other are volitional and emotional as well as intellectual; in other words, persons relate to each other through a variety of perspectives. The form of that personal relationship will be discussed in the next section.

2. The Covenantal Structure of Understanding

If we are dependent on a personal God, what form does our relationship to Him take? In other words, what is the structure of the bond between God and humanity? The answer in brief is *covenant*. The biblical use of the word covenant is not easy to sum up. At the most basic, a covenant means an agreement between two parties. As used in Scripture, a covenant may refer to a negotiated pact between two equals or a unilaterally imposed relationship between a conqueror and his vassals. Divine-human covenants are, of course, of the later type. By way of specific examples, God has explicitly entered into covenant with Noah, Abraham, the nation of Israel, and David. Jeremiah prophesied the coming of a new covenant, Jesus spoke of the last supper in covenantal language, and the author of the *Epistle to the Hebrews* identified the completed work of Christ as the fulfillment of the new covenant promised by God in *Jeremiah*.

The concept of covenant is even more all encompassing in Scripture than the particular examples noted above. It is one of the most pervasive, large-scale descriptions of humanity's relationship to God. The very structure of creation is covenantal, including the original commands to Adam and Eve to populate the earth, to rule over the world, and to subdue the creation. If the cosmic scope of the obligations assigned to our original parents was embedded in a covenantal relationship, then our work as their descendents is also embedded in covenant.

The conclusion that all of humanity's relationship to God is covenantal is not simply an exercise in biblical exegesis or historical analysis. The covenantal connection answers at least one question and entails at least three significant conclusions. If all humankind is not covenantally related to God, then what are its responsibilities in the world? Or, to put it another way, if only the Church stands in covenant with God, then there would be neither a basis on which to hold those outside the covenant community responsible for failing to observe the stipulations of creation nor justification for imposing sanctions on them for their failure to do so.

Our universal human relationship to God through the covenant of creation also entails the conclusion that there is no division between sacred and secular; all of the life of every human being is embedded in covenantal relationship (including the law of contracts). The covenant of creation also relates the extended Scriptural analogies of covenant and kingdom: if the suzerain king rules his vassal people by a covenant, then Christians should see *all* their activities as taking place in God's kingdom. God's kingdom (the sphere over which he rules covenantally) is not limited to His redemptive work (i.e., the Church). The practice of law *is* kingdom service, not merely a platform *for* kingdom service.

Finally, creation understood in terms of covenant entails that the cosmos is subject to God's kingship. If the whole creation is God's covenant kingdom and if God is the king of creation, then God is king over that sphere of life called "law." Neither the law nor lawyering is a neutral, secular activity. A Christian analysis, critique, and theory of the law should not take place without reference to God and His covenantal administration.

A practical atheist finds the meaning of the world and principles of action solely within the world order. A secular approach to the law cannot acknowledge the existence of an independent God who rules a dependent humanity through a covenant of His determination. Ultimatcly, a secular approach to the law concludes that there is no real connection between law and morality. Morality is reduced to emotivism, and the law is diminished to the exercise of power. Rather than seeking to frame the law in terms of an objective criterion of justice, most people see the law as a means by which his or her personal or group interests may be advantaged at the expense of someone else. For many today any connections between law and morality are little more than arbitrary products of human activity. If effective lawyering becomes simply a tool to enhance the client's interests, the notion of *justice* as morality may become a foreign concept.

Human law is ultimately grounded in the divine character; the law of contracts is dependent. Human law is administered on earth; the law of contracts flourishes in God's Kingdom. Human beings dispense human law; the law of contracts is subject to God's kingship. In short, all human knowledge, including knowledge of the law of contracts, is servant knowledge, and the Christian's concern should be to discover what the LORD thinks about this law, to agree with that judgment, and to carry it out in loving obedience.

3. The Law of God

In view of the preceding discussion, one might conclude that the first place to begin a Christian analysis of the law of contracts would be the inscripturated Word of God. Such a conclusion would not necessarily be incorrect. Nevertheless, it might reveal an insufficiently broad understanding of the law of God. The law of God is more than the Ten Commandments, their adumbration in the Pentateuch, or even their elaboration throughout the rest of Scripture. Law is every word by which God subjects His creation to His will. Law may therefore be discovered from the full range of God's revelation including the world around us, our consciences, and human experience as well as the Bible.

The Scriptures relate generally to the study of law in three ways. As God's inspired, infallible, and inerrant Word, the Bible is the "best evidence" of God's will on any topic it addresses. The Scriptures also provide the standard against which all other truth claims must be evaluated because God's Word is His Word of truth. Last, the Bible justifies other means by which the truth about the law of contracts can be discovered. Notwithstanding the primary authority of the Scripture, we may also have confidence that we can discover God's norms for the law of contracts from sources other than the Bible. Non-biblical sources of divine norms are frequently labeled as general revelation. God did not abandon the world after the Fall. God the King continues His covenantal rule over His creation. Correctly interpreted, general revelation in the forms of the testimony of the human conscience, the results of trial and error throughout history, and the empirical sciences, such as economics, can also reveal the mind of God on the law of contracts.

B. The Three Perspectives

I have described three doctrines that I believe are relevant to a Christian understanding of the law of contracts. In order to understand anything accurately we must acknowledge our utter dependence on God; apprehend the personal, covenantal relationship between humanity and God; and submit to the authority of God's law disclosed in special and general revelation. I am now prepared to apply these limiting concepts to the justification of law as a human enterprise.

We must ultimately relate the many "parts" of the law of contracts to the underlying whole described in the three doctrines. This is a big job, to say the least. For example, just how does the creator-creature distinction relate to the "mailbox rule," or what does the covenantal structure of understanding have to do with the Statute of Frauds? Multiperspectivalism describes the way of relating the various aspects of a system to each other and ultimately relating them to the whole (described in the three doctrines). Each element of the system of the law of contracts is perspectivally related to another and to the whole. These three perspectives can be summarized in several ways. We could call them the starting point; the method and the conclusion; or law, object, and subject. Alternatively, we could identify them (as I do) as the normative, the situational, and the existential. First, all human activity is "normed" by the law of God, but the law is not simply "out there"; it is part of the covenantal constitution between the personal independent God and personal dependent human beings. Second, every human application of the law of God must take place in a particular setting; situations differ and provide differing fora or spheres in which to apply the correct norm. Last, the law is applied in a particular situation by and to human beings. All human beings exist equally as image-bearers of God. Yet, not all humans are identical. Our relative abilities to reason, form intentions, exercise our wills, feel passionate emotions, achieve ends, and the like do not provide reasons to apply the law relatively. Yet, these common capabilities suggest something about the nature of the law common to each person, not the least of which is that all are equal before the law.

* * *

II. THE LIBERTY PRINCIPLE

God created human beings in His image and with liberty to exercise dominion by making certain promises enforceable at law when they communicate decisions to act or refrain from acting in some definite way in the future, subject to other stipulations of His covenant(s).

* * *

A. Introduction

One of the first questions that might occur to someone about to study the law of contracts concerns the nature of a contract: just what is a "contract"? *Restatement (Second) of Contracts* defines (or rather describes) the subject as follows: "A contract is a promise or a set of promises for the breach of which the law gives a remedy, or the performance of which the law in some way recognizes as a duty." However, this definition largely begs the question of what a contract *is*. While the authors of the *Restatement* affirm that promising is the presupposition of any contract, they frame the range of promises that rise to the level of contract in terms of what the law will enforce. Yet how does the law *know* which promises to enforce? Moreover, what justifies legal enforcement of *any* promises? At these points, the *Restatement* is agnostic.

* * *

E. Scriptural Resources

The three doctrines supply us with the basis for believing the Christian Scriptures will be relevant to the task of justifying the social practice of contracting. The doctrines of covenant and law, in particular, are pertinent to the law of contracts. Even divine-human covenants have contractual aspects: there are two parties who are bound to undertake actions in the future and sanctions for default. Each of these elements is also found in an ordinary contract. A word of caution is in order, however. The Bible contains virtually no substantive references to executory contracts. While the Scriptures describe and regulate transactions corresponding to agreements enforceable by the writs of covenant,[107] debt,[108] replevin,[109] and detinue,[110] the early biblical economy had apparently not progressed to the point of significant use of executory agreements (agreements where both parties have remaining unperformed obligations). Care must thus be taken when drawing inferences from both the prescriptive and descriptive revelatory data in order to critique the law of contracts as it exists today.

1. The Normative Perspective

The normative perspective can be examined from three scriptural directions: God as our model, specific biblical teachings, and relevant biblical examples. Each of these "perspectives" on the normative will justify the social practice of contracting and, ultimately, its legal enforcement.

i. God as the Model

We can start with the scriptural revelation about the character of God. From the Apostle Paul's Epistle to Titus, we observe that promising is something that takes place within the Godhead: "God, who cannot lie, promised before time began...." If God is the promisor, to whom did he

---

[107] *See, e.g., Genesis* 31:44....
[108] *See generally Leviticus* 25:25ff.; *Deuteronomy* 15:1-6.
[109] *See, e.g., Deuteronomy* 24:10-13; *Ezekiel* 18:12, 16.
[110] *See generally Exodus* 22:7-8, 10-13.

make this promise "before time began"? The answer can only be Himself: the Father made the promise to the Son.

If making promises is part of the nature of God, does the Bible reveal any information about whether God keeps His promises? The answer is an unqualified "yes." One of the most well known examples is from chapter twenty-three of the book of Numbers where Balaam, in his second oracle about the future of the people of Israel, says:

> [16]The LORD met Balaam, put a word into his mouth, and said, "Return to Balak, and this is what you shall say." [17]When he came to him, he was standing beside his burnt offerings with the officials of Moab. Balak said to him, "What has the LORD said?" [18]Then Balaam uttered his oracle, saying:
>
> "Rise, Balak, and hear;
> listen to me, O son of Zippor:
> [19]God is not a human being, that he should lie [fail],
> or a mortal, that he should change his mind.
> Has he promised, and will he not do it?
> Has he spoken, and will he not fulfill it?

Other references to the nature of God to keep His promises are too numerous to quote. The performing of promises by the independent Creator-God serves as a model for created and dependent humanity.

ii. Scriptural Precepts

Promise-keeping by human beings is specifically prescribed in Scripture. Although the Scriptures have little to say directly regarding the social practice of contracting, there are many references to a particular class of promises called *vows*. Vows are promises in the name of God *to* God. Vows are distinguished from ordinary contracts in two respects: they have the significance of an oath ("promises in the name of God") and the promisee is God ("promises...to God"). Individuals typically made vows in the biblical record, although they were sometimes offered on behalf of the nation as a whole. Vows in the Hebrew Scriptures were typically offerings or gifts promised to the LORD for His assistance; when God's aid had been secured, what had been promised was to be promptly offered to Him in thanksgiving. Several biblical texts contain stern reminders that vows were binding and were not to be made rashly or in an ill-considered way. For example, in *Deuteronomy* 23 Moses tells the people of Israel that:

> When you make a vow to the LORD your God, you shall not delay to pay it, for it would be sin in you, and the LORD your God will surely require it of you. However, if you refrain from vowing, it would not be sin in you. You shall be careful to perform what goes out from your lips, just as you have voluntarily vowed to the LORD your God, what you have promised.

Although one cannot simply apply the rules concerning vows to ordinary contracts, the normative significance of keeping one's promises cannot be ignored. Promise-keeping, a fundamental aspect of the law of contracts, is clearly the biblical rule.

iii. Scriptural Examples

Not only does God model promise-keeping, promising represents a practice into which God entered with human beings such as Adam, Noah, Abraham, and numerous others. Moreover, the Bible contains references to the practice of contracting with apparent approval, such as the agreement between Abraham and Abimelech over water rights, and Esau's sale of his birthright to Jacob. Finally, the Apostle Paul acknowledged the significance of contracting (at least obliquely) when he compared the absolute certainly of God's promise with a human covenant: "Brethren, I speak in terms of human relations: even though it is *only* a man's covenant, yet when it has been ratified, no one sets it aside or adds conditions to it."

The normative basis for promising and, by extension, contracting is established by Scripture. The Scriptures reveal that promising is a characteristic of God within Himself; that God made promises to people; that God's law mandates performance of vows; and that people made binding contracts with each other. Therefore, while the maxim *pacta sunt servanda* will turn out to be insufficient to explain the common law of contracts, it is a biblically justifiable presumption from which to start.

2. The Situational Perspective

What does the perspective of office disclose regarding the justification of the social practice of contracting? As we have noted, God endowed humanity with a creational mandate of dominion. The Scriptures do not explicitly identify the practice of contracting as a means by which to exercise dominion. Yet, examples of contracting in connection with the production of wealth justify the conclusion that human beings can legitimately occupy the office of a contracting party. Furthermore, the biblical promise to Israel of economic prosperity tied to commercial lending, a practice based upon contracting, demonstrates that God intended the use of contracts as a means by which to produce wealth and exercise dominion.

The biblical description of division of labor following the creation account also implies that some contractual arrangements were necessary to obtain property or services. Adam is presented as the general handyman of creation, but the biblical record indicates that many of his descendants developed a particular trade or occupation. As persons with particular talents and interests exercised dominion over different aspects of creation, they would have to engage in barter to obtain other items necessary for survival. By the time of the Exodus, the use of money in lieu of barter had become so widespread that it could be used to redeem that which was promised to God as part of a vow. It is only a few steps to proceed from the use of money to the extension of credit for purchasing goods and then to the exchange of promises, which constitutes the core of modern contracts.

The value of the insights of an economic analysis of law should be apparent. Human beings are not merely rational maximizers of self-interest. They are God's image-bearers who are charged with the covenantal duty to exercise dominion by developing the latent potential of creation. To the extent an economic analysis enhances evaluation of the efficiency of the rules of contract law, it enhances the exercise of dominion. Dominion, however, is not a stand-alone concept; it is part of the covenantal relationship between God and humanity. Efficiency is therefore not the *sole* arbiter of appropriate dominion; all of God's law must be consulted. With the establishment of contracting as a means of exercising dominion, it follows that human beings have a right to insist on the performance of the unexecuted portions of contracts. The biblical precepts and examples cited above further justify this conclusion.

3. The Existential Perspective

Even if human beings were truly autonomous, human freedom alone would be an insufficient foundation on which to build ethics or law. Persons are able to make promises as image-bearers of the God who makes promises. They are to keep promises because the God in whose image they were created keeps His promises. These fundamental truths have an ontological basis in the narrative of the biblical creation account and carry epistemological weight as the prescriptions of God's law. The Kantian ethic based on the sole good of the free will is rescued from its own contradiction. There are also several legitimate implications for the law of contracts drawn from humanity's creation in the image of God.

Positively, imaging God justifies human cooperation in the exercise of the dominion mandate. The inter-Trinitarian covenant of redemption involved the cooperation of the Father and Son in the accomplishment of salvation. Reasoning from the greater to the lesser, it follows that human beings can also cooperate through contracts to carry out their goals.

Creation in the image of God suggests three additional implications. First, although human freedom in carrying out the dominion mandate is quite extensive, it is not unlimited. The covenantal relationship with God and His laws both exemplify and put limits on human freedom. While human beings are made in the image of the absolutely sovereign God, no humans individually (nor even groups of human beings collectively) are totally sovereign. The very power to contract—authorized and prescribed by the Bible—greatly limits the legitimate office of the State to bind its citizens to a particular form of dominion.

Second, the biblical concept of freedom of contract is not self-centered; it is covenant enmeshed and circumscribed by the law of God. The fact that the other party to the contract is also a member of the human covenant community constrains the ends to which contracts can be used. Not even Samuel Pufendorf was willing to extend the maxim of *pact sunt servanda* [pacts must be respected] to the enforcement of a contract to commit a crime.

Finally, the fact that others are created in the image of God has a third implication for the law of contracts: the other party to an agreement must be freely acting as an image bearer in order to contract. Thus, those who are incompetent due to age or disability, or who have been the victims of fraud or coercion, have remedies that may involve the cancellation of the contract into which they entered.

F. Conclusion

Taking the three perspectives in reverse order, we see that the ability to freely make promises is part of created human nature. We also observe that promising is a means by which human beings carry out the covenantal dominion mandate. Finally, we observe that keeping promises accords with God's normative standards. This analysis is consistent with human dependence: this understanding of the liberty of contract is based upon the foundation of the independent Creator-God. These conclusions are embedded in humanity's covenantal relationship with God. With this foundation, we can examine a specific doctrine under which the law of contracts is formulated in the common law tradition, the doctrine of consideration.

III. THE JURISDICTION PRINCIPLE

God has delegated to the State the authority to provide remedies for agreements that concern a person's interests in life, liberty or property, subject to other stipulations of his covenant(s).

A. Introduction

No legal system has ever sought to enforce all agreements. The law refuses to provide a remedy for some promises even where there has been mutual consent. The question of which agreements to enforce particularly concerned the common law over the course of the sixteenth century. Then and now, the common law courts have named the fact necessary to turn an agreement into a legally enforceable contract "consideration." Unfortunately, courts have not been as consistent in defining what constitutes consideration.

Consideration: An Historical Excursus

From shortly after the Norman Conquest until early in the nineteenth century, all suits at common law in England had to fit one of the prescribed forms of action. As noted above, for many years the only writs available for contract-like actions were covenant and debt. Assumpsit was one of the last forms of action created by the common law judges, probably in the mid-1300s.

* * *

Assumpsit was not a freestanding writ by which courts could right every wrong brought before them. The plaintiff had to plead the existence of an obligation (*indebitatus*), a subsequent promise (*assumpsit*), a breach of the promise, and that the promise was actionable. It was the last element of the action of assumpsit that judges in the 1500s called consideration. Even 500 years ago, consideration included what today would be called a bargain. However, the early uses of consideration included far more than bargains, too. In fact, judges of the sixteenth century "[b]ent or disregarded the consideration/exchange requirement to enforce promises that we now enforce as promissory estoppel (gratuitous promises unfairly inducing detriment), moral obligation, and quasi-contract/unjust enrichment.... Finally, in some cases, courts granted relief on the basis of mutual assent *without* any consideration...."

By the early part of the twentieth century, however, through the influence of Oliver Wendell Holmes, Jr., most courts had limited consideration to cases of the bargained-for exchange. Today, consideration is still required as an element of a contract....

The promise to make a gift is the paradigmatic case of the common law court's refusal to enforce a promise. A gift promise by definition is not the result of a bargain; thus, it cannot fit the bargained-for exchange model of a contract according to the *Restatement (Second) of Contracts*. It is not the case, however, that unbargained-for promises are always the result of the promisor's altruism.... "[G]ift" promises should be understood to include all promises that are not the product of a conventional bargain. Had the common law adopted a purely promissory basis for contracting, virtually every promise to make a gift would be enforceable.

* * *

E. Scriptural Resources

1. The Normative Perspective

The Normative Perspective on *civil enforcement* of agreements is not founded simply on the promise. With few exceptions promises should be kept. God will ultimately judge all breaches of promises; as Jesus said: "[E]very careless word that men shall speak, they shall render account for it in the day of judgment." Nonetheless, just as the norm of promise-keeping has biblical justification, so too the Normative Perspective on civil enforcement of agreements must be grounded in the Word of God.

No passage in Scripture answers directly the question of which agreements are subject to enforcement by the civil government. The Bible does, however, clearly identify the State as an authorized agent of the vindication of the presently existing rights to life (and liberty) and property. The Sixth and Eighth Commandments provide that "[Y]ou shall not murder" and "[Y]ou shall not steal." Immediately after the revelation of the Ten Commandments on Mount Sinai, God went on to provide for judicial remedies for killing (and associated deprivations of liberty) and theft in the Book of the Covenant. Forty years later, Moses spelled out more details regarding the sanctions for interfering with these standing rights in his second address to the people of Israel on the Plains of Moab.

The presence of State-enforced remedies for violations of the rights of life and property opens the door to judicial vindication of *agreements* founded on these rights. On the one hand, if civil government has no jurisdiction over the subject of an agreement, couching the subject in promissory form should not change the legitimate reach of the State. For example, since modern states cannot compel the worship of any god, they should not be able to enforce an agreement to worship a particular god. On the other hand, even if civil government has jurisdiction over an agreement's subject matter, it does not necessarily follow that it has jurisdiction over a promise relating to that subject matter. However, if no promises received judicial protection then the insights of the three perspectives would be diluted. The Normative Perspective on promise-keeping at least suggests some civil sanction for breach; the usefulness of promises as a tool of dominion (the Situational Perspective) would be seriously undermined if no promise received judicial enforcement; and the failure to provide state protection for all promises would undercut the Existential Perspective on human beings as images of God. It is thus reasonable to start with the proposition that all agreements relating to the subject matter of civil jurisdiction are *prima facie* also within the scope of civil jurisdiction.

i. Agreements About Property

Contracts concerning sales of goods, conveyances of real estate, and licenses of intellectual property make up a large portion of all contracts. The question of whether promises relating to property should receive judicial sanction depends in the first place on whether private property itself deserves civil protection. If all property were the common possession (or available for common use) of humanity, then the civil government should not enforce contracts treating property as something over which the parties have dominion. Yet the fundamental right to own property is biblical:

> The Ten Commandments sanction private property implicitly and explicitly. God forbids stealing, indeed even coveting, the house, land or animals of one's neighbors (Exod. 20:15, 17; Deut. 5:19, 21; *see also* Deut. 27:17; Prov. 22:28). Apparently Jesus likewise assumed the legitimacy of private property. His disciple Simon Peter owned a house that Jesus frequented (Mark 1:29). Jesus commanded his followers to give to the poor (Matt. 6:2-4) and loan money even when there was no reasonable hope of repayment (Matt. 6:24; 5:42; Luke 6:34-35). Such advice would have made little sense if Jesus had not also assumed that the possession of property and money was legitimate so that one could make loans.... [N]ot even the dramatic economic sharing in the first Jerusalem church led to a rejection of private owner-

ship. Throughout biblical revelation the legitimacy of private property is constantly affirmed.

Not only is private property a fundamental biblical right, the passages cited above demonstrate that civil governments should protect it. Thus, given the presumption of judicial enforcement where the subject of an agreement is within the civil jurisdiction, parties to agreements for sale, conveyance or license are entitled to seek the power of the State to vindicate the expectations to property arising under an agreement.

ii. Agreements About Services

Agreements for services ranging from painting a house to teaching at a law school make up another large portion of modern contracts. Rooting civil jurisdiction over service contracts in the commandment "you shall not murder," however, may not be self-evident. Consider, however, that a positive restatement of the prohibition of murder is the vindication of life. According to John Calvin, we vindicate life when we:

> Study faithfully to defend the life of [my] neighbor, and practically to declare that it is dear to [me]; for in that summary [*Leviticus* 19:18] no mere negative phrase is used, but the words expressly set forth that [my] neighbors are to be loved.

Life is a prerequisite to the exercise of dominion. In turn, the goal of dominion is to enhance life. Consistent with the foregoing paragraph, the life enhanced through the exercise of dominion should include not only our own but also that of our neighbor. Given the division of labor inherent in the unfolding of the exercise of dominion, the provision of services between persons becomes necessary for the preservation of life. Thus, there is a fundamental and legally enforceable biblical duty to perform agreements to supply and receive services.

There is also a biblical basis for civil jurisdiction over exchanges of services. The texts cited above, granting civil government the authority to punish wrongful deprivations of life and liberty, provide a general basis for judicial enforcement of agreements relating to services. The previous discussion dealing with judicial protection of promises relating to property is also relevant because services are most often promised in exchange for property (e.g., money). Nonetheless, there are also specific Scriptural prescriptions relevant to this topic. *Deuteronomy* 24:14-15 provides:

> You shall not oppress a hired servant who is poor and needy, whether he is one of your countrymen or one of your aliens who is in your land in your towns. [15]You shall give him his wages on his day before the sun sets, for he is poor and sets his heart on it; so that he may not cry against you to the LORD and it become sin in you.

Moses expressly authorizes the exchange of services for pay, and provision is made for performance of the promised payment. Similarly, Jesus remarks, "[T]he laborer is worthy of his wages." And Paul expressly provides that "to the one who works, his wage is not reckoned as a favor, but as what is due." Not only are the fundamental rights to life and the liberty of the use of one's services in exchange for payment biblically based, civil government should protect those rights as part of its mandate under the Sixth Commandment. The general presumption is that judicial enforcement is appropriate where the subject of an agreement is within the civil jurisdiction. In the case of service contracts, there is also a clear scriptural implication that a party providing services pursuant to an agreement is entitled to seek the power of the State to vindicate her expectation to payment. Together, these biblical norms lead to the conclusion that agreements for services are civilly enforceable contracts.

2. The Situational Perspective

The Bible is replete with examples of the use of agreements for the transfer of property. Beginning with Abraham, there are accounts of purchases and conveyances as tools of dominion. For example, Abraham purchased real estate in which to bury Sarah in *Genesis* 23, and Esau sold his birthright in *Genesis* 25. Service contracts receive their first mention in the lengthy account of Jacob and Laban in *Genesis* 29-30. In the New Testament, the legitimacy of the power to convey property is assumed, and Paul gives very high status indeed to the inviolability of contracts in *Galatians* 3:15. The Bible thus provides examples of valid transfers of property and services. It also ratifies the importance of promising. These two points combined with the mandate of dominion provide ample support for the conclusion that agreements relating to property and services are judicially enforceable contracts.

God has ordained the State, *inter alia*, to protect the lives and property of its residents. In turn, the State commissions particular individuals to an office to carry out its mandate. Among those offices is the judge. While judges in Hebrew society had a broader range of activity than modern judges, among the tasks that Moses assigned the Israelite judge was to preside over trials. Thus the biblical concepts of office and service are consistent with and fortify the conclusion that God's structure for society includes persons with the specific charge of deciding cases and that the coercive power of the civil authority extends to the results of those decisions.

3. The Existential Perspective

The biblical perspective on humans as images of God is consistent with promising. The scriptural examples of promise and assent confirm the validity of inter-human agreements. And the biblical norms related to human liberty and the right to property demonstrate that freedom to contract is in harmony with our creation in God's image.

Questions

1. According to Schutt, what role should Christian lawyers play as citizens of God's kingdom while living in this world?
2. What is Schutt's response to those who say that "religious language and convictions are inappropriate in the public discussion of law and politics?"
3. Colson writes of a battle between two kingdoms. What are they, and why does he believe conflict is inevitable between them?
4. According to Colson, what is Jesus' position on the proper role of the two kingdoms? See Matthew 22:15-22 and John 18:33-37.
5. Does Colson believe the church has any role in political matters?
6. According to Colson, when is it appropriate for Christians to seek passage of a particular law?
7. Would Colson urge a Christian legislator to seek passage of the following laws?
   a. A law prohibiting theft;
   b. A law prohibiting adultery;
   c. A law prohibiting same-sex marriage;
   d. A law requiring citizens to contribute 100 hours annually to serving the poor;

e. A law prohibiting restaurants from serving food containing trans fat;

f. A law requiring convicted criminals to make restitution to the crime victim;

g. A law prohibiting the cloning of human beings for research purposes.

8. Why does Pryor believe that what we know and say about justice and law (including contract law) is dependent on God's view of justice and law?

9. Pryor argues that all humanity, not just the church, is in a covenantal relationship with God. Why does that matter?

10. What insights from scripture does Pryor draw regarding the liberty of contract?

11. What insights from scripture does Pryor draw regarding the doctrine of consideration?

B. Cautions Regarding the Use of Higher Law

Introduction

The authors of each piece in this section believe in a higher law. They also believe that Christians can do—and have at times done—great harm by not applying the higher law appropriately to modern society. They therefore urge caution about the use of higher law.

The author of the first two pieces, Joel Belz, agrees with Christian reconstructionists that God's law has continuing validity today. But he takes a very different approach. While one might call the reconstructionist approach a maximalist approach—God's law should be applied in full to modern society—Belz takes what one might call a minimalist approach. He argues that while God's law should be the source of human law, sinful human beings should apply no more of it than necessary.

Belz is the founder of *World*, a Christian weekly news magazine. *World* seeks to bring a Christian worldview to bear on news and current events. The first two pieces in this section are editorials Belz wrote in April, 1994.

The third piece is an excerpt from John Warwick Montgomery's book, *The Law Above the Law*. Montgomery is barrister-at-law of the

Middle Temple and Lincoln's Inn, England. Much of his practice has been devoted to the protection of international human rights. Montgomery has taught and lectured at numerous universities in both Europe and the United States. From 1980-87 he served as dean of Simon Greenleaf School of Law. Montgomery has written over forty books in five languages and is internationally regarded both as a theologian and a lawyer.

While Montgomery would likely not completely agree with Belz's editorials, the excerpt from his book reveals that Montgomery shares Belz's fear that sinful human beings, even well-intentioned ones, can easily misapply God's law. Montgomery applies this principle to the specific issue of criminal sanctions against witchcraft.

The fourth piece is an excerpt from an article by David Skeel and William Stuntz. Skeel is the S. Samuel Arsht Professor of Corporate Law at the University of Pennsylvania Law School. Skeel received a B.A. from the University of North Carolina and a J.D. from the University of Virginia. Stuntz is the Henry J. Friendly Professor of Law at Harvard Law School. He received a B.A. from the College of William and Mary and a J.D. from the University of Virginia.

In "Christianity and the (Modest) Rule of Law," Skeel and Stuntz argue against what they call "legal moralism," the tendency to respond to moral wrongs through legislation. They argue that legal bans of moral wrongs often are counterproductive. Rather than turning people away from the outlawed behavior, such bans encourage greater lawlessness. To Skeel and Stuntz, our experience with prohibition, the war on drugs, and anti-abortion legislation demonstrates that moral progress must be made through teaching and example rather than through law.

Joel Belz, *Going to God's Law School*[*]

His Law Is The Best There Is But How Are We To Impose It?

If you had all the power in the world, and could snap your fingers and bring to pass whatever you wished, what kind of law would you impose on your fellow human beings—and how much of it?

As a Christian, you're almost certainly inclined to think first of God's law, as well you should. But you probably also have some reservations about just how appropriate that law is for a secular society in the 1990s. One of the worst things people can say about you is that if you really had your way you'd probably establish a theocracy. It puts you in

[*] Joel Belz, *Going to God's Law School*, WORLD, Apr. 9, 1994, at 3. Reprinted with the permission of the author.

the same category with the Ayatollah Khomeni or David Koresh. You're a wacko, an intolerant fundamentalistic ideologue.

Even so, play with the challenge. You're a dictator now—benevolent, to be sure, but with complete power to do what you want. Would you start with the Ten Commandments? And how many of them would you codify into state or federal law? What penalties would you impose for each when it is broken?

It may seem easy to start with the Sixth Commandment: "You shall not kill." Setting aside for the moment the pesky difficulty of deciding who may be killed and who may not, societies everywhere seem to find it necessary to place some sanctions on the willy-nilly taking of other people's lives. I'd be surprised if in your new domain you wouldn't fairly quickly decide that you need rules about murder.

The Eighth Commandment too finds broad acceptance in human society. Perhaps it's just that we're all selfish about our own possessions, but the insistence that "You shall not steal" seems written on our hearts from the time we're little kids. The rule gets blurry sometimes, especially when governments try to distinguish between what's ours and what's theirs, but in some form or another, my guess is you'll move fairly soon toward imposing some form of the Eighth Commandment.

The Ninth Commandment also seems relatively important for preserving public order. The prohibition against "bearing false witness" appears essential if you're not going to give free license to everybody to write bad checks and phony corporate contracts. Working out all the details will admittedly be a challenge, but it's hard to see how a society can function without at least some effort on this front.

But beyond Commandments Six, Eight, and Nine, how much farther will you go with public codification of the law God delivered to Moses? Would you, if you could, impose public sanctions for adultery, for fornication, for a lustful look? How about for covetousness? For publishing a consumer ad that promotes covetousness? For hanging up the week's laundry on Sunday? For using the clothes drier? For taking God's name in vain on prime time TV? For saying "gosh darn it"?

The further you move into the task, the more complicated it gets.

Yet it's instructive to flip the coin over and ask the question from another perspective: If not God's laws, whose? For human beings will be governed by some law, you know. It may be as freewheeling as the law of the jungle, it may be as tight as the law of a dictator, or it may be somewhere in between—but always there is a law of some sort. So the everlasting pair of questions is: Whose law, and how much of it?

Christians, dividing that question, ought to respond with these two answers:

(1) God's law, of course.

(2) Just as little of it as possible.

If that seems surprising, remember that we're not talking here about how people ought to live before God; we're talking instead about how much law ought to be publicly codified and applied to society. There's a huge difference.

Try to see it from God's perspective. Going back to my very first question on this page, we have to keep in mind that God already has all the power in the universe, can choose any set of laws he wants consistent with his own character, and can impose them any way he wants on the people he has created.

So, with all that power at his disposal, what has he actually done?

For starters, he's told us what his law is. In broad strokes, we know the direction he wants us to go. He wants us to love him with everything we've got, and he wants us to love our neighbors just as much as we love ourselves. How can we deny that in his *choice* of law systems, he would choose his own? His law, as David reminds us throughout the Psalms, is perfect. It's impossible to think of his preferring another.

But God's imposition of that perfect law is something else again. Even for serious students of the Bible, the application of God's marvelous standard to public society has remained something of a conundrum. In its best form, it happens by God's Spirit working in people's hearts; it is therefore literally a "spiritual" work—not accomplished by a heavy-handed state, but by God himself remaking and reshaping the inclination of our desires. It's a profound and magnificent piece of work—something no kingdom or state can ever hope to accomplish with any set of codes.

Kingdoms and states must exist, of course, because that work of God's Spirit is a patient, long-term enterprise. God has all of eternity to show us the perfection of his ways, and he's in no hurry. In the meantime, he's ordained the state as one of several stopgap measures to keep a semblance of order. But it's only temporary; true order has to be built into our hearts—and that's a spiritual task.

Christians need to keep that in mind even as they get involved in setting the structure of public policy. Humans are sinful and humans tend to mess up something as beautiful as God's law. When we're obligated to impose it on each other through the force of human codification, we will do so—insisting along the way that what we codify must be consistent with what God has said. But we will never yield to the temptation to try to bring ultimate order to a fallen world through the force of human law—even when it is modeled after God's perfect law.

Our final appeal, however, will always be to God's Spirit, who is the best and gentlest teacher of law that any of us could ever have. In his own words, his yoke is easy, and his burden is light.

Joel Belz, *A Minimal Civil Code*[*]

Christians Could Seize The High Road In The Culture War

In arguing, as I did here a couple of weeks ago, that we should codify just as little of God's law as possible into public legislation, it's easy to be misunderstood. The letters I've begun getting from a number of you demonstrate just how easy. So let me round out the argument a bit.

I start with two main assumptions—one about God and the other about human government.

Concerning God, we assume (because the Bible tells us this) that his main method of bringing human beings into compliance with his law is through the gracious work of his Spirit.

Concerning human government, we assume (both from the Bible and from our experience throughout history) that efforts to micromanage human behavior through public law tend to end up in messy disaster.

Even when Israel was a literal theocracy, and God was governing several million of his people directly as a nation and a civil entity, he had an impressively skinny book of laws. Put your fingers around the entirety of the books of Exodus, Leviticus, Numbers, and Deuteronomy, and you'll find a swatch of printing not a whole lot bigger than your average IRS tax return booklet. I'm not ignoring the possibility that Israel's judges may have started to accumulate a few interpretive tablets on the side—but it's noteworthy that a nation about the size and population of Pennsylvania seems to have run itself pretty well with this slender constitution. Wise judges could take the basics and make things work.

Indeed, this minimal code of civil legislation is clearly based on the far briefer statement of God's laws in the Ten Commandments. And Jesus stressed this point of simplicity by compressing those ten rules down to just two!

But human beings have developed an ironic habit. As they discover that they can neither keep God's laws and patterns for life nor even appreciate the beauty of them, they respond by multiplying and amending those laws *ad infinitum*. People mistakenly suppose that God's law is too broad and too vague, so they refine and correct and footnote and clarify

---

[*] Joel Belz, *A Minimal Civil Code*, WORLD, Apr. 23, 1994, at 3. Reprinted with the permission of the author.

until what started as a fairly digestible code becomes so many roomfuls of heavy volumes that no citizen, however dutiful, can know for sure any longer whether he or she is really law-abiding. Even well-intended laws become mischief-makers.

The civil rights laws of the last generation are a good case in point. Assume for the moment the good intentions behind all of them. But now those efforts to undo blatant and often sinful racial discrimination have launched us into an orbit from which there seems no return. Every group and sub-group and sub-sub-group wants legal protection, and we've arrived at a point where you can't turn around without legally offending someone's rights.

Micromanagement of the tax code is another telling example. Efforts at fairness have produced instead a system so complex that it was impossible for you two weeks ago, when you sent in your tax return, to be sure it was accurate.

So, given our human record at trying to correct things by passing the right laws, there's little room for optimism. Every time we try it, we botch it instead. And that doesn't even count the times when we rebel against the law.

Yet, some people will say, that's because we've always passed the wrong laws. If we only pass godly laws, things will work better. To which I think we must respond: If only we could.

If ever it were humanly possible both to pass and to enforce fairly the laws God gave for the people of Israel, it seems hard to argue that anything could be better. But our very fallenness as human beings makes it impossible for us first to adopt, and then to administer, even something so simple as God's good laws. Indeed, if we were good at that, or even potentially good at it, we wouldn't need God's grace. We wouldn't need the gift of a redeemer.

But, of course, we do need those gifts. We need the rule of God's spirit in us because we have proved so conclusively that we cannot rule ourselves—or even appropriate a good gift like God's law and apply it to our societies without completely messing them up. We haven't shown even in our own churches that we know how to live by God's rules. Are we really ready to tell society at large that the details will fit them well?

That's why I have come increasingly to believe that God's preferred pattern for human beings in our present age is to live with the very least structure of law possible to maintain basic order. It's not a reflection on the perfections of God's law to say that; it's an accurate reflection instead of the inadequacy of sinful humans to apply God's perfect law.

In practical terms, this means that as Christians we won't spend inordinate amounts of time and energy trying to reshape civil law after a biblical pattern. Instead, we will acknowledge our human inadequacies at structuring complex civil systems, and we will push simply for the least and the lightest of all possible civil structures.

This gives us several enormous advantages in the culture war that rages about us:

First, it lifts us above the grungy battle zone in which our opponents are forced to operate. While every other component of society connives legally and politically to force every other component to follow a particular code, we will strive genuinely for no more than a minimal code sufficient to keep order. The rest, we will concede frankly, must come by persuasion—or, more theologically, by God's Spirit, who is a remarkable persuader of people.

Second, it lets us say straightforwardly to our secular and our ungodly opponents: "You don't force us on the fine points, and we won't force you. You don't try to micromanage our lives, and we won't try to micromanage yours." I don't expect an increasingly secular society to live long by such an agreement; they're more likely to resemble Jeremiah's society, which wasn't willing even to extend to him freedom of speech. But at least it puts us on the moral high road with our opponents.

And finally, such a strategic withdrawal opens up all the rest of culture for us to concentrate on. So long as we act as though all of life revolved on the axis of law and politics, we restrict the arena in which God makes himself known. When we say we'll carry his cause into the fields of education, art, entertainment, music, and everything else, the battle gets interesting indeed.

The end result is that Christians would both implicitly and explicitly be challenging the rest of the world to an experiment. "You show us how your gods rule you," we'd be saying. "We'll show you how ours rules us." After all, how much faith do we really have?

John Warwick Montgomery, *The Law Above the Law*[*]

The Question of Legal Remedy

Our examination of the adjective law of the witch trials (procedure and evidence) has thus brought us directly to a central question of substantive law: Should witchcraft have been subject to human legal sanctions at all?

Here the modern critic of Christianity gleefully cites Ex. 22:18 and related Old Testament verses: "Thou shalt not suffer a witch to live." But such passages, though they certainly have been used to rationalize witchcraft persecution, do not necessarily justify it at all. There are many verses in the Bible that pronounce in no uncertain terms a death penalty upon evil, but which do not at all imply that human courts should deliver or carry out that sentence. "The wages of sin is death," declares the Apostle in Rom. 3:23, but the implication is hardly that human tribunals should sentence all sinners to the gallows! And even if one concedes that the Israelites were expected to punish witchcraft with the death penalty, this in no way commits the children of the new covenant to such activity—unless at the same time one would bring the New Testament church under the bondage of Old Testament ceremonial law, dietary rulings, and slaughters of Amalekites, all of which served a special purpose in preparation for the coming of Messiah but which are abrogated after His incarnation (Acts 10, Gal. 2, Col. 2:16-18).

The proper function of human law is to regulate conduct so as to prevent injustice among men; it is not to regulate ideas or to coerce opinions. But, as Rossell Hope Robbins emphasizes in the introduction to his standard *Encyclopedia of Witchcraft and Demonology*: "Witchcraft was not primarily concerned with acts; it was concerned with opinions and ideas." No objection could be raised to prosecuting a witch for murder when adequate evidence was able to be marshalled to show that she had in fact killed someone, but the difficulty lay in showing a connection between her demonic *beliefs* and actual harm to others. Montesquieu, in his *Spirit of the Laws* (bk. XII, chap. v), gives classic expression to the issue:

> It is an important maxim, that we ought to be very circumspect in the prosecution of witchcraft and heresy. The accusation of

[*] JOHN WARWICK MONTGOMERY, THE LAW ABOVE THE LAW 76-82 (1975). Reprinted with the permission of the author.

> these two crimes may be vastly injurious to liberty and productive of infinite oppression, if the legislator knows not how to set bounds to it. For as it does not directly point at a person's actions, but at his character, it grows dangerous in proportion to the ignorance of the people; and then a man is sure to be always in danger, because the most exceptionable conduct, the purest morals, and the constant practice of every duty in life, are not a sufficient security against the suspicion of his being guilty of the like crimes.

Some witchcraft ordinances made the salutary distinction between belief and practice; for example, "the Carolina of 1532 (based on the Bamberg Halsgerichtsordnung of 1507) punishes with death only injurious sorcery." Sad to say, however, examples can be multiplied in the opposite direction. The learned Melchior Goldast, in his *Rechtiliches Bedencken*, cites the Schauenberg Policey-Ordnung of 1615 and other territorial Ordnungen to the effect that whoever makes a pact with the devil shall be burned alive even though he works no evil to anyone; "therefore those, whether Catholic or Protestant, are wholly wrong who teach that witches and sorcerers who give themselves to the devil and renounce God, but do no harm to man or beast, are not to be executed, but, like heretics, are to be received to repentance and absolution, with public church-discipline." Thus the witch trials courts frequently obliterated the distinction between sin and crime and set themselves to the work of a miniature last judgment—but without benefit of divine omniscience.

It is vital, however, not to attribute this grace [sic] jurisdictional mistake solely to spiritual insensitivity or even perversity. Until very recent times, western man has not thought in terms of church-state separation in any serious way, and the assumption that state and church were fundamentally doing the same work lies at the root of much of the excesses of the witch trials. From Constantine's recognition of Christianity as the official religion of the empire in the early fourth century to the minority pleas of the Reformation Anabaptists for separation of Church and State in the sixteenth century—pleas that took another two centuries and more to be acted upon—the most universal rule was "cujus regio, eius religio" [whose rule, his religion]. The operation of this principle was especially powerful in the centuries when the witch trials were most frequent. To be sure, there was halting recognition theologically that something was wrong, as is evidenced by the insistence of the Holy Inquisition that those they found guilty must be turned over to the secular arm for actual punishment. But the great insight of Augustine in separating the City of God from the City of Man and Luther's fundamental distinction between

Law and Gospel and the Two Kingdoms were not brought to bear on the issue of church-state relations or on the vital collateral question of the proper jurisdiction of human courts.

The blending of church and state is of course a spiritual problem in itself. Luther rightly emphasized that whenever Law and Gospel are confused—whenever a mélange of the Two Kingdoms occurs—human pride and works righteousness lie at the root. Man wants to carry out God's functions; he wants to build new towers of Babel to reach heaven. Not satisfied with the areas of civil and legal control given to him ("subdue the earth"—Gen. 1:28), man tries also to subdue hell. In the case of the witch trials, irony is piled upon irony, for in an effort to conquer the devil by whatever means, man falls directly into the clutches of the evil one. It was the primal sin of Lucifer to say, "I will be like the most High" (Isa. 14:12-15). Thus did the son of the morning become the prince of darkness; and thus were the Christians who played God in the witch trials historically tainted with the mark of the beast they endeavored to subdue in an unscriptural way.

Again, the witch trials hold out warning for the contemporary church. We also—with no excuse available by way of established religion, since the separation of church and state is integral to our constitutional law—press for the expansion of remedies in moral and spiritual realms. Evangelicals have a long and sorry history of pushing for the legal enforcement of morals (local option campaigns, Sunday closing laws, and the like). Where, as in the case of literary censorship, the causal connection between wrong belief and direct injury is as hard to establish as it was in the witchcraft trials, are we not doing the Faith a great disservice to press for legal sanctions? Ought we not to keep before us the fundamental distinction between God's tribunal and man's, between His kingdom and ours, between eternal and temporal law? Our task is not to correct every moral failing by human legislation; we are rather to legislate where provable harm to the body politic will arise in the absence of law. Thus we must prosecute stealing, but not profanity; perjury and misrepresentation of the terms of a contract, but not lying in general; child abuse, but not the teaching of atheism; murder, but not belief in witchcraft. God is still in His heaven, and the evils we are powerless to correct in accord with His Word He will most assuredly remedy on the last day.

David Skeel and William Stuntz, *Christianity and the (Modest) Rule of Law*[*]

Notwithstanding legal theorists' optimism about law's ability to teach wisdom or express our society's highest ideals, there is no reason to believe that criminal codes can accomplish these goals. When lawmakers try, the effort usually backfires. Prohibition did not produce an alcohol-free culture any more than contemporary law enforcement crusades have produced a culture that is drug-free. (It seems closer to the truth to say that our culture is drug-*obsessed*, perhaps in response to the law's ceaseless efforts to fine-tune what substances Americans can and cannot consume.) Criminal bans on abortion did not reinforce the social norm against that practice; on the contrary, the norm fell apart while those bans were still in place. Even in the realm of civil justice, legal rules do not seem to move the culture in productive directions. As Michael Klarman's fine book on race and the Supreme Court shows, the greatest effect of *Brown v. Board of Education* was to prompt still greater intransigence on the part of Southern segregationists.

That last example deserves a little elaboration. Plainly, law played a central role in the civil rights movement; equally plainly, law made a difference—a large difference—in American life. It seems fair to say that, at least to some degree, the landmark civil rights legislation of the 1960s taught racial toleration. All of which sounds inconsistent with the claim that law governs best when it seeks only to govern, not to teach people how to live. The inconsistency is smaller than it first appears. Neither *Brown v. Board of Education* nor the Civil Rights Act of 1964 is chiefly responsible for teaching white Americans to treat their black neighbors like equals. The key teaching was done in the decade between those two legal events by Martin Luther King, Jr. and by the movement that he led. King and other civil rights leaders gave violent white segregationists the opportunity to show the world who and what they were. The world watched, and the result was an emerging national consensus in favor of civil rights for African-Americans. The civil rights legislation of the 1960s did not cause that consensus. Actually, causation ran the other way: changed minds and hearts among Northern whites (and more than a few Southern whites, as well) led Congress to conclude that support for civil rights was both morally sound and politically advantageous.

---

[*] David Skeel & William Stuntz, *Christianity and the (Modest) Rule of Law*, 8 U. PA. J. CONST. L. 809, 829-39 (2006). Reprinted with the permission of David Skeel.

To be sure, civil-rights legislation mattered; it was a strong force for good. But the reasons why it worked so well do not suggest optimism about contemporary efforts to use law to advance moral agendas. The most important reason is that the key pieces of legislation—the 1964 Act and the Voting Rights Act of 1965—had direct, tangible consequences that did not depend on discretionary decisions of police officers or prosecutors. Jim Crow laws were invalidated. Voting rules had to be pre-cleared with the Justice Department. Most important of all, victims of discrimination could sue and seek monetary relief from their victimizers.

These tangible consequences meant that the law in action—the law that ordinary citizens experienced, the law that redressed wrongs and punished wrongdoers—was, in all essentials, the same as the law on the books. For the most part, civil rights law functioned as law: defining rights, wrongs, and remedies. That is very different from the role law plays in most regulatory regimes, civil as well as criminal. Not coincidentally, civil rights law also reinforced healthy moral messages that the larger society had already begun to absorb. Perhaps the lesson is this: law can indeed teach, but only when its chief object lies elsewhere. In governance as in life, most people learn by example. Moral messages are more likely to be received, and less likely to be garbled, when the message is acted out, not just written in code books and case reporters.

All of which is to say that law works best when its ambitions are modest. Humility turns out to be a better regulatory strategy than arrogance. Identifying the most destructive wrongs, doing so in terms that allow for fair, accurate adjudication, matching the scope of the criminal code to the resources of the police forces and prosecutors' offices that must enforce it—these are achievable goals. They are also worthy goals: a society whose criminal law meets these objectives is likely to have a criminal justice system that controls crime and does justice. The grander ambitions our law seems to have—to define a code of proper business practice or proper alcohol and drug use and to shape moral norms more generally—are not achievable. They are proper jobs for ethicists and philosophers, or perhaps doctors and economists, but not for lawyers and judges.

Not coincidentally, they are also proper subjects for the moral law about which Jesus preached in the Sermon on the Mount. That law makes for very good morals, but very bad positive law. It is a lesson our secular legal system would do well to learn.

Conservative Christians could stand to learn the same lesson. The New Testament makes abundantly clear that law cannot save souls; salvation must come through other means and from another Source. In the apostle Paul's letters, law is not the mechanism of salvation; rather, law shows the need of it. Paul repeatedly warns Christians about the dangers of converting their faith into a moral code, just as Jesus condemned the Pharisees for doing the same thing to their own faith and thus weighing down the people with burdens too heavy to carry. One might expect professing Christians to be especially attuned to the dangers of legal moralism. Judging from contemporary culture-wars debates, we are not. The heart of the problem is a tendency to confuse God's law with man's. Those of us who believe in a divine moral law are regularly tempted to try to write that law into our much-less-than-divine code books.

Among American evangelicals, this tendency was reinforced by the judicially mandated legalization of abortion in 1973, which galvanized theologically conservative Catholics and Protestants alike and spurred a long, still-ongoing campaign to flip the legal switch back. The reasoning was and is quite straightforward: abortion is a serious wrong. It should therefore be outlawed, not legally protected. Whether or not one finds this logic persuasive, it is bedeviled by a striking irony in the practical world of American politics: the campaign against abortion seems to have been strengthened, not weakened, by the fact that pro-life evangelicals no longer have the law on their side. In the 1960s, abortion was a crime, and its public image was largely defined by the gruesome deaths that women risked when they sought illegal, black-market abortions. Thanks in large part to that image, the campaign to liberalize abortion laws prospered. Since *Roe v. Wade*, the public face of abortion has switched sides. In place of deaths from back-alley abortions, public attention focuses on deaths of almost-born infants in partial birth abortions. Just as the first set of deaths were not representative of ordinary experience under the law that preceded *Roe v. Wade*, partial birth abortions are not representative of the mass of abortions that have taken place since that case. But different laws produce different public scandals.

Different scandals produce different politics. When the public is sharply divided about the rights and wrongs of some class of conduct, both sides of the debate will strive to use extreme and inflammatory cases against one another. But only one side will succeed. The law gives that devastatingly powerful weapon to the side that loses the legal debate, be they abortion rights proponents in the 1960s or pro-life advocates today. When even first-trimester abortions were crimes, partial birth abortions did not exist. Now that abortion is a constitutional right, deaths from back-alley abortions are much less common than they once were. (Even in the 1960s, they were less common than the popular press led people to believe.) Both times, the weapon—the ability of a vocal minority to reference cases or statutes to inflame citizens—played a large role in turning public opinion. Support for legalized abortion grew in the 1960s, just as opposition to it has grown since the early 1990s. The consequences can be seen not just in political rhetoric, but also in practical conduct. The number of abortions rose steeply in the years leading up to *Roe*. That number has *declined* steeply in the years since 1980. The abortion rate could well be lower today than it was the year before *Roe* was decided. When the relevant legal territory is morally contested, the law's weaponry tends to wound those who wield it. Legal victory produces cultural and political defeat.

Evangelicals—especially conservative evangelicals—have been similarly united in opposing gambling and have treated legal prohibitions as the principal tool in the cultural debate on that subject. Evangelicals have comprised much of the opposition to lottery initiatives in South Carolina, Alabama, and elsewhere; they are the most visible opponents of the recent movement to allow racetracks to introduce slot machines. The cover of a recent issue of a publication of the evangelical group, the Pennsylvania Family Institute, warned of the "false promises of funding schools and social programs with casino gambling" and urged its members to circulate citizens' petitions and lobby their lawmakers to oppose Pennsylvania legislation that would authorize racetrack slots.

Judging by the last century of criminal law enforcement, gambling's religious opponents may have bet on the wrong horse. At least since the early twentieth century, federal and state criminal codes have banned most forms of gambling. Those criminal prohibitions may have taught some Americans that gambling is wrong, but they seem to have taught millions of others to ignore the law's commands. Far from disappearing in the face of such proscriptions, gambling simply went underground. Bookmakers and numbers rackets took the place of casinos and legal lotteries. Gambling was too ubiquitous for the government to punish across the board, so the line between what was forbidden and what was tolerated was a matter of prosecutors' discretion. In practice, the line differed depending on the class of the customers. Police might raid the numbers rackets that flourished in poor immigrant and working-class neighborhoods, but they mostly left upscale bookmakers alone. This class-based discrimination was a rational response to limited enforcement resources: it was far easier to police numbers games, which were often out in the open, than to track down more discreet bookmakers and their well-heeled clients. Going after lower-class gambling made sense as a way to get the biggest bang for the buck. But the bang turned out not to be as big as it seemed: the perception that gambling was a crime if you lived in the wrong neighborhood bred contempt for the laws that did the criminalizing. In turn, this contempt eroded the very moral principles on which the prohibition was based.

If evangelicals could assemble a majority coalition in the current environment—resisting or even reversing the expansion of racetrack gambling, for instance, or heading off new lottery initiatives—we might see a similar dynamic at work. Millions of Americans do not believe gambling is immoral, and a wave of new gambling prohibitions could increase that number if those on the margin recoil at the effort to legislate morality or the inconsistent enforcement of the prohibition. This points to another danger in trying to make the statute books mirror the law of God: the enterprise distracts religious believers from other, more limited efforts that might command widespread support. If they were not so closely linked with the campaign to prohibit gambling, evangelicals might speak with greater moral authority when criticizing, say, state governments' all-out efforts to promote their own lotteries. The same states that force welfare recipients to work for their bread also run advertisements featuring lottery winners bragging that "I'll never have to work another day in my life." Religious believers sometimes criticize these cynical campaigns to put more cash in government coffers, but the message is muddled by the not-unfounded perception that their real goal is to use the law's sword to outlaw *all* gambling.

The tendency of legal moralism to backfire extends beyond culturally contentious issues like abortion and gambling. The world of corporate finance tends to prompt a moralism of the left, with politically liberal Christians seeking to enforce God's law in corporate boardrooms. Jim Wallis, editor of the liberal evangelical magazine *Sojourners* and author of the best-selling book *God's Politics*, praises Congress for its recent efforts to promote corporate responsibility:

> The Senate finally passed unanimously a series of accounting and corporate regulatory measures considerably tougher than what the president had suggested. They included, by a 97-to-0 vote, a new chapter in the criminal code that makes any "scheme or artifice" to defraud stockholders a criminal offense.

Wallis then quotes and endorses Senator Patrick Leahy's assessment:

> If you steal a $500 television set, you can go to jail. Apparently if you steal $500 million from your corporation and your pension holders and everyone else, then nothing happens. [The corporate responsibility legislation] makes sure something will happen....

The suggestion is that laws can be used as an instrument to teach the next generation of corporate executives how to behave and reshape corporate culture.

It isn't likely to work out that way. Title 18 of the United States Code already includes several hundred laws banning various kinds of fraud and misrepresentation. Adding a few more is like adding new rules to the tax code: corporate crooks, like rich taxpayers, will pay their lawyers to find new ways to maneuver around the rules. Nearly everyone agrees that there was a serious breakdown in corporate America at the outset of the twenty-first century and that corporate ethics were a large part of the problem. But new criminal prohibitions are more likely to undermine managers' sense of moral responsibility than to promote it. Every parent understands this point: given a choice between saying "don't hurt your sister" and "here is a list of fifteen ways you might hurt your sister—don't do any of these," wise parents opt for the first approach. Most children, when they are presented with a list of fifteen things not to do, will quickly come up with a sixteenth that is not on the list. Detailed codes that try to define misconduct comprehensively tend to produce the same reaction. Complying with the law becomes an exercise in ticket-punching, following mechanical legal formulae. Regulated actors exercise their creativity by looking for ways to evade legal norms—like taxpayers filling out their tax forms every April 15, trying all the while to hold on to every penny they can.

When corporate regulation looks like the tax code, corporate executives respond like taxpayers. Given a list of dos and don'ts, many will find themselves thinking more about what they can get away with and less about what is honorable and right. Rather than cultivating a sense of moral responsibility, a comprehensive set of rules may simply function as an obstacle course, a set of barriers around which corporate officers must maneuver. As with legal efforts to resolve contentious issues in our social life, legal efforts to define and enforce a code of economic morality produce a kind of reverse alchemy, turning the gold of good morals into dross.

It gets worse. Prosecutors cannot hope to enforce white-collar criminal law across the board; they must be selective. The most obvious way to select targets is to investigate every high-profile corporate bankruptcy.

The moral message becomes not "don't lie" but "don't fail"—not the best message to send budding entrepreneurs.

Why do evangelical Christians find it so hard to resist the attractions of legal moralism? One answer is historical. Early in the twentieth century, evangelicals disengaged from American politics, partly in response to the spread of secular modernism and partly in reaction to the debacle of Prohibition and its repeal. Starting in the 1940s, evangelical leaders, many of them connected to *Christianity Today*, the principal voice of conservative evangelicalism, began calling for a renewed commitment on the part of believers to engage and influence the culture around them. "From Carl Henry and Harold Ockenga in the 1940s and 1950s," as Christian Smith puts it, "to Francis Schaeffer and Mark Hatfield in the 1960s and 1970s, to Charles Colson and Anthony Campolo in the 1980s and 1990s, evangelicals have been driven by a vision of redemptive world transformation." If the end is to transform a law-saturated culture like contemporary America's, legal reform seems a natural means. Debates over legal limits on abortion, gambling, and Enron-style corporate immorality become tools for healing a spiritually diseased society.

But the cure risks worsening the disease. A legal culture that invites selective enforcement (or no enforcement at all) of controversial laws makes it all too easy to enact such laws. Religious moralists need not win the culture in order to enact their preferred moral vision into law; on the contrary, culture and law can follow separate paths. Law becomes largely symbolic: the vast federal criminal law of misrepresentation goes unenforced, save for the occasional Martha Stewart or Scooter Libby on whom ambitious prosecutors train their sights. That state of affairs pleases neither moralists nor libertarians.

* * *

In short, legal moralism is nearly always counterproductive. In Christian terms, it is also deeply wrong. Jesus' definitions of adultery and murder proved that immorality and illegality cannot and must not be coextensive. God's law reigns over a broad empire that man's law cannot hope to govern. Good moral principles are often vague and open-ended, and they reach into every nook and cranny of our lives and our thoughts. Legal principles that have these qualities only serve to invite arbitrary and discriminatory enforcement. Arbitrariness and discrimination in turn invite contempt for the law. Moral education becomes an exercise in educating the public in bad morals. The same thing happens if lawmakers choose a long list of rigid rules in place of vague moral principles, as our experience with trying to define and enforce corporate morality proves. Targets of those rules focus on the rules themselves, on maneuvering through legal minefields instead of exercising moral judgment.

The law deters the very thing it seeks to promote. It is hard to avoid the conclusion that the law must draw lines not between right and wrong but between the most destructive and verifiable wrongs, and everything else.

And mixing God's law and man's law may have other unfortunate consequences: distorting religious believers' understanding of the divine law even as it distorts the public's approach to the laws of code books and court decisions. Distortion runs, in other words, in both directions. Even as we try to write morality into the statute books, we may be tempted to turn God's law into a list of purposeless rules, a kind of Biblical version of the Internal Revenue Code. That is precisely the tendency that Christ criticized in the Pharisees of his time—the tendency to focus on rules rather than relationship with the one true God, a tendency that robbed God's law both of its vastness and of its delight.

Conflating God's law and man's law thus does violence to both. It makes far too much of man's law, and far too little of God's. This realization leads to a surprising implication about contemporary American politics: the deep divide between moralists and libertarians may be needless, the result more of theological error than of spiritual disagreement. Libertarians seek to minimize formal legal restraints on private conduct. That agenda should hold some appeal for wise moralists, at least if the moralists are Christian. After all, the rule of law is a moral good in Christian terms. And the rule of law is likely to be honored best where legal restraints are most modest. The rule of good morals, meanwhile, must be honored—if it is to be honored at all—in the hearts and minds of the citizenry. Not in its courthouses.

Questions

1. Belz says we must ask two questions in setting up a system of law. What are they?

2. How does Belz believe Christians should answer these questions?

3. Why does Belz seek to minimize the amount of God's law we apply in modern society? What is his view of human nature?

4. Is it proper to take man's sinfulness into account in deciding whether to impose a portion of God's law on society? Does Matthew 19:3-12 help?

5. Does witchcraft violate God's law? Consider why Montgomery argues that human law should not prohibit witchcraft.

6. According to Montgomery, what types of wrongs should human law prohibit?

7. What do Skeel and Stuntz believe occurs in most cases when individuals codify moral law? Why?

8. Why do they believe "conflating God's law and man's law...does violence to both?"

9. What conclusions do Skeel and Stuntz draw from the experiences of the civil rights and pro-life movements? Do you agree?

10. Would you enact any or all of the following laws as human law?

    a. A law prohibiting theft;

    b. A law prohibiting adultery;

    c. A law prohibiting same-sex marriage;

    d. A law requiring citizens to contribute 100 hours annually to serving the poor;

    e. A law prohibiting restaurants from serving food containing trans fat;

    f. A law prohibiting gambling;

    g. A law prohibiting human cloning for research purposes.

Index